◇全国高等中医药院校汉英[...]

推拿学

第2版

主　编　金宏柱

副主编　韩明舫　王金贵

主　译　李照国

副主译　陈　嘉　蒋建勇

编译委员会（按姓氏笔画排序）

王华兰（河南中医学院）　　　范炳华（浙江中医药大学）
王金贵（天津中医药大学）　　金宏柱（南京中医药大学）
王艳国（天津中医药大学）　　金德锋（贵阳中医学院）
王道全（山东中医药大学）　　周运峰（河南中医学院）
尤永超（贵阳中医学院）　　　胡　赟（贵阳中医学院）
吕　明（长春中医药大学）　　顾一煌（南京中医药大学）
李照国（上海师范大学）　　　蒋建勇（贵阳中医学院）
吴云川（南京中医药大学）　　郭爱松（南通大学）
吴　健（上海中医药大学）　　梅荣军（黑龙江中医药大学）
陈琳琳（上海中医药大学）　　韩明舫（辽宁中医药大学）
陈朝晖（安徽中医学院）　　　程英武（上海中医药大学）
陈　嘉（贵阳中医学院）　　　樊　旭（辽宁中医药大学）

英文主审　赵燕澍（美国）

人民卫生出版社

◇Chinese-English Bilingual Textbooks for International Students of Chinese TCM Institutions

Science of Tuina
2nd edition

Compiler-in-Chief　　　　Jin Hongzhu
Vice Compiler-in-Chief　　Han Mingfang　Wang Jingui
Translator-in-Chief　　　　Li Zhaoguo
Vice Translator-in-Chief　Chen Jia　Jiang Jianyong

Compiling and Translating Committee (Listed in the order of strokes of their Chinese surname)
　　Wang Hualan (Henan College of TCM)
　　Wang Jingui (Tianjin University of TCM)
　　Wang Yanguo (Tianjin University of TCM)
　　Wang Daoquan (Shandong University of TCM)
　　You Yongchao (Guiyang College of TCM)
　　Lu Ming (Changchun University of TCM)
　　Li Zhaoguo (Shanghai Normal University)
　　Wu Yunchuan (Nanjing University of TCM)
　　Wu Jian (Shanghai University of TCM)
　　Chen Linlin (Shanghai University of TCM)
　　Chen Zhaohui (Anhui College of TCM)
　　Chen Jia (Guiyang College of TCM)
　　Fan Binghua (Zhejiang University of CM)
　　Jin Hongzhu (Nanjing University of TCM)
　　Jin Defeng (Guiyang College of TCM)
　　Zhou Yunfeng (Henan College of TCM)
　　Hu Yun (Guiyang College of TCM)
　　Gu Yihuang (Nanjing University of TCM)
　　Jiang Jianyong (Guiyang College of TCM)
　　Guo Aisong (Nantong University)
　　Mei Rongjun (Heilongjiang University of TCM)
　　Han Mingfang (Liaoning University of TCM)
　　Cheng Yingwu (Shanghai University of TCM)
　　Fan Xu (Liaoning University of TCM)

English Reviser　　Michael Zhao (U.S.A.)

People's Medical Publishing House

图书在版编目（CIP）数据

推拿学/金宏柱主编．李照国主译．—2版．—北京：
人民卫生出版社，2007.9
全国高等中医药院校卫生部规划汉英双语教材
ISBN 978-7-117-08638-7

Ⅰ．推… Ⅱ．①金…②李… Ⅲ．推拿学-双语教学-中医学院-教材 Ⅳ．R244.1

中国版本图书馆CIP数据核字（2007）第048154号

本书本印次封底贴有防伪标。请注意识别。

推 拿 学
第 2 版

主　　编：金宏柱　Jing Hongzhu
主　　译：李照国　Li Zhaoguo
出版发行：人民卫生出版社（中继线 010-67616688）
地　　址：北京市丰台区方庄芳群园3区3号楼
邮　　编：100078
网　　址：http://www.pmph.com
E - mail：pmph @ pmph.com
购书热线：010-67605754　010-65264830
印　　刷：保定市中画美凯印刷有限公司
经　　销：新华书店
开　　本：787×1092　1/16　印张：30
字　　数：667千字
版　　次：2000年8月第1版　2007年9月第2版第3次印刷
标准书号：ISBN 978-7-117-08638-7/R·8639
定　　价：48.00元

版权所有，侵权必究，打击盗版举报电话：010-87613394
（凡属印装质量问题请与本社销售部联系退换）

出版说明

1996年,由全国中医药高等教育国际交流与合作学会联合了全国21所中医药高等院校组织编写了全国首套外国进修生教材(汉英双语),并于1998年在我社出版。近十年的教学实践中,本套教材得到了师生的好评,有些院校一直沿用至今。随着当今世界范围内中医药热潮的涌动,中医药在国际上越来越受到人们的关注,逐渐成为中国"输出型"文化而跨出国门,走向世界。因此,来华学习中医药的留学生逐年增多,已形成了一支学习、继承、传播、发展中医药事业不可忽视的力量。为了适应中医药学高水平国际教学的迫切需要,在国家留学基金管理委员会、全国留学生教育管理学会及国家教育部、国家卫生部、国家中医药管理局的关怀指导下,经全国高等医药教材建设研究会、全国中医药高等教育国际交流与合作学会的积极努力,2006年5月开始启动了本套教材的修订工作。

本套教材的修订,在全国高等中医药院校来华留学生卫生部"十一五"规划汉英双语教材编审委员会的指导下,根据留学生教学的实际需要由第一版的6种增补到10种。其编写修订宗旨是:中医基础及临床学科内容的深度和广度适宜、够用,定位在中国中医药学历教育本科段的层次,在"三基"(基础理论、基本知识、基本技能)、"五性"(思想性、科学性、先进性、启发性、实用性)基础上,要求内容更精炼(不涉及学科发展史)、语言更简洁(不引经据典),同时注重突出中医药学科特点;译文准确,名词术语规范,便于汉语水平偏低的留学生学习。

本套教材适用于来华学习中医药的本科生,以及进修生、培训生等。亦适合境内外中医药汉英双语教学使用。

本套教材目录(第一批):

《中医基础理论》(第2版)	主编	柴可夫	主译	张庆荣
《中医诊断学》(第2版)	主编	王天芳	主译	方廷钰
△《中药学》	主编	滕佳林	主译	崔洪江
《方剂学》(第2版)	主编	陈德兴	主译	朱忠宝
△《中医内科学》(第2版)	主编	彭 勃	主译	谢建群
《中医妇科学》	主编	谈 勇	主译	肖 平
《针灸学》(第2版)	主编	沈雪勇 王 华	主译	赵百孝
《推拿学》(第2版)	主编	金宏柱	主译	李照国
《中医养生学》	主编	刘占文 马烈光	主译	刘占文
《医学基础知识导读》	主编	牛 欣	主译	宋一伦

注:△为普通高等教育"十一五"国家级规划教材

Publisher's Note

In 1996, China National Association of International Exchange and Collaboration in TCM Higher Education organized 21 colleges and universities of traditional Chinese medicine in China to compile the first series of textbooks (Chinese-English) for international students. These textbooks were published by the People's Medical Publishing House in 1998 and have been used nearly for ten years to train international students in the colleges and universities of traditional Chinese medicine in China. With the rapid dissemination of traditional Chinese medicine throughout the world, more and more international students come to China every year to study this ancient Chinese system of medicine. To meet the needs of international students of traditional Chinese medicine, the project to revise this series of textbooks began in May 2006 with the support of China Scholarship Council, Chinese Association of Universities and Colleges for Foreign Student Affairs, Ministry of Education of the People's Republic of P.R.C., Ministry of Health of the People's Republic of P.R.C. and State Administration of Traditional Chinese Medicine of P.R.C..

In this revision, four more textbooks were added to the original series so as to equal the level of regular undergraduate education of traditional Chinese medicine in China. The compilation of these textbooks was undertaken on the basis of three essential aspects (essentials of theory, knowledge and techniques), five qualities (theoretical, scientific, advanced, inspiring and practical) and two standards (standard translation and terminology). The contents were concise, excluding much history and quotations from classic texts.

This newly compiled and revised series of textbooks can be used by international students for undergraduate study, advanced study or training purposes in the field of traditional Chinese medicine.

This series of textbook includes the following fascicles (the first set):

Fundamental Theory of Traditional Chinese Medicine (2nd edition)
Compiler-in-Chief: Chai Kefu   Translator-in-Chief: Zhang Qingrong

Diagnostics of Traditional Chinese Medicine (2nd edition)
Compiler-in-Chief: Wang Tianfang   Translator-in-Chief: Fang Tingyu

ΔChinese Materia Medica
Compiler-in-Chief: Teng Jialin   Translator-in-Chief: Cui Hongjiang

Formulas of Traditional Chinese Medicine (2nd edition)
Compiler-in-Chief: Chen Dexing   Translator-in-Chief: Zhu Zhongbao
△**Traditional Chinese Internal Medicine (2nd edition)**
Compiler-in-Chief: Peng Bo   Translator-in-Chief: Xie Jianqun
Gynecology of Traditional Chinese Medicine
Compiler-in-Chief: Tan Yong   Translator-in-Chief: Xiao Ping
Acupuncture and Moxibustion (2nd edition)
Compiler-in-Chief: Shen Xueyong   Translator-in-Chief: Zhao Baixiao
            Wang Hua
Science of Tuina (2nd edition)
Compiler-in-Chief: Jin Hongzhu   Translator-in-Chief: Li Zhaoguo
Health Preservation of Traditional Chinese Medicine
Compiler-in-Chief: Liu Zhanwen   Translator-in-Chief: Liu Zhanwen
            Ma Lieguang
An Introductory Course in Medicine
Compiler-in-Chief: Niu Xin   Translator-in-Chief: Song Yilun

△ The State Eleventh Five-Year Plan Textbooks for Colleges and Universities

全国高等中医药院校来华留学生卫生部"十一五"规划汉英双语教材编审委员会名单

顾问

曹国兴（中华人民共和国教育部国际交流与合作司司长）

张秀琴（国家留学基金管理委员会秘书长　全国高等学校外国留学生教育管理学会会长）

郑守曾（北京中医药大学校长）

方廷钰（北京中医药大学教授　全国政协委员）

胡国臣（人民卫生出版社社长　兼总编辑）

刘振民（全国中医药高等教育学会秘书长）

范永升（浙江中医药大学副校长）

王　华（湖北中医学院院长）

王之虹（长春中医药大学校长）

李佃贵（河北医科大学副校长）

马　骥（辽宁中医药大学校长）

张俊龙（山西中医学院副院长）

刘延祯（甘肃中医学院院长）

左铮云（江西中医学院副院长）

邓家刚（广西中医学院副院长）

王彦晖（厦门大学医学院副院长）

主任委员

吴秀芬（北京中医药大学教授　全国中医药高等教育国际交流与合作学会会长）

副主任委员

彭　勃（河南中医学院院长　教授　全国中医药高等教育国际交流与合作学会理事）

谢建群（上海中医药大学常务副校长　党委书记　教授）

陈盈晖（中华人民共和国教育部科学技术司副司长）

赵灵山（中华人民共和国教育部国际合作与交流司来华留学工作处处长）

呼素华（卫生部教材办公室　人民卫生出版社编审）

委员（按姓氏笔画排序）

　　牛　欣（北京中医药大学国际学院院长　教授　全国中医药高等教育国际交流
　　　　　与合作学会副会长）
　　王洪琦（广州中医药大学国际学院院长　全国中医药高等教育国际交流与合作
　　　　　学会副会长）
　　乐毅敏（江西中医学院国际教育学院院长　教授）
　　朱忠宝（河南中医学院教授）
　　孙　勇（卫生部教材办公室　人民卫生出版社编辑）
　　刘　淼（长春中医药大学国际教育学院院长）
　　刘占文（北京中医药大学教授）
　　刘景峰（辽宁中医药大学国际教育学院副院长）
　　李　军（甘肃中医学院国际处处长）
　　李　沛（福建中医学院国际合作与交流处处长）
　　李照国（上海师范大学教授）
　　应森林（天津中医药大学国际教育学院院长　教授　学会常务理事）
　　张庆荣（辽宁中医药大学教授）
　　尚　力（上海中医药大学国际教育学院院长　教授　全国中医药高等教育国际
　　　　　交流与合作学会副会长）
　　罗　萤（福建中医学院党委书记）
　　周海虹（厦门大学医学院中医系副主任）
　　房家毅（河北医科大学国际教育学院院长）
　　赵　熔（南京中医药大学国际教育学院院长　学会常务理事）
　　赵雪丽（山西中医学院国际教育中心主任）
　　姚洪武（成都中医药大学外事处副处长　讲师　学会常务理事）
　　柴可夫（浙江中医药大学国际教育中心主任　教授）
　　梁　华（黑龙江中医药大学外事处处长　教授　学会常务理事）
　　崔洪江（山东中医药大学外事处处长　副教授　学会常务理事）
　　彭清华（湖南中医药大学国际教育学院院长　教授）
　　傅　萍（湖北中医学院外事处处长）
　　路　玫（河南中医学院海外教育学院处长　教授　学会常务理事）

Editing Committee of Chinese-English Bilingual Textbooks Included in the Eleventh Five-Year Plan of the Ministry of Health of P.R.C. for International Students of Chinese TCM Institutions

Adivisors

Cao Guoxing (Chief of the International Exchange and Cooperation Department, Ministry of Education, P.R.C.)

Zhang Xiuqin (Secretary-General of China Scholarship Council and Chief of Chinese Association of Universities and Colleges for Foreign Student Affairs)

Zheng Shouzeng (President of Beijing University of CM)

Fang Tingyu (Professor of Beijing University of CM and Member of National Political Consultative Committee)

Hu Guochen (President and Editor-in-General of the People's Medical Publishing House)

Liu Zhenmin (Secretary-General of the National Association of TCM Higher Education)

Fan Yongsheng (Vice President of Zhenjiang University of CM)

Wang Hua (President of Hubei College of TCM)

Wang Zhihong (President of Changchun University of TCM)

Li Diangui (Vice President of Hebei Medical University)

Ma Ji (President of Liaoning University of TCM)

Zhang Junlong (Vice President of Shanxi College of TCM)

Liu Yanzhen (President of Gansu College of TCM)

Zuo Zhengyun (Vice President of Jiangxi College of TCM)

Deng Jiagang (Vice President of Guangxi College of TCM)

Wang Yanhui (Vice President of Medical College of Xiamen University)

Dean

Wu Xiufen (Professor of Beijing University of CM and Chairwoman of China National Association of International Exchange and Collaboration in TCM Higher Education)

Deputy-Dean

  Peng Bo (Professor and President of Henan College of TCM and Member of China National Association of International Exchange and Collaboration in TCM Higher Education)

  Xie Jianqun (Professor, CPC Branch Secretary and Vice President of Shanghai University of TCM)

  Chen Yinghui (Deputy Director-General, Department of Science and Technology, Ministry of Education, P.R.C.)

  Zhao Lingshan (Director, Division for International Students, Departement of International Cooperation and Exchanges, Ministry of Education, P.R.C.)

  Hu Suhua (Senior Editor of People's Medical Publishing House and the Textbook Office Affiliated to the Ministry of Health of P.R.C.)

Members (Listed in the order of strokes in their Chinese surname)

  Niu Xin (Professor and President of International College of Beijing University of CM and Vice Chairman of China National Association of International Exchange and Collaboration in TCM Higher Education)

  Wang Hongqi (President of International College of Guangzhou University of CM, Vice Chairman of China National Association of International Exchange and Collabortion in TCM Higher Education)

  Le Yimin (Professor and President of International College of Jiangxi College of TCM)

  Zhu Zhongbao (Professor of Henan College of TCM)

  Sun Yong (Editor of People's Medical Publishing House and the Textbook Office Affiliated to the Ministry of Health of P.R.C.)

  Liu Miao (President of International College of Changchun University of TCM)

  Liu Zhanwen (Professor of Beijing University of CM)

  Liu Jingfeng (Vice President of International College of Liaoning University of TCM)

  Li Jun (Director of International Education Center of Gansu College of TCM)

  Li Pei (Director of International Cooperation and Exchange Department of Fujian College of TCM)

  Li Zhaoguo (Professor of Shanghai Normal University)

  Ying Senlin (President of International Education College of Tianjin University of TCM and Standing Member of the China National Association of International Exchange and Collaboration in TCM Higher Education)

  Zhang Qingrong (Professor of Liaoning University of TCM)

Shang Li (Professor and President of International College of Shanghai University of TCM, Vice Chairman of China National Association of International Exchange and Collaboration in TCM Higher Education)

Luo Ying (CPC Branch Secretary of Fujian College of TCM)

Zhou Haihong (Deputy Director of TCM Department of Xiamen Medical University)

Fang Jiayi (President of International College of Hebei Medical University)

Zhao Rong (President of International Educational College of Nanjing University of TCM and Standing Member of the China National Association of International Exchange and Collaboration in TCM Higher Education)

Zhao Xueli (Director of International Education Center of Shanxi College of TCM)

Yao Hongwu (Lecturer and Deputy Director of International Affairs Department of Chengdu University of TCM and Standing Member of the China National Association of International Exchange and Collaboration in TCM Higher Education)

Chai Kefu (Professor and Director of International Center of Zhejiang University of CM)

Liang Hua (Professor and Director of Personnel Department of Heilongjiang University of TCM and Standing Member of the China National Association of International Exchange and Collaboration in TCM Higher Education)

Cui Hongjiang (Associate Professor and Director of International Affairs Department of Shandong University of TCM and Standing Member of the China National Association of International Exchange and Collaboration in TCM Higher Education)

Peng Qinghua (Professor and President of International College of Hunan University of TCM)

Fu Ping (Dean of Personnel Department of Hubei College of TCM)

Lu Mei (Director of International Education College of Henan College of TCM and Standing Member of the China National Association of International Exchange and Collaboration in TCM Higher Education)

前　言

中医药学以它独特的理论体系和显著的临床效果，在国际上越来越受到人们的关注。近些年随着世界范围的中医药热潮的涌动，来华学习中医药的留学生逐年增多。为了适应中医药国际交流与合作的需要，加快中医药国际化进程，提高来华学习中医药留学生的教学质量，根据教育部、卫生部、国家中医药管理局等上级领导部门的有关精神，全国中医药高等教育国际交流与合作学会研究决定拟启动"全国高等中医药院校外国进修生教材（1997～1998年出版）"的修订工作。此项工作得到了卫生部教材办公室的高度重视，同时得到了国家教育部国际交流与合作司、国家留学基金管理委员会、全国高等院校外国留学生教育管理学会、全国各高等院校，以及人民卫生出版社的大力支持。随即教材的修订纳入了"卫生部'十一五'规划"，并组建了全国高等中医药院校来华留学生卫生部"十一五"规划汉英双语教材编审委员会。本套教材在第一版的基础上，仍然采取汉英两种文字语言的形式出版，即前部分为中文，后部分为中文的英文译文。教材的科目根据留学生教学的需要由原来的6种（《中医基础理论》、《中医诊断学》、《方剂学》、《中医内科学》、《针灸学》、《推拿学》）增补到10种（增加了《中药学》、《中医妇科学》、《中医养生学》、《医学基础知识导读》）。教材的编写针对来华留学生的学习特点及教学需要，以"全国高等中医药院校外国进修生教材（第一版）"为蓝本，参照国内中医药高等院校本科生教学大纲，以及国际中医药从业人员考试大纲和国家中医执业医师考试大纲，同时参考全国高等中医院校五版、七版及二十一世纪课程教材，编写要求坚持"三基"（基础理论、基本知识、基本技能）、"五性"（思想性、科学性、先进性、启发性、适用性）"三特定"（特定的对象、特定的要求、特定的限制）的基本原则，注重继承与创新、传统与现代、理论与实践、中医与西医的关系，力求做到理论系统、重点突出、简明扼要、临床实用。

本套教材的主编、主译经全国高等中医药院校申报、教材编审委员会根据有关条件严格遴选、确定，最后经卫生部教材办公室审核、确认。教材编写实行主编、主译负责制，编写人员大多为多年从事高等中医药对外教育、具有丰富留学生教学经验的著名专家、教授；英文译者大多为从事中医药专业英语教学研究和汉英双语教学的专家。每种教材的编写均经过编写会、统稿会、定稿会，英文部分均聘请外籍专家审核、修改,最后全套教材的英文稿件又进行了集中统稿、定稿,从而确保了本套教材的编写质量和英文的翻译质量。

中医药走向世界,面临众多层面的跨文化沟通与传播问题,但愿我们这套教材能在弘扬中华民族优秀文化、造福人类健康、促进中国与世界科学文化交流的伟大事业中,做出新的、更大的贡献。

全国中医药高等教育国际交流与合作学会
全国高等中医药院校来华留学生卫生部"十一五"规划
汉英双语教材编审委员会
2007 年 7 月

Foreword

Traditional Chinese medicine (TCM) has a unique theoretical system and is clinically effective. Over the past few decades it has been attracting increasing attention from all over the world. More and more overseas students come to China to learn TCM and there has been a huge upsurge in the learning of TCM worldwide. To meet the needs of these students, accelerate the processes of internationalization of TCM, and improve the quality of education available to overseas students coming to China to learn TCM, these textbooks have been compiled by China National Association of International Exchange and Collaboration in TCM Higher Education in accordance with the wishes of the Ministry of Education of P.R.C., the Ministry of Health of P.R.C., and the State Administration Bureau of TCM of P.R.C.. The Textbook Office Affiliated to the Ministry of Health of P.R.C. has attached great importance to the matter. In addition, the compilation of the textbooks has the support of the following important organizations: International Cooperation and Exchange Department of the Ministry of Education of P.R.C., China Scholarship Council, Chinese Association of Universities and Colleges for Foreign Students Affairs, all the colleges and universities of TCM, and the People's Medical Publishing House. This series of textbooks has been brought into the Eleventh Five-Year Plan of the Ministry of Health of P.R.C. and a new organization, the Editing Committee of Chinese-English Bilingual Textbooks Included in the Eleventh Five-Year Plan of the Ministry of Health of P.R.C. for International Students of Chinese TCM Institutions, was established.

The textbooks have been compiled to conform to the standards of the exam syllabus for international licensed TCM professionals, Chinese licensed TCM physicians, and the 21st century textbooks for TCM universities (referencing the 5th, 6th, and 7th editions). The textbooks are bilingual, with content first in Chinese and then in English. The total is ten textbooks: *Fundamental Theory of Traditional Chinese Medicine, Diagnostics of Traditional Chinese Medicine, Chinese Materia Medica, Formulas of Traditional Chinese Medicine, Traditional Chinese Internal Medicine, Acupuncture and Moxibustion, Science of Tuina, Gynecology of Traditional Chinese Medicine, Health Preservation of Traditional Chinese Medicine, An Introductory Course in Medicine*. The compilers of the textbooks adhered to "three points: basic theories, basic knowledge, and basic techniques"; "five features: the ideological, scientific, advanced, enlightening, and practical"; and "three principles: specific readers, specific requirements, and specific levels". Great attention has been paid to the issues of inheritance and innovation, traditional and modern aspects, theory and practice, and Chinese medicine and biomedicine. It is our aim to make the theories of TCM systematic, presenting key points in concise language that will lead to practical clinical applications.

There was a strict procedure for selecting and translators. Names of compilers and translators had to be approved by the Editing Committee of Chinese-English Bilingual Textbooks Included in the Eleventh Five-Year Plan of the Ministry of Health of P.R.C. for International Students of Chinese TCM Institutions, and The Textbook Office Affiliated to the Ministry of Health of P.R.C.. All candidates selected are experts with years of experience teaching TCM to international students.

Each textbook was repeatedly examined and revised to guarantee quality by numerous committees at multiple stages. The English text was thoroughly reviewed by foreign experts.

Introducing TCM to overseas students in China and abroad meets with many challenges of communication and dissemination of material. We hope this series of textbooks will make great contributions to the development of Chinese culture, the improvement of human health, and the promotion of scientific and cultural exchange between China and the rest of the world.

China National Association of International Exchange and Collaboration in TCM Higher Education

Editing Committee of Chinese-English Bilingual Textbooks Included in the Eleventh Five-Year Plan of the Ministry of Health of P.R.C. for International Students of Chinese TCM Institutions

July,2007

编写说明

本教材是"全国高等中医药院校来华留学生卫生部'十一五'规划汉英双语教材"系列之一。

推拿学是研究和阐述推拿理论及其临床应用的一门学科,是中医学的重要组成部分。本教材的编写根据"全国高等中医药院校来华留学生卫生部'十一五'规划汉英双语教材编审委员会"的编写要求,针对来华留学生的学习特点编写而成。

本书执简驭繁地介绍了既包括源流和现代研究、学习方法、经络腧穴、推拿练功、诊断方法等中医推拿学的基础内容,又有重点地介绍了临床防治疾病的推拿常用手法,精要阐述中医推拿中最具特色的小儿推拿内容,着重讲述临床常见的40余种疾病的推拿防治,并以肝、心、脾、肺、肾五脏科学归类,对推拿用于临床保健养生、强身健体的按摩方法进行了归纳和便于学习的编排。

本教材的编写和翻译工作均由教材编译委员会分工完成,其中主编统审中文稿部分,主译统审英文稿部分。

编写中医汉英双语教材,是一项繁重的工作,尽管我们在编译中作了很多努力,但由于经验不足,水平有限,编写和翻译中可能会存在一些问题,希望大家提出宝贵意见,以便不断修订、改进和提高。

《推拿学》编译委员会
2007年7月

Preface

This is one of the Chinese-English TCM Textbooks for international Students studying in the colleges and universities of TCM in China for the 11th five Year Plan organized by the Health Ministry.

Tuina is a branch of traditional Chinese medicine (TCM) with systemic theories and rich clinical experiences. The compilation of this book is, guided by the Compiling and Approving Committee of TCM Bilingual Textbooks, based on the needs of international students.

In compiling this textbook, we have tried to introduce the essentials of Tuina to the students, such as modern studies, learning methods, meridians and Acupoints, special exercises and diagnostic methods; the commonly used methods for preventing and treating diseases for adults, women and children; the methods used for cultivating health and strengthening the body.

As it is known to all, it is a great challenge to compile bilingual textbook of TCM. So there must be some errors in this book and we will try to improve it in the next edition.

Compiling and Translating Committee of Tuina
July, 2007

目 录

1 总论 ·· 3
1.1 推拿学简史 ··· 3
1.2 推拿学的发展和研究 ·· 5
1.3 怎样学习推拿 ··· 6

2 推拿学的作用原理 ··· 7
2.1 调整阴阳 ··· 7
2.2 补虚泻实 ··· 7
2.3 活血化瘀 ··· 8
2.3.1 促进血液流通 ·· 8
2.3.2 改善血液流变 ·· 8
2.3.3 降低血流阻力 ·· 8
2.3.4 改善心脏功能 ·· 9
2.3.5 促进微循环建立 ··· 9
2.4 舒筋通络 ··· 9
2.5 理筋整复 ··· 10

3 经络腧穴 ··· 11
3.1 经络腧穴的基本理论 ·· 11
3.1.1 十二经脉 ··· 11
3.1.2 奇经八脉 ··· 13
3.1.3 十五络脉 ··· 13
3.1.4 十二经别 ··· 13
3.1.5 十二经筋 ··· 14
3.1.6 十二皮部 ··· 14
3.2 常用腧穴 ··· 15

4 推拿常用检查方法 …… 23

4.1 头面部检查 …… 23
4.1.1 望诊 …… 23
4.1.2 触诊 …… 24

4.2 胸腹部 …… 25
4.2.1 望诊 …… 25
4.2.2 触诊 …… 25

4.3 脊柱部 …… 26
4.3.1 望诊 …… 26
4.3.2 触诊 …… 26
4.3.3 运动检查 …… 26
4.3.4 特殊检查 …… 27

4.4 上肢部 …… 28
4.4.1 肩部 …… 28
4.4.2 肘部 …… 30
4.4.3 腕掌指部 …… 31

4.5 下肢部 …… 32
4.5.1 髋部 …… 32
4.5.2 膝部 …… 33
4.5.3 踝部 …… 34

5 推拿基本练功法 …… 36

5.1 推拿练功法的特点和作用 …… 36
5.1.1 推拿练功法的特点 …… 36
5.1.2 推拿练功对机体的作用 …… 37

5.2 易筋经练习法 …… 38
5.3 少林内功练习法 …… 44

6 推拿手法 …… 53

6.1 成人推拿基本手法 …… 54
6.1.1 一指禅推法 …… 54
6.1.2 㨰法 …… 55
6.1.3 揉法 …… 57
6.1.4 摩法 …… 58
6.1.5 擦法 …… 59
6.1.6 推法 …… 60
6.1.7 抹法 …… 63
6.1.8 扫散法 …… 63

6.1.9	搓法	64
6.1.10	振法	64
6.1.11	抖法	65
6.1.12	按法	66
6.1.13	压法	67
6.1.14	点法	67
6.1.15	捏法	68
6.1.16	拿法	68
6.1.17	捻法	69
6.1.18	拨法	69
6.1.19	拍法	70
6.1.20	击法	70
6.1.21	弹法	72
6.1.22	摇法	72
6.1.23	拔伸法	76
6.1.24	背法	79
6.1.25	扳法	79

6.2 成人复式推拿手法 …… 86

- 6.2.1 按揉法 …… 86
- 6.2.2 拿揉法 …… 87
- 6.2.3 推摩法 …… 87

7 成人疾病的推拿治疗 …… **89**

7.1 骨伤科病症 …… 89

- 7.1.1 落枕 …… 89
- 7.1.2 颈椎病 …… 90
- 7.1.3 急性腰扭伤 …… 95
- 7.1.4 慢性腰肌劳损 …… 99
- 7.1.5 退行性脊柱炎 …… 100
- 7.1.6 第三腰椎横突综合征 …… 101
- 7.1.7 腰椎间盘突出症 …… 102
- 7.1.8 胸胁屏伤 …… 105
- 7.1.9 骶髂关节错缝 …… 106
- 7.1.10 梨状肌综合征 …… 108
- 7.1.11 腰背肌筋膜炎 …… 109
- 7.1.12 肩关节周围炎 …… 111
- 7.1.13 肱骨外上髁炎 …… 112
- 7.1.14 腕管综合征 …… 114
- 7.1.15 腕关节扭挫伤 …… 115

- 7.1.16 髂胫束劳损 ······ 116
- 7.1.17 膝关节骨性关节炎 ······ 117
- 7.1.18 膝关节侧副韧带损伤 ······ 119
- 7.1.19 踝关节扭挫伤 ······ 121
- 7.1.20 颞颌关节功能紊乱症 ······ 123

7.2 内妇五官科病症 ······ 125
- 7.2.1 胃脘痛 ······ 125
- 7.2.2 泄泻 ······ 126
- 7.2.3 便秘 ······ 128
- 7.2.4 高血压病 ······ 129
- 7.2.5 冠心病 ······ 130
- 7.2.6 头痛 ······ 131
- 7.2.7 失眠 ······ 133
- 7.2.8 中风后遗症 ······ 135
- 7.2.9 痛经 ······ 136
- 7.2.10 更年期综合征 ······ 138
- 7.2.11 阳痿 ······ 140
- 7.2.12 牙痛 ······ 141
- 7.2.13 耳聋 ······ 142
- 7.2.14 郁证 ······ 143
- 7.2.15 月经不调 ······ 144

8 小儿常见疾病推拿治疗　**147**

8.1 小儿推拿基本手法 ······ 147
- 8.1.1 推法 ······ 147
- 8.1.2 揉法 ······ 148
- 8.1.3 按法 ······ 149
- 8.1.4 摩法 ······ 149
- 8.1.5 掐法 ······ 150
- 8.1.6 捏法 ······ 150
- 8.1.7 运法 ······ 151
- 8.1.8 捣法 ······ 151

8.2 小儿复式操作手法 ······ 152
- 8.2.1 黄蜂入洞 ······ 152
- 8.2.2 双凤展翅 ······ 152
- 8.2.3 按弦走搓摩 ······ 153
- 8.2.4 猿猴摘果 ······ 153
- 8.2.5 水底捞月 ······ 153
- 8.2.6 打马过天河 ······ 154

8.2.7 运土入水	154
8.2.8 运水入土	155
8.3 小儿推拿特定穴	155
8.3.1 坎宫	156
8.3.2 天门	156
8.3.3 太阳	157
8.3.4 耳后高骨	158
8.3.5 天柱骨	158
8.3.6 乳根	158
8.3.7 乳旁	158
8.3.8 胁肋	158
8.3.9 腹	159
8.3.10 脐	159
8.3.11 丹田	159
8.3.12 肚角	159
8.3.13 肺俞	160
8.3.14 脊柱	160
8.3.15 七节骨	160
8.3.16 龟尾	161
8.3.17 脾经	161
8.3.18 肝经	161
8.3.19 心经	162
8.3.20 肺经	162
8.3.21 肾经	162
8.3.22 小肠	162
8.3.23 大肠	163
8.3.24 肾顶	163
8.3.25 四横纹	163
8.3.26 小横纹	163
8.3.27 掌小横纹	163
8.3.28 胃经	164
8.3.29 板门	164
8.3.30 内劳宫	164
8.3.31 小天心	164
8.3.32 内八卦	165
8.3.33 总筋	165
8.3.34 大横纹	165
8.3.35 左端正	166
8.3.36 右端正	166

- 8.3.37 五指节 ······ 166
- 8.3.38 二扇门 ······ 166
- 8.3.39 上马 ······ 167
- 8.3.40 威灵 ······ 167
- 8.3.41 精宁 ······ 167
- 8.3.42 膊阳池 ······ 167
- 8.3.43 一窝风 ······ 167
- 8.3.44 三关 ······ 168
- 8.3.45 六腑 ······ 168
- 8.3.46 天河水 ······ 169
- 8.4 小儿常见病症 ······ 169
  - 8.4.1 小儿病治疗特点 ······ 169
  - 8.4.2 咳嗽 ······ 170
  - 8.4.3 发热 ······ 171
  - 8.4.4 哮喘 ······ 173
  - 8.4.5 呕吐 ······ 174
  - 8.4.6 泄泻 ······ 176
  - 8.4.7 厌食 ······ 177
  - 8.4.8 便秘 ······ 178
  - 8.4.9 夜啼 ······ 179
  - 8.4.10 遗尿 ······ 180
  - 8.4.11 小儿肌性斜颈 ······ 182
  - 8.4.12 小儿桡骨头半脱位 ······ 183

9 自我推拿保健 ······ 184

- 9.1 自我推拿保健对人体的作用 ······ 184
- 9.2 自我推拿保健操作方法 ······ 184
  - 9.2.1 疏肝理气法 ······ 184
  - 9.2.2 宁心安神法 ······ 185
  - 9.2.3 健脾和胃法 ······ 186
  - 9.2.4 宣肺解表法 ······ 186
  - 9.2.5 固肾增精法 ······ 187

Contents

1 **Introduction** ··· **191**

   1.1 History ··· 191

   1.2 Academic studies and development of Tuina ············ 194

   1.3 How to study Tuina ································· 195

2 **Mechanism of Tuina** ································· **196**

   2.1 Regulating Yin and Yang ····························· 196

   2.2 Improving deficiency and reducing excess ············· 196

   2.3 Activating blood and resolving stasis ················· 197

      2.3.1 Promoting blood flow ························ 197

      2.3.2 Improving blood rheology ···················· 198

      2.3.3 Reducing resistance of blood flow ············· 198

      2.3.4 Improving functions of heart ················· 198

      2.3.5 Promoting the establishment of

             microcirculation ··························· 199

   2.4 Relaxing sinews and dredging collaterals ············· 199

   2.5 Regulating sinews for repair ························· 200

3 **Meridians and Acupoints** ···························· **201**

   3.1 Essentials of meridians and acupoints ················ 201

      3.1.1 The twelve regular meridians ················· 202

      3.1.2 Eight extraordinary meridians ················ 204

      3.1.3 The fifteen major collaterals ················· 204

      3.1.4 The twelve meridian branches ················ 205

      3.1.5 The twelve musculatures ···················· 205

      3.1.6 Twelve cutaneous regions ··················· 206

   3.2 Commonly used Acupoints ·························· 206

4 Commonly Used Examination Methods ... 220

4.1 Examination of the head and face ... 220
4.1.1 Inspection ... 220
4.1.2 Palpation ... 222

4.2 Examination of the chest and abdomen ... 222
4.2.1 Inspection ... 222
4.2.2 Palpation ... 223

4.3 Spine ... 224
4.3.1 Inspection ... 224
4.3.2 Palpation ... 224
4.3.3 Motor examination ... 225
4.3.4 Special examination ... 225

4.4 The upper limbs ... 227
4.4.1 The shoulders ... 227
4.4.2 Elbow ... 230
4.4.3 Wrist, palm and fingers ... 232

4.5 Lower limbs ... 234
4.5.1 Hip ... 234
4.5.2 Knees ... 236
4.5.3 Malleolus ... 237

5 Basic Exercises for Manipulation Practice ... 239

5.1 Characteristics and actions of manipulation exercises ... 239
5.1.1 Characteristics ... 239
5.1.2 Effect of Tuina exercises on the body ... 240

5.2 Exercise of Yi Jin Jing (Change of tendons) ... 241

5.3 Shao Lin Nei Gong (Shao Lin internal exercise) ... 249

6 Manipulations for Tuina ... 262

6.1 Basic manipulations for adult Tuina ... 263
6.1.1 Yi Zhi Chan Fa (One-finger pushing manipulation) ... 263
6.1.2 Rolling manipulation ... 264
6.1.3 Rou Fa (Kneading manipulation) ... 266
6.1.4 Mo Fa (Circular-rubbing or stroking manipulation) ... 267
6.1.5 Ca Fa (To-and-fro rubbing manipulation) ... 268
6.1.6 Tui Fa (Pushing manipulation) ... 269
6.1.7 Mo Fa (Wiping manipulation) ... 271
6.1.8 Sao San Fa (Cleaning and dissipating manipulation) ... 272
6.1.9 Cuo Fa (Palm-twisting manipulation) ... 273

6.1.10	Zhen Fa (Vibrating manipulation)	274
6.1.11	Dou Fa (Shaking manipulation)	275
6.1.12	An Fa (Point-pressing manipulation)	275
6.1.13	Ya Fa (Suppressing manipulation)	276
6.1.14	Dian Fa (Point-pressing manipulation)	276
6.1.15	Nie Fa (Pinching manipulation)	277
6.1.16	Na Fa (Grasping manipulation)	278
6.1.17	Nian Fa (Finger-twisting manipulation)	278
6.1.18	Bo Fa (Plucking manipulation)	279
6.1.19	Pai Fa (Patting manipulation)	279
6.1.20	Ji Fa (Hitting manipulation)	280
6.1.21	Tan Fa (Flipping manipulation)	281
6.1.22	Yao Fa (Rotating manipulation)	282
6.1.23	Ba Shen Fa (Pulling-extending manipulation)	284
6.1.24	Bei Fa (Back-carrying manipulation)	287
6.1.25	Ban Fa (Pulling manipulation)	287

6.2 Compound Tuina Manipulation for Adults ... 292
    6.2.1 An Rou Fa (Pressing and kneading manipulation) ... 292
    6.2.2 Na Rou Fa (Grasping and kneading manipulation) ... 293
    6.2.3 Tui Mo Fa (Pushing and rubbing manipulation) ... 293

7 Tuina Treatment for Adult Diseases ... 295

7.1 Disorders in oesteonosus and traumatism ... 295
    7.1.1 Stiff neck ... 295
    7.1.2 Cervical Spondylopathy ... 297
    7.1.3 Acute Lumbar Sprain ... 305
    7.1.4 Chronic lumbar muscle strain ... 310
    7.1.5 Retrograde spondylitis ... 312
    7.1.6 Third Lumbar Transverse Process Syndrome ... 314
    7.1.7 Lumbar intervertebral disc protrusion ... 316
    7.1.8 Chest and hypochondrium trauma ... 319
    7.1.9 Shifted sacroiliac joint ... 322
    7.1.10 Piriformis syndrome ... 324
    7.1.11 Lumbospinal myofascitis ... 326
    7.1.12 Scapulohumeral periarthritis ... 329
    7.1.13 Lateral humeral epicondylitis ... 331
    7.1.14 Carpal tunnel syndrome ... 333
    7.1.15 Sprain of wrist joint ... 335
    7.1.16 Strain of iliotibial tract ... 338

7.1.17	Ostcoarthritis of knee joint	339
7.1.18	Injury of the collateral ligament of knee joint	342
7.1.19	Contusion and sprain of ankle joint	345
7.1.20	Dysfunction syndrome of the temporomandibular joint	348

7.2 Diseases in internal medicine, gynaecology and otolaryngology ... 351

7.2.1	Stomachache	351
7.2.2	Diarrhea	353
7.2.3	Constipation	355
7.2.4	Hypertension	357
7.2.5	Coronary heart disease	359
7.2.6	Headache	360
7.2.7	Insomnia	363
7.2.8	Apoplexy sequelae	365
7.2.9	Dysmenorrhea	368
7.2.10	Menopause syndrome	370
7.2.11	Impotence	373
7.2.12	Toothache	375
7.2.13	Deafness	377
7.2.14	Depression syndrome	378
7.2.15	Irregular menstruation	380

8 Tuina Therapy for Commonly Encountered Infantile Diseases ... 384

8.1 Basic manipulations for infantile Tuina ... 384

8.1.1	Pushing manipulation	384
8.1.2	Kneading manipulation	385
8.1.3	Pressing manipulation	386
8.1.4	Mo Fa (Circular rubbing manipulation)	386
8.1.5	Nipping manipulation	387
8.1.6	Pinching manipulation	387
8.1.7	Circularly pushing manipulation	388
8.1.8	Pounding manipulation	389

8.2 Compound manipulations for infantile Tuina ... 389

8.2.1	Huang Feng Ru Dong (Wasp entering the hole)	389
8.2.2	Manipulation of Shuang Feng Zhan Chi (Two phoenixes spreading wings)	389
8.2.3	An Xuan Zou Cuo Mo (Twisting and rubbing like plucking string)	390
8.2.4	Yuan Hou Zhai Guo (Manipulation of ape picking fruits)	390
8.2.5	Manipulation of Shui Di Lao Yue (Scooping the

		moon from the bottom of water) ·································	390
8.2.6		Manipulation of Da Ma Guo Tian He (Beating the horse to cross the heaven river) ·····························	391
8.2.7		Manipulation of Yun Tu Ru Shui (Carrying earth into water) ············	391
8.2.8		Manipulation of Yun Shui Ru Tu (Carrying water into earth) ············	391
8.3	Specific acupoints for infantile tuina ································		392
	8.3.1	Kangong ··	392
	8.3.2	Tianmen (Heaven gate) ·····································	392
	8.3.3	Taiyang (EX-HN 5) ··	393
	8.3.4	Erhougaogu (Prominent bone behind the ears) ················	393
	8.3.5	Tianzhugu (Cervical column) ································	394
	8.3.6	Rugen (ST 18) ···	394
	8.3.7	Rupang (Region lateral to the breast) ························	394
	8.3.8	Xielei (Hypochondrium) ····································	394
	8.3.9	Fu (Abdomen) ···	395
	8.3.10	Qi (Umbilicus) ···	395
	8.3.11	Dantian (Lower abdomen) ···································	396
	8.3.12	Dujiao (Side of abdomen) ···································	396
	8.3.13	Feishu (BL 13) ···	396
	8.3.14	Jizhu (Spinal column) ······································	397
	8.3.15	Qijiegu (Seven lumbrosacral vertebrae) ·······················	397
	8.3.16	Guiwei (Coccyx) ···	398
	8.3.17	Pijing (Spleen meridian) ····································	398
	8.3.18	Ganjing (Liver meridian) ····································	399
	8.3.19	Xinjing (Heart meridian) ····································	399
	8.3.20	Feijing (Lung meridian) ·····································	399
	8.3.21	Shenjing (Kidney meridian) ·································	400
	8.3.22	Xiaochang (Small intestine) ·································	400
	8.3.23	Dachang (Large intestine) ···································	401
	8.3.24	Shending (Tip of the small finger) ···························	401
	8.3.25	Sihengwen (Four transverse creases) ·························	402
	8.3.26	Xiaohengwen (Small transverse crease) ·······················	402
	8.3.27	Zhangxiaohengwen (Small palmar transverse crease) ···········	402
	8.3.28	Weijing (Stomach meridian) ·································	403
	8.3.29	Banmen (Major thenar) ·····································	403
	8.3.30	Neilaogong (Inner part of palm) ······························	404
	8.3.31	Xiaotianxin (Small heaven center) ····························	404
	8.3.32	Neibagua ··	405
	8.3.33	Zongjin (Great tendon) ·····································	405

- 8.3.34 Dahengwen (Major transverse crease) ········ 406
- 8.3.35 Zuoduanzheng (Left upright) ········ 406
- 8.3.36 Youduanzheng (Right upright) ········ 407
- 8.3.37 Wuzhijie (Interphalangeal joints of five fingers) ········ 407
- 8.3.38 Ershanmen (Double gate) ········ 407
- 8.3.39 Shangma (Climbing upon the horse) ········ 408
- 8.3.40 Weiling (Powerful and magic) ········ 408
- 8.3.41 Jingning (Essence and tranquility) ········ 409
- 8.3.42 Boyangchi (Pool of Yang on the arm) ········ 409
- 8.3.43 Yiwofeng (A cave of wind) ········ 409
- 8.3.44 Sanguan (Triple pass) ········ 410
- 8.3.45 Liufu (Six Fu-organs) ········ 410
- 8.3.46 Tianheshui (Heaven river water) ········ 411
- 8.4 Commonly encountered infantile diseases ········ 411
  - 8.4.1 Characteristics in treating infantile diseases ········ 411
  - 8.4.2 Cough ········ 413
  - 8.4.3 Fever ········ 416
  - 8.4.4 Asthma ········ 419
  - 8.4.5 Vomiting ········ 421
  - 8.4.6 Diarrhea ········ 424
  - 8.4.7 Anorexia ········ 427
  - 8.4.8 Constipation ········ 429
  - 8.4.9 Night Crying ········ 431
  - 8.4.10 Enuresis ········ 434
  - 8.4.11 Infantile Myogenic Torticollis ········ 436
  - 8.4.12 Infantile subluxation of radial head ········ 437

9 Self-Healthcare Tuina ········ 440

- 9.1 The effect of self-healthcare Tuina on human body ········ 440
- 9.2 The methods of Self-healthcare Tuina ········ 440
  - 9.2.1 Soothing the liver to regulate Qi ········ 440
  - 9.2.2 Tranquilizing the heart and calming the mind ········ 441
  - 9.2.3 Strengthening the spleen and regulating the stomach ········ 443
  - 9.2.4 Dispersing the lung and relieving superficies ········ 444
  - 9.2.5 Strengthening the kidney and benefiting essence ········ 445

推 拿 学

1 总 论

推拿是以中医理论为指导,推拿医生运用推拿手法或借助于一定的推拿工具作用于患者体表的特定部位或穴位来治疗疾病的一种治疗方法,属于中医外治法范畴。推拿学是研究用推拿疗法治疗疾病的一门系统科学,数千年来,推拿医学为人类的卫生保健事业发挥了极其重要的作用。今天在人们重新认识天然药物疗法和非药物疗法的优越性时,推拿这一传统的不药而愈的治疗方法越来越为社会所重视。

1.1 推拿学简史

推拿起源于生活劳动。人类在生活劳动造成跌仆折骨之类的损伤时,就会本能地以手按以止血,摩以消肿止痛。经过漫长的日积月累,终于总结出一些原始的推拿方法,而使之成为人们治疗疾病的常用方法之一。

有关早期推拿的记载,出现在中国上古时期,距今已有3千多年的殷墟文化的甲骨卜辞及以后的长沙马王堆汉墓医书中,甲骨卜辞里不仅有多条按摩师用推拿治疗疾病的记载,而且甲骨卜辞中有许多字还与推拿治疗有关,说明当时的殷人主要治病手段是推拿。另外,马王堆帛简医书中以《五十二病方》涉及推拿治病最多,该书中的推拿疗法有下列两个显著特点:一是记载了推拿发展史上最早的药摩和膏摩;二是推拿时运用了许多富有特色的工具,如用一种"药巾"来治疗某些性功能障碍或进行养生保健。推拿最早最原始的工具是砭石。砭石有很多种类,不同的砭石其功用也不同,推拿工具的使用,使推拿治疗效果更为显著。

秦汉时期是推拿历史发展的重要阶段。据《汉书》记载,我国推拿史上第一部推拿专著《黄帝岐伯按摩十卷》与《黄帝内经》同时问世。从分类来看,此书应以记载保健按摩为主;从医学源流来看,此书与《黄帝内经》应出于同一个医学流派。很可能《黄帝内经》以论病为主将针灸作为治病的主要手段;《黄帝岐伯按摩十卷》则是以养生为主,将推拿作为主要保健方法。因各种原因,本书早已佚失,但在《黄帝内经》中却记载了大量的推拿文献。综观《黄帝内经》全书,可以看出,秦汉时期推拿独特的治疗体系已经形成,这部巨著中许多条文是对殷商以来推拿疗法的理论总结。《黄帝内经》指出了我国推拿发源地在我国中央地区,相当于现今河南洛阳一带。望、闻、问、切诊是推拿学中最重要的诊断方法,将推拿手法运用到切诊中,以加强疾病诊断的准确性,在《黄帝内经》中比比皆是。《黄帝内经》充分肯定了推拿的治疗作用,认为推拿具有行气活血、散寒止痛、疏经通络、退热宁神等作用,同时提出推拿要注意补泻,注重与针灸、药物等其他疗法的协同配合。《黄帝内经》中记载的手法也很丰富,有按、摩、切、扪、循、扪、弹、抓、推、压、屈、伸、摇等方法,这些方法中以按摩二法运用最多,故而当时以按摩称之。《黄帝内经》中还对推拿者提出了要求,认为从事推拿必须要有健康的体魄和强有力的双手。《黄帝内经》中的主要推拿工具是九针中的圆针和提针,圆针用于泻法,提针用于补法。总之,《黄帝内经》对推拿学的贡献和影响,远远不止以上这些。最重要的是,《黄帝内经》奠定了中医基本理论。其中的主要内容,如脏腑经络学说、阴阳五行、气血津液学说、诊断方法、治疗原则等,也都成为推拿学中最重要的指导原则。

汉代名医张仲景所著《金匮要略》中,首次将膏摩疗法列为预防保健方法之一,还介绍了一首用于推拿治疗头风的摩散,方仅附子与盐两味。张仲景在这部以内科为主的传世著作中还详细记载了推拿救治自缢方法,此法被医学界公认为世界上最早的救治缢死的科学记载。汉末名医华佗倡导的"五禽戏",使得导引按摩向仿生学靠拢,为后世提供了一套行之有效的保健方法,其治病善用膏摩,是第一位将膏摩广泛用于临床的医家。

总之,推拿自本能按摩行为,经历漫长岁月的不断积累,至《黄帝岐伯按摩十卷》和《黄帝内经》成书,终于发展成为一门具有独特治疗体系的临床学科,不仅在理论上得到总结和提高,而且经当时名医扁鹊、张仲景、华佗等倡导和运用在临床,也更成熟和广泛,而且富有特色。因此秦汉时期既是推拿独特治疗体系的形成时期,又是推拿发展史上第一个承前启后的鼎盛时期。

隋唐之际,隋太医署首次设立了按摩博士。唐太宗则在隋代已有的基础上,建立了规模更大,设置更加完备的太医署,并在其中设立了按摩科,将推拿医生分为按摩博士、按摩师和按摩工,按摩博士在按摩师和按摩工的辅助下,教按摩生使用按摩的方法。自我推拿在这一时期得到了广泛的重视,在葛洪《肘后备急方》、孙思邈《备急千金要方》中都记载了许多自我推拿的方法。巢元方在《诸病源候论》的每一章节,均附有养生导引法,尤其重视摩腹养生之术。自我推拿的广泛开展,说明推拿疗法开始注重预防保健,注意发挥病人与疾病作斗争的主观能动性。药物与手法相得益彰的按摩疗法又有了很大发展。葛洪十分重视膏摩的运用,是第一位系统论述膏摩,使膏摩证、法、方、药齐备的医家。《肘后方》记载了葛洪常备膏摩方有8首,这些膏方多出名医之手。《外台秘要》在《刘涓子鬼遗方》膏摩催产的基础上,又增添了盐摩与汤摩两种催产方法。该书中罗列诸多膏摩名方,且多有出处。这一时期推拿治疗范围也逐渐扩大,如《唐六典》说推拿可除八疾,即风、寒、暑、湿、饥、饱、劳、逸。推拿也正是这一时期传入朝鲜、日本、印度、阿拉伯及欧洲。

宋金元时期,推拿运用范围更加广泛,并注重手法的分析。《圣济总录》首列"按摩"专论,对按摩疗法进行总结和归纳,是现存最早最完整的推拿专论。在这一时期,膏摩疗法又有了新的发展。《太平圣惠方》记载了六首治疗目疾的摩顶膏,为膏摩治疗眼病的最早记载,该书还首次记载了摩腰膏,是历代医书中记载膏摩方最多的医书,对后世膏摩发展影响巨大。金元四大家中,对推拿介绍最多的,首推张从正。他在其著作《儒门事亲》中将按摩列为汗法之一。《世医得效方》中所载肩关节脱位的坐凳架梯法、髋关节脱位的倒吊复位法和脊椎骨折的悬吊复位法等都可以替代拔伸手法,是推拿史上的重大发明。

明清时期,是推拿发展史上的又一个鼎盛时期。小儿推拿专著纷纷面世,如四明陈氏的《保婴神术》乃现存最早的推拿专著,为杨继洲之《针灸大成》所收录;太医龚云林的《小儿推拿方脉活婴秘旨全书》(又称《小儿推拿全书》)属单行本流行最早者;周于藩的《小儿推拿秘诀》描述小儿推拿八法最为精彩;熊应雄的《小儿推拿广意》附录儿科常用方药,被誉为清代最善之本;夏禹铸的《幼科铁镜》匠心独运,与诸书存异处甚多,更作"推拿代药赋",令人耳目一新;骆如龙的《幼科推拿秘书》最为详细,条理清楚,是小儿推拿之入门捷径;徐谦光的《推拿三字经》朗朗上口,烂熟于胸,必临症应手;张振鋆的《厘正按摩要术》博采众家之长,独创体例,成为一本集光绪十四年之前小儿推拿疗法大成之专著,屡经翻印。该书首次提出小儿推拿八法,即"按、摩、掐、揉、推、运、搓、摇",这标志着小儿推拿独特治疗体系的形成。其次,成人推拿也得到了很大发展,可谓百花齐放,流派纷呈,诸如正骨推拿、点穴推拿、一指禅推拿、眼科推拿、外科推拿、内功推拿、保健推拿,等等。

民国时期,是推拿发展史上承上启下,形成流派的关键阶段,这些流派包括一指禅推拿、经络脏腑推拿、点穴推拿、腹诊推拿、内功推拿、滚法推拿、胃病推拿等。这些推拿学术流派的发展多是"以师带徒,口授心传"的方式继承和传授,并且有着独特的见解。这一时期出版的一些推拿学术著作图文并茂,通俗易懂。1933年出版的黄汉如著《黄氏医话》是目前见到的第一本推拿医话。该书记载了作者数十年间运用推拿治疗疾病的验案和心得,介绍了一指禅推拿的来源和特点,可惜未及具体手法,使后学者无法窥得其中奥秘之处。

1.2 推拿学的发展和研究

中华人民共和国成立后,推拿医学进入了一个全面发展的新时期。

第一,推拿古籍得到全面的发掘和整理,并出版了大量推拿新著。这一阶段整理再版了大量推拿专著。推拿新著有以基础理论与临证知识相结合的通俗著作;有以临证专科形式出现;有以流派和独到的经验见长;有专论手法,功法也有集大成之类的巨制。综观这些著作,其共同特点是推拿理论的科学性和逻辑性增强,在推拿原理方面有所突破,增加现代研究的佐证,在疾病的治疗方面多结合西医学的诊断和解剖知识。

第二,推拿实践及临床经验的总结日趋科学化。推拿医师已掌握了一整套辨证论治的理论,理、法、方、术,择善而从之。全国各类期刊发表了数以千计的推拿论文,对推拿各方面进行了科学总结,对推拿临床起到了重要的指导作用。

第三,推拿教学体系日趋完善。自1956年10月上海卫生学校开办了推拿训练班起,推拿教学就从过去师带徒形式走上了正规教育的途径。全国各中医院校相继成立推拿专业,完善推拿专业专科、本科、硕士研究生和外国留学生教育体系,为中医推拿培养了大量的高级人才。随着推拿学科的发展,教材也分为《推拿学基础》、《推拿治疗学》、《推拿手法学》、《推拿练功学》、《小儿推拿学》等课程。

第四,推拿科研发展迅速。从20世纪50年代起,推拿科研人员运用现代科学和现代医学知识对推拿作用机制进行了广泛的临床和实验研究,取得了令人兴奋的进展。如运用神经生理学中闸门控制学说,较为完满地解释了推拿镇痛原理;推拿前后血液及淋巴管液循环速度差异明显,可能是推拿消肿化瘀的作用原理之一;推拿降血压,效果稳定,推拿后血液中 5-HT 含量增加;捏脊疗法明显促进小肠的吸收功能等。

第五,总结和创造出许多新的推拿疗法,如耳穴推拿、足穴推拿、第二掌骨推拿法、运动推拿、推拿麻醉等。

1.3 怎样学习推拿

推拿学是一门理论性和实践性都比较强的中医临床学科。推拿医生不仅要通晓中西医基础知识、诊断及辨证论治方法、推拿专业理论知识,而且还要具备能适应推拿临床工作的身体素质和熟练的手法操作技能。所以推拿学习者,除了要学习中西医基础理论课程,还要系统学习专业课,并且要进行严格的身体素质锻炼和手法操作技能的训练。

在医学基础理论方面,要特别强调中医的阴阳五行、脏腑经络、营卫气血、病因病机、四诊八纲、辨证论治和西医的解剖、生理、病理生理、病理解剖、物理诊断等内容的学习。尤其要熟知人体的解剖结构、运动生理、神经节段和十四经络的循行、常用穴的位置、作用等,这些在推拿临床尤其有实用价值。

在专业技能方面,首先要根据本书"练功"卷所介绍的常用功法及其练习方法,按步骤进行认真练功。在练功过程中,不仅要注意力量、耐力、柔韧性等身体素质的锻炼,而且还要加强心理素质的培养。即在锻炼身体素质的同时,培养自己吃苦耐劳、坚韧不拔的精神,为将来长期从事推拿工作打下良好的基础。其次,在老师的指导下,认真学习和练习本教材手法篇中所介绍的各种手法,严格按照动作要求循序渐进、持之以恒、保质保量、按步骤地完成米袋练习、人体练习与常见病操作练习三个基本阶段的训练。第三,认真学习本教材有关推拿治疗的内容,并随时找机会临证锻炼,理论与实践相结合将大大提高学习效果。

思 考 题

- 推拿体系形成于何时?
- 唐朝中国推拿的发展有什么特点?

2 推拿学的作用原理

2.1 调整阴阳

人体内部的一切矛盾斗争与变化均可以阴阳概括,气血不和、营卫失调等病理变化均属于阴阳失调的范畴,阴阳的失调是疾病的内在根本,贯穿于一切疾病发生、发展的始终。人体在疾病过程中,会出现各种各样的病理变化。无论外感病或内伤病,其病理变化的基本规律不外乎阴阳的偏盛或偏衰。推拿要根据证候的属性来调节阴阳的偏盛或偏衰,使机体转归于"阴平阳秘",恢复其正常的生理功能,从而达到治愈疾病的目的。这种调整阴阳的功能,主要是通过经络、气血而起作用的,因为经络遍布全身,内属脏腑,外络于肢节,沟通和联系人体所有的脏腑、器官、孔窍皮毛、筋肉、骨骼等组织,再通过气血在经络中运行,组成了整体的联系。推拿手法作用于局部,在局部通经络、行气血、濡筋骨,并通过气血、经络影响到脏器及其它部位。如对肠蠕动亢进者,在腹部和背部使用适当的手法,可使亢进受到抑制而恢复正常;反之,肠蠕动功能减退者,亦可通过手法促其蠕动,恢复正常。

2.2 补虚泻实

一般说来,人体物质之不足或某一组织功能低下则为虚,邪气有余或某一组织功能亢进则为实。而推拿可以通过手法作用于人体某一部位,使人体气血津液、脏腑经络起到相应的变化,补虚泻实,达到治疗的目的。

现代生理研究表明:对某一组织来说,弱刺激能活跃、兴奋其生理功能,强刺激能抑制其生理功能。临床上治疗脾胃虚的患者,在脾俞、胃俞、中脘、气海等穴用轻柔的一指禅推法进行较长时间的有节律的刺激,可取得好的疗效;胃肠痉挛患者,则在其背部相应的俞穴,用点、按等较强的手法作短时间刺激,痉挛即可缓解。对高血压病的治疗也是如此,由于肝阳上亢而致的高血压病,可在桥弓穴用推、按、揉、拿等手法作重刺激,平肝潜阳,降低血压;由于痰湿内阻而致的高血压病,则可在腹部及背部脾俞、肾俞用推摩等手法,作较长时间的轻刺激,健脾化湿,从而降低血压。以上例子可以看出,推拿虽无直接补、泻物质进入体内,但从本质上看,依靠手法在体表一定的部位刺激,可起到促进机体功能或抑制其亢进的作用。

在推拿治疗中,手法的频率和方向对补虚泻实亦起着重要的作用,手法的频率在一定范围内变化,仅是量的变化,但超过一定范围的变化,则出现了从量变到质变的飞跃,如一般频率的一指禅推法,仅具有舒通经络、调和营卫的作用,但高频率的一指禅推法则具有活血消肿,托脓排毒的作用,临床上常用来治疗痈疖等疾病。因高频率的手法,能量扩散少,能有效地渗透于组织中起到"清、消、托"等作用,称之为泻,反之则为补。手法的方向在特定的治疗部位有不同的补泻作用,如在腹部摩腹,手法操作方向与治疗部位移动的方向为顺时针时,有明显的泻下作用;若手法的操作方向为逆时针,而治疗部位的移动方向为顺时针时,则有增加肠胃的消化功能,起到补的作用。

2.3 活血化瘀

瘀血是因血行失度而使机体某一局部的血液凝聚而形成的一种病理产物,而这一产物在机体内又会成为某些疾病的致病因素,推拿可以通过适当的手法消除瘀血。

2.3.1 促进血液流通

现代医学研究已表明微循环障碍是形成瘀血的主要原因之一。现代医学认为,促使血液流动的一个主要因素就是动脉与静脉之间保持了一定的压力差,如果这一个压力差达不到一定的数值,血液流动减慢,甚至停留,形成瘀血。推拿手法虽然作用于体外,但手法的压力能传递到血管壁,使血管壁有节律地被压下、复原,在压下时,在按压处的近侧端,由于心脏的压力和血管壁的弹性,局部压力急骤增高,急速放松压迫,则血液以短暂的较大的冲击力向远端流去,由于动脉内的压力较高,不容易压瘪,而静脉内又有静脉瓣的存在,血液不能逆流,故实际上是驱动微循环内的血液从小动脉流向小静脉。由于血液中物质的交换是在微循环过程中完成的,故推拿对微循环中血液流通的促进意义重大。这是其活血化瘀作用的一个方面,有人通过实验发现在肩部进行推拿时,手指的甲皱微循环明显加快,对流速提高有明显的意义,可以促使指端血管容积增加,而这一容积的增加,在推拿停止后一段时间开始出现。

2.3.2 改善血液流变

瘀血与血液的流变有很大的关系,血液的粘稠度越高,越不容易流动,血液的粘稠度并不是固定不变的,它与血液流动速度有关,血液流速越快,粘稠度越低,流速越慢,粘稠度越高,当流速减低到一定程度时,血液就会聚集、凝固。而推拿通过手法挤压的作用,可以提高流速,改善血液的流变。现代实验研究已证明,推拿对瘀血症患者的血液流变有一定的影响,无论是在高切速下,还是低切速下,全血比的粘稠度均有一定程度的下降,值得注意的是红细胞的变形能力亦得到增强,血液流速得到明显提高。血液成分的改变对血液流变亦会产生一定的影响,推拿的研究表明,推拿之后,健康人白细胞总数增加,淋巴细胞比例升高,白细胞的噬菌能力有较大幅度的增强。对贫血患者的推拿显示,红细胞及血红蛋白数量增加。

2.3.3 降低血流阻力

血流阻力是血液流通的一个重要环节,与小血管管径有密切的关系。根据流体力学计算,血管的阻力与管径的四次方成反比,因此,即使血管管径的微小变化,亦可较大幅度地降低血液流通的阻力。推拿手法的直接作用,可以松弛血管的平滑肌,扩大管径。另外,研究亦表明,通过使用手法一方面降低交感神经的兴奋性,另一方面促进血液中游离肾上腺素、去甲肾上腺素的分解、排泄,从而促进小动脉管径扩张,而降低血流阻力。

由于手法对躯体外表的压力和手法操作时产生的摩擦力,可大量地消耗和祛除血管壁上的脂类物质,从而对恢复血管壁的弹性,改善管道的通畅性,降低血流阻力起到良好的作用。研究已显示,推拿同时改善了淋巴循环。

2.3.4 改善心脏功能

心脏有节律的搏动是形成血液循环的主要因素,心脏每搏输出量是衡量循环功能的主要标志,研究表明,通过适当部位的推拿,可以改善患者的心功能,有人选用内关、心俞两穴进行推拿,发现推拿后心率减慢,心肌舒张期延长,血液灌注也随之增多,提高了心肌的供氧,左心室舒张末压降低,左心室收缩功能明显增强。

2.3.5 促进微循环建立

在机体中,血管网是血液与组织进行物质交换的主要部位,在安静情况下,平均仅有 8%～16% 的毛细血管是开放的。在推拿前后有人进行了对比,发现推拿局部毛细血管的开放量增加。据此又进一步进行动物实验,对家兔跟腱切断再缝合,缝合后行局部推拿治疗,发现推拿局部毛细血管的开放量最高增加到 32%,发现治疗组跟腱断端有大量小血管生成,形成新的血管网,而对照组动物仅跟腱周围组织中有一些管壁增厚并塌陷的小血管,血管中还有许多血栓形成,呈瘀血状态。由于有新的血管网的建立,推拿组断裂跟腱的修复较未推拿组快。

2.4 舒筋通络

肌肉的紧张直至痉挛、经络不通、局部麻木不仁、疼痛是推拿临床的常见症状。推拿可以通过舒筋通络,消除上述症状,从而起到一定的治疗作用。

在组织损伤后,损伤部位可以发出疼痛刺激,通过人体正常的反射作用,该刺激可以使机体有关组织处于警觉状态,肌肉收缩,紧张直至痉挛是这一状态的表现,其目的是为了减少肢体的活动,防止过度地运动而牵拉受损处,从而引起疼痛或再损伤。此时如不及时治疗或治疗不彻底,肌肉紧张、痉挛不能得到较好的缓解,痉挛的肌肉压迫穿行于其间的血管,致使肌肉的供血量明显减少,而痉挛状态的肌肉所需的血量远较松弛状态的肌肉为高,因此,代谢产物大量堆积,引起炎性疼痛,肌肉的长期的、慢性的缺血、缺氧,使损伤组织形成不同程度的结缔组织增生,以至粘连,纤维化或疤痕化,长期发出有害刺激,从而加重疼痛和肌肉的紧张、痉挛,形成恶性循环,推拿能打破这一恶性循环,加速损伤组织的修复和恢复。

生理研究表明,调节肌肉张力的神经组织有位于肌腹的肌梭感受器和位于肌腱的腱梭感受器,前者兴奋时可使肌肉加强收缩,后者兴奋时可抑制肌肉收缩。运动生理研究证实,受累的肌肉充分拉长后可使腱梭感受器兴奋。推拿可通过运动关节类手法拉长受损的肌肉,从而消除肌紧张、痉挛。

局部组织温度的升高,亦可使肌紧张、痉挛得到缓解,《黄帝内经》中有"按之热气至"的记载,实验显示,推拿后,局部温度有明显的提高,而其他相关部位温度亦升高了。

推拿还可起到镇静、镇痛作用,缓解疼痛导致的肌紧张、痉挛,达到舒筋通络的目的。

推拿极有效的镇痛作用目前在推拿临床上得到公认,推拿可以通过提高机体痛阈和减低刺激量从而达到止痛作用。

推拿的现代研究证实,推拿的舒筋通络作用还表现在对肌电图的影响,对颈、腰、腿痛患者推拿治疗后,经肌电图检查证实紧张性肌电活动已明显减少或消失。

2.5 理筋整复

因各种原因,造成的有关组织解剖位置异常的一系列疾病,都可以通过手法外力的直接作用得到纠正,而使经络顺接,气血运行流畅。

推拿对关节脱位者,可以通过运动关节类手法使关节回复到正常的解剖位置,如肩关节的脱位,可嘱患者取坐位,作跨肩关节的拔伸,即可令肩关节回复正常;骶髂关节半脱位者,因关节滑膜的嵌顿挤压和局部软组织的牵拉而出现疼痛,可通过斜扳、伸屈髋膝等被动运动,将脱位整复,疼痛亦随之减轻、消失。又如临床上常见的腰椎间盘突出症患者,由于突出物对神经根的压迫而引起腰部疼痛及下肢的放射痛,应用强迫直腿抬高、斜扳、牵引等手法,可以改变突出物与神经根的位置,从而解除突出物对神经根的压迫,消除疼痛。

对软组织错位者,推拿也可以通过手法外力作用使之回复正常。如肌腱滑脱者,在滑脱部位可以摸到条索样隆起,关节活动严重障碍,推拿中可使用弹拨或推扳手法使其回复正常。肌肉肌腱、韧带完全断裂者,必须用手术缝合才能重建,但对部分断裂者,可使用适当的理筋手法,使组织抚顺,然后加以固定。

总之,推拿可以通过手法直接力的作用进行理筋整复,使各种组织各守其位,经络关节通顺,从而达到治疗作用。

思 考 题

- 推拿的作用原理有哪些?
- 推拿是怎样起到活血化瘀作用的?

3 经络腧穴

3.1 经络腧穴的基本理论

经络腧穴是组成人体的重要结构，与推拿学有着密切的联系。推拿疗法针对病位讲究点线面结合运用，"点"指相应腧穴，"线"指相应经络，而"面"便指相应的经筋及皮部。

经络，是经脉和络脉的总称。经，有路径的意思，经脉是经络系统的纵行干线。络，有网络的意思，络脉是经脉的分支，纵横交错，网络全身，无处不至。经络是运行全身气血，联络脏腑支节，沟通上下内外，调节体内各部分的通路。通过经络在全身有规律的循行和错综复杂的联络交会，把人体的五脏六腑、四肢百骸、五官九窍、皮肉筋脉等组织器官联结成一个有机的统一整体。

经络是由经脉和络脉组成，其中经脉包括十二经脉和奇经八脉，为经络系统的主要部分。络脉包括别络、浮络和孙络。别络较大，共有十五。其中十二经脉与任、督二脉各有一支别络，再加上脾之大络，合为"十五别络"。别络有本经别走邻经之意，其功能是加强表里阴阳两经的联系与调节作用。络脉中行于浅表部位的称为"浮络"。络脉最细小的分支称为"孙络"。此外，还有十二经别、十二经筋和十二皮部。十二经别是十二经脉别出的正经，加强了十二经脉在体内的联系，并能通达某些正经未能行经的器官与形体部位，以补正经之不足。十二经筋，是十二经脉循行部位上分布的筋肉系统的总称，有连缀百骸、维络周身、主司关节运动的作用。十二皮部，是十二经脉在体表一定皮肤部位的反应区。由于十二经筋与十二皮部的分区，基本上和十二经脉在体表的循行部位一致，因此它们都是按照十二经脉命名的。

腧穴是人体脏腑经络之气输注于体表的特殊部位。腧与"输"相通，有转输的含义，穴有孔隙的意思。

人体的经络和腧穴是密切相连的，腧穴与经络、脏腑和气血密切相关。经穴分别归属于各经脉，经脉又隶属于一定的脏腑，这样，腧穴—经络—脏腑成为一个不可分割的整体。当人体的脏腑发生病变时，在相应的腧穴上就会有一定的反应；同样，通过推拿手法刺激一定的腧穴，使其信息通过经络传导到相应的脏腑，就可以改变脏腑的病理状态，达到治疗作用。

3.1.1 十二经脉

名称分类

十二经脉是手三阳经、足三阳经和手三阴经、足三阴经总称，是经络系统的主体。

十二经脉的名称是根据各经所联系内脏的阴阳属性及其在肢体循行位置的不同而予以命名。阳经属腑,行于四肢的外侧;阴经属脏,行于四肢的内侧。手经行于上肢,足经行于下肢。十二经脉对称地分布于头面、四肢和躯干,纵贯全身。

四肢部:阴经隶属于五脏,行于四肢的内侧,太阴在前,少阴在后,厥阴在中;阳经隶属于六腑,行于四肢的外侧,阳明在前,太阳在后,少阳在中。躯干部:足三阳经分布于躯干的外侧,足三阴经分布于胸腹部。手六经中,手三阳经过肩上颈部,除手厥阴在侧胸部有较短的分布外,手太阴、手少阴由胸内直接出于腋下。头面部:阳经都上行头面部而联系五官,但分布复杂,规律不明显;阴经多行于头颈的深部而联系喉咙、舌、目等器官。

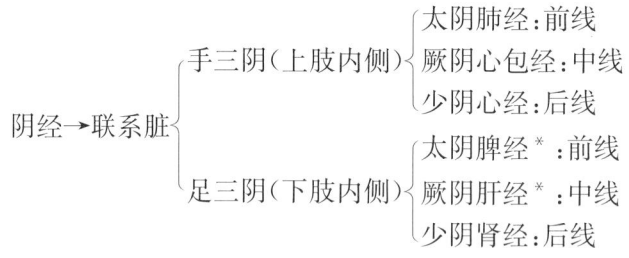

$$
阴经→联系脏 \begin{cases} 手三阴(上肢内侧) \begin{cases} 太阴肺经:前线 \\ 厥阴心包经:中线 \\ 少阴心经:后线 \end{cases} \\ 足三阴(下肢内侧) \begin{cases} 太阴脾经^*:前线 \\ 厥阴肝经^*:中线 \\ 少阴肾经:后线 \end{cases} \end{cases}
$$

* 小腿下半部和足背部,肝经在前,脾经在中线。至内踝上八寸处交叉之后,脾经在前,肝经在中线。

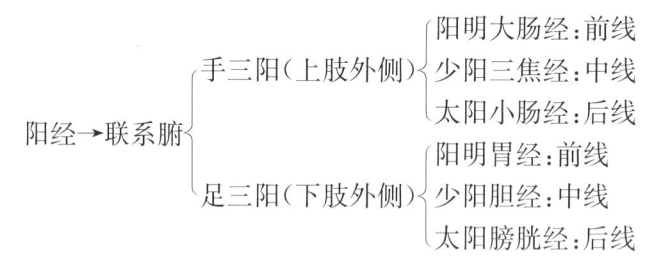

$$
阳经→联系腑 \begin{cases} 手三阳(上肢外侧) \begin{cases} 阳明大肠经:前线 \\ 少阳三焦经:中线 \\ 太阳小肠经:后线 \end{cases} \\ 足三阳(下肢外侧) \begin{cases} 阳明胃经:前线 \\ 少阳胆经:中线 \\ 太阳膀胱经:后线 \end{cases} \end{cases}
$$

走向和交接规律

手足三阴三阳经脉的走向和相互交接的规律是:手三阴从胸走手,交手三阳;手三阳从手走头,交足三阳;足三阳从头走足,交足三阴,足三阴从足走腹,交手三阴。这样就构成了一个"阴阳相贯,如环无端"的循环径路。

表里关系及流注次序

十二经脉分别络属于相应的脏腑,从而构成了脏腑阴阳的表里相合关系,即:手阳明大肠经与手太阴肺经为表里;手少阳三焦经与手厥阴心包经为表里;手太阳小肠经与手少阴心经为表里;足阳明胃经与足太阴脾经为表里;足少阳胆经与足厥阴肝经为表里;足太阳膀胱经与足少阴肾经为表里,构成"六合"。在循行路线上,凡具有表里关系的经脉,均循行分布于四肢内外两个侧面的相对位置(足厥阴肝经与足太阴脾经在下肢内踝上八寸处,交叉变换前后位置),并在手或足相互交接。十二经脉存在着这种表里关系,所以在生理上是彼此相通的,在病变时也是相互影响的。

十二经脉分布在人体内外,经脉中的气血运行是循环贯注的。即从手太阴肺经开始,依次传至足厥阴肝经,再传至手太阴肺经,首尾相贯,如环无端。流注规律是:手太阴肺经→手阳明大肠经→足阳明胃经→足太阴脾经→手少阴心经→手太阳小肠经→足太阳膀胱经→足少阴肾经→手厥阴心包经→手少阳三焦经→足少阳胆经→足厥阴肝经。

3.1.2 奇经八脉

奇经八脉是督脉、任脉、冲脉、带脉、阴跷脉、阳跷脉、阴维脉和阳维脉的总称。由于它们与脏腑没有直接相互"络属"的关系，分布不像十二经脉那样规则，相互之间也没有表里配合，与十二正经不同，故称"奇经"。

奇经八脉交叉贯穿于十二经脉之间，具有加强经脉之间的联系，调节十二经脉气血的作用。当十二经脉中气血满溢时，则流注于奇经八脉，蓄以备用；不足时，也可由奇经给予补充。奇经与肝、肾等脏及女子胞、脑、髓等奇恒之府的关系较为密切，这对奇经的生理病理均有一定意义。

督脉 为阳脉之海。主要功能是统摄全身阳气及维系人身之气。十二经脉中的手三阳与足三阳均会于督脉，故有调整和振奋全身阳气的重要作用；同时因督脉由下向上入脑，贯脊属肾，故它对脑、脊髓和肾的功能有密切影响。

任脉 为阴脉之海，三阴经脉、阴维脉与冲脉均会于任脉，故有总调人身阴经经气的功能。另外，任脉起于胞中，与女子妊娠有关，又称为"任主胞胎"。

冲脉 总领诸经气血的要冲，能调节十二经的气血。故冲脉有"十二经脉之海"之称。冲脉同妇女的月经有密切联系，又称为"血海"。

带脉 有约束躯干部各条经脉，使经气通畅的功能。循行于下肢的经脉都受带脉约束，故对这些经脉具有统带作用，所以有"诸脉皆属于带"的说法。

阴跷脉、阳跷脉 跷，有轻健跷捷的意思。阳跷脉主一身左右之阳；阴跷脉主一身左右之阴。同时还有濡养眼目，司眼睑的开合和下肢运动的作用。

阴维脉、阳维脉 维，有维系的意思。阴维脉维系手、足三阴经；阳维脉维系手、足三阳经。

3.1.3 十五络脉

十二经脉和任、督二脉各自别出一络，加上脾之大络，共计十五条，称为"十五络"。它们的作用主要是加强互为表里的两条经的沟通、联系，统率其它的络脉，灌渗气血以营养全身。

十五络脉的分布特点是：十二经脉的别络从本经的络穴处别出后，均走向其表里的经脉（阴经别络于阳经，阳经别络于阴经）；任脉的别络散布于腹部，以沟通腹部的经气，督脉别络散布于头部，别走足太阳膀胱经，以沟通背部的经气；脾之大络散布于胸胁。

此外，还有孙络与浮络。孙络是从别络分出的细小络脉。分布在皮肤表层能看到的络脉称为浮络。它们难以数计，遍布全身，其作用主要是输布气血于经筋和皮部。

3.1.4 十二经别

十二经别，是十二正经离合出入的别行部分，故称"经别"。它们的作用主要是加强人体表里、内外及脏腑间的联系，扩大了经穴主治范围。

十二经别的分布特点是：十二经别多从肘、膝以上的正经别出，经过躯干，深入内脏，在头、项浅出体表后，阴经经别合于相表里的阳经经脉，阳经经别合于本经而上抵头面，故有"六合"之称。足太阳、足少阴经别，从腘窝分出，入走肾与膀胱，上出于项，合于足太阳膀胱经。足少阳、足厥阴经别从下肢分出，行至毛际，入走肝胆，上系于目，合于足少阳胆经。足阳明、足太阴经别从髀部分出，入走脾胃，上出鼻颏，合于足阳明胃经。手太阳、手太阴经别从腋部分出，入走心与小肠，上出目内眦，合于手太阳小肠经。手少阳、手厥阴经别分别从所属的正经分出，进入胸中，入走三焦，上出耳后，合于手少阳三焦经。手阳明、手太阴经别分别从所属的正经分出，入走肺与大肠，上出缺盆，合于手阳明大肠经。手足三阴经腧穴之所以能治头面范围的疾病，主要是因为经别与经脉有其内在联系。例如偏、正头痛，可取太渊、列缺治疗。

3.1.5 十二经筋

十二经筋，即筋肉系统，包括筋膜、肌腱、肌肉等，是十二经脉之气结聚散络于肌肉关节的体系。其主要作用是联结筋肉、骨骼，保持人体正常的运动功能。

十二经筋是十二经脉的外周连属部分，十二经筋的分布与十二经脉的体表通路基本一致，其循行走向都是从四肢末端走向头身，行于体表，不入内脏，结于关节、骨骼部。其规律为：手三阳经筋起于手指，循臑外上行结于角（头部）；手三阴经筋起于手指，循臑内上行结于贲（胸部）；足三阳经筋起于足趾，行股外上行结于𬵪（面部）；足三阴经筋起于足趾，循股内上行结于阴器（腹部）。另外，各经在循行中，还在踝、膝、股、髀、腕、肘、臂、腋、肩、颈等关节或筋肉丰盛处结聚，特别是足厥阴经筋，除结于阴器外，并能总络诸筋。十二经筋是筋肉受相应经络支配的部分，其主要作用是约束骨骼，利于关节屈伸活动，保持人体正常的运动功能。经筋的病变，多表现为拘挛、强直和抽搐。

经筋除附于骨骼外，还满布于躯体和四肢的浅部，因此经筋对周身各部分的脏器组织还能起到一定的保护作用。

从上述经筋的分布和联结的情况来看，可见经筋同肌肉系统的关系是相当密切的。这就说明经筋能约束骨骼，利于关节的屈伸活动。

3.1.6 十二皮部

十二皮部是十二经脉机能活动反映于体表的部位，也是络脉之气的散布所在。

十二皮部的分布区域，是以十二经脉在体表的分布范围为依据的。由于皮部居于人体的最外层，是机体的卫外屏障。当机体卫外功能失常时，病邪可通过皮部深入络脉、经脉以至脏腑，这是外邪由表入里的一个方面。反之，当机体内脏有病时，亦可通过经脉、络脉而反应于皮部。如脾脏有病、消化不良的患者，多在足太阴脾经的皮部出现皮损（真皮上部血管变化、血管周围炎性浸润等）。同样经脉或内脏有病变时可取皮部进行治疗。推拿手法在皮部进行刺激，可以通过络脉、经脉，起到对内脏的调整作用，如用推拿手法作用于手太阴肺经的皮部，可以有效地治疗胸闷、咳嗽等与肺脏相关的病症。由此可见，皮部与内脏也是密切相关的。

3.2 常用腧穴

腧穴又称穴位、穴道。"腧"具有转输和输注的意思,"腧穴"具有空隙和聚集的意思。凡是有一定的名称和一定部位,按照十四经排列的腧穴也称为"经穴";没有列入十四经,而从临床实践中逐渐发现的经验穴,称为经外奇穴;无一定名称和位置,是以压痛点而定穴的称为阿是穴,又称天应穴。

腧穴的治疗作用不只限于局部或浅表,常可治疗邻近、远端或体内的疾病。

取穴时可以运用人体体表标志、骨度分寸、指寸法等不同的方法。取穴正确与否能直接影响治疗效果。在临床上除用以上方法取穴外,往往还可以根据特殊体表和肢体活动时所出现肌肉皱纹、筋腱关节凹陷等标志取穴,这就要求我们除了熟悉一些显露的体表标志外还要对骨性、肌肉、筋腱标志进行观察、揣摩,以掌握骨骼、关节、肌肉、筋腱的隆突凹陷等特点。

选穴和配穴可依据腧穴的主治和所属经络而采用邻近、远端、前后、上下、左右等方法。常用腧穴见表3-1。

表3-1 常用腧穴手法功能主治

经络	穴名	位置	主治	常用手法
手太阴肺经	中府	前正中线旁开6寸,平第一肋间隙处	咳喘、胸闷、肩背痛	一指禅推、按、揉、摩
	尺泽	肘横纹中,肱二头肌腱桡侧	肘臂挛痛、咳喘、胸胁胀痛、小儿惊风	按、揉、拿
	孔最	在尺泽与太渊连线上,腕横纹上7寸	咳嗽、咯血、音哑、咽喉痛、肘臂痛	按、揉、拿
	列缺	桡骨茎突上方,腕横纹上1.5寸	咳嗽、气急、头项强痛、牙痛	一指禅推、按、揉
	太渊	腕横纹桡侧端,桡动脉桡侧凹陷中	咳嗽、气喘、乳胀、咽喉痛、手腕痛	按、揉、掐
	鱼际	第一掌骨中点,赤白肉际	胸背痛、头痛、眩晕、喉痛、发热恶寒	按、揉、掐
	少商	拇指桡侧指甲角旁约0.1寸	中风昏仆、手指挛痛、小儿惊风	掐
手阳明大肠经	合谷	手背,第一、二掌骨之间,约平第二掌骨中点处	头痛、牙痛、发热、喉痛、指挛、臂痛、口眼㖞斜	拿、按、揉
	阳溪	腕背横纹桡侧,两筋之间	头痛、耳鸣、齿痛、咽喉肿痛、目赤、手腕痛	掐、按、拿、揉
	偏历	在阳溪与曲池的连线上,阳溪上3寸处	鼻衄、目赤、耳聋、耳鸣、手臂酸痛、喉痛、水肿	按、揉、拿
	温溜	在阳溪与曲池的连线上,阳溪上5寸	腹痛、呃逆、喉舌痛、头痛	一指禅推、按、掐、拿

续表

经络	穴名	位置	主治	常用手法
手阳明大肠经	手三里	曲池穴下2寸	肘挛、屈伸不利、手臂麻木酸痛	拿、按、揉、一指禅推
	曲池	屈肘,当肘横纹外端凹陷中	发热、高血压、手臂肿痛、肘痛、上肢瘫痪	拿、按、揉
	肩髃	肩峰前下方,举臂时呈凹陷处	肩膀痛、肩关节活动障碍、偏瘫	一指禅推、按、揉
	迎香	鼻翼旁0.5寸,鼻唇沟中	鼻炎、鼻塞、口眼㖞斜	掐、按、揉、一指禅推
足阳明胃经	四白	目正视,瞳孔直下,当眶下孔凹陷中	口眼㖞斜、目赤痛痒	按、揉、一指禅推
	地仓	口角旁0.4寸	流涎、口眼㖞斜	一指禅推、按、揉
	大迎	下颌角前1.3寸骨陷中	口噤、牙痛	掐、按
	颊车	下颌角前上方一横指凹陷中,咀嚼时咬肌隆起处	口眼㖞斜、牙痛、颊肿	一指禅推、按、揉
	下关	颧弓与下颌切迹之间的凹陷中,合口有孔,张口即闭	面瘫、牙痛	一指禅推、按、揉
	头维	额角发际直上0.5寸	头痛	抹、按、揉、扫散法
	人迎	喉结旁开1.5寸	咽喉肿痛、喘息、瘰疬颈肿、气闷	拿、缠
	水突	人迎穴下1寸,胸锁乳突肌的前缘	胸满咳喘、项强	拿、缠
	缺盆	锁骨上窝中央,前正中线旁开4寸	胸满喘咳、项强	按、弹拨
	天枢	脐旁2寸	腹泻、便秘、腹痛、月经不调	揉、摩、一指禅推
	髀关	髂前上棘与髌骨外缘连线上,平臀沟外	腰腿痛、下肢麻木痿软、筋挛急、屈伸不利	按、拿、弹拨、捻
	伏兔	髌骨外上缘上6寸	膝痛冷麻、下肢瘫痪	滚、按、揉
	梁丘	髌骨外上缘上2寸	膝痛冷麻	滚、按、点、拿
	犊鼻	髌骨下缘,髌韧带外侧凹陷中	膝关节酸痛、活动不便	点、按
	足三里	犊鼻穴下3寸,胫骨前棘外一横指处	腹痛、腹泻、便秘、下肢冷麻、高血压	按、点、一指禅推
	上巨虚	足三里穴下3寸	夹脐痛、腹泻、下肢痿痹	拿、滚、按、揉
	下巨虚	上巨虚穴下3寸	小腹痛、腰脊痛、乳痛、下肢痿痹	拿、滚、按、揉

续表

经络	穴名	位置	主治	常用手法
足阳明胃经	丰隆	外膝眼与外侧踝尖连线中点	头痛、咳嗽、肢肿、便秘、狂痫、下肢痿痹	一指禅推、按、揉
	解溪	足背踝关节横纹中央,拇长伸肌腱与趾长伸肌腱之间	踝关节扭伤、足趾麻木	按、拿、掐、点
	冲阳	解溪穴下1.5寸,足背最高处,有动脉应手	口眼㖞斜、面肿、上齿痛、胃痛、足缓不收、狂痫	按、揉、点、掐
足太阴脾经	太白	第一跖骨小头后缘,赤白肉际	胃痛、腹胀、肠鸣、泄泻、便秘、痔瘘	掐、按、揉
	公孙	第一跖骨底前缘,赤白肉际	胃痛、呕吐、食不化、腹痛、泄泻、痢疾	掐、按、揉
	三阴交	内踝上3寸,胫骨内侧面的中央	失眠、腹胀纳呆、遗尿、小便不利、妇科病	按、点、拿
	地机	阴陵泉下3寸	腹痛、泄泻、水肿、小便不利、遗精	拿、按、揉
	阴陵泉	胫骨内侧髁下缘凹陷中	膝关节酸痛、小便不利	点、拿、按、一指禅推
	血海	髌骨内上方2寸	月经不调、膝痛	拿、按、点
	大横	脐中旁开4寸	虚寒泻痢、大便秘结、小腹痛	一指禅推、摩、揉、拿
手少阴心经	极泉	腋窝正中	胸闷胁痛、臂肘冷麻	拿、弹拨
	少海	屈肘,当肘横纹尺侧端凹陷中	肘关节痛、手颤肘挛	拿、弹拨
	通里	神门穴上1寸	心悸、怔忡、头晕、咽痛、暴暗、舌强不语、腕臂痛	掐、按、揉、拿
	阴郄	神门穴上0.5寸	心痛、惊悸、骨蒸盗汗、吐血衄血、暴暗	掐、按、揉、拿
	神门	腕横纹尺侧端,尺侧腕屈肌腱的桡侧凹陷中	惊悸、怔忡、失眠、健忘	拿、按、揉
手太阳小肠经	少泽	小指尺侧指甲角旁约0.1寸	发热、中风昏迷、乳少、咽喉肿痛	掐
	后溪	第五掌指关节后尺侧、横纹头赤白肉	头项强痛、耳聋、咽痛、齿痛、目翳、肘臂挛痛	掐
	腕骨	手背尺侧,豌豆骨前凹陷中	头痛、肩臂挛痛、腕痛指挛、黄疸、热病无汗	掐
	养老	尺骨小头桡侧缘凹陷中	目视不明、肩臂腰痛	掐、按、揉
	支正	前臂伸侧面尺侧,腕上5寸处	颈项强、手指拘挛、头痛、目眩	拿、按、揉

续表

经络	穴名	位　置	主　治	常用手法
足太阳小肠经	小海	屈肘，当尺骨鹰嘴与肱骨内上髁之间凹陷中	牙痛、颈项痛、上肢酸痛	拿
	肩贞	腋后皱襞上1寸	肩关节酸痛、活动不便、上肢瘫痪	拿、按、揉、㨰
	天宗	肩胛骨冈下窝的中央	肩背酸痛、肩关节活动不便、项强	一指禅推、㨰、按、揉
	秉风	肩胛骨冈上窝中	肩胛疼痛、不能举臂，上肢酸麻	一指禅推、按、揉、㨰
	肩外俞	第一胸椎棘突下旁开3寸	肩背酸痛、颈项强急、上肢冷痛	一指禅推、按、揉
	肩中俞	大椎穴旁开2寸	咳嗽、气喘、肩背疼痛、视物不清	一指禅推、按、揉
	颧髎	目外眦直下，颧骨下缘凹陷中	口眼㖞斜	一指禅推、按、揉
足太阳膀胱经	睛明	目内眦旁0.1寸	眼病	一指禅推、按
	攒竹	眉头凹陷中	头痛失眠、眉棱骨痛、目赤痛	一指禅推、按、揉
	天柱	哑门穴旁开1.3寸，当斜方肌后外缘凹陷中	头痛、项强、鼻塞、肩背痛	一指禅推、按、拿
	大杼	第一胸椎棘突下，旁开1.5寸	发热、咳嗽、项强、肩胛酸痛	一指禅推、㨰、按、揉
	风门	第二胸椎棘突下，旁开1.5寸	伤风、咳嗽、项强、腰背痛	一指禅推、㨰、按、揉
	肺俞	第三胸椎棘突下，旁开1.5寸	咳嗽气喘、胸闷、背肌劳损	一指禅推、㨰、按、揉、弹拨
	心俞	第五胸椎棘突下，旁开1.5寸	失眠，心悸	一指禅推、㨰、按、揉、弹拨
	膈俞	第七胸椎棘突下，旁开1.5寸	呕吐、噎膈气喘、咳嗽、盗汗	一指禅推、㨰、按、揉
	肝俞	第九胸椎棘突下，旁开1.5寸	胁肋痛、肝炎、目糊	一指禅推、㨰、按、揉、弹拨
	胆俞	第十胸椎棘突下，旁开1.5寸	胁肋痛、口苦、黄疸	一指禅推、点、按、揉
	脾俞	第十一胸椎棘突下，旁开1.5寸	胃脘胀痛、消化不良、小儿慢脾惊	一指禅推、点、按、揉、㨰、弹拨
	胃俞	第十二胸椎棘突下，旁开1.5寸	胃病、小儿吐乳、消化不良	一指禅推、点、按、揉、㨰、弹拨

续表

经络	穴名	位置	主治	常用手法
足太阳膀胱经	三焦俞	第一腰椎棘突下,旁开1.5寸	肠鸣、腹胀、呕吐、腰背强痛	一指禅推、按、揉、滚
	肾俞	第二腰椎棘突下,旁开1.5寸	肾虚、腰痛、遗精、月经不调	一指禅推、按、揉、滚
	气海俞	第三腰椎棘突下,旁开1.5寸	腰痛	一指禅推、按、揉、滚
	大肠俞	第四腰椎棘突下,旁开1.5寸	腰腿痛、腰肌劳损、肠炎	一指禅推、按、揉、滚、弹拨
	关元俞	第五腰椎棘突下,旁开1.5寸	腰痛、泄泻	一指禅推、按、揉、滚
	八髎	在第一、二、三、四骶后孔中（分别为上髎、次髎、中髎、下髎）	腰腿痛、泌尿生殖系疾患	点、按、揉、擦
	秩边	第四骶椎下,旁开3寸	腰臀痛、下肢痿痹、小便不利、便秘	滚、拿、弹、拨、按
	殷门	臀沟中央下6寸	坐骨神经痛、下肢瘫痪、腰背痛	点、压、拍、滚、拿
	昆仑	外踝与跟腱之间凹陷中	头痛、项强、腰痛、踝关节扭伤	按、拿、点
	申脉	外踝下缘凹陷中	癫狂痫、腰腿痠痛	掐、点、按
	金门	申脉前下方,骰骨外侧凹陷中	癫痫、腰痛、外踝痛、下肢痹痛	掐、点、按
	京骨	第五跖骨粗隆下,赤白肉际	癫痫、头痛、项强、腰腿痛、膝痛脚挛	拿、掐
足少阴肾经	涌泉	足底中、足趾跖屈时呈凹陷处	偏头痛、高血压、小儿发热	擦、按、拿
	太溪	内踝与跟腱之间凹陷中	喉痛、齿痛、不寐、遗精、阳痿、月经不调	一指禅推、拿、按、揉
	大钟	太溪下0.5寸,跟腱内缘	腰脊强痛、足跟痛、气喘、咳血	一指禅推、按、揉
	水泉	太溪直下1寸	月经不调、痛经、小便不利、目昏花	按、揉、点
	照海	内踝下缘凹陷中	月经不调	按
	交信	内踝上2寸,胫骨内侧缘	月经不调、泄泻、便秘、睾丸肿痛	按、揉
	筑宾	太溪直上5寸	癫狂、疝痛、足胫痛	点、按、揉、拿

续表

经络	穴名	位置	主治	常用手法
手厥阴心包经	曲泽	肘横纹中,肱二头肌腱尺侧缘	上肢酸痛颤抖	拿、按、揉
	郄门	腕横纹上5寸,掌长肌腱与桡侧腕屈肌腱之间	心痛、心悸、呕吐	拿、按、揉
	内关	腕横纹上2寸,掌长肌腱与桡侧腕屈肌腱之间	胃痛、呕吐、心悸、精神失常	一指禅推、按、揉、拿
	大陵	腕横纹中央,掌长肌腱与桡侧腕屈肌腱之间	心痛、心悸、胃痛、呕吐、癫痫、胸胁痛	按、揉、弹拨
	劳宫	手掌心横纹中,第二、三掌骨之间	心悸、颤抖	按、揉、拿
手少阳三焦经	中渚	握拳第四、五掌骨小头后缘之间凹陷中	偏头痛、掌指痛屈伸不利、肘臂痛	点、按、揉、一指禅推
	阳池	腕背横纹中、指总伸肌腱尺侧缘凹陷中	肩臂痛、腕痛、疟疾、消渴、耳聋	一指禅推、按、揉
	外关	腕背横纹上2寸,桡骨与尺骨之间	头痛、肘臂手指痛、屈伸不利	一指禅推、㨰、按、揉
	会宗	腕背横纹上3寸,尺骨桡侧缘	耳聋、痫证、臂痛	㨰、按、揉
	肩髎	肩峰外下方,肩髃穴后寸许凹陷中	肩臂酸痛、肩关节活动不便	一指禅推、按、揉、㨰、拿
足少阳胆经	风池	胸锁乳突肌与斜方肌之间,平风府穴	偏正头痛、感冒项强	按、拿、一指禅推
	肩井	大椎穴与肩峰连线的中点	项强、肩背痛、手臂上举不便	拿、㨰、一指禅推、按、揉
	居髎	髂前上棘与股骨大转子连线的中点	腰腿痛、髋关节酸痛、骶髂关节炎	㨰、点、压、按
	环跳	股骨大转子与骶裂孔连线的外1/3与内2/3交界处	腰腿痛、偏瘫	㨰、点、压、按
	风市	大腿外侧中间,腘横纹水平线上7寸	偏瘫、膝关节酸痛	㨰、点、按、压
	阳陵泉	腓骨小头前下方凹陷中	膝关节酸痛、胁肋痛	拿、点、按、揉
	外丘	外踝上7寸,腓骨前缘	胸胁支满、痿痹、癫痫呕沫	㨰、按、揉
	光明	外踝上5寸,腓骨前缘	膝痛、下肢痿痹、目痛、夜盲、乳胀	㨰、拨、揉
	悬钟	外踝上3寸,腓骨后缘	头痛、项强、下肢酸痛	拿、按

续表

经络	穴名	位　置	主　治	常用手法
足少阳胆经	丘墟	外踝前下方,趾长伸肌腱外侧凹陷中	踝关节痛、胸胁痛	按、点、拿
	足临泣	足背,第四、五趾间缝纹端上1.5寸	瘰疬、胁肋痛、足跗肿痛、足趾挛痛	掐、点、按
足厥阴肝经	太冲	足背,第一、二跖骨底之间凹陷中	头痛、眩晕、高血压、小儿惊风	拿、按、揉
	蠡沟	内踝上5寸,胫骨内侧面的中央	小便不利、月经不调、足胫痿痹	擦、拿、按、揉
	中都	内踝上7寸,胫骨内侧面的中央	腹痛、泄泻、疝气、崩漏、恶露不尽	擦、拿、按、揉
	章门	第十一肋端	胸胁痛、胸闷	摩、揉、按
	期门	乳头直下、第六肋间隙	胸胁痛	摩、揉、按
任脉	关元	脐下3寸	腹痛、痛经、遗尿	一指禅推、摩、揉、按
	石门	脐下2寸	腹痛、泄泻	一指禅推、摩、揉、按
	气海	脐下1.5寸	腹痛、月经不调、遗尿	一指禅推、摩、揉、按
	神阙	脐的中间	腹痛、泄泻	摩、揉、按
	中脘	脐上4寸	胃痛、腹胀、呕吐、消化不良	一指禅推、摩、揉、按
	鸠尾	剑突下,脐上7寸	心胸痛、反胃、癫痫	按、揉
	膻中	前正中线,平第四肋间隙处	咳喘、胸闷胸痛	一指禅推、摩、按、揉
	天突	胸骨上窝正中	喘咳、咯痰不畅	按、压、一指禅推
	承浆	颏唇沟的中点	口眼㖞斜、牙痛	按、揉、掐
督脉	长强	尾骨尖下0.5寸	腹泻、便秘、脱肛	按、揉、点
	腰阳关	第四腰椎棘突下	腰脊疼痛	擦、一指禅推、按、揉、擦、扳
	命门	第二腰椎棘突下	腰脊疼痛	擦、一指禅推、按、揉、擦、扳
	身柱	第三胸椎棘突下	膝脊强痛	擦、一指禅推、扳、按
	大椎	第七颈椎棘突下	感冒、发热、落枕	一指禅推、擦、按、揉

续表

经络	穴名	位 置	主 治	常用手法
督脉	风府	后发际正中直上1寸	头痛项强	点、按、揉、一指禅推
	百会	后发际正中直上7寸	头痛头晕、昏厥、高血压、脱肛	按、揉、一指禅推
	人中	人中沟正中线上1/3与下2/3交界处	惊风、口眼㖞斜	掐
经外奇穴	印堂	两眉头连线的中点	头痛、鼻炎、失眠	抹、一指禅推、按、揉
	太阳	眉梢与目外眦之间向后约1寸处凹陷中	头痛、感冒、眼病	按、揉、抹、一指禅推
	鱼腰	眉毛的中点	眉棱骨痛、目赤肿痛、眼睑颤动	抹、一指禅推、按
	腰眼	第四腰椎棘突下,旁开3.3寸凹陷处	腰扭伤、腰背酸楚	滚、按、拿、擦
	夹脊	第一胸椎至第五腰椎,各椎棘突下旁开0.5寸	脊柱疼痛强直、脏腑疾患及强壮作用	滚、擦、压、推、一指禅推
	十七椎	第五腰椎棘突下	腰腿痛	扳、滚、按
	十宣	十手指尖端,距指甲0.1寸	昏厥	掐
	鹤顶	髌骨上缘正中凹陷处	膝关节肿痛	按、揉、点
	阑尾穴	足三里穴下约2寸处	阑尾炎、腹痛	按、拿、揉、点
	肩内陵	腋前皱襞顶端与肩髃穴连线中点	肩关节酸痛、运动障碍	一指禅推、滚、拿、按、揉
	桥弓	耳后翳风到缺盆成一线	头痛、头晕	推、揉、拿
	胆囊穴	阳陵泉直下1寸	胆绞痛	按、揉、点

思 考 题

- 试述经筋、皮部在推拿治疗中的作用。
- 十二经脉的循行有什么特点?

4 推拿常用检查方法

推拿疗法的治疗范围广,涉及骨伤、内、外、妇、儿各科疾病。临床上通过四诊及必要的物理检查、实验室检查及影像学检查等手段,全面了解患者的全身情况和局部症状,通过辨证对疾病进行综合分析,分清主次,判断病情并得出正确诊断,并在此基础上,以辨证施治和辨病施治相结合的原则为指导,选择相应的治疗部位和手法进行治疗。

4.1 头面部检查

4.1.1 望诊

主要观察头面部的神色和形态变化。

望神

神是人体生命活动的总称,亦是对人体精神意识、思维活动以及气血、脏腑功能外在表现的高度概括。察神可判断正气的盛衰和疾病过程中的转化情况。

察眼神的变化是望神的重要内容之一。如患者双目灵活,明亮有神,鉴识精明,神志清楚,反应灵敏,语言清晰者,称为"有神",表示正气未伤,脏腑功能未衰,即使病情较重,预后亦多良好。如患者表现为目光晦暗,瞳仁呆滞,精神萎靡,反应迟钝,呼吸气微,甚至神识昏迷,循衣摸床,撮空理线,或猝倒而目闭口开、手撒尿遗等,均称为"失神",表示正气已伤,病情严重,预后不佳。如久病、重病、精气极度衰弱的患者,突然出现精神转"佳"等虚假现象,称为"假神",通常比喻为"回光返照",是病危的表现,应予以特别注意。

望色

主要是察面部的气色,即望面部的颜色和光泽。面部的色泽是脏腑气血盛衰的外在表现。色与泽两方面的异常变化,是人体不同病理变化的表现。不同的色反映着不同的病证。而泽则反映着机体精气盛衰,所以察面部肤色的润泽与否,对诊断疾病的轻重和推断病情的进退有较重要的意义。一般而言,病人气色鲜明、荣润的,说明病变轻浅,气血未衰,其病易治,预后良好;面色晦暗、枯槁的,说明病变深重,精气已伤,预后欠佳。

如为创伤患者,通过观察患者面部表情,可初步推知伤情之轻重:轻伤神志清楚,言语如常;重伤则面色苍白,表情淡漠或神志昏迷。

望头面部形态

额骨及颞骨双侧凸出,顶部扁平,呈方形,俗称方头,多见于佝偻病患儿,头发多稀疏不华。小儿头倾向患侧,颜面转向健侧,呈倾斜状态,大多见于小儿肌性斜颈。头轻度前倾位,姿势牵强,多为"落枕"、颈椎病。一侧不能闭眼,额部皱纹消失,作露齿动作时,口角斜向健侧,鼻唇沟消失,多为面神经麻痹。中枢性的面瘫主要表现为颜面下半部瘫痪,口角歪向患侧。头部不自主地震颤,可见于震颤麻痹患者或老年人。下颌关节强直,如发生于单侧,则颈部偏斜于患侧,面部不对称,患侧丰满,健侧扁平;如病发生于双侧,自幼得病者,则整个下颌骨发育不良,颏部后缩,形成下颌畸形;成年得病者,则畸形不显著,但张口困难。

望舌

大体上说,舌质的情况多反映气血的变化,舌苔的情况多反映脾胃、津液的变化。

1. 舌质　正常人舌质一般为淡红色。

(1) 淡白舌:舌质淡白,为气血虚弱,或为阳气不足而伴有寒象。

(2) 红绛色:舌质红绛为热证,或为阳证。舌质鲜红,深于正常,称为舌红;若进一步发展成为深红者为绛色。两者均主有热,而绛者热势更甚。多见于里热实证、感染发热、创伤或大手术后。

(3) 青紫色:舌质青紫,多为伤后气血运行不畅,瘀血凝聚。若舌之局部紫斑,表示血瘀程度较轻,或局部有瘀血。若全舌青紫表示血瘀程度较重。

2. 舌苔　正常舌苔为薄白而润滑。观察舌苔的变化,可鉴别病患是在表,还是属里;舌苔的过多或过少标志着正邪两方面的虚实。

(1) 舌苔的厚薄:它与邪气的盛衰成正比。舌苔过少或无苔表示脾胃虚弱。舌苔厚腻为湿浊内盛,舌苔越厚则邪越重。从舌苔的消长和转化可测知病情的发展趋势,如由薄增厚为病进;由厚转薄称为"苔化",为病退。舌红光剥无苔属胃气虚或阴液伤,如老年人股骨颈等骨折时多见。

(2) 苔白:白苔一般主寒。舌苔厚白而滑为损伤伴有寒湿或寒痰等兼证;厚白而腻为湿浊;薄白而干燥表示湿邪化热、津液不足;厚白而干燥表示湿邪化燥;白如积粉为创伤感染、热毒内蕴之象。

(3) 苔黄:黄苔一般主热证,或里热证,故在创伤感染、瘀血化热时多见。若由黄色转为灰黑苔时,表示病邪较盛,多见于严重创伤感染伴有高热或津枯等。

4.1.2 触诊

触诊是切诊的一部分,就是用医者的手触摸病人体表的一定部位,分辨其寒、温、润、燥、肿胀、疼痛,并观察病人对按压的反应。

婴儿囟门检查　两手掌分别放在左右颞部,拇指按在额部,用中指和食指检查囟门。正常前囟门可触及与脉搏一致的跳动,囟门与颅骨平齐,稍有紧张感。如前囟隆起,除外小儿哭叫时,多见于高热、颅内出血等颅内压增高的疾病。前囟门如迟闭,见于佝偻病等。如前囟凹陷,多见于吐泻后津液大伤的患儿。

张口度测定　张口时,上下颌牙齿之间的距离,相当于自己中、食、无名指三指并拢时末节的宽度,如下颌关节病变,则宽度减小或牙关紧闭。

落枕、颈椎病患者,常可在颈项部触摸到肌肉强硬痉挛。

外伤患者检查 对头部外伤患者,如外观无明显改变,要认真细致地触诊,重点要摸清颅骨有无塌陷,特别要注意有皮下血肿者深层是否有骨折存在。有无头皮撕脱伤,有无皮下血肿,其颅骨有无凹陷畸形等。下颌关节脱位时,关节窝空虚,其前方可触到隆起的髁状突。

4.2 胸腹部

4.2.1 望诊

应注意胸腹壁有无局部皮肤红肿、有无包块、有无皮下青筋暴露。若乳房红肿变硬有明显压痛,并伴有发热者,多为乳腺炎所致。腹部青筋暴露(静脉曲张),伴有腹水、脾肿大者,多为肝病所致的门脉高压症;小儿骨瘦如柴,腹大如鼓,并见青筋暴露,多为疳积。胸腹部望诊还要注意观察胸廓及腹部的形状。"桶状胸",多见于肺气肿及支气管哮喘患者,整个胸廓表现为高度扩大,尤其是前后径扩大,外形像桶状。"扁平胸"一般见于瘦长体型的人,也可由肺结核等慢性消耗性疾病引起,胸部的前后径不到左右径的一半,呈扁平状。"鸡胸"见于佝偻病,表现为胸骨(尤其是下部)显著前突,胸廓的前后径扩大,横径缩小。

脊柱畸形可引起胸廓变化,如脊柱结核或老年驼背,造成脊柱后凸,使胸椎变短,肋骨互相接近或重迭,胸廓牵向脊柱;如发育畸形、脊柱的某些疾患或者脊柱旁一侧肌肉麻痹,使脊柱侧凸,脊柱突起的一侧胸廓膨隆,肋间隙加宽,而另一侧胸廓下陷,肋骨互相接近或重迭,两肩不等高。

站立时,如见上腹凹陷,而脐部及下腹部隆起,多为胃下垂患者。正常腹部不能看到蠕动波,只有极度消瘦者因腹壁较薄,可能看到。幽门梗阻或肠梗阻时,则出现明显的胃或肠蠕动波,且常伴有胃型或肠型。

4.2.2 触诊

胸腹部触诊要注意压痛点。一般来说,内脏病变按照该脏器的解剖位置,在相应的体表上有疼痛反应及压痛。

胸壁有皮下气肿时,用手按压可有握雪或捻发感,多由于胸部外伤后,使肺或气管破裂,气体逸至皮下所致。

胸廓挤压试验 检查肋骨是否骨折,其方法是患者坐位或站立位,医生两手在胸廓一侧的前后对称位或胸廓两侧的左右对称位作轻轻挤压胸廓动作,如有肋骨骨折,则骨折部位出现疼痛,有的可伴有骨擦音,为阳性征。

腹壁反射,其检查方法是:患者仰卧,下肢屈曲,嘱患者放松腹肌,检查者用钝尖物轻而迅速地划其两侧季肋部、脐平面和髂部腹壁皮肤,划的方向由外向内。正常时可见到腹肌收缩。反射中心,上腹壁在胸髓7～8,中腹壁在胸髓9～10,下腹壁在胸髓11～12。一侧腹壁反射消失见于锥体束损害,某一水平的腹壁反射消失提示相应节段的脊髓损害。

提睾反射 用火柴杆或钝头竹签由下向上轻划股内侧上方皮肤,可引起同侧提睾肌收缩,睾丸上提。一侧反射减弱或消失见于锥体束损害,双侧反射消失见于腰髓1~2节病损。

4.3 脊柱部

4.3.1 望诊

脊柱部的望诊,首先要注意脊柱的正常生理曲线是否改变,脊柱有无畸形。正常脊柱有四个生理弯曲,即颈曲(前凸)、胸曲(后凸)、腰曲(前凸)和骶曲(后凸)。观察姿势有无异常,如脊柱侧弯或倾斜、驼背、腰前凸增大或减小、骨盆歪斜等。

根据脊柱的解剖结构是否发生改变,脊柱侧弯分为功能性和结构性两类:功能性脊柱侧弯本身无结构性异常,这类凸出为可逆性的,可用下述方法予以鉴别:卧位时侧弯消失者为功能性侧弯;令患者双手悬垂于单杠之上,脊柱侧弯消失者为功能性侧弯;脊柱前屈试验,当患者脊柱前屈80°时,功能性侧弯可以消失,而结构性侧弯则依然存在。结构性侧弯由于椎骨、韧带、椎间盘、神经或肌肉等组织结构产生病变,为不可逆性,不能用改变姿势体位的办法纠正。此类侧弯较重,曲度皆较固定,侧弯凸侧脊柱旋转突出,脊柱前屈时更加明显,严重的侧弯往往伴有胸廓畸形。大多由于姿势不良、下肢不等长、肩部畸形、腰椎间盘纤维环破裂症、小儿麻痹症及慢性胸腔或胸廓病变引起;姿势不良引起的侧突畸形,可在平卧及弯腰时消失。

望诊时还要注意观察脊柱区的皮肤颜色、汗毛,两侧软组织是否对称,局部有无肿胀、充血、瘀血、挫伤、肌痉挛、肌萎缩、色素斑、丛毛、包块等。如背腰部不同形状的咖啡色斑点,反映了神经纤维瘤或纤维异样增殖综合征的存在;腰骶部汗毛过长、皮肤色浓,多有先天性骶椎裂;腰部中线软组织肿胀,多为硬脊膜膨出;一侧腰三角区肿胀,多为流注脓肿。

4.3.2 触诊

触诊寻找压痛点,检查脊柱部压痛点,要分别浅、深压痛和间接压痛。浅压痛表示浅部病变,如棘上、棘间韧带等浅层组织。深压痛和间接压痛表示深部病变,如椎体、小关节和椎间盘等组织。腰背部的软组织劳损,大多能在病变部位找到压痛,如棘间韧带劳损在棘突之间有压痛;棘上韧带劳损在棘上有压痛;腰背部肌筋膜炎多在腰部有特定的压痛点,如果腰部只有痠痛,压痛点不明确,或者根本没有压痛点,用拳叩击腰部反觉舒适,往往是子宫后倾、肾下垂、神经衰弱等的症状性腰痛。背腰部的压痛点,亦应注意区别是否为内脏疾病在背腰部的反射性疼痛点。如心脏疾患有时可在右侧心俞处有压痛,肝、胆疾患则可表现为右侧肝、胆俞处压痛。因此临床上必须注意详细、全面地诊察。

4.3.3 运动检查

正常脊柱有前屈、后伸、左右侧屈及旋转的功能。颈椎和腰椎的正常活动幅度如下:

颈部运动检查时,嘱患者坐位,头正直,固定双肩,使躯干不参与颈椎的运动,然后再做各方向活动。颈椎前屈35°~45°,后伸35°~45°,左右侧屈各45°,左右旋转各60°~80°。

腰部中立位为直立,腰伸直自然体位,腰椎前屈90°,后伸30°,左右侧屈各30°,左右旋转各30°。

检查时重点观察运动是否自如,有无运动障碍,要排除代偿动作。对疑有骨折脱位者,不要做运动检查,防止造成脊髓、神经或血管损伤。

4.3.4 特殊检查

叩顶试验 患者正坐,先令患者将头向患侧倾斜,检查者左手掌平放于患者头顶部,右手握拳轻叩击手背部,使力量向下传递。如有根性损害,则由于椎间孔的狭小而出现颈部疼痛或肢体放射性疼痛,即为阳性,提示脊神经受压。对根性疼痛剧烈者,检查者仅用双手叠放于患者头顶向下加压即可诱发或加剧症状。

臂丛神经牵拉试验 患者颈部前屈,医者以一手抵住患侧头部,一手握患肢腕部,反方向牵拉,患肢有疼痛或麻木感为阳性,提示臂丛神经受压。

深呼吸试验 患者端坐,两手置于膝部,先比较两侧桡动脉搏动力量,然后让患者尽力后伸颈部做深吸气,并将头转向患侧,同时下压肩部,再比较两侧脉搏或血压,往往患侧脉搏减弱或消失、疼痛加重。相反,抬高肩部,头面转向前方,则脉搏恢复,疼痛缓解。主要用于检查有无颈肋和前斜角肌综合征。

超外展试验 用于超外展综合征的检查,即锁骨下动脉是否被喙突及胸小肌压迫。患者站立或坐位,将患肢被动地从侧方外展高举过肩过头,若出现桡动脉脉搏减弱或消失,即为阳性。

旋颈试验 又称椎动脉扭曲试验,主要用于判定椎动脉状态。具体操作方法为,患者头部略向后仰,自主作向左、向右旋颈动作,如出现眩晕等椎-基底动脉供血不足症时,即为阳性。该试验有时可引起患者呕吐或猝倒,故检查者应密切观察以防意外。

屈颈试验 患者仰卧,医生一手置于病人头部枕后,一手置于病人胸前,然后将患者头部前屈,若出现腰痛及坐骨神经痛即为阳性征。颈部前屈时可使脊髓在椎管内上升1~2cm,神经根亦随之受到牵拉,出现放射性疼痛。常用于腰椎间盘突出症的检查。

挺腹试验 患者仰卧,当挺腹使腰部及骨盆离开床面,而出现腰及下肢放射性疼痛或挺腹的同时屏气咳嗽而出现腰及下肢疼痛为阳性,提示腰部神经根受压。

直腿抬高和足背屈试验 患者仰卧,两腿伸直,在保持膝关节伸直的情况下,分别做直腿抬高动作。测量抬高时无痛的范围(抬高肢体与床面的夹角)。如有神经根受压时,可出现直腿抬高明显受限,一般多在60°以下,即出现受压神经分布区疼痛,为直腿抬高试验阳性。然后将下肢降低5°~10°至疼痛消失,并突然将足背屈,坐骨神经痛再度出现称为加强试验阳性。后者较前者对腰椎间盘纤维环破裂症的诊断更有临床价值。因为髂胫束及腘绳肌紧张时直腿抬高试验亦可出现阳性。而足背屈试验阳性是单纯坐骨神经受牵拉紧张的表现。

股神经牵拉试验 患者俯卧,检查者一手固定患者骨盆,另一手握患肢小腿下端,膝关节伸直或屈曲,将大腿强力过伸,如出现大腿前方放射样疼痛,即为阳性。

骨盆回旋试验 患者仰卧位,医生极度屈曲两侧髋、膝关节,使臀部离床,腰部被动前屈,若腰骶部出现疼痛则为阳性征。常见于下腰部的软组织劳损及腰骶椎的病变。

骨盆分离、挤压试验 患者仰卧位,医生用两手将两侧髂嵴翼向外侧相对挤压,称为骨盆分离试验。同样体位,两手将两侧髂嵴翼向中心相对挤压,称为骨盆挤压实验。如有疼痛者为阳性。提示骶髂关节病变,或骨盆骨折等。

"4"字试验 患者仰卧,健侧下肢伸直,患肢屈曲外旋,使足置于健侧膝上方,医者一手压住患侧的膝上方,另一手压住健侧髂前上棘,使患侧骶髂关节扭转,产生疼痛为阳性。如无髋关节病变即为骶髂关节有病变。

床边试验 患者仰卧,患侧臀部靠床边,健侧下肢屈膝屈髋,以固定骨盆。医者将其患肢移至床外并使之尽量后伸,使骶髂关节牵张和移动。若骶髂关节疼痛,则提示有病变。

跟臀试验 患者俯卧,两下肢伸直,肌肉放松。医者握其足部,使其屈膝,足跟触到臀部。如腰骶关节有病变,则引起腰骶部疼痛,骨盆甚至腰部也随着抬起。

4.4 上肢部

4.4.1 肩部

临床上有些内脏疾病,可以通过神经反射表现为体表某些区域疼痛,因此遇到肩部疼痛的病人,首先要排除因内脏疾病而引起的疼痛。如左肩疼痛要排除心脏疾病;右肩疼痛要排除肝胆疾病。另外有些肩痛是由于颈椎病而引起的,所以对肩部疼痛进行整体检查是十分必要的。

望诊

肩部望诊时两肩要裸露,以便对比检查。首先对比两肩是否等高,皮肤颜色情况,对比两侧三角肌的发育及锁骨上、下窝的深浅是否对称,肌肉有否萎缩,有无畸形、肿胀、窦道、肿块及静脉怒张;背面检查,要对比两肩胛骨高低是否一致,肩胛骨内缘与脊椎距离是否相等,肩胛冈的上下肌肉有无萎缩。并通过肩关节主动或被动运动来观察其肌肉及关节的形态和功能状况,如果发现两侧不对称,则应进一步检查。若肩胛骨高耸,多为先天性肩胛骨高耸症;若肩胛骨内缘向后突起,尤在用手抵墙时更为明显,则为前锯肌瘫痪,又称"翼状肩";对于急性损伤患者,如果在肩后部有明显肿胀,则提示可能有肩关节脱位或肩胛骨骨折。三角肌膨隆消失成"方肩",多提示肩关节脱位。对比两肩,看锁骨外端是否高突,患肩是否向下、前、内移位,前者说明肩锁关节脱位或锁骨外端骨折,后者则为胸锁关节脱位或锁骨骨折。此外,臂丛神经损伤或偏瘫造成的肩部肌肉麻痹,也会出现垂肩畸形。

触诊

肩部触诊时,用拇指详细地按压检查,寻找有无压痛点,并注意关节结构是否正常,活动时有无异常状态及弹响、摩擦感等,并应注意排除骨折。对肩部压痛点,须和肩关节功能检查结合,来判断病变的部位。如压痛点在肩峰前下方,一般是肱骨小结节附近的病变;压痛点在肩峰外侧,多见于肱骨大结节附近的病变。

在望诊时如发现两侧上肢不等长,肌肉萎缩,需进行测量。上肢的长度一般测量从肩峰至中指尖的长度,两侧对比;测量上肢周径时一般选择两臂相应的部位,并标明该部位距肩峰或尺骨鹰嘴突的长度。

运动检查

肩部活动功能检查时,应固定肩胛骨下角,避免肩胛骨一起参与活动造成假象,肩关节的正常活动度如下:

前屈运动:正常可达90°,检查时一手固定患侧肩部,嘱其向前抬起上肢,参与前屈运动的主要肌肉是三角肌前部和喙肱肌。

后伸运动:正常可达45°,检查时嘱患者将上肢后伸,参与后伸运动的主要肌肉是背阔肌和大圆肌。

外展运动:正常可达90°,检查时嘱患者屈肘90°,然后作上臂外展运动,参与外展运动的主要肌肉是三角肌和冈上肌。

内收运动:正常可达45°,检查时嘱患者屈肘,上臂置胸前向内移动,参与内收运动的主要肌肉是胸大肌。

外旋运动:正常可达30°,检查时嘱患者屈肘90°,检查者一手扶肘部,一手扶腕部,使上臂作外旋动作,参与外旋运动主要肌肉是冈下肌和小圆肌。

内旋运动:正常可达80°,检查时屈肘90°,前臂内收到胸前,或将前臂绕到背后部摸到对侧肩胛下角为正常,参与内旋运动主要肌肉是肩胛下肌和背阔肌。

上臂上举:上举是一个比较复杂的动作,能够完成此动作就说明肩部功能基本良好。

环转运动:即上臂以肩肱关节为中心作划圈动作。环转运动可以沿着冠状面、矢状面及横面任何一个面进行。

特殊试验

搭肩试验(Dugas征) 患者屈肘,患肢手搭在对侧肩部,肘关节能贴近胸壁为正常,若患者不能完成上述动作,或仅能完成两动作之一者为阳性,提示肩关节脱位。

直尺试验 正常人肩峰位于肱骨外上髁与肱骨大结节连线之内侧。检查者用直尺边缘贴于患者上臂外侧,一端贴肱骨外上髁,另一端能与肩峰接触则为阳性,说明肩关节脱位。

落臂试验 患者站立,先将患肢被动外展90°,然后令其缓慢地向下放,如果不能慢慢放下,出现突然直落到体侧则为阳性,说明冈上肌损伤。

疼痛弧试验 嘱患者肩外展或被动外展患肢,当外展到60°~120°范围时,冈上肌腱在肩峰下摩擦,肩部出现疼痛为阳性征,这一特定区域的外展痛称疼痛弧,见于冈上肌腱炎。

冈上肌腱断裂试验 嘱患者肩外展,当外展到30°~60°时可以看到患侧三角肌用力收缩,但不能外展上举上肢,越用力越耸肩。若检查者被动外展患肢越过60°,则患者又能主动上举上肢。这一特定区外展障碍为阳性征,说明有冈上肌腱的断裂或撕裂。

叶加森(Yergason)试验　又称肱二头肌抗阻试验。患者屈肘90°,检查者一手扶其肘部,一手扶其腕部,嘱患者用力作屈肘及前臂旋后动作,同时检查者给予阻力,如出现肱二头肌腱滑出,或结节间沟处产生疼痛为阳性征,前者为肱二头肌长头腱滑脱,后者为肱二头肌长头肌腱炎。

4.4.2　肘部

望诊

肘部望诊需两肘裸出,两侧对比检查,首先观察肘关节有无肿胀和变形。

对肘关节有明显肿胀的患者,检查时必须认真区分是关节内肿胀还是关节外肿胀,是全关节肿胀还是局限性肿胀,是外伤性肿胀抑或是病理性(化脓感染、结核等)肿胀。关节内有积液时,早期表现为尺骨鹰嘴突两侧正常的凹陷消失,而变得饱满。当有大量积液时,关节肿胀明显,且呈半屈曲状态。

外伤患者如出现局限性肿胀,常常提示某一局部的损伤。如以肘内侧肿胀为著,可能为肱骨内上髁骨折;以肘外侧肿胀为著,则有肱骨外上髁或桡骨小头骨折的可能;如以肘后方肿胀为主则有尺骨鹰嘴突骨折可能。此外局部软组织挫伤,肿胀亦较局限。神经麻痹时,可引起广泛的肌萎缩。

正常肘关节伸直位时,有5°～7°的携带角,一般女性比男性度数稍大。携带角增大为肘外翻,减小或前臂尺偏则为肘内翻。

肘关节的形态如有改变,应注意有否骨折和脱位。肘关节脱位或髁上骨折时,患肢常处于半屈肘位;肱骨髁上伸直型骨折或肘关节后方脱位时,鹰嘴后突明显;小儿桡骨小头半脱位者,以前臂旋前畸形多见。

触诊

肱骨内髁、外髁和尺骨鹰嘴是肘关节触诊的重要骨性标志。此三点所构成的"肘直线"和"肘三角"有无改变,对鉴别肘关节脱位和骨折有实际意义。触诊时要注意压痛点的位置。肱骨外上髁有前臂伸肌群附着,外上髁炎时(网球肘),该处压痛明显;肱骨内上髁有前臂屈肌群附着,也可因炎症而有明显压痛;鹰嘴部可因骨折或滑囊炎等而有压痛或肥厚感;桡骨头可于肘后桡侧窝处触及,同时旋转前臂,可触到桡骨头转动的感觉,骨折时此窝鼓起并有压痛;尺骨粗隆在肘前不易摸到,需要以拇指在肘前深压,骨折时该处可有压痛;尺神经位于肘后尺侧,如尺神经有病变,局部可有肥厚感,并有压痛和窜麻等现象。肱骨外上髁、内上髁、桡骨小头和鹰嘴骨折时,除局部肿胀和压痛外,可触到骨擦感和异常活动。若前臂外展或内收活动受限,则表示内、外侧前臂屈、伸肌起点或侧副韧带的损伤,或内、外上髁撕脱骨折。肘关节脱位或骨折时,可出现异常的外展和内收活动。

运动检查

肘关节活动以屈伸为主,活动的关节主要在肱尺关节,屈曲140°,过伸0°～10°。前臂的旋转则依赖于尺桡上、下关节和骨间膜的相互活动,其旋前(掌心向下)90°,旋后(掌心向上)90°。肱桡关节虽参与屈伸和旋转活动,但处于次要位置。肘伸直位无侧方活动,但当侧副韧带损伤时,会出现异常的侧方活动。

特殊检查

网球肘试验(Mill试验)　前臂稍弯曲,手半握拳,腕关节尽量屈曲,然后将前臂完全旋前,再将肘伸直。如在肘伸直时,肱桡关节的外侧发生疼痛,即为阳性。

前臂屈、伸肌紧张(抗阻力)试验　患者握拳、屈肘,检查者以手按压患者手背,患者抗阻力伸腕,如肘外侧疼痛则为阳性,提示肱骨外上髁有炎性病灶;或患者伸手指和背伸腕关节,检查者以手按压患者手掌,患者抗阻力屈腕,肘内侧痛为阳性,则提示肱骨内上髁的病变。

前臂(收展)试验　本试验用于判断是否有肘关节侧副韧带损伤。检查时患者与检查者对面坐,上肢向前伸直,检查者一手握住肘部,一手握腕部并使前臂内收,握肘部的手推肘关节向外,如有外侧副韧带断裂,则前臂可出现内收运动。若握腕部的手使前臂外展,而拉肘关节向内,出现前臂有外展运动,则为内侧副韧带损伤。

4.4.3　腕掌指部

望诊

腕、指部的望诊应强调两侧对比检查,观察骨的轮廓有无畸形、软组织有无肿胀及肌萎缩等。

手的自然体位(休息位)是自然半握拳状态,手部各组拮抗肌张力相互平衡。腕轻度背伸约15°,拇指靠近食指旁边,其余四指屈曲,从第二至第五指各指的屈曲度逐渐增大,而诸指尖端指向舟状骨。当手部受伤,由于肌力不平衡,即可出现手部功能位的异常。

在手的功能位上能快速地握拳和完全伸开手指,表明手的功能正常。

桡骨远端骨折可见到银叉状畸形或枪刺状畸形。远端尺桡关节脱位时尺骨茎突向背侧凸出。非急性损伤所引起的畸形多为神经血管损伤所致。桡神经损伤出现腕下垂;正中神经损伤,拇指不能作对掌、外展动作,拇指和食指不能弯曲,亦不能过伸,大鱼际萎缩,呈猿手畸形;尺神经损伤后,拇指不能内收,其余四指不能作内收和外展运动,第四、五手指指掌关节不能屈曲,远端指间关节不能伸直,骨间肌、小鱼际肌萎缩,呈爪形手。此外,前臂屈肌群缺血坏死,疤痕挛缩所引起的缺血性挛缩患者也可有爪形手畸形。因骨间肌收缩,骨折端向背侧成角。近节指骨骨折或中节指骨骨折时(骨折线位于屈指浅肌腱止点远端),骨折端向掌侧成角。末节指骨基底部骨折或伸肌腱远端断裂时,手指末节呈下垂位。

此外还应注意软组织肿胀的部位和范围。鼻烟窝处饱满多为舟状骨骨折。两侧近端指间关节呈对称性梭形肿胀,多为类风湿性关节炎。沿肌腱的肿胀多为腱鞘炎或肌腱周围炎。整个手指呈杵状指,多为肺原性心脏病、支气管扩张或发绀型先天性心脏病等疾患。

手指震颤,多见于甲状腺功能亢进、震颤麻痹、慢性酒精中毒等。震颤性麻痹患者,运动时震颤减轻或消失,静止时出现。如震颤轻微,可叫病人闭眼,双手前平举,在其双手背上放一张纸,可见到纸的抖动。

3岁以下的婴幼儿疾病,望指纹(在食指掌面桡侧的浅表静脉)的颜色可作为辨别病情轻重的参考。食指第一节为风关,第二节为气关,第三节为命关。正常指纹,色呈浅红,隐现于风关之内。如纹色鲜红为感受外邪,色紫为热感,色青为惊风,色淡多属虚寒证。纹色见于风关为病轻,至气关为病重,透过命关则病笃。

触诊

腕掌指部的触诊应注意压痛点、肿块和叩击痛。桡骨茎突处压痛,多系拇短伸肌、拇长展肌腱鞘炎;掌指关节掌侧处压痛,多见于第1、2、3、4指腱鞘炎;掌侧腕横纹中央区压痛且伴手指放射痛和麻木感,为腕管综合征,提示正中神经受压;"鼻烟窝"肿胀和压痛,表示舟状骨骨折。下尺桡关节处压痛,尺骨茎突高凸且有松弛感,为下尺桡关节分离;远侧和近侧指间关节侧方压痛或伴有侧向活动,为侧副韧带损伤。腕掌部的骨折多在骨折断端有明显肿胀、压痛、畸形和骨擦音,轴心叩击痛,临床上应仔细检查。

腕部背侧触及局限性肿块,且肿块可顺肌腱的垂直方向轻微移动,但不能平行移动者,通常为腱鞘囊肿。

运动检查

腕关节有内收、外展、背伸和掌屈的功能。腕关节的正常活动度为:背伸35°~60°,掌屈50°~60°,桡偏25°~30°,尺偏30°~40°。

特殊检查

握拳试验　患手握拳(拇指在里、四指在外),腕关节尺偏,出现桡骨茎突处疼痛为阳性,提示桡骨茎突狭窄性腱鞘炎。

屈腕试验　将患者腕关节极度屈曲,即引起手指麻痛,为腕管综合征的体征。

腕三角软骨挤压试验　判断是否有三角软骨损伤。检查时嘱患者屈肘90°,掌心向下,医者一手握住前下端,另一手握住手掌部,使患手向尺侧被动偏斜,然后伸屈腕关节,使尺腕关节部发生挤压和研磨,如有明显疼痛加重即为阳性。

4.5　下肢部

4.5.1　髋部

望诊

首先要患者脱去外衣行走,前面观察要注意两侧髂前上棘是否在同一水平,腹股沟区是否对称,有无高凸饱满或空虚,前者多系髋关节肿胀,后者往往提示股骨头有严重破坏。然后观察下肢有无过度内收、外展和短缩等畸形。

侧面观察要注意大腿有无屈曲畸形,特别是有无腰椎过度前凸。如有腰生理前凸加大,臀部明显后凸,髋部呈现屈曲位,则可能是髋关节后脱位(陈旧性),或系小儿先天性髋脱位和髋关节屈曲性强直。

后面观察,应注意有无臀大肌萎缩,髋关节疾病由于长期负重量减少和运动障碍,可出现废用性肌萎缩;小儿麻痹后遗症,则有神经性肌萎缩。对比观察两侧臀横纹是否对称,如有单侧横纹皱褶增多,而且加深,并有升高,为单侧先天性髋关节脱位;若有两侧股骨大转子向外突出,会阴部增宽,为双侧先天髋关节脱位。

触诊

病人仰卧,检查者两拇指用同样力量触压两腹股沟韧带中点下 2cm 处,观察病人的反应。或用拳叩击大转子或足跟,若引起髋关节痛,说明髋关节有病变。触摸腹股沟部时,注意淋巴结是否有肿大,局部有无饱满肿胀、压痛等。外侧大转子浅表压痛,往往提示大转子滑囊炎。对髋关节的活动痛须仔细检查,判定其疼痛的位置。检查旋转痛有两种方法:一种是髋关节伸直旋转试验,以检查关节面摩擦痛;另一种为髋关节屈曲旋转试验,髋关节屈曲位时,髂腰肌松弛,如有轻微旋转即出现疼痛,则为关节面摩擦痛,可以排除髂腰肌的牵扯痛;如小幅度旋转无疼痛,幅度增大时出现疼痛,提示髂腰肌等软组织的病变。

如发现下肢不等长,肌肉有萎缩,须进行测量,下肢长度应测量从髂前上棘至股骨内髁或内踝的距离;下肢周径的测量应取两下肢相应的部位,写明该部距髌骨上缘或下缘的长度,并须两侧对比。

运动检查

髋关节有屈曲、后伸、内收、外展、内旋和外旋的活动功能。髋关节的正常活动幅度为:屈曲 145°,后伸 40°,外展 30°～45°,内收 20°～30°,外旋 40°,内旋 40°。

特殊检查

掌跟试验　患者仰卧,下肢伸直,足跟放在医者的掌面上。正常情况下,下肢呈中立位直竖在掌面上。但股骨颈骨折、髋关节脱位或截瘫患者,则足倒向一侧呈外旋位。

髋关节过伸试验　患者俯卧,两下肢伸直。医者一手压住其骶后部以固定骨盆,另一手提起患侧小腿,使髋关节过伸,如髋关节或骶髂关节有病变,用力后伸时,则骨盆随之抬起,髋或骶髂关节疼痛。

髋关节屈曲试验　患者仰卧,将健侧髋、膝关节极度屈曲,置骨盆于前倾体位,患髋即表现出屈曲畸形,大腿与床面的夹角即为畸形角度。

足跟叩击试验　患者仰卧,两下肢伸直。医者用一手将患肢抬起,另一手以拳击其足跟。若髋关节处疼痛为阳性,常提示髋关节病变。

屈膝屈髋分腿试验　患者两下肢屈曲外旋,两足底相对,两下肢外展外旋。股内收肌综合征患者,大腿不易完全分开,若被动分开即产生疼痛。

4.5.2　膝部

望诊

观察膝部有无畸形。正常膝关节仅有 5°的过伸,大腿和小腿有 5°～8°的轻度外翻;如外翻超过或者小于 5°～8°则为外翻或内翻畸形;观察膝关节是否肿胀,轻度肿胀表现为两侧膝眼饱满,严重时髌上滑囊及整个膝周均隆起肿大。髌上滑囊区的肿块可能是滑囊炎、关节积液。胫骨和股骨髁部及干骺端的肿大可能是骨肿瘤。引起膝关节运动障碍,股四头肌内侧头即很快萎缩,因此,此肌萎缩与否对判断膝关节有无病变有较大意义。

触诊

患者仰卧,两腿伸直。髌骨软化症向下按压髌骨,使髌骨轻轻移动,可出现明显的疼痛反应。胫骨结节骨骺炎,局部能触到高凸坚硬的包块,压痛明显。髌下脂肪垫肥厚，在髌韧带两侧可触到饱满柔韧的硬性包块。膝关节间隙压痛，可能为半月板损伤。侧副韧带损伤，在侧副韧带附着点有压痛。髌下韧带损伤，在髌骨下端有压痛。

此外，对于肿块应进一步鉴别其性质、压痛，有否波动感、乒乓球感，或搏动感等。

运动检查

膝关节的正常活动幅度为：屈曲145°，过伸10°。膝关节被动活动受限，常提示膝关节的病变。检查膝关节的主动活动，可测知股四头肌伸膝力和腘绳肌屈膝力。

特殊检查和神经反射

浮髌试验 患者平卧，患肢伸直放松。医者一手将髌骨上方髌上囊内液体向下挤入关节腔；另一手食指按压髌骨，一压一放，反复数次。如有波动感即表示关节腔内有积液。

膝关节侧向挤压试验 患者仰卧，患膝伸直，股四头肌放松，作膝关节被动内翻或外翻活动，正常时无侧方活动，亦无疼痛。如韧带完全撕裂，则出现侧方异常活动；如韧带损伤或部分撕裂则引起疼痛。

抽屉试验 又称推拉试验。患者仰卧，屈膝至90°，肌肉放松，足平放于床上，医者双手握小腿上端将其向前和向后反复拉推。向前活动度增大，提示前交叉韧带损伤；向后活动度增大，则表示后交叉韧带损伤。

膝关节回旋挤压试验 又称麦氏征试验。是临床诊断半月板损伤最常用的试验方法，检查时患者取仰卧位，双下肢伸直，如检查内侧半月板损伤，检查者一手扶患膝，另一手握住足踝部，先将膝关节屈曲到最大限度时，然后使膝外旋，小腿内收，并逐渐伸直膝关节，这样使膝关节内侧间隙产生挤压力和研磨力。如发生弹响和明显疼痛，即为阳性。如使小腿外展，膝内旋，可以检查外侧半月板损伤。

研磨提拉试验 本试验是鉴别侧副韧带损伤与半月板破裂的方法。患者俯卧，膝关节伸直，患膝屈曲至90°，医者将其大腿固定，用双手握住患足，挤压膝关节，并旋转小腿，引起疼痛者为阳性，提示半月板损伤；反之，将小腿提起，使膝关节间隙增宽，并旋转小腿，如引起疼痛，则为侧副韧带损伤。

膝腱反射 坐位检查时，病员坐于床沿，双小腿自然悬垂，在卧位时病人仰卧，检查者以左手托起其膝部，使稍屈曲，约20°～30°，然后轻叩膝下股四头肌腱，反应为伸膝动作，其反射中心在$L_{2\sim4}$。

4.5.3 踝部

望诊

观察有无畸形，如足下垂、内翻足、外翻足、扁平足和高弓足。有无肿胀、皮下瘀血等。

触诊

踝部软组织较薄，往往压痛点就是病灶的位置。踝、足部压痛点多位于关节间隙，以及骨端和肌腱附着处。如果压痛在跟腱上，可能是腱本身或腱旁膜的病变；在跟腱的止点处，可能是跟腱后滑囊炎；如果8～12岁儿童，跟部后下方压痛，可能是跟骨骨骺炎（塞渥病）。压痛点在跟骨的跖面正中偏后，可能是跟骨棘或脂肪垫的病症，靠前部可能是跖腱膜的疼痛。压痛点在跟骨的内外侧，可能是跟骨本身的病变。压痛点在跟骨两侧靠内、外踝的直下方,则可能是距下关节病变。

肿胀一般多有压痛,检查时应注意有无波动感及实质感。软性肿块常属滑膜、腱鞘病变,硬性者为骨病变。此外足背和胫后动脉的触诊对了解血液循环情况,有重要的临床意义。

运动检查

踝关节有背屈和跖屈的功能,正常活动度为:背伸 20°～30°,跖屈 40°～50°,足内翻约 45°,足外翻约 25°。

特殊检查

足内、外翻试验　检查者一手固定小腿,另一手握足,将踝关节极度内翻或外翻,如同侧疼痛,提示有内或外踝骨折可能,如对侧痛则多属副韧带损伤。

踝反射(跟腱反射)　患者卧位,髋关节外旋,膝关节屈曲,医者一手推足底,使踝关节略背屈,另一手用叩诊锤轻叩跟腱,其反应是足跖屈。如不易引起时,可让患者跪在床边,医者一手推足底使其背屈,另一手用叩诊锤轻叩跟腱。其反射中心在 S_{1-2}。

踝阵挛常与跟腱反射亢进同时存在。检查者一手托住腘窝,一手握足,用力使其踝关节突然背屈,然后放松,可以产生踝关节连续交替的伸屈运动,提示有锥体束损害。

巴宾斯基征　检查时用钝尖物轻划患者足底外缘。由后向前。阳性者拇趾缓缓背屈,其它各趾轻度外展,提示有锥体束损害。

弹趾试验　轻叩足趾的基底部或用手将足趾向背面挑动,如引起足趾跖屈为阳性,提示有锥体束损害。

思 考 题

- 试述腰部的特殊检查。
- 臂丛神经牵拉试验如何操作?其临床意义是什么?
- 试述膝关节在触诊时在其周围必须注意的压痛点。

5 推拿基本练功法

5.1 推拿练功法的特点和作用

5.1.1 推拿练功法的特点

推拿练功法有很好的健身强体、防治疾病的作用,它对人体肌肉力量以及内脏机能都有一个明显的锻炼和提高,具有如下的一些特点。

动作明确,锻炼全面

推拿医生必须具备良好的身体素质和指力、臂力及腰腿的力量,这也就需要一个自我锻炼的过程。推拿练功法中选取的徒手与器械练功方法,对身体素质和力量锻炼作用很明显,练功中针对性很强。如徒手练功法中,首先强调步型、档势,要求通过下肢各种屈曲、起伏,使下肢肌肉、韧带以及腹肌、腰肌、背肌等都得到一个全面的锻炼,长期练习,可使下肢肌肉充实,力量大增,有了扎实而坚强的下肢力量,是练功顺利进行的良好基础。

徒手练功法中还有许多动作都是以掌为主要动作基础,掌从胁肋下擦推而出,徐徐有力,两手起落多有螺旋翻转,使前臂肌肉产生一个拧转裹抱的过程,形成拧劲、争劲、螺旋劲等,再兼之以握力器、拉力器、杠铃和哑铃这些针对性更强的器械练功,通过各部肌肉的伸展收缩,相互争衡,从而使指掌、上肢肌肉力量得到更大的锻炼。

注重"意气",强调"内劲"

推拿练功法中强调蓄养气机,充实精血,而要达到这种良好的生理机能状态,则需经过诸如推拿武术的"外练筋骨皮,内练一口气",以及气功"呼吸精气,独立守神,肌肉若一"等等的锻炼过程。进行这些锻炼时,由于高度的意念活动,可有效地促生、转化人体"精、气、血"类物质,提高其功能、质量。进而"以意领气,以气贯力",使人体产生所谓的"内劲"。这种"内劲"的产生,可以说是人体功能态的最好发挥,其不仅有益自身的生命机能,更可以在对他人进行推拿手法治疗时产生积极的康复作用。

医练结合,增强疗效

推拿临床工作中,不仅重视疾病的治疗,而且更加注意预防疾病的发生和发展,推拿练功法中亦有着很好的体现。推拿练功法中一些动作,很适合患者练习,有利于消除疾病,是一种扶正祛邪和调动病员积极性的好方法。如徒手练功法中"前推八匹马,倒拉九头牛"一类动作,两手自胁肋两侧向前推出,使气机蓄行出于中焦,故能健脾和胃,促进胃肠功能,使摄纳增加,化生有源,气血由是充沛。

5.1.2 推拿练功对机体的作用

祖国医学对推拿练功的作用认识是疏通经络，畅旺气血。外柔四肢百骸，内养五脏六腑，现代医学和科研则对其有了进一步的认识，主要表现在如下几个方面：

推拿练功对血液和循环系统的作用

血液和循环系统包括血液、心脏和血管，这两个系统的作用是运送体内新陈代谢过程中所需要的养料和产生的代谢产物。推拿练功可以使心肌发达，心脏收缩力加强。一般人的心脏每次收缩能输出血液60～70ml，经常从事推拿练功，心脏每次收缩能输出血液80～100ml，甚至还要多一些，心脏容量增大比一般不参加练功的健康人多出三分之一左右。推拿徒手练功动作有起有伏，姿势有高有低，器械练功运动量尤其较大。因此，经常进行练功，心脏功能可得到较大的加强。

进行推拿练功还可以使血液中的白细胞、红细胞和血红蛋白增加，红细胞和血红蛋白增加了，可以提高人体的营养水平和代谢能力；白细胞有吞噬细菌和异物的作用，可以增强对传染病的抵抗能力。

推拿练功对呼吸系统的作用

呼吸系统的功能是吸收外界的氧气和排出体内的二氧化碳，保证人体新陈代谢的进行。推拿练功者有着较大的运动强度，从而使机体能量消耗增加，需要大量的氧气供给，同时也要大量地排出二氧化碳，这就促进呼吸频率加快，呼吸幅度加深，呼吸器官加强工作，使其功能得到更好的提高。例如，经常进行推拿练功，人的胸廓活动范围增大，肺活量增加。常进行推拿练功者，呼吸频率在安静时减少到每分钟8～12次，他们呼吸深而慢，这就使呼吸器官有较多的休息时间，不易疲劳，也不致大口喘气。

推拿练功对神经系统的作用

人体的复杂而又多种多样的活动都是在神经系统调节下进行的，推拿练功对神经系统能产生良好的调节作用，并能使其机能有序化。如在练功过程中，许多动作都有动有静，有起有伏，有虚有实，这些特点对改善有机体的控制能力起到锻炼作用。中枢神经就随着这些动作的变化而迅速准确地变换，一下兴奋，一下抑制，从而提高了中枢神经的调节机能，达到中枢神经、内脏呼吸器官和手、眼、身、步的协调一致。

推拿练功对消化系统的作用

推拿练功时，消化器官中的腺体分泌更多的消化液，胃肠道的蠕动加强，利于消化和吸收食物；另一方面，经常从事推拿练功，由于膈肌和腹肌的大幅度活动，对胃肠可起一个按摩作用，这对改善胃肠血液循环和增强其功能都有良好的作用。

推拿练功对肌肉、骨骼系统的作用

推拿练功可以使肌纤维增多、变粗，肌原及肌红蛋白储量增加，从而使肌肉发达，强壮有力，同时练功可使骨骼增粗，骨皮质加厚，关节活动灵活，能够承受较大的负荷。练功还能改善血液循环和新陈代谢，减轻关节骨质增生和韧带肌肉的退行性变化，推迟肌肉酸痛关节僵直、动作呆滞以及容易发生骨折等老年性变化。

推拿练功对内分泌系统和皮肤的作用

推拿练功对人体内分泌系统也有着很大的作用，它能增强肾上腺皮质功能，从而对人体内部蛋白质、脂肪、无机盐和水等各种物质代谢有利,它能通过甲状腺素来提高细胞的新陈代谢,它还能通过脑垂体所分泌的促生长激素加速蛋白质的合成和骨的成长,此外,推拿练功尚可刺激胰岛素的分泌,有利于增进糖的氧化过程,交感和副交感神经兴奋性,对心跳、呼吸、血压等都有一个良好的调节作用。另外,推拿练功还可以通过改变皮肤的结构和功能达到提高身体对冷、热的适应能力;同时,还能促进皮肤的血液循环,加强营养物质和氧气的供给,从而提高新陈代谢水平,改善皮肤功能,进一步增强防御"外邪"入侵的能力,保障皮肤的健康。

5.2 易筋经练习法

易筋经,是我国民间早已流传的健身锻炼方法,亦是骨伤和推拿科医生常用的练功内容之一。从易筋经三字来理解,"易"是改变之意,"筋"为肌腱,"经"指方法。由此可见,易筋经是一套通过锻炼来改变筋骨功能,使之强健的功法。主要作用在于强筋壮骨。

"易筋经"的特点是始终采用静止性用力。呼吸以舒适自然为宜,呼吸有顺式和逆式两种。吸气时腹部凹下,胸部外展,称为"逆式呼吸";相反,吸气时腹部凸出,胸部收缩,呼气时腹部内收,称为"顺式呼吸"。这两种呼吸都可用。但开始锻炼时,以用顺式呼吸为宜,因为逆式呼吸活动比较剧烈。

在练易筋经前,要做好准备工作,换穿宽松的衣服、练功鞋或软底布鞋等。练功时,要求松静自然,刚柔相济,意守丹田。松静自然就是肌肉放松,意念也要放松,保持安静。刚柔相济,即指用力要适度,切不可用僵力。意守丹田即微微用意,内视脐下附近,别的暂时不想。练习完毕或中间休息时,不可当风,可作适当活动,如散步、活动关节等,但不应作剧烈运动。

锻炼时可视每人的具体情况,选其中若干动作或整套进行,但必须循序渐进,持之以恒,练功的时间和次数及动作的强度,都要因人、因时、因地而宜,一般以练至微微汗出为好,不可勉强过量,每天至少锻炼一次,体质特别虚弱者,不宜练习易筋经。

第一势 韦驮献杵

【预备】 两脚贴靠并拢立正,全脚掌着地;两腿髋、膝关节放松,伸直并立;头如顶物,两目平视前方,下颌微向里收,口微开,舌尖轻抵上腭;两肩关节放松,手臂自然下垂于身体两侧,五指并拢,中指贴近裤缝;挺胸收腹,直腰拔背,蓄臀收二阴;排除杂念、自然呼吸。

【动作】

1. 左脚向左平跨出一步与肩平,两膝微挺,五趾着地。两臂同时外展至水平,掌心向下。注意:肘腕不可硬挺。

2. 两掌心向前,慢慢合拢。曲肘,两臂与腕徐徐内收,腕、肘、肩相平,十指朝天。

3. 两臂内旋,指尖对胸(与天突穴相平)。

4. 两肩徐徐拉开,双手在胸前成抱球状,略垂肘,掌心内凹,十指微屈,指端相对,约距4~5寸。身体微前倾。

5. 收势 先深吸一口清气,然后徐徐呼出,并徐徐放下两手。

【要领】 本势两足之距等肩,内侧穴档要立成长方形。全身放松,上身端正直立略前倾,两肩松开。两目平视,半开半闭,这样可起到澄心、敛神的作用,如果眼上视则心神上浮,下视则心神下降,不得平衡。头如顶物,口微开,舌尖顶上腭,紧吸慢呼,臀部微收,少腹含蓄,两胭空松,两掌心相对,这样能使肺脏上下、左右位置适中,升降开合自如,从而达到气定的要求,气定则心境澄清,神意内敛。

【按语】 本势锻炼重点在三角肌、上臂肱三头肌、前臂旋后肌群、伸肌群、肛门内外括约肌。久练能增强臂力。在临床上可增强悬劲和持久力,为锻炼蓄力最重要的一环。病者锻炼此势则可使气机协调,血脉畅达,以提高疗效。如痔疮、高血压病人等坚持锻炼此势则可祛病延年。本势须意守丹田。本势初练3分钟,一周后,每周加2分钟,至10分钟后,每周加1分钟。以后再据实际情况,酌情加减,一般在30分钟左右。体弱、病者减半。

第二势　横担降魔杵

【预备】 同韦驮献杵。

【动作】

1. 左脚向左平跨一步,与肩等宽,两手用力下按,掌心朝地,指端向前,肘须挺直,两目平视。

2. 两手翻掌上提至胸,拇指外侧着力,徐徐向前推出,高与肩平。

3. 两手同时向左右分开,以拇指外侧着力为主。两臂伸直,一字平开。肩、肘、腕相平。翻掌,掌心向下。

4. 两膝挺直,足跟提起,前掌着地,两目圆睁,咬牙切齿。

5. 收势　先深吸气,然后徐徐呼出,并慢慢放下两手及两足跟,闭目片刻。

【要领】 本势两手平开,与肩一字平,两足跟提起,脚尖着力是关键。这样就会觉得两肩沉重,如负重担。功夫深了就可以只用蹯趾点地。在此动作中,心念一定要寄托在掌心与趾尖,才能心平气静,其外部征象就是目瞪口呆。如果两目乱视,口动气粗,那就会适得其反,甚至导致站立不稳,徒劳无功。

【按语】 本势可与韦驮献杵势相接。即紧接第一势动作后,徐徐抬起两肘与肩平,同时翻掌,并向前伸出即成本势动作。本势锻炼重点在三角肌、小腿三头肌、伸趾肌群、股四头肌、肛门内外括约肌、咬肌、眼轮匝肌等。久练之能增强肌力、协调气机、强壮身体。本势对身体的平衡性起很好的调节作用,故即使小脑共济失调者练之,亦有改善症状之功。本势初练3分钟,一周后每周增加2分钟,至20分钟后酌情加减,一般30分钟左右。病者、体弱者减半。

第三势　掌托天门

【预备】 同韦驮献杵。

【动作】

1. 左脚向左横跨一步,与肩同宽,平心息气。

2. 两手同时上提至胸前,旋腕转掌,四指并拢,掌心向下,内凹,指端相距1~2寸,不高于肩。

3. 两手上举过头,同时翻掌,掌心朝天,指端相距约1寸,四指并拢,拇指外分,微触或对着天门处,两虎口相对成四边形。

4. 头向后仰,两目注视掌背,两膝微挺,足跟提起,前掌着实,咬牙致耳根有振动感。

5. 收势　同韦驮献杵。

【要领】　本势中两目上视掌背,实指内视之,不需过分仰头,必须从天门观两手背。初学者一时难以做到,这需要一个过程。如果不守此意,过分仰头,势必头昏脑胀,且站立不稳。脚尖着地的要求至足跟不能再升为止,但初练者可不抬足跟。足跟抬起时要微微向两侧分开些,使阴跷收合而阳跷开,使三阳脉之气血上升,合络督脉。督脉阳气均衡,背后三关自然流畅,姿势也就平稳了。此外全身充分放松,使气血随心所指。两臂切忌贯力,否则不能持久,提肛、咬牙、舌抵上腭以通督任脉。

【按语】　本势主要增强上肢各肌群、小腿三头肌、提肛肌的力量,提高整体的稳定协调性,更重要的是本势能使大脑血液灌注量明显增加,血管弹性提高,从而使气血供应充分,起到提神醒脑之功。久练之,可延年益寿。高血压患者忌练此功,但低血压病人坚持练此功,则有明显的升压效果。本势初练3分钟,一周后每周加2分钟,一般30分钟左右即可。体弱减半。

第四势　摘星换斗

【预备】　同韦驮献杵。

【动作】

1. 右足向前跨半步,两足相隔一拳,成前丁后八式。双手同时动作,左手握空拳,靠于腰眼(十四椎两旁),右手垂于右大腿内侧。

2. 左腿弯曲下蹲,右足尖着地,足跟提起离地约2寸,身体不可前倾后仰,不可左右歪斜。

3. 右手五指微握如钩状,屈腕沿胸向上举起,至身体右侧,离右额约一拳。

4. 指端向右略偏,头同时略向右侧抬起,双目注视掌心,紧吸慢呼,使气下沉,两腿前虚后实,但须虚中带实,实中带虚。

5. 收势　紧吸慢呼,同时还原至预备姿势。左右交换,要求相同。

【要领】　本势单手高举,五指须微微捏齐,曲腕如钩状,离前额约一拳。肘向胸前,指端向外,头微偏,松肩。两目注视掌心是关键。舌抵上腭,口微开。呼吸调匀,臀微收。前腿虚中带实,约负重量30~40%,后腿实中求虚,约负重量60~70%。换步时,前足向后退半步,动作左右相同。

【按语】　本势较其他各势为难,在推拿练功中占重要地位。练时应神注于掌心,勿使肌肉紧张,上松下实,以意运气,以气随意,务令沉着,使全身气血得以畅达。这样使身体各部分保持充分潜力,为临床应用手法打下良好基础。练时要循序渐进,切勿操之过急。本势能增加屈腕肌群、肱三头肌、下肢屈伸肌群及提肛肌的张力。本势久练之,会自觉掌心发热、发麻。初练2分钟,一周后每周增加1分钟,至7分钟后,每两周加1分钟,至10分钟后,应据具体情况而增加,一般15分钟即可。体弱多病者莫练此功。

第五势　倒拽九牛尾

【预备】　同韦驮献杵。

【动作】

1. 左腿向左平跨一步（距较比肩宽），足尖内扣，屈膝下蹲成马裆势，两手握拳护腰。随势上身略前俯，松肩，直肘，昂头，目前视。

2. 两拳上提至胸前，由拳化掌，成抱球势（上身势同韦驮献杵），随势直腰，肩松肘屈，肘略低于肩，头端平，目前视。

3. 旋转两掌，使掌心各向左右（四指并拢朝天，拇指外分，成八字掌）。随势徐徐向左右平分推，至肘直。松肩，挺肘，腕背屈，肩、肘、腕相平。

4. 身体向右转侧，成右弓左箭（面向右方）。两上肢同时动作，右上肢外旋，屈肘成半圆状，手握空拳用力，拳心对面，高不过肩，双目注拳，拳高约与肩平。肘不过膝，膝不过足尖。左上肢内旋向后伸，作螺旋劲，上身正直，塌腰收臀，鼻息调匀。

5. 收势　深呼吸，徐徐呼气，同时还原至预备姿势。左右交换，姿势相同。

【要领】　两腿前弓后箭，前肘拳微屈，似半弧形，高不过眉，肘不过膝，膝不过足，后肘微屈拳向内旋。两肩松开蓄劲用力内收，作螺旋劲，即如绞绳状，双目注于拳中（内视劳宫），上身微向前俯，重心下沉，口微开，舌抵上腭，鼻息调匀，少腹藏气含蓄，运气归纳丹田。换步时向左转，左右相同。

【按语】　本势练习中要思想集中，神志合一，内外相应，能增强两臂潜力。久练之，可增强两臂旋后肌群、旋前肌群和五指的力量。

本势顺着"左阴右阳"之规律，做时以右手领先，不可反之。两拳空握尽力，气机集中于劳宫穴，心念只想掌中，如同拽着九条牛的尾巴向后拉一样。本势初练3分钟（即左右各1分半钟），一周后每周增加1分钟，一般至8分钟左右即可。可据体质情况酌情加减。

第六势　出爪亮翅

【预备】　见韦驮献杵。

【动作】

1. 护腰势　两手握拳提至腰侧，掌心向内。

2. 两拳缓缓上提至胸变掌，拇指外侧着力，掌心向上，向前推出，掌侧相距2寸，高与肩平，两手缓缓旋腕翻掌，拇指相接，四指并拢，肩、肘、腕、掌相平。两手十指用力外分，使劲贯于指端，两目平视，头如顶物。

3. 十指用力上翘外分，肘直腕曲，两目视指端，挺胸，足踏实，膝含蓄，气欲沉，握拳七次，用力收回。

【要领】　握拳护腰，伸掌向前，拇指外侧着力，高与肩平，开始时轻如推窗，继而推到极点则重如排山倒海，这时要挺胸拔背，两目睁开，不许眨眼，集中心念于两掌中，如观明月。功夫深了，当会感觉有月在前，不可追求。用力握拳七次，用力收回。收拳时要吸气，推掌要呼气，犹如海水还潮，落汐归海。

【按语】　本势旨在锻炼两臂屈伸肌群和十指功夫，久练之会气行随意，使劲由肩臂循肘腕贯于指端，以增加推拿治病的效果。

本势初练时推收可快些，以后逐渐变缓，观掌初练1分钟，一周后每周增加1分钟，至7分钟后酌情增加，一般增至15分钟后即可。

第七势　九鬼拔马刀

【预备】　见韦驮献杵。

【动作】

1. 右手上举过头,掌心朝天,肘关节伸直,指端向左,右手下按,掌心向地,指端向前。

2. 左手旋臂向后背下按,掌心朝地,指端向右。

3. 右手屈肘旋腕,掌心向下,抱住颈项,头略向前俯,左手翻掌,掌心向背。

4. 颈部用力上抬,使头后仰,右手掌用力下按,肘弯欲尽力向上,使二力抗争,两目向左平视,背后五指欲紧按。

5. 收势　深呼吸,随呼收回。左右交换,要求相同。

【要领】　上举下按,肘部欲直,上举之掌,指端向对侧,掌心朝天,旋腕翻掌,抱颈用力下按,头后抬用力与之抗争,目须平视对侧。下按之掌,指端向前,掌心朝地,而后按后背则指端向对侧,五指紧按背部。左右轮换,身宜气静。

【按语】　本势旨在锻炼上肢伸肌(肱三头肌)、项肌、肩胛提肌及掌指的力量。

本势另一锻炼方法为同时提起足跟,这须功力深厚后才行,否则站立不稳,影响全身的姿势,甚或导致气乱,达不到锻炼的目的。从第一动作起就须气沉丹田,不可升降,轻呼吸(胸式),这样才能使颈、胸、肩特别放松,气机才能平静,然后意念集中后背心(后丹田)。高血压患者勿练此势。本势初练1分钟,一周后每周加1分钟,至5分钟后可据具体情况酌情增加。一般10分钟即可。

第八势　三盘落地

【预备】　见韦驮献杵。

【动作】

1. 左足向左横开一步,两足之距较肩为宽,足尖微向内收。屈膝下蹲,两手叉腰。

2. 两掌心朝上如托物,沿胸徐徐上托与肩平,高不过眉,两手相距1尺左右。

3. 两掌翻转掌心朝下,慢慢下覆,五指自然分开,虎口朝内,如握物状,悬空于膝盖上部(或虚掌置于膝盖),上身稍向前俯。

4. 上身转内正直,前胸微起,后背如弓,两肩松开,两肘向里裹,两目直视,口裂牙啮,提肛。

5. 收势　深呼吸,随呼收势。

【要领】　前胸微挺,后背如弓,两肘略向里内旋,头如顶物,两目直视,舌抵上腭,口微开,鼻息调匀,提肛,重心放在两脚,屈膝90°,不过足尖。意守丹田。

【按语】　本势锻炼得法能使神贯于顶,气注丹田,全身气血周流不息,故能使两臂沉静,腋力充沛,尤其能使股四头肌、腰背肌力量加强。这是推拿医生的必修功法之一。本势初练2分钟,一周后增加1分钟,至8分钟即可。

第九势　青龙探爪

【预备】　左腿向左平跨一步,两足之宽约与肩等宽,两手成仰拳护腰势。身立正直,头端平,目前视。

【动作】

1. 左上肢仰掌向右前上方伸探,掌高过顶,随势身略向右转侧,面向右前方,松肩直肘,腕勿屈曲,右拳仍作仰拳护腰势。目视于掌,两足踏实勿移。

2. 由上势，左手大拇指向掌心屈曲，双目视大拇指。

3. 左臂内旋，掌心向下，俯身探腰，随势推掌至地。膝直，足跟勿离地，昂首，目前视。

4. 左掌离地，围左膝上收至腰，成仰拳护腰势。左右交换，要求相同。

5. 收势。

【要领】 两手握拳在腰侧，左从右出拳化掌，目注掌平勿过眉，拇指内屈四指并。肩松肘直气实掌，俯身探腰推及地，围收过膝足勿移，左右轮换要求同。

【按语】 本势是专练肺、肝胆、带脉的动作，久练之可起疏肝利胆，宣肺束带之功，故此功法是肺、肝胆系统疾患和妇科带脉弛张等自身锻炼的好方法，健康人锻炼之可强身益寿。此功法练时须意守丹田，神贯拇指。推拿医生练之旨在增加两臂的蓄劲和手指的功夫，是一指禅推法的入门功法之一。本势初练3分钟，每周增加1分钟，至7分钟后，每二周增加1分钟，至10分钟后，可据情况适当增加。

第十势 饿虎扑食

【预备】 见韦驮献杵。

【动作】

1. 左足向左跨出一大步，右足稍向左偏斜，前弓后箭成左弓步。

2. 两手向前，五指着地，掌心悬空，后足跟略微提起，头向上抬。

3. 前足收回，足背放于后足跟之上，胸腹微收，抬头。

4. 全身后收，臀部突起，两肘挺直，头昂起，向前运行，约离地2寸。此时两肘弯曲，右足尖着地，全身向前，然后臀部突出，成波浪形往返动作，势如饿虎扑食。

5. 收势 随呼吸徐徐起立。左右交换，要求相同。

【要领】 头向上抬，不可过高或过低，两目注视前方，两肘和两膝伸直时不能硬挺，切忌用力过猛，应蓄力待发，吸气时全身向后收缩，臀部突出，胸腹内收，以一般柔和的悬劲，在呼气时将身向前推送（吸起呼落），力求平衡，往返动作，切勿屏气，应量力而行，紧吸慢呼，换步时，左右相同。

【按语】 本势能强筋健骨，增加手指功夫、上肢屈伸肌肉的力量、脚尖的蓄劲，亦可起到锻炼腰腹肌群的作用。本势初练时掌心可与五指同时着地，经过一个时期的锻炼后，在臂力增强的基础上，再用五指着地，掌心悬空，并逐渐减为三指着地（拇、食、中指）、二指、一指着地。练本势左右各起伏4次，以后每周增加2次，至10次即可。体弱者勿练此功。

第十一势 打躬击鼓

【预备】 见韦驮献杵。

【动作】

1. 左足向左横开一步，足尖内扣，宽与肩平。两手仰掌徐徐向左右而上，成左右平举势。头如顶物，目向前视，松肩直肘，腕勿屈曲，立身正直，腕、肘、肩相平。

2. 由上势屈肘，十指交叉相握，从掌心抱持后脑。勿挺腹凸臀。

3. 由上势，屈膝下蹲成马裆势。

4. 直膝弯腰身俯，两手用力使头尽向胯下，两膝不得屈曲，足跟勿离地，与此同时鸣天鼓左右各24次。

5. 收势　直腰,松手随呼吸放下。

【要领】　两手掌心抱头,十指相握,力与项争,足勿移,膝不屈。两腿下蹲,上身欲挺,打躬前俯,使头向胯,两膝勿挺,力在肘弯,舌抵上腭,气不可屏,与此同时左右各鸣天鼓 24 次。

【按语】　本势有数种练法,一为并步势,一为八字势,一为蹲裆势。此为锻炼腰、腿、项、臀的基础功,对临床应用按、抖两法很有帮助。本势初练 2 分钟,一周后每周增加 1 分钟,至 10 分钟即可。高血压者禁练此势。

第十二势　掉尾摇头

【预备】　见韦驮献杵。

【动作】

1. 两手仰掌由胸前徐徐上举过顶,双目视掌,随掌上举而渐移。身立正直。
2. 由上势,十指交叉相握,旋腕反掌上托,掌心朝天,两肘欲直,目向前平视。
3. 由上势,仰身,腰向后弯,上肢随之而往,目上视。
4. 由上势俯身向前,推掌至地,昂首瞪目,膝直,足跟勿离地。
5. 收势　随呼吸徐徐收势。

【要领】　十指交叉相握,上举肘须直,身向前俯,掌须直推至地,以膝直、肘直为要,昂首,瞪目。

【按语】　本势能舒松经络,强健筋骨,增强腰和手臂的功夫,为锻炼易筋经中的主要基础功。本势是易筋经的结束功法,看起来简单,实际上能使全身十二经脉、奇经八脉通达调和,达到舒通气血的作用,使人练功后有种轻松愉快的感觉。初练往返 3 次,每周增加 2 次,至 15 次后视具体情况增减。

易筋经十二势可按序全套练习,总时限以半小时左右为宜,也可根据各人具体情况,选取个别动作练习,以达到健身祛病的目的。

5.3　少林内功练习法

少林内功是内功推拿的组成部分,相传亦是达摩根据少林武术动作所衍化。少林内功的锻炼方法有别于一般气功,它不强调吐纳意守,而是讲求以力贯气,所谓"炼气不见气,以力带气,气贯四肢",在锻炼中要求两下肢用"霸力",就是用足力气,以五趾抓地,足跟踏实,下肢挺直,脚尖内收,两股用力内夹,躯干要挺拔,做到挺胸,收腹,含颔。上肢在进行各种锻炼时,要求凝劲于肩、臂、肘、腕、指,呼吸自然,与动作相协调,练时力达于四肢腰背,气随力行,注于经脉,使气血循行畅通,荣灌四肢九窍、五脏六腑,使阴阳平复,气血充盈,因而能扶正健体,祛除病邪。少林内功锻炼时,还必须注意的是虽然周身肌肉静止性用劲,但呼吸要自然,不能屏气,即所谓"外紧内松",运动时要做到刚中有柔,刚柔相济。

少林内功锻炼时全身紧张用力,久之习练,可使食欲增加,睡眠沉实。现代科学认识到这种功法可以促进新陈代谢,增强消化功能,并使神经系统的功能得到调节。

（一）站势

【动作】

1. 立正,左足向左平跨一步,宽于肩部,足尖略收成内八字,五趾着地,运用霸力,劲由上贯下注足。

2. 前胸微挺,后臀要蓄,两手后伸,挺肘伸腕,肩腋莫松,四指并拢,拇指外分,两目平视,头勿左右盼顾,精神贯注,呼吸随意。

【要领】 三直四平。三直:臀、腰、腿;四平:头、肩、掌、脚,两脚内扣,运用霸力。夹肩、挺肘、伸腕、翻掌、立指。挺胸收腹,舌抵上腭,呼吸自然,两目平视。

【按语】 本势为锻炼少林内功的主要基本站桩功,它要求下肢足尖略收成内八字站立,五趾着地,外分,两大腿以内侧肌群,如耻骨肌、股薄肌、长收肌、短收肌以及大收肌等为主,收缩夹紧,运用霸力,劲由上贯下注足。上肢以背阔肌、大圆肌、三角肌后束为主,使两臂后伸,以斜方肌使两肩胛靠拢,并通过前臂后肌群如桡侧腕长伸肌等使手腕背伸,拇长伸肌和指总伸肌等使手指伸直,总之要凝劲于四末,使气贯四肢。四肢末端乃十二经脉之本,练习本势可通调十二经脉气血,使其循行畅通,外荣四肢百骸,内灌五脏六腑,从而调和阴阳,疏通气血,调整脏腑功能,起到扶正祛邪的作用。

(二) 马裆势

【动作】

1. 立正,左足向左平开一步,屈膝下蹲,两足距离较肩为宽,两膝和脚尖微向内扣,两脚跟微向外蹬,足尖成内八字形。

2. 两手后伸,肘直腕伸,拇指分开,四指并拢,或两手平放两胯处,虎口朝内。上身挺胸,收腹微微前倾,重心放在两腿之间,头如顶物,目须平视,呼吸随意。

【要领】 沉腰屈膝,挺胸收腹,两目平视,呼吸自然。

【按语】 本势是锻炼下部的基本功,所谓练"架力"的功夫,它要求以半腱肌、半膜肌、股二头肌、缝匠肌、股薄肌以及腓肠肌为主,使两膝屈曲下蹲并使膝部和脚尖微向内扣,以其拮抗肌即股四头肌收缩,保持马步姿势。并通过骶棘肌和腹直肌、腹外斜肌、腹内斜肌和腹横肌等的作用,以挺胸收腹,将重心放在两腿之间,从而达到健腰补肾之功。

(三) 弓箭裆势

【动作】

1. 立正,身向右旋,右足向右前方跨出一大步,距离可根据自己身体高矮取其自然;右腿在前,屈膝半蹲,膝与足成垂直线,足尖微向内扣;左腿在后,膝部挺直,足略向外撤,脚跟必须着地,成前弓后箭之势。

2. 上身略向前俯,重心下沉,臀须微收,两臂后伸,挺肘伸腕,掌根蓄劲(或两手叉腰),虎口朝内,蓄势待发,全神贯注,虚领顶劲,呼吸随意。

【要领】 前弓后箭,重心下沉,挺胸收腹,呼吸随意。

【按语】 本势是锻炼裆势的重要"运动"之一。要求成前弓后箭之势。即以髂腰肌、股直肌、阔筋膜张肌、缝匠肌以及半腱肌、半膜肌、股二头肌和腓肠肌为主,使前腿屈髋屈膝;以股四头肌为主使后腿挺直。锻炼时要用劲后沉,使势有待发之态,练至一个阶段就可结合上肢动作。

(四) 磨裆势

【预备】 右弓步,上身略向前俯,重心下沉,臀微收,两手仰掌护腰。
【动作】

1. 左手化俯掌屈肘向右上方推出,掌根及臂外侧运动徐徐向左方磨转,同时身随其向左旋转,右弓步演变成左弓步,左手变仰掌护腰。

2. 右手化俯掌屈肘向左上方推出,掌根及臂外侧运动徐徐向右方磨转,同时身随其向右旋转,左弓步演变成右弓步,右手变仰掌护腰。

【要领】 前弓后箭,重心下沉,上肢蓄力,徐徐磨转。
【按语】 本势下肢要求呈前弓后箭势,上肢要求由仰掌化俯掌,屈肘向右(左)上方推出,并以上肢肌群尤以三角肌、冈上肌、冈下肌、小圆肌为主,蓄力于掌根、臂外,徐徐向左(右)方磨转,同时身随其转,右弓步演变成左弓步。左右同。

(五)亮裆势

【预备】 同弓箭裆势。
【动作】

1. 两手由后向上亮掌,指端相对,掌心朝上,目注掌背,上身略前俯,重心下沉。

2. 换步时向后转,两掌收回由腰部向后,左右同之。

【要领】 上举亮掌,目注掌背,换步后转,两掌收回。
【按语】 本势预备姿势为弓箭裆,要求以冈上肌、三角肌、斜方肌和前锯肌为主,蓄力上举亮掌,当换步后转时,两掌收回后伸。

(六)并裆势

【动作】

1. 立正,两足跟微微向外蹬,足尖并拢,五趾着实,用力宜匀。

2. 两手挺肘伸腕,微向后伸,掌心朝下,四指并拢,拇指外分,目须平视。

【要领】 同站裆势。

(七)大裆势

【动作】

1. 左足向左分开一大步,膝直足实。

2. 两手后伸,虎口相对,四指并拢,肘直腕伸。

【要领】 同站裆势。

(八)悬裆势

【动作】

1. 左足向左横开一大步,屈膝半蹲,两足距离较马裆宽。

2. 两手后伸,肘直腕伸,四指并拢,拇指外分,动作与马裆相同,故又称大马裆。

【要领】 同马裆势。

(九)低裆势

【动作】

1. 立正,足尖相拢,五趾着地,足跟外蹬,呈内八字。

2. 屈膝下蹲,上身下沉,臀部后坐不可着地,故有蹲裆之称,同时两手握拳前举,肘要微屈,掌心相对,目须平视。

【要领】 屈膝下蹲,上身下沉,臀不着地,握拳上举,拳心相对,两肘微屈。

【按语】 本姿势要求以半腱肌、半膜肌、股二头肌、缝匠肌、股薄肌、腓肠肌以及髂腰肌、股直肌、阔筋膜张肌和缝匠肌为主,屈膝屈髋,使上身下沉,并同时以其拮抗肌,即股四头肌以及臀大肌、股二头肌、半腱肌和半膜肌收缩,使身体保持低档势。

(十) 坐档势

【动作】

1. 两脚交叉,盘膝而坐,脚外侧着地,上身微向前俯,故称之为坐盘功架。

2. 两手掌心朝下,腕要伸,使身平衡,两目平视。

【要领】 盘膝而坐,脚侧着地,上身微前俯。

【按语】 本势要求在屈膝屈髋的基础上,再以臀中肌、臀小肌的后部肌束以及梨状肌等收缩,使髋关节外旋,呈坐档势。

基本动作

第一势 前推八匹马

【预备】 站好站档或指定的档势

【动作】

1. 两手屈肘,直掌于两胁。

2. 两掌心相对,拇指伸直,四指并拢,蓄劲于肩臂指端,使两臂徐徐运力前推,以肩与掌成直线为度。胸须微挺,臂略收,头勿盼顾,两目平视,呼吸随意。

3. 手臂运动,拇指上翘,指端力求与手臂成直线,慢慢屈肘,收回于两胁。

4. 由直掌化俯掌下按,两臂后伸,回原档势。

【要领】 指臂蓄力,立指运气慢推,两目平视,呼吸自然。

【按语】 本势为内功推拿的基础功法,前推时要求蓄力于肩臂指端,两臂运力,其中尤以肱三头肌为主,徐徐向前推动。

第二势 倒拉九头牛

【预备】 站好站档或指定的档势。

【动作】

1. 两手屈肘,直掌于两胁。

2. 两掌沿两胁前推,边推边将前臂渐渐内旋,手臂完全伸直时,虎口正好朝下。四指并拢,拇指用力外分,腕、肘伸直,力求与肩平。

3. 五指向内屈收,由掌化拳如握物状,劲注拳心,旋腕拳眼朝上,紧紧内收,化直掌于两胁,身微前倾,臀部微收。

4. 由直掌化俯掌下按,两臂后伸,恢复原档势。

【要领】 直掌旋推,劲注拳心,肘腕伸直,力求肩平,紧紧后拉。

【按语】 本势前推时,要以肩胛下肌、胸大肌、背阔肌及大圆肌为主,边推边将前臂内旋,当手臂伸直时,虎口正好朝下,再化掌握拳,拳眼朝上,以肱二头肌、肱肌、肱桡肌以及旋前圆肌收缩,劲注拳眼,紧紧内收,犹如倒拉九头牛之势。

第三势 单掌拉金环

【预备】 站好站档或指定的档势。

【动作】

1. 两手屈肘,直掌于两胁。

2. 右手前推,边推边将前臂内旋,虎口朝下,掌心朝外,四指并拢,拇指外分,臂欲蓄劲,掌侧着力,肘腕伸直,松肩,身体正直,两目平视,呼吸随意。

3. 五指内收握拳,使劲注掌心,旋腕,拳眼朝上,紧紧内收,化直掌护胁。左手动作与右手相同。

4. 由直掌化俯掌下按,两臂后伸,恢复原档势。

【要领】 同倒拉九头牛。

【按语】 同倒拉九头牛。

第四势 凤凰展翅

【预备】 站好弓箭档或指定的档势。

【动作】

1. 两手屈肘上行,徐徐至上胸成立掌交叉。

2. 由立掌化为俯掌,缓缓用力向左右外分,两臂尽力伸直,形如展翅,四指并拢,拇指外分,指欲翘,头如顶物,两目平视,上身微倾,切勿抬肩,呼吸随意。

3. 两掌旋腕,屈肘内收,两侧蓄劲着力,徐徐收回,使掌心逐渐相对,处于胸前交叉立掌。

4. 由上胸之立掌化俯掌下按,两臂后伸,恢复原档势。

【要领】 立掌交叉,用力外展,颈如开弓,肩肘腕平,蓄劲内收。

【按语】 本势外展时,以桡侧腕屈肌、尺侧腕屈肌、掌长肌、指浅屈肌和指深屈肌为主,化立掌为俯掌,并通过三角肌、冈上肌等上臂肌群的收缩,使两臂用力缓缓向左右外分,其形如凤凰展翅。

第五势 霸王举鼎

【预备】 站好弓箭档势或指定的档势。

【动作】

1. 两手屈肘,仰掌于腰部。

2. 仰掌缓缓上托,掌心朝天,过于肩部掌根外展,指端由左右向内旋转,虎口相对,犹托重物,徐徐上举,肘部要挺,指端相对,四指并拢,拇指外分,两目平视,呼吸自然。

3. 旋腕翻掌,指端朝上,掌侧相对,拇指外分,蓄力而下,渐渐收回腰部。

4. 在腰部之仰掌化俯掌下按,两臂后伸同原档势。

【要领】 仰掌上托,过肩旋腕翻掌,指端相对,挺肘上举,回收旋腕翻掌直下,指端朝上,掌侧相对。

【按语】 本势上举时,要求过肩旋腕翻掌,以桡侧腕长伸肌、桡侧腕短伸肌、尺侧腕伸肌及所有伸指肌收缩,使腕关节尽量皆伸,挺肘缓缓上举。

第六势 顺水推舟

【预备】 站好马档或指定的档势。

【动作】

1. 两手屈肘,直掌于两胁。

2. 两直掌运动徐徐向前推出,边推边掌根外展,虎口朝下,四指并拢,拇指外分,由外向内旋转,指尖相对,肘欲伸直,腕欲屈曲,似环之形,头勿低,身勿倾,力求掌肘肩平。

3. 五指慢慢向左右外旋,恢复直掌,四指并拢,拇指运劲后翘,指端着力,屈肘蓄力而收,置于两胁。

4. 由直掌化俯掌下按,两臂后伸,同原裆势。

【要领】 直掌运劲慢推时,旋腕指尖相对,挺肘形似推舟。

【按语】 本势直掌前推时,要求以肩胛下肌、胸大肌、背阔肌、大圆肌及上臂肌群蓄力,边推边内旋前臂,同时通过桡侧腕长伸肌、桡侧腕短伸肌、尺侧腕伸肌及所有伸指肌的收缩,背伸腕关节,待推出后其形似环。

第七势　怀中抱月

【预备】 站好悬裆或指定的裆势。

【动作】

1. 两手屈肘,仰掌于腰部。

2. 两仰掌由腰部上提,化立掌在上胸交叉,缓缓向左右外分,肘欲直,指端朝左右,掌心朝前须与肩平。

3. 两指端向下,掌心朝内,慢慢蓄劲,上身略前倾,两手势如抱物,由上而下,再由下而上徐徐抄起,仍直掌回收上胸交叉。

4. 由上胸立掌化俯掌下按,两臂后伸,同原裆势。

【要领】 仰掌上提,立掌交叉,左右外分,掌心朝前,腕肘肩平,指端向下,掌心朝内,上身略向前倾,同时以胸大肌、背阔肌、大圆肌以及肱二头肌等为主,将两臂由下而上徐徐抄起,其势如抱月。

第八势　仙人指路

【预备】 站好并裆势或指定的裆势。

【动作】

1. 两手屈肘,仰掌于腰部。

2. 右仰掌上提至胸前立掌而出,四指并拢。拇指伸直,手心内凹成瓦楞掌,肘臂运劲立掌向前推出,力要均匀。

3. 推直后屈腕握拳,蓄劲内收,边收边外旋前臂,仰掌于腰部,左掌动作与右掌相同。

4. 由仰掌化俯掌下按,两臂后伸,同原裆势。

【要领】 仰掌上提,立掌胸前,手心内凹,如同瓦楞,臂指运劲,用力前推,旋腕握拳后拉。

【按语】 本势前推时,要求立掌,并通过骨间掌侧肌、拇长伸肌,以及蚓状肌等,使四指并拢,拇指伸直,手心内凹成瓦楞掌,肘臂运力,向前推出。

第九势　平手托塔

【预备】 站好大裆或指定的裆势。

【动作】

1. 两手屈肘,仰掌于胁部。

2. 两仰掌慢慢向前运劲推出,边推边拇指向左右外侧倾斜,保持掌平运行,犹如托物在手,推足后手与肩平。

3. 拇指运劲向左右外侧倾斜,四指齐着力,屈肘缓缓蓄劲收回,处于两胁。

4. 由仰掌化俯掌下按,两臂后伸,同原裆势。

【要领】 仰掌运劲前推,大指外下倾斜,肘直掌平托物。

【按语】 本势前推时,要求以冈下肌、小圆肌为主,使前臂外旋,保持手掌平行,慢慢向前推出。

第十势 运掌合瓦

【预备】 站好大裆或指定的裆势。

【动作】

1. 两手屈肘,仰掌于腰部。

2. 右手由仰掌化俯掌,运劲于臂,贯指向前推足,肩欲松开,肘欲伸直,指端朝前,掌心向下,蓄力待发。

3. 右手旋腕变仰掌徐徐收回,待近胸时左仰掌即变俯掌在右仰掌上交叉,掌心相合,慢慢向前推出,掌心向下,右仰掌收回腰部。

4. 左手旋腕变仰掌徐徐收回,并两手化俯掌下按,两臂后伸,同原裆势。

【要领】 仰掌运劲前推,肩松肘直,指端朝前。

【按语】 本势前推时,通过旋前圆肌,旋前方肌和肱桡肌的收缩,使仰掌化俯掌,而后再运力向前推出。

第十一势 风摆荷叶

【预备】 站好弓箭裆或指定的裆势。

【动作】

1. 两手屈肘,仰掌于腰部。

2. 两手掌心向上,四指并拢,拇指伸直,向前上方推出,至胸部左掌在右掌上相迭,运劲向前推足,然后即缓缓向左右外分,肩肘掌须平成直线形,拇指外侧着力含蓄,使两手平托成水平线,头如顶物,目欲平视,呼吸随意。

3. 两仰掌慢慢合拢,右下左上,交叉相迭,再收于腰部。

4. 由仰掌化俯掌下按,两臂后伸,同原裆势。

【要领】 仰掌交叉前推,外旋挺肘拉开,肩肘腕掌平齐。

【按语】 本势仰掌于腰部,通过肱三头肌等的收缩,运劲向前推足,然后以三角肌、冈上肌等上臂肌群为主,缓缓向左右外分,使两手平托成水平线。

第十二势 两手托天

【预备】 站好悬裆或指定的裆势。

【动作】

1. 两手屈肘,仰掌于腰部。

2. 两仰掌上托,掌心朝天,缓缓上举。指端着力,肩松肘直,两目平视,头如顶物。

3. 掌根外旋,四指并拢分向左右,蓄力徐徐而下,至胸部旋腕变仰掌,收回护腰。

4. 由仰掌化俯掌下按,两臂后伸,同原裆势。

【要领】 仰掌上托,掌心朝天,指端运劲,松肩挺肘,两目平视。

【按语】 本势仰掌上托时,以三角肌、冈上肌、斜方肌、前锯肌等为主,蓄力上举,犹如托天。

第十三势　单凤朝阳

【预备】 站好并档或指定的档势。

【动作】

1. 两手屈肘,仰掌于腰部。

2. 左仰掌旋腕变俯掌,屈肘向胸之左上方运力外展,再缓缓运向右下方,屈肘运动上抄作半圆形,收回护腰。

3. 右手动作与左手相同,唯方向相反。

4. 由仰掌化俯掌下按,两臂后伸,同原档势。

【要领】 旋腕化掌,蓄力外展,缓缓下运,形似半圆。

【按语】 本势由仰掌化俯掌,以三角肌、冈上肌及手臂肌群运力向左上外展,推足后再以胸大肌、背阔肌、三角肌、肱三头肌长头等为主,缓缓运向右下方,屈肘上抄作半圆形。

第十四势　海底捞月

【预备】 站好大档或指定的档势。

【动作】

1. 两手屈肘,仰掌于腰部。

2. 两手仰掌上提,经胸徐徐高举,并向左右推分,旋腕翻掌,掌心朝下,同时腰向前俯,腿不可屈,脚用霸力,两掌由上而下逐渐相拢,掌心向上似抱物,蓄劲待发。

3. 两臂运劲,掌心指端着力,慢慢抄起,用抱力缓缓提到胸部成仰掌护腰,上身随势而直,目须平视。

4. 由仰掌化俯掌下按,两臂后伸,同原档势。

【要领】 仰掌上提,胸上高举,左右分推,旋腕翻掌,腰俯腿直,掌心向上,似如抱月,两臂运劲,指端着力,慢慢抄起。

【按语】 本势仰掌以冈上肌、三角肌、前锯肌、斜方肌为主,将两臂缓缓上提,并通过三角肌和冈上肌等使两臂向左右推分,旋腕翻掌后以腹肌的收缩,使身体微向前俯,同时以胸大肌、背阔肌、大圆肌等蓄力,将两掌由上而下,再由下而上慢慢抄起,形似海底捞月。

第十五势　顶天抱地

【预备】 站好大档或指定的档势。

【动作】

1. 两手屈肘,仰掌于腰部。

2. 仰掌上托,过于肩部旋腕翻掌,掌根外展,指端内旋相对,徐徐上举,待推足后,旋腕翻掌,慢慢向左右外分下抄,同时身向前俯,两掌逐渐合拢,拇指外分,两掌相叠(右掌在上),掌背尽量靠底待发。

3. 两掌如抬重物缓缓提到胸部成仰掌护腰,上身随势而直,目须平视。

4. 两仰掌化俯掌下按,两臂后伸,同原档势。

【要领】 仰掌上托,过肩旋腕翻掌,掌心朝上,指端相对,两翻掌外分下抄,身向前俯,两掌合拢相迭,如抱物上提。

【按语】 本势仰掌上托时,要求过肩旋腕翻掌,以桡侧腕长伸肌、桡侧腕短伸肌、尺侧腕伸肌及所有伸指肌的收缩,使腕关节尽量背伸,挺肘缓缓上举,推足后以桡侧腕屈肌、尺侧腕屈肌、掌长肌、指浅屈肌、指深屈肌和拇指屈肌等为主,旋腕翻掌,再徐徐向左右外分抄,同时身向前俯,两掌合拢相叠,缓缓提起,通过骶棘肌的作用,身体随势而直。

第十六势　力劈华山

【预备】 站好弓箭裆或指定的裆势。

【动作】

1. 两手屈肘,在上胸部成立掌交叉(左在右上或右在左上)。

2. 两立掌缓缓向左右分推,两肩松开,肘部微曲,四指并拢,拇指后翘,掌心向前,力求成水平线。

3. 两臂同时用力下劈,连续三次,头勿转侧摇动,两目平视,待劈完最后一次,仰掌护腰。

4. 由仰掌化俯掌下按,两臂后伸,同原裆势。

【要领】 立掌交叉,左右分推,用力下劈,两目平视。

【按语】 本势立掌交叉,向左右分推,当两臂成水平线向下劈时,要求以斜方肌、背阔肌、胸大肌、大圆肌、肩胛下肌以及上臂肌群等蓄力,连续用力劈砍三次。

思 考 题

- 试述推拿练功的作用。
- 站裆势的要求有哪些。

6 推拿手法

推拿手法是操作者用手或肢体其他部分刺激治疗部位和活动肢体的规范化的技巧动作。由于刺激方式、强度、时间的不同,形成了许多操作方法不同的基本手法,如推法、按法、揉法等,基本手法是推拿手法的主要组成部分;两个以上基本手法结合起来操作形成复合手法,如按揉法、推摩法等;小儿推拿中还存在着一些复式手法,以一连串动作组合起来操作,并冠以特定名称,如"打马过天河"、"黄蜂入洞"等。推拿手法刺激机体的不同部位,具有疏通经络、行气活血、滑利关节、调节脏腑功能等作用。

推拿手法是推拿治疗的手段,良好的推拿手法是取得临床疗效的关键。推拿手法的基本要求是:持久,有力,均匀,柔和,深透。"持久",是要求手法操作能持续一定的时间,且动作规范不变形;"有力",是要求手法必须具有恰当的力量,力量的大小应根据病人的体质、病情和治疗部位的不同进行调整,切忌使用拙力、暴力;"均匀",是要求手法动作有节奏性,速度、压力在一定范围内维持恒定;"柔和",是要求手法轻柔缓和,不能生硬粗暴;"深透",是指手法作用达到组织深层。只有符合持久、有力、均匀、柔和要求的手法才能深透。成功的手法应以柔为先、和为贵。

推拿基本手法有多种分类方式。根据手法动作形态可分为摆动类、摩擦类、振动类、按压类、叩击类、活动关节类手法;根据作用组织不同可分为软组织推拿手法、关节整复推拿手法;根据推拿流派分为一指禅推拿手法、㨰法推拿手法、正骨推拿手法等;根据作用途径可分为刺激性手法,矫正性手法,松动性手法等。本书采用基本手法和复式手法的分类方法来叙述。

推拿手法的练习主要是练习动作技巧及锻炼指、腕、臂力。可先在沙袋上练习,然后再在人体上练习。沙袋练习时,备棉布袋一只,长约8寸,宽约5寸,内装洗净黄沙(最好掺些碎海绵,使沙袋具有弹性),另外用一只棉布袋作套以利换洗。开始练习时,袋可扎得稍紧些,以后随着手法的熟练,将袋逐渐放松。各种基本手法经过沙袋上的练习,动作技巧比较熟练后,可到人体头面及颈项部、上肢部、下肢部、肩背部、腰臀部、胸胁部、腹部几个部位进行基本手法综合操作练习。被操作者分别取坐位、俯卧位、仰卧位、侧卧位等不同体位。

除手法操作技巧练习外,推拿医师还应进行指、腕、臂力等专项练习,可采用徒手和器械的方法,具体如俯卧撑、哑铃、握力器等。同时推拿练功是推拿医师的必修课,通过功法锻炼不仅可提高推拿师的身体素质,而且可使推拿手法质量提高。

6.1 成人推拿基本手法

推拿基本手法是指由单一动作成分为基本结构单元的推拿手法,基本推拿手法数量较多,注重技巧,具有稳定的动力构型,是组成复式推拿手法的基本成分。

6.1.1 一指禅推法

以拇指指端或罗纹面着力,前臂摆动,使所产生的功力通过拇指持续不断的作用于施术部位或穴位上,称为一指禅推法。一指禅推法是一指禅推拿流派的代表手法。

【操作方法】

术者手握空拳,腕掌悬屈,拇指自然伸直,盖住拳眼,用拇指指端或末节罗纹面着力于体表上,沉肩、垂肘、悬腕,运用前臂的主动摆动带动腕部的横向摆动及拇指关节的屈伸活动,使功力轻重交替、持续不断地作用于经络穴位上,频率每分钟120~160次(图6-1)。

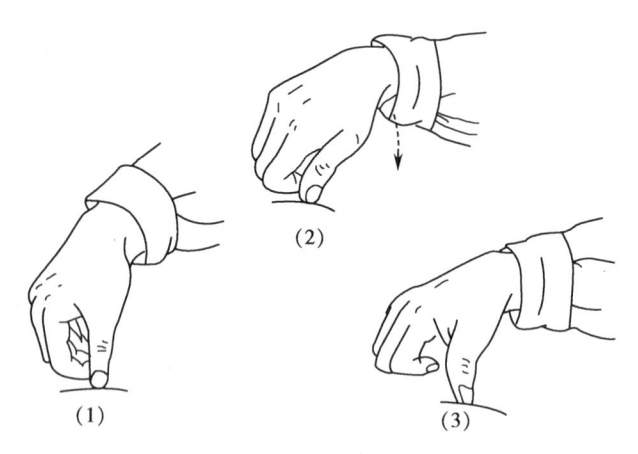

图 6-1 一指禅推法

Fig. 6-1 One-finger pushing manipulation

【动作要领】

1. 沉肩 肩关节放松,肩胛骨自然下沉,保持腋下空松,能容纳一拳的距离,不要耸肩用力。

2. 垂肘 肘关节自然下垂,略低于腕部。肘部不要向外支起,亦不宜过度内收。

3. 悬腕 腕关节屈曲,自然悬垂,在保持腕关节放松的基础上,尽可能屈腕至90°。

4. 指实 拇指指端或罗纹面自然着实,吸定于施术部位或穴位上,但不可拙力下压。

5. 掌虚 除拇指外的其余四指及手掌放松,握虚拳,做到蓄力于掌,发力于指。

6. 紧推慢移 一指禅推法在体表移动过程中的操作要领。紧推指一指禅推法的摆动频率相对较快,维持在每分钟120~160次;慢移是拇指指端或罗纹面在吸定于体表的基础上,可沿经络或特定的路径缓慢移动,同时不可滑动或摩擦。

【注意事项】

1. 一指禅推法操作时宜气定神敛,心神和宁,专注于手法操作。姿势端正,要领正确,肩、肘、腕各部位贯穿一个"松"字,且松而不懈,与躯干整体协调,才能使手法形神俱备。

2. 一指禅推法有拇指指间关节屈伸和不屈伸两种不同术式,若术者拇指指间关节较僵硬,活动范围较小或治疗时需要较柔和的刺激,可采用屈伸拇指指间关节的操作;若术者拇指指间关节较柔软,宜选用不屈伸拇指指间关节的操作。

3. 一指禅推法在体表操作时应遵循"推经络,走穴道"的原则,循经取穴施治。

附:一指禅推法的衍变

1. 一指禅偏峰推法 以拇指偏峰处(少商穴)着力,拇指伸直并内收,其余掌指伸直,腕关节微屈,前臂主动摆动,带动腕关节轻度摆动的一指禅推法,称为一指禅偏峰推法(又称"少商劲")(图 6-2)。刺激轻快柔和,常用于颜面部操作。

2. 一指禅屈指推法 拇指屈曲,以拇指指间关节桡侧或背侧着力,做一指禅推法,称为一指禅屈指推法(又称"跪推法")(图 6-3),着力较稳,刚劲有力,常用于项枕部、关节骨缝处。

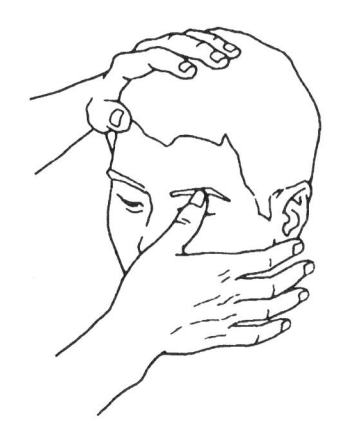

图 6-2 一指禅偏峰推法
Fig. 6-2 Yi Zhi Chan Pian Feng Tui Fa(lateral-pushing of one-finger pushing manipulation)

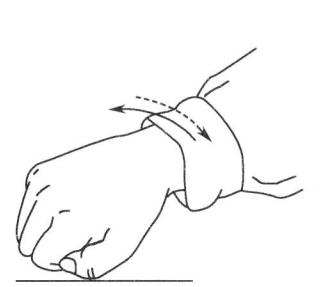

图 6-3 一指禅屈指推法
Fig. 6-3 Yi Zhi Chan Qu Zhi Tui Fa(one-finger pushing manipulation performed with flexed thumb)

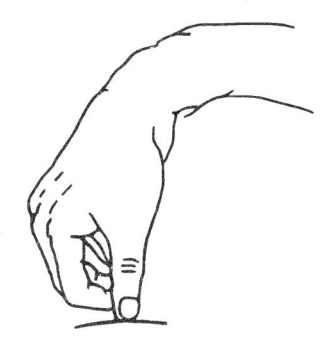

图 6-4 缠法
Fig. 6-4 Chan Fa(Twining manipulation or quick pushing manipulation)

3. 缠法 缩小一指禅推法拇指指端或偏峰的接触部位面积,减少前臂摆动幅度,降低拇指对体表的压力,提高摆动频率至每分钟 220~250 次,称为缠法(取缠绵不休之意)(图 6-4)。缠法具有较强的消散作用,常用于实热证及痈疖等外科病证的治疗。

6.1.2 㨰法

以尺侧手背为接触面,前臂摆动带动腕关节屈伸,手背在体表施术部位滚动,称为㨰法。㨰法是㨰法推拿流派的代表手法。

【操作方法】

术者拇指自然伸直,手握空拳,小指、无名指的掌指关节自然屈曲约90°,其余手指掌指关节屈曲角度依次减小,使手背沿掌横弓排列成弧面,以手掌部近小指侧部分贴附于治疗部位上,前臂主动摆动,带动腕关节较大幅度的屈伸和前臂旋转的协同运动,使手背尺侧在治疗部位上作持续不断的来回滚动(图6-5),摆动频率每分钟120次左右。

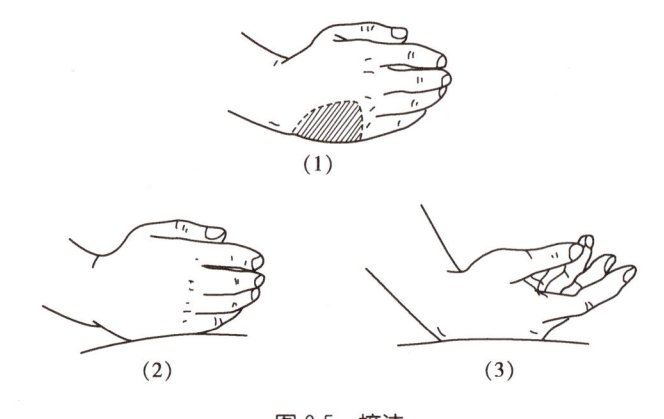

图 6-5 滚法

Fig. 6-5　Gun Fa(Rolling Manipulation)

【动作要领】

1. 沉肩,垂肘,肘关节自然屈曲140°,距胸壁一拳左右,松腕,手握空拳,小指至食指掌指关节屈曲角度依次减小,手背呈弧形,吸定于治疗部位。

2. 腕关节屈伸幅度要在120°左右,即外摆时屈腕约80°,回摆时伸腕约40°,使手掌背部分的二分之一面积依次接触治疗部位。外摆的同时前臂外旋,回摆时前臂内旋。

3. 刺激轻重交替,前滚同回滚时着力重轻之比为3∶1,即"滚三回一"。

4. 滚法在体表移动时应在吸定的基础上,保持手法的固有频率,移动速度不宜过快。

5. 滚法在临床应用时经常配合患者肢体的被动运动,可在一手滚法同时,另一手协同肢体作被动运动,两手要协调,被动运动要"轻巧、短促、随发随收"。

【注意事项】

1. 滚法操作应尽量做到腕关节最大幅度的屈伸,避免出现前臂旋转为主、腕关节屈伸幅度不足的错误方式。

2. 滚法宜吸定,不宜拖动、跳动或旋转摆动。避免出现手背与体表的撞击感。在移动过程中,注意避免在体表的拖动。

3. 避免在脊椎棘突或其他各部关节的骨突处施术,带来不适感。

附:滚法的衍变

1. 掌指关节滚法　以掌指关节骨突为接触部位,用腕关节单纯伸屈运动代替腕关节屈伸与前臂旋转的复合运动,称为掌指关节滚法(图6-6)。压力和刺激强度较滚法更大,多用于腰臀及下肢肌肉特别丰厚坚实的部位。

2. 前臂滚法　用前臂尺侧着力于治疗部位,作来回往返的滚动,称为前臂滚法(图6-7)。其接触面积大,刺激柔和舒适,多用于较肥胖的患者或施治部位范围较广的腰背及下肢部。

图 6-6　掌指关节㨰法

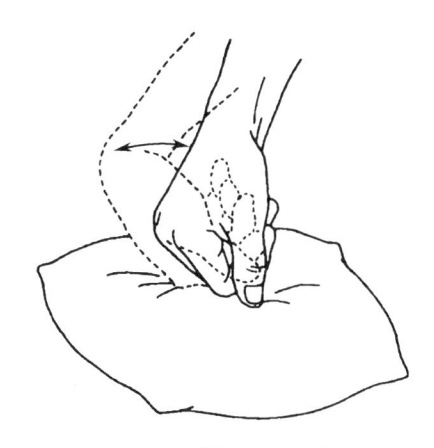

Fig. 6-6　Zhang Zhi Guan Jie Gun Fa (Manipulation of rolling with palm and phalangeal joints)

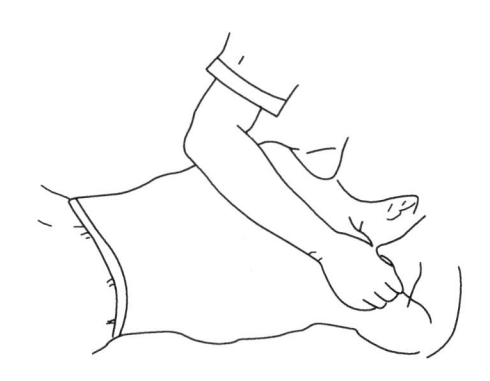

图 6-7　前臂㨰法

Fig. 6-7　Qian Bi Gun Fa (manipulation of rolling with forearm)

6.1.3　揉法

以指、掌的某一部位着力吸定于体表上,带动该处的皮下组织作轻柔缓和的环旋揉动,称为揉法,是推拿常用手法之一。根据操作时接触面的不同可分为掌根揉法、大鱼际揉法和指揉法。

【操作方法】

1. 大鱼际揉法　术者以手掌大鱼际部着力,肘关节微屈120°～140°,以肘关节为支点,前臂作主动摆动,带动大鱼际在治疗部位揉动摆动,频率每分钟120～160次左右。(图6-8)

2. 掌根揉法　术者以掌根部分着力,手指自然弯曲,腕关节略背伸,肘关节微屈作为支点,前臂作主动摆动,带动掌根在治疗部位揉动,频率为每分钟120～160次左右。(图6-9)

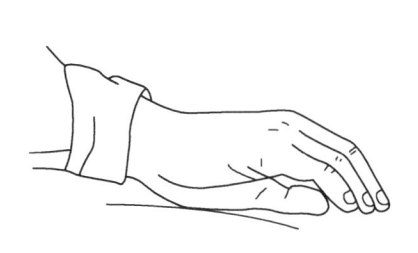

图 6-8　大鱼际揉法

Fig. 6-8　Da Yu Ji Rou Fa(Major thenar kneading manipulation)

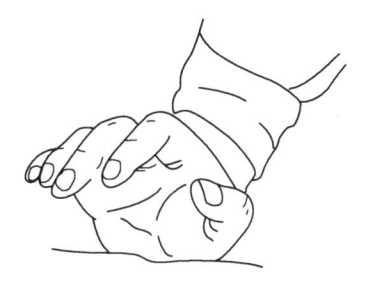

图 6-9　掌根揉法

Fig. 6-9　Zhang Gen Rou Fa(Palm base kneading manipulation)

3. 拇指揉法　以拇指罗纹面着力,其余手指扶持于合适部位,腕关节微屈或伸直,前臂做小幅度摆动,带动拇指在施术部位上作环转运动,频率为每分钟120～160次(图6-10)。

4. 中指揉法　以中指罗纹面着力,中指指间关节伸直,掌指关节微屈,以肘关节为支点,前臂作小幅度主动运动,带动中指罗纹面在施术部位作环转运动,频率为每分钟 120～160 次(图 6-11)。

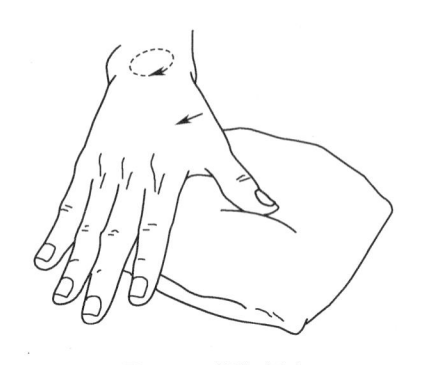

图 6-10　拇指揉法
Fig. 6-10　Mu Zhi Rou Fa(Thumb kneading manipulation)

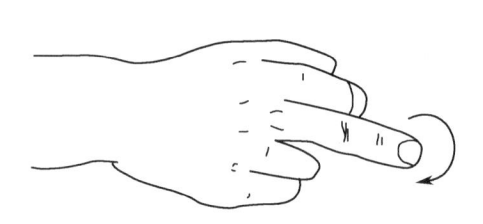

图 6-11　中指揉法
Fig. 6-11　Zhong Zhi Rou Fa(Middle finger kneading manipulation)

以食指或食、中、无名指并拢作指揉法分称为食指揉法和三指揉法,操作要领同中指揉法。

【动作要领】

1. 揉法要做到沉肩、垂肘、腕关节放松,以前臂小幅度的主动摆动,通过腕关节传递,带动接触部位回转运动。

2. 揉法操作时要带动皮下组织一起运动,动作要灵活协调而有节律。

3. 揉法所施压力要适中,以受术者感到舒适为度。

【注意事项】

1. 揉法操作时,接触部位不可和体表之间有相对摩擦运动。

2. 揉法的功力要通过放松的腕关节传递,注意在作指揉法的时候,腕关节应在放松的基础上,保持一定的紧张度,不可使腕关节过分僵硬。

6.1.4　摩法

以指、掌面为接触部位,在体表作环形而有节奏的摩擦运动,称为摩法。

【操作方法】

1. 掌摩法　术者手指并拢,手掌自然伸直,腕关节微伸,将手掌平放在体表上,以肘关节为支点,前臂作主动运动,带动手掌在体表施术部位作环旋摩擦运动(图 6-12)。频率为每分钟 100～120 次,顺逆时针均可。

2. 指摩法　以食、中、无名、小指末节指面为接触部位,四指并拢,手掌自然伸

图 6-12　掌摩法
Fig. 6-12　Zhang Mo Fa(Palm-rubbing manipulation)

直,腕关节微屈,以肘关节为支点,前臂做主动运动,带动四指指面在施术部位作环形摩擦运动。频率为每分钟 100～120 次,顺逆时针均可。

【动作要领】

1. 摩法应肩关节放松,以前臂主动摆动为主,带动放松的腕关节作环转运动。指摩法时腕关节在放松的基础上可保持一定的紧张度,但要紧而不僵。

2. 摩法用力要轻重得宜,速度均衡,做到轻而不飘,重而不滞。指摩法较轻快,掌摩法稍重缓。

【注意事项】

1. 摩法宜轻缓,不宜急重。

2. 根据病情的虚实决定手法的方向。传统认为虚证宜用顺时针方向的摩法,实证宜用逆时针方向的摩法,临床还应结合施术部位的解剖结构和病理状况选择使用不同方向的摩法。

3. 摩法应用时,常根据病情,涂以各种性能的药膏,称为膏摩(见"膏摩")。也可在应用摩法时,涂以葱姜汁、冬青膏、松节油等推拿介质,以加强摩法的作用。

4. 注意揉法和摩法的区别:揉法着力较重,操作时指掌吸定一个部位,带动皮下组织,和体表没有摩擦动作;摩法则着力较轻,操作时指掌在体表作环旋摩擦,而不带动皮下组织。临床上两者常结合使用,揉中兼摩,摩中兼揉。

6.1.5 擦法

术者以手掌的大鱼际、掌根或小鱼际着力于施术部位,作直线往返摩擦运动,使摩擦产生的热量透过体表渗透至深层,称为擦法。可分为掌擦法、大鱼际擦法和小鱼际擦法。

【操作方法】

1. 掌擦法 术者以手掌掌面紧贴皮肤,腕关节平直,以肩关节为支点,上臂做主动运动,使手掌掌面在体表作直线往返的摩擦运动(图 6-13)。频率为每分钟 100～120 次,多用于胸胁及腹部。

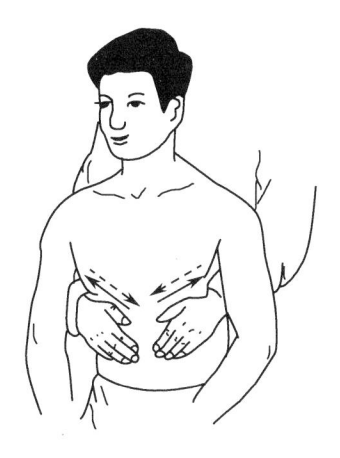

图 6-13　掌擦法
Fig. 6-13　Zhang Ca Fa(To-and-fro rubbing manipulation with palm)

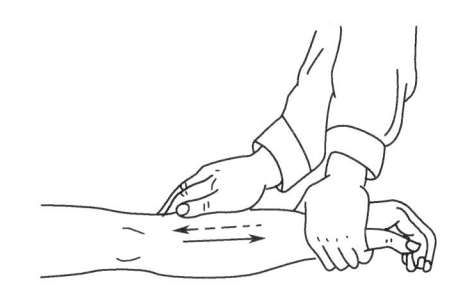

图 6-14　大鱼际擦法
Fig. 6-14　Da Yu JiCa Fa(To-and-fro rubbing manipulation with palm major thenar)

2. 大鱼际擦法 术者以大鱼际着力贴于体表,腕关节平直,以肩关节为支点,上臂做主动运动,使大鱼际在体表作直线往返的摩擦运动(图 6-14)。频率为每分钟 100~120 次,多用于胸腹、腰背和四肢部。

3. 小鱼际擦法 术者以小鱼际着力贴于体表,立掌,腕关节平直,以肩关节为支点,上臂做主动运动,使小鱼际在体表作直线往返的摩擦运动(图 6-15)。频率为每分钟 100~120 次,多用于肩背、腰臀及下肢部。

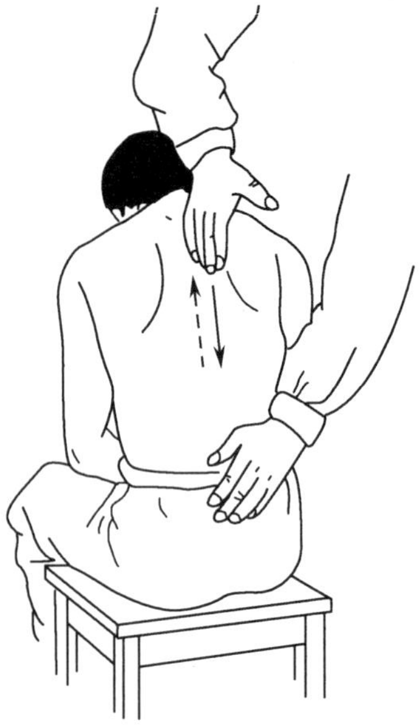

【动作要领】

1. 擦法运行路线宜直、长。不论是上下或左右摩擦,都要直线往返,不可歪斜,而且往返距离要拉长且连续,如拉锯状,不能间歇停顿。

2. 擦法手掌应与受术者体表接触平实,向下的压力要保持均匀,以摩擦时不使皮肤起皱褶为度,动作频率也应均匀。

【注意事项】

1. 术者在操作时呼吸要自然,不能屏气。

2. 擦法产生温热刺激,掌擦法的热效应较温和;小鱼际擦法产生的热量较高;大鱼际擦法产生的热量中等。临床使用擦法宜患者自觉透热为度。

3. 擦法操作时,多在施术部位涂些润滑剂(如冬青膏、麻油之类),既可保护皮肤,又有利于热量渗透到体内。

4. 擦法需直接在体表操作,应注意室内保暖。

5. 擦法操作后,一般不宜在该施术部位再使用其他手法,避免皮肤损伤。

图 6-15 小鱼际擦法
Fig. 6-15 Xiao Yu Ji Ca Fa(To-and-fro rubbing manipulation with minor thenar)

6.1.6 推法

用指掌或其他部位着力与人体一定部位或穴位上,作单方向直线或弧线的移动,称为推法。可分为平推法、直推法、旋推法、分推法、合推法等。

【操作方法】

1. 平推法 根据着力部位的不同,有拇指平推法、掌平推法和肘平推法三种。

(1) 拇指平推法:术者用拇指面着力紧贴体表,其余四指分开助力,肘关节屈伸带动拇指按经络循行或肌纤维平行方向作单方向沉缓推动(图 6-16),连续操作 5~15 遍。

(2) 掌平推法:术者用手掌按于体表,以掌根部(或全掌)为着力点,肘关节屈伸带动手掌向一定方向沉缓推动(图 6-17),连续操作 5~15 遍。

(3) 肘平推法:术者屈肘,以肘尖(尺骨鹰嘴)部着力于一定部位,沿肌纤维走行方向作直线缓慢推动(图 6-18)。

2. 直推法 术者用拇指桡侧面或食、中两指罗纹面着力于一定部位或穴位上,作单方向的直线推动(图 6-19)。

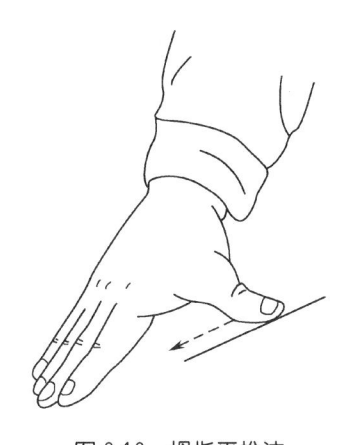

图 6-16　拇指平推法
Fig. 6-16　Mu Zhi Ping Tui Fa (Flat pushing Manipulation with Thumb)

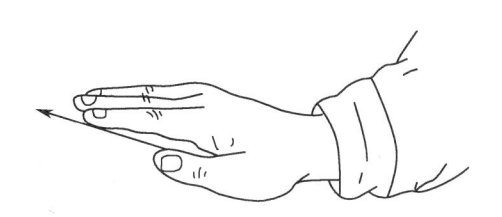

图 6-17　掌平推法
Fig. 6-17　Zhang Ping Tui Fa(Flat pushing Manipulation with Palm)

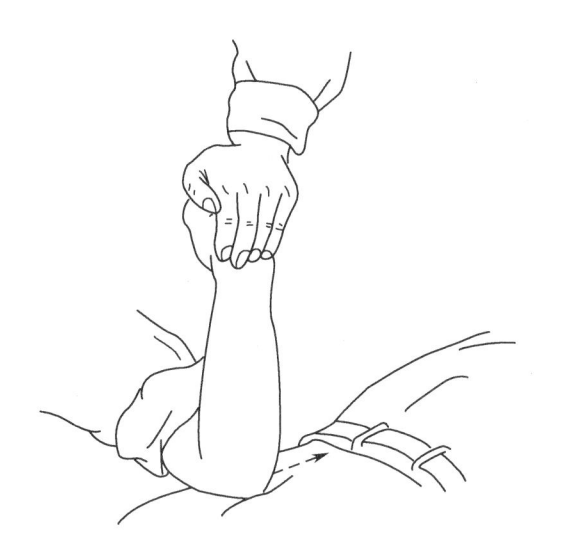

图 6-18　肘平推法
Fig. 6-18　Zhou Ping Tui Fa(Flat Pushing Manipulation with Elbow)

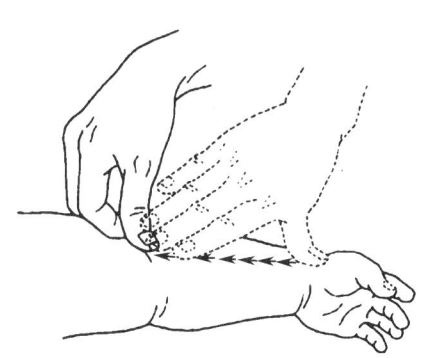

图 6-19　直推法
Fig. 6-19　Zhi Tui Fa(Straight Pushing Manipulation)

3. 旋推法　术者用拇指罗纹面在穴位上作螺旋形推动(图 6-20)，频率为每分钟 200～240 次左右。

4. 分推法　术者用双手拇指罗纹面或掌面紧贴在体表上，自中心部位分别向左右两侧单方向推开(图 6-21)，频率为每分钟 120 次。

5. 合推法　术者用双手拇指罗纹面或掌面紧贴体表，自穴位两旁推向穴位中间(图 6-22)。合推法是与分推法相对而言，也称合法或和法。

【动作要领】

1. 平推法是推法中着力较大的一种，推的时候需用一定的压力，用力要平稳，推进速度要缓慢，要沿直线作单方向运动。

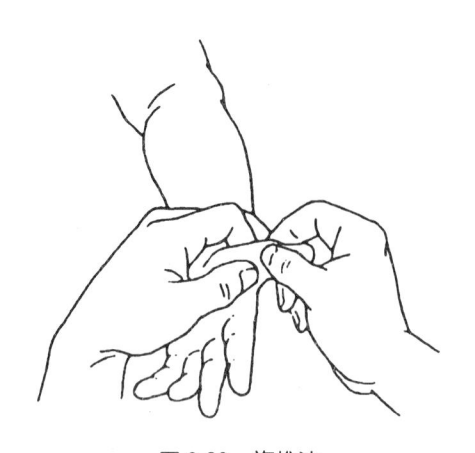

图 6-20　旋推法
Fig. 6-20　Xuan Tui Fa(Spiral Pushing Manipulation)

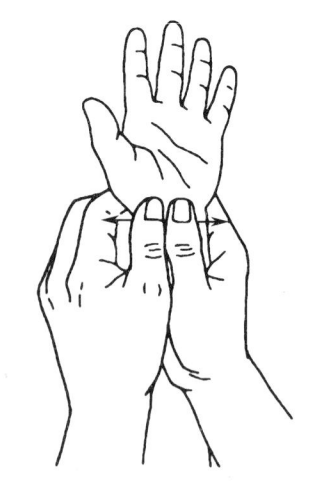

图 6-21　分推法
Fig. 6-21　Separate Pushing Manipulation

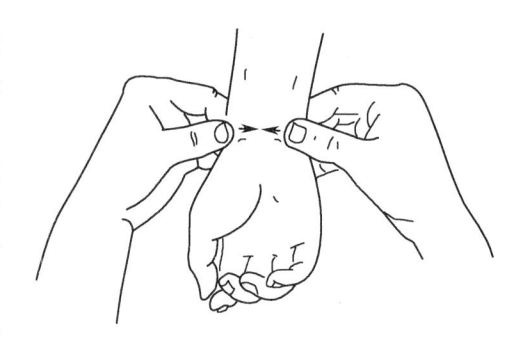

图 6-22　合推法
Fig. 6-22　He Tui Fa(Coalescent Pushing Manipulation)

（1）拇指平推法肘关节屈伸幅度较小，以拇指及腕臂部主动用力，向拇指端方向作短距离单方向直线推动。

（2）掌推法操作时，以掌根部（或全掌）着力，腕关节略背伸，肩关节为运动支点，上臂主动用力，带动肘关节屈伸，使手掌向前作单方向推动。

（3）肘平推法借助躯体力量推动，刺激较强。

2. 直推法以肘关节的伸屈带动腕、掌、指，作单方向的直线运动，所用压力较平推法为轻，动作要求轻快连续，一拂而过，如帚拂尘之状，以推后皮肤不发红为佳。

3. 旋推法要求肘、腕关节放松，仅靠拇指作小幅度的环旋运动，不带动皮下组织运动，类似指摩法。

4. 分推法操作时，要求两手用力均匀，动作柔和协调一致，向两旁分推时既可作直线推动，也可沿弧形推动。

5. 合推法的操作要领同分推法，只不过方向相反。在腕阴阳和腹阴阳穴常与分推法配合使用。一分一合，起到相辅相成的作用。

【注意事项】

1. 推法是单方向的直线或弧线运动，忌往返擦动。
2. 操作时应贴紧体表，用力平稳，均匀适中，推动的速度不宜过快。
3. 推法在体表操作时，可在施术部位涂冬青膏、滑石粉或沾葱姜汁等推拿介质。

6.1.7 抹法

以拇指罗纹面贴紧皮肤,沿上下、左右或弧形路径往返推动,称为抹法。分为指抹法和掌抹法两种。

【操作方法】

1. 指抹法　术者用单手或双手拇指罗纹面着力于体表,其余四指扶持助力,拇指略用力,缓慢地作上下、左右或直线或弧线的往返移动(图 6-23)。

2. 掌抹法　术者用单手或双手掌面着力于体表,腕关节放松,前臂与上臂协调用力,带动手掌掌面在体表作上下、左右或直线或弧线的往返移动(图 6-24)。

图 6-23　指抹法
Fig. 6-23　Zhi Mo Fa(Finger wiping Manipulation)

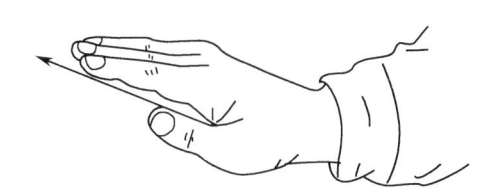

图 6-24　掌抹法
Fig. 6-24　Zhang Mo Fa(Palm wiping Manipulation)

【动作要领】

1. 抹法操作时,拇指罗纹面或手掌掌面应贴紧体表。
2. 抹法用力要均匀,动作要和缓,在施术区域内来回抹动的距离应尽量拉长,做到轻而不浮,重而不滞。

【注意事项】

1. 抹法刺激较表浅,操作时不宜带动皮下深部组织。
2. 抹法易与推法相混淆。推法是单向、直线的运动,而抹法可上可下,或直线往来,或曲线运转,应用较灵活。
3. 指抹法在头面部使用时,有较固定的操作程序。

6.1.8 扫散法

用拇指桡侧和食、中、无名、小指指端在患者颞部沿少阳经自前向后,作来回推擦运动,称为扫散法。是内功推拿流派的主要手法之一。

【操作方法】

术者一手扶患者头部,一手拇指桡侧面及其余四指指端,同时贴于头颞侧部,稍用力向耳后沿少阳经循行路线作快速来回抹动(图 6-25)。频率为每分钟 250 次左右。

【动作要领】

1. 术者应沉肩、垂肘、肘关节屈曲90°～120°，腕关节放松。

2. 以肘关节为支点，前臂作主动摆动，带动腕关节摆动，使着力手指在颞侧来回推擦。

【注意事项】

1. 扫散法操作时，手指着力部位稍用力紧贴头皮，向前推擦时用力稍重，回返时用力稍轻。做到轻而不浮，重而不滞。

2. 扫散时，扶持手应固定好患者头部，避免晃动，产生不适。

3. 扫散法应自前向后循经操作，每次推擦的距离不应太长。

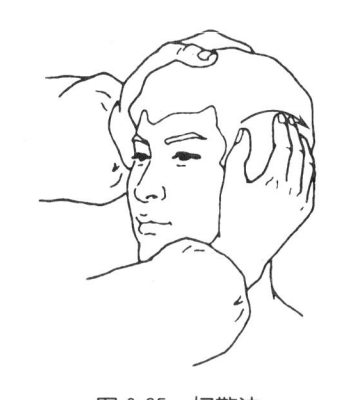

图 6-25 扫散法
Fig. 6-25 Sao San Fa(Cleaning and dissipating Manipulation)

6.1.9 搓法

用双手掌面夹住躯干或肢体一定部位，相对用力交替或往返快速搓动，称为搓法。

【操作方法】

1. 肩及上肢部搓法 患者取坐位，肩臂放松，自然下垂，术者站于其侧，上身略前倾，双手掌分别夹其肩前后部，相对用力快速搓揉，同时自上而下沿上肢移动至腕部(图6-26)，往返3～5遍。

2. 胁肋部搓法 患者坐位，两臂略外展，术者站其身后，以两掌分别夹其两胁肋，自腋下搓向腰部两侧数遍。

3. 下肢搓法 患者取仰卧位，屈膝约60°，术者站于床侧，以双手掌夹其大腿两侧，自上而下搓揉至小腿部。

【动作要领】

1. 做搓法时，操作者应蓄腹收臀，双掌对称用力，劲要含蓄；患者肢体宜放松，不可绷紧。

2. 搓法应紧搓慢移，即搓动要快，上下移动要慢。

【注意事项】

图 6-26 肩及上肢部搓法
Fig. 6-26 Jian Ji Shang Zhi Bu Cuo Fa(Palm twisting Manipulation on Shoulders and Upper Extremities)

1. 搓法时力不可过重，搓夹太紧会造成手法呆滞。

2. 搓法是一种辅助手法，常用于肩及上肢部，多在推拿治疗结束时使用。

6.1.10 振法

用手指或掌面按压在人体一定的穴位或部位上，做连续不断的快速振动，称为振法，也称振颤法。分为指振法和掌振法。

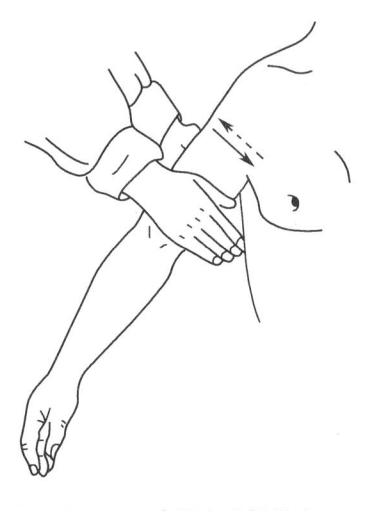

【操作方法】

1. 指振法　术者垂腕,用中指端置于治疗部位上,手指伸直,食指可叠加于中指背面以助力,肘微屈,前臂和手部静止性用力,肌肉交替性收缩,使手臂发出的振颤通过中指传递到机体(图6-27)。振动频率为每分钟300～400次。

2. 掌振法　术者腕关节略背伸,手指自然伸直,以手掌面轻按患者体表(也可两手掌叠加按于体表),肘微屈,前臂和手部静止性用力,肌肉交替性收缩,使手臂发出的振颤通过手掌传递到机体(图6-28)。振动频率为每分钟300～400次。

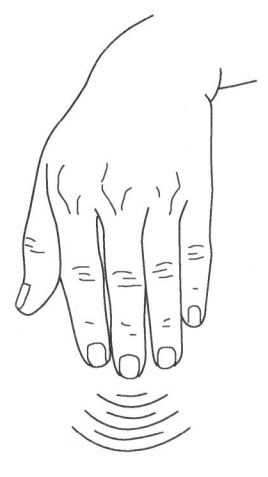

图 6-27　指振法
Fig. 6-27　Zhi Zhen Fa(Finger-vibrating manipulation)

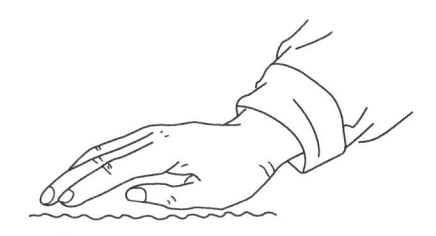

图 6-28　掌振法
Fig. 6-28　Zhang Zhen Fa(Palm-vibrating manipulation)

【动作要领】

1. 指振法和掌振法操作时,均取肩关节外展30°左右,肘关节屈曲140°左右的体位。

2. 静止性用力是将手部与前臂肌肉绷紧,但不作主动运动。但在手与前臂肌肉绷紧的基础上,手臂做主动运动,可使作用时间持久。

3. 注意力应高度集中于掌指部,做到"意到气到"。

【注意事项】

1. 振法要求肌肉静止性用力,操作过程中应保持呼吸自然,不可屏气。

2. 振法肌肉收缩方式较消耗体力,术者要使手臂产生振颤,需经过较长时间的锻炼。少林内功的练习可有效提高振法的质量。

6.1.11　抖法

以双手或单手握住患肢远端,做小幅度的上下或左右的连续抖动,称为抖法。

【操作方法】

术者用手握住上肢或下肢的远端(腕部或踝部),将被抖动的肢体抬高一定的角度(上肢在坐位下外展约60°,下肢在仰卧位下抬离床面约30°),在稍用力牵引状态下,作小幅度的、连续的上下抖动,使患者肢体的软组织产生颤动并传达到肢体近端(图6-29)。

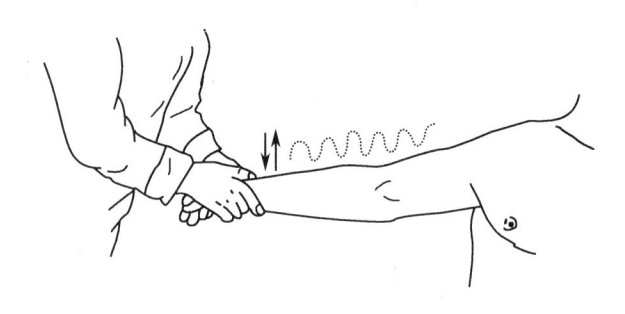

图 6-29　抖法

Fig. 6-29　Dou Fa(Shaking Manipulationa)

【动作要领】
1. 患者被抖动肢体要自然伸直放松,术者呼吸自然,不可屏气。
2. 抖动的幅度要小,频率要快。

【注意事项】
1. 下肢抖法时,因下肢较重,抖动的幅度可比上肢大些,频率低些。
2. 抖法常用作结束手法,上肢抖法较为常用。

6.1.12　按法

用手指或手掌面着力于体表特定的穴位或部位上,逐渐用力下压,称为按法。

【操作方法】

1. 指按法　拇指伸直,用拇指指端或罗纹面按压体表经络穴位上,其余四指张开,扶持在旁相应位置上以助力,单手指力不足时可用另一手拇指重叠按压其上,使拇指指面用力向下按压(图 6-30)。

2. 掌按法　用掌根、鱼际或全掌着力按压体表,单手力量不足时,可用双手掌重叠按压(图 6-31)。

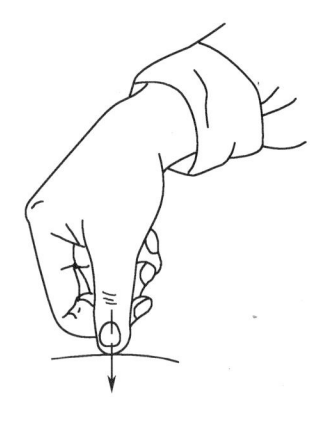

图 6-30　指按法

Fig. 6-30　Zhi An Fa(Finger-pressing Manipulation)

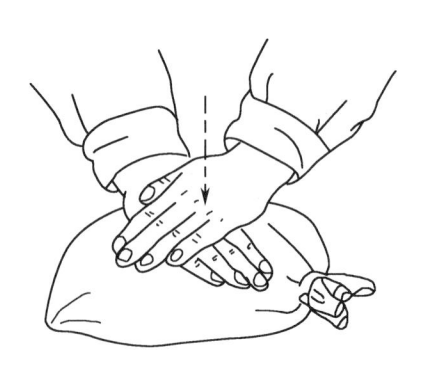

图 6-31　掌按法

Fig. 6-31　Zhang An Fa(Palm vibrating manipulation)

【动作要领】

1. 按压方向要垂直,用力要由轻到重,稳而持续,使刺激充分透达到机体组织的深部,然后逐渐减轻压力,遵循从轻到重再到轻的原则。

2. 按法如需较大刺激时,可略前倾身体,借助躯干的力量增加刺激。

【注意事项】

1. 切忌用迅猛的爆发力,以免产生不良反应。

2. 按法用力有节律变化,注意和较长时间持续用力的压法区别。按法在临床上常和揉法结合使用,形成复合手法按揉法。

6.1.13 压法

用拇指面、掌面或肘关节鹰嘴突起部着力于体表特定的穴位或部位上,持续用力下按,称为压法。

【操作方法】

术者用拇指罗纹面、手掌或屈肘以肘部前臂上段垂直向下按压体表,按压时也可在体表上逐渐滑动。肘部前臂上段按压又称为肘压法(图6-32)。

【动作要领】

按法和压法两者动作相似,故常混称为"按压法"。若严格区分,按法偏动,压法偏静;按法持续时间短,压法持续时间长;按法压力小、刺激轻,压法压力大、刺激强。

【注意事项】

1. 压法在背腰部使用时,注意控制用力大小,避免产生不良反应。

2. 肘压法的刺激较强,多用于体格健壮者的腰臀部肌肉丰厚处。

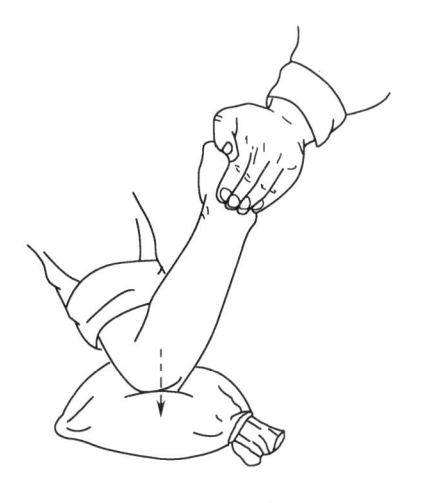

图 6-32 压法
Fig. 6-32 Ya Fa(Supressing Manipulation)

6.1.14 点法

以指端或关节突起部点压一定的穴位或部位,称为点法,临床上可分为指点法和肘点法。

【操作方法】

1. 指点法 术者手握空拳,拇指伸直并靠近食指中节,以拇指端着力或拇指屈曲,以拇指指间关节背侧着力或以中指指端着力,食指末节叠压于中指背侧助力,由轻而重,平稳施力,按压一定的穴位或部位(图6-33)。

2. 肘点法 术者屈肘,以尺骨鹰嘴突起部着力,身体略前倾,用身体上半身的重量通过肩关节、上臂传递至肘部,持续点压(图6-34)。

【动作要领】

点法是由按法衍化而来,要领基本相同,只不过接触面积较小,刺激较强。

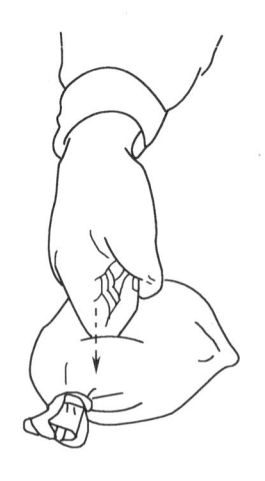

图 6-33 指点法
Fig. 6-33 Zhi Dian Fa(Finger-pointing Manipulation)

图 6-34 肘点法
Fig. 6-34 Zhou Dian Fa(Elbow-pointing Manipulation)

【注意事项】

1. 点法接触面较小,刺激强度大,刺激时间短,多用于止痛,又称"指针"。点按后应用揉法舒缓气血,避免局部软组织损伤。

2. 年老体弱、久病虚衰者慎用点法。

3. 肘点法和肘压法的施力部位不同,前者用尖锐的尺骨鹰嘴突起部着力,后者以肘部平钝的前臂上段着力。

6.1.15 捏法

用拇指和其他手指对称用力,挤压施术部位,称为捏法。用以脊柱的捏法称为"捏脊",多用于小儿推拿,参见小儿推拿手法相关条目。

【操作方法】

用拇指与食、中指指面或拇指与其余四指指面夹住施术部位,相对用力挤压,随即放松,重复上述动作并循序移动(图6-35)。

【动作要领】

拇指与其余手指用力要对称,均匀柔和,动作连贯,富有节奏。

【注意事项】

1. 以手指掌面着力,不可用指端着力。

2. 捏法对指力要求较高,尤其是拇指与其他四指的对合力,可采用相应功法练习以提高指力。

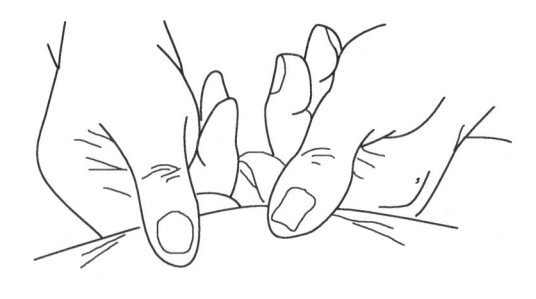

图 6-35 捏法
Fig. 6-35 Nie Fa(Pinching Manipulation)

6.1.16 拿法

用拇指与其他四指相对用力,提捏或夹持肢体或肌肤,称为拿法。分三指拿法和五指拿法。

【操作方法】

术者腕关节放松，以拇指与食、中指或其余手指的罗纹面相对用力夹紧治疗部位，将肌肤提起，并作轻重交替而连续的揉捏动作(图6-36)。

【动作要领】

1. 腕关节放松，手指伸直，以平坦的指腹着力挟住治疗部位，与拇指相对手指掌指关节屈曲，做类似剪刀式相对用力提捏皮肤及皮下软组织。

2. 用力缓慢柔和而均匀，由轻到重，再由重到轻，揉捏动作连贯。

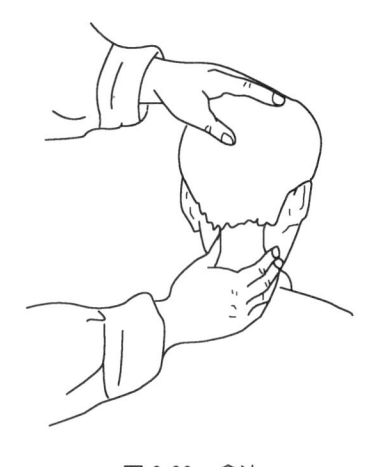

图 6-36　拿法
Fig. 6-36　Na Fa(Grasping Manipulation)

【注意事项】

1. 拿法操作时，应避免手指的指间关节屈曲，形成指端夹持肌肤或指甲抠掐的动作。

2. 拿法操作时，应根据临床需要尽可能多地捏拿皮下软组织，避免手指在体表滑移。

3. 拿法操作后，可用轻柔的揉摩法以舒缓气血。

6.1.17　捻法

用拇指和食指指面相对夹住施术部位，作对称的揉捏捻动，称为捻法。

【操作方法】

术者用拇指的罗纹面及食指桡侧面相对用力，夹住治疗部位，拇指与食指稍用力作较快速的揉捏捻动，如捻线状(图6-37)。

【动作要领】

1. 捻法要动作要连贯灵活，柔和有力。

2. 捻动的速度稍快，在施术部位上的移动速度宜慢。

图 6-37　捻法
Fig. 6-37　Nian Fa(Finger-twisting Manipulation)

【注意事项】

捻法为辅助手法，多用于指、趾关节部。

6.1.18　拨法

以拇指指腹深按于施术部位，做与筋腱、肌肉等组织走行相垂直的来回拨动，称为拨法，又称"弹拨法"。

【操作】

拇指伸直，以拇指指端或罗纹面着力，其余四指置于相应的位置以助力，拇指深

推拿手法

69

按至有酸胀感后,再做与肌纤维或筋腱走行方向垂直的来回拨动(图6-38)。单手指力不足时,可双手拇指叠加操作。

【动作要领】

1. 拨法操作时,拇指不能和体表皮肤有相对摩擦移动,应带动皮下肌纤维或筋腱韧带一起拨动。

2. 拨法用力宜由轻渐重,以患者能忍受为度。

【注意事项】

1. 拨法常用在压痛点上操作,取"以痛为腧"之意。

2. 拨法刺激较强,操作后宜用轻柔的揉摩法以舒缓气血。

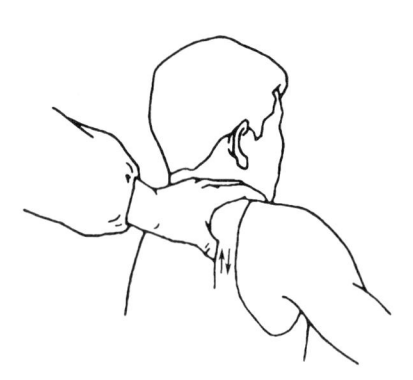

图6-38 拨法
Fig. 6-38 Bo Fa(Plucking Manipulation)

6.1.19 拍法

用虚掌在体表有节律地拍打,称为拍法。

【操作】

术者五指并拢,掌指关节微屈,掌心凹陷呈虚掌,有节奏地拍打治疗部位(图6-39)。击打频率为每分钟100～120次。

【动作要领】

1. 拍法操作时,肩关节宜松沉,腕关节放松,击打要轻快而平稳,手掌着实后即抬起,动作富有节律,拍打次数以皮肤出现微红充血为度。

2. 可单手或双手操作,双手操作时两手应交替进行。

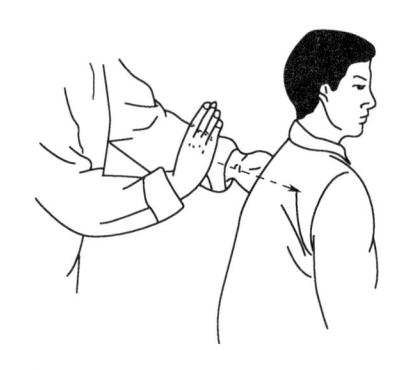

图6-39 拍法
Fig. 6-39 Pai Fa(Patting Manipulation)

【注意事项】

1. 手掌落在体表上应平实,不能在体表有拖抽的动作。

2. 注意拍法的适应症,结核、严重的骨质疏松、骨肿瘤、冠心病患者禁用拍法。

6.1.20 击法

用掌根、掌侧小鱼际、拳背、指尖或桑枝棒等有节奏地击打治疗部位,称为击法。分掌根击法、侧击法、拳击法、指尖击法和棒击法。

【操作方法】

1. 掌根击法 手指自然伸展,腕关节略背伸,以掌根部击打体表(图6-40)。

2. 侧击法 手指自然伸直,腕关节略背伸,以双手手掌小鱼际部交替击打体表(图6-41)。

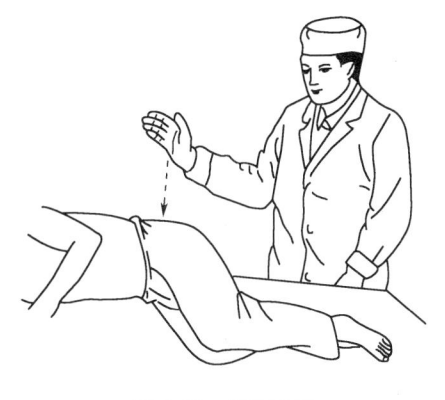

图 6-40　掌根击法

Fig. 6-40　Zhang Gen Ji Fa(hitting Manipulation with palm base)

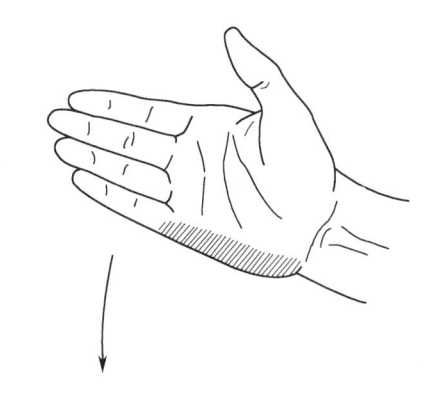

图 6-41　侧击法

Fig. 6-41　Ce Ji Fa(hitting manipulation with lateral side of palm)

3. 拳击法　术者手握拳,腕关节平直,以拳背平击体表(图6-42),一般每次击打3～5下。

4. 指尖击法　以手之五指指端合拢呈梅花状或散开呈爪状轻快敲击治疗部位(图6-43)。

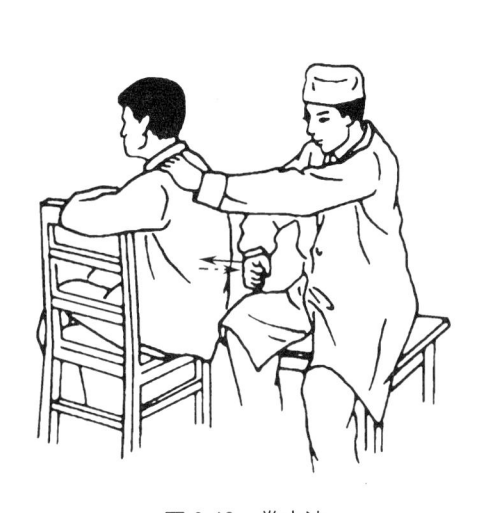

图 6-42　拳击法

Fig. 6-42　Quan Ji Fa(hitting manipulation with a fist)

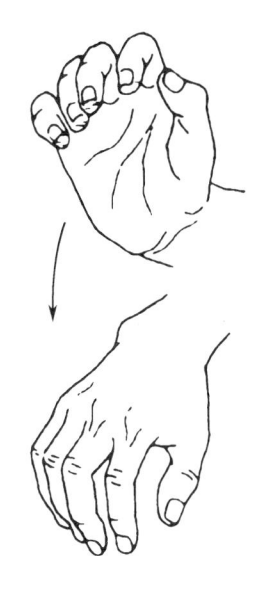

图 6-43　指尖击法

Fig. 6-43　Zhi Jian Ji Fa (Fingertip-hitting Manipulation)

5. 棒击法　用特制的桑枝棒前段约1/2部着力,击打体表(图6-44)。

【动作要领】

1. 击法用劲要快速而短暂,垂直叩击体表,频率均匀有节奏。

2. 掌根击法以掌根为着力点,运用前臂的力量击打,手臂挥动的幅度可较大,一般每次击打3～5下。

3. 侧击法可单手或双手合掌操作,以肘关节为支点,前臂主动运动,击打时手掌小鱼际应与肌纤维方向垂直,动作轻快有节奏。

4. 拳击法以肘关节为支点,运用肘关节的屈伸和前臂的力量击打,着力宜平稳。

5. 指尖击法操作时,腕关节放松,运用腕关节的小幅度屈伸,以指端轻击体表,频率快如雨点落下。

6. 棒击法以手握桑枝棒下段的1/3,前臂做主动运动,使桑枝棒前段有节奏地击打施术部位。

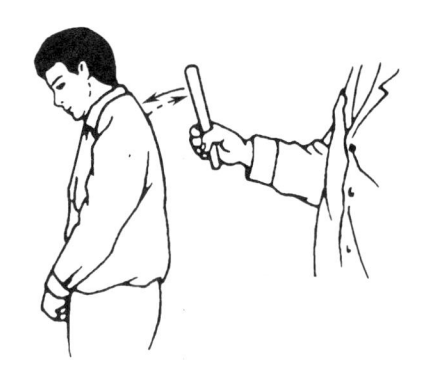

图 6-44 棒击法
Fig. 6-44 Bang Ji Fa(Stick-hitting Manipulation)

【注意事项】

1. 击法操作时,应注意击打的反弹感,一触施术部位即弹起,不可在体表停顿或拖抽。

2. 严格掌握各种击法的适应部位和病症,忌暴力击打。

3. 拳击法主要用于大椎、腰骶部;掌击法可用于百会、环跳;指尖击法常用于头部;桑枝棒击法击打时要用棒体平击,不用棒尖。除腰骶部外,其它部位应用顺棒(棒体纵轴与肌纤维方向平行)击打。

6.1.21 弹法

用中指指腹紧压食指背侧,用力快速弹出,连续弹击某一部位或穴位,称为弹法。

【操作方法】

将食指屈曲,以中指罗纹面紧压食指背侧,然后迅速弹出,击打患处(图6-45),频率为每分钟120~160次左右。

【动作要领】

操作要均匀连续,刺激强度以不引起疼痛为度。

【注意事项】

本法常作为头面部操作的辅助手法使用。

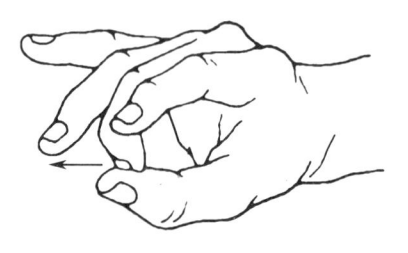

图 6-45 弹法
Fig. 6-45 Tan Fa(Flipping Manipulation)

6.1.22 摇法

在关节或半关节的生理活动范围内作关节或半关节的被动运动的手法,称为摇法。摇法是推拿常用手法之一,用于不同的部位摇法有着不同的操作方法。

【操作方法】

1. 颈部摇法 患者坐位,颈项放松。术者站于侧方,用一手扶住其头后顶部,另一手托住下颏,双手以相反方向缓缓地使头作顺逆时针的摇转各数次(图6-46)。

2. 肩部摇法 患者坐位。有三种操作方式:

(1) 托肘摇肩法:患者肩部放松,屈肘,术者站于侧方,取弓步势,上身略为前屈,

(1) (2)

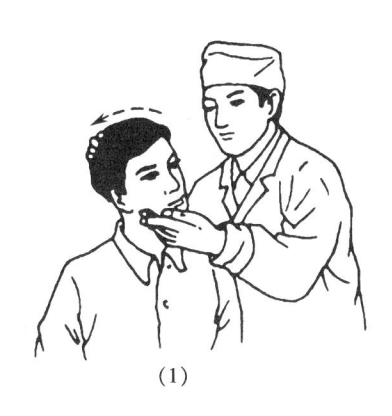

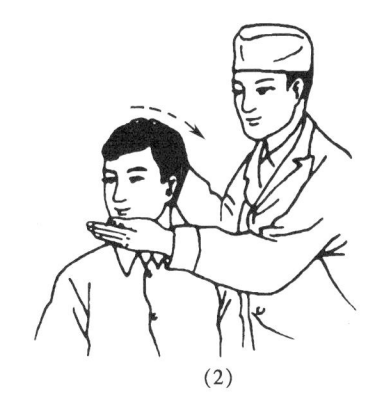

图 6-46 颈部摇法
Fig. 6-46 Jing Bu Yao Fa (Neck-rotating Manipulation)

用一手扶住患者肩胛骨上部,使其固定,另一手托起患肢肘部,作顺时针或逆时针方向运转各数次(图 6-47)。

(2) 握腕摇肩法:患者肩部放松,上肢伸直自然下垂,术者一手扶住其肩胛骨上部,另一手握住患肢腕部,作顺时针或逆时针方向运转各数次(图 6-48)。

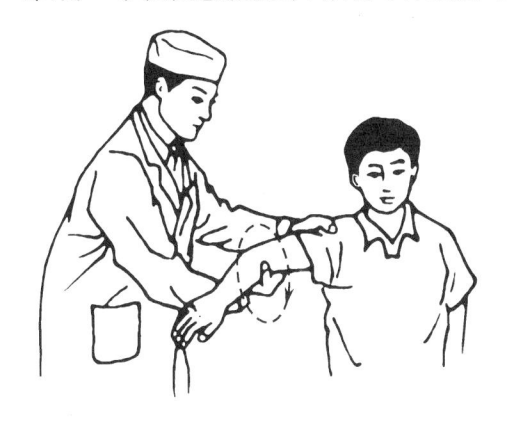

图 6-47 托肘摇肩法
Fig. 6-47 Tuo Zhou Yao Jian Fa (Shoulder-rotating Manipulation by Supporting the Elbow)

图 6-48 握腕摇肩法
Fig. 6-48 Wo Wan Yao Jian Fa (Shoulder-rotating Manipulation by Holding the Elbow)

(3) 大幅度摇肩法:患者上肢自然下垂,术者站于侧方,取丁字步,用一手握住患者腕部,另一手以掌背抵住患者的前臂部,将其上肢上举至160°幅度时,医者将掌背反过来用手握住其腕部,而原握住患者腕部的手向下滑移,扶按肩部,此时略作停顿,两手协调用力(按于肩部之手略向前下按压,握腕之手略上提,使肩关节伸展),然后使患肢向后作大幅度运转(图 6-49)。反方向环转时,则动作相反。

3. 肘部摇法 患者坐位或仰卧位,术者一手握患肢肘部,另一手握患肢腕部,作肘关节的环转摇动(图 6-50),顺逆时针各数次。

4. 腕部摇法 术者一手握患肢腕关节的上端,另一手握其手掌部,在轻拔伸腕关节的基础上,作腕关节的环转摇动(图 6-51),顺逆时针各数次。

(1)   (2)

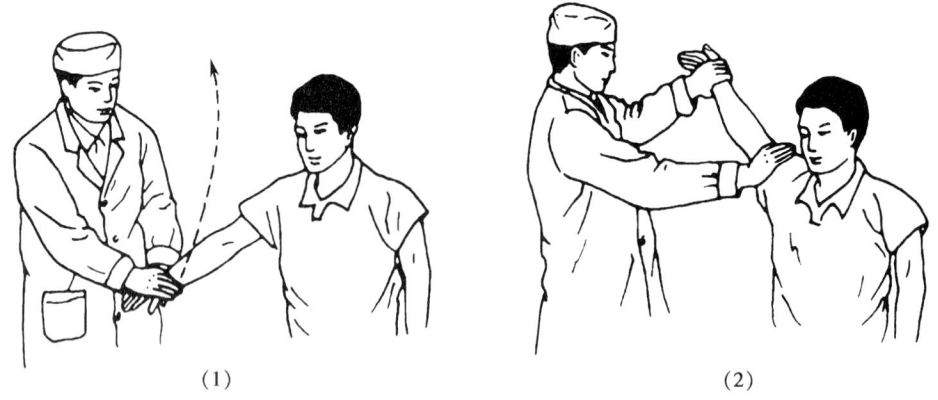

图 6-49　大幅度摇肩法

Fig. 6-49　Da Fu Du Yao Jian Fa(Shoulder-rotating Manipulation in a Great Amplitude)

图 6-50　肘部摇法

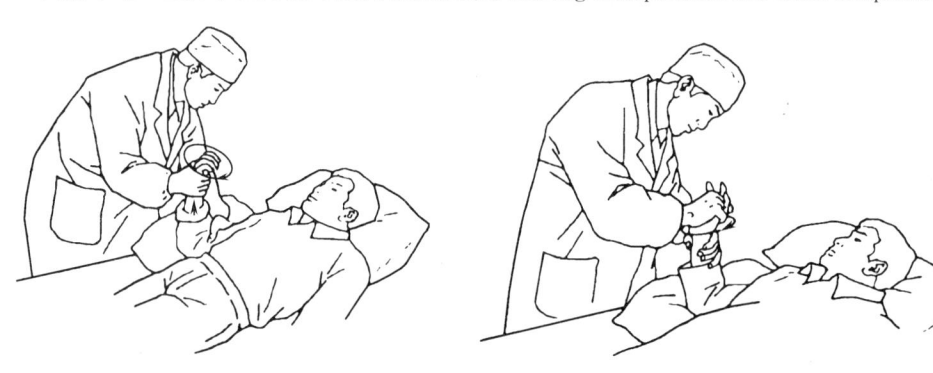

Fig. 6-50　Zhou Bu Yao Fa(Elbow-rotating Manipulation)

图 6-51　腕部摇法

Fig. 6-51　Wan Bu Yao Fa(Wrist-rotating Manipulation)

5. 腰部摇法　有两种操作方式：

（1）患者坐位，腰部放松。术者站其后方，一手扶住其一侧腰部，另一手扶住对侧肩部，两手协调用力，将患者的上身由左向右或由右向左作连续的前后左右俯仰侧弯，使腰部作环转动作(图 6-52)，顺逆时针各数次。

（2）患者仰卧位，屈膝屈髋，术者一手按于两膝部并使之合拢，另一手托起两小腿下端或握两踝部，然后作两下肢环转摇动，带动腰部运动，顺逆时针各数次(图 6-53)。

6. 髋部摇法　患者仰卧，患肢屈膝屈髋，健侧下肢伸直，术者站于侧方，用一手扶其膝部，另一手托住其足跟，两手协同使其髋关节屈曲到90°，然后两手协调用力，使髋关节做环转运动，顺逆时针各数次(图 6-54)。

7. 膝部摇法　患者仰卧，患肢屈膝屈髋，术者一手扶膝部上方固定，另一手握起足踝部环转摇动膝关节，顺逆时针各数次(图 6-55)。可边摇边缓慢将膝关节伸直。

8. 踝部摇法　患者仰卧，患肢自然伸直，医者位于其足后方，用一手握住小腿下端，另一手握住其足背前部环转摇动踝关节，顺逆时针各数次(图 6-56)。

图 6-52 腰部摇法
Fig. 6-52 Yao Bu Yao Fa (Waist-rotating Manipulation)

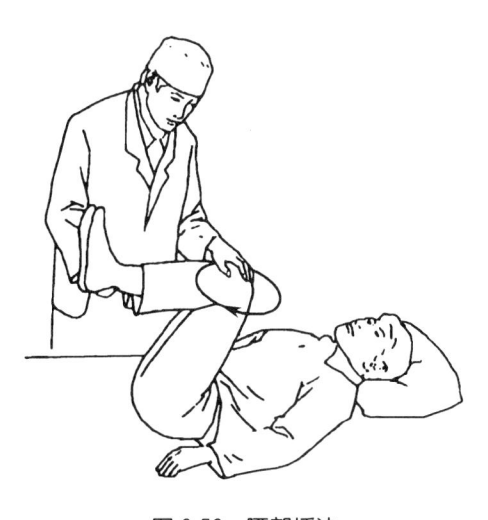

图 6-53 腰部摇法
Fig. 6-53 Yao Bu Yao Fa (Waist-rotating Manipulation)

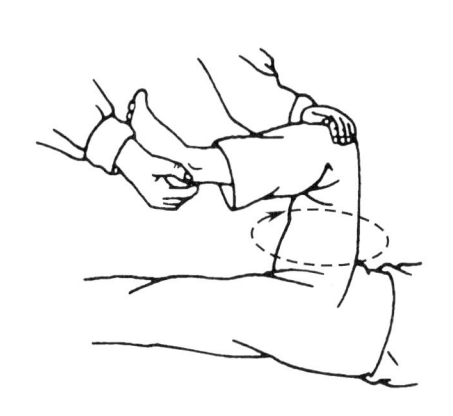

图 6-54 髋部摇法
Fig. 6-54 Kuan Bu Yao Fa (Hip-rotating Manipulation)

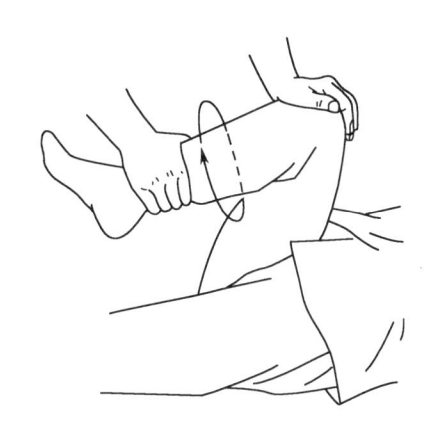

图 6-55 膝部摇法
Fig. 6-55 Xi Bu Yao Fa (Knee-rotating Manipulation)

【动作要领】

1. 摇法动作要缓和，用力要稳，转动速度宜缓慢均匀，动作初起时更宜缓慢。

2. 摇转的幅度宜由小渐大，并根据病情适当掌握，一般不超过其关节的生理活动范围，但可略超过关节的病理限制位。

【注意事项】

1. 摇法应禁止粗暴和违反正常生理活动的运动，对于关节功能障碍者在做摇法时，应顺势利导。

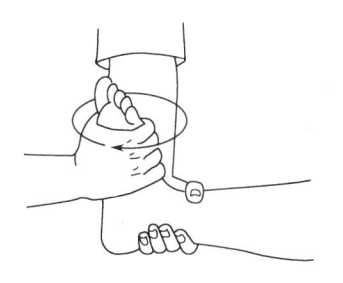

图 6-56 踝部摇法
Fig. 6-56 Huai Bu Yao Fa (Ankle-rotating Manipulation)

推拿手法

2. 掌握好使用宜忌,关节有骨折、脱位等损伤者,禁止使用摇法;椎动脉型颈椎病禁用颈部摇法、脊髓型颈椎病慎用颈部摇法;颈项肌过于紧张者,可取仰卧位摇颈。

3. 肩关节摇法常用于肩关节功能改善。托肘摇肩法、握腕摇肩法的活动幅度相对较小,适用于肩关节疼痛及活动障碍明显者,如肩周炎早期。大幅度摇肩法适用于肩关节活动已大部改善者,如肩周炎恢复期。

6.1.23 拔伸法

固定肢体或关节的一端,持续用力地牵拉肢体或关节的另一端,使关节的间隙拉开,称为拔伸法,又称"牵引法"。可用于不同的关节部位。

【操作方法】

1. 颈部拔伸法 分为掌指托拔伸法、肘托拔伸法和仰卧位拔伸法。

（1）掌指托颈拔伸法:患者取坐位,术者站其身后,双手拇指抵住患者枕骨后方（风池穴）,其余四指及手掌托住其下颌骨处,两前臂分置患者肩部。手臂协调用力,双手上托头颈,前臂下压肩部,缓慢向上拔伸颈部（图 6-57）。

（2）肘部托颈拔伸法:患者取坐位,头部略前倾,术者站其侧后方,一手从患者颈前绕过,用肘弯部托住其下颌部,另一手虎口张开托住其枕部,然后两手同时沿颈椎纵轴向上缓慢作颈部拔伸（图 6-58）。

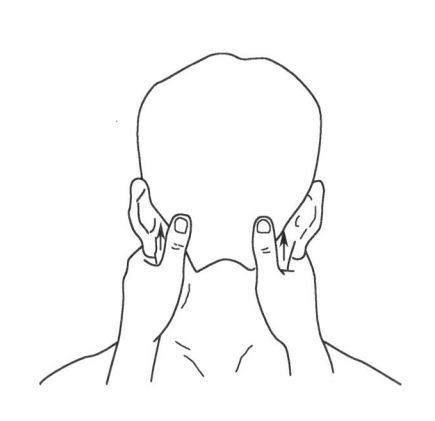

图 6-57 掌指托颈拔伸法
Fig. 6-57 Zhang Zhi Tuo Jing Ba Shen Fa (Pulling-extending Manipulation with palm and finger holding the neck)

图 6-58 肘部托颈拔伸法
Fig. 6-58 Zhou Bu Tuo Jing Ba Shen Fa (Pulling-extending Manipulation with elbow supporting the neck)

（3）仰卧位拔伸法:患者取仰卧位,术者坐方凳于其头前端,一手置头颈下扶托枕后部,另一手掌托下颌部,两手协调用力,沿颈椎纵轴方向拔伸（图 6-59）。

2. 肩部拔伸法 肩部拔伸法有两种操作方式：

（1）上举拔伸法：患者坐于低凳上，患肢放松，术者站其侧后方，双手握其腕部，缓慢上举至最大限度，然后沿上肢纵轴持续牵引，拔伸肩部（图6-60）。

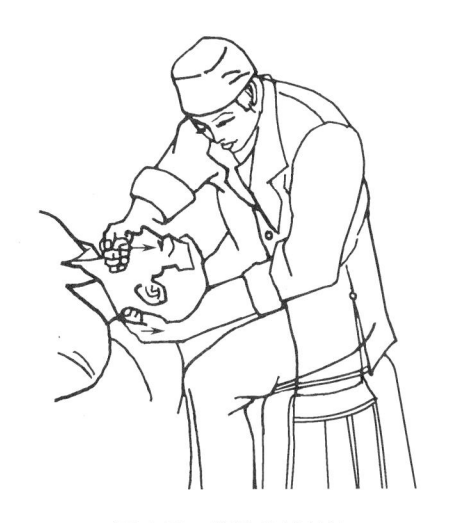

图 6-59 仰卧位拔伸法
Fig. 6-59 Yang Wo Wei Bo Shen Fa (Pulling-extending Manipulation in supine position)

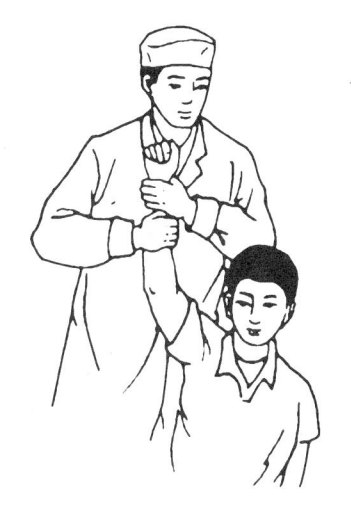

图 6-60 上举拔伸法
Fig. 6-60 Shang Ju Ba Shen Fa (Up-lifting Pulling-extending Manipulation)

（2）外展拔伸法：患者取坐位，患肢放松，外展45°～60°，助手立其健侧，双手从腋下抱住患者躯干以固定，术者站其患侧，双手握腕逐渐用力沿上肢纵轴牵拉（图6-61）。

3. 肘部拔伸法 患者取坐位，术者一手固定患肢肘关节近端（或用助手固定），另一手握其前臂远端，两手对抗用力拔伸肘关节。

4. 腕部拔伸法 患者取坐位，术者一手握患肢腕部近端，另一手握其指掌部，对抗用力拔伸腕部（图6-62）。

5. 手指拔伸法 术者一手握患指腕部，另一手食、中指屈曲，以食、中指中节夹住患指，对抗用力拔伸（图6-63）。

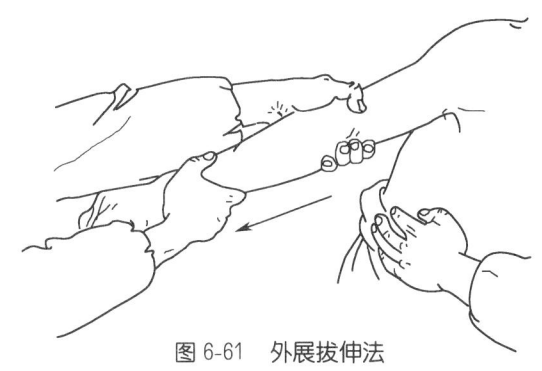

图 6-61 外展拔伸法
Fig. 6-61 Wan Zhan Ba Shen Fa (Pulling-extending Manipulation by abduction)

6. 腰部拔伸法 患者取俯卧位，助手立于床头前，双手抓住其腋下，以固定其身体（或患者双手用力抓住床头），术者站其足后方，双手分别握其两踝，逐渐用力向后持续牵拉（图6-64）。

7. 髋部拔伸法 患者仰卧位，术者立其患侧，助手用双手按其髂前上棘以固定，患肢屈膝屈髋，术者一手扶其膝，另一上肢屈肘以前臂托其腘窝部，同时用胸胁部抵压其小腿，两手臂及躯体协调用力，沿大腿纵轴向上拔伸患者髋关节。

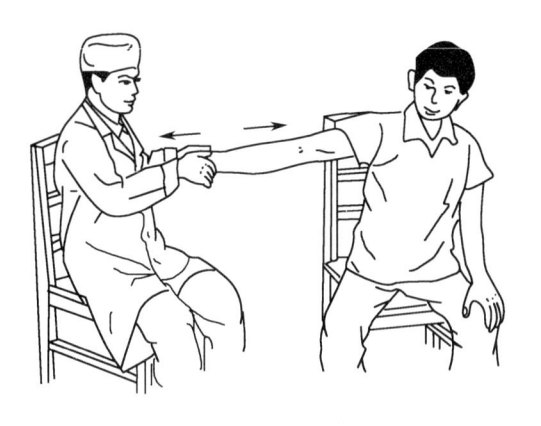

图 6-62 腕部拔伸法
Fig. 6-62 Wan Bu Ba Shen Fa(Pulling-extending Manipulation of the Wrist)

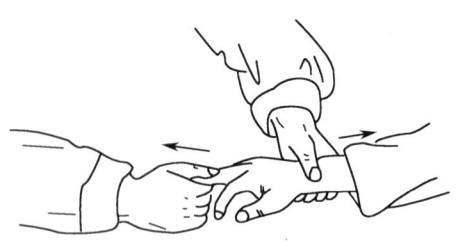

图 6-63 手指拔伸法
Fig. 6-63 Shou Zhi Ba Shen Fa(Pulling-extending Manipulation of the fingers)

8. 膝部拔伸法 患者俯卧位，患肢屈膝 90°，术者站于患侧，以一侧膝部跪按于患肢大腿后侧下端，双手握其踝部，沿小腿纵轴向上拔伸膝关节。

9. 踝部拔伸法 患者仰卧位，术者一手托握患足跟部，另一手握跖趾部，沿胫骨纵轴牵拉踝部（图 6-65）。

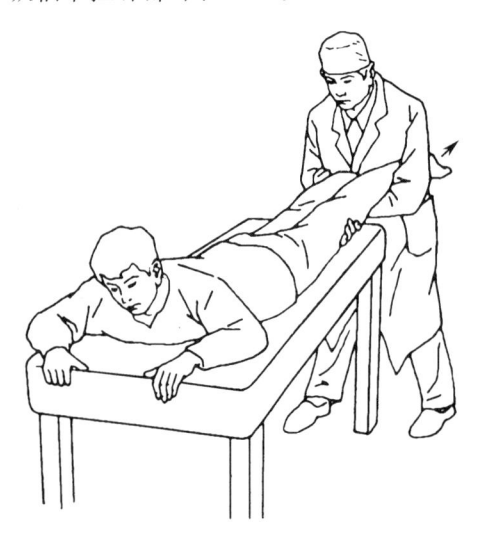

图 6-64 腰部拔伸法
Fig. 6-64 Yao Bu Ba Shen Fa(Pulling-extending Manipulation of the Waist)

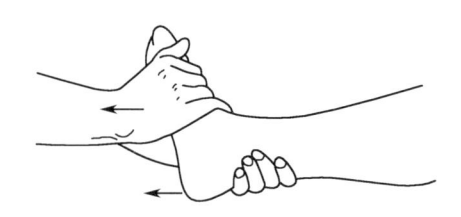

图 6-65 踝部拔伸法
Fig. 6-65 Huai Bu Ba Shen Fa(Pulling-extending Manipulation of the Ankle)

【动作要领】

1. 拔伸法动作要平稳柔和，力量由小渐大，牵拉到一定程度后，应维持稳定的牵拉力一段时间。
2. 掌握好拔伸的角度，牵拉方向应顺应肢体的纵轴线。

【注意事项】

1. 忌用突发性暴力和违背关节生理活动方向的操作。

2. 颈部拔伸法操作时注意避免挤压颈部两侧的颈动脉窦,引起不良反应。

6.1.24 背法

将患者背起后对腰椎进行牵引和振动的方法,称为背法。

【操作方法】

术者与患者背靠背站立,用双肘挽住患者的肘弯部,然后弯腰、屈膝、挺臀,将患者背起,使其双脚离地,略使患者身体下滑,使术者臀部对准患者腰骶部。然后术者用臀部左右摆动,待患者肌肉松弛后,做一突发性伸膝、屈髋、挺臀的动作(图6-66)。

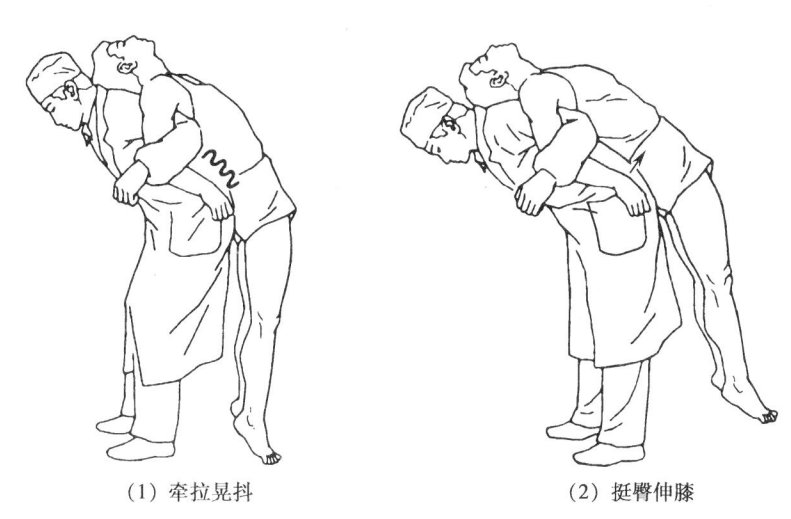

(1) 牵拉晃抖　　　　　(2) 挺臀伸膝

图 6-66　背法

Fig. 6-66　Bei Fa(Back-carrying Manipulation)

【动作要领】

1. 患者应全身放松,呼吸自然,被术者背起后,头后仰,整个身体靠于术者背部,利用下半身的重量牵伸腰椎。
2. 术者左右摇摆和伸膝挺臀动作要协调连贯。

【注意事项】

注意衡量患者的体重与术者自身的力量比,避免因负荷过重影响动作完成,甚至损伤术者。

6.1.25 扳法

用双手相反方向或同一方向用力协调扳动关节,使病变关节产生伸展、屈曲、或旋转等形式运动的手法,称为扳法。扳法是正骨推拿的常用手法,应用于颈、腰及四肢不同部位时,其操作方法各不相同。

【操作方法】

1. 颈部扳法　　颈椎扳法常用的三种操作方式:

(1) 颈部斜扳法:患者取坐位,颈微前屈或中立位,颈项部肌肉放松。术者站于其侧方,一手扶住其头顶,另一手托住下颏,使头作向左或向右旋转,在旋转到受限侧有弹性限制时(有阻力感),略作停顿,随即再做一有控制的、小幅度的、迅速而轻巧的扳动,常可听到"咔嗒"复位声响(图 6-67)。

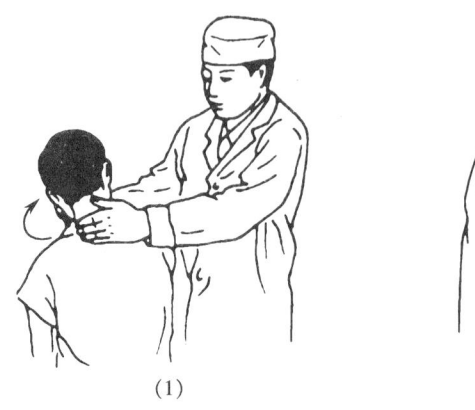

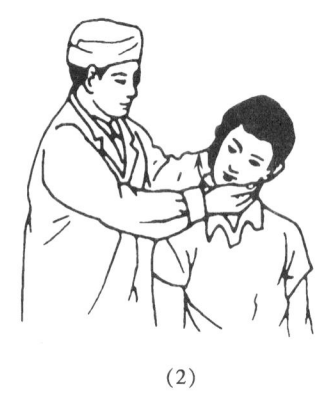

图 6-67 颈部斜扳法

Fig. 6-67 Jing Bu Xie Ban Fa(Manipulation for Obliquely-pulling the Neck)

(2) 颈椎旋转定位扳法:患者取坐位,颈椎前屈 15°～30°,以向左旋转扳动为例:术者站于其左侧后方,以右手拇指面顶按患椎棘突或横突旁,左手托起下颏,使患者头部在维持固定前屈角度下慢慢向左旋转,至感到有弹性阻力时,略作停顿,随即向旋转方向做一有控制的、小幅度的、迅速而轻巧的扳动,在扳动的同时,顶按棘突的拇指协调用力向对侧推压(图 6-68),关节整复成功时,常可听到"咔嗒"声响,有时虽无关节复位的"咔嗒"声响,但拇指下可有棘突的"跳动"感。

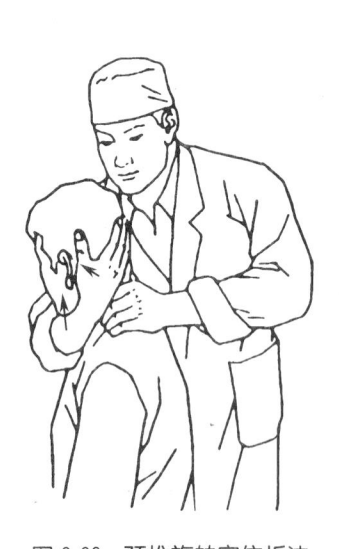

图 6-68 颈椎旋转定位扳法

Fig. 6-68 Jing Zhui Xuan Zhuan Ding Wei Ban Fa(Pulling Manipulation for Rotating and Locating Cervical Vertebrae)

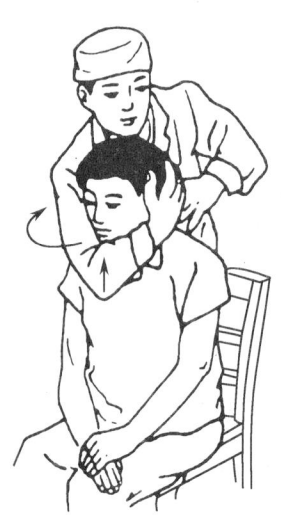

图 6-69 环枢关节旋转扳法

Fig. 6-69 Huan Shu Guan Jie Xuan Zhuan Ban Fa(Pulling and rotating manipulation on atlantoaxial joint)

(3) 环枢关节旋转扳法：患者坐于低凳上，术者站于其侧方，用一手拇指按于第二颈椎棘突旁，另一手以肘部兜托患者下颏，手掌绕过对侧耳部，扶住枕骨，令患者缓慢屈颈至拇指下感觉患椎棘突刚有滑动时，维持此颈屈角度，稍用力沿颈椎纵轴方向向上拔伸，在拔伸的基础上向棘突偏歪侧旋转至弹性限制位，略作停顿，然后做一有控制的、小幅度的、迅速而轻巧的扳动，同时拇指向另一侧推顶棘突(图6-69)。

2. 胸椎扳法 胸椎扳法常用的两种操作方式：

(1) 胸椎对抗复位法：患者坐位，双手十指交叉相扣，抱于枕部，术者站于其背后，以一足踏于患者坐椅，膝部抵住患处胸椎棘突，两手经患者腋下，从前臂和上臂之间穿过，扣握住其前臂下段，术者双手下压患者前臂，两前臂用力上抬，使患者颈椎略前屈，同时将脊柱向后上牵引，略停片刻，术者双手、两臂协同用力，做一有控制的、小幅度的、迅速而轻巧的扳动，同时膝部突然前顶，常可闻及关节复位的"咔嗒"声响。(图6-70)。

(2) 胸椎按压复位法：患者俯卧位，术者将双臂交叉，以掌根豌豆骨分置于患椎左右横突上下，令患者深呼吸，待呼吸协调后，于其吸气末适时用肘关节发力，做一有控制的、突发的顿挫按压，常可闻及关节复位的"咔嗒"声响(图6-71)。

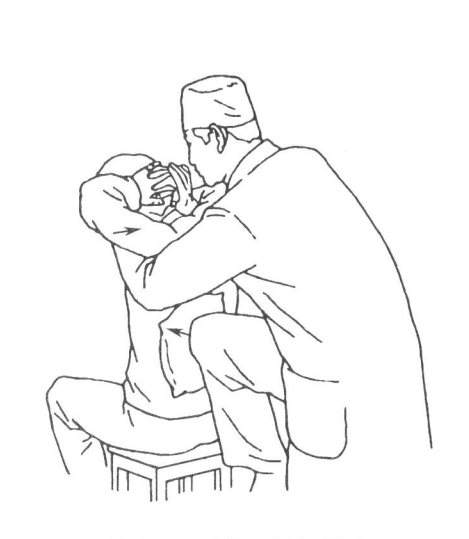

图 6-70 胸椎对抗复位法
Fig. 6-70 Xiong Zhui Dui Kang Fu Wei Fa (Counter-reduction of Thoracic Vertebrae)

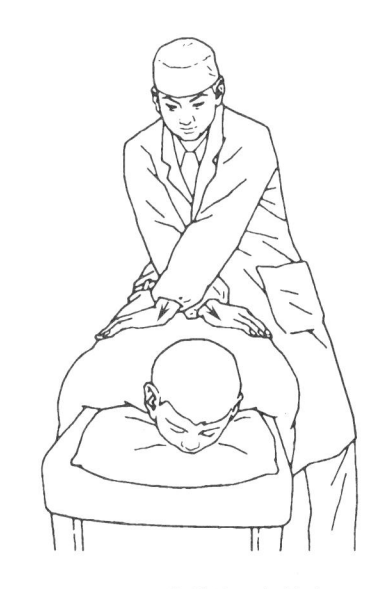

图 6-71 胸椎按压复位法
Fig. 6-71 Xiong Zhui An Ya Fa Wei Fa (Pressing Reduction of Thoracic Vertebrae)

3. 腰部扳法 腰椎扳法常用的三种操作方式：

(1) 腰椎斜扳法：患者侧卧位，健侧下肢在下自然伸直，患肢在上，膝髋关节屈曲，踝关节置于健侧下肢腘窝处。术者面对患者，两肘部(前臂上段)分别置于患者的肩前部及臀部，以相反方向缓缓用力，使腰部扭转到有弹性阻力时，再做一有控制的、小幅度的、迅速的扳动,常可听到"喀嗒"复位声响(图6-72)。

(2)腰椎旋转定位扳法:以右侧旋扳为例。患者坐位,腰部放松,助手站在患者侧前方,双手固定住患者膝部,术者坐于患者侧后方,用左手的拇指按住偏歪的棘突,右手从患者右腋下穿过扣按其项后部,然后右手掌下压,令患者缓慢前屈,至拇指下感到

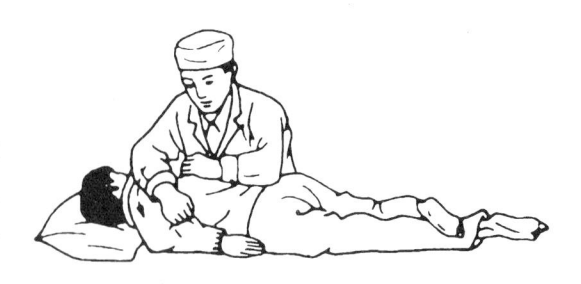

图 6-72 腰椎斜扳法

Fig. 6-72 Yao Zhui Xie Ban Fa(Obliquely Pulling Manipulation of the Lumbar Vertebrae)

棘突间隙分开时,维持此前屈角度,右手臂缓慢用力,以患椎棘突为支点,向右侧作脊柱侧屈,然后右旋至弹性限制位,略作停顿,术者右手掌下压,肘部用力上抬,同时拇指向对侧推顶棘突,做一有控制的、小幅度的、迅速的扳动,常能听到"咔嗒"复位声响,拇指下也有棘突的跳动感(图6-73)。

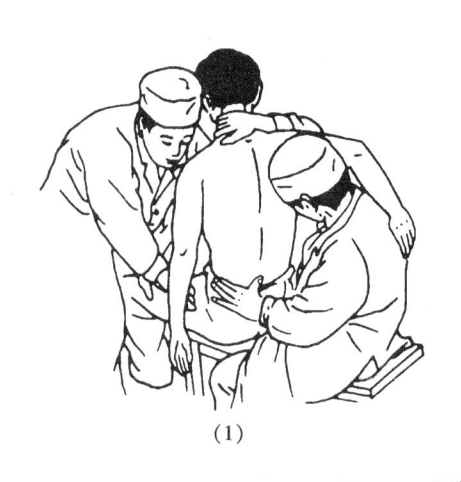

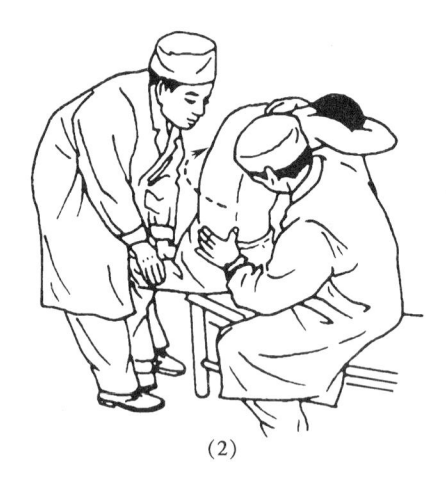

图 6-73 腰椎旋转定位扳法

Fig. 6-73 Yao Zhui Xuan Zhuan Ding Wei Ban Fa(Pulling Manipulation for Rotating and Locating Lumbar Vertebrae)

单人操作时,可令患者骑坐于治疗床头,固定骨盆及下肢。

(3)腰部后伸扳法:患者俯卧位,医者站于侧方,用一手按压其腰部,另一手将患侧下肢或双下肢托起至限制位,两手协调相对用力使腰椎后伸,做一有控制的、小幅度的、迅速的向后扳动(图6-74)。

4. 肩部扳法 肩部扳法按肩关节的运动分为上举、内收、后伸、外展四个方向:

(1)肩上举扳法:患者取坐位,两臂自然下垂,术者立于其后方,以身体固定患者躯干,以一手握住患肢前臂下段自前屈位缓缓上举,至120°～140°时,以另一手握其前臂近腕关节处,两手协调用力,向上逐渐牵引,至有阻力时,做一有控制的、小幅度的、迅速的向上扳拉,随即放松,可重复操作3～5次。

(2)肩内收扳法:患者坐位,将患肢屈肘放于胸前,术者站在患者后面紧靠其背,

稳定身体,用自己与患肩同侧的手扶住患肩以固定,另一手托住患肢肘部作内收至有阻力时,做一有控制的、小幅度的、迅速的内收扳动,随即放松,可重复操作3～5次(图6-75)。

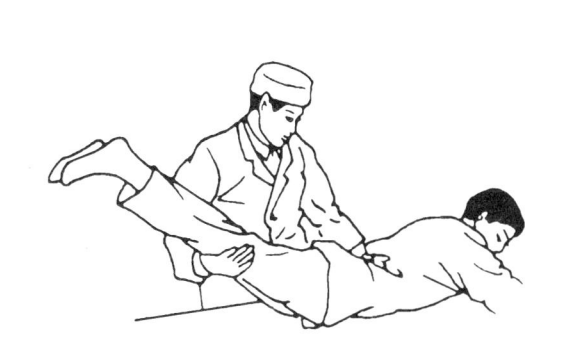

图6-74　腰部后伸扳法
Fig. 6-74　Yao Bu Hou Shen Ban Fa(Pulling Manipulation of the Waist)

图6-75　肩内收扳法
Fig. 6-75　Jian Nei Shou Ban Fa(Pulling Manipulation in Adducting the Shoulder)

(3) 肩后伸(内旋)扳法:患者坐位,患肢自然下垂。术者站在其侧后方,一手扶住患肩以固定,另一手握住其腕部使上肢后伸并屈肘,手背贴于背部,上拉至有阻力时,再做一突发性有控制的小幅度向上拉动,随即放松,可重复操作3～5次(图6-76)。

(4) 肩外展扳法:患者坐位,术者略半蹲位站于其患肩的侧方,患者上肢伸直外展,术者一手前臂经患者上臂下,穿过腋窝,经患肩前方同另一手交叉相扣于肩上,按住患肩,以患肩为支点,缓慢立起,同时轻轻摇晃患者上臂,将患肢外展至有阻力时,做一有控制的、小幅度的、迅速的外展扳动,随即放松,可重复操作3～5次(图6-77)。

5. 肘部扳法　患者取仰卧,术者一手握住其上臂下端,另一手握住其前臂下端,反复伸屈肘关节,至疼痛限制位时,做一突发性有控制的、小幅度的或屈或伸的扳动(图6-78)。

6. 腕部扳法　术者一手握住患者前臂下端固定,一手握住手掌拔伸,在此基础上,屈伸或侧屈腕关节至疼痛限制位,做一突发性有控制的、小幅度的或伸或屈或侧屈的扳动。

7. 骶髂关节扳法　骶髂关节扳法常用的两种操作方式:

(1) 骶髂关节后伸扳法:患者俯卧位,术者站于健侧,一手掌根按住髂后上棘,另一手托住患侧大腿下端前方,令患侧膝关节屈曲,然后将患侧下肢后伸至弹性限制位,配合患者咳嗽,待咳出肌肉松弛时,做一突发有控制的后伸扳动,扩大下肢后伸幅度3°～5°,同时按髂后上棘的手作一短促的向下按压(图6-79)。

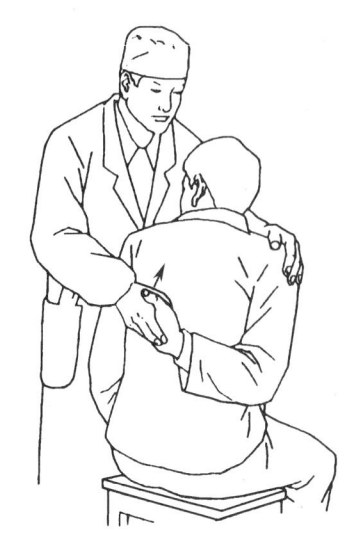

图 6-76 肩后伸（内旋）扳法
Fig. 6-76 Jian Hou Shen (Nei Xuan) Ban Fa (Pulling Manipulation for Backward Extending or Adducting the Shoulder)

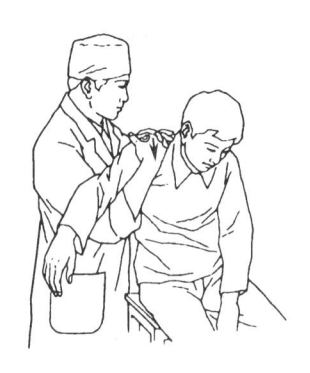

图 6-77 肩外展扳法
Fig. 6-77 Jian Wai Zhan Ban Fa (Pulling Manipulation for Abducting the Shoulder)

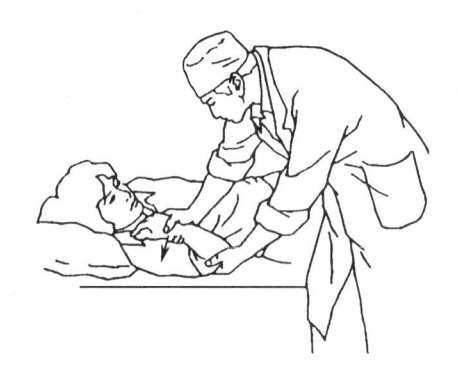

图 6-78 肘部扳法
Fig. 6-78 Zhou Bu Ban Fa (Pulling Manipulation of the Elbow)

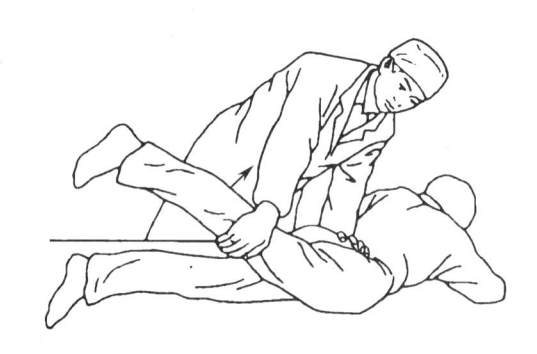

图 6-79 骶髂关节后伸扳法
Fig. 6-79 Di Ge Guan Jie Hou Shen Ban Fa (Backward Extending and Pulling Manipulation of Sacro-iliac Articulation)

（2）骶髂关节斜扳法：患者健侧卧位，患侧在上，健侧下肢伸直，略屈髋，患侧下肢屈膝屈髋。术者一手推肩部，使上半身躯干向后旋转，另一手按患者膝部外侧令腰骶向前旋转，当脊柱扭转至弹性限制位后，两手协调用力，做一有控制的、小幅度的、迅速扳动（图 6-80）。

8. 膝关节扳法 膝关节扳法常用的两种操作方式：

（1）膝关节伸膝扳法：患者取仰卧位，术者站其侧方，一手扶按患肢膝上方，另一手置于患肢小腿下段后侧，两手相对协调用力，伸膝至有阻力时，做一有控制的、小幅度的、迅速扳动（图 6-81）。

图 6-80 骶髂关节斜扳法
Fig. 6-80 Di Ge Guan Jie Xie Ban Fa (Obliquely Pulling Manipulation of Sacro-iliac Articulation)

图 6-81 膝关节伸膝扳法
Fig. 6-81 Xi Guan Jie Shen Xi Ban Fa (Pulling Manipulation for Extending Knee Joint)

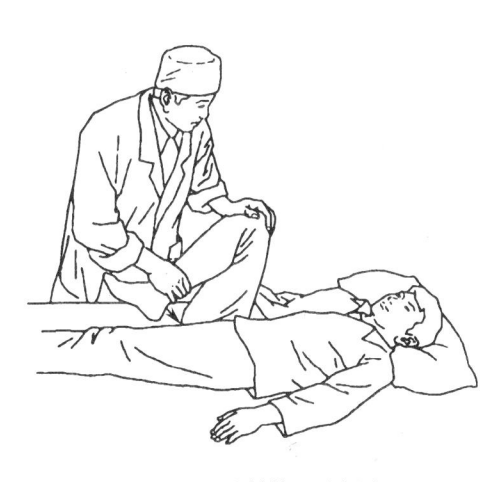

（2）膝关节屈膝扳法：患者取俯卧位，术者站其侧方，一手按股后部固定大腿，另一手握患肢踝部，使患肢膝关节屈曲至有阻力时，做一有控制的、小幅度的、迅速扳动（图 6-82）。

9. 踝部扳法　患者仰卧，医者用一手托住其足跟，另一手握住跖趾部，两手协调用力，将踝关节屈伸或内、外翻至疼痛限制位，做一突发性有控制的、小幅度的或屈或伸或内外翻的扳动（图 6-83）。

【动作要领】

1. 扳法操作应顺应关节的生理活动，将关节先调至弹性限制位是手法成

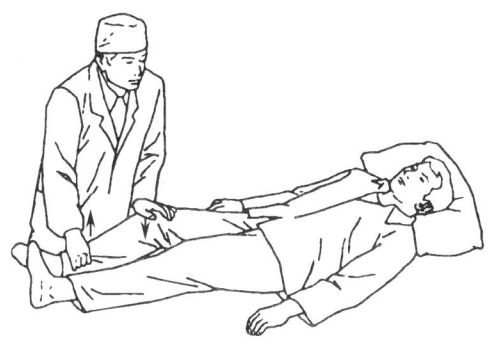

图 6-82 膝关节屈膝扳法
Fig. 6-82 Xi Guan Jie Qu Xi Ban Fa (Pulling Manipulation for Flexing Knee Joint)

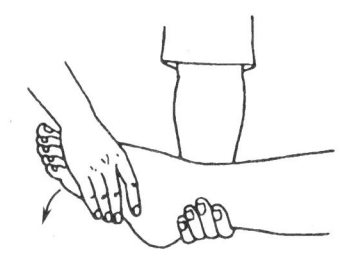

图 6-83 踝部扳法
Fig. 6-83 Huai Bu Ban Fa (Pulling Manipulation of the Ankle)

功的重要一环。

2. 扳法的发力动作宜轻巧、短促、随发随收。

3. 患者尽可能保持放松状态,有时需配合呼吸以调整。

【注意事项】

1. 扳法的力量应控制恰当,切忌突发暴力扳动。

2. 扳动的幅度要根据关节的生理活动范围及病理状况适当掌握,不得超越关节运动的生理位。

3. 扳法成功时常可听到关节复位时的"咔嗒"弹响声,应掌握"到位即有效"的原则,切忌追求关节复位弹响的操作,以免造成损伤或意外。

4. 严格掌握各种扳法的适应症,对于有关节骨折、脱位、肿瘤等禁忌存在者,严禁使用扳法。

6.2 成人复式推拿手法

由两个或两个以上运动学特征相近或作用部位相同的基本手法结合起来操作,构成复式推拿手法。

6.2.1 按揉法

由按法和揉法叠加复合而成的推拿手法,称为按揉法。分为指按揉法和掌按揉法两种。

【操作方法】

1. 指按揉法 用单手或双手拇指罗纹面着力,其余手指置于相应的位置以助力,腕关节微悬屈,拇指和前臂主动施力,作有节律的按压揉动(图 6-84)。

2. 掌按揉法 以一掌根部着力,其余手指自然伸直,前臂主动摆动,进行有节律的按压揉动。叠掌按揉可增加刺激量,操作时以肩关节为支点,上肢施力,带动手掌作有节律的按压揉动(图 6-85)。

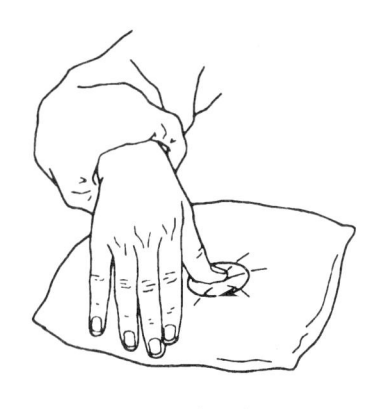

图 6-84　指按揉法
Fig. 6-84　Zhi An Rou Fa(pressing and kneading manipulation with fingers)

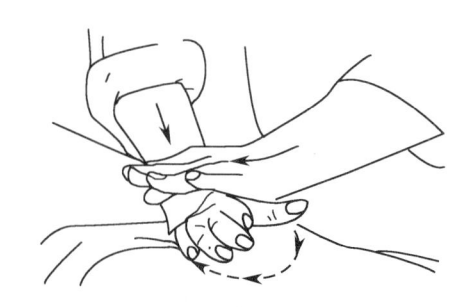

图 6-85　掌按揉法
Fig. 6-85　Zhang An Rou Fa(pressing and kneading manipulation with palm)

【动作要领】

1. 按揉法是按法和揉法的有机结合，在揉法的基础上，增加了按压的力量，按揉并重，刚柔相济。

2. 按揉法的频率较揉法稍慢，操作富有节奏性。

3. 沉肩垂肘，肩、肘、腕关节放松，使术者整体的力量渗透至患者皮下深层组织。

【注意事项】

1. 注意掌握按压的力量，过小则失之轻浮，过重则流于涩滞。

2. 指按揉法的动作酷似拿法，区别是指按揉法拇指之外的手指仅起扶持助力的作用，而拿法则是拇指和其余手指相对用力操作。

6.2.2 拿揉法

在做拿法的同时增加手法的揉动成分，称为拿揉法。

【操作方法】

操作方法同拿法相似，在拿法的基础上增加拇指与其他手指的旋转揉动(图6-86)。

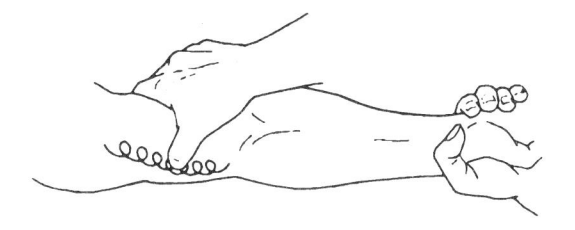

图 6-86 拿揉法
Fig. 6-86 Na Rou Fa(Grasping and Kneading Manipulation)

【动作要领】

1. 拿揉法以拿法为主，揉法为辅。

2. 可边拿揉边沿肢体移动，移动的速度不宜过快。

【注意事项】

拿揉法增加了手指的旋转揉动，减小了拇指和其他手指的相对合力，手法更趋柔和，操作时应较拿法更轻灵流畅。

6.2.3 推摩法

在拇指作一指禅推法的同时，其余手指作指摩法的复式手法，称为推摩法。是一指禅推法的衍变手法，常用于胸腹及背部。

【操作方法】

以拇指端偏峰侧着力，前臂摆动作一指禅推法，同时其余四指伸直并拢以指面作摩法(图6-87)。

【动作要领】

沉肩、垂肘的要领同一指禅推法，悬腕的幅度减小，腕关节微屈，拇指着实，其余四指以指面着力，作指摩法。

【注意事项】

1. 拇指置于主穴，其余四指置于辅助用穴施治。

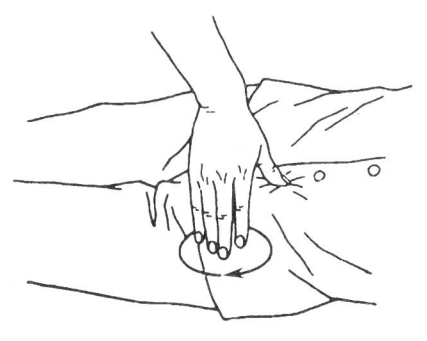

图 6-87 推摩法
Fig. 6-87 Tui Mo Fa(Pushing and Rubbing Manipulation)

2. 一指禅推法应与指摩法协调操作，不可偏废。

> **思 考 题**
>
> - 推拿手法的要求是什么？
> - 试述一指禅推法、滚法、按法、揉法、推法、拿法的操作方法。
> - 扳法的注意事项是什么？

7 成人疾病的推拿治疗

7.1 骨伤科病症

7.1.1 落枕

落枕又名"失枕",多由于患者素体虚弱或疲劳,加之睡姿不良,枕头高低不适或过硬,使头颈部肌肉长时间处于过伸或过屈状态,导致颈项部肌肉尤其是胸锁乳突肌、斜方肌和肩胛提肌被牵张而导致肌肉痉挛;过度牵拉颈部肌肉,促使局部血供下降,组织代谢障碍,代谢产物聚积,使颈部肌肉痉挛与疼痛。经常低头伏案工作,在无意识下突然用力转动头颈部,使颈项部的肌肉骤然强烈收缩而引起局部出血、水肿、渗出,产生疼痛和活动障碍。亦可见于颈项部感受风寒侵袭,致寒凝血滞,筋络痹阻,局部血管收缩,而使颈项部肌肉代谢障碍,引起痉挛。症状特点以酸胀、疼痛、颈椎呈僵直、斜颈或强迫性体位等一系列症状。轻者4~5天可自愈。重者疼痛剧烈,并向头部及上肢部放射,迁延数周不愈。

本病多见于青壮年,男性多于女性,冬春季发病率较高。

【临床表现】

多数患者在晨起时突然感觉颈项部疼痛不适,呈强迫体位,头部常偏向患侧。严重者疼痛可向肩背部或一侧上臂放射。常以颈项部一侧的斜方肌、胸锁乳突肌或肩胛提肌痉挛疼痛和僵直为主;若两侧肌肉同时受损,症状一般也有轻重之分。颈部活动受限明显,不能自由转动、俯仰,动则痛甚。用手碰触患部肌肉时,疼痛剧烈,昼轻夜重。由外感风寒所致者,遇风寒刺激后症状加重,舌质青紫或有瘀斑,苔薄或薄白;脉弦或紧。

【诊断要点】

1. 颈项部肌肉张力明显增高,常发生在胸锁乳突肌、斜方肌或肩胛提肌等处,可触及条索状、紧张或肿胀的肌束。

2. 颈部常有明显的压痛点,常分布在肌肉的起止处和肌腹部。胸锁乳突肌痉挛者,在胸锁乳突肌腹处和乳突处有压痛;斜方肌痉挛者,在锁骨外1/3或肩井穴或颈胸椎棘突旁有压痛;肩胛提肌痉挛者,在上位颈椎棘突旁和肩胛骨内上角处有压痛。

3. 颈部转动、俯仰等活动受限,头部常偏向患侧,呈强迫体位,动则加重。

4. 颈部各项试验无神经根压迫症状。

5. X线检查一般无特殊发现。

【推拿治疗】

1. 治疗原则 舒筋活血,温经通络。

2. 取穴和部位 风池、秉风、肩井、天宗、肩中俞、肩外俞、曲池、合谷、阳陵泉等穴以及颈项部和肩部等。

3. 操作

(1) 患者取坐位,先点揉天宗、曲池、合谷、阳陵泉穴,每穴约半分钟。在点揉天宗时,告诉患者尽可能地主动进行颈部的转动、俯仰活动,以此来稍微缓解患者颈部肌肉的痉挛和疼痛,为下步手法治疗作好准备。

(2) 医生立于其后外侧,一手把持住头顶,另一手先用轻柔的掌揉法在疼痛部位的周围,反复操作3～5遍,力量应以患者能够承受为度。依次用㨰法和一指禅推法在两侧的颈项及肩部施术,先健侧后患侧,以患侧为重点,操作约3～5分钟,直至患者感到疼痛明显缓解为止。

(3) 医生用拇指指腹按揉或用一指禅定点推法在风池、秉风、肩井、天宗、肩中俞、肩外俞等穴上操作,每穴10秒钟左右,以起到通经活络、进一步缓解痉挛的作用。

(4) 医生用单手拇指指腹与食、中两指指腹相对用力依次拿揉风池半分钟,拿揉颈项2～3遍,双手五指提拿肩井穴2～3次,然后弹拨紧张的肌肉,力量由小到大,使痉挛的肌肉彻底放松,时间为2～3分钟。

(5) 嘱患者自然放松颈项部肌肉,医生一手持续托起下颌,一手扶持后枕部,使颈略前屈,下颌内收。然后双手同时用力向上提拉,并缓慢左右旋转患者头部10次左右,以活动颈椎小关节。摇动旋转之后,在颈部微前屈的状态下,迅速向患侧加大幅度的扳动,手法要稳而快,手法的力度和旋转的角度必须掌握在患者可以耐受的限度内,切忌暴力蛮劲,以防发生意外。

(6) 采用摇法使患者被动地进行颈部的前屈、后伸和左右旋转运动,最后用小鱼际轻叩肩背部,用擦法擦颈项及肩背部,以透热为度,时间为2～3分钟。

【注意事项】

1. 推拿治疗本病过程中,手法宜轻柔,力量由轻到重,切忌施用强刺激手法和突然使用暴力,防止发生意外;治疗要先从疼痛部位的远端开始操作,逐渐向其靠近,使患者的机体有一个适应的过程。

2. 疼痛较重的患者,应该先点按远处的穴位以缓解疼痛再用其他方法进行治疗。

3. 睡卧时垫枕高低要适当,枕头的软硬要适中。

4. 经常发生落枕的患者,注意颈项部不要过度疲劳和注意颈项部的保暖。

7.1.2 颈椎病

颈椎病又称颈椎综合征,是由于颈椎间盘退行性改变、颈椎骨质增生以及损伤等原因引起颈椎内、外平衡失调,稳定性较差,颈椎发生功能或结构上的改变,使颈神经根、椎动脉、脊髓或交感神经等受到刺激或压迫,从而相应引起的一系列综合征候群。轻者头、颈、肩臂疼痛、麻木,重者可致肢体酸软无力,甚至大小便失禁、瘫痪等。病变累及椎动脉及交感神经时则可出现头晕、心慌等相应的临床表现。

本病属中医学"项筋急"、"项肩痛"、"眩晕"等范畴。本病以40岁以上多见,是中老年人的常见病、多发病,男性多于女性。但是,随着学习、工作和生活习惯的改变,发病年龄有提前趋势,30岁发病者也不少见。

【临床表现】

颈椎病主要是一种颈椎退行性改变。颈椎间盘退变是本病的内因,各种急慢性颈部外伤是导致本病的外因。临床上根据病变的部位及其产生的症状不同,常把颈椎病分为颈型、神经根型、脊髓型、椎动脉型、交感神经型和混合型六型。

1. 颈型颈椎病 颈型颈椎病由于颈椎过度运动、外伤或长期不良姿势,而造成椎旁软组织劳损,颈椎活动节段轻度错位,颈椎稳定性的下降,从而造成椎间盘代偿性退变,此为退变的早期阶段。可有椎间盘纤维环结构的部分破坏、椎间盘组织的轻度膨出及椎骨骨质的轻度增生,膨出及增生的结构尚未构成对神经、血管组织的压迫,但可刺激分布于其间的椎窦神经感觉纤维。后者则向中枢发放传入冲动,经脊髓节段反射及近节段反射的途径,导致颈项部和肩胛骨间区肌肉处于持续紧张的状态,出现该区域的刺激症状。舌质青紫或有瘀斑,苔薄或薄白,脉弦或紧。

症状表现为患者颈部前屈、旋转幅度明显减小,颈夹肌、半棘肌、斜方肌等出现肌紧张性疼痛。颈部有僵硬感,易于疲劳,肩胛肩区有疲痛感和沉重感,劳累后症状加重,休息后症状减轻。

2. 颈神经根型颈椎病 颈神经根型颈椎病由于颈椎钩椎关节、关节突骨质增生,颈椎椎骨之间结构异常及软组织损伤肿胀等原因,造成对神经根的机械压迫和化学刺激而引起典型的神经根症状。

症状表现为肩背或颈枕部呈阵发性或持续性的隐痛或剧痛,受刺激或压迫的颈神经根疼痛及向上肢传导的放射痛,伴针刺样或过电样麻感。当颈部活动、腹压增高时,上述症状加重。受压神经根所支配的皮肤在急性期可能出现痛觉过敏,出现烧灼样或刀割样剧痛,后期则表现为感觉的减退、手指麻木、肢冷,伴有患侧上肢沉重无力,握力减弱或持物坠落等症状。颈部活动有不同程度受限或僵硬感,向患侧旋转及侧屈,则可能导致放射性神经痛的加重,呈疼痛性斜颈畸形。舌质淡红,苔薄或薄白,脉弦紧。

3. 脊髓型颈椎病 脊髓型颈椎病是由于膨出的颈椎间盘组织、椎体后缘的骨质增生、向下滑脱的椎体、增厚的黄韧带和椎管内肿胀的软组织等,对脊髓造成压迫;或由于血管因素的参与,导致脊髓缺血、变性坏死,引起颈部以下身体感觉、运动和大小便功能等异常。

症状表现为上肢症状往往不明显,有时仅表现为沉重无力;下肢症状明显,可出现双下肢僵硬无力、酸胀、烧灼感或麻木感和运动障碍,呈进行性加重的趋势。重者活动不便、走路不稳、大小便功能障碍,甚至出现瘫痪。颈部活动受限,可出现强迫性颈椎强直,勉强活动时症状加重。患者有时伴有头胀、头痛、头昏等症状。舌质淡,苔薄白,脉沉细。

4. 椎动脉型颈椎病 椎动脉型颈椎病是由于椎间盘退变及上位颈椎错位、横突孔骨性非连续管道扭转而引起椎动脉扭曲,或因椎体后外缘、钩突的骨质增生而导致椎动脉受压,或因椎动脉交感神经丛受刺激而导致动脉终末支痉挛等,造成一侧或双侧的椎动脉供血不足。

症状表现为持续性眩晕、恶心、耳鸣、耳聋、记忆力减退、后头部麻木等症状；有时伴有视物模糊、视力减退、精神萎靡、乏力嗜睡等。头部过伸或旋转时，可出现位置性眩晕、恶心、呕吐等急性发作症状。可出现猝然摔倒，摔倒时神志多清醒。舌质红，苔薄白，脉弦细。

5. 交感神经型颈椎病 交感神经型颈椎病是由于颈椎的骨质增生、痉挛的椎前肌群、失稳的颈椎及炎症介质等刺激了颈交感神经纤维或精神因素，引起交感神经兴奋性的异常增高或抑制，出现身体上相应区域内的腺体、血管、内脏功能活动失调。

症状表现为持续性头痛或偏头痛、眼部胀痛，额部及眉棱骨处疼痛明显。常伴有头沉或头晕，或伴有耳鸣耳聋等。心跳加快或减慢，心前区可出现胸闷或疼痛，咽喉不适、干渴和异物感、嗳气等；有时可出现血压升高，肢体可发凉、局部皮温降低，遇冷时有刺痒感，继而出现红肿、疼痛加重，偶可出现指端发红、发热、疼痛或痛觉过敏。疲劳、精神紧张时症状加重，休息后减轻。舌质淡红，苔薄黄，脉弦数。

6. 混合型颈椎病 混合型颈椎病指的是出现两型或两型以上症状者。临床上多以混合型颈椎病出现，而单一型颈椎病临床少见。

【诊断要点】

临床上对颈椎病的患者，首先要仔细询问患者发病原因和病史，了解目前表现出的症状并分清主次，进行相应的查体和临床辅助检查。颈神经根型颈椎病的常规检查为拍摄颈椎正、侧位，左、右前斜位和过伸、过屈位X线片，必要时可CT或MRI的检查；椎动脉型颈椎病可做脑血流图、脑电图检查，必要时可作椎动脉造影检查；脊髓型颈椎病以CT、MRI检查或脊髓造影检查；交感神经型颈椎病可做心电图检查。

1. 颈型颈椎病

（1）有颈部劳损史，反复出现"落枕"现象。

（2）平时肩胛骨内上角和内侧缘常有酸胀疼痛感。发病时颈椎活动受限，颈部肌张力增高，肩胛提肌、菱形肌、冈下肌、大小圆肌处往往可触及条索状改变及压痛。

（3）神经系统检查不能发现明确的定位体征。

（4）臂丛神经牵拉试验、叩顶试验阴性。

（5）排除颈肩软组织风湿及颈椎外伤。

（6）颈椎平片可见退行性变化，但X线检查并不与患者的症状完全一致。

2. 神经根型颈椎病

（1）在病变节段间隙、棘突旁及其神经分布区可出现压痛，颈部肌肉张力增高，局部有条索状或结节状反应物。

（2）符合神经根型颈椎病的临床表现。

（3）臂丛神经牵拉试验阳性，叩顶试验阳性，患侧上肢肱二头肌或肱三头肌反射可减弱。

（4）X线侧位片可见颈椎生理前凸减少或消失，椎体后缘和（或）小关节增生，椎间孔相对狭窄。正位片可见颈椎出现侧凸畸形，椎间隙变窄。X线显示与受害神经根的症状相一致。

（5）排除脊髓内、神经丛、神经干病变的可能性和排除颈椎结核、肿瘤、胸廓出口综合症、肩关节周围炎、网球肘等疾病。

3. 脊髓型颈椎病

(1) 脊髓受压,从上至下,波及全身为中央型;从下至上,波及全身为周围型。

(2) 肢体张力增高,肌力减弱,四肢不完全瘫痪。低头后可诱发肢体症状加重。

(3) 出现明显的感觉障碍平面,感觉障碍不平衡,一般是痛、温觉感觉障碍明显而触觉障碍较轻或正常,下肢感觉障碍较重而躯干部感觉障碍较轻。

(4) 腹壁反射和提睾反射减弱或消失。肱二、三头肌肌腱及膝、跟腱反射亢进,同时还可出现髌阵挛及踝阵挛。

(5) 霍夫曼征和巴宾斯基征阳性。

(6) X线侧位片上可见颈椎生理曲度变直或反弓,椎体后缘增生,项韧带钙化,椎间隙变窄,椎管矢状径变窄;CT或MRI检查可见骨质增生和(或)软组织压迫脊髓,脊髓出现受压切迹;脊髓造影也可见脊髓受压影,脑脊液流通不畅。

(7) 排除椎管内外占位性病变、脊髓损伤、肌肉萎缩型侧索硬化症、多发性神经根炎和末梢神经炎等疾病。

4. 椎动脉型颈椎病

(1) 病变节段横突部压痛。

(2) 出现颈性眩晕等椎动脉供血不足的症状,症状表现为"猝倒"。

(3) 旋颈试验阳性:颈椎旋转到一定的方位即出现眩晕,改变位置时,症状即可消失。

(4) 脑血流图、脑电图可出现异常,仅供临床参考;椎动脉造影可见椎动脉受压或扭曲,可作为确切诊断。

(5) X线片可见颈椎生理曲度减小或消失,可出现侧凸畸形;钩椎关节侧方或关节突关节部骨质增生,横突肥大。

(6) 排除耳源性眩晕、眼源性眩晕、椎动脉瘤等动脉本身的病变、锁骨下动脉盗血综合症、颅内肿瘤、神经官能症等疾病。

5. 交感神经型颈椎病

(1) 有慢性头痛史。

(2) 两侧颈椎横突前压痛点明显。

(3) 可出现身体上部的头晕、眼花、耳鸣、心动过速或减慢、心前区疼痛等交感神经功能紊乱症状和体征。部分患者出现霍纳征。

(4) 心电图无或轻度异常。

(5) X光片检查颈椎生理曲度改变,椎体和钩椎关节骨质增生,横突肥厚等。

(6) 排除心脏、眼等器官的器质性病变。

6. 混合型颈椎病

兼具以上两种或两种以上颈椎病的诊断要点。

【推拿治疗】

1. 治疗原则 舒筋活血,解痉止痛,松解粘连。

2. 取穴和部位 风池、风府、颈夹脊、肩井、天宗、曲池、手三里、合谷、阿是穴等穴和枕后部、颈肩背及患侧上肢部。

3. 操作

(1) 基本操作

1) 患者取坐位,医生立于其后外侧,一手固定头顶部,另一手拇指指腹与食、中指指腹对称用力拿揉颈项两旁的软组织由上而下操作3~5遍,力量由轻到重;然后用一指禅推法推颈后部正中及两侧,操作5分钟;随后用𢮦法、掌按揉法放松患者颈肩部、上背部及上肢的肌肉,反复操作3~5遍。

2) 按揉或一指禅推风池、风府、颈夹脊、肩井、天宗、曲池、手三里、合谷、阿是穴等穴,每穴10秒钟左右。

3) 接着做颈项部拔伸法,医生两前臂尺侧放于患者两侧肩部并向下用力,双手拇指顶按在风池穴上方,其余四指及手掌托住下颌部,嘱患者身体下沉,术者双手向上用力,前臂与手同时向相反方向用力,边牵引边使头颈部前屈、后伸及左右旋转。

4) 五指拿头部五经、三指拿颈项,双手拿提患者两侧的肩井穴。时间为2~3分钟。

5) 拿揉患肢,以肱二头肌和肱三头肌为主,用多指横拨腋下臂丛神经分支,使患者手指有窜麻感为宜。时间为2~3分钟。

6) 牵抖患侧上肢2~3次,最后拍打肩背部和上肢,使患者有轻快感为宜。

(2) 辨病加减

1) 颈型颈椎病:以局部肌肉松解和颈椎小关节调整为主,可加用弹拨压痛点和痉挛的颈部肌肉,用以缓解颈部疼痛和肌肉的痉挛;用颈椎斜扳法或旋转定位扳法纠正颈椎小关节紊乱,来减少对颈部椎窦神经感觉纤维的刺激;前后左右活动并摇动颈部,是为了调整颈部肌肉和颈椎小关节紊乱。

若治疗后患者的肩胛骨内上角或内侧缘仍感到酸痛,可从病变节段所在的横突后结节开始,以轻柔的拇指按揉法或一指禅推法循序逐渐向下推移到酸痛所在部位,使该紧张肌纤维松弛而症状缓解。

2) 神经根型颈椎病:常规操作基础上再用一指禅推法和拇指按揉法在患肢沿放射性神经痛路线循序推移,由上到下,操作3~5遍,以消除因神经根受压所引起的神经干炎性反应和由运动神经受刺激、肌肉反射性紧张引起的应力性筋膜劳损;按揉和弹拨颈部压痛点,以松解局部粘连和缓解局部的疼痛;用颈椎斜扳法或旋转复位扳法来纠正颈椎小关节紊乱,减轻对病变神经根的刺激;从上至下搓动患肢2~3遍,理五指一遍,可以促进患肢的血液循环,加速病变神经炎症的消散和吸收。治疗前,采用坐位或卧位颈椎持续牵引,重量3~5kg,20~30分钟,可以扩大椎间孔的上下径和拉伸痉挛的颈部肌肉,有利于缓解病变神经根的压迫和颈部肌肉的痉挛,为治疗做好准备。

3) 脊髓型颈椎病:治疗前,采用坐位或卧位颈椎持续牵引,重量3~5kg,40~60分钟,可以增大椎间隙和拉伸痉挛的颈部肌肉,有利于缓解病变颈椎间盘的机械压迫和颈部肌肉的痉挛,为治疗做好准备;颈椎拔伸下用颈椎微调手法进行颈椎调整,纠正紊乱的颈椎,可防止颈部软组织代偿性损伤;下肢同上肢的治疗,用以改善下肢肌肉痉挛症状,以及缓解下肢酸痛和无力症状。

4) 椎动脉型椎病:常规操作基础上再以指揉法在眼眶周围及头的两侧,用一指禅"∞"字推法推眼眶周围和一指禅推太阳穴、前额、头顶,用抹法在前额、眼眶周围操作,用扫散法在头的两侧治疗,以醒脑开窍,促进头部血液循环,从而消除头面部的症状;适当选择颈椎斜扳法或旋转定位扳法,缓解紧张与痉挛和防止颈部软组织代偿性损伤;在颈部适当使用摇法,以不加重症状和患者能忍受为度,起到调整颈部肌肉和关节的作用;治疗前根据情况适当牵引,牵引的力量宜小,一般为3kg左右,以拉伸痉挛的颈部肌肉,缓解颈部肌肉的痉挛。

5) 交感神经型颈椎病:常规操作基础上,再以轻巧的推揉手法在颈前两侧椎前肌群处从上到下,循序推揉,使痉挛的椎前肌群放松,从而减轻对交感神经干或结的刺激;以轻柔的一指禅推法或拇指弹拨法沿前斜角肌、胸小肌推移到胸大肌及诸肋间隙,以掌擦法至左侧胸壁,加按揉内关、心俞、三焦俞等穴,以调整失常的心率和调节交感神经的兴奋性;摇颈项以放松颈部的肌肉,调整颈椎的小关节紊乱,减轻对交感神经干或结的刺激。

若患者伴有慢性头痛,则以轻柔的一指禅推法自枕后沿足少阳胆经的路线推移至两颞侧部、前额部,以一指禅偏峰推法治疗两眼眶内缘和扫散头的两侧;若患者伴有视力降低,则以一指禅"∞"字推法推眼眶周围,一指禅偏峰推法刺激两眼眶内缘,用抹法在前额、眼眶周围操作;若患者伴有慢性咽喉疼痛、异物感,可以轻柔的一指禅推法推气管两侧和咽喉部。

6) 混合型颈椎病:根据所包括的不同类型颈椎病,采取相应的手法进行治疗。

【注意事项】

1. 颈椎病的推拿治疗前,要清楚是急性期还是缓解期。急性期手法宜轻柔,避免使用颈椎斜扳法或旋转定位扳法;缓解期手法力量宜稍重,但要注意以患者能够承受为度。

2. 颈椎病的推拿治疗时,要遵循循序渐进的治疗原则,在做被动运动时,动作应缓慢,切忌暴力、蛮力和动作过大,以免发生意外。

3. 注意低头位工作不宜太久,避免头顶、手持重物,避免不正常的工作体位。

4. 睡眠时枕头不宜过高、过低、过硬,最好另用一只小枕头,垫放在颈项部。

5. 推拿治疗期间和治疗后1~2周,可戴颈项围领。

6. 注意颈肩部的保暖。

7. 注意治疗期间和治疗后的颈部功能锻炼,有目的地练习颈部前后肌群。

8. 对脊髓型颈椎病有进行性加重趋势,应考虑综合治疗或建议手术治疗。

7.1.3 急性腰扭伤

急性腰扭伤是指劳动或运动时腰部肌肉、筋膜、韧带、椎间小关节、腰骶关节的急性损伤,多为突然承受超负荷牵拉或嵌压等间接外力所致。人们常称为"闪腰"、"岔气"。急性腰扭伤是临床中常见病,多发病。青壮年和体力劳动者、平素缺少参加体力劳动锻炼的人,偶然参加劳动时,用力不当亦易发生损伤。男性多于女性。急性腰扭伤若处理不当,治疗不及时,或不治疗者,亦可使症状缓解或形成慢性的发病过程。

造成急性腰扭伤的因素不一,常与劳动强度、动作技巧、腰背部健康状况、疲劳甚至气候、季节有关。大部分患者能清楚讲述受伤时的体态,指出疼痛部位。下列因素易造成腰部损伤。①腰部用力不当,如在膝部伸直弯腰提取重物时,重心距离躯干中轴较远,因杠杆作用,增加了肌肉的承受力,容易引起腰部肌肉的急性扭伤。②行走失足,行走不平坦的道路或下楼梯时不慎滑倒,腰部前屈,下肢处于伸直位时,亦易造成腰肌筋膜的扭伤或撕裂。③动作失调,两人搬抬物体,动作失于协调,身体失去平衡,重心突然偏移,或失去控制,致使腰部肌肉在无准备的情况下,骤然强力收缩,引起急性腰扭伤。④对客观估计不足,思想准备不够,如倒水、弯腰、猛起,甚至打喷嚏等无防备的情况下,也可发生"闪腰岔气"等。

急性腰扭伤临床常见于急性腰肌筋膜损伤、急性腰部韧带损伤和急性腰椎后关节紊乱等。

【临床表现】

急性腰肌筋膜损伤:急性腰肌筋膜损伤是一种较常见的腰部外伤。多因弯腰提取重物用力过猛,弯腰转身突然闪扭,致使腰部肌肉强烈的收缩,而引起腰部肌肉和筋膜受到过度牵拉、扭捩、甚至撕裂。本病在中医伤科统归于跌扑闪挫所致。损伤时因受力大小不同,组织损伤程度亦不一样。常见者为骶棘肌由骶骨起点部骨膜撕裂,或筋膜等组织附着点撕裂。筋膜损伤,血脉破损,必然会造成腰部瘀血凝滞,气机不通,则产生瘀血肿胀、疼痛、活动受限等临床表现。

症状表现为损伤时患者常感到腰部有一响声或有组织"撕裂"感。随即感到腰部一侧或两侧剧烈疼痛,不能直腰,屈伸俯仰、转身起坐则疼痛加剧,整个腰部多不能活动,呈强直状,严重者起床、用力、咳嗽、喷嚏时疼痛加剧。轻者伤时疼痛轻微,尚能坚持继续劳动,数小时后或次日症状加重。患者为减轻腰部疼痛,常用两手扶住并固定腰部。疼痛多位于腰骶部,有时感到一侧或两侧臀部及大腿后部疼痛,部位和性质较模糊,多胀痛、酸痛。舌质紫或有瘀斑,苔薄,脉迟或弦。

体征检查扭伤早期,肌肉、筋膜和韧带的撕裂可引起疼痛,引起肌肉的保护性痉挛,腰椎生理前凸减小;不对称性的肌痉挛可引起脊柱生理性侧弯等改变。待疼痛等症状缓解后,以上症状亦自行缓解或消失。

多数患者均有明显的局限性的压痛点,发生的部位多在腰骶关节、第三腰椎横突尖和髂棘后部。压痛点既是组织损伤部位,又是诊断本病的部位之一。另因损伤而致骶棘肌和臀大肌疼痛刺激所引起的一种保护性反应。

X线检查对于严重的腰扭伤患者,应拍腰骶部正、侧位X线片,必要时拍斜位片。一般软组织扭伤,X线片不显示任何病理性腰椎峡部骨折、骨质增生、肿瘤或结核等。

【诊断要点】

(1) 有突然腰部损伤的外伤史。

(2) 腰部剧烈疼痛,活动受限,咳嗽、喷嚏时腰痛加重。

(3) 腰部的棘突上、棘突间、椎间隙旁、骶髂关节附近有明显压痛点,叩击时疼痛加重,腰肌痉挛,有时可触及棘突偏歪,棘间隙变宽,脊柱侧弯。

(4) 站立或腰微前弯时,骶棘肌和臀大肌痉挛明显。

(5) 一般无下肢痛,有时在臀部、大腿后部或大腿根部前内有反射性疼痛区。

(6) X线检查多无异常发现或仅见腰椎屈度变直或侧弯,骨关节畸形或退行性变等。

急性腰部韧带损伤：腰部的主要韧带有前纵韧带、后纵韧带、黄韧带、棘间韧带、棘上韧带、横突间韧带及脊椎各关节囊、韧带。而临床常见的韧带损伤，主要是棘上韧带、棘间韧带和髂腰韧带。腰部韧带在正常情况下，皆由骶棘肌的保护而免受损伤，当人体弯腰搬物、动作失调时，骶棘肌处于松弛状态，臀部肌肉和大腿后部肌肉收缩，韧带无保护，棘上韧带、棘间韧带极易损伤，尤以腰骶部最多见。再则腰部受外力直接挫伤，均可造成腰部韧带的损伤。此种损伤往往较重，多合并骨折、脱位或神经受伤。舌质红紫，苔薄白，脉弦紧。

棘突上、棘间韧带损伤常发生在弯腰工作时。患者自觉腰部有一清脆响声或撕裂样感觉。随即局部突然疼痛，常呈现断裂样、针刺样或刀割样疼痛，局部可出现瘀斑肿胀，坐卧困难，伴有下肢放射性疼痛。腰部肌肉痉挛，各方向活动受限，尤以前屈时疼痛明显加重。在损伤的棘突和棘突间有明显压痛。局部封闭治疗后疼痛可减轻或消失。有棘突上、棘间韧带断裂者，触诊可见棘突间的距离加宽。X线检查：韧带损伤者，无异常表现，如有棘突上、棘间韧带断裂者，其棘突间距离可增大。

【诊断要点】
（1）有明显外伤史。
（2）伤后腰骶部有撕裂感，剧痛，活动受限，屈曲时疼痛加重。
（3）棘突上、棘突间处压痛明显，棘突间距可增宽。
（4）普鲁卡因局部封闭后疼痛减轻或消失，也可确定损伤的性质和部位。
（5）严重损伤者，拍X线片，了解有否骨折或脱位。

急性腰椎后关节滑膜嵌顿：亦称腰椎后关节紊乱症或腰椎间小关节综合征。腰椎后关节为上位椎骨的下关节突及下位椎骨的上关节突所构成。每个关节突是互成直角的两个面，一是冠状位，一是矢状位，所以侧弯和前后屈伸运动的范围较大。腰骶关节，则为小关节面介于冠状和矢状位之间的斜位，由直立面渐变为近似水平面，上下关节囊较宽松，其屈伸和旋转等活动范围增大。当腰部在突然无准备的弯腰前屈和旋转时，腰椎后关节后缘间隙张开，使关节内产生负压，吸入滑膜。此时如脊椎突然后伸时，滑膜就可能退出不及而被嵌夹在关节面之间，形成腰椎后小关节滑膜嵌顿，或关节突关节面的软骨相互错位，可引起腰部剧烈疼痛。若有先天性腰骶关节突不对称，一侧关节突发生斜向运动，使骨膜更易嵌入，或关节突错位。

本病以往对其发病机理的认识不十分清楚，多被误诊为急性腰肌筋膜损伤或急性腰肌纤维组织炎等，而延误治疗，产生慢性腰痛。现认为是临床上的一种常见病，是引起急性腰痛的常见原因之一。其发病年龄以青壮年为多见，男性多于女性。其机理多在轻度急性腰扭伤或弯腰猛然起立时，致使关节突扭动，滑膜嵌插于关节内，脊椎活动受限。

临床多有腰部扭伤或弯腰后立即直腰的病史。损伤后腰部立即发生剧烈疼痛，活动更加明显，尤其惧怕任何搬动。腰部呈现紧张僵硬状态，功能活动基本丧失。检查腰部呈僵直屈曲位，后伸活动明显受限，一般无神经根刺激性体征。触诊未发现患椎棘突偏歪，棘突间隙无变化。$L_{4～5}$或$L_5～S_1$棘突间和椎体旁有明显压痛点。X线检查部分患者可显示后关节排列方向不对称，或有腰椎后突和侧弯，椎间隙左右宽窄不等。舌紫伴有瘀斑,苔薄黄,脉沉紧。

【诊断要点】

(1) 有急性腰部扭闪外伤史,或慢性腰部劳损史。

(2) 主诉腰部剧痛,活动更加明显。腰椎后关节错位或滑膜嵌顿时,腰部正常生理曲线异常,站、坐和过伸活动时疼痛加剧。

(3) 腰部紧张、僵硬,紧张、痉挛缓解后,患椎棘突或关节突部位压痛也逐渐消失。

(4) 卧床休息翻身时痛剧,轻微活动或改变体位后疼痛减轻,直腿抬高受阻,一般无神经刺激性体征。

(5) 整复或嵌顿解除后,腰部疼痛可缓解。

【推拿治疗】

1. 治疗原则 舒筋活血。

2. 取穴和部位 肾俞、大肠俞、环跳、殷门、委中、承山、阳陵泉、昆仑、阿是穴等穴位及腰背部。

3. 操作

(1) 急性腰肌筋膜损伤

1) 患者取俯卧位。用滚法在压痛点周围治疗,逐渐移至疼痛处,然后在伤侧顺骶棘肌纤维方向用滚法操作,往返3～4遍,配合腰部后伸被动活动,幅度由小到大,手法压力由轻到重,时间为5分钟左右。

2) 患者俯卧位。滚法、揉肾俞、大肠俞、环跳、殷门、承山、阳陵泉、昆仑、阿是穴,拿委中,以酸胀为度,再在压痛点上、下方,用弹拨法治疗,弹拨时手法宜柔和深沉,时间为5分钟左右。

3) 患者俯卧位。在受伤一侧,沿骶棘肌纤维方向,进行直擦,以透热为度。时间为3分钟左右。

4) 患者侧卧位。患侧在上作腰部斜扳。

(2) 急性腰部韧带损伤

1) 在"急性腰肌筋膜损伤"治疗的基础上,松解粘连。患者站立或端坐位,医生立于患者背后,嘱患者前屈弯腰,以双手拇指触摸、剥离病变的棘上韧带。术后卧硬板床休息。避免腰部旋转活动,暂不作身体屈曲动作。时间为5分钟左右。

2) 患者俯卧位,医生用按、揉手法治疗脊柱两侧,并用一手拇指指腹在患部棘上韧带做与其呈垂直方向的弹拨、按揉治疗,最后做腰背部督脉上直擦,以透热为度。时间为5分钟左右。

(3) 急性腰椎后关节滑膜嵌顿

1) 在"急性腰肌筋膜损伤"治疗的基础上,松解粘连。

2) 选用弯腰旋转扳法。

【注意事项】

1. 治疗后,嘱患者卧床休息,短期内勿做腰部前屈及旋转活动。

2. 急性症状经治疗后可即刻缓解,但疼痛及腰部僵硬感并未消失,所以可配合局部导入,症状可逐渐缓解、消失。

3. 腰背伸肌功能锻炼,有助于巩固疗效和预防。
4. 腰部保暖。

7.1.4 慢性腰肌劳损

慢性腰肌劳损系指腰部积累性的肌肉、筋膜、韧带、骨与关节等组织的慢性损伤。本病因长期蹲位弯腰工作,腰背部经常性过度负重、疲劳,或工作时姿势不正确,或有腰部解剖特点和缺陷等所致,但亦可因腰部急性损伤治疗不及时、治疗不当,或反复受伤后遗留为慢性腰痛的。

长期从事腰部持力或弯腰活动工作,长期的腰部姿势不良等,都可引起腰背肌肉筋膜劳损,或者筋膜松弛,或慢性的撕裂伤,以致腰痛难愈。亦有腰部急性扭挫伤之后,未能获得及时而有效的治疗,或治疗不彻底,或反复轻微损伤,肌肉筋膜发生粘连,迁延而成为慢性腰痛。亦有平素体虚,肾气虚弱,外感风、寒、湿邪,留滞肌肉筋脉,以致筋脉不和,肌肉筋膜拘挛,经络阻闭,气血运行障碍而致慢性腰痛。再者腰椎有先天性畸形和解剖缺陷者,如腰椎骶化、椎弓根崩裂与腰椎滑脱,以及骨折、脱位所致的腰椎后突畸形等,都可引起腰背部肌力平衡失调,亦可造成腰部肌肉筋膜的劳损。

腰部劳损是腰痛中最常见的一种,临床根据发病部位、损伤组织的不同则分有腰肌劳损和韧带劳损两种。

【临床表现】

腰肌劳损主要是指腰部肌肉慢性劳累性损伤。自诉腰痛,疼痛多为隐痛,时轻时重,经常反复发作,休息后减轻,劳累后加重,适当活动或变动体位时减轻,弯腰工作困难,若勉强弯腰则腰痛加剧,常喜用双手捶腰,以减轻疼痛,少数患者有臀部的大腿后上部胀痛。天气变化、劳累后疼痛加剧。舌质淡红,舌苔薄白,脉浮紧。

检查脊柱外观正常,俯仰活动多无障碍,一侧或两侧骶棘肌处、髂骨嵴后部或骶骨后面腰背肌止点处有压痛。病情严重时疼痛较重,活动稍有受限。神经系统检查多无异常。X线检查:有时可见脊柱生理弓的改变,如腰椎侧弯、腰前凸度减弱或消失,或见第5腰椎骶化、第1骶椎腰化、隐性脊柱裂等先天变异,或见有骨质增生等。

临床中应与棘上韧带劳损相互鉴别。

【诊断要点】

1. 有长期腰痛史,反复发作。
2. 腰部痠痛不舒,在劳累后或阴雨天加重。
3. 直腿抬高试验多接近正常,腰部运动受限制不明显。
4. X线检查,仅提示腰骶椎先天变异或骨质增生,余无异常发现。

【推拿治疗】

1. 治疗原则 舒筋活血,温经通络。
2. 取穴和部位 肾俞、大肠俞、关元俞、秩边、环跳、委中;腰背部和腰骶部。
3. 操作
(1) 患者取俯卧位,医生用双手掌推、按、揉脊柱两侧的竖脊肌。时间为5分钟。
(2) 再用双手指点、拨骶棘肌数遍。而后,用拇指端重点推、按、拨压痛点。时间为5分钟。

(3) 医生用双手指指端、指腹按、揉、振肾俞、大肠俞、关元俞、秩边、环跳、委中等穴,每穴各半分钟即可。

(4) 患者取仰卧位,横擦腰背部带脉。时间为3～5分钟。

【注意事项】

1. 保持良好的姿势,注意纠正习惯性姿势不良,维持脊柱正常的生理弧度。
2. 加强体育锻炼,增强腰肌功能。

7.1.5 退行性脊柱炎

退行性脊柱炎又称为"增生性脊柱炎"、"肥大性脊柱炎"、"脊椎骨关节炎"、"老年性关节炎"等,是以腰椎软骨的退行性改变、骨质增生为主要特点的骨关节病变。本病多见于中老年人,男性多于女性。体态肥胖者、体力劳动者及运动员等发病较早,是一种慢性腰椎骨关节炎,患者可出现慢性腰腿疼痛。

本症分为原发性和继发性两种:原发性主要为老年人的生理退行性改变,患者大多在中老年以上,人体各组织器官,随着年龄的增长逐渐衰退,骨质开始出现退行性改变。这种改变主要表现在机体各部组织细胞所含水分和胶质减少,而游离钙质增加,其生理功能也随之衰退老化,腰椎椎体边缘产生不同程度的骨质增生,椎间盘发生变性,椎间隙变窄,椎间孔缩小,压迫刺激神经根,而引起腰腿疼痛;继发性主要继发于各种损伤、慢性炎症、贫血、新陈代谢障碍,或内分泌紊乱等。因为这些病症,都会影响到骨关节软骨板的血液循环和营养供给,从而导致软骨的炎性改变和软骨下骨反应性的骨质增生,而引起腰腿痛。

本病主要的病理机制为关节软骨的变性,椎间盘的退行性改变。人体在中壮年以后,椎体周围关节的软骨弹性降低,其边缘、关节囊、韧带等附着处,逐渐形成保护性的骨质增生。髓核内的纤维组织增多,但仍保持其原有的膨大和胶质状态,在中老年以后,髓核的变性逐渐达到后期,椎间盘萎缩性变化广泛,椎间隙变窄,椎间孔变小。此时软骨板的变性也已明显,液体的交换减少,促进了髓核和纤维环的变性和坏死。脊柱曲线凹侧(椎体后侧)的椎体缘,由于杠杆作用,所受压力较大,随年龄增长,椎体所受压迫和磨损的时间越长,因此骨质增生形成的机会越多。椎间盘变性后,椎间隙变窄,并失去其"水垫"或水力学性能,椎体两端不断受到震荡、冲击和磨损。在椎间盘变性的同时,也会发生老年性的骨质疏松现象,削弱了椎体对压力的抵抗。

【临床表现】

中老年以后逐渐出现腰痛,但不伴有全身症状。45～55岁之间,是退行性脊柱炎腰痛现象的高峰期。随着年龄的增长,椎间盘逐渐萎缩,且其稳定性增加。因此,在60岁以后,腰痛便逐渐减轻。舌苔薄白或白腻,脉象沉紧或濡缓。

一般腰痛并不剧烈,或仅感腰部酸痛不适,不太灵活,或有束缚感。在晨起或久坐站起时,腰痛明显,而稍事活动后,疼痛减轻或消失,但过度疲劳之后又会加重。腰痛有时可放散至臀部或大腿部。阴雨天气或受风着凉时,腰痛加重。脊柱变形,腰椎的生理前突也减小或消失,脊柱运动受限。有时腰椎棘突出现叩击痛,两侧腰肌紧张、压痛。在臀上神经和坐骨神经的径路上,也可出现压痛,甚至出现坐骨神经刺激症状。直腿抬高试验阳性,腱反射减弱,屈颈压腹试验阳性。X线片可显示骨质增生的程度。

【诊断要点】

1. 慢性下腰部痛,腰腿痛,符合本病疼痛特征。
2. 脊柱常无明显畸形。如有滑脱,腰前凸可增大。腰活动一般无明显受限,或仅有轻度受限。直腿抬高试验呈假阳性。
3. 腰部常无固定压痛点,或在两侧腰肌及 $L_3\sim L_4$、$L_4\sim L_5$ 腰椎处压痛。
4. X线片诊断　腰椎体边缘有骨质增生,椎体前缘呈唇形变,或骨刺形成。椎体间隙变窄或不规则,关节突模糊不清,可伴有老年性骨萎缩。

【推拿治疗】

1. 治疗原则　行气活血,舒筋通络。

2. 取穴和部位　命门、阳关、气海俞、大肠俞、关元俞、夹脊、委中、阳陵泉、承山;腰部。

3. 操作

(1) 患者取俯卧位,医生用㨰法施术于腰部病变处及腰椎两侧,其力度由轻至重。时间为3～5分钟左右。

(2) 用指按命门、阳关、气海俞、大肠俞、关元俞,或掌根按脊椎两旁夹脊,接着再用㨰法从腰部到臀部治疗。有下肢牵痛时,用捏、拿、按揉法沿股后面向下至小腿,点、按揉委中、承山、阳陵泉等穴位。同时配合下肢后抬腿活动,时间为10分钟左右。

(3) 最后用擦法施术于腰背部及相关部位,可配合热敷治疗。

【注意事项】

1. 卧硬板床,注意腰部保暖。
2. 应注意适宜的功能锻炼,如前屈、后伸及左右旋转腰部等。

7.1.6　第三腰椎横突综合征

第三腰椎横突综合征是以第三腰椎横突部明显压痛为特征的慢性腰痛。亦称为第三腰椎横突周围炎,或第三腰椎横突滑囊炎。它是腰肌筋膜劳损的一种类型,由于第三腰椎居全腰椎之中心,活动度大,其横突较长,抗力大,劳损发病率较高,故易产生腰痛和臀部痛。本病多见于青壮年,尤以体力劳动者最为多见。

腰椎横突位于腰椎两侧,无骨性组织保护,其中以第三腰椎横突最长,上为腰大肌、腰方肌起点,并附有腹横肌、背阔肌的深部筋膜。当腰、腹部肌肉强力收缩时,该处所承受的拉应力最大,因此,第三腰椎横突上附着的肌肉容易发生牵拉损伤,引起局部组织的炎性肿胀、充血、液体渗出等病理变化,继而发生滑膜、纤维组织、纤维软骨等的增生,邻近腰脊神经后支的外侧支受到刺激,日久神经纤维可发生变性,产生腰痛和臀部痛,引起腰骶部肌肉痉挛。外邪、外伤亦可使第三腰椎周围的肌肉筋膜撕裂,出现损伤性炎症,若治疗不当,可引起横突周围瘢痕粘连,筋膜增厚,肌腱挛缩等病理变化,并产生相应的症状。

【临床表现】

腰部常有疲劳、不适感、疼痛等,呈弥漫性疼痛,并向大腿后侧至腘窝平面扩散。

劳累后、天气变化、晨起或弯腰时加重,稍事活动疼痛减轻,腰痛多呈持续性。少数患者可出现间歇性酸胀乏力,疼痛可向臀部或大腿外侧放散。在第三腰椎横突部有明显压痛,有时可触及纤维性结节状或条索状硬结。$L_{2\sim3}$椎间隙旁常有麻木区或过敏区。腰部肌张力减弱,运动基本正常。舌淡嫩,苔白,脉沉细。

检查时在骶棘肌外缘第3腰椎横突尖端处有局限性压痛,有时可触及一纤维性软组织硬结,常可引起同侧下肢反射痛,直腿抬高试验可为阳性。X线检查:X线摄片除可见第3腰椎明显过长外,有时左右横突不对称,或向后倾斜。

【诊断要点】

1. 多伴轻重不等的腰部损伤史。
2. 疼痛为腰部一侧或双侧,晨起或劳累后加重,弯腰活动时加重,症状重者可沿大腿向下肢放射。
3. 第三腰椎横突顶端处明显压痛,且有结节状纤维硬化。
4. X线片显示第三腰椎横突过长,远端边缘部有钙化阴影,或两侧横突不对称。

【推拿治疗】

1. 治疗原则　行气活血,舒筋通络。

2. 取穴和部位　环跳、承扶、殷门、委中、承山;腰背部。

3. 操作

(1) 患者取俯卧位,医生用两手掌根或肘尖,由胸椎自上而下反复地推、揉、按、点脊柱两侧的骶棘肌,直至骶骨背面或臀部的股骨大转子附近,并以两手拇指分别反复按、揉环跳、承扶、殷门、委中、承山,时间为5分钟左右。

(2) 医生用一手拇指在第三腰椎横突处做与结节样或条索状硬块垂直方向弹拨,弹拨要由浅到深,由轻到重,然后用拇指或肘尖在该处反复揉、摩,以缓解疼痛,时间为3分钟左右。

(3) 医生用掌根沿患侧骶棘肌自上而下地推、摩、按、揉。同时结合擦法,做反复的治疗。最后沿骶棘肌纤维方向自上而下的推、擦法,并配合腰部后伸被动活动,时间为2分钟左右。

【注意事项】

1. 病变和治疗期间,应卧硬板床。
2. 注意保温,防止外邪的侵袭,而影响治疗效果。治疗期间,可用热敷,以提高疗效。
3. 根据病变的情况,尽量避免容易导致腰部劳累的劳动。
4. 纠正不良姿势。

7.1.7　腰椎间盘突出症

腰椎间盘突出症,又称"腰椎间盘纤维环破裂髓核突出症",是指腰椎间盘发生退行性变后,因外力作用,使纤维环部分或完全破裂,髓核向外膨出或突出,压迫神经根,或刺激脊髓,而引起腰腿痛等一系列症状。本病是腰腿痛的常见病之一,多见于青壮年体力劳动者。以工人发病率为高,好发于20~40岁之间。临床以$L_4\sim L_5$的椎间盘最易发生病变,$L_5\sim S_1$的椎间盘次之,$L_3\sim L_4$之间的椎间盘偶有发生,$L_2\sim$

L_3 和 L_1～L_2 的椎间盘极为少见。本病的发生原因有内因和外因两个方面，内因是椎间盘本身的退行性改变，或椎间盘发育上的缺陷；外因有损伤、劳损以及风寒侵袭等。

腰椎间盘位于相邻二个椎体之间，构成脊椎骨的负重关节，为脊柱活动的枢纽。椎间盘由纤维环、髓核、软骨板所组成。纤维环是由坚韧致密的弹性纤维在软骨基质中交织而成，与上下椎体紧密相连。髓核是一种含水分较多的胶状物，纤维环与上下椎体面上的软板，把髓核限制在一个球形腔内。随着年龄的增长，以及不断遭受挤压、牵拉和扭转等外力作用，使椎间盘逐渐发生退化，髓核含水量逐渐减少，而失去弹性，使椎间隙变窄，周围韧带松弛，或产生裂隙，形成腰椎间盘突出症的内在原因。在外力作用下，后部压力增加，容易发生纤维环破裂和髓核向后外侧突出，刺激、压迫脊神经或脊髓，引起明显的神经痛症状。亦有患者无明显外伤史，而于受凉后而发病，由于腰部着凉后腰肌痉挛，促使已有退行性变的椎间盘突出，神经根发生充血、水肿、变性，日久可有周围组织的增生肥厚，甚至与突出的椎间盘发生粘连。多数腰椎间盘突出症为单侧发病，髓核自后纵韧带一侧突出压迫脊髓或神经根，产生同侧症状。另有髓核自后纵韧带突出，直接刺激和压迫脊髓，出现的双侧下肢同时或交替样症状。

【临床表现】

腰椎间盘突出症根据髓核突出的位置、程度、方向、退变程度与神经根的关系及不同的影像学检查，有多种分型方法，归纳起来有病理分型，部位分型，形态分型，临床症状分型和中医学分型五种。但现在常用的分型，多依据髓核突出的方向和髓核突出的程度。其主要症状，是腰部疼痛和下肢（坐骨神经痛）的放射性疼痛。

腰痛常局限于腰骶部附近，在 L_4～L_5、L_5～S_1 或 L_3～L_4 棘突间有局限性深压痛，并向患侧下肢放射，坐骨神经痛常为单侧，并沿患侧的大腿后侧向下放射至小腿外侧、足跟部或足背外侧。若椎间盘突出较大或位于椎管中央时，可为双侧疼痛。咳嗽、喷嚏、用力排便时，均可使神经根更加紧张而加重症状，步行、弯腰、伸膝起坐等牵拉神经根的动作也使疼痛加剧，屈髋、屈膝卧床休息时疼痛减轻。疼痛多数为间歇性，少数为持续性。经休息，特别是卧床后可明显减轻，但容易在轻微损伤后复发。病程长者，其下肢放射部位感觉麻木，按中医学分型为瘀血型腰痛，症见腰部疼痛如锥刺，痛处固定不移，拒按，轻则俯仰不便，重则不能转侧，舌紫黯，或有瘀点、瘀斑，脉沉涩。

临床检查：腰部畸形。发病时，腰部僵硬，患者可有功能性脊柱侧弯，腰椎生理前凸减弱或消失。脊椎侧弯可以侧向患侧，也可侧向健侧，当椎间盘突出在受压神经根的内下方时，则脊柱侧向健侧，受压神经根可得到缓解；椎间盘突出在受压神经根的外上方时，则脊柱侧向患侧，受压神经根可得到缓解。前屈受限明显，后伸受限较少。侧弯则根据畸形方向而出现疼痛或受限，一般弯向凹侧，疼痛减轻，弯向凸侧，疼痛将加重。有明显压痛点。屈颈试验阳性；挺腹试验阳性；直腿抬高试验阳性；腱反射减弱或消失。

X线摄片检查：应常规拍摄 X 线正侧位片。有时正位片可显示腰椎侧凸，侧位片可见腰椎生理前凸消失，病变的椎间隙可能变窄，相邻椎体边缘有骨质增生。X 线检查时腰椎间盘突出症的诊断只作参考，其重要性在于排除腰椎其他病变，如结核、肿瘤、骨折、腰骶椎先天畸形等。

电子计算机断层扫描:采用CT测定腰椎椎管的形态和管径,对诊断腰椎间盘突出症有重要的价值,可以显示出腰、骶神经根受嵌压方式的因素。通过CT的立体动力显示器还可展现出椎间盘突出的程度和部位。

【诊断要点】

1. 有腰部外伤、慢性劳损或受寒湿史。大部分患者在发病前有慢性腰痛史。
2. 常发生于青壮年。
3. 腰痛向臀部及下肢放射,腹压增加(如咳嗽、喷嚏)时疼痛加重。
4. 脊柱侧弯,腰生理弧度消失,病变部位椎旁有压痛,并向下肢放射,腰活动受限。
5. 下肢受累神经支配区有感觉过敏或迟钝,病程长都可出现肌肉萎缩,直腿抬高等试验阳性,膝、跟腱反射减弱或消失,踇趾背伸力减弱。
6. X线摄片检查:脊柱侧弯,腰椎生理前凸消失,相邻边缘有骨质增生。CT、MRI检查可显示椎间盘突出的部位及程度。

【推拿治疗】

1. 治疗原则 舒筋通络,松解粘连。

2. 取穴和部位 腰阳关、大肠俞、环跳、居髎、承扶、殷门、委中、承山、阳陵泉、绝骨、丘墟及腰背、下肢部。

3. 操作

(1) 患者俯卧位,医生用㨰、按、揉手法在患者脊柱两侧膀胱经及臀部和下肢后外侧施术3~5分钟,以腰部为重点。然后医生用双手掌重叠用力,沿脊柱由上至下按压腰骶部,此法作用在于改善血液循环,缓解腰背肌肉痉挛,促进炎症的吸收,时间为5分钟左右。

(2) 患者俯卧位,医生先用拇指指腹或肘尖点、按、揉腰阳关、大肠俞、环跳、居髎、承扶、殷门、委中、承山、阳陵泉、绝骨、丘墟及阿是穴,以解痉止痛,时间为5~10分钟左右。

(3) 医生再用双手拇指指腹重叠推按或肘尖按压患处,向健侧推,促使突出的髓核对周围组织的刺激与压迫减轻,时间为3~5分钟左右。

(4) 患者取俯卧位,医生用点、按、揉、弹拨手法作用于腰部及患侧坐骨神经分布区。其作用是改善局部组织的血液循环,促进因损伤所致炎症的吸收,进而使萎缩的肌肉和麻痹的神经组织,逐渐恢复其功能,时间为1~3分钟左右。

(5) 最后根据突出的部位、程度,分别选用弯腰旋转扳法、单肢体后伸扳法、双肢体后伸扳法,以调整后关节紊乱,松解粘连,改变突出物与神经根的位置,增加椎间盘外周的压力,减轻疼痛,逐步恢复其功能。

【注意事项】

1. 睡硬板床。睡硬板床可以减少椎间盘承受的压力。
2. 注意腰间保暖,尽量不要受寒。避免着凉和贪食生冷之物,不要长时间在空调下,加强腰背部的保护。
3. 不要做弯腰又用力的动作(如拖地板等),注意劳动姿势,避免长久弯腰和过度负重,以免加速椎间盘的退行性病变。

4. 急性发作期尽量卧床休息，疼痛期缓解后也要注意适当休息，不要过于劳累，以免加重疼痛。

5. 平时的饮食上，多食含钙量高的食物。牛奶、奶制品、海产品等含有丰富的钙，也有利于钙的补充。注意营养结构。

7.1.8 胸胁屏伤

胸胁屏伤多由于外伤、暴力的撞击或挤压，但又不足以使肋骨骨折；或因姿势不良、用力不当等所形成的胸胁部气机壅塞，出现以胸部扳紧、掣痛，胸闷不舒为主要症状的一种病症。临床上把胸胁屏伤分为三种类型，即伤气型、伤血型和气血两伤型。伤气型是由于间接暴力扭转、牵拉等原因，造成胸廓的关节、软组织的损伤，但局部无明显的压痛，俗称"岔气"、"胁痛"；伤血型是由于直接暴力的撞击等，造成胸廓组织出血，阻塞气机，而表现为损伤处有明显的压痛，痛处固定不移；气血两伤型是由于直接和间接暴力，如挤压、撞击伴有牵拉等，造成胸廓组织出血和广泛性损伤，兼具伤气和伤血两种类型的临床特征。

本病为临床常见多发病之一，推拿疗法对伤气型胸胁屏伤有显著的疗效。

【临床表现】

患者一般都有明显的外伤史。受伤后即出现一侧胸肋部疼痛，可牵扯肩背部疼痛，咳嗽或呼吸时疼痛加重。由于患者施以保护性措施，故出现减少呼吸运动幅度的浅表急促呼吸，同时伴有胸闷不适。"气伤痛，形伤肿"，筋肉损伤，气血互阻，症见舌质青紫或有瘀斑，苔稍厚，脉迟涩；气血损伤较重者，可见舌淡有瘀斑，苔薄，脉细涩。根据不同的损伤类型，可出现不同的临床特征。

伤气型：痛时走窜不定，局部无明显压痛，呼吸、说话时有牵掣性疼痛，甚者不能平卧，不敢俯仰转侧。若伴肋椎关节半脱位的患者，其受累关节处可有小范围的压痛。

伤血型：痛有定处，局部肿胀明显。若胸壁附着肌拉伤，可出现损伤部位的明显肿胀，局部明显压痛；若胸壁固有肌群撕裂或痉挛，在相应的肋间隙可见肿胀、压痛、肋间隙稍窄等现象。

气血两伤型：兼具以上两种症状特点，疼痛范围广泛，局部也有明显的压痛点。临床上较单独伤血型多见。

【诊断要点】

临床上除查体之外，X线摄片被列为胸胁屏伤的常规检查，主要是判断有无肋椎关节半脱位和排除肋骨骨折。

1. 一般患者都有明显的外伤史。要仔细询问受伤原因，了解直接或间接暴力损伤的方式，用以初步判断胸胁屏伤的类型。

2. 触诊以判定是否有明显的压痛点和肋椎关节半脱位，以及确定肿胀的部位、程度和累及的大致范围。伤气型患者常不能明确指出疼痛部位，或在局部伤处可有小范围的压痛；伤血型和气血两伤型患者可见损伤部位有青紫瘀斑和肿胀，局部压痛明显，拒按。

3. 患者呼吸、说话时有牵掣性疼痛，甚者不能平卧，不敢俯仰转侧，动则疼痛难忍。

4. 胸廓挤压试验阴性。

5. 肋骨骨折患者则有肿痛显著,肋骨有挤压痛,或有肋骨移位畸形,或兼痰中带血,或见呼吸困难等症,胸廓挤压试验阳性,应加以鉴别。

6. 胸部 X 线片可见肋椎关节半脱位,单发或多发横断形或斜形肋骨骨折影;胸片可发现气胸、肺挫伤、血胸、皮下或纵隔气肿等病理表现。

7. 还应排除单纯性肋间神经痛、胸部带状疱疹早期、胸椎结核、肿瘤、胸膜炎、肋软骨炎等疾病。

【推拿治疗】

1. 治疗原则 活血散瘀,行气止痛,理筋整复。

2. 取穴和部位 重点取膻中、中府、云门、章门、期门、大包、日月和背部膀胱经腧穴以及患侧胸胁部、肩背部为主。

3. 操作

(1) 患者仰卧位,医生先用拇指指腹点按膻中、中府、云门、章门、期门、大包、日月等穴各 10 秒左右,以疏通经络,行气活血,稍微缓解局部疼痛。然后以掌揉、摩胸胁部患处 3~5 分钟,力量由轻到重,以解除肌肉痉挛,缓解疼痛。

(2) 患者取坐位,医生先用手掌按揉胸痛相应的背部,使之局部肌肉放松;接着沿着患侧背部的膀胱经作一指禅推法,从上至下操作,约 3~5 分钟;再以大拇指指腹按揉相应背部的膀胱经腧穴,以行气止痛。

(3) 患者取坐位,嘱患者全身肌肉放松,不可屏气,医生立其患侧的后外侧,面对患者,一手自患侧插入,用手反把持住患者肩的前上部,另一手扶住患侧上臂外侧,两手共同用力,将患侧肩部向上提拉,起到牵引患肩的作用,然后,在其吸气末期,再作一小幅度的、有控制的向上提拉动作,如果有肋椎关节半脱位或滑膜嵌顿者,可使其复位。操作完后,慢慢地放下患者肩部。

(4) 如果复位未成功,可再用扩胸牵引扳法或胸椎对抗扳法进行治疗。

(5) 最后用擦法擦背部膀胱经及患部,以透热为度,以起到温经活络的作用。

【注意事项】

1. 急性期禁用较重的推拿手法、热疗等,防止出血或渗出,进一步加重病情,可以服用止痛药物,暂时止痛。

2. 如果伴有胸椎小关节功能紊乱者,可直接用扩胸牵引扳法或胸椎对抗扳法进行治疗。

3. 治疗期间患者宜睡硬板床,避免重体力劳动。

7.1.9 骶髂关节错缝

骶髂关节错缝,主要是暴力损伤所致。如突然跌倒,单侧臀部着地,地面的作用力通过坐骨结节向上传导,而躯体向下的冲击作用力通过骶髂关节向下传导,二作用力在骶髂关节汇合,将髂骨推向上向内错移,而产生骶髂关节错缝。同样的机理,单侧下肢的突然负重,如跳跃、坠跌等,也可引起骶髂关节错缝。

下蹲位持重站立时扭伤,或身体向前、向后跌仆,使骶髂关节过度前后旋转,将髂骨推向内、上方而产生错移,致骶髂关节错缝。腹直肌的强烈收缩,髂骨关节面可在骶骨上向前旋转;而股后肌收缩时,使髂骨关节面在骶骨上向后旋转。由于这种旋转作用力的存在,可使骶髂关节交锁在一不正常的位置,而产生错缝,引起疼痛发生。

女性在妊娠期和产后,因内分泌的作用,使骶髂关节松弛,如受到扭转、牵拉、碰挫、滑跌等而产生错缝。

严重的骶髂关节错缝,可使关节周围的肌筋、韧带等产生撕裂,使关节的稳定性降低,负重或活动时有加重错缝的可能。轻微的错缝,有自行恢复的可能。如骶髂关节反复的错缝损伤或关节错缝未能得到及时正确的治疗,局部出血、机化、瘢痕形成,充填关节的空隙,造成复位困难和关节不稳,久之引起顽固性的持续下腰部疼痛。

本病临床较为常见,是腰腿痛的常见病因之一。本病好发于青壮年,以女性尤为多见,若治疗不当,可引起持续性的下腰痛。

【临床表现】

患者大多有外伤史,下腰部疼痛,并有单侧或双侧骶髂关节处疼痛,有的单侧或双侧下肢交替发生类似坐骨神经样疼痛。患侧骶髂关节周围有肌肉痉挛、下肢活动受限,且不能负重,行走须拄拐或者跛行,弯腰、翻身、仰卧等均可引起疼痛加剧,故患者往往不能穿鞋、袜,并且不敢大声咳嗽与谈笑,因腹压的增加亦可引起患侧骶髂关节疼痛加剧。患侧下肢痠痛无力,可有下肢放射性疼痛,偶有麻木感,自觉下肢有延长和缩短。行走时往往需用手掌保护患肢少受震动,上下楼梯需患肢先行,上下床铺需人作牵引扶持,否则疼痛难忍。舌淡,苔薄白,脉弦紧。

检查可见患侧骶髂关节肿胀,较健侧突起。患侧髂后下棘的内下角有压痛、叩击痛,有时可触及痛性筋结。双侧对比触摸髂后上棘时,可感觉患侧髂后上棘有凸起或凹陷。双下肢量比检查:观察双下肢足跟量比差,有学者认为量比差0.3厘米以上有诊断意义;量比差1厘米以上有确诊意义,通常不超过2厘米。患侧下肢缩短,髂后上棘凸起,为向后错缝移位。反之,患侧下肢变长,髂后上棘凹陷,为向前错缝移位。骨盆分离试验及"4"字试验、床边试验等均为阳性。

X线检查:拍摄骨盆X线片,一般无明显变化。有的患侧骶髂关节间隙略有增宽变窄,耻骨联合略有上下移动;陈旧性者则可见骶髂关节上下边缘出现骨质增生现象。

本病应与骶髂关节扭挫伤、腰椎间盘突出症和骶髂关节结核相鉴别。

【推拿治疗】

1. 治疗原则 疏通经络,松解粘连。

2. 取穴和部位 肾俞、大肠俞、承山、八髎、秩边、环跳、委中;腰背部及骶髂关节。

3. 操作

(1) 患者取俯卧位,擦、按、揉等法于骶棘肌和骶髂关节及臀部治疗5分钟左右,然后在患侧骶髂关节处重点施拇指按、揉、点、拨八髎、环跳、秩边等穴,以酸胀为度,达到解痉止痛之目的。

(2) 下肢疼痛者,捏、拿、按、揉下肢大腿、小腿等部位。然后擦热患处,或配合湿热敷。

(3) 整复向前扭转错位的方法：①患者健侧卧位，身体靠近床边，健侧下肢伸直，患侧屈膝屈髋，医生一手按住患肩向后固定其躯体，另一手按住患膝向前向下作最大限度按压，借助杠杆作用，可使骶髂关节错动而复位。②患者仰卧位，医者站于患侧，在作髋膝关节屈曲至最大限度的同时，于屈髋位作快速伸膝和下肢拔伸动作，反复3～5次。

【注意事项】

1. 推拿治疗后，症状可立即缓解，但因骶髂关节韧带损伤需要修复过程，故在两周内不宜作腰部、下肢部大幅度的活动。

2. 治疗期间，宜卧床休息，并注意保暖。

7.1.10 梨状肌综合征

梨状肌综合征是指因梨状肌直接或间接受损伤，致使梨状肌撕裂、出血、渗出、粘连，肌肉呈保护性痉挛；或受风、寒、湿邪的侵袭，致梨状肌痉挛、增粗，局部炎性渗出、水肿、张力增高，刺激、压迫穿越其肌腹的坐骨神经，出现以坐骨神经痛为主的一系列临床症状。本病又称梨状肌损伤综合征、梨状肌痉挛综合征。临床上以臀部疼痛，沿大腿后侧、小腿前外侧、外踝、足背至足趾放射为特点。任何年龄均可发病，以青壮年多见。

由于梨状肌的变异，当臀部遭受风、寒、湿邪的侵袭，使梨状肌痉挛、增粗，局部非特异性炎性渗出、水肿，局部张力增高，刺激、压迫穿越其肌腹的坐骨神经或腓总神经时，则出现坐骨神经痛。本病属中医伤科足少阳经筋病，伤及足少阳经筋所络，结骶尻部，以致经筋拘结，故臀痛。

【临床表现】

患者常在下肢外展、外旋位突然用力，或外展、外旋蹲位突然起立，负重情况下，髋关节突然内收、内旋用力的受伤史，部分患者有臀部受凉史。主要表现为一侧臀部疼痛，亦可有两侧同时发病，呈"针刺样"或"刀割样"疼痛，向同侧沿大腿后侧、小腿前外侧、外踝、足背至足趾放射，撅臀跛行，久行、劳累或遇阴雨天疼痛往往加剧，腹压增高时，如咳嗽、解便、喷嚏时疼痛加剧。

患侧臀部梨状肌体表投影区有明显压痛，可触及梨状肌呈条索状痉挛，按压时可引起同侧下肢放射痛。日久，臀部肌肉出现轻度萎缩。直腿抬高在小于60°时疼痛明显，大于60°时疼痛反而减轻。梨状肌紧张试验阳性。X线骨盆平片一般无异常改变。

本病日久聚结不散，气血瘀滞，经筋失于调达，流窜于下，筋肌挛急而腿痛，舌淡红，苔白，或薄白，脉弦，或弦紧。

【诊断要点】

1. 臀部有损伤史或受凉史。

2. 患臀疼痛，撅臀跛行。

3. 患侧臀部梨状肌压痛并可触及条索状痉挛，疼痛向同侧下肢放射。

4. X线检查无异常。

【推拿治疗】

1. 治疗原则 舒筋通络,活血止痛。

2. 取穴和部位 肾俞、大肠俞、环跳、秩边、居髎、承扶、委中、阳陵泉、足三里、承山;腰部、臀部。

3. 操作

(1) 患者取俯卧位,术者立于患侧,在患侧臀部施㨰、按、揉法治疗,重点在梨状肌体表投影区,手法宜深沉缓和,时间约5分钟。

(2) 患者取俯卧位,医生在腰部,患侧腰三横突周围施柔和的㨰、按、揉手法3～5分钟,配合点按肾俞、大肠俞,以酸胀为度,缓解肌肉紧张痉挛。

(3) 患者取俯卧位,医生用双手指指腹在腰三横突尖端作与条索状硬块垂直方向的按、揉、弹拨,弹拨的力度要由轻到重、由浅入深,手法要柔和深透,并配合搓、揉以解痉止痛,松解粘连。

(4) 同上法,沿患侧髋部及大腿后外侧、小腿外侧施以捏、拿、按揉法3～5分钟,配合点、按、弹拨环跳、秩边、委中、承山等穴位,以舒筋通络,活血散瘀。

(5) 按、揉、弹拨督脉和足太阳膀胱经3～5分钟,并配合腰部后伸被动运动。最后直擦督脉和足太阳膀胱经,横擦腰骶部带脉,以透热为度。可配合湿热敷。

【注意事项】

1. 腰部束宽皮带护腰,对防止过度损伤有一定作用。
2. 治疗期间,避免腰部过多地屈伸和旋转活动。
3. 注意局部保暖,防止过度劳累。

7.1.11 腰背肌筋膜炎

腰背肌筋膜炎又称"功能性腰痛",俗称"腰肌劳损",是慢性腰腿痛中常见的疾病之一,主要指腰背部肌肉、筋膜、韧带等软组织的慢性损伤,导致局部无菌性炎症,从而引起腰背部一侧或两侧的弥漫性疼痛。

中医认为,本病以肾气亏虚为本,复感风、寒、湿邪,致使经络痹阻,气血瘀滞,筋脉失去濡养而致背腰部的疼痛,所以把该病称之为肾虚腰痛。多见于青壮年,有时外伤史不明显,常与职业和工作环境有一定关系。

【临床表现】

腰背肌筋膜炎主要由于腰部肌肉疲劳过度,如长时间的弯腰工作,或由于习惯性姿势不良,或由于长时间处于某一固定体位,致使肌肉、筋膜及韧带持续牵拉,使肌肉内的压力增加,血液循环障碍,肌纤维在收缩时消耗的氧及营养得不到有效的补充,组织内形成无氧代谢而产生大量乳酸,加之代谢产物得不到及时清除,积聚过多,而引起炎症、粘连,日久即可导致组织变性、增厚及挛缩,并刺激相应的神经而引起慢性腰痛;或因腰部软组织急性损伤后,未作及时治疗或治疗不彻底或因反复多次损伤,局部发生纤维变性或疤痕组织增生,加之微循环障碍,乳酸等代谢产物堆积,这些病变组织和病理产物压迫或刺激神经而形成慢性腰痛;由于先天性畸形,如两侧腰椎间小关节发育不对称或先天性脊柱裂、腰椎骶化或骶椎腰化等,使腰骶部两侧活动度不一致,脊柱不稳而易造成腰骶部软组织劳损。

临床表现为一侧或两侧腰背部疼痛,长期反复发作,呈钝性胀痛或酸痛,时轻时重、缠绵难愈。休息、适当活动或经常改变体位姿势可使症状减轻;劳累、阴雨天气、受风寒湿影响则症状加重。患者腰背部有时感觉减退,喜暖怕凉;常觉腰背部板滞不舒,常喜双手捶击,以减轻症状。腰部活动基本正常,一般无明显功能障碍,但有时有牵掣不适感。不能久坐久立、弯腰工作,弯腰稍久,便直腰困难。急性发作时,诸症明显加重,可有明显的肌痉挛,甚至出现腰脊柱侧弯,下肢牵掣作痛等症状。舌红或有瘀斑,少苔,脉细数。

【诊断要点】

1. 可有急性外伤史、受凉史;亦可无外伤史,但有劳损史。

2. 腰背部酸痛或胀痛,并具有反复发作、时轻时重、腰部活动受限不明显的典型特征。

3. 根据劳损的不同部位,可有较广泛的压痛,压痛一般不明显,无放射痛,压痛点多在骶髂关节背面、骶骨背面和腰椎横突等处,轻者压痛多不明显,重者伴随压痛可有一侧或双侧骶棘肌痉挛僵硬。

4. 腰椎生理曲度可减少或消失,病程长者,可有明显的一侧或两侧腰背部肌肉萎缩,有时可以在腰骶部触摸到结节样或条索样改变。

5. 急性发作者一侧或两侧腰背部肌肉张力升高,脊柱侧弯明显,伴有不同程度的功能障碍。

6. X线检查:少数可发现腰骶椎先天性畸形,老年患者椎体骨质可见退行性改变,大部分患者腰骶椎无异常改变。

【推拿治疗】

1. 治疗原则　舒筋通络,温经活血,解痉止痛。

2. 取穴和部位　肾俞、腰阳关、大肠俞、八髎、秩边、委中、阳陵泉、承山、昆仑、太溪等穴及腰背部及臀部。

3. 操作

(1) 患者俯卧位,医生先用深沉而柔和的㨰法,后用手掌或掌根沿两侧足太阳膀胱经从上向下反复操作,各施术约3～5遍,以疼痛部位为重点,力量由轻到重,目的是放松局部肌肉,初步缓解局部疼痛。

(2) 医生以双手拇指或肘尖依次按揉脊柱两侧的肾俞、腰阳关、大肠俞、八髎、秩边等穴和双下肢的委中、阳陵泉、承山、昆仑、太溪等穴,每穴10秒钟左右,以酸胀为度,从而达到提高痛阈、解痉止痛的目的。

(3) 医生用拇指在痛点、肌肉痉挛或结节处,运用弹拨手法对其施术,反复3～5遍,以达到松解粘连,提高痛阈,解痉止痛的目的。

(4) 医生双手桡侧缘并拢,用两手拇指与食、中指指腹提拿两侧的腰眼,操作2～3次,以松解腰骶部软组织的粘连。

(5) 医生立于患者的头侧,双手或单手沿着脊柱两侧的足太阳膀胱经从上向下反复推动,施术约2～3遍,力量要适中,达到捋顺腰背部肌肉的目的。

(6) 患者侧卧位,医生与患者面对面,施腰部斜扳法,左右各1次。患者改仰卧位,医生对患者作屈髋屈膝运腰运动,顺、逆时针各2～3次,和抱膝滚腰运动2～3次,以调整腰椎后关节及腰骶关节的紊乱。

(7) 患者俯卧位,医生用掌擦法直擦腰背部两侧的膀胱经,横擦腰骶部,以透热为度。

(8) 最后医生双手握空拳,交替叩击患者的背腰部及骶部,从上至下,约2~3遍,结束治疗。

【注意事项】

1. 治疗期间宜用宽皮带或腰围保护腰部,减少意外的发生。
2. 宜睡板床,防止脊柱变形。
3. 注意休息和局部保暖,节制房事。

7.1.12 肩关节周围炎

肩关节周围炎是指因关节囊及关节周围组织无菌性炎症引起关节广泛性粘连,或因肩关节的急、慢性损伤,致关节周围韧带、肌腱、关节囊广泛性充血、渗出、水肿、增厚、粘连,发生非特异性炎症,限制了肩关节活动的一种症状。上肢其他部位的骨折、脱位后的复位固定,使肩部长期处于不活动状态,也可引起肩周炎。本病又称"五十肩"、"肩凝症"、"漏肩风"。临床上以肩关节周围疼痛、活动功能障碍、后期肌肉萎缩为特点。本病以单侧发病为主,少见有双侧发病,好发于年龄在50岁左右,女性发病略高于男性,多见于体力劳动者。

本病中医称肩凝症、漏肩风。筋络节,节属骨,骨为肾所主。人值中年之后,形体渐退,肾气将衰,肾气衰则不足以生精养髓,骨疏节弛,髓不足以养肝,则筋纵。若因动之太过,或跌仆闪挫,或劳伤筋节,气血瘀滞,筋拘节挛,日久,则筋肌节窍滞僵,或因气血失于疏导而瘀滞,或为风寒湿邪所客,寒凝气聚,气血痹阻,筋肌节窍失于濡养,筋肌拘结而不得舒展,节窍粘涩不得屈伸而僵固。脉络不通,不通则痛。久之筋脉失养,拘挛不用,发为本病。

【临床表现】

发病缓慢,呈渐进性发作,少数患者可为急性发病,一般都有肩部慢性劳损或感受风、寒、湿邪病史,部分患者因肩部急性损伤、脱位,或上肢部位骨折、脱位固定后引起。主要表现为疼痛、活动功能受限、后期肌肉萎缩三大症状。

初起感肩部酸楚疼痛,常因天气变化、劳累、受凉而诱发,局部怕冷,僵滞感,害怕活动,以后逐渐加重,发展到持续性疼痛,疼痛累及整个肩关节,可向颈部和肘部放射。患者白天疼痛较轻,夜间疼痛加剧,影响睡眠,不敢患侧侧卧。当肩部受牵拉时,可引起剧烈疼痛。

早期的功能受限常因疼痛引起,后期功能受限则因关节粘连引起,当关节粘连形成时则疼痛明显减轻,关节主动活动和被动活动功能均受到限制,影响梳头、穿脱衣服、洗脸、叉腰、提物等日常生活。日久,三角肌、冈上肌出现萎缩,萎缩的程度与病情时间长短有关。

肩关节周围均有广泛性压痛,肩髃、肩髎、秉风、肩贞等穴,三角肌前、后部有不同程度的压痛。肩部前屈、后伸、外展、内收、旋内、旋外活动均受限,尤以上举、旋内、后弯摸背功能障碍明显。病情较久者,肩部肌肉萎缩,肩峰凸起,呈典型的"扛肩"征象。X线摄片主要是排除骨质病变可能,多数患者无异常,部分患者可有骨质疏松,有时可见关节周围软组织有不规则的钙化阴影。本病舌淡白,或淡红,苔白,或薄白,脉弦紧或紧涩。

【诊断要点】

1. 缓慢起病,有肩部慢性劳损或受风寒史。
2. 广泛性压痛,随关节运动则压痛点不固定。
3. 活动功能障碍,各个方向活动均有受限。
4. 病程较久时,出现肌肉松弛、僵滞、萎缩。

【推拿治疗】

1. 治疗原则　活血散瘀,舒筋通络,松解粘连。

2. 取穴和部位　肩井、肩髎、肩髃、肩贞、天宗、臂臑、曲池;肩关节周围、三角肌部。

3. 操作

(1) 患者取坐位,医生用一手托患肢手臂约60°,用按、揉、摩或一指禅推法在肩前部、肩外侧、肩后部、上臂往返治疗。配合患肢外展、后伸和旋转被动活动,时间约5分钟。

(2) 按、揉肩井、肩髎、肩髃、肩贞、天宗、臂臑、曲池穴,每穴1分钟。同时在肩前部、肱二头肌短头腱处、冈下肌、肩后大圆肌、小圆肌处按、揉、点、弹拨手法治疗,手法宜深沉缓和,约2分钟。

(3) 在肩胛部、肩背部用㨰、按、揉、点、拨法等交替治疗;捏、拿、按、揉肩井、三角肌部,约5分钟。

(4) 医生一手扶住患肩部,另一手托住其肘部,作肩关节环旋摇动,幅度由小至大,或用大幅度摇肩法,约1分钟。

(5) 医生立于患肩背后侧,以一手前臂置于患肩腋下,另一手托其肘部并使肘关节屈曲,利用杠杆原理,一手向上抬,另一手将肘部向内推,以松解关节内粘连,增加关节活动度。

(6) 最后在肩关节周围施擦法,以透热为度,并做肩部至前臂用搓法往返搓动3～5次。患肩外展60°,抖动肩部。

【注意事项】

1. 注意患肩保暖,避免风寒湿邪侵袭。
2. 急性期肩部应尽量少活动,以免炎性渗出增加;粘连期应积极功能锻炼,持之以恒。

7.1.13　肱骨外上髁炎

肱骨外上髁炎是指因前臂过度旋转,用力伸腕过猛,或肘部慢性劳损,致使前臂桡侧伸腕肌腱附着处牵拉损伤,发生非特异性炎症,刺激神经末梢或骨膜所产生的一系列临床症状。本病又称"网球肘"、"肱骨外上髁综合征"、"肱桡滑囊炎"等。临床上以肱骨外上髁部肿胀、疼痛、活动受限为主要特点。本病因好发于网球运动员而得名,右侧发病多于左侧,长期从事前臂旋转作业者易发本病。

在前臂旋前位,腕关节作主动背伸的突然猛力动作,可使桡侧伸腕肌强烈收缩,牵拉肌腱附着处造成急性损伤；长期从事前臂旋前单一动作作业，使前臂桡侧伸腕肌处于单调的紧张牵拉状态，则造成慢性劳损。其病理变化可有以下途径：①伸腕肌腱附着处发生撕裂。②伸腕肌腱附着处骨膜下出血、肿胀、血肿机化，导致骨膜炎，骨膜下张力增高。③环状韧带的创伤性炎症或纤维组织炎。④肱桡关节滑囊炎或肱桡关节滑膜被嵌挤所引起的炎症。

本病属中医伤科筋节损伤范畴。肘节外廉为手阳明经筋所络结，其结络之处急、慢劳伤，累及阳明经筋；或风寒湿邪客于筋络，致使气血瘀滞，积聚凝结，筋络粘连，壅肿作痛，筋肌挛拘，节隙粘涩，则屈伸回旋掣痛而失利。

【临床表现】

急性发病者有明显的扭伤或拉伤病史，一般无明显外伤史，发病缓慢。主要表现为患肘后外侧酸痛，同时可沿伸腕肌向下牵制痛，前臂旋转、握物无力，每遇过劳或阴雨天肘部酸痛往往加剧。作前臂旋转、腕背伸，或提、拉、端、推动作时疼痛加剧，以拧毛巾动作不能最为典型。局部可有轻微肿胀。患者舌淡红，苔薄白；脉弦或弦涩。

肱骨外上髁局部轻度肿胀，少数患者可触及一小滑液囊。肱骨外上髁压痛，根据压痛部位的不同，其损伤的组织也不相同。肱骨外上髁压痛，为桡侧腕短伸肌起点损伤；肱骨外上髁上方压痛，为桡侧腕长伸肌起点损伤；桡骨小头附近压痛，可能为环状韧带合并桡侧副韧带损伤。伸肌紧张试验阳性，密耳（Miil）试验阳性。肘部 X 线摄片一般无异常改变，部分患者可见肱骨外上髁部毛糙或密度增高。

【诊断要点】

1. 有急性损伤或慢性劳损史。
2. 肱骨外上髁疼痛、压痛，牵掣前臂桡侧酸、胀痛。
3. 提物无力，拧毛巾动作时疼痛加剧。
4. 密耳（Miil）试验阳性。

【推拿治疗】

1. 治疗原则 活血祛瘀，舒筋通络。

2. 取穴和部位 曲池、曲泽、手三里、合谷，肱骨外上髁、前臂桡侧肌群。

3. 操作

（1）患者取仰卧位或坐位。医生自肘部桡侧至前臂桡侧用㨰法往返治疗。以拇指按、揉、点、拨曲池、曲泽、手三里、合谷等穴，每穴 1 分钟，时间约 5 分钟。

（2）医生在肱骨外上髁部用一指禅推法、按、揉、点法作重点治疗，并与弹拨法交替进行，约 5 分钟。

（3）医生一手拇指按压肱骨外上髁痛点处，其余四指握住内上髁，另一手握住腕部作对抗牵引拔伸肘关节片刻，然后缓缓屈曲肘关节，使前臂旋前至最大幅度时，做快速后伸伸直前臂顿拉，连续 3 次。此法目的使滑液囊撕破，以利渗出液吸收。

（4）用拇指自肱骨外上髁向桡侧伸腕肌作推揉，然后沿前臂桡侧至外上髁用擦法，以透热为度。

【注意事项】

1. 治疗期间应避免前臂过度旋转和腕部用力背伸动作。
2. 注意局部保暖。

7.1.14 腕管综合征

腕管综合征是指因腕部劳损,或直接外伤,腕部骨折、脱位、畸形愈合、骨质增生、腕横韧带肥厚、腱鞘囊肿、脂肪瘤压迫等因素,致使管内压力增高,压迫从管内通过的正中神经、屈指肌腱,所产生的一系列临床症状,又称"腕管卡压综合征"。临床上以三个半手指麻木,感觉异常,腕部无力为主要特点。本病好发于中老年人,女性多于男性。

中医学认为,本病由于急性损伤或慢性劳损,血瘀经络,或寒湿淫筋,风邪侵肌,致气血流通受阻而引起。

【临床表现】

起病缓慢,部分患者有急、慢性损伤史。初起感手腕无力、酸胀,逐渐出现正中神经受压症状,表现为患手拇指、食指、中指及环指桡侧(桡侧三个半手指)有感觉异常、麻木、刺痛,可向肘部、肩部放射。症状以晨起、夜间较重,当手部温度升高、劳累、手下垂时加重,作腕关节活动、甩手或上举手部,可使症状缓解。患侧手指可有胀、僵、凉的感觉,皮肤颜色可见苍白或紫绀,舌淡白,或淡红,苔白,或薄白;脉弦紧或紧涩。

腕管部明显压痛,并向手指放射;叩击腕管时可引起正中神经分布区手指(桡侧三个半手指)放射性触电样刺痛。作腕关节屈掌90°,40秒钟可见症状加剧。后期患者可出现大鱼际萎缩、麻痹、肌力减弱,桡侧三个半手指感觉明显减退或消失,对掌功能障碍。肌肉萎缩的程度与病程长短有密切关系。X线摄片一般无异常,可排除骨性病变。

【诊断要点】

1. 腕部疼痛,伴桡侧三个半手指疼痛、麻木。
2. 正中神经分布区域皮肤感觉异常。
3. 叩击腕管时有正中神经支配区域触电样放射性麻木、刺痛。
4. 屈腕压迫试验阳性。

【推拿治疗】

1. 治疗原则 活血消肿、舒筋通络。

2. 取穴和部位 大陵、内关、曲泽、鱼际部、腕管部。

3. 操作

(1) 按揉大陵、内关、曲泽、腕管部,每穴1分钟,以酸胀为度,并作大鱼际部按揉。

(2) 用拇指按揉腕管部,与屈指肌腱作垂直方向的弹拨,配合腕部各方位的摇动、拔伸手法,交替进行,约5分钟。

(3) 医生用捏、拿、按、揉法沿前臂屈肌群至腕部往返操作,重点在腕管部,使前臂肌肉放松,时间约5分钟。

(4) 患肢屈肘约45°,术者一手握患手固定于腕部,另一手拇指从腕管向前臂屈肌方向作推抹法,使腕管内渗出液推至前臂肌肉,缓解管内压力,约2分钟。

(5) 患者取坐位,前臂置旋前位,手背向上,术者两手的四指握住患腕的掌侧,两拇指平放于腕关节的背侧,以拇指指端按入腕关节背侧的间隙内,先作腕关节拔伸,在拔伸状态下摇晃腕关节,然后,在拇指按压下将手腕背伸至最大幅度,随即屈腕,并左右旋转其手腕,反复数次,时间约5分钟,搓揉腕关节结束治疗。

【注意事项】

1. 每次推拿后,局部可加用湿热敷,每日2次。
2. 治疗期间避免过度用腕。
3. 注意腕部保暖,必要时可用护腕保护。

7.1.15 腕关节扭挫伤

腕关节扭挫伤是指腕部受直接或间接外力作用,或由于腕关节过度扭转,超过腕部韧带所能承受的能力,导致关节周围韧带、肌腱、关节囊的损伤,影响关节的功能活动。临床上以腕关节周围疼痛、肿胀、活动功能受限为主要特点。任何年龄均可发病,以青壮年好动者多见。而腕关节受直接暴力或间接暴力损伤,易引起腕部骨折,应予以区别。

中医认为本病由"筋脉受损,气血凝滞"所致,属中医"骨错缝,筋出槽"范畴。腕节为多气少血之节,为手三阴、手三阳经筋起循之处,急慢性劳伤,伤筋伤节,筋或弛或拘,腕节或粘或错,活动受限,气滞血瘀而作痛。

【临床表现】

一般多有较明确的外伤史,如不慎跌仆,手掌撑地、劳动或运动时腕部扭挫、持物过重、长期用腕超负荷劳作等。轻者一般疼痛不甚,仅感腕部不灵活,作大幅度活动时可有疼痛;重者,伤后即感疼痛,腕部不能活动。腕部有不同程度的肿胀,重者皮下有瘀血,早期呈青紫色,后期呈紫黄相兼或土黄色。活动受限,急性损伤活动明显受限,甚至不能活动;慢性损伤则受限不明显,或只有向某一个方向活动受限,劳累后或阴雨天症状加重。

损伤部位疼痛、压痛、活动受限方向对明确诊断有很大帮助。

1. 压痛 腕背侧韧带损伤,压痛点常在桡腕背侧韧带部位;腕掌侧韧带损伤,压痛点常在桡腕掌侧韧带部位;腕桡侧副韧带损伤,压痛点常在桡侧鼻咽窝处;腕尺侧副韧带损伤,压痛点常在尺骨小头处;腕三角软骨盘损伤,压痛点常在桡尺下关节间隙及腕关节尺侧部。

2. 活动受限 腕背侧韧带损伤,做腕掌屈时疼痛,活动受限;腕掌侧韧带损伤,做腕背伸时疼痛,活动受限;腕桡侧副韧带损伤,做腕尺侧屈时疼痛,活动受限;腕尺侧副韧带损伤,做腕桡侧屈时疼痛,活动受限;腕三角软骨盘损伤,做腕关节内外旋转时疼痛,活动受限。本病表现为舌淡红,苔薄白;脉弦涩,或弦紧。

X线摄片对腕关节扭挫伤诊断十分重要,单纯腕关节扭挫伤,X线检查一般无明显改变,对瘀血、肿胀明显者,有排除骨折、脱位作用。常见的有桡、尺骨远端骨折、舟状骨骨折、月骨骨折、月骨脱位、三角骨背侧撕脱骨折、舟骨及月骨无菌性坏死等,应注意鉴别。

【诊断要点】

1. 有腕部急、慢性损伤史。
2. 腕关节疼痛,疼痛与损伤部位相一致。

3. 腕关节肿胀,慢性损伤不明显,急性损伤肿胀明显,皮下有血肿瘀紫。
4. 活动功能受限,活动受限方向与损伤部位呈相反方向。
5. X线摄片检查,排除骨折、脱位可能。

【推拿治疗】

1. 治疗原则 舒筋活血,祛瘀通络。

2. 取穴和部位 外关、阳溪、阳谷、阳池、合谷、太渊、少海、尺泽、曲池、神门、列缺、大陵、腕骨、通里及损伤部位。根据不同的损伤部位选择应用。

3. 操作

推拿治疗应在X线摄片检查后排除骨折、脱位的情况下进行。急性损伤瘀血肿胀明显的,应在伤后24～48小时后方可推拿治疗。

(1) 腕掌侧损伤,可选用手少阴心经的少海、通里、神门等穴;腕掌桡侧损伤,可选用手太阴肺经的尺泽、列缺、太渊等穴;腕桡侧背面损伤,可选用手阳明大肠经的曲池、阳溪、合谷等穴,其他部位损伤可选用相关穴位。应用按、揉、点法,手法要求轻重交替,逐渐用力,以酸胀为度。每穴1分钟。

(2) 患者取坐位,医生用指按、揉、点、拨法在损伤部位施术。手法宜轻柔缓和,操作应先在损伤附近进行,然后在损伤部位操作。时间约5分钟。

(3) 被动运动手法的应用,作腕关节背伸、掌屈,左、右侧偏及环绕运动,拔伸、摇腕手法。以解除痉挛,分解粘连,改善关节功能。时间约5分钟。

(4) 在腕关节损伤部位用擦法治疗,以透热为度。时间约2分钟。

【注意事项】

1. 急性损伤有皮下出血的,应予冰敷止血为先,防止出血不止。
2. 损伤严重的,应作X线摄片,排除骨折、脱位的可能。
3. 治疗期间应注意局部保暖,可戴护腕保护。
4. 合并有脱位、撕脱性骨折的,应按脱位、骨折处理。固定6～8周,或骨折临床愈合后,可考虑推拿,以恢复关节功能。

7.1.16 髂胫束劳损

髂胫束劳损是指因髂胫束后缘或臀大肌前缘与股骨大转子长期摩擦引起髂胫束劳损或臀大肌前缘增厚,髋关节在主动屈伸活动或行走时,髂胫束在股骨大转子上滑动而发生的弹响。本病又称"弹响髋"、"髋关节弹响症"等。临床上以行走时髋关节弹响,一般无特殊不适症状为特点。本病多见于女性,单侧发病居多,也有双侧同时发病的。

本病属中医伤科节伤范畴。髀为虚窍,机关之室,为真气所过,血络所游。急慢劳伤,气血凝滞,络节筋肌,或拘或弛,拘则疼痛,弛则筋翻弹响。

【临床表现】

一般无明显损伤病史。患者仅感髋部不适,在髋关节作屈曲、内收、内旋,或髋关节主动弯曲、伸展时,髋部出现弹响,而被动屈伸髋时一般不会有弹响现象。同时伴有大转子滑囊炎渗出增多时,在大转子后方可有疼痛,并向大腿后外侧放射,患者有酸胀、重滞、无力等感觉。触诊时可以感到弹响处的组织变硬或呈条索状物,作主动屈伸髋时,可触及髂胫束从大转子上滑过,并发出弹响声。髋关节X线摄片无明显异常发现。

本病最大危害是因为一动一弹响,患者精神紧张,心理压力较大。本病表现为舌淡红,苔薄白;脉平,或弦紧。

【诊断要点】

1. 无急、慢性损伤史。
2. 髋部弹响。
3. 无疼痛,无活动功能障碍。
4. X线摄片无明显异常。

【推拿治疗】

1. 治疗原则 舒筋活血,疏经通络。

2. 取穴和部位 居髎、环跳、承扶、风市、髀关,大转子部位。

3. 操作

(1) 用拇指按揉居髎、环跳、承扶、风市、髀关等穴位,每穴1分钟,股骨大转子部用掌揉法,时间为3分钟。

(2) 患者取俯卧位,医生立于患侧,用捏、拿、按、揉法沿臀大肌及髂胫束的方向治疗,同时配合髋关节后伸、外展的被动活动,使局部肌肉放松,时间约3分钟。

(3) 患者取侧卧位(患侧在上),用按、揉、点、拨法在阔筋膜张肌及大腿外侧治疗5分钟。然后在股骨大转子上与条索状物成垂直方向的弹拨法,时间为3分钟。

(4) 患者取卧位,术者一手扶握患侧膝部,另一手握住患侧小腿下端,作患肢的屈膝屈髋运动10~15次,然后自大腿上端至膝部用搓法,上下反复,时间为3分钟。

(5) 接上势,在髋部条索状物处至大腿外侧用擦法,以透热为度,时间为3分钟。

【注意事项】

1. 向患者正确解释本病,解除心理压力。
2. 局部保暖,谨防受寒。
3. 避免髋部过多活动,如长期行走等。

7.1.17 膝关节骨性关节炎

膝关节骨性关节炎是指因胫股关节、髌股关节骨质增生、机械性磨损等非炎症性退行性病变,引起关节内平衡失调,功能紊乱所产生的一系列临床症状,排除软组织因素所致的关节炎症。本病又称"退行性关节炎"、"骨关节炎"、"肥大性关节炎"、"老年性膝关节炎"等。临床上以膝关节疼痛、活动功能受限和关节畸形为主要特点。好发于老年人,以女性、肥胖者多见。

本病的病因目前尚未十分明了,一般认为,膝关节慢性积累性损伤、机械性牵拉和刺激是主要原因。鉴于本病多发于老年人,有人认为与代谢有关。按病因可分为原发性和继发性两种。原发性骨性关节炎与年龄有关,随着年龄的增长,结缔组织发生退行性变,软骨随着年龄增长及磨损,进而侵犯骨质,形成骨质增生。继发性骨关节病是由创伤、畸形等所造成的软骨损害,日久导致骨性关节炎。

膝关节活动时,增生物直接刺激关节内容物或关节面产生疼痛。由于增生使膝关节间隙逐渐变窄,滑膜非特异性炎症渗出,关节腔内压增高,出现关节肿胀,关节囊呈纤维化增厚,滑膜肥厚。后期关节内滑液反而减少,关节间隙干涩,摩擦增加,髌骨软骨面龟裂、剥脱。上述因素均可刺激局部血管、神经,使症状进一步加重,膝关节周围肌肉出现粘连,萎缩,活动受限。

本病属中医骨痹范畴。膝关节乃诸筋之会,多气多血之节。年老体弱,肝肾亏虚,气血失荣,肝亏则筋弛,肾虚则骨疏,动之不慎伤节,或复感风寒湿邪,凝聚节窍,发为痹症,滞留不去,为肿为痛。骨疏则为赘,筋挛则为拘,节窍屈而不伸,伸而不屈。

【临床表现】

多见于中老年人发病。起病缓慢,常有膝关节劳损史。初起仅感膝关节乏力,逐渐出现行走时疼痛,开始先以一侧发病,以后逐渐发展至两侧发病,两侧同时发病的较少。疼痛可呈双侧交替性发作,忽左忽右,时轻时重,表现为"游走"性。患者早晨起床或从坐位起立、上下楼梯时,疼痛特别明显,稍微活动以后症状可缓解,但活动过度,疼痛又会加重。以后诱发疼痛的行走距离越来越短,而且疼痛持续的时间也逐渐变长,甚至发展到休息后也不能缓解。疼痛的性质起初以酸痛为主,随着病程的发展,逐渐变成胀痛、刺痛、麻痛,行走或上下楼时,关节内有一步一刺痛的感觉,心理压力明显增加。舌淡白,或淡红,苔白,或薄白;脉弦紧或紧涩。

膝关节活动逐渐受限,屈伸范围变小,患侧膝关节不能伸直,屈膝达不到生理功能范围。关节活动时可听到关节内弹响或摩擦音。炎性渗出明显者,两侧膝眼饱满,髌上滑囊积液。个别严重者可发生关节僵直。部分患者因膝关节功能减退,其部分功能由髋、踝关节来代偿,以致髋、踝关节也发病。

检查胫股关节炎时,两侧膝眼深压痛,腘窝部压痛;髌股关节炎时,髌骨周缘压痛,髌骨内面与股骨滑车有明显摩擦音,浮髌试验阳性。股四头肌有不同程度的萎缩。①实验室检查:血沉正常,抗"O"、类风湿因子阴性。②X线摄片检查:可见胫骨平台髁间突明显增生变尖,或髌骨边缘骨质增生,关节间隙变窄,韧带钙化阴影,同时可排除其他骨性病变。

【诊断要点】

1. 中老年发病,有膝关节慢性劳损史。
2. 膝关节内疼痛,进行性加重,上下楼梯时尤为明显。
3. 膝关节活动功能障碍,关节内有摩擦音,肌肉萎缩。
4. X线摄片有明显骨质增生,关节间隙变窄。
5. 实验室检查,排除类风湿性关节炎。

【推拿治疗】

1. 治疗原则 舒筋活血,解痉止痛,通利关节。

2. 取穴和部位 犊鼻、膝眼、鹤顶、血海、梁丘、风市、委中、阳陵泉、阴陵泉、承山;髌骨周围。

3. 操作

(1) 患者取仰卧位,医生立于患侧,沿股四头肌至髌骨及髌骨两侧用捏、拿、按、揉等手法往返治疗,重点在髌骨两侧;然后按、揉小腿前外侧。时间约5分钟。

(2) 根据患者疼痛明显的部位,选择性地按揉犊鼻、膝眼、鹤顶、血海、梁丘、委中、阳陵泉、阴陵泉、承山等穴位，每穴1分钟。

（3）患者取俯卧位，医生立于患侧，在腘窝部、大腿下端、小腿上端用捏、拿、按、揉等手法往返治疗，重点在腘窝部（委中穴），并与膝关节被动屈伸活动配合进行，再点按委中、承山穴，时间约5分钟。

（4）患者取俯卧位，屈患膝呈45°，在两侧膝眼用按、揉等手法，反复操作。操作时，用拇指尺侧偏峰着力向髌韧带方向推动，右手推患者右侧膝眼，左手推患者左侧膝眼。并用拇指或手掌按、揉髌骨周缘及关节间隙。操作时应根据治疗部位的需要，推移髌骨暴露治疗部位，如按揉髌骨内侧缘时，把髌骨向内侧推移；按揉外侧缘时，把髌骨向外侧推移；按揉髌骨下缘时，把髌骨向下推移，以充分显露治疗部位，使手法直接作用于治疗部位。

（5）在膝关节两侧、髌骨周围、关节间隙用擦法，以透热为度，然后搓揉、摇膝关节，结束治疗。

【注意事项】

1. 注意膝部保暖，在家可自行做湿热敷，水温在45～50°左右。
2. 疼痛、肿胀明显时，应注意休息，减少膝关节活动。
3. 患膝避免过度负重支撑，以减少膝关节负担。可用护膝加以保护。
4. 平时注意膝关节功能锻炼，防止肌肉萎缩和关节粘连。
5. 配合作膝关节的自我按摩，每日2次。

7.1.18 膝关节侧副韧带损伤

膝关节侧副韧带损伤包括胫侧副韧带损伤和腓侧副韧带损伤，是指因膝关节突然遭受外翻或内翻应力作用，引起内侧或外侧副韧带损伤，其损伤可分为部分撕裂、完全断裂、合并半月板或十字韧带损伤三种类型，严重时可伴有撕脱性骨折。临床上以膝关节损伤侧疼痛、瘀肿、活动功能受限为主要特点。

1. 胫侧副韧带损伤 膝关节生理上呈轻度外翻，当膝关节微屈（约130～150°）时，其稳定性相对较差，此时来自膝关节外侧的暴力作用于膝外侧，使小腿突然外翻、外旋；或足部固定不动，大腿突然强力内收、内旋，即可造成膝关节胫侧副韧带牵拉损伤。若损伤作用机制进一步加大，则可造成韧带部分撕裂和完全断裂。

韧带损伤后，局部毛细血管出血、肿胀。韧带撕裂常局限于韧带附着处，完全断裂常合并有内侧半月板及关节囊撕裂、股骨内侧髁及胫骨内侧髁撕脱性骨折。

2. 腓侧副韧带损伤 膝关节半屈曲位时，腓侧副韧带变得松弛，其稳定性差。当小腿突然用力内收、内旋，或大腿过度强力外展、外旋，使膝关节急骤内翻，导致腓侧副韧带在松弛状态下突然绷紧牵拉形成撕裂损伤；或跑、跳运动时，因场地不平，不慎内翻捩足，使膝关节过度内翻，牵拉腓侧副韧带损伤。此外，直接暴力作用于此韧带也可以引起损伤。

此韧带损伤可分为部分撕裂和完全断裂两种。完全断裂常位于关节囊、肌腱与肌纤维交界处损伤，严重时可伴有十字韧带损伤。韧带撕裂在腓骨小头处，可伴有撕脱性骨折，严重时造成腓总神经损伤或受压。

临床上以膝关节胫侧副韧带损伤多见，常由运动损伤所致。

膝为诸筋之会,内为足三阴经筋所结之处,外为足少阳经筋,足阳明经筋的支筋所络结。急慢劳伤,损伤筋结,气血瘀滞,致筋脉拘挛,屈伸不利,伤处为肿为痛。

【临床表现】

患者都有明显外伤史。伤后即感损伤侧疼痛,轻者踮足跛行,局部肿胀不明显;重者不能行走,损伤侧局限性肿胀明显,关节伸屈活动受限。伤后2~3天皮下瘀斑出现,瘀斑的大小与损伤的程度和出血量的多少有关,初起为青紫色,5~7天后呈紫黄色,以后逐渐转为土黄色,肿胀也开始逐渐消退,瘀血吸收。舌淡红,苔白,或薄白;脉弦,或弦紧。

检查

胫侧副韧带损伤:膝关节内侧压痛明显,其压痛点常在股骨侧髁韧带附着处。做侧向运动试验时,膝关节内侧疼痛加剧。胫侧副韧带完全断裂时,可触及断裂韧带之间隙,侧向运动试验时,关节内侧有被"拉开"和"合拢"的感觉。X线摄片检查,部分撕裂伤者一般无明显异常,韧带完全断裂者,膝关节外翻位片可见内侧关节间隙增宽;合并撕脱骨折者,可见有撕脱的小骨片;合并半月板损伤者,需作CT或关节腔造影才能明确诊断。

腓侧副韧带损伤:膝关节外侧压痛明显,其压痛点常在股骨外侧髁和腓骨小头处。作侧向运动试验时,膝关节外侧疼痛加剧。腓侧副韧带完全断裂者,侧向运动试验时,关节外侧有被"拉开"和"合拢"的感觉。X线摄片检查,部分撕裂者一般无明显异常,韧带完全断裂者,膝关节内翻位片可见外侧关节间隙增宽,合并撕脱骨折者,可见腓骨小头撕脱的小骨片。

【诊断要点】

1. 有明显的膝关节外伤史。
2. 膝关节内侧或外侧疼痛、肿胀,损伤部位明显压痛。
3. 关节活动功能受限,膝关节伸直时疼痛加剧。
4. 侧向运动试验阳性。
5. X线摄片检查,可见关节间隙增宽改变,合并骨折的,可见有撕脱的小骨片。

【推拿治疗】

1. 治疗原则 活血祛瘀,消肿止痛,理筋通络。

2. 取穴和部位 胫侧副韧带损伤:血海、曲泉、阴陵泉、膝眼、膝关节内侧;腓侧副韧带损伤:膝阳关、阳陵泉、犊鼻、梁丘、膝关节外侧。

3. 操作

胫侧副韧带损伤

(1) 患者取仰卧位,患肢外旋伸膝位。医生在其大腿内侧至膝内侧用捏、拿、按、揉等手法反复治疗。然后沿股骨内侧髁至胫骨内侧髁用掌按、揉法治疗。手法宜轻柔,先损伤周围,后损伤部位,切忌粗暴。时间约10分钟。

(2) 用拇指按揉血海、曲泉、阴陵泉、膝眼等穴,每穴1分钟。

(3) 用拇指做与韧带纤维呈垂直方向的轻柔快速的按、揉、弹拨理筋手法,并配合膝关节被动屈伸运动,时间约3分钟,手法应循序渐进。

(4) 在损伤部位用掌摩法,然后与韧带纤维平行方向施擦法,以透热为度。再搓揉膝关节结束治疗。时间约3分钟。

腓侧副韧带损伤

（1）患者取健侧卧位，患肢微屈，术者在其大腿外侧下部至小腿外侧上部用捏、拿、按、揉等手法治疗。然后自股骨外侧髁至腓骨小头处用掌按、揉法治疗。手法宜轻柔，先损伤周围，后损伤部位，切忌粗暴。时间约10分钟。

（2）用拇指按揉膝阳关、阳陵泉、犊鼻、梁丘等穴，每穴1分钟。

（3）用拇指作与韧带纤维呈垂直方向的轻柔快速的按、揉、弹拨理筋手法，并配合膝关节被动屈伸运动，约3分钟。手法应循序渐进，不宜死扳硬拉。

（4）在损伤部位用掌摩法，然后与韧带纤维平行方向施擦法，以透热为度。再搓揉膝关节结束治疗。时间约3分钟。

【注意事项】

1. 急性损伤有出血肿胀者，视出血程度，应在伤后24～48小时才能推拿。损伤即刻宜用冰敷。

2. 损伤严重者，应作X线摄片检查，在排除骨折和韧带完全断裂的情况下才能推拿。

3. 每次推拿后局部加用湿热敷，可加速瘀肿吸收。

4. 防止股四头肌萎缩，可采取仰卧位作股四头肌绷紧、放松的练习，每天2次，每次约5分钟。

5. 恢复膝关节功能训练，可采用仰卧位作膝关节主动屈曲、伸直蹬腿练习，每天2次，每次约3分钟。

7.1.19 踝关节扭挫伤

踝关节扭挫伤包括内侧副韧带损伤和外侧副韧带损伤，是指因踝关节突然遭受扭挫，使足呈内翻位或外翻位牵拉韧带及周围组织所致的损伤。其损伤可分为部分撕裂、完全断裂、严重时可伴有撕脱性骨折。临床上以踝关节损伤侧疼痛、瘀肿、活动功能受限为主要特点。

1. 踝关节外侧副韧带损伤 造成外侧副韧带损伤有以下三个因素：①外踝长，内踝短，外侧副韧带比较薄弱，容易导致内翻位损伤。②使足外翻、背屈的肌肉（第三腓骨肌）不如内翻背屈的肌肉（胫前肌）强大，因此，使足向外的力量不如向内的力量大。③踝穴并非是完全坚固，位于胫腓骨之间的胫腓横韧带纤维斜向外、下方向，同时外踝内面的关节面比较倾斜，因此，腓骨下端能向上或向外作适当的活动。当路面场地不平，跑、跳时失足，或下楼梯、下坡时足跖屈位突然向内翻转，身体重心偏向一侧，导致外侧副韧带突然受到强大的张力牵扯损伤。损伤后，轻者韧带附着处骨膜撕裂，骨膜下出血；重者韧带部分撕裂；更甚者韧带完全断裂，常伴有撕脱性骨折或距骨半脱位。

2. 踝关节内侧副韧带损伤 踝关节突然外翻是造成内侧副韧带损伤的主要原因。在跑、跳运动中，由于落地不稳，身体重心移至足内侧，踝关节突然向外侧捩扭，致使内侧副韧带撕裂损伤。如果外翻的作用力继续增强，可造成内侧副韧带撕脱，胫腓下联合韧带撕裂，或胫腓骨下端分离，胫踝撕脱骨折。

临床上以外侧副韧带损伤多见,常由运动损伤所致。

踝为足之枢纽,足之三阴、三阳经筋所结。因足跗用力不当,经筋牵抻过度,致使经筋所结之处撕掇,阳筋弛长,阴筋拘挛,气血离经,为瘀为肿,活动牵掣,屈伸不利,伤处作痛。

【临床表现】

患者都有明显外伤史。伤后即感损伤侧疼痛,轻者跛足跛行,局部轻度肿胀;重者不能行走,损伤侧局限性肿胀明显,关节伸屈活动受限。伤后2~3天皮下瘀斑出现,损伤严重时,瘀斑扩散到对侧关节。瘀斑的大小与损伤的程度和出血量的多少有关,初起为青紫色,5~7天后呈紫黄色,以后逐渐转为土黄色,肿胀也开始逐渐消退,瘀血吸收,瘀斑颜色的变化对损伤时间长短的判断有重要意义。本病为血瘀气滞,故舌淡红,苔薄白;脉弦,或弦紧。

外侧副韧带损伤:外踝前下方压痛明显,其压痛点常在距腓前韧带处(故又称距腓前韧带损伤)。作足内翻动作时,外踝前下方疼痛加剧。当距腓前韧带和距腓中韧带均断裂时,侧向运动试验时,关节外侧有被"拉开"和"合拢"的感觉。有外踝撕脱性骨折时,可摸到骨折碎片。X线摄片检查,可明确是否有骨折、脱位存在。韧带断裂时,作足部强力内翻位摄片,可见胫骨下关节面与距骨上关节面之切线交角大于15°。

内侧副韧带损伤:踝关节内侧压痛明显,其压痛点常在内踝下方,胫腓下联合韧带损伤时,该处有压痛。作足外翻动作时,内踝下疼痛加剧。内踝撕脱性骨折时,可摸到骨折碎片。X线摄片检查,可明确是否有骨折、脱位。胫腓下联合韧带断裂时,内外踝之间的距离变宽。

【诊断要点】

1. 有明显的踝关节扭挫伤史。
2. 踝关节内侧或外侧疼痛、肿胀,损伤部位明显压痛。
3. 关节活动功能受限,尤其是重复损伤机制时疼痛加剧。
4. X线摄片检查,排除骨折、脱位等。

【推拿治疗】

1. 治疗原则 消肿止痛,活血祛瘀,理筋通络。

2. 取穴和部位 外侧副韧带损伤:足三里、阳陵泉、解溪、丘墟、申脉、金门、外踝前下方;内侧副韧带损伤:三阴交、商丘、照海、太溪、内踝下方。

3. 操作

外侧副韧带损伤

(1) 患者取仰卧位,术者在其小腿前外侧至踝外侧用捏、拿、按、揉手法,反复治疗,时间约5分钟。

(2) 在外踝前下方用拇指或大鱼际按揉法,先按揉损伤周围,待疼痛稍缓解后再在损伤处作重点按揉。手法宜轻柔缓和,时间约5分钟。

(3) 用按、揉、点、拨或一指禅推法治疗足三里、阳陵泉、解溪、丘墟、申脉、金门穴,每穴1分钟。

(4) 医生以一手托住患肢足跟部,另一手握住其足趾部作牵引拔伸片刻,再在拔伸状态下轻轻摇动踝关节,并配合足部逐渐向内翻牵拉,然后再外翻足部。

(5) 最后在损伤部位用擦法,以透热为度,自上而下施理筋手法结束治疗,时间约 2 分钟。

内侧副韧带损伤

(1) 患者取健侧卧位,患肢伸直,健肢屈曲。医生沿小腿内侧、内踝下至内侧足弓部施推法或按、揉等手法反复治疗,时间约 5 分钟。

(2) 在内踝下方先按、揉损伤周围,待疼痛稍缓解后再在损伤处作重点按、揉、点、拨。手法宜轻柔缓和,时间约 3 分钟。

(3) 用按、揉或一指禅推法治疗三阴交、商丘、照海、太溪等穴位,每穴 1 分钟。

(4) 施拔伸摇法。医生以一手托住患肢足跟部,另一手握住其足趾部作牵引拔伸片刻,再在拔伸状态下轻轻摇动踝关节,并配合足部逐渐向外翻牵拉,然后再内翻足部。

(5) 最后在损伤部位用擦法,以透热为度,自上而下施理筋手法结束治疗,时间约 2 分钟。

【注意事项】

1. 急性损伤有出血肿胀者,视出血程度,应在伤后 24～48 小时推拿治疗。损伤即刻宜用冰敷。

2. 损伤严重者,应作 X 线摄片检查,在排除骨折和韧带完全断裂的情况下才能推拿。

3. 急性期患足宜固定休息,患肢抬高,以利消肿。

4. 恢复期加强功能锻炼,作膝关节屈伸练习,每天 2 次,每次约 3 分钟;踝关节屈伸练习,每天 2 次,每次约 3 分钟;踝关节顺时针、逆时针方向的转踝练习,每天 2 次,每次约 3 分钟。

7.1.20 颞颌关节功能紊乱症

颞颌关节紊乱症又称"弹响颌",是由于颞颌关节周围关节囊、关节盘、韧带、肌肉等软组织或关节本身病变,引起该关节出现关节疼痛、关节区弹响、运动异常或障碍等一系列综合症候群。颞颌关节紊乱症发病原因目前尚未完全阐明,可能是由于暴力打击、喜吃硬性食物、关节发育不对称、寒冷侵袭、关节周围炎症、习惯性单侧咀嚼及有工作紧张、咬牙习惯或长时间的张口等因素造成的。

本病常发生在一侧颞颌关节,亦可累及双侧。好发于 20～40 岁的青壮年。

【临床表现】

颞颌关节功能紊乱症的患者,多数有外伤或感寒凉病史,或与关节周围肌肉过度兴奋或过度抑制、牙咬合关系紊乱和关节先天性畸形等有关。其临床主要表现为:颞颌关节弹响,一般是由于关节盘扭伤后引起肥厚、折叠或撕裂变化。在运动过程中,关节结节和下颌头发生摩擦而造成弹响,弹响时可伴有不适感或疼痛。部分患者在开口初期和闭口末期出现弹响;有的则发生在开口末期和闭口初期;关节软骨面和骨质破坏的患者,在开闭口运动时可出现连续性的似揉玻璃纸样的杂音。颞颌关节周围疼痛,患者疼痛不明显或仅有酸痛。咀嚼运动、张口运动或作下颌前伸、侧方运动时可诱发疼痛;部分患者可伴有闭口肌群痉挛。开口运动异常,有的患者因疼痛而开口受限;也有患者因韧带、关节囊松弛或翼外肌功能亢进而开口度过大,或颞颌关节半脱位造成开口困难;有的患者因咀嚼肌群痉挛而出现牙关紧闭;部分单侧颞颌关节发病的患者有开口型侧偏现象。少数患者可因颞神经和鼓索神经被髁突刺激或压迫而发生听觉障碍、眩晕、头痛以及放射性疼痛的症状。还有感受外邪或外伤所致的以上症状,并有舌红或有瘀斑,少苔,脉细弦等。

【诊断要点】

1. 可有颞颌关节损伤或先天发育不良的相关病史。

2. 面部外形可有异常,长期一侧颞颌关节紊乱的患者或习惯单侧咀嚼者,常可出现面部不对称,牙齿对合不齐等。

3. 有的患者在一侧或两侧颞颌关节区有压痛点,压痛点可能在乙状切迹和上颌结节后方,也可能在颞颌关节后区或关节结节处和髁突前斜面。有闭口肌群痉挛的患者,可以触摸到紧张痉挛的肌肉。

4. 有的患者作咀嚼或张口运动时,可有颞颌关节弹响。

5. 张口运动异常或张口功能受限。一侧受限,则下颌偏向患侧;双侧受限,则下颌不偏或偏向受限严重的一侧。

6. X线片检查可见先天性发育畸形、颞颌关节的退变和半脱位等,并可以用来鉴别颞颌关节部的骨折、脱位程度和骨病等。

【推拿治疗】

1. 治疗原则 舒筋活血、理筋整复。

2. 取穴及部位 上关、下关、翳风、颊车、合谷等穴及一侧或两侧的颞颌关节部。

3. 操作

(1) 患者正坐或侧卧位,患侧在上,医生点按患侧上关、下关、翳风、颊车、合谷等穴,每穴约10秒钟,以缓解局部痉挛和疼痛。

(2) 医生用指揉法或大鱼际揉法从颞颌关节周围慢慢向中心揉动,力量由轻到重,反复操作。目的是放松局部的肌肉,为下步手法做准备。时间约2~3分钟。

(3) 医生用指按、揉法和一指禅推法在肌肉上及颞颌关节周围操作时,可嘱患者闭口,使咬肌自然松弛;在关节囊上操作时,可嘱患者张口,使下颌关节轻度分离,便于手法操作和力量的渗透,从而起到舒筋活络、止痛的作用。时间约3~5分钟。

(4) 下颌骨向健侧偏歪,咬合关节异常者。患者取坐位,医生立于患者背后,一手掌大鱼际按在患者患侧颞部和髁突处,另一手掌按在健侧的下颌部,令患者作张口和闭口运动,与此同时,医生两手相对用力挤按,即可恢复其正常的咬合关系。治疗时间依患者的治疗情况而定。

(5) 医生用指摩法在颞颌关节部轻轻摩动,以调和局部的经气,使患者有轻松感,时间约2~3分钟。

(6) 颞颌关节半脱位者,可采用整复手法:患者正坐,医生两手拇指按住患者两侧的颊车穴,其余四指扣托住下颌骨的下缘,两手拇指按揉颊车穴,同时两手轻微活动下颌,使下颌头自动弹入关节窝中。如果不成功,医生可以用一手中、食二指(包有消毒纱布)伸入口腔内按压住患侧的下牙床,拇指相对置于下颌底处,相对用力夹持住下颌骨,令其摇晃,同时另一手拇指在髁突部作揉捻动作,其余四指扶住下颌骨。摇揉下颌骨1分钟后,嘱患者张大口,口腔中的食、中二指也随着向前下方用力下压,然后迅速拿出食、中二指,并用手掌托其下颌部,向后上方端提,同时让患者闭口,此时按于髁突拇指也同时将髁突向后上方挤按,令其复位。

【注意事项】

1. 推拿治疗需要用颞颌关节整复手法时,要注意选择合理的复位手法,掌握好恰当的力量;复位后需要进行一段时间的下颌关节的固定,进食和治疗时松开,以防止再脱位和为组织修复创造条件,但不宜固定时间过久。

2. 患病时应忌食生冷、硬性食物,避免造成对颞颌关节区的刺激。

3. 面部注意保暖,避免寒冷刺激。

4. 纠正不良的咀嚼习惯,避免患侧肌肉的过度疲劳。

7.2 内妇五官科病症

7.2.1 胃脘痛

胃脘痛简称胃痛,是指上腹部近心窝处,经常发生疼痛的一种病症。与西医学的胃痉挛、急慢性胃炎、胃及十二指肠溃疡、胃肠神经官能症、胃癌等所有消化系统疾病有相似之处。

【临床表现】

胃脘痛在临床上分病邪阻滞和脏腑失调两类。但不论是病邪阻滞或脏腑失调的胃脘痛,只要未经彻底治疗,日久不愈,均可形成瘀血内停。

1. 病邪阻滞

(1) 寒邪犯胃:胃脘痛暴作,隐痛或绞痛,局部得温则痛减,遇寒加剧,口不渴或渴喜热饮,苔薄白,脉弦紧。

(2) 食滞:胃脘胀闷,甚者疼痛,嗳腐吞酸或呕吐不消化食物,吐后或矢气后痛减,厌食,大便不爽,苔白腻或黄腻,脉滑。

2. 脏腑失调

(1) 肝气犯胃:胃脘胀满,攻撑作痛,脘痛连胁,嗳气频繁,大便不畅,每因情绪因素而痛作,苔薄白,脉弦。

(2) 脾胃虚寒:胃痛隐隐,泛吐清水,喜暖喜按,得暖得按痛减,空腹痛甚,得食痛减,纳差,神疲,甚则手足不温,大便溏薄,苔白,脉虚弱或迟缓。

以上胃脘痛诸症,病邪阻滞者多为急性疼痛;脏腑失调者多为慢性疼痛。在临床中,上述诸症,往往不是单纯出现或一成不变的,虚实并见,寒热错杂的并不少见。

【诊断要点】

1. 胃脘部疼痛,常伴痞闷或胀满、嗳气、泛酸、嘈杂、恶心呕吐等症。

2. 发病常与情志不畅、饮食不节、劳累、受寒等因素有关。

3. 上消化道钡餐X线检查、纤维胃镜及组织病理活检等,可见胃、十二指肠黏膜炎症、溃疡等病变。

4. 大便或呕吐物隐血试验阳性者,提示并发消化道出血。
5. B超、肝功能、胆道X线造影有助于鉴别诊断。

【推拿治疗】
1. 治疗原则　理气止痛。
2. 取穴和部位　中脘、天枢、气海、足三里、膈俞、肝俞、脾俞、胃俞、三焦俞、肩井、手三里、内关、合谷及胁肋部。
3. 操作
(1) 患者仰卧位,医生先用轻柔的一指禅推法、摩法在胃脘部治疗,使热量渗透于腹部,然后按、揉中脘、气海、天枢等穴,同时配合按、揉足三里。时间约5分钟。
(2) 患者俯卧位,医生用一指禅推法,从背部脊柱两旁沿膀胱经顺序而下至三焦俞,往返4~5次,然后用轻重交替的按、揉法于膈俞、肝俞、脾俞、胃俞、三焦俞,时间约5分钟。
(3) 患者取坐位,医生用捏、拿肩井循臂肘而下,在手三里、内关、合谷等穴作较强的按、揉刺激。然后搓、揉肩臂使经络畅通,再搓、抹两胁部,由上而下往返数次。时间为5~10分钟。
4. 辨证治疗
(1) 寒邪犯胃用较重的点、按法治疗脾俞、胃俞,时间约2分钟。用擦法在左侧背部治疗(T_7~T_{12}),以透热为度。
(2) 食滞用顺时针方向摩腹,重点在中脘、天枢穴。按、揉脾俞、胃俞、大肠俞、八髎、足三里。时间为5分钟。
(3) 肝气犯胃用轻柔的一指禅推或揉法,自天突向下至中脘穴治疗,重点在膻中穴,然后轻柔地按揉两侧章门、期门。时间约3分钟。用较重的手法按揉背部肝俞、胆俞、膈俞。
(4) 脾胃虚寒用轻柔的按揉法在气海、关元、足三里治疗,每穴约2分钟,在气海穴治疗时间可适当延长。直擦背部督脉,横擦左侧背部(T_7~T_{12})及腰部肾俞、命门穴,以透热为度。
(5) 疼痛剧烈者在背部脾俞、胃俞附近压痛点,用较重的点、按法,连续刺激2分钟左右,待疼痛缓解后,再辨其证而治之。

【注意事项】
1. 对胃、十二指肠溃疡出血的患者,一般不宜手法治疗。
2. 患者生活要有规律,注意精神和饮食的调摄。
3. 患者切忌暴饮暴食,或饥饱不匀,一般可少食多餐,以清淡易消化的食物为宜,忌食烈酒及辛辣刺激性食物。
4. 胃痛持续不止者,应在一定时间内进流质或半流质食物。

7.2.2　泄泻

泄泻,是指大便次数增多,粪便清稀,甚至泻出如水样而言,以大便溏薄而势缓者为泄,以大便清稀如水而直下者为泻。本证一年四季均可发生,但以夏秋二季多见。本证与西医学的急慢性肠炎、胃肠神经功能紊乱、慢性非特异性溃疡性结肠炎等疾病相近。

【临床表现】

1. 急性泄泻

（1）湿邪侵袭：发病急骤，大便稀薄或夹粘液，每日数次或者十余次，腹痛肠鸣，肢体酸痛，苔白腻或黄腻，脉濡或滑数。

（2）伤食：有暴饮暴食或不洁的饮食史。发病突然，脘腹胀痛，泄下粪便，臭如败卵，泻后痛减，嗳腐吞酸，舌苔垢腻，脉濡或滑数。

2. 慢性泄泻

（1）脾胃虚弱：大便时溏时稀，完谷不化，反复发作，稍食油腻则大便次数增多，食欲不振，舌淡苔白，脉缓弱。

（2）脾肾阳虚：症多发作于黎明之前，脐周作痛，肠鸣即泄，泻后痛减，并有腹部畏寒，腰酸肢冷，舌淡苔白，脉沉细。

（3）肝气乘脾：泄泻每因精神因素，情绪波动而诱发，平时有腹痛肠鸣，胸胁痞满，嗳气食少，苔薄，脉弦细。

【诊断要点】

1. 大便稀薄或如水样，次数增多，可伴腹胀腹痛等症。
2. 急性暴泻起病突然，病程短，可伴有恶寒、发热等症。
3. 慢性久泻起病缓慢，病程较长，反复发作，时轻时重。
4. 饮食不当、受寒凉或情绪变化可诱发。
5. 大便常规可见少许红、白细胞，大便培养致病菌阳性或阴性。
6. 必要时作 X 线钡剂灌肠或纤维肠镜检查。

【推拿治疗】

1. 治疗原则　　健脾和胃，温肾壮阳，疏肝理气。

2. 取穴与部位　　中脘、天枢、气海、关元、脾俞、胃俞、肾俞、大肠俞、长强。

3. 操作

（1）患者取仰卧位，医生用轻重交替的一指禅推法由中脘开始向下移至气海、关元，往返操作 5～6 遍；用掌摩法逆时针摩腹，时间约 8 分钟。

（2）患者取俯卧位，用㨰法沿脊柱两旁从脾俞到大肠俞治疗，每穴约 1 分钟；然后按揉脾俞、胃俞、大肠俞、长强，往返 3～4 次；再在左侧背部用擦法治疗，以透热为度，时间约 10 分钟。

4. 辨证治疗

（1）寒湿泻：揉神阙、气海，以腹内有温热感为度；按、揉足三里、内关。每穴约 1 分钟；左侧背部及腰骶部用擦法，以透热为度。

（2）伤食泻：以摩腹为主治疗，摩法及其在腹部移动均以顺时针方向进行。

（3）脾胃虚弱：在气海、关元、足三里用轻柔的按、揉法治疗，每穴约 2 分钟，在气海穴治疗的时间可适当延长；摩腹，重点在胃脘部，摩法以逆时针方向进行，往下至腹部时则按顺时针方向进行。

（4）脾肾阳虚：用轻柔的按、揉法在气海、关元治疗，每穴约 3 分钟；直擦背部督脉，横擦腰骶部肾俞、命门及骶部八髎穴，以透热为度。

(5) 肝郁乘脾:用轻柔的按揉法在两侧章门、期门治疗,时间约5～10分钟;斜擦两胁,以两胁微热为度;用轻柔的手法,按、揉背部肝俞、胆俞、膈俞及太冲、行间。

【注意事项】

1. 泄泻期间忌食含淀粉和脂肪过多的食物,以及一切生冷刺激与不易消化的食物。

2. 注意保暖,不宜过度疲劳,注意情志和饮食的调摄。

7.2.3 便秘

便秘是指大便干燥,排出困难,或排便间隔时间延长,或欲大便而临厕努挣乏力,艰涩不畅的一种病证。本证可单独发病或见于其他疾病中。本症主要是由于大肠传导功能失常,粪便在肠内停留时间过久,水分被过量吸收,而使粪质干燥、坚硬所致。

【临床表现】

一般为大便干燥,排便困难,经常三、五日或七、八日排便一次;或有的大便次数正常,但粪质干燥,坚硬难排;或少数患者,时有便意,但排出艰难。便秘日久,腑气不通,浊气不降,可引起腹胀,甚至腹痛,头晕头胀,食欲减退,睡眠不安等。长期便秘,可导致痔疮或肛裂。

1. 胃肠积热 大便干结不通,腹部痞满,心烦,面红身热,口干,口臭,口苦,小便短赤,舌苔黄燥,脉滑实。

2. 气机郁滞 大便秘而不干结,腹胀痛连及两胁,嗳气频作,口苦,目眩,舌质偏红,舌苔薄白稍腻,脉弦。

3. 气血亏损

(1) 气虚便秘:大便不畅,临厕努挣乏力,便后疲乏汗出,短气,便下并不干结,舌淡苔薄,脉虚软。

(2) 血虚便秘:大便秘结,面色少华,头晕目眩,心悸,唇舌淡,脉细。

4. 阴寒凝滞 大便难涩不易排出,面色(㿠)白,畏寒肢冷,喜热,喜温喜按,腹中冷痛,腰背酸冷,小便清长,舌淡苔白,脉沉迟。

【诊断要点】

1. 排便时间延长,两天以上一次,粪便干燥坚硬。

2. 重者大便艰难,干燥如粟,可伴少腹胀满,神倦乏力,胃纳减退等症。

3. 排除肠道器质性疾病。

【推拿治疗】

1. 治疗原则 和肠通便,调理气机。

2. 取穴及部位 中脘、天枢、大横、关元、腹部、肝俞、脾俞、胃俞、肾俞、大肠俞、八髎、长强;腹部及背部。

3. 操作

(1) 患者取仰卧位,医生用轻柔的一指禅推法施于中脘、天枢、大横治疗,每穴约1分钟;然后用掌摩法以顺时针方向摩腹约8分钟。

(2) 患者取俯卧位,医生用轻柔的一指禅推法在脊柱两侧从肝俞、脾俞到八髎穴往返施术,时间约 5 分钟;然后用轻柔的按、揉法在肾俞、大肠俞、八髎、长强穴治疗,往返 2~3 遍。

(3) 最后则以搓法在背部操作,时间约 5 分钟。

4. 辨证治疗

(1) 胃肠积热:横擦八髎,以透热为度;按、揉足三里、大肠俞,以酸胀为度。

(2) 气机郁滞:按、揉胸胁部的中府、云门、膻中、章门、期门;背部的肺俞、肝俞、膈俞,均以酸胀为度,不宜刺激太重;横擦胸上部,以透热为度;斜擦两胁,以微有热感为度。

(3) 气血亏虚:横擦胸上部、左侧背部及骶部八髎穴,均以透热为度;按、揉足三里、支沟穴各 1 分钟。

(4) 阴寒凝滞:横擦肩背部及腰部肾俞、命门穴,骶部八髎穴,均以透热为度;直擦背部督脉,以透热为度。

【注意事项】

1. 指导病人养成每日定时排便的习惯,不论有无便意,皆按时去厕所作排便动作,日久成习惯,届时大便即可自下。

2. 调整饮食结构,宜多喝开水,多吃含粗纤维的食物,如蔬菜、水果、粗粮等。忌用辛辣、刺激性食物,少食肥甘厚味之物。

3. 进行适当的户外活动,在病情允许时,可作腹部肌肉锻炼,以加强腹肌,有助于排便。

7.2.4 高血压病

高血压病是一种常见的慢性疾病,又称"原发性高血压病",以动脉血压持续性增高为其主要临床表现。晚期可导致心、脑、肾等器官病变。本病发病率高,与年龄、职业、家族史有一定关系。

高血压病是以血压经常性增高为主要临床表现的一种疾病,在临床上高血压有 80%~90% 是本病引起。继发性高血压是某些疾病发生过程中,作为症状之一而出现的高血压,高血压在这些疾病中可有可无,可暂时性或为持久性,这类高血压患者约占临床高血压的 10%~20%。一般认为,收缩压≥140mmHg 和(或)舒张压≥90mmHg 就是高血压,根据血压升高水平,又可分为 1、2、3 级。

【临床表现】

高血压病的临床表现,轻重程度相差很大,部分患者可无自觉症状,常在体检时偶然发现有高血压。一般症状有眩晕、头痛、面红、目赤、口苦、惊悸、便秘、舌红、脉弦。

本病根据病程进展快慢可分为缓进型和急进型两类。临床上以缓进型多见。

1. 缓进型

(1) 早期主要有头痛、头昏、失眠、记忆力减退、注意力不集中、烦闷、乏力、心悸等。症状轻重与血压增高的程度未必成正比。

(2) 后期主要决定于心、脑、肾的病变情况。

2. 急进型

(1) 可有数年缓进型后突然迅速发展,或一开始即发展迅速。

(2) 多见于40岁以下的青年和中年人,血压显著升高,舒张压持续在130～140mmHg以上,症状明显。

(3) 数月或1～2年内出现肾、心脏病变。

(4) 本型极易出现高血压脑病、心力衰竭,肾功能急剧减退。

【诊断要点】

1. 根据1999年世界卫生组织高血压专家委员会(WHO/ISH)确定的标准和中国高血压防治指南(1999年10月)的规定,18岁以上成年人高血压定义,是指在未服用降压药物情况下收缩压≥140mmHg和(或)舒张压≥90mmHg。

2. 患者既往有高血压史,目前正服用抗高血压药物,即使血压已低于140/90mmHg,仍诊断为高血压。

【推拿治疗】

1. 治疗原则　平肝安神,化痰降浊。

2. 取穴及部位　桥弓、印堂、发际、太阳、百会、风池、头维、公孙、攒竹、大椎、关元、气海、神阙、中脘、大横、肾俞、命门、涌泉;头面及颈项部。

3. 操作

(1) 患者取坐位,医生用双手指指腹自上而下推抹颈项部桥弓,每侧约1分钟;用一指禅推法,从印堂直线向上到发际;再沿眉弓至太阳;然后从印堂到一侧睛明,绕眼眶治疗,两侧交替进行。时间约4分钟。用揉法在额部治疗,从一侧太阳穴至另一侧太阳穴,再用扫散法在头侧胆经循行部位,自前上方向后下方治疗;然后用抹法在前额及面部治疗,配合按角孙、睛明、太阳,时间约3分钟。在头顶部用五指拿法,至颈项部改用三指拿法,沿颈椎两侧拿至大椎两侧,配合按、揉、捏、拿百会、风池及颈项部,用一指禅推法,由风府沿颈椎向下到大椎往返治疗,再在颈椎两侧膀胱经用一指禅推法往返治疗,时间约4分钟。最后回至面部用分法自前额至迎香往返操作,时间约3～5分钟。

(2) 患者取仰卧位,医生用摩法在患者腹部治疗,摩法按顺时针方向操作,腹部移动也按顺时针方向进行,在摩腹过程中配合按、揉上述穴位,时间约10分钟。

(3) 横擦腰部肾俞、命门及腰骶部的督脉,以透热为度;直擦足底涌泉穴,以透热为度。

【注意事项】

1. 生活要有规律,不能过度疲劳,但要在医生指导下进行适当的体育锻炼,忌食油腻烈酒。

2. 避免精神刺激。

3. 推拿适宜于缓进型高血压,急进型高血压则可作配合治疗。

7.2.5 冠心病

冠心病是指由于冠状动脉循环改变引起冠状血流与心肌之间的供需平衡遭到破坏,而导致心肌受损的疾病,又叫缺血性心脏病。引起冠状循环障碍的原因可以是功能性的,如冠状动脉痉挛等;也可以是器质性的,如冠状动脉粥样硬化等。

【临床表现】
临床以前胸部阵发性或持久性的压榨样疼痛或剧痛,甚则心律失常,休克或心力衰竭为特征;亦可无任何症状而在体检时发现心电图有心肌缺血表现者。

1. 胸阳痹阻 胸前绞痛,或痛闷交作,痛发时可引及左肩、左臂,爪甲暗淡,唇舌紫黯,或呕吐痰涎,舌边有瘀血点,苔薄白或白腻,脉弦或细滑。

2. 阳气虚衰 心胸隐痛或胸闷气短,头晕,心悸,神疲懒言,畏寒肢冷,面色苍白,动则汗出,舌淡胖边有齿印,脉沉细或结、代。

【诊断要点】
1. 前胸部阵发性或持久性的压榨样疼痛或剧痛,也可无症状。
2. 心电图有心肌缺血的改变。
3. 胸阳痹阻型,以痛发时可引及左肩、左臂,爪甲暗淡,唇舌紫黯,舌暗边有瘀血点为辨证要点,苔薄白或白腻,脉弦或细滑。
4. 阳气虚衰型,以头晕,心悸,神疲懒言,畏寒肢冷,面色苍白,动则汗出为辨证要点,舌淡胖,边有齿印,脉沉细或结、代。

【推拿治疗】
1. 治疗原则 补心温阳,宣痹止痛。

2. 取穴及部位 膻中、心俞、厥阴俞、内关穴,胸部任脉循行部位及背部督脉、太阳经循行部位。

3. 操作

(1) 患者取坐位或仰卧位,以一指禅推法结合指按、指揉法在膻中、内关穴操作;横擦前胸部,以透热为度。时间约3~5分钟。

(2) 患者取坐位或俯卧位,以一指禅推法结合指按、指揉法在心俞、厥阴俞操作;侧擦背部,透热为度。时间约3~5分钟。

(3) 患者取坐位,医生用双手拇指指腹,交替推抹颈项部桥弓穴,时间约3~5分钟。

4. 辨证治疗

(1) 胸阳痹阻:上述手法操作时用力宜重,重推背部太阳经肺俞至膈俞,以泻为主。

(2) 阳气虚衰:上述手法操作时用力宜轻,轻摩心俞、厥阴俞,10~20分钟,以补为主。

【注意事项】
1. 患者生活要有规律,注意精神和饮食调摄。
2. 推拿手法对缓解期或轻症病人效果较好,对急性发作期或重型病人宜配合药物综合进行治疗。

7.2.6 头痛

头痛是颅内、颅外病变刺激疼痛敏感组织引起头颅上半部的疼痛,是临床上比较常见自觉症状,可出现于多种急慢性疾患中。引起头痛的疾病有四类:颅内病变、颅外病变、全身性疾病、神经官能症。

本节论述的头痛,是中医内科疾病的范畴,以头痛为主要症状者。若属外伤及一些疾病过程中所出现的兼症,则主病去,头痛亦自除。

【临床表现】

1. 风寒头痛　多发于吹风受寒之后引起头痛,头痛时作,有时痛连项背,恶风寒,肢节酸楚,喜裹头,口不渴,苔薄白,脉浮或紧。

2. 风热头痛　头胀痛,甚则如裂,恶风发热,面红目赤,口渴欲饮,咽红肿痛,尿黄或便秘,苔薄黄或舌尖红,脉浮数。

3. 暑湿头痛　头痛如裹,脘闷纳呆,肢体倦怠,沉重疼痛,身热汗出,心烦口渴,苔腻,脉濡数。

4. 肝阳头痛　头痛眩晕,两侧偏重,心烦易怒,睡眠不安,面红口干苦,两胁胀痛,苔薄黄或舌红少苔,脉弦有力或弦细数。

5. 痰浊头痛　头痛头胀,胸膈支满,纳呆倦怠,口吐涎津,恶心,苔白腻,脉滑。

6. 血虚头痛　头痛头晕,劳累更剧,神疲乏力,面色少华,食欲不振,心悸气短,舌淡,脉细无力或涩。

7. 肾亏头痛　头脑空痛,神疲倦怠,耳鸣目眩,健忘失眠,腰酸腿软,遗精带下。阳虚者四肢作冷,舌淡胖,脉沉细无力;阴虚者口干少津,舌质红,脉细数。

8. 瘀血头痛　头痛反复发作,经久不愈,痛处固定,痛如锥刺,或头部有撞击史,舌质紫黯或见瘀斑,脉涩。

【诊断要点】

1. 以头痛为主症,或前额、额颞、巅顶、顶枕部或全头部头痛,头痛性质多为跳痛、刺痛、胀痛、昏痛、隐痛等。有突然而作,其痛如破而无休止者;也有反复发作,久治不愈,时痛时止者;头痛每次发作可持续数分钟、数小时、数天或数周不等。

2. 因外感、内伤等因素,突然而病或有反复发作的病史。

3. 应查血常规、测血压,必要时做脑脊液、脑电图检查,有条件时做经颅多普勒、颅脑 CT 和 MRI 检查,有助于排除器质性疾病,明确诊断。

【推拿治疗】

1. 治疗原则　疏经通络,行气活血。

2. 取穴及部位　印堂、头维、太阳、鱼腰、攒竹、阳白、百会、四神聪、肩井、风池;头面、颈项部。

3. 操作

(1)患者取坐位,医生用一指禅推法沿颈部两侧膀胱经向下,往返治疗约 3 分钟左右,然后按揉风池、风府、天柱等穴,再拿两侧风池穴、肩井穴,各约 1 分钟,沿颈部两侧膀胱经自上向下操作 4～5 次。

(2)患者取坐位。医生用一指禅推法从印堂穴开始,向上沿发际至头维、太阳穴,往返 3～4 次。配合按印堂、鱼腰、太阳、百会等穴,然后用五指拿法从头顶拿至风池穴处,改用三指拿法,沿膀胱经拿至大椎两侧,往返 3～4 次。

4. 辨证治疗

(1)风寒头痛:用㨰法在项背部治疗 2～3 分钟,配合按揉肺俞、风门;再拿两侧肩井,直擦背部两侧膀胱经,以透热为度。

（2）风热头痛：按揉大椎、肺俞、风门等穴各1分钟，再拿两侧肩井穴；按、拿两侧曲池、手三里、合谷，以酸胀为度；拍击背部两侧膀胱经，以皮肤微红为度。

（3）暑湿头痛：按揉大椎、曲池，配合拿肩井、合谷；拍击背部两侧膀胱经，以皮肤微红为度；提捏印堂及项部皮肤，以皮肤透红为度。

（4）肝阳头痛：推桥弓，自上而下，每侧各20余次，两侧交替进行；用扫散法在头侧胆经循行部自前上方向后下方操作，两侧交替进行，各数十次，配合按角孙穴；按揉两侧太冲、行间，以酸胀为度，再擦两侧涌泉穴，以透热为度。

（5）痰浊头痛：用一指禅推法及摩法在腹部治疗，重点在中脘、天枢穴，时间6～8分钟；按揉脾俞、胃俞、大肠俞，然后在左侧背部横擦，以透热为度；按揉两侧足三里、丰隆、内关。

（6）血虚头痛：摩腹6～8分钟，以气海、中脘、关元为重点；横擦左侧背部及直擦背部督脉，以透热为度；按揉两侧心俞、膈俞、足三里、三阴交，以微微酸胀为度。

（7）肾亏头痛（肾阳不足）：摩腹6～8分钟，以气海、关元为重点；横擦背部督脉，横按腰部肾俞、命门及腰骶部，均以透热为度。

（8）瘀血头痛：按、揉、抹太阳、攒竹穴及前额、头侧胆经循行部位；擦前额及两侧太阳穴部位，以透热为度。

【注意事项】

1. 推拿手法对颅内疾病中的脑脓肿、脑血管疾病急性期、颅内占位性疾病、脑挫裂伤、外伤性颅内血肿等不宜治疗。

2. 外感头痛须注意保暖，避风寒，适当休息。

3. 肝阳头痛应经常测量血压，需注意血压的波动及对心脏的影响。

4. 血虚头痛和肾虚头痛应注意节制房事。

5. 各种头痛均忌烟酒刺激。

7.2.7 失眠

失眠是指经常不能获得正常的睡眠为特征的一种病症。一般包括睡眠时间、深度及恢复体力的不足。轻者入眠困难，或眠而不酣，时寐时醒，醒后不能再寐，严重者可整夜不眠。本症可单独出现，也可以与头痛、眩晕、心悸、健忘等症同时出现。失眠多见于西医学的神经官能症、更年期综合征等。

【临床表现】

本证临床要辨其虚实。虚证多由阴血不足而引起；实证多由肝郁化火、痰热内扰、壅遏胃腑而引起。

1. 心脾两虚 多梦易醒，忽寐忽醒，甚至彻夜不眠，心悸健忘，神疲乏力，饮食无味，面色少华，舌淡苔薄，脉细弱。

2. 阴虚火旺 心烦失眠，头晕耳鸣，口干津少，五心烦热，或有梦遗，健忘，心悸，腰酸等症，舌质红，脉细数。

3. 痰热内扰 失眠多梦，心烦意乱，急躁易怒，胸闷头重目眩，两胁胀痛，不思饮食，口渴喜饮，目赤口苦，小便黄赤，大便秘结，舌质红，苔黄腻，脉弦而滑数。

4. 肝郁化火 失眠，性情急躁易怒，不思饮食，口渴喜饮，目赤口苦，小便黄赤，大便秘结,舌质红,苔黄,脉弦而数。

【诊断要点】

1. 以睡眠障碍为几乎唯一的症状,其他症状均继发于失眠,包括难以入睡、睡眠不深、易醒、多梦、早醒、醒后不易再睡、醒后感不适、疲乏或白天困倦。

2. 上述睡眠障碍每周至少发生三次,并持续一个月以上。

3. 不是任何一种躯体疾病或精神障碍症状的一部分。

【推拿治疗】

1. 治疗原则 调理脏腑,镇静安神。

2. 取穴及部位 印堂、神庭、太阳、睛明、攒竹、鱼腰、角孙、百会、风池、肩井、中脘、气海、关元、心俞、肝俞、脾俞、胃俞、肾俞、命门;头面、颈肩部、腹部。

3. 操作

(1) 患者取坐位或仰卧位,医生用一指禅推法或揉法,从印堂开始向上至神庭穴;再从印堂向两侧沿眉弓推至太阳穴;然后用一指禅推法沿眼眶周围治疗。时间约5分钟。

(2) 再从印堂沿鼻两侧向下经迎香沿颧髎,至两耳前。治疗过程中按、揉印堂、神庭、睛明、攒竹、太阳等穴位。时间约5分钟。

(3) 沿上述治疗部位,用双手按、揉睛明、鱼腰,时间约3分钟。

(4) 用扫散法在头两侧胆经循行部位治疗,配合按角孙;从头顶开始用五指拿法,到枕骨下部转用三指拿法,配合按拿两侧肩井。时间约3分钟。

(5) 医者用掌摩法先顺时针方向摩腹,同时配合按揉中脘、气海、关元。时间约5分钟。

4. 辨证治疗

(1) 心脾两虚:按揉心俞、肝俞、胃俞、小肠俞、足三里,每穴约1分钟;横擦左侧背部及直擦背部督脉,以透热为度。

(2) 阴虚火旺:推桥弓穴,先推一侧桥弓,再推另一侧桥弓穴;横擦肾俞、命门部,以透热为度,再擦两侧涌泉穴以引火归原。

(3) 痰热内扰:沿背部脊柱两侧用㨰法治疗,重点在脾俞、胃俞、心俞,手法要轻柔,时间约5分钟。再按揉上述穴位;再摩腹时配合按揉中脘、气海、天枢、神阙、足三里、丰隆;横擦左侧背部及骶部八髎穴,以透热为度。

(4) 肝郁化火:指按揉肝俞、胆俞、期门、章门、太冲,每穴1~2分钟;搓两胁,时间约1分钟。

【注意事项】

1. 失眠常见于神经衰弱,但某些器质性病变也可出现本症,须注意鉴别,如为器质性病变引起的失眠,应重病因治疗。

2. 患者睡前不要吸烟、饮酒、喝茶和咖啡,避免看有刺激性的书和电影,每日用温水洗脚。

3. 适当参加体力劳动和体育锻炼,增强体质。

4. 注意劳逸结合,特别是房事要有所节制;平时生活起居要有规律,早睡早起。

5. 嘱患者消除烦恼,解除思想顾虑,避免情绪波动,心情要开朗、乐观。

7.2.8 中风后遗症

中风后遗症又称"偏枯"或"半身不遂",是指以半侧肢体肌肉萎缩,软弱无力,不能随意运动为主的一种临床病证,且多伴有口眼㖞斜、语言不利等,多见于脑卒中之后,亦可见于其他脑部疾患之后。临床上其他脑与脊髓疾患(如肿瘤、脑炎、外伤等)遗留有类似症状而出现偏瘫、截瘫或肢瘫时,可参考治疗。

【临床表现】

1. 半身不遂 以单侧上下肢瘫痪无力,口眼㖞斜,舌强语涩等为主症。初期患者肢体软弱无力,知觉迟钝或稍有强硬,活动功能受限,以后逐渐趋于强直挛急,患者肢体姿势常发生改变和畸形等。

2. 口眼㖞斜 口角及鼻唇沟歪向健侧,两腮鼓起漏气,但能作皱额蹙眉和闭眼等动作。

检查

1. 半身不遂 患者肢体肌张力增高,关节挛缩畸形,感觉略减退,活动功能基本丧失,患侧上肢肱二头肌、肱三头肌腱反射亢进,下肢膝腱和跟腱反射均为亢进,健侧正常。

2. 血压 脑出血和脑血栓形成患者血压偏高,蛛网膜下腔出血的患者有脑膜刺激征阳性,脑栓塞可出现神经系统体征。

3. 脑脊液检查 脑出血和蛛网膜下腔出血患者脑脊液为血性,而脑血栓形成和脑栓塞患者均为正常。

【诊断要点】

1. 既往有高血压、心脏病和头痛、眩晕的病史。

2. 卒然仆倒,不省人事,或静止状态下逐渐出现半身不遂、口眼㖞斜、舌强语涩等症。

【推拿治疗】

本病宜早期治疗为主,一般在中风后两星期,适宜用推拿治疗。

1. 治疗原则 舒筋通络,行气活血。

2. 取穴与部位 天宗、肝俞、胆俞、膈俞、肾俞、环跳、阳陵泉、委中、承山、风市、伏兔、膝眼、解溪、尺泽、曲池、手三里、合谷、印堂、睛明、太阳、角孙、风池、风府、肩井;背部、四肢部、头面部。

3. 操作

(1)患者取俯卧位,医生用按法治疗背部脊柱两侧,自上而下,点、按、揉天宗、肝俞、胆俞、膈俞、肾俞。再在脊柱两侧用㨰法治疗,并向下至臀部、股后部、小腿后部,以腰椎两侧、环跳、委中、承山及跟腱部为重点治疗部位。同时配合腰后伸和患侧髋后伸的被动活动。时间约5分钟。

(2)患者取健侧卧位法。患侧在上,自然侧臀部沿大腿外侧经膝部至小腿外侧用㨰法治疗,以髋关节和膝关节作为重点治疗部位。时间约3分钟。

(3)患者取仰卧位。医者站在侧面,用㨰法在患侧下肢,自髂前上棘向下沿大腿前面,向下肢踝关节及足背部治疗,点、按、揉伏兔、膝眼、解溪。同时配合髋关节、膝关节、踝关节的被动伸屈活动和整个下肢内旋动作。再拿患侧下肢,委中、承山、大腿内侧中部及膝部周围。时间约 5~10 分钟。

(4) 患者仰卧位。用㨰法自患侧上臂内侧至前臂进行治疗,肘关节及其周围为重点治疗部位。在进行手法的同时,配合患肢外展和肘关节伸屈的被动活动。按、揉尺泽、曲池、手三里、合谷。继之在患肢腕部、手掌和手指用㨰法治疗,同时配合腕关节及指间关节伸屈的被动活动,手指关节可配合捻法。时间约 5 分钟。

(5) 患者取坐位。用㨰法施于患侧肩胛周围及颈项两侧,在进行手法时,配合患肢向背后回旋上举及肩关节外展内收的被动活动;然后用拿法自肩部拿至腕部,配合活动肩、肘、腕关节;最后用搓法自肩部搓至腕部往返治疗。时间约 3 分钟。

(6) 医生用抹法自印堂至太阳往返治疗,同时配合按揉睛明、太阳;再用扫散法在头侧胆经循行部位自前上方向后下方操作,配合按、揉角孙。时间约 2 分钟。

口眼㖞斜:医生用一指禅推法自印堂、阳白、睛明、四白、迎香、下关、颊车、地仓往返治疗,再配合应用轻柔的擦法治疗。医生用一指禅推法施于风池及项部,随后拿风池、合谷结束治疗。

【注意事项】

1. 由于本病病程的长短与康复有直接的关系,所以尽早对本病进行治疗是十分重要的。一般在中风后,病情基本稳定便可以接受推拿治疗。

2. 病程在半年以内治以活血化瘀为先,半年以上则治以补益气血为重,以期扶正固本,强筋健骨。其手法操作基本相同,但应加强患者肢体关节的被动活动。

3. 患者应保持情绪的稳定,生活要有规律,禁忌烟、酒、辛辣等刺激性食物和脂肪过多的食品,保持身体清洁,加强褥疮的护理与防治。可适当配合中药、针灸、理疗、药膳等康复手段进行治疗。

4. 恢复期间,要进行全身性锻炼与轻便的活动,加强患侧肢体的功能锻炼,如滚健身球、握健身圈、拉滑轮、体后拉肩、大小云手、股四头肌舒缩活动、蹬空增力、搓滚舒筋等,但不可过量,更不可过度疲劳。

7.2.9 痛经

痛经是指女性在经期或行经前后出现周期性的小腹疼痛或腰部疼痛,甚至剧痛难忍,常伴有面色苍白、恶心呕吐、头面冷汗淋漓、手足厥冷等症,并随着月经周期发作,又称"经行腹痛",多见于未婚的青年女性。

西医学认为,原发性痛经多见于青年妇女,自初潮起即有痛经,与植物神经功能紊乱、子宫痉挛有关,也可由于子宫发育不良、子宫颈狭窄、子宫过度屈曲等,影响经血畅行而致。继发性痛经常继发于生殖器官器质性病变,如炎症、子宫肌瘤或子宫内膜异位症等。

【临床表现】

痛经的主要临床表现是经行小腹疼痛,可掣及全腹或腰骶,或出现外阴及肛门的坠痛。若疼痛剧烈者,可出现面色苍白,冷汗淋漓,手足厥冷,甚至昏厥虚脱等症状,并随月经周期而发作。应根据疼痛发作的时间、疼痛的性质,辨其寒热虚实。以经前、经期痛者为实,经后痛者为虚;痛时拒按为实,喜按为虚;得热则痛减为寒,得热而痛剧为热;而痛甚于胀,血块排出而疼痛减轻者为血瘀,胀甚于痛则为气滞。

1. 气滞血瘀 每于经前一、二日或经期中出现小腹胀痛、拒按、经量少或经行不畅,经色紫黯有块,血块排出时疼痛减轻,常伴胸胁、乳房胀痛不适,舌质黯或见瘀点,脉沉弦。

2. 寒湿凝滞 经前数日或经期出现小腹冷痛,得热痛减,按之痛甚,经色黯黑有血块,或畏寒身痛,舌苔白腻,脉沉紧。

3. 气血虚弱 经后或经期小腹部隐隐作痛,按之痛减,经色淡而清稀,或神疲乏力,面白无华,或纳少便溏,舌淡苔薄,脉虚细。

4. 肝肾虚损 经后一、二日内出现小腹部绵绵作痛,腰部酸胀,经血黯淡、量少而稀薄,或伴有耳鸣、头晕、眼花,或腰骶酸痛,小腹空坠不温,或潮热颧红,舌淡,苔薄白或薄黄,脉沉细。

【诊断要点】
1. 经期或经行前后小腹疼痛,痛及腰骶,甚则昏厥。呈周期性发作。
2. 好发于青年未婚女子。
3. 排除盆腔器质性疾病所致腹痛。

【推拿治疗】
1. 治疗原则 通调气血,温经散寒。
2. 取穴及部位 气海、关元、肾俞、八髎,腹部、小腹部、腰背部。
3. 操作
(1) 患者取仰卧位,医生用摩法按顺时针方向在小腹部治疗;然后用一指禅推法或按、揉气海、关元等穴位,每穴约5分钟。
(2) 患者取俯卧位,医生用㨰法在腰部脊柱两侧及腰骶部治疗;然后用一指禅推法或按、点法治疗肾俞、八髎,以酸胀为度;再在腰骶部及八髎穴用擦法治疗,以透热为度。时间约5分钟。

4. 辨证加减
(1) 气滞血瘀:先按揉章门、期门、肝俞、膈俞,拿血海、三阴交,以酸胀为度。
(2) 寒湿凝滞:先直擦背部督脉,再横擦腰骶部肾俞、命门,以透热为度;然后按揉血海、三阴交。
(3) 气血虚弱:先直擦背部督脉,再横擦两侧背部,以透热为度;然后摩腹并按揉中脘穴;最后按揉脾俞、胃俞、足三里等穴位。
(4) 肝肾虚损:先直擦背部督脉,再横擦腰部肾俞、命门,以透热为度;按、揉照海、太溪、肝俞、肾俞、涌泉等穴。

5. 实证痛经的特殊治疗方法 实证痛经,第三腰椎或第四腰椎(大部分在第四腰椎)有棘突偏歪及轻度压痛者:对偏歪棘突用旋转复位或斜扳的方法纠正棘突偏歪。直擦背部督脉及横擦腰骶部八髎穴,以透热为度。

在月经来潮前一周,治疗两次,以后每月在月经前一周治疗两次,连续3个月治疗六次为一疗程。

【注意事项】
1. 在经期注意保暖,避免寒冷,注意经期卫生。

2. 适当休息,不要过度疲劳。
3. 情绪安宁,避免暴怒、忧郁。
4. 推拿手法对器质性病变所引起的痛经,远期疗效尚不满意。

7.2.10 更年期综合征

更年期综合征又称围绝经期综合征,是指妇女在从生育年龄向老年过渡时期因卵巢功能减退、雌激素水平下降引起的以植物神经功能紊乱和代谢障碍为主的一系列症候群。

本病的发生与绝经前后的生理特点有密切关系。女性49岁前后,肾气由盛渐衰,天癸由少渐至衰竭,冲任二脉也随之而衰少,在此生理转折时期,受内、外环境的影响,如素体阴阳有所偏胜偏衰,素性抑郁,宿有痼疾,或家庭、社会等环境改变,易导致肾阴阳失调而发病。"肾为先天之本",故肾阴阳失调,易波及其他脏腑,而其他脏腑病变,久则必然累及于肾,故本病之本在肾,常累及心、肝、脾等多脏、多经,致使本病证候复杂。

【临床表现】

发病年龄多在45～55岁。要注意发病前有无工作、生活的特殊改变。有精神创伤史及双侧卵巢切除手术或放射治疗史。早期症状为潮热、汗出和情绪改变。潮热从胸前开始,涌向头部、颈部和面部,继而出汗,汗出热退,这个过程持续时间长短不定,短者数秒,长者数分钟,每日发作次数也没有规律;情绪改变表现为易激动,烦躁易怒,或无故悲伤啼哭,不能自我控制。此外,尚有头晕头痛,失眠心悸,腰酸背痛,月经紊乱等。晚期症状则有阴道干燥灼热,阴痒,尿频急或尿失禁,皮肤瘙痒等。

检查

1. 妇科检查 晚期可有阴道、子宫不同程度的萎缩,宫颈及阴道分泌物减少。

2. 实验室检查 阴道脱落细胞涂片检查显示雌激素水平不同程度的低落,血清垂体促卵泡生成素(ESH)水平增高而雌二醇(E_2)水平下降,对本病的诊断有参考意义。

【诊断要点】

1. 更年期综合征临床症状繁多,主诉杂乱,但体征极少,且易与其他疾病相混淆,诊断必须谨慎,必须在排除其他器质性疾病时才能确定。

2. 多发生在40岁以上,月经不规则或闭经、潮热、出汗、心悸、易激动、失眠或抑郁等症状。

3. 生殖器官及第二性征有不同程度萎缩。

4. 尿、血雌激素降低,促卵泡素及黄体生成素明显升高。

5. 子宫颈、子宫体变小,阴道穹隆变浅。

6. 子宫颈管内缩,子宫内膜萎缩。

7. 阴道黏膜变薄,表层细胞缺如。

8. 阴道内pH值增高。

9. 阴道干燥、弹性消失。

【推拿治疗】

1. 治疗原则 调和阴阳,调理冲任。

2. 取穴及部位 膻中、中脘、气海、关元、中极。腰背部:厥阴俞、膈俞、肝俞、脾俞、肾俞、命门、背部督脉、背部膀胱经第一侧线;头面及颈肩部:太阳、攒竹、四白、迎香、百会、风池、肩井;腹部、颈项部及背部。

3. 操作

(1) 患者取仰卧位,医生用一指禅推法分别施治于膻中、中脘、气海、关元、中极穴,每穴2~3分钟,接着用顺时针揉、摩胃脘部及小腹部,分别约5分钟。

(2) 患者取俯卧位,医生用一指禅推法或拇指按、揉法施于厥阴俞、膈俞、肝俞、脾俞、肾俞、命门穴,每穴2分钟;然后用小鱼际擦法擦背部督脉经和背部膀胱经第一侧线及肾俞、命门穴,以透热为度。

(3) 患者坐位,医生捏、拿风池及颈项部2分钟;捏、拿头部(由前发际向后发际移动)5~10次;用一指禅推法或鱼际揉法施术于前额部5分钟;用分抹法施于前额、目眶及鼻翼两旁5~10次;两拇指同时按揉太阳、攒竹、四白、迎香穴各0.5分钟;拇指按、揉百会0.5分钟;拿肩井5~10次。

4. 辨证加减

(1) 肝肾阴虚:先揉、按志室、血海、阴陵泉、三阴交、太溪、太冲各半分钟;然后交替推桥弓穴。

(2) 心肾不交:先揉、按通里、内关、合谷、肺俞、心俞、血海、三阴交、太溪各半分钟;再搓擦涌泉,以透热为度。

(3) 脾肾阳虚:先揉、按天枢、曲池、合谷、足三里、阳陵泉、丰隆、悬钟、委中、承山、昆仑各半分钟;再掌振关元,横擦八髎,以透热为度。

(4) 心脾两虚:先揉按劳宫、通里、内关、合谷、心俞、血海、足三里、阴陵泉、悬钟、三阴交各半分钟;再搓擦涌泉,以透热为度。

(5) 阴阳俱虚:先揉按合谷、足三里、阳陵泉、血海、阴陵泉、三阴交、太溪、太冲、悬钟各半分钟;再横擦八髎,搓擦涌泉,以透热为度。

(6) 阴血亏虚:先按揉劳宫、通里、内关、合谷、心俞、血海、足三里、悬钟、三阴交、太冲各半分钟;再搓擦涌泉,以透热为度。

(7) 肝郁脾虚:先揉按内关、足三里、阳陵泉、丰隆、悬钟、三阴交、太冲各半分钟;再搓擦涌泉,横擦八髎,以透热为度。

(8) 冲任不固:先揉按合谷、足三里、阳陵泉、三阴交、太溪、太冲各半分钟;再掌振关元,横擦八髎,搓擦涌泉,以透热为度。

(9) 气郁痰结:先揉按支沟、合谷、足三里、天突、丰隆、三阴交、太溪、太冲各半分钟;再横擦八髎,搓擦涌泉,以透热为度。

【注意事项】

1. 更年期是每个妇女都必须经过的时期,是一个正常的生理过程。开导患者以客观、积极的态度对待这时期所出现的植物神经功能紊乱症状,消除忧虑。

2. 推拿治疗本病的疗效肯定,适合各种症状。

7.2.11 阳痿

阳痿是指青壮年时期,由于虚损、惊恐或湿热等原因,使宗筋失养而弛纵,引起阳事不举,或临房举而不坚的病证。西医学认为阳痿是男子性功能障碍的一种,常与早泄、遗精、性欲降低或无性欲等成为一组临床证候,多有大脑皮层功能紊乱、脊髓性中枢功能紊乱和生殖器官器质性病变等原因引起。

【临床表现】

1. 命门火衰 阳事不举,精薄清冷,头晕耳鸣,目眩,精神萎靡,面色㿠白,腰膝酸软,畏寒肢冷,舌质淡,苔白,脉沉细。

2. 心脾两虚 阳事不举,精神不振,夜寐不安,面色不华,食少纳呆,舌质淡,苔薄腻,脉细。

3. 湿热下注 阴茎痿软,勃而不坚,阴囊腥臭,下肢酸困,小便黄赤,余沥不尽,舌质红,苔黄腻,脉濡数。

4. 恐惧伤肾 阳痿不振,举而不坚,胆怯多疑,心悸失眠,苔薄腻,脉弦细。

【诊断要点】

1. 已婚男子阴茎不能勃起或勃而不坚,致使不能行房事,此为本病的主要临床表现。

2. 阳痿有原发性和继发性两种,又有器质性和功能性之分。原发性阳痿表现为阴茎从未能进入阴道进行性交;继发性阳痿则有过性交,但后来发生障碍。器质性阳痿表现为阴茎任何时候都不能勃起,既不能在性兴奋时勃起(如睡梦中和膀胱充盈时),亦无自发性勃起;功能性阳痿则有自发的勃起,但临房勃起又失败。

3. 本病绝大多数由精神心理因素所致。因此,患者都不同程度地处于紧张、恐惧、抑郁、焦虑和苦恼等精神状态中。

4. 排除功能性的阳痿,应结合其他体征,追踪原发病。如因糖尿病继发者,应做血、尿糖常规检查。

【推拿治疗】

1. 治疗原则 益肾壮阳。

2. 取穴及部位 神阙、气海、关元、中极、心俞、脾俞、肾俞、命门、腰阳关、三阴交、腹部、腰部、下肢部。

3. 操作

(1) 患者取仰卧位,医生用掌根揉神阙穴5分钟左右;然后用一指禅推法推气海、关元、中极穴各2分钟左右;再用掌摩其小腹,以温热为度;最后掌振小腹部。

(2) 患者取俯卧位,医生用指按、揉心俞、脾俞、肾俞、命门,每穴约2分钟;擦腰阳关穴,以透热为度。

(3) 同时用指按、揉法按揉三阴交,约2分钟;最后交替捏、拿双下肢3~5分钟。

4. 辨证加减

(1) 命门火衰:指按、揉肾俞、命门,每穴约5分钟;用直擦督脉及脊柱两侧膀胱经,横擦肾俞、命门、八髎穴,均以透热为度。

(2) 心脾两虚:指按、揉内关、足三里、血海,每穴约1~2分钟;指按揉心俞、脾俞,每穴约 3~5 分钟。

(3) 湿热下注:指按、揉天枢、丰隆、足三里、阴陵泉、大肠俞、膀胱俞,每穴约 2 分钟;掌摩小腹部,约 5 分钟。

(4) 恐惧伤肾:分抹前额 10 余次;指按、揉太阳、神门、大陵、胆囊穴,每穴 1~2 分钟;再交替捏、拿上肢部,约 2 分钟。

【注意事项】
1. 正确引导患者消除紧张恐惧心理,保持心情愉快舒畅。
2. 鼓励患者树立战胜疾病的信心,特别是夫妻之间要互相关怀体贴。
3. 要劳逸结合,适当参加体育锻炼和体力劳动。
4. 生活要有规律,戒除烟酒。
5. 清心寡欲,戒除手淫,节制房事。

7.2.12 牙痛

牙痛是指牙齿因各种原因引起的疼痛而言,为口腔疾患中常见的症状之一。遇冷、热、酸、甜等刺激使牙痛发作或加剧,可见于西医学的龋齿、牙髓炎、根尖周围炎和牙本质过敏等。

【临床表现】
本病在临床中不受任何年龄限制,也无明显的季节差异。

1. 风热牙痛 牙齿疼痛,呈阵发性,遇风发作,患处遇冷痛减,遇热则痛重,牙龈红肿,全身伴有发热、恶寒、口渴、舌质红,苔白而干,脉浮数。

2. 胃火牙痛 牙齿疼痛剧烈,牙龈红肿较甚,甚至渗血、出脓,肿连腮颊,头痛,口渴引饮,口气臭秽,大便秘结,舌苔黄腻,脉洪数。

3. 虚火牙痛 牙齿隐隐作痛或微痛,牙龈微红、微肿,久则龈肉萎缩,牙齿浮动,咬物无力,午后痛甚。全身可见腰背酸痛,头晕眼花,口干不欲饮,舌质红嫩,无苔,脉多细数。

【诊断要点】
凡以牙齿疼痛为主要症状者,均可诊断为牙痛。

1. 风热牙痛 以牙痛为主证,以患处遇冷痛减,遇热则痛重,牙龈红肿,发热、恶寒、口渴为辨证要点,舌质红,苔白而干,脉浮数。

2. 胃火牙痛 以牙痛为主证,以牙龈红肿较甚,肿连腮颊,头痛,口渴引饮,口气臭秽,大便秘结为辨证要点,舌苔黄腻,脉洪数。

3. 虚火牙痛 以牙痛为主证,以隐痛,牙龈微红、微肿,久则龈肉萎缩,牙齿浮动,咬物无力,午后痛甚为辨证要点。全身可见腰背酸痛,头晕眼花,口干不欲饮,舌质红嫩,无苔,脉多细数。

【推拿治疗】
1. 治疗原则 疏风清火,消肿止痛。
2. 取穴及部位 合谷、下关、颊车、内庭、太溪、行间、太冲;面部。
3. 操作
(1) 用点、按、揉内庭、太溪、行间、太冲等穴治疗,其压力应以重刺激为主,治疗时间约在3分钟左右。

(2) 用一指禅推法或按、揉面部的下关、颊车等穴治疗,压力由轻至重,时间约3分钟。

(3) 按、揉、捏、拿合谷穴,时间约1分钟。

(4) 最后捏、拿、按、揉病变牙龈的局部,结束治疗。

4. 辨证加减

(1) 风热牙痛:一指禅推太阳穴,拿风池、曲池、外关。

(2) 胃火牙痛:按揉二间、三间、内庭。

(3) 虚火牙痛:一指禅推肾俞,按、揉太溪、行间。

【注意事项】

1. 牙痛无论何种原因所致,必须养成良好的卫生习惯,坚持餐后漱口或刷牙。

2. 本病在面部治疗的过程中,手法必须固定一点,不可带有任何的摩擦动作。以防止出现红、肿等改变。

3. 龋齿、牙髓炎、根尖炎等疾病乃属于急性的炎症改变,推拿治疗时可配合消炎药物治疗,以提高临床疗效。

7.2.13 耳聋

耳聋是指听力异常的一种症状,以听力减退或听力丧失为主症,耳聋往往由耳鸣发展而来。西医学认为内耳性疾病、某些药物导致听神经损伤或先天听觉障碍可致耳聋。

【临床表现】

1. 实证

主症:暴病耳聋,或耳中觉胀,鸣声隆隆不断,按之不减。兼见头胀,面赤,咽干,烦躁善怒,脉弦,为肝胆火盛;畏寒,发热,脉浮,为外感风邪。

2. 虚证

主症:久病耳聋,耳中如蝉鸣,时作时止,劳累则加剧,按之鸣声减弱。兼见头晕,腰膝酸软,乏力,遗精,带下,脉虚细,为肾气亏;五心烦热,遗精盗汗,舌红少津,脉细数,为肝肾阴虚。

【诊断要点】

1. 以听力下降为主要症状,或伴耳鸣及轻度眩晕。

2. 常有恼怒、劳累、外感等诱因,或使用了耳毒性药物,或年老体衰、营养不良等因素致病。

3. 耳部检查时鼓膜无明显变化,或有混浊、内陷、增厚、粘连、钙质沉着等表现。

4. 听力检查呈感音神经性聋或传音性聋。

5. 应与耳胀、耳闭、耳眩晕、听神经瘤相鉴别。

【推拿治疗】

1. 治疗原则　通窍聪耳,清肝泻火。

2. 取穴及部位　耳门、听宫、听会、翳风、百会、哑门、风池、风府;头、耳部周围。

3. 操作

(1) 捏、拿头部五经；捏、拿、按、揉颈项部；按、揉百会、哑门、风池、风府。时间约5分钟。

(2) 一指禅偏峰推耳门、听宫、听会；按、揉翳风穴。时间约5分钟。

(3) 以双手食中两指夹持两耳前后推擦，以透热为度。时间约5分钟。

(4) 指振或掌振两耳，结束治疗。

4. 辨证治疗

(1) 肝胆火盛：点按太冲、行间、胆俞、三焦俞，以酸胀为度；搓胁肋1分钟左右；用拿法拿大腿内侧肌肉2分钟。

(2) 外感风邪：用擦法在项背部治疗2～3分钟，按揉太阳、大椎、肺俞、风门，再拿两侧肩井；直擦背部两侧膀胱经，以透热为度。再拿两侧肩井穴，拍击背部两侧膀胱经，以皮肤微红为度。

(3) 肾气亏虚：用轻柔的按揉法在气海、关元治疗，每穴1分钟；直擦背部督脉，横擦腰骶部肾俞、命门及骶部八髎穴，以透热为度。

(4) 肝肾阴虚：按揉肾俞、气海、关元、三阴交，每穴约2分钟；轻擦腰部，擦涌泉穴，以透热为度。

【注意事项】

1. 推拿治疗耳聋具有增加脑血流量，改善病损听神经组织的血氧供应，使血管弹性增强，血流阻力减少而产生恢复听神经功能的作用，有一定疗效。但对鼓膜损伤致听力完全丧失者疗效不佳。

2. 引起耳聋的原因十分复杂，在治疗中应明确诊断，配合原发病的治疗。颈性耳聋可参见颈椎病章节。

3. 生活规律和精神调节对耳聋患者的健康具有重要意义，应避免劳倦，调适情绪，保持耳道清洁。

7.2.14 郁证

郁证是由于情志抑郁，气机郁滞所引起的疾病总称。以心情抑郁、情绪不宁，胸部满闷，胁肋胀痛，或易怒易哭，或咽中如有异物梗阻等为主要症状。

郁证的范围相当广泛，包括由于外感六淫，情志不舒，以及饮食、痰浊积滞所引起的脏腑功能不调，可出现血瘀、痰结、食积、火郁等证。与西医学神经官能症中神经衰弱、癔病、反应性精神病以及更年期综合征等，大致属于本证范畴。推拿治疗主要是因情志不舒、气机郁滞所引起的气郁证。

【临床表现】

1. 肝气郁结 精神抑郁，胸闷，善太息，胸胁胀痛，或痛无定处，不思饮食，或腹痛呕吐，或嗳气频频，大便不调，苔薄白略腻、脉弦紧。

2. 气郁化火 性情急躁易怒，胸胁胀满，口苦而干，或头痛、目赤、耳鸣，或嘈杂吞酸，大便秘结，舌红，苔黄，脉弦数。

3. 气滞痰郁 精神抑郁，咽中作梗，如有炙脔，咯之不出，吞之不下，胸胁胀闷，苔薄白，脉弦滑。

4. 心神失养 烦闷忧郁、精神恍惚，甚至哭笑无常，时时欠伸，苔薄白，脉弦细。

5. 心脾两虚 多思善虑,头晕神疲,心悸胆怯,失眠健忘,食少纳呆,面色不华,舌质淡,苔薄白,脉细。

6. 心肾阴虚 头晕耳鸣,心悸少寐,心烦易怒,腰腿酸软,男子遗精,妇女月事不调,舌质红少苔,脉弦细数。

【诊断要点】

1. 精神症状以情感高涨或低落为主,伴有思维奔逸或迟滞。
2. 病程呈发作性特点,间歇期精神状态基本正常。
3. 躯体、神经系统和实验室检查一般无阳性所见。

【推拿治疗】

1. 治疗原则 疏肝理气,解郁化痰。

2. 取穴及部位 肝俞、脾俞、胃俞、章门、期门;背部、胁肋部、腹部。

3. 操作

(1) 患者俯卧位,医生用滚法在背腰部脊柱两侧膀胱经施术,时间约5分钟;用一指禅推法或指按、揉肝俞、脾俞、胃俞,每穴约2分钟。

(2) 患者取仰卧位,医生用指按、揉章门、期门各1分钟左右;用指、掌摩胁肋、腹部各约3分钟。

4. 辨证治疗

(1) 肝气郁结:用点法或按法在太冲、行间处施术,每穴约2分钟;搓胁肋1分钟左右。

(2) 气郁化火:用点法或按法在胆俞、三焦俞处施术,每穴约2分钟;用拿法拿大腿内侧肌肉约5分钟。

(3) 气滞痰郁:用点法或按法在肺俞、胆俞、天突穴施术,每穴约2分钟;掌揉中脘穴约3分钟。

(4) 心神失养:指按揉心俞、足三里,每穴约2分钟;用拿法拿下肢内侧和前侧的肌肉,约5分钟。

(5) 心脾两虚:指按揉心俞、内关、外关、足三里,每穴约1分钟;掌揉中脘穴3分钟左右。

(6) 心肾阴虚:指按揉肾俞、气海、关元、三阴交,每穴约2分钟;擦涌泉穴,以透热为度。

【注意事项】

1. 郁证多由情志所伤,故在治疗中,必须注意精神治疗,正确地引导患者,减少忧思郁虑。
2. 保持室内安静,禁止喧哗,病室光线宜暗,避免强烈光线刺激。
3. 饮食以蔬菜和营养丰富的鱼、瘦肉、乳类、豆制品为宜,忌食辛辣、烟酒,少食肥甘厚味。
4. 注意劳逸结合,保证有充足的睡眠时间。

7.2.15 月经不调

月经不调是一种常见的妇科疾病,是女性月经周期出现异常的总称。本病以月经周期、经期、经量、经色、经质的异常为主要特点,包括月经先期、月经后期或月经先后不定期。临床上称月经先期者为月经周期提前了7天,甚至一月两至者,又称"经早",月经后期为月经周期延后7天,甚至四、五十日一至者,又称"经迟",月经先后不定期为月经不按周期来潮,或提前或延后7天以上者,又称"经乱"。

现代医学认为体内雌激素分泌失调、植物神经功能紊乱、精神刺激、寒冷疲劳和某些全身性疾病等,都可以导致此病的发生。

【临床表现】

月经不调主要表现在月经的周期、经量、经色、经质等方面的异常。周期的紊乱表现为月经的先期、后期、先后不定期、经期缩短或延长;经量的异常表现为月经过多或过少;经色的异常则可表现为月经粘稠或清稀、有瘀血块及气味臭秽等;还可兼有少腹不适,胀满疼痛,乳房或胁肋胀痛及头痛、恶心、呕吐、二便不调等症。

1. 经早 月经先期而至,甚则一月经行二次。实热症者可见量多,色紫而粘稠心胸烦闷,苔薄黄,脉浮数;阴虚血热者见量少色红,面赤,手足心热,舌红苔黄,脉细数;肝郁化热者可见经血夹有瘀血块,胸胁、乳房及少腹胀痛,烦躁易怒,脉弦;气虚者则见月经量少色淡,质清稀,神疲气短心悸、小腹坠胀感,舌质淡,苔薄脉虚等症。

2. 经迟 月经周期延后。实寒者见月经量少色黯红,小腹绞痛,得热则痛减,面青肢冷,舌苔薄白,脉沉紧;虚寒者见月经量少色淡,腹痛喜按喜暖,面色苍白,舌淡苔白,脉沉迟无力;气郁者见量少小腹胀痛,精神郁闷,胸胁痞满不舒,嗳气则痛减,舌苔黄,脉弦涩;血虚者则见小腹空痛,面色萎黄,皮肤不润,心悸眼花,舌淡苔薄,脉虚细弱。

3. 经乱 经期或先或后。肝郁者见经行不畅,胸胁、乳房、小腹胀痛,精神抑郁,胸闷不舒,善太息,脉弦;肾虚者则见经量少,色淡质清稀,面色晦暗,头晕耳鸣,腰膝酸软,夜尿频多,舌淡苔薄,脉沉弱。

【诊断要点】

1. 经早 月经周期提前7天以上,甚至半月余一行,连续两个月经周期以上。

2. 经迟 月经周期超过35天,连续两个月经周期以上。妇科检查,B超或气腹造影,以排除子宫及卵巢器质性疾病。

3. 经乱 月经周期或前或后,均逾7天以上,并连续两个月经周期以上。妇科检查及B超等排除器质性病变。测基础体温,阴道涂片、宫颈粘液结晶检查以了解卵巢功能情况。

【推拿治疗】

1. 治疗原则 调和气血,疏肝理气。

2. 取穴及部位 关元、气海、中极、脾俞、肝俞、肾俞、三阴交、太冲、太溪,腹部、腰背部、下肢部。

3. 操作

(1)患者取仰卧位。医生用一指禅推法或揉法于气海、关元,中极等穴,每穴约1分钟,以得气为度,然后用摩法顺时针方向摩小腹治疗,时间约10分钟。

(2)患者取俯卧位。医生用一指禅推法施术于背部两侧膀胱经,重点在脾俞、肝俞、肾俞等处,时间约3~5分钟;然后用按、揉法于脾俞、肝俞、肾俞等穴,每穴约1分钟,以得气为度。

(3) 患者取仰卧位,医生用双手拇指按、揉三阴交、太冲、太溪等穴,每穴约1分钟,以酸胀为度。

4. 辨证加减

(1) 血热:用拇指按揉法施术于大敦、行间、隐白、三阴交、解溪、血海等穴,每穴操作约1分钟,以得气为度;或用拇指或食指、中指按揉肝俞、胃俞、大肠俞,操作3~5分钟。

(2) 血寒:用掌按法施术于神阙穴,持续按压3~5分钟,使患者下腹部出现发热感;然后用掌擦法,施术于背部督脉和肾俞、命门部位,反复摩擦1~2分钟,以皮肤透热为度。

(3) 气血虚:在患者腹部用掌按法,施术于患者中脘、气海,每穴持续按压3分钟,使腹部出现发热感,然后用拇指按揉足三里、三阴交,每穴约3分钟,以得气为度,然后用拇指按揉法施术于脾俞、胃俞,每穴操作1分钟;最后用掌擦法施术于背部脾胃俞,以透热为度。

(4) 肝郁:用拇指按揉法施术于章门、期门穴约2分钟;然后用拇指按揉膈俞、肝俞,操作3~5分钟。

(5) 肾虚:用指按法施术于关元穴,操作3~5分钟,以热深透下腹为度;然后用拇指按揉双侧涌泉穴,持续施术1分钟,然后沿足底纵轴用掌擦法,反复摩擦,以透热为度;最后用擦法施术于背部督脉和足太阳膀胱经两侧,反复摩擦5~7遍,然后擦肾俞、命门、白环俞,以透热为度。

【注意事项】

1. 推拿宜在经期前后进行。注意调节饮食,避免暴饮暴食,或过食肥甘厚味、生冷寒凉、辛辣之品。

2. 注意气候环境的变化,不要着凉,但亦不宜过热。

3. 保持心情舒畅,避免情志过极,扰及冲任而发本病。

4. 注意休息,不宜过度疲劳,避免房劳过度。

思考题

- 试述颈椎病、急性腰扭伤、慢性腰肌劳损、腰椎间盘突出症、梨状肌综合征、腰背肌筋膜炎、肩关节周围炎、膝关节侧副韧带损伤的诊断和推拿治疗。
- 试述胃脘痛、便秘、头痛、失眠、更年期综合征、郁证、月经不调的诊断和推拿治疗。

8 小儿常见疾病推拿治疗

8.1 小儿推拿基本手法

8.1.1 推法

用拇指或食、中二指指面附着于施术部位或穴位上进行直线或环旋移动的方法称推法。根据施术方向的不同可分为直推法、旋推法、分推法、合推法等。

【操作方法】

直推法 用拇指桡侧或指面,或食、中二指指面在穴位上作直线推动(图8-1)。

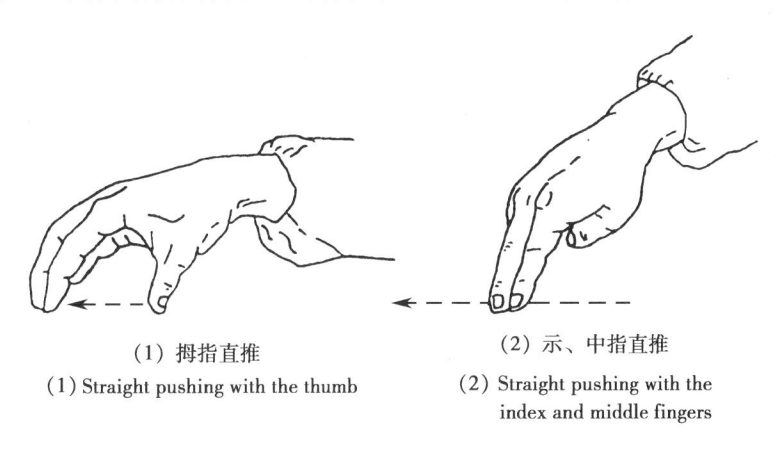

(1) 拇指直推
(1) Straight pushing with the thumb

(2) 示、中指直推
(2) Straight pushing with the index and middle fingers

图 8-1 直推法
Fig. 8-1 Straight pushing manipulation

旋推法 以拇指指面在穴位上作顺时针或逆时针方向的旋转推动(图8-2)。

分推法 用两手拇指桡侧或指面,或食、中二指指面自穴位两旁分向推动,或作"八"字形推动称分推法(图8-3)。

合推法 医者双手拇指伸直,四指分开,用拇指罗纹面或手掌面紧贴治疗部位,分别自穴位两旁向中间合向推动(图8-4)。

【动作要领】

直推法 术者肩、肘、腕关节放松,伸直拇指或食、中二指。用拇指桡侧缘做直推法时主要依靠拇指做主动的内收或外展活动,用食、中指指面做直推法主要依靠肘关节的屈伸活动。动作要求轻快连续,频率约每分钟200次左右。

旋推法 术者肩、肘、腕关节放松,以拇指指面在皮肤表面摩擦,不带动皮下组织,

图 8-2 旋推法
Fig. 8-2　Rotational pushing manipulation

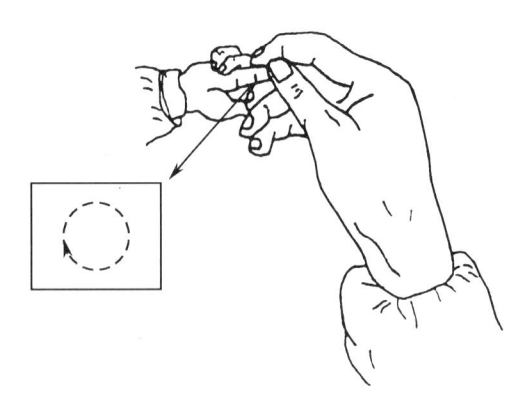

图 8-3　分推法
Fig. 8-3　Separate-pushing manipulation

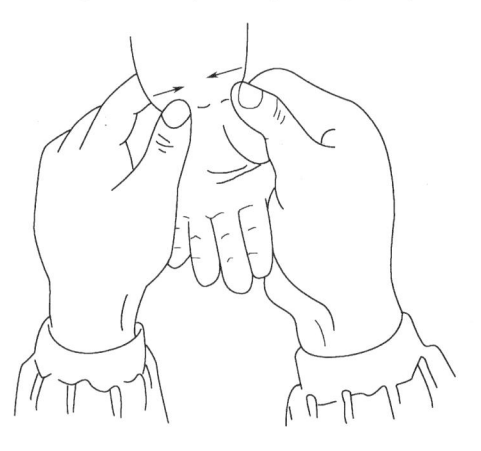

用力均匀柔和，频率每分钟约 160～200 次。

分推法　两手向两旁分推时用力要均匀、柔和，动作应轻快并协调一致。操作时既可作直线移动，也可顺体表作弧形移动，频率为 120～160 次/分。

合推法　合推法的动作与分推法相似，只是推动方向相反，推动幅度较小。

【注意事项】

1. 做直推法时，注意手法的方向、轻重、快慢，以期获得补、泻的不同。

2. 为防止推伤小儿皮肤和增加疗效，应适当加用介质如葱汁、姜汁、麻油等。

3. 推法操作要用力均匀，操作平稳。

图 8-4　合推法
Fig. 8-4　Combined pushing manipulation

8.1.2　揉法

以中指或拇指罗纹面、或鱼际部，吸定于一定部位或穴位上，作环转运动的手法为揉法。根据施术部位的不同可分为中指揉法、拇指揉法、鱼际揉法等。

【操作方法】

1. 指揉法　单指、双指或三指指面或指端吸定于治疗部位或穴位上，带动皮下组织，作轻柔、小幅度的环转运动。

2. 掌根揉法　以掌根吸附于治疗部位上，腕部放松，稍用力下压，以肘关节为支点，前臂作主动运动，带动着力部位作轻柔、小幅度的环旋揉动。

3. 鱼际揉法　以大鱼际部着力于施术部位，腕部放松，前臂主动运动，通过腕关节带动该处皮肤作轻快柔和的环旋运动。

【动作要领】

1. 术者肩、肘、腕关节放松，手指自然伸开。

2. 用力持续、均匀、协调而有节奏性,作到旋而不滞,转而不乱。
3. 揉法的幅度由小到大,力量由轻渐重,频率为每分钟 200~300 次。

【注意事项】
1. 手法操作用力柔和,着力点吸定,严禁出现局部滑动或摩擦。
2. 揉法不可用力按压。

8.1.3 按法

以手指或手掌在一定部位或穴位上逐渐用力,向下按压,称为按法。根据不同的治疗部位,分为指按法、掌按法。

【操作方法】

1. 掌按法 腕关节背伸,五指伸直放松,用掌面或掌根着力于治疗部位,垂直用力,向下按压,持续一定时间,然后放松,再逐渐用力向下按压,如此反复操作。

2. 指按法 用拇指或中指罗纹面为着力部,垂直用力,向下按压。余同掌按法。

【动作要领】
1. 气沉丹田,自然呼吸,不可屏气用力。
2. 按而不动,用力平稳,力量逐渐由轻到重。

【注意事项】
1. 按而留之,不宜突然松手,忌粗暴施力。
2. 掌按法接触面积大,按压力稍重而刺激要缓和。
3. 指按法接触面积较小,刺激要轻柔。

8.1.4 摩法

以手掌或食、中、无名指指面附着于一定部位或穴位上,以腕关节连同前臂作顺时针或逆时针方向环形运动,称为摩法。

【操作方法】

1. 掌摩法 指掌自然伸直,腕关节微背伸,用掌面着力,轻附于治疗部位上,腕关节放松,前臂主动运动,手掌随腕关节连同前臂作顺时针或逆时针方向的环形摩动。

2. 指摩法 食指、中指、无名指、小指四指并拢伸直,腕部微悬屈,以指面着力于治疗部位或穴位上,前臂主动运动,通过腕关节带动作环形摩动。

【动作要领】
1. 肩、肘、腕关节放松,肘关节微屈。
2. 掌摩时,腕部放松,手掌自然伸直;指摩时,腕部微悬屈,掌指关节微屈。
3. 操作时,用力应自然,动作缓和协调,摩动频率约为每分钟 120~160 次。

【注意事项】
1. 在操作过程中应避免带动皮下组织。
2. 手指应随手法一起做环形运动,不能出现冲击敲打动作。

8.1.5 掐法

用拇指指甲着力,按压穴位或一定部位的手法,称掐法。

【操作方法】

医者手握空拳,拇指伸直,以拇指指甲着力,吸定在治疗的穴位或部位上,逐渐用力进行重按切掐(图 8-5)。

【动作要领】

1. 操作时,应垂直用力,力量逐渐加重,也可间歇性用力以增强刺激,取穴宜准。

2. 操作次数一般掌握在 3~5 次,或中病即止,不宜反复长期使用;若用于急救则用力要重,以患儿清醒为度。

【注意事项】

掐法是强刺激手法之一,不宜反复长时间应用,施术时为避免刺破皮肤,可在施术部位上置一薄布。掐后常继用揉法,以缓和刺激,减轻局部的疼痛或不适感。

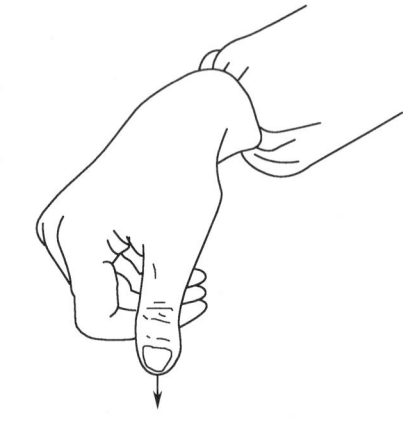

图 8-5　掐法
Fig. 8-5　Qia Fa(Nipping manipulation)

8.1.6 捏法

以双手拇指与食、中、环三指指腹为着力部,夹持住患儿的肌肤或肢体,相对用力挤压做连续的交替提拿动作,称捏法。

【操作方法】

小儿捏法以捏脊法为主:

1. 三指捏　用拇指指面顶住皮肤,食、中两指前按,三指同时对称用力提拿,双手一紧一松交替挤压,移动向前(图 8-6)。

2. 两指捏　食指屈曲,以中节指骨桡侧面顶住皮肤,拇指前按,两指同时对称用力提捏,双手交替移动向前(图 8-7)。

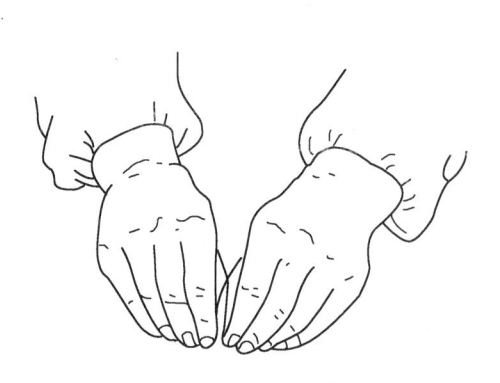

图 8-6　三指捏法
Fig. 8-6　Three-finger pinching

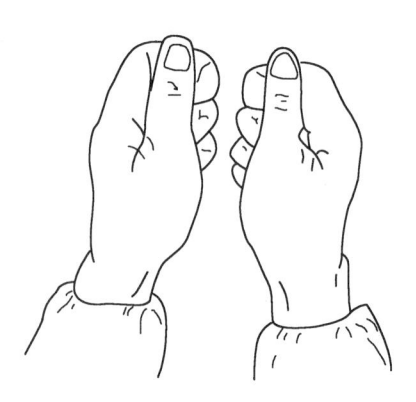

图 8-7　两指捏法
Fig. 8-7　Two-finger pinching

【动作要领】

1. 前臂静止发力,以腕关节活动为主,带动掌指关节作连续灵活轻快的捻转活动。

2. 手法操作顺序是:先捏住皮肤,再提起、捻动、推移,再捏住皮肤,进行下一循环的动作,周而复始,连绵不断。

3. 移动缓慢,用力柔和,动作要灵活,均匀而有节律性。

【注意事项】

1. 动作不可断续、跳跃,捏起皮肤多少及捏拿的力量要适当。

2. 捏动时不可拧转、用指甲掐压皮肤,捻动向前时,要作直线前进,不可歪斜。

8.1.7 运法

以拇指或中指罗纹面在一定穴位上由此至彼作弧形或环形推动的手法,称运法。

【操作方法】

用拇指或中指的罗纹面,轻附于治疗部位,作由此穴向彼穴的弧形推动,或在穴位周围作周而复始的环形推动(图8-8)。

【动作要领】

1. 腕部自然伸平,拇指伸直,余指屈曲,虎口张开;以拇指端桡侧着力,或拇、食、环、小指屈曲,中指伸直,以中指端着力。

2. 以拇指掌指关节或腕关节为主,带动拇指或中指端作弧形或环形移动。

3. 手法宜轻不宜重,操作时仅有皮肤表面的摩擦感,频率一般每分钟80~120次。

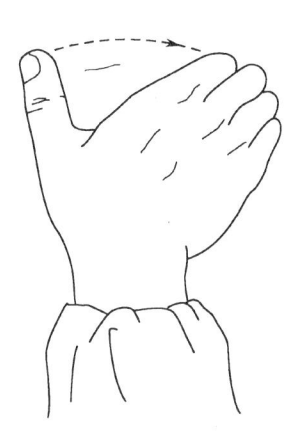

图8-8 运法
Fig. 8-8 Yun Fa(Circularly pushing Manipulation)

【注意事项】

1. 操作时,勿带动深层组织,其用力较推法和摩法都轻。

2. 操作时可配合使用润滑剂作为介质,以保护患儿皮肤。

8.1.8 捣法

用中指端或屈曲的食、中指的指间关节着力,做有节奏的叩击穴位的手法,称为捣法。

【操作方法】

肩、肘、腕放松,指端对准穴位,以腕关节带动叩击,击打后立即抬起,一般捣5~20次(图8-9)。

【注意事项】

1. 操作时指间关节要放松,腕关节主动屈伸。

2. 捣击时位置要准确,用力要有弹性。

3. 捣击时不要用暴力,操作前要剪指甲,以免损伤小儿皮肤。

(1)　　　　　　　　　　　　　　(2)

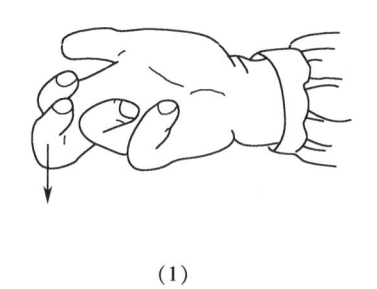

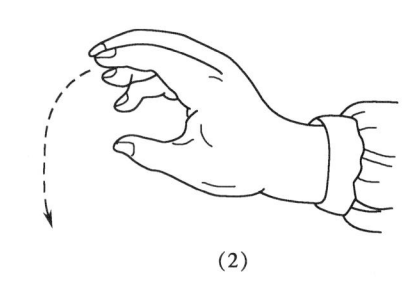

图 8-9　捣法

Fig. 8-9　Dao Fa(Pounding Manipulation)

8.2　小儿复式操作手法

8.2.1　黄蜂入洞

【操作方法】

以一手轻扶患儿头部,使患儿头部相对固定,另一手食、中指的指端着力,紧贴在患儿两鼻孔下缘处,以腕关节主动运动,带动着力部分作反复揉动 50～100 次(图 8-10)。

【作用】

发汗解表,宣肺通窍。用于治疗外感风寒的发热无汗及急慢性鼻炎的鼻塞、呼吸不畅等病症。

图 8-10　黄蜂入洞

Fig. 8-10　Huang Feng Ru Dong (Wasp Entering the Hole)

8.2.2　双凤展翅

【操作方法】

医者先用两手食指、中指,夹患儿两耳,并向上提 3～5 次后,再用一手或两手拇指端,按、掐眉心、太阳、听会、人中、承浆、颊车诸穴,每穴按、掐各 3～5 次(图 8-11)。

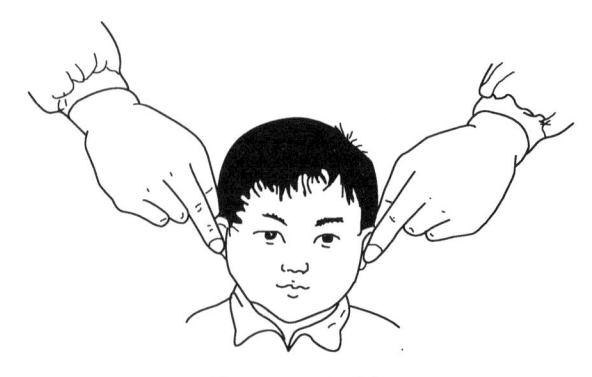

图 8-11　双凤展翅

Fig. 8-11　Shuang Feng Zhan Chi(Two Phoenixes Spreading Their Wings)

【作用】

祛风散寒,温肺通经,止咳化痰。用于外感风寒,咳嗽多痰等上呼吸道疾患。

8.2.3 按弦走搓摩

【操作方法】

患儿坐位或家长将患儿抱坐怀中,将患儿两手交叉搭在对侧肩上,医者坐于患儿身后。用双手掌面着力,轻贴在患儿两侧胁肋部,呈对称性搓摩,并自上而下搓摩至肚角处 50~500 次(图 8-12)。

【作用】

理气化痰,健脾消食。用于治疗痰积,胸胁不畅,咳嗽气喘,腹痛、腹胀、饮食积滞等病症。

8.2.4 猿猴摘果

【操作方法】

患儿坐位或仰卧位,医者坐其身前。用两手拇指、食指捏患儿螺蛳骨上皮,一扯一放,反复多次(图 8-13)。

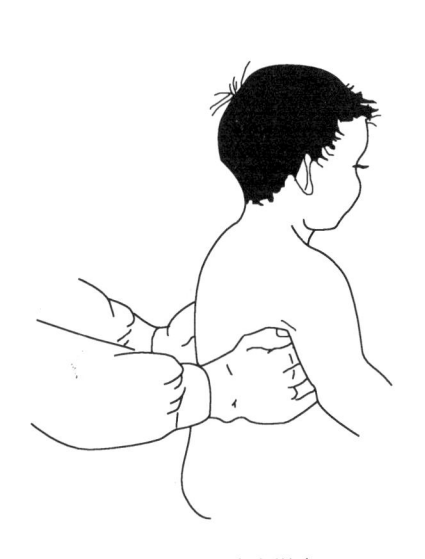

图 8-12 按弦走搓摩
Fig.8-12 An Xuan Zou Cuo Mo (Twisting and Rubbing like Plucking the String)

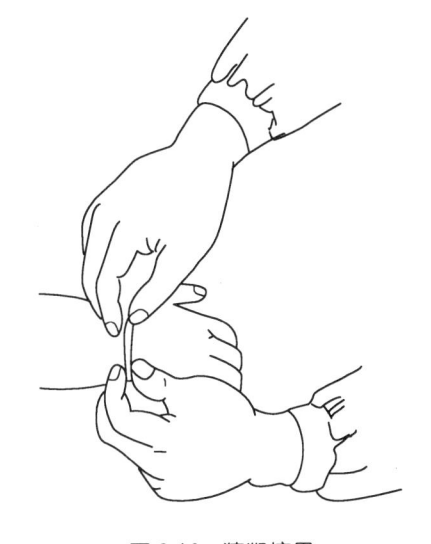

图 8-13 猿猴摘果
Fig. 8-13 Yuan Hou Zhai Guo (Manipulation of Ape Picking Fruits)

【作用】

健脾化痰。用于治疗食积、寒痰、寒热往来等病症。

8.2.5 水底捞月

【操作方法】

患儿坐位或仰卧位,医者坐其身前。用一手握住患儿四指,将掌面向上,用冷水滴入患儿掌心,用另一手拇指罗纹面着力,紧贴患儿掌心并作旋推法,后自小指根沿手掌边缘经坎宫运至内劳宫,边推边用口对其掌心吹凉气,反复操作 3～5 分钟(图 8-14)。

【作用】

本法大寒大凉,有清热凉血、宁心除烦之功。用于治疗高热神昏、热入营血,烦躁不安,便秘等实热病症。

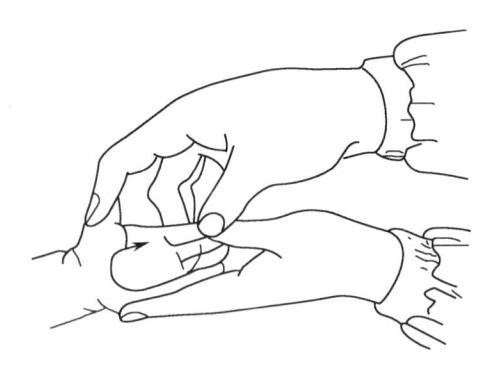

图 8-14 水底捞月

Fig. 8-14 Shui Di Lao Yue(Scooping the Moon from the Bottom of Water)

8.2.6 打马过天河

【操作方法】

患儿坐位或仰卧位,医者坐其前。用一手捏住患儿四指,将掌心向上,用另一手的中指指面运内劳宫后,再用食指、中指、无名指三指由总筋起沿天河水弹打至洪池穴,弹击约 20～30 次(图 8-15)。

【作用】

清热凉血通络,用于治疗高热烦躁,神昏谵语,上肢麻木抽搐等病症。

8.2.7 运土入水

【操作方法】

患儿坐位或仰卧位,医者坐其身前。用一手握住患儿食指、中指、无名指、小指四指,使掌面向上,另一手拇指外侧缘着力,自患儿脾土穴推起,沿手掌边缘,经小天心、掌小横纹,推运至小指端肾水穴止,呈单方向反复推运 100～300 次左右(图 8-16)。

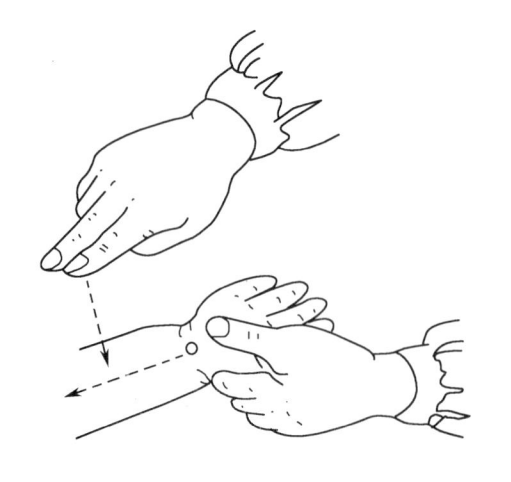

图 8-15 打马过天河

Fig. 8-15 Da Ma Guo Tian He(Beating the Horse to Cross the Heaven River)

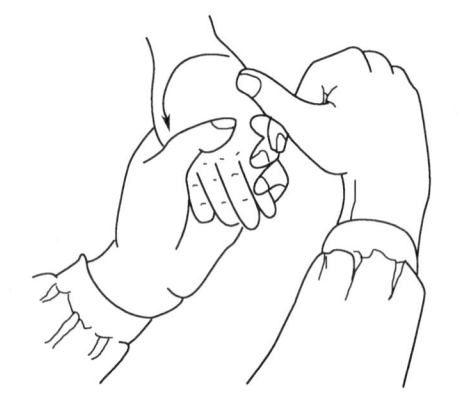

图 8-16 运土入水

Fig. 8-16 Yun Tu Ru Shui (Carrying Earth into Water)

【作用】

清脾胃湿热,利尿止泻,滋补肾水。用于治疗小便赤涩,频数,小腹胀满,泄泻等病症。

8.2.8 运水入土

【操作方法】

患儿坐位或仰卧位,医者坐其身前。用一手握住患儿食指、中指、无名指、小指四指,使掌面向上,另一手拇指外侧缘着力,自患儿肾水穴推起,沿手掌边缘,经掌横纹、小天心,推运至拇指端脾土穴止,呈单方向反复推运 100～300 次左右(图 8-17)。

图 8-17 运水入土

Fig. 8-17 Yun Shui Ru Tu(Carrying Water into Earth)

【作用】

健脾助运,润燥通便。用于治疗脾胃虚弱引起的消化不良、食欲不振、便秘、腹胀、泄泻等病症。

8.3 小儿推拿特定穴

小儿推拿特定穴是指小儿推拿特有的穴位(图 8-18、8-19、8-20),这些穴位不仅

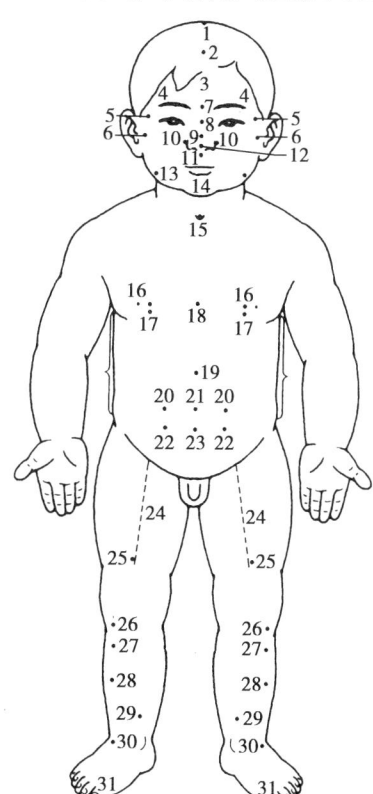

图 8-18 正面穴位图

Fig.8-18 Points on the front of the body

1. 百会 Baihui(GV 20) 2. 囟门 Xinmen 3. 攒竹 Cuanzhu 4. 坎宫 Kangong 5. 太阳 Taiyang(EX-HN 5) 6. 耳门 Ermen 7. 眉心 Meixin 8. 山根 Shangen 9. 延年 Yannian 10. 迎香 Yingxiang(LI 20) 11. 人中 Renzhong(GV 26) 12. 准头 Zhuntou 13. 牙关 Yaguan 14. 承浆 Chengjiang(CV 24) 15. 天突 Tiantu(CV 22) 16. 乳旁 Rupang 17. 乳根 Rugen(ST 18) 18. 膻中 Danzhong(CV 17) 19. 中脘 Zhongwan(CV 12) 20. 天枢 Tianshu(ST 25) 21. 脐(神阙)Qi(Shenque,CV 8) 22. 肚角 Dujiao 23. 丹田 Dantian(Elixir Field) 24. 箕门 Jimen 25. 百虫(血海)Baichong(Xuehai,SP 10) 26. 膝眼 Xiyan(EX-LE 5) 27. 足三里 Zusanli(ST 36) 28. 前承山 Qianchengshan 29. 三阴交 Sanyinjiao(SP 6) 30. 解溪 Jiexi(ST 41) 31. 大敦 Dadun(LR 1)

图 8-19 背面穴位图

Fig.8-19 Points on the back of the body

1. 耳后高骨 Erhougaogu 2. 肩井 Jianjing(GB 21) 3. 十宣 Shixuan(EX-UE 11) 4. 天柱骨 Tianzhugu 5. 大椎 Dazhui(GV 14) 6. 风门 Fengmen(BL 12) 7. 肺俞 Feishu(BL 13) 8. 脊 Ji(Spine) 9. 脾俞 Pishu(BL 20) 10. 肾俞 Shenshu(BL 23) 11. 腰俞 Yaoshu(GV 2) 12. 七节骨 Qijiegu 13. 龟尾 Guiwei 14. 委中 Weizhong(BL 40) 15. 丰隆 Fenglong(ST 40) 16. 后承山 Houchengshan 17. 昆仑 Kunlun(BL 60) 18. 仆参 Pucan(BL 61) 19. 涌泉 Yongquan(KI 1)

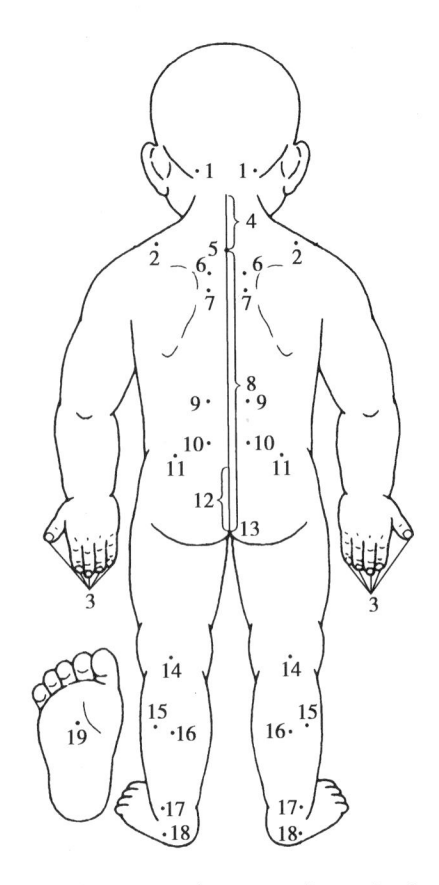

有"点"状、还有"线"状及"面"状,且以两手居多,正所谓"小儿百脉汇于两掌"。为了便于学习及应用,其中"次数"一项,仅做6个月～1周岁患儿,在临床应用时参考。临诊时还要根据患儿年龄大小,身体强弱,病情轻重等情况而有所增减。上肢部特定穴位,一般不分男女,习惯于推拿左手。小儿推拿操作的顺序,一般是先头面,次上肢,再胸腹、腰背,最后是下肢。亦可根据患儿病情轻重缓急或体位,灵活掌握。

8.3.1 坎宫

定位:自眉头起沿眉向眉梢成一横线。

操作:两拇指自眉心向眉梢作分推,称推坎宫,又称推眉弓。30～50次。

作用:疏风解表,醒脑明目,止头痛。

主治:外感头痛、发热、目赤痛、惊风、近视等。

应用:常用于外感发热、头痛,多与推攒竹、揉太阳等合用;若用于治疗目赤痛,多与清肝经、掐揉小天心、清天河水等合用。

8.3.2 天门

定位:两眉中间至前发际成一直线。

操作:两拇指末节面自下而上交替直推,称开天门,又称推攒竹。30～50次。

作用:发汗解表,镇静安神,开窍醒神。

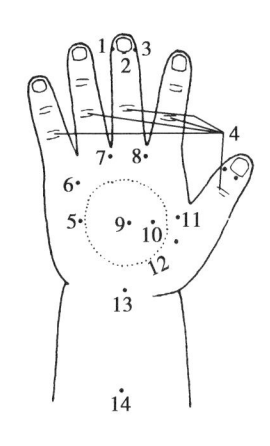

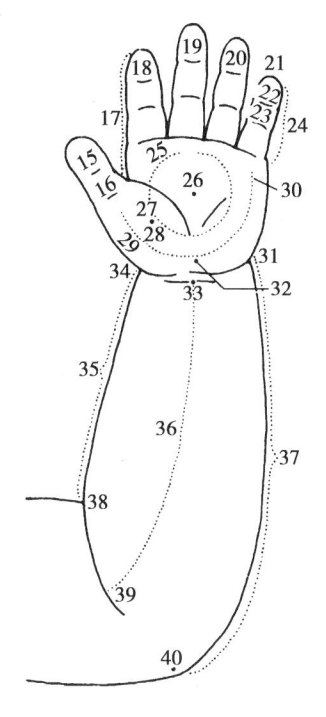

图 8-20 上肢穴位图
Fig.8-20 Points on the upper limbs

1. 右端正 Youduanzheng 2. 老龙 Laolong 3. 左端正 Zuoduanzheng 4. 五指节 Wuzhijie 5. 精宁 Jingning 6. 二马 Erma 7,8. 二扇门 Ershanmen 9. 外劳宫 Wailaogong 10. 威灵 Weiling 11. 合谷 Hegu(LI 4) 12. 外八卦 Waibagua 13. 一窝风 Yiwofeng 14. 膊阳池 Boyangchi 15. 脾经 Pijing 16. 胃经 Weijing 17. 大肠 Dachang 18. 肝经 Ganjing 19. 心经 Xinjing 20. 肺经 Feijing 21. 肾顶 Shending 22. 肾经 Shenjing 23. 肾纹 Shenwen 24. 小肠 Xiaochang 25. 内八卦 Neibagua 26. 内劳宫 Neilaogong(PC 8) 27. 板门 Banmen 28. 运水入土 Yunshuirutu 29. 运土入水 Yunturushui 30. 掌小横纹 Zhangxiaohengwen 31. 阴池 Yinchi 32. 小天心 Xiaotianxin 33. 总筋 Zongjin 34. 阳池 Yangchi 35. 三关 Sanguan 36. 天河水 Tianheshui 37. 六腑 Liufu(the Six Fu-Organs) 38. 曲池 Quchi(LI 11) 39. 洪池 Hongchi 40. 抖肘 Douzhou

主治：头痛、感冒、头晕、夜啼、失眠等。

应用：常用于风寒感冒，头痛、无汗、发热等症，多与推坎宫、揉太阳等合用；若惊惕不安，烦躁不宁多与清肝经、捣小天心、掐揉五指节、揉百会等合用。

8.3.3 太阳

定位：眉后凹陷处。

操作：用中指端或拇指端揉之，称揉太阳或运太阳；向眼前方向揉为补，向耳后方向揉为泻。以拇指桡侧由前向后直推，称推太阳。各30～50次。

作用：解表、明目、止头痛。

主治：头痛、头晕、感冒、发热、目赤痛。

应用:外感表实头痛用泻法;外感表虚、内伤头痛用补法;推太阳主要用于外感发热等。

8.3.4 耳后高骨

定位:耳后入发际高骨下凹陷中。
操作:两拇指或中指端揉之,称揉耳后高骨。30~50次。
作用:疏风解表,安神除烦。
主治:头痛、烦躁不安、感冒等。
应用:感冒头痛(风寒表实证),本穴常配合开天门、推坎宫、揉太阳一起使用,以上四穴惯称为小儿推拿四大手法。

8.3.5 天柱骨

定位:颈后发际正中至大椎穴成一直线。
操作:用拇指或食、中指末节面自上向下直推,称推天柱骨。推100~500次。
作用:降逆止呕,祛风散寒。
主治:恶心呕吐、感冒、发热、咽痛、项僵。
应用:呕恶多与横纹推向板门、揉中脘等合用;治疗外感发热、颈项强痛,多与拿风池、掐揉二扇门等同用。

8.3.6 乳根

定位:乳下2分。
操作:中指端揉,称揉乳根。20~50次。
作用:宽胸理气,止咳化痰。
主治:胸闷、咳喘、胸痛。
应用:见乳旁穴。

8.3.7 乳旁

定位:乳外旁开2分。
操作:中指端揉,称揉乳旁。20~50次。
作用:宽胸理气,止咳化痰。
主治:胸闷、痰鸣、咳嗽、呕吐。
应用:主要治疗胸闷、咳嗽、痰鸣、呕吐等症。临床上常用乳根、乳旁两穴配用,以食、中两指端同时操作。

8.3.8 胁肋

定位:从腋下两胁至天枢处。
操作:以两手掌从两胁腋下搓摩至天枢处,称搓摩胁肋。50~100次。
作用:顺气化痰,除胸闷。
主治:胸闷、痰喘气急、胁痛等。

应用:本穴性开而降,多用于小儿由于食积、痰壅、气逆所致的胸闷、腹胀等。

8.3.9 腹

定位:腹部。

操作:沿肋弓角边缘或自中脘至脐两旁作分向推动,称分推腹阴阳;以掌或四指摩称摩腹(图8-21)。分推100～200次;摩3～5分钟。

作用:健脾和胃,理气消食。

主治:腹泻、腹胀、腹痛、便秘、恶心呕吐等。

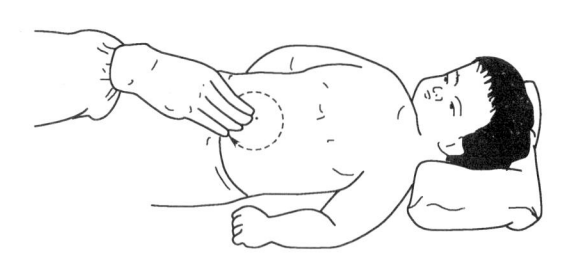

图8-21 摩腹
Fig. 8-21 Rubbing Abdomen

应用:对于小儿泄泻、便秘、腹胀、厌食等实证,应做顺时针摩揉腹部(泻法);脾虚泄泻等虚证用逆时针操作(补法);摩腹常与捏脊、按揉足三里合用;伤食呕吐者,分推腹阴阳为主,配合横纹推向板门、推天柱骨等使用。另外,本穴还常作为小儿保健穴。

8.3.10 脐

定位:肚脐。

操作:用指摩或掌摩称摩脐;拇指端或中指端或掌根揉,称揉脐。揉100～300次;摩3～5分钟。

作用:逆时针摩揉之能温阳散寒、补益气血;顺时针则消食导滞通便等。

主治:腹痛、便秘、腹胀、食积、泄泻等。

应用:临床上揉脐多与摩腹、推上七节骨、揉龟尾配合应用。逆时针摩揉肚脐用于小儿泄泻、肠鸣腹痛等虚证、寒证;顺时针摩揉之用于小儿便秘、腹胀等实证。

8.3.11 丹田

定位:小腹部,或脐下2寸与3寸之间。

操作:揉法或摩法,称揉丹田或摩丹田。揉50～100次;摩3～5分钟。

作用:培肾固本,温补下元,分清别浊。

主治:遗尿、腹痛等。

应用:多用于小儿先天不足,寒凝少腹及腹痛、遗尿等症,常与补肾经、推三关、揉外劳等合用。

8.3.12 肚角

定位:脐下2寸(石门)旁开2寸大筋。

操作:用拇、食、中三指作拿法,称拿肚角;或用中指端按,称按肚角。3～5次。

作用:止腹痛。

主治:腹痛、泄泻。

应用:对各种原因引起的腹痛均可应用,特别是对寒痛、伤食痛效果更好。为防止患儿哭闹影响手法的进行,可在诸手法推毕,再拿此穴。

8.3.13 肺俞

定位:第三胸椎棘突下,旁开1.5寸。

操作:一手食、中指端或两拇指端揉之,称揉肺俞;两拇指端分别自肩胛骨内缘由上而下做分向推动,称推肺俞或分推肩胛骨。揉50～100次;分推100～300次。

作用:分推肩胛骨能降肺气、止咳喘;揉肺俞则调肺气、补虚损。

主治:咳嗽、哮喘、胸闷、胸痛、痰鸣、咽痛、感冒、发热、背痛等。

应用:本穴多用于小儿呼吸系统病症,常与推揉膻中、揉乳根、揉乳旁、推肺经、运内八卦、揉天突、揉掌小横纹、推小横纹等合用。

8.3.14 脊柱

定位:大椎至长强成一直线。

操作:用捏法自下而上捏之,称为捏脊。每捏三下再将脊背皮提一下,称为捏三提一法。用食、中二指末节面自上而下做直线推动,称推脊。推100～300次,捏3～5次遍。

作用:捏脊能调阴阳、理气血、和脏腑、通经络、培元气;推脊能清热。

主治:泄泻、腹痛、呕吐、便秘、发热、夜啼等。

应用:捏脊是小儿保健常用主要穴位之一。临床上多与补脾经、补肾经、推三关、摩腹、按揉足三里等配合应用,治疗先、后天不足的一切虚弱病症,均有一定效果。本法单用名捏脊疗法。

推脊柱常用于小儿发热,多与清天河水、退六腑、推涌泉等合用。

8.3.15 七节骨

定位:第四腰椎至尾椎骨端(长强)成一直线。

操作:用拇指桡侧面或食、中二指面自下向上或自上向下作直推,分别称为推上七节骨和推下七节骨(图8-22)。推100～300次。

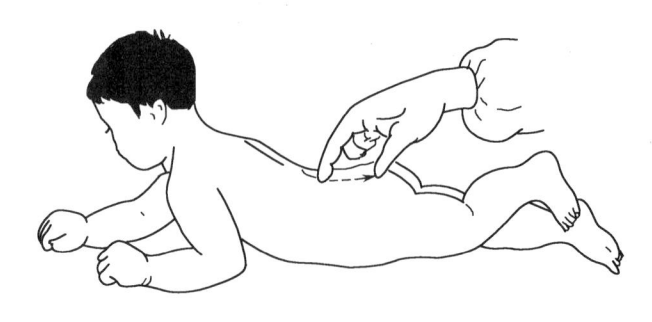

图 8-22 推下七节骨
Fig. 8-22 Pushing Qijiegu

作用:温阳止泻、泻热通便。

主治:泄泻、便秘、发热等。

应用:推上七节骨能温阳止泻。多用于虚证寒证腹泻、腹痛等症,临床上常与补大肠、推三关、按揉百会、揉丹田等合用。若属湿热泻,则不宜用本法,用后多令小儿腹胀或出现其他变症。

推下七节骨能泻热通便。多用于肠热便秘、发热等症。

8.3.16 龟尾

定位:尾椎骨端与肛门之间。

操作:拇指端或中指端揉,称揉龟尾(图8-23)。揉100～300次。

作用:调理大肠。

主治:便秘、泄泻、遗尿等。

应用:本穴即督脉经之长强穴,揉之能通调督脉之经气。穴性平和,能止泻,也能通便。多与揉脐、推七节骨配合应用,以治泄泻、便秘等症。

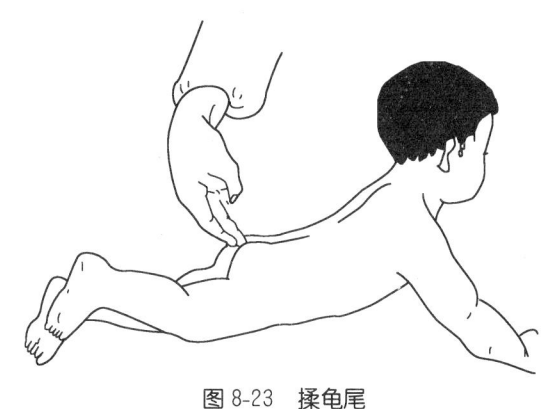

图8-23 揉龟尾
Fig. 8-23 Rubbing Guiwei

8.3.17 脾经

定位:拇指桡侧缘,指尖至指根成一线。

操作:将患儿拇指屈曲,循拇指桡侧缘向指根方向直推为补,称补脾经(图8-24)。反之为清,称清脾经。各100～500次。

作用:补脾经可健脾胃,补气血;清脾经可清热利湿,化痰止呕。

主治:泄泻、便秘、腹胀、痢疾、食欲不振、湿热黄疸等。

应用:补脾经用于脾胃虚弱,气血不足而引起的食欲不振、肌肉消瘦、消化不良等症。小儿脾胃薄弱,在一般情况下,脾经穴多用补法。

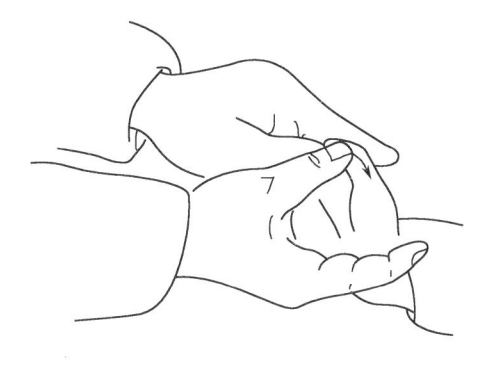

图8-24 补脾经
Fig. 8-24 Reinforcing Pijing
(spleen meridian)

8.3.18 肝经

定位:食指末节罗纹面。

操作:自指尖向指根方向直推为补,称补肝经;反之为清,称清肝经。推100～500次。

作用:清肝经能清肝泻火,熄风镇惊,解郁除烦。

主治:目赤、口苦、咽干、惊风、烦躁不安、五心发热等。

应用:清肝经常用于肝火上炎所致目赤肿痛、惊风、烦躁不安等证,常与清心经、清天河水等合用。肝经宜清不宜补,若肝虚应补时以补肾经代之,称为滋肾养肝法。

8.3.19 心经

定位:中指末节罗纹面。

操作:自指尖向指根方向直推为补,称补心经。反之为清,称清心经。推100~500次。

作用:清心经可清心泻火;补心经可养心安神。

主治:口舌生疮、小便短赤、高热神昏、手足心热等。

应用:清心经常用于心火旺盛而引起的高热神昏、面赤口疮、小便短赤等,多与清天河水、清小肠等合用。本穴宜用清法,不宜用补法,恐动心火之故。

8.3.20 肺经

定位:无名指末节罗纹面。

操作:自指尖向指根方向直推为补,称补肺经;反之为清,称清肺经。推100~500次。

作用:补肺经能补益肺气;清肺经则宣肺清热,疏风解表,化痰止咳。

主治:感冒、咳嗽、气喘痰鸣、自汗、盗汗、面白、脱肛、遗尿、大便秘结等。

应用:补肺经用于肺气虚损,咳嗽气喘,虚汗怕冷等肺经虚寒证;清肺经用于感冒发热及咳嗽、气喘、痰鸣等肺经实热证。

8.3.21 肾经

定位:小指末节罗纹面。

操作:自指根向指尖方向直推为补,称补肾经;反之为清,称清肾经。推100~500次。

作用:补肾经可补肾益脑,温养下元;清肾经可清利下焦湿热。

主治:先天不足、久病体虚、五更泄泻、遗尿、咳嗽、喘息、目赤、小便淋浊刺痛。

应用:补肾经用于先天不足、久病体虚、肾虚久泻、多尿、遗尿、虚汗喘息等症。清肾经用于膀胱蕴热,小便赤涩等症。临床上肾经穴一般多用补法,需用清法时,多以清小肠代之。

8.3.22 小肠

定位:小指尺侧边缘,自指尖到指根成一直线。

操作:自指尖直推向指根为补,称补小肠;反之为清,称清小肠。推100~300次。

作用:清热利尿,泌别清浊,滋阴补虚。

主治:小便赤涩、水泻、口舌生疮、午后潮热等。

应用:清小肠可泌清别浊,多用于小便短赤不利等症。若心经有热,移热于小肠,以本法配合清天河水,能加强清热利尿的作用。若属下焦虚寒,多尿、遗尿则宜用补小肠。

8.3.23 大肠

定位:食指桡侧缘,自食指尖至指根成一直线。

操作:从食指尖直线推向指根为补,称补大肠;反之为清,称清大肠。推 100~300 次。

作用:补大肠能温中涩肠止泻;清大肠则清热利湿通便。

主治:泄泻、痢疾、便秘、腹痛等。

应用:补大肠多用于虚寒泄泻等病症。清大肠多用于湿热、积食滞留肠道、身热腹痛、痢下赤白、湿热泄泻、大便秘结等症。

8.3.24 肾顶

定位:小指顶端。

操作:以中指或拇指端按揉,称揉肾顶。揉 100~500 次。

作用:收敛元气,固表止汗。

主治:盗汗、自汗、解颅。

应用:揉肾顶对自汗、盗汗或大汗淋漓不止等症均有一定的疗效。

8.3.25 四横纹

定位:掌面食、中、无名、小指第一指间关节横纹处。

操作:拇指甲从食指依次掐揉至小指横纹,称掐四横纹;四指并拢,从食指横纹处,推向小指横纹处,称推四横纹。掐各 3~5 次;推 100~300 次。

作用:掐之能退热除烦,散瘀结;推之能调中行气,和气血,消胀满。

主治:消化不良,腹胀腹痛,气血不和,气喘,口唇破裂。

应用:临床上多用于腹胀、气血不和、消化不良等症。常与补脾经、揉中脘等合用。也可用毫针或三棱针点刺本穴出血以治疗疳积。

8.3.26 小横纹

定位:掌面食、中、无名、小指掌指关节横纹处。

操作:以拇指甲掐,称掐小横纹;拇指侧推,称推小横纹。掐各 3~5 次;推 100~300 次。

作用:退热,消胀,散结。

主治:口唇破裂、口疮、腹胀、发热、烦躁等症。

应用:推掐本穴主要用于脾胃热结、口唇破烂及腹胀等症。临床上用推小横纹治疗肺部干性啰音久不消失者,有一定疗效。

8.3.27 掌小横纹

定位:掌面小指根下,尺侧掌纹头。

操作:中指或拇指端按揉,称揉掌小横纹。揉 100~500 次。

作用:清热散结,宽胸宣肺,化痰止咳。

主治:口舌生疮、流涎、肺炎及一切痰壅喘咳。

应用:主要用于喘咳、口舌生疮等,为治疗肺炎的要穴。临床上用揉掌小横纹配合揉上马治疗肺部湿性啰音,有一定的疗效。

8.3.28 胃经

定位:大鱼际桡侧赤白肉际处。

操作:自拇指根向掌根方向直推为补,称补胃经;反之为清,称清胃经。推100~500次。

作用:清胃经可清中焦湿热,和胃降逆,泻胃火,除烦止渴;补胃经可健脾胃,助运化。

主治:恶心呕吐、呃逆、嗳气、食欲不振、腹胀、口臭、便秘等症。

应用:清胃经多与清脾经、推天柱骨、横纹推向板门等合用,治疗脾胃湿热、胃气不和所引起的呕恶、腹胀等症;若系发热烦渴、便秘等实证,多与清大肠、退六腑、揉天枢、推下七节骨等合用。补胃经多与补脾经、揉中脘、摩腹、按揉足三里等合用,治疗脾胃虚弱、消化不良、纳呆等虚寒症。

8.3.29 板门

定位:手掌大鱼际平面。

操作:指端揉,称揉板门;用推法自指根推向腕横纹,称板门推向横纹,反之称横纹推向板门。揉30~50次,推100~300次。

作用:消食化滞,止泻,止呕。

主治:食欲不振、乳食内伤、呕吐、泄泻、腹胀、气喘、嗳气。

应用:揉板门能消食化滞。多用于乳食停积,食欲不振或嗳气、腹胀、腹泻、呕吐等症,多与顺运内八卦、摩中脘等合用。板门推向横纹能止泻;横纹推向板门能止呕吐。

8.3.30 内劳宫

定位:掌心中,屈指时中指、无名指之间中点。

操作:中指端揉,称揉内劳宫;自小指根掐运起,经掌小横纹、小天心至内劳宫,称运内劳宫。揉100~300次;运10~30次。

作用:清热除烦,清虚热。

主治:发热、烦渴、口疮、便血、齿龈糜烂、虚烦内热。

应用:揉内劳用于心经有热而致口舌生疮、发热、烦渴等症。运内劳为运掌小横纹、揉小天心、运内劳宫的复合手法,对心、肾两经虚热最为适宜。

8.3.31 小天心

定位:大小鱼际交接处凹陷中。

操作:中指端揉,称揉小天心;拇指甲掐,称掐小天心;以中指尖或屈曲的指间关节捣,称捣小天心。揉100~300次;掐、捣5~20次。

作用:清热、镇惊、利尿、明目。

主治:抽搐、夜啼、小便赤涩、目赤肿痛、口舌生疮、斜视等症。

应用:揉小天心主要用于心经有热而致目赤肿痛、口舌生疮、惊惕不安或心经有热,移热于小肠而见小便短赤等症。另外对小儿癃闭等症亦有良效。掐、捣小天心主要用于夜啼等症。

8.3.32 内八卦

定位:以掌中心为圆心,从圆心至中指根横纹内2/3处为半径,画一圆圈,八卦穴即在此圆圈上。对小天心者为坎卦,对中指根者为离卦,在拇指侧离至坎半圆的中点为震卦,在小指侧半圆的中点为兑卦,共八个方位即乾、坎、艮、震、巽、离、坤、兑。

操作:用拇指端自乾向坎运至兑卦为一遍,在运至离卦时轻轻而过,称顺运内八卦(图8-25)。若从兑卦运至乾卦,称为逆运内八卦。各100～300次。

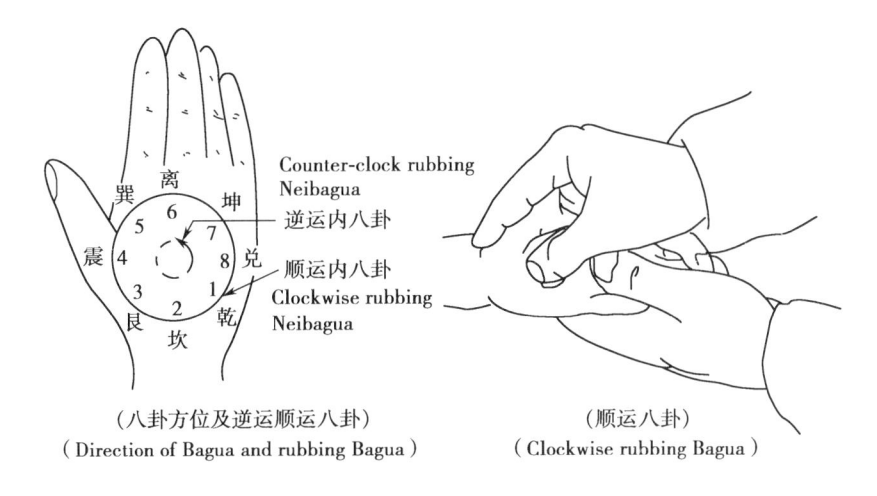

（八卦方位及逆运顺运八卦）
（Direction of Bagua and rubbing Bagua）

（顺运八卦）
（Clockwise rubbing Bagua）

图 8-25 顺运内八卦
Fig. 8-25 Clockwise rubbing Neibagua

作用:顺运内八卦能宽胸理气,止咳化痰,行滞消食;逆运则降气平喘。

主治:胸闷、咳嗽、气喘、呕吐、泄泻、腹胀、食欲不振、呃逆、发热、恶寒等症。

应用:顺运内八卦主治胸闷、咳嗽、腹胀、食欲不振等,多与运板门等合用;逆运内八卦能降气平喘,用于痰喘呕吐甚者,多与推膻中、推天柱骨等合用。

8.3.33 总筋

定位:掌后腕横纹中点。
操作:按揉本穴,称揉总筋;用拇指甲掐,称掐总筋。揉100～300次;掐3～5次。
作用:清心经热,散结止痉,通调周身气机。
主治:口舌生疮、潮热、夜啼、牙痛等症。
应用:揉总筋临床上多与清天河水、清心经配合,治疗口舌生疮、潮热、夜啼等实热证。操作时手法宜快,并稍用力。

8.3.34 大横纹

定位:仰掌,掌后横纹。近拇指端称阳池,近小指端称阴池。

操作:两拇指自掌后横纹中(总筋)向两旁分推,称分推大横纹,又称分阴阳;自两旁(阴池、阳池)向总筋合推,称合阴阳。推30~50次。

作用:平衡阴阳,调和气血,行滞消食,行痰散结。

主治:寒热往来、泄泻、呕吐、食积、身热不退、烦躁不安、胸闷、喘嗽等症。

应用:分阴阳多用于阴阳不调,气血不和而致寒热往来,烦躁不安,以及乳食停滞、腹胀、泄泻、呕吐等症。在操作时,如实热证阴池宜重分,虚寒证阳池宜重分。合阴阳多用于喘嗽、胸闷等症。

8.3.35 左端正

定位:中指甲根桡侧赤白肉际处,称左端正。

操作:用拇指甲掐或拇指罗纹面揉称掐、揉左端正。掐5次;揉50次。

作用:升阳止泻。

主治:水泻、痢疾等。

应用:揉左端正主要用于水泻、痢疾等症,多与补大肠、推上七节骨等合用。

8.3.36 右端正

定位:中指甲根尺侧赤白肉际处,称右端正。

操作:用拇指甲掐或拇指罗纹面揉称掐、揉右端正。掐5次;揉50次。

作用:降逆止呕。

主治:止呕吐、降逆、止血。

应用:揉右端正主要用于胃气上逆而引起的恶心呕吐等症。掐右端正多用于治疗小儿惊风,常与清肝经等配合。同时本穴对鼻衄有效,方法用细绳由中指第三节横纹起扎至指端,扎好后患儿静卧即可。

8.3.37 五指节

定位:手背五指第一指间关节横纹处。

操作:拇指甲掐,称掐五指节;用拇、食指揉搓称揉五指节。掐各3~5次;揉搓30~50次。

作用:安神镇惊,祛风痰,通关窍。

主治:咳嗽风痰、吐涎、惊惕不安等症。

应用:掐五指节主要用于惊惕不安等症,多与清肝经合用;揉五指节主要用于胸闷、痰喘、咳嗽等症,多与运内八卦、推揉膻中等合用。

8.3.38 二扇门

定位:掌背中指根本节两侧凹陷处。

操作:拇指甲掐,称掐二扇门;拇指偏峰按揉,称揉二扇门。掐5次;揉100~300次。

作用:发汗透表,退热平喘。

主治:伤风、感冒、发热无汗、痰喘气粗等症。

应用:掐、揉二扇门是发汗效法。揉时要稍用力,速度宜快,多用于风寒外感。本法与揉肾顶、补脾经、补肾经等配合应用,适宜于平素体虚外感者。

8.3.39 上马

定位:手背无名及小指掌指关节后凹陷中。
操作:拇指端揉或拇指甲掐,称揉上马或掐上马。掐3～5次;揉100～300次。
作用:滋阴补肾,顺气散结,利水通淋。
主治:小便赤涩、腹痛、遗尿、消化不良、喘促、牙痛等症。
应用:临床上用揉法为多,主要用于阴虚阳亢、潮热烦躁、盗汗、牙痛、小便赤涩等症。本法对体质虚弱,肺部感染有干性啰音,久不消失者配揉小横纹;湿性啰音配揉掌小横纹。

8.3.40 威灵

定位:手背二、三掌骨歧缝间。
操作:用掐法,称掐威灵。掐3～5次,或醒后即止。
作用:开窍醒神。
主治:急惊暴死、昏迷不醒、头痛等。
应用:急惊暴死、昏迷不醒时,多配合掐人中、掐十宣等合用。

8.3.41 精宁

定位:手背第四、第五掌骨歧缝间。
操作:用掐法,称掐精宁。掐3～5次,或醒后即止。
作用:行气、破结、化痰。
主治:痰食积聚、气吼痰喘、干呕、疳积、惊厥等症。
应用:多用于痰食积聚,气吼痰喘,干呕等症。本法于体虚者慎用,如必须应用时则多与补脾经、推三关、捏脊等同用,以免元气受损。
用于急惊昏厥时,本法多与掐威灵配合,能加强开窍醒神的作用。

8.3.42 膊阳池

定位:在手背一窝风上3寸处。
操作:拇指甲掐或指端揉,称掐膊阳池或揉膊阳池。掐3～5次;揉100～300次。
作用:通大便,利小便,止头痛。
主治:大便秘结,小便赤涩,感冒头痛。
应用:特别对大便秘结,多揉之有显效,但大便滑泻者禁用;用于感冒头痛,或小便赤涩短少多与其他解表、利尿穴配用。

8.3.43 一窝风

定位:手背腕横纹正中凹陷处。
操作:指端揉,称揉一窝风。揉100～300次。

作用:温中行气,止痹痛,利关节,宣通表里。
主治:腹痛肠鸣、风寒感冒、急慢惊风、关节屈伸不利等。
应用:常用于受寒,食积引起的腹痛等症,多与拿肚角、推三关、揉中脘等合用。本法对寒滞经络引起的痹痛或感受风寒等症也有良效。

8.3.44 三关

定位:前臂桡侧缘,阳池至曲池成一直线。
操作:用食中指末节面,自腕横纹推向肘横纹,称推三关(图8-26)。推100～300次。
作用:温阳散寒,益气活血,发汗解表。
主治:腹痛腹泻、畏寒、四肢乏力、病后体虚及风寒感冒等一切虚、寒病症。
应用:本穴性温热,主治一切虚寒病症,对非虚寒病症者宜慎用。临床上治疗气血虚弱,命门火衰,下元虚冷,阳气不足引起的四肢厥冷、面色无华、食欲不振、吐泻等症。多与补脾经、补肾经、揉丹田、捏脊、摩腹等合用。

8.3.45 六腑

定位:前臂尺侧缘,阴池至肘横纹成一直线。
操作:用拇指面或食、中指指面,自肘横纹推向腕横纹,称退六腑或推六腑(图8-27)。推100～300次。

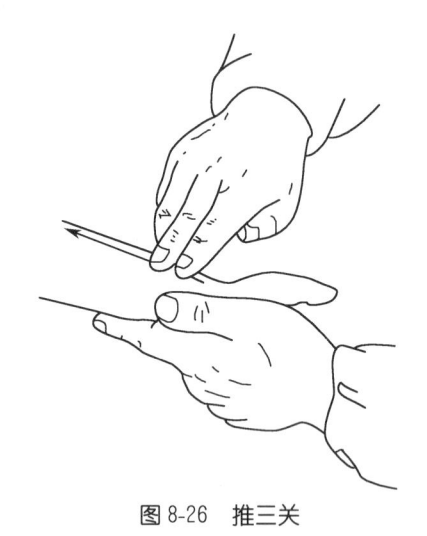

图8-26 推三关
Fig. 8-26 Pushing triple pass

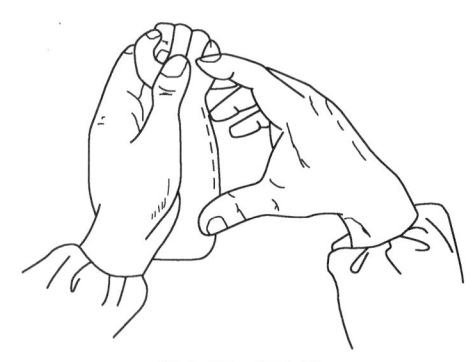

图8-27 退六腑
Fig. 8-27 Purging the six Fu-organs

作用:清热,凉血,解毒。
主治:高热、烦渴、惊风、咽痛、大便秘结等一切实热证。
应用:本穴性寒凉,对温病热入营血,脏腑郁热积滞而致壮热烦渴、便秘等实热证均可应用。本穴与补脾经合用,有止汗的效果。若患儿平素大便溏薄,脾虚腹泻者,本法慎用。
本法与推三关为大凉大热之法,可单用,亦可合用。若患儿气虚体弱,畏寒怕冷,可单用推三关,如高热烦渴、发斑等可单用退六腑。而两穴合用能平衡阴阳,防止大凉大热,伤其正气。如寒热夹杂,以热为主,则可以退六腑三数,推三关一数之比推之;若以寒为重,则可以推三关三数,退六腑一数之比推之。

8.3.46 天河水

定位:前臂内侧正中,总筋至洪池(曲泽)成一直线。

操作:用食、中二指末节面自腕横纹推向肘横纹,称清(推)天河水。推100~300次。

作用:清热解表,泻心火,除烦躁,润燥结。

主治:一切热症。外感发热、内热、潮热、烦躁不安、口渴、口舌生疮、咳嗽、痰喘、咽痛等症。

应用:本穴性微凉,较平和,主要用于治疗热性病症,清热而不伤阴分,多用于五心烦热、口燥咽干、唇舌生疮、夜啼等症。对于感冒发热、头痛、恶风、汗微出、咽痛等外感风热者,也常与推攒竹、推坎宫、揉太阳等合用。本穴善清卫、气分之热。

8.4 小儿常见病症

8.4.1 小儿病治疗特点

小儿推拿学是推拿学的一个重要分支。小儿推拿是在中医基本理论指导下,根据小儿的生理病理特点,在其体表特定的穴位或部位施以手法,以防治疾病或助长益智的一种外治疗法。

小儿推拿强调从小儿的生理病理特点出发。小儿具有脏腑娇嫩、形气未充和生机蓬勃、发育迅速的生理特点。小儿出生后,五脏六腑娇柔嫩弱,其形态结构、四肢百骸、筋骨肌肉、气血津液、气化功能都不够成熟和相对不足。祖国医学依此提出了"稚阴稚阳"的观点,认为小儿"稚阳未充,稚阴未长",无论在物质基础和生理功能方面都是幼稚和不完全的,是处在不断生长发育过程之中的。另一方面,小儿机体生长发育迅猛,年龄越小,生长越快,对于营养的需求越迫切。小儿还有抵抗力差、容易发病、传变迅速和脏气清灵、易趋康复的病理特点。小儿由于体质和功能均较脆弱,易受外界环境变化的影响,因此抗病能力差,加上小儿寒暖不能自调,饮食不能自节,故外易为六淫所侵,内易为饮食所伤。在临床发病方面,也以肺、脾二脏疾患为多。总之,小儿寒热虚实变化,比成人更为迅速而错综复杂。若调治不当,容易轻病变重、重病转危。而脏气清灵、易趋康复是指小儿机体生机蓬勃、活力充沛、气血反应灵敏,在疾病过程中,其组织再生和修补能力也是旺盛的。故儿科疾病如能准确诊断,及早治疗,往往能够较好痊愈或减少后遗症的发生。小儿推拿辨证也是在四诊八纲的基础上进行的。在四诊中,乳儿不会说话,因此问诊常是间接的,较大儿童虽能言语,但也往往不能确切诉说病情,加之婴儿气血未充,经脉未盛,脉象难凭;闻诊虽能反映一些情况,但也不够全面;只有望诊不受条件限制,反映病情比较可靠,尤其是小儿指纹的望诊,应予重视。

由于小儿发病特点以外感疾病和饮食内伤居多,辨证以阳证、实证、热证为多,因此在推拿治疗上,常用的也以解表法、消导法为多;小儿推拿的穴位除常用的少数经穴、奇穴外,多数穴位为小儿特定穴位,而且多分布在两肘以下,与成人不同,这些特有穴位的分布特点,给临床治疗带来了很多方便。

小儿推拿手法要求轻柔深透,适达病所而止。小儿推拿手法操作的时间,一般来说以推法、揉法次数为多,而摩法时间较长,掐法则重、快、少,在掐后常继用揉法,而按法和揉法也常配合应用。

小儿推拿治疗时应注意以下几点:(1)医者的指甲须修剪圆滑。(2)天气寒冷时,保持双手温暖。(3)推拿顺序在临床上一般有三种方法,可根据情况灵活应用:①一般先推头面部穴位,依次推上肢、胸腹、腰背、下肢部穴位。②先推主穴,后推配穴。③先推配穴,后推主穴(如捏脊等)。不管采用哪种方法,无论主穴、配穴,运用掐、拿、捏等强刺激手法,应最后操作,以免刺激患儿哭闹,影响后来的操作进行和治疗效果。④推拿的时间,应根据患儿年龄大小、病情轻重、体质强弱及手法的特性而定,一般不超过20分钟,亦可根据病情灵活掌握,通常每日治疗1次,高热等急性病可每日治疗2次。⑤上肢部穴位,习惯只推左侧,无男女之分;其他部位的双侧穴位,两侧均可治疗。⑥治疗时应配合推拿介质,如滑石粉等,其目的是润滑皮肤,防止擦破皮肤,又可提高治疗效果。⑦小儿过饥过饱,均不利于推拿疗效的发挥,最佳的小儿推拿时间宜在饭后1小时进行。

8.4.2 咳嗽

咳嗽是肺脏疾病的主要症状之一。本病一年四季皆可发生,以冬春季节为多发,婴幼儿发病率较高,本节所述咳嗽仅指以咳嗽为主的急、慢性支气管炎等症。

本病主要病因有外感和内伤两种,病位主要在肺脾两脏。肺为娇脏,开窍于鼻,外合皮毛,主一身之表,外感邪气,首当犯肺,肺气不宣,清肃失职,肺气上逆,而致咳嗽;或感受燥邪,气道干燥,咽喉不利,肺津受灼,痰涎粘结,肺气上逆,而致咳嗽。内伤咳嗽多因平素体虚,或肺阴虚损,肺气上逆,或脾胃虚寒,健运失职,水湿停滞,酿湿为痰,上扰肺络,失于肃降,而为咳嗽。

西医学认为理化刺激、感染和过敏原是本病外在病因,而机体抵抗力下降、过敏体质和呼吸道免疫能力下降是内因。小儿呼吸道的免疫能力较差,且小儿的咳嗽反射和气道平滑肌收缩功能及纤毛运动功能均较差,难以有效地清除吸入的尘埃及异物颗粒,故易患呼吸道感染。

【临床表现】

1. 风寒咳嗽 咳嗽频作,伴痰少清稀色白,鼻塞流清涕,或有恶寒无汗,头身疼痛,苔薄白,脉浮紧,指纹浮红。

2. 风热咳嗽 咳嗽不爽,伴痰稠色黄,或有鼻流浊涕,恶风,微汗出,发热,口渴,咽痛,小便黄,大便干,舌尖红,苔薄黄,脉浮数,指纹鲜红或紫红。

3. 内伤咳嗽 久咳不愈,身微热或干咳少痰,或咳嗽痰多,食欲不振,神疲乏力,形体消瘦,舌红少苔,脉细数,指纹淡紫等。

【推拿治疗】

1. 风寒咳嗽

治法：疏风散寒，宣肺止咳。

处方：推攒竹、推坎宫、揉太阳、揉耳后高骨、推揉膻中、揉乳根、揉乳旁、揉肺俞、分推肩胛骨、清肺经、顺运内八卦。

方解：推攒竹、推坎宫、揉太阳、揉耳后高骨能疏风解表止头痛；揉膻中、揉乳根、揉乳旁可以化痰理气，宣肺止咳；推揉肺俞、分推肩胛骨可以调肺理气，化痰止咳；清肺经能疏风解表，宣肺止咳；运内八卦能宽胸利膈，理气化痰。

若风寒无汗，流清涕甚者，掐揉二扇门、揉迎香、黄蜂入洞、揉外劳宫；若痰多咳喘，有干、湿性啰音者，加推小横纹、揉掌小横纹、双凤展翅。

2. 风热咳嗽

治法：疏风清热，宣肺止咳。

处方：开天门、推坎宫、揉太阳、推揉膻中、揉乳根、揉乳旁、推脊柱、揉肺俞、清肺经、清天河水、运内八卦。

方解：开天门、推坎宫、揉太阳可以疏风解表；揉膻中、揉乳根、揉乳旁可以宽胸理气，化痰止咳；清肺经能疏风解表，宣肺止咳；清天河水可以清热解表；运内八卦能宽胸利膈，理气化痰。

若痰多喘咳，加揉丰隆、擦背部脾胃区；肺内有干性啰音加揉小横纹，湿性啰音加揉掌小横纹；咳嗽身热痰多并伴有大便干结，可配合退六腑、清大肠。

3. 内伤咳嗽

治法：健脾养肺，止咳化痰。

处方：补脾经、补肺经、运内八卦、推揉膻中、揉乳根、揉乳旁、揉中脘、揉肺俞、按揉足三里。

方解：补脾经、按揉足三里能健脾胃，化痰涎；补肺经能补益肺气；运内八卦、推揉膻中、揉乳旁、揉乳根能宽胸理气，止咳化痰；揉中脘能健脾和胃；揉肺俞能调肺气，止咳嗽。

若阴虚咳嗽加揉上马；久咳体虚喘促者，加补肾经、推三关、捏脊；痰涎壅盛者，加揉丰隆、揉天突、按弦走搓摩。

【护理】

1. 治疗期间，饮食宜清淡，禁食生冷酸甜以及辛辣、鱼腥类食品，以防加重咳嗽。
2. 适当休息，多饮开水，注意气候变化，避风寒，防止重感。
3. 改善居住环境，保持室内空气流通，避免烟尘、油气等不良刺激。

8.4.3 发热

发热是指体温异常升高，是小儿常见的一种病症。临床上可见外感发热、肺胃实热、阴虚内热、气虚发热等证型。外感发热，一般是指感冒而言。本病一年四季皆可发生，多发于冬春季节，年龄越小越易发生。对于体弱患儿，由于得病后容易出现兼症，应予注意。

该病的病因主要是由于小儿体质虚弱，抗邪能力不足，加之家长护理不周，易为风寒或风热之邪侵袭体表，卫外之阳被郁而致发热；或由于外感误治或乳食内伤而致肺胃实热；或小儿先天不足，后天营养失调，久病伤阴，阴液亏损而致阴虚内热；或患儿素体脾胃虚弱，久病气虚，阳浮于外致气虚发热。

西医学认为小儿时期免疫力差，易发生上呼吸感染而致发热；并且小儿全身含水量占体重的比重较成人高，旺盛的新陈代谢使得小儿排水量相对较大，易发生水代谢紊乱，体温调节活动因之紊乱，而出现体温升高。

【临床表现】

1. 外感发热 发热无汗，畏寒，头痛，周身疼痛，鼻塞，流清涕，手足不温，苔薄白，指纹鲜红者，为风寒；发热微汗出，鼻流黄涕或浊涕，咽喉肿痛，口干，舌尖红苔薄黄，指纹红紫者，为风热。

2. 肺胃实热 发热，热势较高，汗出较多，渴而引饮，食欲减退，面红赤，气促，便秘烦躁，舌红苔黄燥，指纹深紫。

3. 阴虚发热 午后发热，热势较低，伴五心烦热，盗汗颧红，食欲减退，形体瘦弱，脉细数，舌红少苔或无苔，指纹淡紫。

4. 气虚发热 劳累后发热，低热，语声低微，懒言乏力，动则自汗，食欲不振，形体消瘦或食后即泻，舌质淡，苔薄白，脉虚弱或沉细无力，指纹色淡。

【推拿治疗】

1. 外感发热

治法：清热解表，发散外邪。

处方：开天门、推坎宫、运太阳、清天河水、清肺经。风寒者加推三关、揉二扇门、拿风池、推天柱骨；风热者多清天河水，加推脊、揉大椎。若兼咳嗽、痰鸣气急者，加推揉膻中、揉肺俞、运内八卦、推小横纹、揉丰隆；加清肝经、掐揉小天心、掐揉五指节。兼鼻塞流涕者，加黄蜂入洞；兼高热烦躁加打马过天河；兼惊惕不安、睡卧不宁者，加清肝经、掐揉小天心。

方解：开天门、推坎宫、运太阳可以疏风解表；清肺经能宣肺清热，疏风解表；清天河水能清热解表，泻火除烦；风寒者加推三关、掐揉二扇门、拿风池、推天柱骨可以发汗解表；风热者加推脊柱从上至下、揉大椎，有清热解表的作用。

2. 肺胃实热

治法：清泻里热，理气消食。

处方：清肺经、清胃经、清大肠、揉板门、运内八卦、清天河水、退六腑、揉天枢。若大便干燥难排者，加推下七节骨、顺时针摩腹、揉脐阳池、搓摩胁肋等。

方解：清肺经、清胃经可以清肺、胃两经实热，配清大肠、揉天枢，疏调肠腑结滞，以通便泻火；清天河水、退六腑，清热除烦；揉板门、运内八卦，理气消食。

3. 阴虚内热

治法：滋阴清热。

处方：揉上马、清天河水、水底捞月、补脾经、补肺经、揉足三里、推擦涌泉。若盗汗自汗，加揉肾顶、捏脊、补肾经；烦躁不眠者，加清肝经、揉百会、开天门、掐揉五指节、捣小天心。

方解：揉上马、推擦涌泉、水底捞月，能滋阴清虚热；清天河水能清热泻火除烦；补脾经、补肺经、揉足三里能健脾肺，补气养血清热。

4. 气虚发热

治法:健脾益气,佐以清热。

处方:补脾经、补肺经、运内八卦、摩腹、分手阴阳、揉足三里、揉脾俞、揉肺俞、清天河水、捏脊。

方解:补脾经、补肺经、揉足三里、揉脾俞、摩腹、揉肺俞能健脾肺,补气养血清热;运内八卦、分手阴阳可以平衡阴阳,调和气血;清天河水能清热泻火;捏脊能调和阴阳气血、益气清热。

若腹胀、纳呆者,加揉板门、摩中脘、分推腹阴阳;若大便稀薄,夹有不消化食物残渣者,加逆时针摩腹、补大肠、推上七节骨、板门推向横纹;若恶心呕吐,加推天柱骨、横纹推向板门、推中脘、揉右端正。

【护理】

1. 居室保持空气流通、清洁。
2. 饮食宜清淡、富有营养。
3. 注意体温变化,常用温水洗浴,可帮助发汗降温。

8.4.4 哮喘

哮喘是小儿常见的一种呼吸道疾病。临床常以阵发性呼吸困难、呼气延长、喉间有哮鸣音,甚至张口抬肩,不能平卧为特征。本病好发于冬春季节,气候突变、寒温失宜、饮食不当等为本病诱发因素。

小儿哮喘形成有内因和外因两个方面。内因与肺、脾、肾三脏有关:肺气不足,卫表不固,痰邪内伏,气逆而喘;脾气素虚,运化失司,积湿生痰并贮于肺,肺失清肃,上逆而喘;肾气不足,摄纳无力,则少气而喘。外因多为气候突变、寒温失常、风寒外邪侵袭肺卫,宣降失常,气逆而喘。素有特异体质的小儿感受风寒或饮食不当,或接触异物等,触动伏痰,痰气上阻气道,肺气升降失司,致哮喘发作。若哮喘反复发作可耗散肺气,久病及肾,出现肾阳虚亏、肾不纳气的证候。

西医学认为本病的发生,主要由机体过敏状态所致,由于接触过敏原(如花粉、油漆、鱼虾等)致使细小支气管平滑肌痉挛产生一系列症状。过度疲劳、情绪激动、气候变化等也常为本病的诱发因素。

【临床表现】

1. 寒性哮喘 咳嗽气喘,呼吸困难,喘息时有哮鸣声,甚者张口抬肩,不能平卧,吐清稀痰,色白多沫,形寒无汗,面色苍白或青紫,四肢不温,口不渴或渴喜热饮,小便清长,舌质淡红,苔薄白,脉濡数或浮滑,指纹淡红。

2. 热性哮喘 咳嗽气促,呼吸憋气,喘息时有哮鸣音,痰稠色黄,面红发热,胸闷膈满,烦躁不安,渴喜冷饮,小便黄赤,大便干燥,舌质红,苔薄黄,脉浮数,指纹深红。

3. 肾不纳气兼阳虚 气喘,呼吸困难,喘息时有哮鸣声,兼面色青灰,口不渴,倦怠乏力,食少纳呆,张口抬肩,端坐喘息,肢冷形寒,腰腿酸软,小便清长而频,舌质淡,苔薄白,脉沉细无力,指纹淡白。

【推拿治疗】

1. 寒性哮喘

治法:降气平喘,宣肺散寒。

处方:清肺经、推揉膻中、揉天突、搓摩胁肋、揉肺俞、运内八卦、按揉风池、推三关、揉外劳宫、揉乳旁、揉乳根、推脊、合阴阳、按揉三阴交。

方解:清肺经、推揉膻中、揉天突、搓摩胁肋、揉肺俞宽胸行气降逆;运内八卦、按揉风池、推三关驱风散寒,宣肺平喘;揉外劳宫、揉乳旁、揉乳根、推脊、合阴阳、按揉三阴交宽胸宣肺,降气平喘化痰。

2. 热性哮喘

治法:清热降气,宣肺平喘。

处方:清天河水、清肺经、掐总筋、分阴阳、清大肠、退六腑、推天柱、推脊、揉丰隆、揉肺俞、运内八卦。

方解:清天河水、清肺经可清肺热,降气平喘;掐总筋、分阴阳、清大肠、退六腑清热泻火,退热降气;分推膻中、推天柱、推脊、揉丰隆、揉肺俞、运内八卦宽胸降逆,化痰平喘。

3. 肾不纳气兼阳虚

治法:纳气平喘,补肾温阳。

处方:补肺经、推小肠、推揉膻中、揉天突推三关、按弦走搓摩、摩中脘、揉丹田、揉肾俞、补肾经、补脾经、运内八卦、揉乳旁、揉乳根、揉中脘、揉肺俞、按揉足三里。

方解:补肺经、推小肠补土纳气;推揉膻中、揉天突、推三关、按弦走搓摩宽胸降逆;摩中脘、揉丹田、揉肾俞、补肾经、补脾经补益脾肾,健中纳气;运内八卦、揉乳旁、揉乳根、揉中脘、揉肺俞、按揉足三里健脾宽胸,降逆化痰。

【护理】

1. 体弱或有佝偻病者应适当补充营养。
2. 注意保暖,防止外邪侵袭。
3. 少食辛辣香燥炙烤食物及肥甘厚味,防止内伤乳食。
4. 哮喘发作时应注意休息。不发作时可加强户外活动,增强体质。

8.4.5 呕吐

呕吐是指由于胃气上逆,至胃内容物从口中排出,是临床上小儿常见的症状,可伴于多种疾病中。另外,小儿胃腑娇嫩,贲门松弛,如喂乳过多,或喂养姿势不当,吸入过多空气,出现乳后有少量乳汁倒流口腔,溢出口角,此称为溢乳,不属于病态。

中医学认为胃为水谷之海,以降为和。小儿脾胃娇弱,如外感六淫之气,侵扰脾胃;或饥饱不节,恣食生冷瓜果、油腻之物致停滞不化,积于胃脘;或跌仆惊恐,气机逆乱,伤及脾胃,运化失司,胃失和降,气逆于上,发为呕吐。

西医学认为呕吐是机体的一种本能反射,可将胃内有害物质排出,起到有利保护作用。但频繁剧烈呕吐,会妨碍饮食,日久导致脱水、电解质紊乱、酸碱平衡失调、营养障碍等。小儿呕吐还常伴发于其他系统的疾病,故必须详细询问病史,综合分析。

【临床表现】

1. 寒吐 多食即吐,时发时止,呕吐物不甚酸臭,面色苍白,四肢欠温,腹痛喜暖喜按,大便溏薄,舌淡苔薄白,指纹色红。

2. **热吐** 食入口即吐,吐物酸臭,烦躁不安,口渴身热,大便秘结或臭秽,小便赤黄,唇干舌红,苔黄腻,指纹色紫。

3. **伤食吐** 呕吐酸馊频繁,口气臭秽,厌食,肚腹胀痛,便溏酸臭,舌红苔厚腻,脉滑实,指纹色紫或红。

4. **惊恐吐** 受惊吓后呕吐暴作,或频吐清涎,神态紧张,昼惊惕不安,夜卧不宁,易啼哭,山根青,指纹青,脉乍来乍数。

【推拿治疗】

1. **寒吐**

治法:和胃降逆,温中散寒。

处方:揉中脘、补脾经、补胃经、横纹推向板门、推天柱骨、揉外劳、推三关。

方解:揉中脘、补脾经、补胃经健脾和胃,降逆止呕,温中散寒;推天柱骨祛寒止呕,祛寒止呕,配横纹推向板门善止一切呕吐;揉外劳宫、推三关温阳散寒以加强温中作用。

2. **热吐**

治法:清热降逆,和胃止呕。

处方:清脾胃、退六腑、清大肠、横纹推向板门、运内八卦、推天柱骨、推下七节骨。

方解:清脾胃配推天柱骨可清中焦积热,和胃降逆以止呕吐,退六腑加强清热;运内八卦、横纹推向板门宽胸理气,和胃止呕;推下七节骨、清大肠泄热通便,使胃气得以通降下行。

3. **伤食吐**

治法:消食导滞,和中降逆。

处方:补脾经、揉中脘、按揉足三里、揉板门、运内八卦、分腹阴阳、横纹推向板门、按弦走搓摩。

方解:补脾经、揉中脘、按揉足三里健脾和胃,以助中焦运化;运内八卦、揉板门消食导滞,宽胸理气;分腹阴阳、横纹推向板门以降逆止吐;按弦走搓摩以健脾消食,理气化痰。

4. **惊恐吐**

治法:镇惊止吐。

处方:按揉天突、揉乳旁、清肝经、揉小天心、掐揉五指节、分腹阴阳、推天柱骨、运内八卦、横纹推向板门、揉右端正。

方解:按揉天突、揉乳旁降逆止吐;掐揉五指节、清肝经、揉小天心以镇惊疏肝;分腹阴阳、推天柱骨以降逆止呕;横纹推向板门、运内八卦、揉右端正消导积滞,镇惊安神。

【护理】

1. 调节饮食,忌时饥时饱、过凉过热。

2. 呕吐严重者可使患儿呈呼吸暂停的窒息状态,应密切观察,防止呕吐物吸入产生吸入性肺炎等呼吸道病变。

3. 反复呕吐可致脱水、酸中毒等,此时应配合中西医综合治疗。

8.4.6 泄泻

泄泻是小儿每日大便次数增多,且粪便溏薄,甚至稀如水样。以一周岁以下的小儿较为多见,本病四季皆可发生,多发生在夏秋季节。

泄泻可分为急性和慢性两大类,病变主要与脾和大小肠有关,盖脾主运化,小肠分清泌浊,大肠为传导之官,若发生病变可致泄泻。泄泻易耗气伤血,发病后如不及时诊治,迁延日久可影响小儿营养吸收、生长发育,甚至造成气虚液脱的危象。

西医学认为婴幼儿消化系统发育不成熟,功能尚不完善,神经调节功能差,胃酸与消化酶分泌较少,消化酶活力低等是本病内因,外因可由饮食不当或感受寒凉或由肠道内感染致病性大肠杆菌、病毒、真菌等造成,严重者可造成水和电解质紊乱,引起脱水和酸中毒等危症。

【临床表现】

1. 寒湿泻 大便稀而多沫,色淡不臭,小便清长,呕恶、胸闷、纳差、肠鸣腹痛,恶寒、微发热、手足发凉,口不渴,苔白腻,脉濡,指纹红。

2. 湿热泻 泻下稀薄或粘滞,色黄而臭,小便短赤,口渴烦躁,发热较高,舌红,苔黄腻,脉数,指纹紫暗。

3. 伤食泻 腹痛胀满,泻后痛减,大便量多酸臭,纳呆嗳气,口渴,不思乳食,夜卧不安,手足心发热,苔厚脉滑,指纹深紫。

4. 脾虚泻 久泻不愈,大便稀薄,食后即泻或食油腻即泻,色白不臭,夹有未消化物,面色萎黄,神疲倦怠,肢冷,舌淡苔白,脉濡,指纹淡红。

5. 脾肾阳虚 大便呈水样,次数多,完谷不化,面黄神萎,肢软无力,四肢厥冷,苔白脉细。无论何种泄泻,严重时均会造成阴竭于内,阳越于外的虚脱危候,故必须认真对待。

【推拿治疗】

1. 寒湿泻

治法:温中散寒,健脾止泻。

处方:补脾经、补大肠、揉外劳宫、揉左端正、推三关、摩脐、揉中脘、推上七节骨、揉龟尾、按揉足三里。

方解:推三关、揉外劳宫温阳散寒,配补脾经、揉中脘、摩脐与按揉足三里能健脾化湿,温中散寒;补大肠、揉左端正、推上七节骨、揉龟尾温中升阳止泻。

腹痛、肠鸣重者加揉一窝风、拿肚角;体虚加捏脊;惊惕不安加清肝经、掐揉五指节。

2. 湿热泻

治法:清热利湿,调中止泻。

处方:清脾胃、清小肠、清大肠、退六腑、揉天枢、揉龟尾、推下七节骨。

方解:清脾胃以清中焦湿热;揉天枢、清大肠以清利肠腑湿热积滞;清小肠、退六腑清热利小便除湿;配揉龟尾以理肠止泻;推下七节骨泻热通便。

3. 伤食泻

治法:消食导滞,和中助运。

处方：拿肚角、补脾经、清大肠、运内八卦、揉板门、揉中脘、摩腹、揉天枢、揉龟尾。

方解：拿肚角消食去滞，补脾经、揉中脘健脾助运，揉板门、运内八卦、摩腹健脾和胃，行滞消食；清大肠、揉天枢疏调肠腑积滞；配揉龟尾以理肠止泻。

4. 脾虚泻

治法：健脾益气，温阳止泻。

处方：补脾经、补大肠、推三关、摩腹、揉天枢、揉脐、推上七节骨、揉丹田、揉龟尾、捏脊、运水入土。

方解：补脾经、补大肠健脾益气，固肠实便；推三关、揉丹田、揉天枢、摩腹、揉脐、捏脊以温阳补中；配揉龟尾、推上七节骨以温阳止泻；运水入土以健脾止泻。

肾阳虚者加补肾经、揉外劳宫；腹胀加运内八卦；久泻不止者加按揉百会。

【护理】

1. 注意饮食卫生，防止病从口入。

2. 乳贵有时，食贵有节，节制乳食，忌过凉过热、时饥时饱。

3. 泄泻期间，应食宜消化和清淡之品，不食油腻之物；并要勤换尿布，多翻身，防止逆行性尿路感染或继发性肺炎等并发症。

8.4.7 厌食

厌食是指小儿长期食欲不振，厌恶进食。但在外感或内伤等其他疾病过程中出现的食欲不振不属此症范畴。以1岁～6岁儿童多见，学龄儿童发病明显减少，城市儿童发病率较高。无明显季节性。

厌食的发病主要与脾胃功能及饮食习惯有关。小儿因饮食不节，喂养不当，或长期偏食，伤及脾胃，致使脾失健运，胃不受纳，而成厌食；又或因素体阴虚，或热病伤阴致胃阴不足，失于濡润，而成厌食；亦可因小儿素禀不足，或病后体弱，脾胃虚损，不能受纳；此外，小儿也可因受惊吓、打骂，情志不遂，致使气机逆乱，肝郁伤脾，而成厌食。

西医学认为热量及蛋白质不足，维生素B族缺乏，某些微量元素缺乏，或摄入过多蛋白质、糖、脂肪及维生素D或维生素A均可引起厌食。此外，家长强求小儿进食，影响小儿情绪，或多次补喂，打乱进食习惯，也可引起厌食。儿童本身的紧张、忧惧、兴奋亦可影响食欲。

【临床表现】

1. 脾失健运 乳食不进或不思乳食，食而无味，面色少华，形体偏瘦，舌淡，苔薄白或腻，脉濡缓。

2. 胃阴不足 不欲进食，纳少喜饮，口干舌燥，面色欠华，皮肤失润，便干溲黄，舌红少津，苔少或花剥，脉细数。

3. 脾胃虚弱 不欲纳食，面色萎黄，形体偏瘦，神疲乏力，倦怠懒言，易出汗，大便夹有不消化食物残渣，舌淡，苔薄白，脉虚弱。

4. 肝郁气滞 纳差不食，情志抑郁，脘闷嗳气，胸胁痞满，善太息，舌淡，苔花剥，脉弦缓。

【推拿治疗】

1. 脾失健运

治法:调脾助运。

处方:清补脾经(先清后补)、清大肠、揉板门、推四横纹、揉天枢、摩腹、揉中脘、按揉足三里、推大横纹。

方解:清补脾经健脾利湿;清大肠泻热通便;推大横纹、揉板门消食导滞;摩腹、揉天枢、揉中脘、按揉足三里健脾和胃;推四横纹调中行气。

2. 胃阴不足

治法:滋养胃阴。

处方:补脾经、运内八卦、揉板门、揉上马、清大肠、清天河水、水底捞月、运土入水、揉脾俞、揉胃俞。

方解:清天河水、清大肠、水底捞月、运土入水清胃肠热;补脾经、揉脾俞、揉胃俞补益脾胃;揉上马滋阴润燥;运内八卦、揉板门行气消食。

3. 脾胃虚弱

治法:健脾益气。

处方:补脾经、补胃经、运内八卦、运水入土、推三关、摩中脘、摩腹、揉丹田、揉脾俞、揉胃俞、捏脊、揉足三里。

方解:补脾经、补胃经、运水入土补益脾胃;推三关、揉丹田温阳补气;揉脾俞、揉胃俞、捏脊、揉足三里、摩中脘健脾消食;运内八卦、摩腹行气消食。

4. 肝郁气滞

治法:行气疏肝。

处方:清肝经、补脾经、运内八卦、揉板门、按弦走搓摩、揉肝俞、揉脾俞、揉胃俞。

方解:清肝经、按弦走搓摩、揉肝俞疏肝行气;补脾经、揉脾俞、揉胃俞健脾和胃;运内八卦、揉板门行气消食。

【护理】

1. 正确喂食,定时进食,规律生活,纠正不良饮食习惯。
2. 勿强行予食,增加小儿对进食的反感。
3. 按儿童年龄,予多样化、易消化食品,增加儿童进食兴趣,并减轻胃肠负担。

8.4.8 便秘

便秘是指大便秘结不通,排便时间延长,或欲大便而艰涩不畅。小儿便秘发病率为3%~8%,其中90%~95%为功能性便秘,城市的发病率高于农村,女童高于男童,无季节性。

小儿便秘可分为实秘和虚秘两大类,主要与胃肠两脏及气、血、津液的盛衰情况有关。实秘多因过食辛甘厚味,或热病伤阴,致使胃肠燥热,津液失于输布,不能下润,而致大便干结;又或因乳食积滞,或缺少活动,致使气机郁滞,胃肠传导功能失常,而成便秘。虚秘则多因先天体弱,或病后体虚,气虚则大肠传送无力,血虚则津少不能滋润大肠,而成便秘。便秘日久,因其腑气不通,浊气不降,可引起腹胀腹痛、头晕头胀、食欲减退、睡眠不安等症。长期便秘,会引起痔疮、肛裂等。

西医学认为小儿便秘可分为功能性便秘和肠道畸形所致便秘两种。临床多为功能性便秘。其原因主要有以下几种:①生活无规律,没有养成按时排便的习惯,导致排便反射弱,肠管肌肉无力,形成便秘。②食用过多精细食品,缺乏渣滓,或食物中缺乏足量碳水化合物,而导致便秘。③肛周病变如痔疮、肛裂等在排便时发生疼痛,致使粪便贮留。④营养不良如佝偻病,使肠管功能失调,腹肌软弱或麻痹,导致便秘。

【临床表现】

1. 实秘 大便干结,欲便不得,小便短赤,面赤身热,胁腹痞满,腹部胀痛,纳食减少,口干心烦,舌红,苔黄,脉数,指纹紫。

2. 虚秘 大便不畅,临便努挣,便后汗出气短,便下不干,面色少华,神疲气怯,形倦乏力,舌淡,苔薄,脉虚细,指纹淡。

【推拿治疗】

1. 实秘

治则:清热通便,行气导滞。

处方:清大肠、清胃经、运内八卦、按揉膊阳池、退六腑、摩腹、揉天枢、按弦走搓摩、推下七节骨、揉龟尾、按揉足三里。面赤身热,口干,心烦甚者加推脊、水底捞月;痞满腹胀甚者加分腹阴阳、推四横纹。

方解:清大肠、清胃经、退六腑清热泻火利湿;按揉膊阳池、推下七节骨、揉龟尾行气通便;运内八卦、按弦走搓摩行气导滞;摩腹、揉天枢、按揉足三里健脾消食。

2. 虚秘

治则:益气养血,滋阴润燥。

处方:补脾经、清大肠、揉上马、按揉膊阳池、推三关、揉肾俞、揉龟尾、捏脊、按揉足三里。气虚甚者加揉关元、运水入土;阴血亏虚甚者加揉支沟、揉膈俞。

方解:补脾经、推三关、捏脊、按揉足三里健脾益气,和中通便;揉龟尾、按揉膊阳池、清大肠行气通便;揉上马、揉肾俞滋阴润肠通便。

【护理】

1. 养成定时排便习惯。
2. 多食水果蔬菜、粗粮,忌食辛辣厚味。
3. 适当进行户外运动。

8.4.9 夜啼

夜啼是指小儿入夜啼哭,或每夜定时啼哭,而白天如常。轻者哭后仍能入睡,重者彻夜啼哭,通宵达旦。此症持续时间少则数日,多则数月,多见于1岁内的婴儿,一年四季均可发病。

夜啼的发生主要与脾、胃、心三脏有关。盖脾本属太阴,又小儿素禀虚弱,脾常不足,或因寒邪内侵,潜伏于脾,或因脾寒内生,值入夜阴盛之时,两阴相合,致使寒邪凝滞,气血不通,作腹痛而啼;又或乳食不节,致使胃肠积滞,内伤脾胃,因胃不和而啼哭不眠;又或因乳母恣食肥甘,致使胎儿热结心脾,值入夜阳衰之时,抗邪无力,邪热乘心,烦躁而啼;又或小儿忽闻异声或突视异物,因其神气不足,心气怯弱,致心神不安,神志不宁,因惊而作啼。

西医学认为,小儿长期夜间啼哭,多因消化系统疾病及营养缺乏症所致。消化系统疾病多为肠道感染或肠道功能紊乱导致消化不良,肠平滑肌痉挛产生腹痛而哭闹。

营养不良,微量元素缺乏,佝偻病及婴儿手足搐搦症均可导致夜啼。

【临床表现】

1. 脾脏虚寒 入夜啼哭,时哭时止,哭声低弱,面色㿠白,睡喜伏卧,腹喜温熨,四肢不温,食少便溏,小便色青,唇淡白,舌淡红,指纹淡红,脉沉细。

2. 乳食积滞 夜间烦躁啼哭,手足心热,厌食吐乳,嗳腐泛酸,脘腹胀满,大便酸臭,舌红,苔厚腻,指纹紫滞,脉滑。

3. 心经积热 哭声响亮,恶见灯火,面赤唇红,身腹俱暖,烦躁不安,小便短赤,大便秘结,舌尖红,苔黄,指纹红紫,脉数有力。

4. 惊骇恐惧 夜间突然啼哭,似见异物状,神情不安,时作惊惕,紧偎母怀,面色乍青乍白,舌脉正常,指纹青。

【推拿治疗】

1. 脾脏虚寒

治法:温中健脾。

处方:补脾经、推三关、运水入土、摩腹、揉中脘、捏脊。

方解:补脾经、运水入土、摩腹、揉中脘健脾温中;推三关温通阳气;捏脊理气血,培元气。

2. 乳食积滞

治法:消食导滞。

处方:清补脾经(先清后补)、清大肠、揉板门、推四横纹、摩腹、揉中脘、揉天枢、推下七节骨、按弦走搓摩、捏脊。

方解:清补脾经健脾利湿;清大肠、推下七节骨泻热通便;揉板门、猿猴摘果、按弦走搓摩消食导滞;摩腹、揉中脘、揉天枢、捏脊健脾和胃;推四横纹调中行气。

3. 心经积热

治法:清心导赤。

处方:清心经、清小肠、清天河水、揉总筋、揉内劳宫、水底捞月、推脊。

方解:清心经、揉总筋、揉内劳宫、水底捞月清心泻火除烦;清小肠清热利尿;清天河水、推脊清热除烦。

4. 惊骇恐惧

治法:镇惊安神。

处方:推攒竹、清肝经、捣小天心、掐威灵、掐精宁、揉五指节。

方解:推攒竹、捣小天心、揉五指节、掐威灵、掐精宁镇惊安神;清肝经疏肝解郁安神。

【护理】

1. 衣着适宜,脾寒者注意保暖,防止受凉;心热者勿过于保暖。
2. 乳贵有时,食贵有节,节制乳食,忌过凉过热、时饥时饱。
3. 孕妇、乳母忌过食寒凉、辛辣、热性食物。
4. 保持室内安静,忌受惊吓。

8.4.10 遗尿

遗尿是指3岁以上的小儿在睡眠中不知不觉的将小便尿在床上。3岁以下的儿童,由于脑髓未充,智力未健,排尿的自控能力尚未形成而产生尿床者不属病态。

遗尿症必须及早治疗,如病延日久,会妨碍儿童的身心健康,影响发育。

遗尿与肺、脾、肾三脏气化功能失常有关,其中肾脏与遗尿关系更为密切。小便正常的排泄,有赖于膀胱与三焦功能的健全。而三焦气化,上焦以肺为主,中焦以脾为主,下焦以肾为主。以上三脏功能失常,皆会发生遗尿。另外肝主疏泄,肾主闭藏。由于肝经郁热影响肾的闭藏作用,使肾关开合约制失力,膀胱不藏而发生遗尿。

现代医学认为,小儿的排尿受植物神经系统的调节,而大脑皮层对其有效的控制尚未建立。三岁以上,膀胱的排尿功能开始受大脑皮层的有效控制,如果大脑皮层解除对脊髓排尿中枢的抑制,膀胱逼尿肌收缩而产生排尿。

【临床表现】

睡眠中不自主排尿,如白天疲劳,天气阴雨时更易发生,轻则数夜遗尿一次,重则每夜遗尿一至二次,甚或更多,有些患儿白天也有遗尿情况发生。遗尿病久可见患儿面色萎黄,智力减退,精神不振,头晕腰酸,四肢不温等症。年龄较大儿童有怕羞或精神紧张。

1. 肾气不足 睡中遗尿,醒后方觉,一夜 1~2 次或更多,较大儿童能主诉神疲乏力,腰腿酸软,肢冷形寒,小便清长,或伴有头晕,甚者见肢冷畏寒,蜷卧而睡。舌淡,苔薄白,脉沉细无力。

2. 肺脾气虚 睡中遗尿,尿频量少,面色无华,气短自汗,纳少便溏,形瘦乏力。舌质淡,苔薄白,脉缓无力。

3. 肝经郁热 遗尿,漫黄短赤,频数不能自忍,性情急躁,手足心热,面赤唇红,口渴喜饮,甚至目暗红赤。舌质红,苔黄腻,脉弦数。

【推拿治疗】

1. 肾气不足

治法:益气补肾,固涩下元。

处方:补肾经、补小肠、推三关、按揉百会、揉丹田、揉龟尾、按揉肾俞、擦腰骶部、按揉三阴交。

方解:补肾经、补小肠、按揉肾俞、揉丹田、揉龟尾、擦腰骶部以温补肾气,壮命门之火,固涩下元;按揉百会、推三关、温阳升提;按揉三阴交以通调水道。

2. 肺脾气虚

治法:益气固涩。

处方:补脾经、补肺经、按揉百会、揉中极、按揉膀胱俞、按揉足三里。

方解:补脾经、补肺经、按揉足三里以补脾肺而益气;按揉百会、推三关温阳升提;揉中极、按揉膀胱俞以调膀胱气化,固涩水道。

3. 肝经郁热

治法:清肝泻热。

处方:清肝经、清心经、补脾经、揉小天心、揉上马、揉三阴交、揉涌泉。大便溏者加补大肠、摩腹;食欲不振者加运内八卦;自汗出者加揉肾顶。

方解:清肝经、清心经以清热除烦;揉小天心、揉上马、揉三阴交、揉涌泉以壮水制火,引热下行;补脾经以健脾扶正。

【护理】

1. 使儿童养成按时排尿的卫生习惯及安排合理的生活制度,不使其过度疲劳。

2. 对遗尿患儿,除给予积极的治疗外,要适当地增加营养,并注意休息。临睡前两小时最好不要饮水;少吃或不吃流质类食品。

3. 夜间入睡后,家长应定时叫其起床排尿,培养良好的生活习惯。

4. 家长做好患儿心理工作,消除紧张情绪。

8.4.11 小儿肌性斜颈

小儿肌性斜颈一般系指一侧胸锁乳突肌痉挛或挛缩造成的以头向患侧斜倾、前倾,面部旋向健侧为特点的疾病。本病如超过1年,且畸形明显者,应考虑外科手术治疗。

肌性斜颈的病理为患侧的胸锁乳突肌发生纤维性挛缩,病理可见纤维细胞增生和肌纤维变性,最终全部被结缔组织所代替。其病因尚未完全肯定。

1. 多数认为与损伤有关。分娩时一侧胸锁乳突肌因受产道或产钳挤压受伤出血,血肿机化,形成挛缩。

2. 认为分娩时胎儿头位不正,阻碍一侧胸锁乳突肌血运供给,引起肌肉缺血性改变,肌纤维水肿、甚至坏死及继发性纤维增生,最后引起肌肉挛缩,造成肌性斜颈。

3. 认为由于胎儿在子宫内头部向一侧偏斜所致,阻碍一侧胸锁乳突肌血运供应,引起该肌肉缺血性改变所致,而与生产过程无关。

【临床表现】

1. 在出生后,颈部一侧发现有梭形肿物,以后患侧的胸锁乳突肌逐渐挛缩紧张,突出物呈条索状。

2. 患儿头部向患侧倾斜,而面部旋向健侧。

3. 少数患儿仅见患侧胸锁乳突肌在锁骨的附着点周围有疣样改变的硬块物。

4. 病久患侧的颜面部发育受影响,健侧一半的面部也会发生适应性改变,使颜面部不对称。晚期患儿,一般伴有代偿性的胸椎侧凸。

【推拿治疗】

治法:舒筋通络,软坚消肿。

处方

1. 患儿取坐位或仰卧位,医者于患侧的胸锁乳突肌施用推揉法,可用拇指罗纹面揉,或食、中、无名指罗纹面揉之约4～5分钟。

2. 揉捏患侧胸锁乳突肌往返约3～5分钟,用力宜轻柔。

3. 牵拉扳颈法:医者一手扶住患侧肩部,另一手扶住患儿头顶,使患儿头部渐渐向健侧肩部牵拉倾斜,逐渐拉长患侧胸锁乳突肌,幅度由小渐大,在生理范围内反复数次。

4. 拿揉胸锁乳突肌:于患侧胸锁乳突肌施拿揉法约3～5分钟。

5. 最后配合轻拿肩井5～6次结束。

方解:推揉及拿捏患侧胸锁乳突肌,能舒筋通络活血,改善局部血运供给,缓解肌肉痉挛,促使肿物消散;伸展牵拉患侧胸锁乳突肌,能改善和恢复颈部活动功能。

【护理】

1. 家属可经常在患儿患侧胸锁乳突肌作被动牵拉伸展。
2. 在生活中采用与头面畸形相反方向的动作加以矫正，如喂奶、睡眠的枕垫或用玩具吸引患儿的注意力等，均有利于纠正姿势。

8.4.12 小儿桡骨头半脱位

小儿桡骨头半脱位是由桡骨头与环状韧带的位置不正常所致，多发生于五岁以下的儿童，是临床中常见的肘部损伤。

肱桡关节的韧带前下较薄弱，桡骨头小关节平面略向前后方、远端倾斜与桡骨干的纵轴不完全垂直；旋后位时矢状径较长，极度旋前时桡骨小头略离开尺骨的桡骨切迹，其前外侧边缘较低平并位于偏远端。当幼儿在肘关节伸直时腕部受到牵拉时，如穿衣、走路跌倒时腕部被成人握住，肘部突然受牵拉，肱桡关节间隙加大，关节内负压骤增，关节囊和环状韧带吸入关节间隙，环状韧带卡住桡骨头，阻碍回复而形成桡骨头半脱位。

【临床表现】

多发生于幼儿，患肢有牵拉损伤史。患侧肘部疼痛，肘关节呈半屈曲，前臂呈旋前位，桡骨小头处压痛，局部无明显肿胀或畸形，患手不肯取物和肘部活动，拒绝触碰。肱骨外上髁、肱骨内上髁及尺骨鹰嘴三者的位置无异常，X线检查不能显示病变。

【推拿治疗】

治法　理筋整复止痛。

处方　家长抱患儿正坐，术者与患儿相对。以右侧为例，术者左手拇指放在桡骨头外侧处，右手握其腕上部，并慢慢地将前臂旋后，一般半脱位在旋后过程中常可复位。若不能复位，将前臂稍向远端牵引并作旋后运动或将前臂向近端推进即可使挤压的环状韧带复位，可听到清脆的响声，疼痛立即消失，患肘可自由活动。或可屈肘90°向旋后方向来回旋转前臂，也可复位。复位后患儿肘部疼痛立即消失，停止哭闹，屈肘自如，能上举取物。

【护理】

1. 无明显肿胀的患儿，一般不外敷药物，可用颈腕吊带悬吊于屈肘位2～3天。
2. 注意避免牵拉患肢，以防形成习惯性脱位。

思考题

- 简述推法、摩法、运土入水、打马过天河的操作方法和作用。
- 试述坎宫、天门、耳后高骨、腹、脊柱、七节骨、脾经、四横纹、掌小横纹、上马、三关、六腑、天河水等穴的定位、操作和作用。
- 简述咳嗽、发热、泄泻、厌食、夜啼、遗尿、小儿肌性斜颈、小儿桡骨头半脱位的推拿治疗。

9 自我推拿保健

9.1 自我推拿保健对人体的作用

自我推拿保健是指本人掌握推拿的一些基本手法,在体表一定部位进行主动推拿以及活动肢体,达到早期治疗或保健强身的一种方法,是养生的常用方法。

自我推拿保健,一方面可刺激全身各部的经络、穴位,对身体的一些重要组织、器官的功能进行调整,促其旺盛,从而提高机体的抗病能力;另一方面,通过推拿可激发人体正气,促进气血运行和化生,提高机体免疫功能。

自我推拿保健的种类繁多,内容丰富,适用于各种年龄层次的人进行保健、防病治病等。

9.2 自我推拿保健操作方法

9.2.1 疏肝理气法

肝为魂之处,肝在五行中属木,主动、主升。肝的主要生理功能是主疏泄和主藏血,表现在能够调畅气机,使经络和利,并促进各脏腑器官的生理活动发挥正常,更能推动全身气血津液的运行及增强脾胃的运化功能。肝开窍于目,主筋,其华在爪,在志为怒,在液为泪。若肝气充足,则筋强力壮,爪甲坚韧,眼睛明亮;否则筋软弛缩,视物不清。另一方面,肝与胆,不仅是足厥阴肝经与足少阳胆经相互络属于肝胆之间,而且肝与胆本身也直接相连,互为表里。因此,经常施行疏肝利胆法进行保健推拿,对于肝胆范畴病变有很好的防治作用。

疏肋间:坐位,两手掌横置两腋下,手指张开,指距与肋骨的间隙等宽,先用左掌向右分推至胸骨,再用右掌向左分推至胸骨,由上而下,交替分推至脐水平线,重复9次。注意手指应紧贴肋间,用力要稳、均匀,以肋间有温热感为度。

揉膻中:坐位,用左手或右手,四指并拢置于膻中穴,稍用力作顺时针、逆时针方向的揉动各36次。

擦胁肋:坐位,两手五指并拢置于胸前平乳头,左手在上,右手在下,从胸前横向沿肋骨方向擦动并逐渐下移至浮肋,然后换右手在上,左手在下操作,以胁肋部有透热感为度。

拨阳陵:坐位,两手拇指分别按置于两侧阳陵泉穴上,余四指辅助,先行按揉该穴1分钟,再用力横向弹拨该处肌腱3～5次,以酸麻放射感为度。

掐太冲：坐位，用两手拇指的指尖置于两侧太冲穴上，稍用力按掐，以酸麻为度，约1分钟，换用拇指的罗纹面轻揉该穴位。

擦少腹：坐或卧位，双手掌分置于两胁肋下，同时用力斜向少腹推擦至耻骨，往返36次。

点章门：用两手的中指指尖分别置于两侧的章门穴上，稍用力点按，约1分钟，以有酸麻为度。

揉期门：坐或卧位，用左手的掌根置于右侧的期门穴位上，用力作顺时针、逆时针方向，各揉动36次，然后换右手操作左侧，动作相同。

拿腰肌：坐位，双手虎口卡置于两侧腰胁部肌肉，由上往下至髂部捏拿腰胁肌肉，往返36次。

运双目：坐位，端正凝视，头正腰直，两眼球先顺时针方向缓缓旋转9次，然后瞪大眼睛前视片刻，再逆时针方向如前法操作。

9.2.2 宁心安神法

心的主要生理功能是主血脉，为人体生命活动的关键所在。心主血脉的功能健全，血液才能在脉管中正常运行，周流不息，营养全身而保障生命的正常活动。心脏在体内有经脉和小肠相联系，其功能的盛衰在体表可以通过人的精神、意识、思维活动以及脉象和舌象表现出来。如心气旺盛，血脉充盈，则可见人的精神振奋，思维敏捷，动作灵活，脉搏和缓有力，舌质淡红润泽；反之，则见人的精神萎靡，反应迟钝以及脉涩不畅，节律不整，舌质紫暗或苍白等。经常进行宁心安神的保健推拿法，可以对中医所说的心系范畴的各类疾病有较好的防治作用。

振心脉：站立位，两足分开同肩宽，身体自然放松，两手掌自然伸开，以腰转动带肘臂，肘部带手，两臂一前一后自然甩动。到体前时，用手掌面拍击对侧胸前区，到体后时，以掌背拍击对侧背心区。初做时，拍击力量宜轻，若无不适反应，力量可适当加重，每次拍击36次左右。

摩胸膛：右掌按置两乳正中，指尖斜向前下方，先从左乳下环行推摩心区复原，再以掌根在前，沿右乳下环行推摩，如此连续呈"∞"(横8字)形，操作36次。

勾极泉：先以右手四指置左侧胸大肌处，用掌根稍作按揉，然后用虎口卡住腋前壁，以中指置于腋窝极泉穴位处，稍用力用指端勾住该处经筋，并向外作拨动，使之产生酸麻放射感，操作9次，然后换手如法做右侧。

捏中冲：先以右手拇、示指挟持左手中指尖（中冲穴所在处），稍用力按捏数次，随之拔放，操作9次。再换手法如法进行。

揉血海：坐位，两手分别按置左、右膝关节上方，用拇指点按血海穴1分钟左右，然后再施以轻柔缓和的揉法36次。

拿心经：右手拇指置于左侧腋下，余四指置上臂内上侧，边做拿捏，边做按揉，沿上臂内侧渐次向下操作到腕部神门穴，如此往返操作9次，再换手操作右侧。

揉神门：坐位，用右手示、中指相叠，示指按压在左手的神门穴位，按揉1分钟，换手操作。

挤内关：坐位，用右手拇指按压在左手的内关穴位上，余四指在腕背侧起到辅助作用,稍用力用拇指指端向上、下挤按内关穴9次。再换左手如法操作右侧。

鸣天鼓:双手掌分按于两耳上,掌根向前,五指向后,以示、中、环指叩击枕部3次,双手掌骤离耳部1次,如此重复9次。

搅沧海:舌在口腔上、下牙龈外周从左向右,从右向左各转9次,产生津液分3口缓缓咽下。

9.2.3 健脾和胃法

脾的主要生理功能是运化,有消化、吸收、运输营养物质和促进水液代谢的重要作用。人体各脏器功能的发挥,身体的健康程度,大多取决于脾的这种功能,所以中医称"脾为后天之本"。脾还能统摄血液使其不致溢出脉外,脾在体内在经络和胃相联系,表里相关。其功能的盛衰在体表从四肢肌肉、口唇、口腔气味上表现出来。脾健运则饮食精微不断吸收,化生气血,营养充足,口唇红润光泽;反之,则形体消瘦,肌肉痿软,口淡无味或异味,口唇淡白无光泽。采用健脾益胃的保健推拿按摩法,可对脾胃病范畴的病症有良好的防治作用。

摩脘腹:用左手或右手手掌置于中脘部,先逆时针,从小到大摩脘腹36圈,然后再顺时针,从大到小摩36圈。

荡胃腑:取仰卧位,两下肢屈曲,左右手相叠于中脘穴上,采用顺腹式呼吸,呼气时用叠掌掌根向上推荡,吸气时放松,往返36次。

分阴阳:坐或仰卧,两手相对,全掌置于剑突下,稍用力从内向外沿肋弓向胁肋处分推,并逐渐向小腹移动,操作9次。

按三里:双手拇指或示、中指置于足三里穴位上,稍用力作按揉,使局部有酸胀感,约3分钟。

揉天枢:坐位或仰卧位,用双手的示、中指同时按揉天枢穴,顺、逆时针各36次。

按脘腹:左手或右手并拢四指放置于中脘穴上,采用顺腹式呼吸,吸气时稍用力下按,呼气时作轻柔的环形揉动,如此操作36次。

揉血海:取坐位,两手分别置于大腿部,拇指点按于血海穴,作顺、逆时针方向的揉动各36次。

9.2.4 宣肺解表法

肺的主要生理功能是"主气、司呼吸",是指肺为体内外气体交换的场所。通过不断的呼浊吸清,吐故纳新,促进气的生成,调节气的升降出入运动,从而保证了人体新陈代谢的正常运行。肺还有"宣发、肃降、通调水道"的作用。这些功能的正常,可使人体呼吸、营养、水液代谢保持良好的状态,从而使人体保持健康;反之,则出现呼吸不利、胸闷、咳喘,甚至水肿等病症。肺在体内有经脉和大肠联系,其功能的盛衰在体表可通过皮肤的润泽、病变以及鼻部正常与否表现出来。因此,采用此保健推拿法,对肺系范畴的各种疾病有很好的防治作用。

舒气会:双手手掌相叠,置于两乳中间的膻中穴,上下推擦36次。

畅气机:坐位,先用右手虚掌置于右乳上方,适当用力拍击并渐横向左侧移动,来回9次;再以两手掌交叉紧贴乳上下方,横向用力往返擦动36次;最后两手掌虎口卡置于两肋下,由上沿腰侧向下至髂骨,来回推擦,以热为度。

振胸膺:坐位,先用右手从腋下捏拿左侧胸大肌9次,再换左手如法操作。然后双手十指交叉抱持于后枕部,双肘相平,尽力向后扩展,同时吸气,向前内收肘呼气,一呼一吸,操作9次。

揉中府:坐位,两手掌交叉抱于胸前,用两手中指指端置于两侧的中府穴位上,稍用力作顺时针、逆时针方向的揉动,各36次。

勾天突:用示指指尖置于天突穴处,向下勾点,揉动1分钟。

理三焦:坐或卧位,两手四指交叉,横置于膻中穴,两掌根按置两乳内侧,自上而下,稍用力推至平关元穴处,操作36次。

疏肺经:坐位或立位,右掌先置左乳上方,环摩至热后,以掌沿着肩前、上臂内侧前上方、前臂桡侧至腕、拇、示指背侧(肺经的循行路线),做往返的推擦36次,然后换左手操作右侧。

捏合谷:坐位,右手拇、示指相对捏、拿左侧合谷穴1分钟,然后换左手操作右侧。

擦迎香:坐位,用双手大鱼际或示指桡侧缘分别按置两侧迎香穴处,上下擦动,边擦边快速呼吸,以有热感为度。

9.2.5 固肾增精法

肾在人体中是极为重要的脏器,中医称肾为"先天之本",是人体生命的动力源泉。肾的主要功能是贮藏人体的精气,主管人体的生殖与发育,并可调节人体的水液代谢,使清者上升于肺而宣发全身,浊者下降于膀胱而排出体外,此外,肾的纳气功能对人体呼吸亦有重要意义。肾功能的盛衰在体表可从骨骼的坚韧、毛发的荣枯、人外在的精神状态以及耳的听觉等表现出来。选用固肾益精法的推拿保健可以加强巩固肾脏功能,并在一定程度上对肾系病症有较好的防治作用。

搓涌泉:盘膝而坐,双手掌对搓发热后,从三阴交过踝关节至大趾根外一线往返摩擦至透热为止,然后左右手分别搓涌泉穴至局部发热。搓揉时要不缓不急,略有节奏感。

摩肾府:两手掌紧贴肾俞穴,双手同时按从外向里的方向作环形转动按摩,共转动36次(此为顺转,为补法;反之为泻。肾俞穴宜补不宜泻,转动时要注意顺逆),如有肾虚、腰痛诸病者,可以增加转动次数。

揉命门:以两手的示、中两指点按在命门穴上,稍用力作环形的揉动,顺逆各36次。

擦腰骶:身体微前倾,屈肘,两手掌尽量置于两侧腰背部,以全掌或小鱼际着力,向下至尾骶部快速来回擦动,以透热为度。

摩关元:用左或右掌以关元穴为圆心,作逆时针和顺时针方向摩动各36次,然后随呼吸向内向下按压关元3分钟。

擦少腹:双手掌分置两胁肋下,同时用力斜向少腹部推擦至耻骨,往返操作以透热为度。

振双耳:先用双手掌按于耳上作前后推擦36次,然后双手拇、示指捏住两耳垂抖动36次,再将两示指插入耳孔,作快速的振颤数次后,猛然拔出,重复操作9次。

缩二阴:处于安静状态下,全身放松,用顺腹式呼吸法(即吸气时腹部隆起,呼气时腹部收缩),并在呼气时稍用力收缩前后二阴,吸气时放松,重复36次。

Science of Tuina

1 Introduction

Tuina, one of the external therapeutic methods used in TCM (traditional Chinese medicine), is a therapeutic method performed by using the doctor's hands or certain tools to press or rub certain regions or Acupoints of the patient.

1.1 History

Tuina was developed by Chinese people in ancient times. When they hurt themselves in doing physical work, they would naturally press the affected part of the their body to allay swelling and stop pain. After years of practice, they summarized some primitive ways to perform Tuina.

The records about Tuina can be found in the inscriptions on bones or tortoise shells of the Shang Dynasty (16th~11th century B. C.) and the medical materials unearthed from a tomb of the Han Dynasty in a place called Mawangdui in Changsha City, Hunan Province. This shows that Chinese people used Tuina to treat diseases three thousand years ago. In the medical materials known as Prescriptions for Fifty-Two Diseases unearthed from the ancient tomb in Mawangdui, we can find that Chinese people in the Han Dynasty used medicated ointment and various unique tools to perform Tuina. For instance, they used a sort of material called medicated handkerchief to treat sexual disorder. Stone needle was the commonly used tool to perform Tuina in ancient times. There were various stone needles for different purposes.

Qin and Han Dynasties witnessed the most important development of Tuina. According to Han Shu (history book about the Han Dynasty), Huang Di Qi Bo An Bo Shi Juan (Ten Volumes On Tuina Therapies Developed by Yellow Emperor and Qi Bo), the first monograph about Tuina, appeared at the same time with Huang Di Nei Jing (Yellow Emperor's Canon of Medicine). In terms of classification, this book mainly deals with Tuina and health cultivation; in terms of medicine, this book is of the same origin as that of Huang Di Nei Jing (Yellow Emperor's Canon of Medicine). Unfortunately, this book was lost in history. However, Huang Di Nei Jing (Yellow Emperor's Canon of Medicine) has preserved much content of Tuina.

From Huang Di Nei Jing (Yellow Emperor's Canon of Medicine), we can see that the system of Tuina was already well established in the Qin and Han Dynasties. According to this great canon, Tuina therapy originated from Luoyang area in Henan Province, the central region in China. The four diagnostic methods, namely inspection, smelling and listening, inquiry, pulse-taking and palpation, are the basic methods for diagnosis in Tuina. This great canon, though mainly deals with the basic theory and acupuncture therapy, extends its discussion to Tuina, believing that Tuina is effective for promoting Qi flow and blood circulation, dissipating cold, stopping pain, dredging meridians and collaterals, allaying fever and calming the spirit. It points out that attention must be paid to reinforcing and reducing techniques in performing Tuina. It advocates the practice of combining the therapy of Tuina with other therapeutic methods, such as acupuncture and drugs.

Huang Di Nei Jing (Yellow Emperor's Canon of Medicine) has mentioned some of the commonly used manipulations for Tuina, such as pressing, rubbing, nailing, searching, stroking, flicking, grasping, pushing, bending, stretching and shaking. Usually these manipulations are used in combination. Besides, this great canon has also provided us with quite a number of exercises for practicing Tuina. As to the tools for Tuina, the so-called round needle and sword-shaped needle are usually used for Tuina purpose. Other theoretic discussions in this great canon are also important for the practice of Tuina.

In Jin Kui Yao Lue (Synopsis of Gold Chamber), an important medical book written by Zhang Zhongjing, a great doctor in the Han Dynasty, has described ointment massage as one of the methods for health cultivation. For instance, the book has mentioned a kind of powder for treating headache by means of Tuina. This powder is composed of only two ingredients, Fuzi (Radix Aconiti Lateralis) and salt. In this great book on internal medicine, Zhang Zhongjing also introduced the methods of Tuina for saving those who hung themselves. Hua Tuo, another important doctor in the Han Dynasty, developed a sort of physical exercise known as Wuqinxi (five animals frolics) which is still practiced now as an effective way to cultivate health. Hua advocated the use of ointment in performing Tuina and was then regarded as the first one to apply Tuina therapy with ointment to clinical practice.

In the Jin Dynasty, there were specialists of Tuina worked in the Imperial Hospital. In the Tang Dynasty, specialty of Tuina was set up in the Imperial Hospital. Those who practiced Tuina were classified into three levels, Tuina specialist, Tuina doctor and Tuina worker. Tuina doctor and Tuina worker worked as the assistants of Tuina specialist. Education of Tuina was started at that time. Another important development in Tuina then was the advocacy of self massage. Methods for such practice of Tuina were mentioned in Zhou Hou Bei Ji Fang (A Handbook of Prescriptions for Emergencies) compiled by Ge Hong and Qian Jin Fang (Valuable Prescriptions) compiled by Sun Simiao. In each chapter in Zhu Bing Yuan Hou Lun (Treatise on Causes and Symptoms of Diseases) compiled by Cao Yuanfang, there is a part devoted to Daoyin (the early term for Tuina) and health cultivation, specially the methods for rubbing the abdomen.

The practice of self massage showed that the therapeutic methods of Tuina were already used for preventing disease and cultivating health. The combined use of Tuina and drugs was another important development in this period of time in history. Ge Hong paid much attention to Tuina with ointment. He was the first one to systematically study the use of ointment in Tuina. His book Zhou Hou Fang (Handy Book of Prescriptions for Emergencies) has mentioned eight prescriptions for preparing ointment for Tuina. In Wai Tai Mi Yao (Medical Secrets of An Official) added two more methods for combined use of drugs and Tuina, namely Tuina with salt and Tuina with decoction. During this period of time, the use of Tuina was further extended. According to Tang Liu Dian (Six Canons in the Tang Dynasty), Tuina was used to treat eight kinds of diseases, namely diseases due to wind, cold, heat, dampness, hunger, overeating, overstrain and easy life. Also during this period of time, Tuina was introduced to Korea, Japan, India, Arabian and European countries.

In the Song and Jin Dynasties, the application of Tuina was further extended and much attention was paid to the study of manipulations. In Sheng Ji Zong Lu (Complete Records of Holy Benevolence), a special chapter was devoted to Tuina and trials were made to differentiate the two Chinese characters An (press) and Mo (massage). The authors of this book carefully defined Tuina and described the right ways to perform this therapy. The description was also extended to cover the aspects of clinical application and therapeutic effect. In a book entitled Tai Ping Sheng Hui Fang (Taping Sacred Remedies), there were six prescriptions developed for preparing ointment to be used to treat eye problems with Tuina. This book also mentioned a special ointment for massaging the waist. Among the four great medical schools in the Jin and Yuan Dynasties, Zhang Congzheng paid more attention to Tuina therapy. In his book entitled Ru Men Shi Qin (The Scholars' Care of Their Parents), he described Tuina as one of the sweating therapies. In another book entitled Shi Yi De Xiao Fang (Effective Formulas Tested by Physicians For Generations) described different ways for reduction, such as sitting on a stool and climbing upon a ladder for treating dislocation of shoulder joint, reverse hanging for treating dislocation of hip joint and suspending for dealing with spinal fracture.

In the Ming and Qing Dynasties, quite a number of monographs on infantile Tuina were published. The earliest one in history about infantile Tuina therapy was Bao Ying Shen Shui (Magic Ways to Protect Infants) compiled by Chen and collected by Yang Jizhou in his book Zhen Jiu Da Cheng (A Great Compendium of Acupuncture and Moxibustion). Other monographs include Xiao Er Tui Na Mi Jue (Secret Ways for Infantile Tuina) by Zhou Yufan, Xiao Er Tui Na Fang Mai Huo Ying Mi Zhi Quan Shu (A Complete Book on Secret Ways for Infnatile Tuina, Prescriptions and Pulse Examination) by Gong Yunlin, Xiao Er Tui Na Guang Yi (General Introduction to Infantile Tuina) by

Xiong Yingxiong, You Ke Tie Jing (Iron Mirror of Pediatrics) by Xia Yuzhu, You Ke Tui Na Mi Shu (Secret Book on Infantile Tuina) by Luo Rulong, Tui Na San Zi Jing (Three-Character Verse on Tuina) by Xu Qianguang and Li Zheng An Mo Yao Shu (Key Manipulations of Authentic Tuina) by Zhang Zhenjun. Li Zheng An Mo Yao Shu (Key Manipulations of Authentic Tuina) by Zhang Zhenjun put forward eight manipulations, which are still popularly used now. These eight manipulations include An (press), Mo (stroke), Qia (pinch), Rou (rub), Tui (push), Yun (feel), Cuo (knead) and Yao (shake). During this period of time, Tuina therapies for adults also developed fast and different schools appeared, such as bone-setting Tuina, Acupoint Tuina, Tuina with one finger, Tuina for ophthalmology, internal medicine and healthcare.

In the period of China Republic, Tuina continued to develop and more shcools appeared, such as Tuina with one finger, Acupoint Tuina, rolling Tuina, stomachache Tuina, abdominal examination Tuina and Tuina with intrinsic power. The theory and practice of these different schools of Tuina were taught by means of apprenticeship. Some illustrated popular books about Tuina were published. Huang Shi Yi Hua (Huang's Medical Stories), compiled by Huang Hanru and published in 1933, was the first book about the stories concerning the development of Tuina. In this book, the author also described his experience in treating diseases with Tuina and introduced the origin of some manipulations.

1.2 Academic studies and development of Tuina

As a medical specialty, Tuina has developed greatly since the founding of the People's Republic of China. Such a development can be summarized from the following aspects.

Firstly, measures have been taken to recompile, collect and publish classics about Tuina. Quite a number of classics have been carefully studied and published. Academic studies with the aid of multiple modern sciences have been conducted to summarize the theory and practice of Tuina.

Secondly, trials have been made to promote scientific studies on the clinical application of Tuina. Doctors in this specialty are encouraged, based on the theory and practice of TCM, to adopt scientific methods to perform Tuina therapy. Thousands of articles have been published in various medical and science journals on the theoretic studies and clinical research of Tuina.

Thirdly, the system of education in Tuina has been completed. Since 1956, training classes for Tuina were started in Shanghai Medical School. Ever since then, this specialty has been taught and studied in all the colleges and universities of TCM in China. In recent years, quite a number of Tuina doctors with master degree and doctor degree graduated from the colleges and universities of TCM. To promote the education of Tuina, concerned textbooks have been compiled and published, including Essentials of Tuina, Therapeutics of Tuina, Manipulations of Tuina, Exercises for Infantile Tuina.

Fourthly, scientific studies on Tuina have developed significantly. Since 1950s, researchers have studied this classical specialty with modern science and technology, trying to reveal the mechanism of this old therapy. They have made it clear why Tuina can relieve pain according to neurophysiology. They have found that the reason that Tuina can subdue swelling and resolve stasis is that it can promote blood and lymph circulation. Through experiments, they have discovered that Tuina can lower blood pressure and increase the content of 5-HT and that pinching the spine can promote the absorbing functions of the small intestine.

Fifthly, remarkable innovations have been made in the field of Tuina, such as ear Acupoint Tuina, foot Acupoint Tuina, the second metacarpal bone Tuina, sports Tuina and Tuina anesthesia.

1.3　How to study Tuina

Tuina is a clinical specialty in TCM, emphasizing both theory and practice. As a doctor specializing in Tuina, one has to be familiar with the essentials, diagnostics, therapeutic methods of both TCM and WM (Western medicine). Clinically Tuina is performed with various manipulations. To be familiar with these manipulations, one has to train himself or herself with special physical exercises.

In TCM, the essentials include the theories of Yin and Yang, five elements, nutrient-Qi, defensive-Qi, Qi, blood, etiology, pathogenesis, four diagnostics, eight principles and treatment based on syndrome differentiation. In WM, the essentials cover the aspects of anatomy, physiology and physical diagnostics. To be familiar with the structure of human body, motor physiology, nerve sections, circulation of the fourteen meridians and locations of Acupoints are very important for one to study Tuina.

In doing physical training, one has to practice arduously according to the theory, methods and exercises introduced in this book, trying to train one's intrinsic power, tolerance and physical flexibility.

Review Questions

- When was the system of Tuina developed?
- What were the characteristics of Tuina in the Tang Dynasty?

2 | Mechanism of Tuina

2.1　Regulating Yin and Yang

The interactions inside the body can be explained according to the relationships between Yin and Yang. Both disharmony between Qi and blood and imbalance between nutrient-Qi and defensive-Qi can cause disorder of Yin and Yang which, in turn, leads to various diseases and pathological changes.

A disease, no matter caused by internal factors or external factors, is exclusively due to relative predominance or relative decline of Yin or Yang. To use Tuina therapy to treat diseases, one has to be clear about the state of Yin and Yang, trying to take measures to balance Yin and Yang so as to normalize the physiological functions of the body. Meridians play a very important role in physiological activities and functions of the body. In fact the state of Yin and Yang is adjusted through meridians. Meridians are distributed all over the body to connect all the viscera together and to relate the internal part of the body with the external part. Through such a neat connection, the body becomes an integral whole. So to apply manipulations of Tuina to one specific part of the body may exert effect on many other organs or regions, and consequently promoting the flow of Qi and blood, dredging the meridians and collaterals, and reinforcing the tendons and bones.

For instance, to apply manipulations to the abdomen and back can inhibit hyperactivity of intestinal peristalsis. However, if intestinal peristalsis becomes weak, manipulations can invigorate it and normalize it.

2.2　Improving deficiency and reducing excess

Generally speaking, lack of sufficient substances or hypofunction of an organ means deficiency while excessive pathogenic factors or hyperfunction of an organ means excess. The manipulations of Tuina can help us adjust such morbid state to improve deficiency and reduce excess by means of normalizing the flow of Qi and blood.

Modern physiological researches indicate that, to some tissues, mild stimulation excites their physiological functions while strong stimulation inhibits their physiological functions. Clinically, patients with spleen and stomach deficiency can be effectively treated by means of softly kneading Pishu (BL 20), Weishu (BL 21) and Qihai (CV 6) with one-finger pushing manipulation. Patients with gastric and intestinal spasm can be treated by kneading the related Acupoints located on the back with the manipulation of knocking with finger for strong stimulation. Patients with hypertension also can be treated in such a way. Hypertension caused by hyperactivity of liver Yang can be treated by pushing, pressing and kneading manipulations over the region known as Qiaogong for harmonizing the liver and suppressing Yang. Hypertension due to retention of phlegm and dampness inside the body can be treated by kneading Pishu (BL 20) and Shenshu (BL 23) located on the abdomen and back with mild stimulation for a long period of time. Such a way of treatment can strengthen the spleen and resolve dampness. These examples show that Tuina can effectively stimulate certain region of the body to promote the functions or inhibit hyperfunction of certain organs and tissue, though it does not directly add anything to the body or reduce anything from the body.

In performing Tuina, the frequency and direction of manipulations are key to reinforcement of deficiency and reduction of excess. The change of manipulations within a certain range means quantitative change while the change of manipulations exceeding a certain range indicates qualitative change. For instance, one-finger pushing manipulation with normal frequency can only dredge the meridians and adjust nutrient-Qi and defensive-Qi. But if it is performed with high frequency, it can activate blood to subdue swelling and drain pus to reduce toxin. Clinically such a manipulation with high frequency is used to deal with skin diseases, such as carbuncle and sores. Generally speaking, manipulations with high frequency can restrict the dissipation of energy and work directly on the deeper regions to exert clearing, resolving and draining effects. Such a way of manipulation means reducing. Naturally the opposite to perform manipulations means reinforcing. Under certain conditions, the direction of manipulations also means reinforcing or reducing. For instance, stroking over the abdomen clockwise means reducing while stroking counter-clockwise means reinforcing.

2.3 Activating blood and resolving stasis

Blood stasis is a morbid substance caused by slow flow of blood due to certain pathological changes. Once blood stasis is caused, it will lead to other diseases. Such a morbid condition can be improved by Tuina therapy.

2.3.1 Promoting blood flow

Modern medical research indicates that disorder in blood circulation is a key factor responsible for blood stasis. To maintain a certain pressure difference between blood in the veins and blood in the artery is an essential factor for promoting blood circulation. If such a difference fails to maintain at a certain level, it will slow down blood circulation or even lead to stoppage of blood circulation, consequently causing blood stasis, which can be relieved by Tuina therapy. Manipulations used in Tuina can work on the walls of the vessels. In applying these manipulations, the walls of vessels are pressed and then relieved. Such a pressure induced by manipulation, together with the pressure of the heart and the plasticity of the wall of vessels, will promptly increase local pressure. While immediate relief of such a sudden pressure can invigorate the blood to flow. Since pressure inside the artery is high and there are valves in the veins, blood cannot flow reversely. So the effect of manipulations on blood circulation is to propel the blood in the microcirculation to flow from the small arteries to the small veins. This is the way how manipulations can activate blood to resolve stasis. Experiments of manipulations applied to the shoulders have proved that manipulations can evidently promote microcirculation in the fingers, speed up blood circulation, and increase blood volume in the fingertips after the application of manipulations.

2.3.2 Improving blood rheology

Blood stasis is closely related to blood rheology. If the viscosity of blood is high, it will be difficult for the blood to flow. The viscosity of blood is not fixed, it varies with the speed of blood circulation. The quicker the blood circulation, the lower the viscosity of the blood. When the speed of blood circulation is reduced to a certain degree, the blood begins to coagulate and stop. Under the pressure and pinching of manipulations, the flow of blood will be improved. Modern experimental researches indicate that manipulations can influence blood rheology in patients with blood stasis, reducing the viscosity of the whole blood, reinforcing the power of red cells and promoting blood circulation. Studies show that manipulations can increase the number of white cells, elevate the ratio of lymph cells and strengthen the phagocytic function of the white cells in healthy people. For those with anemia, manipulations can increase the number of red cells and hemoglobin.

2.3.3 Reducing resistance of blood flow

Resistance of blood flow is related to the diameter of small vessels. Thus the subtle change of vascular diameter may greatly reduce the resistance of blood flow. Tuina therapy can relax the smooth muscles and dilate the diameter of blood vessels. Studies indicate that manipulations can reduce excitation of sympathetic nerve and promote wandering adrenalin in the blood and decomposition and discharge of noradrenalin, and consequently dilating the diameter of small arteries and reducing the resistance of blood flow.

The pressure and friction induced by manipulations on the surface of the body can consume and remove lipoid over the vascular wall, improve circulation of blood, reduce resistance of blood flow and ameliorate lymph circulation.

2.3.4 Improving functions of heart

Rhythmic beating of heart is a key factor in blood circulation. The output of blood from the heart is an index to evaluate the circulating function of the heart. Studies indicate that application of manipulations to a certain region can improve the functions of heart. Application of manipulations to the Acupoints like Neiguan (PC 6),Xinshu (BL 15) can slow heart rate, extend diastolic phase of heart muscles, increase infusion of blood, elevate oxygen supply of the heart muscles and reinforce the function of contraction of the left ventricle without reducing the diastolization of the left ventricle.

2.3.5 Promoting the establishment of microcirculation

In the human body, the vascular net is the major place where blood and tissues exchange substances. Under quiet condition, about 8%~16% blood capillaries are open. Comparison made before and after the application of Tuina shows that Tuina can promote regional blood capillaries to open. Animal experiments indicate that application of Tuina therapy can increase the openness of regional blood capillaries to 32% among domestic rabbits after suture of Achilles tendon, and eventually forming new vascular net. However in the control group, only some tissues around the Achilles tendon the wall of small vessels became thick and depressed with the formation of some thrombus. Such an experiment shows that manipulations can promote repair of Achilles tendon because of the formation of new vascular net.

2.4 Relaxing sinews and dredging collaterals

Clinically manipulations are used to deal with the symptoms of vascular contraction, tension and spasm, regional numbness and pain by relaxing sinews and dredging collaterals.

When a tissue is impaired, it will become painful. Pain will restrict movement of the limbs so as to prevent damage of the affected part. Delayed or incomplete treatment will fail to relieve tension and spasm of muscles, leading to evident reduction of blood supply to the muscles and accumulation of metabolic substance which, in turn, resulting in inflammatory pain and hyperplasia, or even adhesion, fibrosis and scarring of connective tissues due to chronic ischemia and hypoxia. Tuina therapy can prevent such a sequela and promote the repair of the affected tissues.

Physiological studies show that the neural tissues that can adjust muscle tone include muscle spindle receptor of muscle belly, the excitation of which can reinforce the contraction of muscles, and tendon spindle receptor, the excitation of which can inhibit the contraction of muscles. Motor physiological experiments indicate that sufficient extension of the affected muscles can excite tendon spindle receptor. Manipulations for activating joints can pull the affected muscles and relieve muscular tension and spasm.

According to the description in Huang Di Nei Jing (Yellow Emperor's Canon of Medicine), elevation of temperature in the regional tissues also can relieve muscular tension and spasm. Experiments show that the temperature of the related regions has been significantly elevated after application of manipulations.

Tuina therapy also can tranquilize the mind, stop pain and relieve muscular tension and spasm due to pain by relaxing sinews and dredging collaterals through increasing threshold of pain and reducing stimulation.

Modern researches have proved that the therapeutic effect of Tuina therapy can be evaluated by electromyogram which shows that tonic muscular activity has disappeared after application of manipulations to the regions like neck, waist and legs.

2.5 Regulating sinews for repair

Various diseases due to abnormal changes certain tissues can be effectively treated by Tuina therapy through regulating sinews and promoting flow of blood and Qi.

Tuina therapy is commonly used to deal with dislocation of joints. For instance, dislocation of shoulder joint can be rectified by pulling the shoulder in a sitting position and semi-dislocation of articulatio sacroiliaca can be treated by obliquely pulling, stretching and bending the knee. Clinically pain due to protrusion of lumbar vertebral disc can be relieved by raising, obliquely pulling and stretching the lower limbs to remove pressure on the nerve root.

Besides Tuina therapy is effective for dealing with transposition of soft tissues. For instance, slipped tendon, usually marked by streak-like eminence and severe dysfunction of joints, can be rectified by flicking or pushing and pulling manipulations. However, for broken muscles, sinews and ligaments, manipulations have to be resorted to only after operational suture.

Review Questions

- What is the mechanism of Tuina?
- Why does Tuina therapy can activate blood and resolve blood stasis?

3 Meridians and Acupoints

3.1 Essentials of meridians and acupoints

Meridians and acupoints are important structures in the human body, closely related to the science of Tuina.

Meridians refer to the routes that transport Qi and blood. Meridians are composed of two parts, meridians and collaterals. The former is the longitudinal trunk parts of the meridian, while the latter is the branches of meridians. Collaterals can be further divided into sub-collaterals. The shallow collaterals are called superficial collaterals distributing all over the body. In this way meridians and collaterals form a net connecting all parts of the body, including the viscera, five sensatory organs, four limbs and the skeleton, into an organic whole.

The system of meridians consists of meridians and collaterals. The meridians include the twelve regular meridians and the eight extraordinary vessels. The collaterals include subsidiary collaterals, superficial collaterals and minute collaterals. Altogether there are fifteen major collaterals. Each of the fourteen regular meridians has one major collateral. The spleen meridian has an extra major collateral. The function of the subsidiary collaterals is to strengthen the internal and external connection between the Yin and Yang meridians. Besides, there still exist the so-called twelve branches of meridians, twelve sinews of meridians and twelve skin divisions of meridians. The twelve branches of meridians stem from the regular meridians to strengthen the connection of the twelve meridians in the surface of the body. The function of the twelve sinews of meridians is to connect the skeleton and govern the joints. The twelve skin divisions of meridians refer to the reactive regions over the surface of the body. The distribution of the twelve sinews and skin divisions is basically the same as the running route of the twelve meridians over the surface of the body.

Acupoints are the regions where Qi and blood from the viscera and meridians effuse and infuse in the body surface. Acupoints are usually located in the interstices in the thick muscles or between tendons and bones.

The meridians and Acupoints are connected with each other. The Acupoints, closely related to the viscera, Qi and blood, pertain to different meridians that are connected with different viscera. If any disease occurs, there must be some pathological changes reflected over the related Acupoints which can be improved through stimulation of

Tuina.

3.1.1 The twelve regular meridians

Categorization

The twelve regular meridians include the three Yang meridians of hand, three Yang meridians of foot, the three Yin meridians of hand and the three Yin meridians of foot. They are named according to the viscera that they are connected with and Yin or Yang that they belong to nature. Yang meridians are connected with the Fu-organs, running along the lateral side of the limbs; while Yin meridians with the Zang-organs, running along the median side of the limbs. The meridians of hand run along the upper limbs while the meridians of foot run along the lower limbs. The twelve regular meridians run symmetrically over the head, face, four limbs and the trunk, all through the body.

In the four limbs: the Yin meridians, connected with the five Zang-organs and running along the median side of the limbs, run in a regular order in which the Taiyin meridian runs in the anterior region, the Shaoyin meridians in the median region and the Jueyin in the posterior region; the Yang meridians, connected with the six Fu-organs and running along the lateral side of the limbs, run also in a regular order in which the Yangming meridians run in the anterior region, the Taiyang meridians in the posterior region and the Shaoyang meridians in the median region. In the trunk: the three Yang meridians of foot run along the lateral side while the three Yin meridians of foot run in the chest and abdomen. Among the six meridians of the hand, the three Yang meridians run over the shoulder and neck; while the three Yin meridians run somewhat differently, a small part of the Jueyin meridian that runs to the lateral side of the chest, the Taiyin and Shaoyin meridians all run in the chest and emerge from the armpits. In the head and face: all the Yang meridians run upwards to the head and face to connect with the five sensory organs with irregular distribution; most of the Yin meridians run in the deep region of the head and neck to connect with the throat, tongue and eyes.

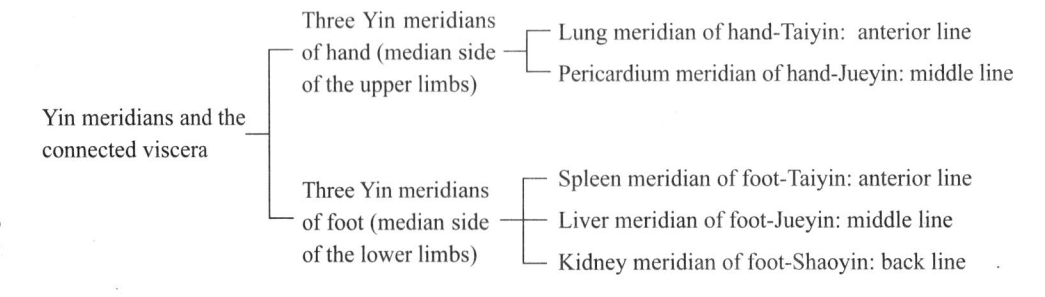

Yin meridians and the connected viscera:
- Three Yin meridians of hand (median side of the upper limbs)
  - Lung meridian of hand-Taiyin: anterior line
  - Pericardium meridian of hand-Jueyin: middle line
- Three Yin meridians of foot (median side of the lower limbs)
  - Spleen meridian of foot-Taiyin: anterior line
  - Liver meridian of foot-Jueyin: middle line
  - Kidney meridian of foot-Shaoyin: back line

*Over the lower part of the shank and the dorsum of foot, the liver meridian runs in the front while the spleen meridian runs in the median region. When these two meridians run to the point 8 cun above the external ankle, they cross and then change the way that they run. From then on the spleen meridian runs in the anterior region while the liver meridian runs in the median region.

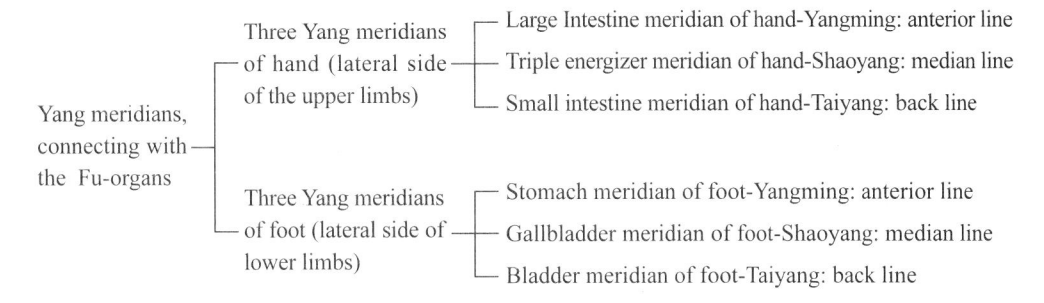

Yang meridians, connecting with the Fu-organs
- Three Yang meridians of hand (lateral side of the upper limbs)
  - Large Intestine meridian of hand-Yangming: anterior line
  - Triple energizer meridian of hand-Shaoyang: median line
  - Small intestine meridian of hand-Taiyang: back line
- Three Yang meridians of foot (lateral side of lower limbs)
  - Stomach meridian of foot-Yangming: anterior line
  - Gallbladder meridian of foot-Shaoyang: median line
  - Bladder meridian of foot-Taiyang: back line

Distribution and convergence

The three Yin meridians of hand run from the chest to the hand and then connect with the three Yang meridians; while the three Yang meridians run from the hand to the head and then connect with the three Yin meridians. The three Yang meridians of the foot run from the head to the foot; while the three Yin meridians of the foot run from the foot to the abdomen and then communicate with the three Yin meridians of the hand. In such a way the twelve regular meridians form a circulatory system.

Internal and external relationship and circulating order

The twelve meridians are connected with the Zang-organs and Fu-organs respectively, and therefore forming several pairs of internal and external relationships, namely the internal and external relationship between the large intestine meridian of hand Yangming and the meridian of hand Taiyin, the internal and external relationship between the triple energizer meridian of hand Shaoyang and the pericardium meridian of hand Jueyin, the internal and external relationship between the small intestine meridian of hand Taiyin and the heart meridian of hand Shaoyin, the internal and external relationship between the stomach meridian of foot Yangming and the spleen meridian of foot Shaoyin, the internal and external relationship between the liver meridian of foot Jueyin and the gallbladder meridian of foot Shaoyang, the internal and external relationship between the bladder meridian of foot Taiyang and the kidney meridian of foot Shaoyin. Each pair of meridians run along the median and lateral side of the limbs except that of the liver and spleen as mentioned in the previous note.

The Qi in the twelve regular meridians flows in a cyclical order: the lung meridian of hand-Taiyin → large intestine meridian of hand-Yangming → the stomach meridian of foot-Yangming → the spleen meridian of foot-Taiyin → the heart meridian of hand-Shaoyin → the small intestine meridian of hand-Taiyang → the bladder meridian of foot-Taiyang → the kidney meridian of foot-Shaoyin → the pericardium meridian of hand-Jueyin → the triple energizer meridian of hand-Shaoyang → the gallbladder meridian of foot-Shaoyang → the liver meridian of foot-Jueyin.

3.1.2 Eight extraordinary meridians

The eight extraordinary meridians are the governor vessel, conception vessel, thoroughfare vessel, belt vessel, Yang heel vessel, Yang link vessel and Yin link vessel. The reason why they are called extraordinary meridians is that they run in an irregular way.

The eight extraordinary meridians run among the twelve regular ones to intensify the connections of the meridians and regulate the Qi and blood in the twelve regular meridians. When Qi and blood in the twelve regular meridians are full, they flow into the eight extraordinary ones. When Qi and blood in the twelve regular meridians are deficient, they will be supplemented by the eight extraordinary ones. These eight meridians are closely related to the liver, kidney, uterus and brain.

Du Mai (Governor Vessel) is the sea of the Yang meridians and commands Yang Qi all through the body. The three Yang meridians of both hand and foot in the twelve meridians are all connected with the Du Mai. That is way it can invigorate and regulate Yang Qi in the whole body. Since it penetrates through the kidney and runs into the brain, it is close to the kidney and the brain.

Ren Mai (Conception Vessel) is the sea of the Yin meridians and is connected with the three Yin meridians of both hand and foot. That is why it can regulate Yin Qi in the whole body. Since it originates from the uterus, it is closely related to pregnancy.

Chong Mai (Thoroughfare Vessel) commands Qi and blood in all the meridians. It is closely related to menstruation.

Dai Mai (Belt Vessel) controls all the meridians over the trunk of the body and the lower part of the body.

Yang Qiao Mai (Yang-Heel Vessel) governs Yang in the whole body while Yin Qiao Mai (Yin-Heel Vessel) manages Yin all through the body. They all invigorate the eyes and are responsible for opening eyelids and moving the lower limbs.

Yin Wei Mai (Yin-Link Vessel) is connected with the three Yin meridians of both and foot while Yang Wei Mai (Yang-Link Vessel) is connected with the three Yang meridians of both hand and foot.

3.1.3 The fifteen major collaterals

The twelve regular meridians and the Du Mai and Ren Mai possess one major collateral respectively. Besides, the spleen has one special major collateral. Altogether there are fifteen major collaterals. Their function is to intensify the connection between two meridians that are internally and externally related to each other.

The fifteen major collaterals stem from the Luo-connective Acupoint of the meridian, and run to the internally and externally related meridians. The collateral of the Yin meridian stems from the related Yang meridian and vice versa. The collateral of the Ren Mai distributes over the abdomen and the collateral of the Du Mai runs upwards to distribute in the head and downwards to the bladder meridian. The collateral of the spleen runs to distribute in the chest and hyponchondrium.

Besides, the collaterals can be further divided into smaller ones known as minute collaterals and superficial collaterals distributing in the surface of the body.

3.1.4 The twelve meridian branches

The twelve branches of the twelve regular meridians intensify the connection between the internal and external parts of the body as well as the internal organs.

These branches usually stem from above the elbows and knees, then running into the viscera and emerging from the head and neck. Then the branches of the Yang meridians merge with the Yin Meridians while the branches of the Yang meridians merge with their meridians proper. The branches of bladder meridian and kidney meridian stem from the poplitea fossa, running into the kidney and bladder, emerging from the neck and merging with the bladder meridian. The branches of gallbladder meridian and liver meridian stem from the lower limbs, running to the pubic region, entering the liver and gallbladder, connected with the eyes and merging with the bladder meridian. The branches of the stomach meridian and spleen meridian stem from the thigh, running into the spleen and stomach, emerging from the nose and forehead and merging with the stomach meridian. The branches of small intestine meridian and the lung meridian stem from the armpits, running into the heart and small intestine, emerging from the inner canthus and merging with the small intestine. The branches of San Jiao (Triple Energizer) meridian and the pericardium meridian stem from their meridians proper, running into the chest and San Jiao, emerging from behind the ears and merging with the San Jiao meridian. The branches of the large intestine meridian and the lung meridian stem from meridians proper, running into the lung and the large intestine, emerging from the clavicular fossa and merging with the large intestine. The Acupoints located on the three Yin meridians of hand and foot can be used to treat disorders of head and face because their branches are connected with the viscera. For instance, migraine and headache can be treated by choosing Taiyuan (LU 9) and Lieque (LU 7).

3.1.5 The twelve musculatures

The twelve musculatures, including membrane, tendon and muscle, are the places where Qi from the twelve meridians accumulates, retains and disperses. They are the external parts of the twelve meridians and distribute in the same way as that of the twelve meridians. They run from the end of the four limbs to the head and body, only distributing over the surface of the body, connected with joints and skeleton. The musculatures of the three Yang meridians of hand start from fingers, run along the inner side of arms to reach the head; the musculatures of the three Yin meridians start from the fingers, running along the inner side of arms to reach the chest; the musculatures of the three Yang meridians of hand start from toes, running along the lateral side of the thigh and reaching the face; the musculatures of the three Yin meridians of foot start from toes, running along the inner side of the thigh and reaching the abdomen. They usually appear thick over the ankles, knees, thighs, wrists, elbows, arms, armpits, shoulders and neck. The musculature of the liver meridian distributes over the external genitals and is connected with all the musculatures. The musculatures are under the control of the related meridians, functioning to control bones and smooth joints. The disorders of musculatures are usually spasm, stiffness and convulsion.

Musculatures are not only attached to the skeleton, but also distribute all parts of the body and limbs to protect the internal organs.

3.1.6 Twelve cutaneous regions

The cutaneous regions are the areas that reflect the functional activities of the twelve regular meridians and the places where Qi of the collaterals distributes.

The distribution of the cutaneous regions follows that of the twelve regular meridians over the body surface. Since the cutaneous regions are the superficial part of the body tissues, they function to protect the organism. When the protecting function of the cutaneous regions is in disorder, it will give rise to invasion of exogenous pathogenic factors from the skin into the collaterals, meridians and viscera. If the viscera are in disorder, it will be manifested over the skin from the meridians and collaterals. For instance, skin lesions (vascular changes on the top of the true skin, inflammatory infiltration around the vessels) can be found in the cutaneous region of the spleen meridian in patients with spleen disorder and indigestion. Treatment of disorders of the meridians and viscera can be concentrated on the related cutaneous regions. Manipulations in Tuina can stimulate the cutaneous regions through collaterals and meridians to regulate the viscera. For instance, application of manipulations to the cutaneous region of the lung meridian can effectively treat chest oppression and cough.

3.2 Commonly used Acupoints

Acupoints located on the fourteen regular meridians are called meridian Acupoints. Acupoints that are located not on the fourteen regular meridians are called extraordinary Acupoints. And the Acupoints without definite names and locations, usually decided by tenderness, are called reflecting Acupoints.

Acupoints not only can be used to treat local or superficial disorders, but also adjacent, distal or internal disorders.

Acupoints are usually located according to anatomical landmarks, proportional measurement and finger measurement. Clinically Acupoints also can be located according to the creases, depressions and other features of the muscles and joints.

The location and combination of Acupoints can be done according to the following table.

Table 3-1 Action and indication of the commonly used Acupoints

Meridian	Acupoint	Location	Indication	Manipulations
Lung Meridian of Hand-Taiyin	Zhongfu (LU 1)	6 cun lateral to the midline of the chest, at the same level of the 1st intercostal space	Asthma, panting, chest fullness and pain in the shoulder and back	One-finger pushing, pressing, kneading and massaging
	Chize (LU5)	On the cubital crease, at the lateral side of the tendon of m.biceps brachii	Spasmodic pain in the elbow and arm, cough, asthma, distending pain of the chest and rib-side, infantile convulsion	Pressing, kneading and grasping
	Kongzui (LU 6)	7 cun above the wrist crease, on the line joining Taiyuan (LU 9) and Chize (LU 5)	Cough, hemoptysis, hoarseness, sore-throat and pain in the elbow and arm	Pressing, kneading and grasping
	Lieque (LU 7)	1.5 cun above the transverse crease of the wrist, above the styloid process of the radius	Cough, shortness of breath, rigid neck and headache, toothache	One-finger pushing, pressing and kneading
	Taiyuan (LU 9)	At the radial end of the transverse crease of the wrist and in the depression on the radial side of the radial artery	Cough, asthma, distension of breast, sore-throat and pain of the wrist	Pressing, kneading and pinching
	Yuji (LU 10)	On the midpoint of the 1st metacarpal bone, at the junction of the white and red skin	Pain in the chest and back, headache, dizziness, sore-throat, fever and aversion to cold	Pressing, kneading and pinching
	Shaoshang (LU 11)	On the radial side of the thumb, 0.1 cun posterior to the corner of the nail	Faint due to apoplexy, spasmodic pain in the fingers and infantile convulsion	pinching
Large Intestine Meridian of hand-Yangming	Hegu (LI 4)	Between the 1st and 2nd metacarpal bones, on the midpoint of the 2nd metarcarpal bone	Headache, toothache, fever, sore-throat, spasmodic pain of fingers, pain of arm and distorted face	Grasping, pressing and kneading
	Yangxi (LI 5)	On the radial side of the wrist and between the tendons of m. extensor pollicis brevis and longus	Headache, tinnitus, toothache, sore-throat, redness of eyes and wrist pain	Pinching, pressing, grasping and kneading
	Pianli (LI 6)	3 cun above Yangxi (LI 5) and on the line between Yangxi (LI 5) and Quchi (LI 11).	Nosebleed, redness of eyes, deafness, aching pain of the arm, sore-throat and edema	Pressing, kneading and grasping
	Wenliu (LI 7)	5 cun above the line between Yangxi (LI 5) and Quchi (LI 11)	Abdominal pain, hiccup, pain of the throat and tongue, headache	One-finger pushing, pressing, pinching and grasping

Continued

Meridian	Acupoint	Location	Indication	Manipulations
Large Intestine Meridian of hand-Yangming	Shousanli (LI 10)	2 cun below Quchi (LI 11)	Spasm of elbow, difficulty in stretching and bending the arm, numbness and aching pain of the arm	Grasping, pressing, kneading and one-finger pushing
	Quchi (LI 11)	In the depression lateral to the elbow crease when the elbow is bent	Fever, hypertension, swelling and pain of the arm and paralysis of the upper limbs	Grasping, pressing and kneading.
	Jianyu (LI 15)	In the depression below the acromion when the arm is raised	Pain of the shoulder, dysfuction of the shoulder joints and paralysis	One-finger pushing, pressing and kneading
	Yingxiang (LI 20)	0.5 cun lateral to the nose and in the naso-labial groove	Rhinitis, nasal obstruction and distorted face	Pinching, pressing, kneading and one-finger pushing
Stomach Meridian of Foot-Yangming	Sibai (ST 2)	Directly below the pupil and in the depression at the infraorbital foramen when looking straight forward	Distorted face, redness and itching of eyes	Pressing, kneading and one-finger pushing
	Dicang (ST 4)	0.4 cun lateral to the corner of mouth	Drooling and distorted face	One-finger pushing, pressing and kneading
	Daying (LI 5)	In the depression 1.3 cun anterior to the mandible	Lockjaw and toothache	Pinching and kneading
	Jiache (ST 6)	In the depression one finger above the mandible and at the prominence of m. maseter when the teeth are clenched	Distorted face, toothache and facial swelling	One-finger pushing, pressing and kneading
	Xiaguan (ST 7)	In the deprssion between thezygomatic arch with mandibular notch which is visible when the mouth is open and invisible when the mouth is closed	Facial paralysis and toothache	One-finger pushing, pressing and kneading
	Touwei (ST 8)	0.5 cun directly above the anterior hairline at the corner of the forehead	headache	mopping, pressing, kneading, cleaning and dissipating
	Renying (ST 9)	1.5 cun lateral to the Adam's apple	sore-throat, panting, scrofula, swollen neck and Qi oppression	grasping, wrapping

Continued

Meridian	Acupoint	Location	Indication	Manipulations
Stomach Meridian of Foot-Yangming	Shuitu (ST 10)	1 cun below Renying (ST 9) and at the anterior margin of sternocleidomastoid muscle	Chest fullness, cough, panting and stiff neck	grasping, wrapping
	Quepen (ST 12)	In the center of the supraclavicular fossa and 4 cun lateral to the front midline	Chest fullness, cough, panting and stiff neck	pressing, flicking
	Tianshu (ST 25)	2 cun lateral to the navel	diarrhea, constipation, abdominal pain, irregular menstruation	kneading, stroking, one-finger pushing
	Biguan (ST 31)	On the anterior side of the thigh and on the line connecting the anterosuperior iliac spine and the superolateral corner of the patella, on the level of the perineum	Lumbago, leg ache, numbness and flaccidity of the lower limbs, spasm of tendons and inflexibility of limbs	pressing, grasping, flicking, rolling
	Futu (ST 32)	6 cun above the inferior border of the patella	Aching knees and paralysis of the lower limbs	rolling, pressing, kneading
	Liangqiu (ST 34)	2 cun above the superolateral border of the patella	Aching, cold and numb knees	rolling, pressing, knocking with finger, grasping
	Dubi (ST 35)	In the depression lateral to the patellar ligament and below the lower border of the patella	Aching pain and restricted movement of the knee joints	knocking with finger, pressing
	Zusanli (ST 36)	3 cun below Dubi (ST 35) and one finger-breadth lateral to the anterior border of the tibia	abdominal pain, diarrhea, constipation, cold numbness of the lower limbs and hypertension	pressing, knocking with finger, one-finger pushing
	Shangjuxu (ST 37)	3 cun above Zusanli (ST 36)	Pain round the navel, diarrhea and flaccidity of the lower limbs	grasping, rolling, pressing, kneading
	Xiajuxu (ST 39)	3 cun below Shangjuxu (ST 37)	Lower abdominal pain, pain of the spine and waist, breast pain and paralysis of the lower limbs	grasping, rolling, pressing, kneading
	Fenglong (ST 40)	On the middle of the line between the lateral part of the knee and the external ankle	Headache, cough, swollen limbs, constipation, mania and epilepsy, and paralysis of the lower limbs	one-finger pushing, pressing, kneading

Continued

Meridian	Acupoint	Location	Indication	Manipulations
Stomach Meridian of Foot-Yangming	Jiexi (ST 41)	On the dorsum of the foot at the transverse malleolus crease, between the tendons of m. extensor digitorum longus and hallucis longus	sprain of ankle and numbness of toes	pressing, grasping, pinching, knocking with finger
	Chongyang (ST 42)	1.5 cun below Jiexi (ST 41) with pulsation	distorted face, facial swelling, upper toothache, stomachache, flaccidity of foot, mania and epilepsy	pressing, kneading, knocking with finger, pinching
	Taibai (SP 3)	Posterior and inferior to the 1st metatarso-phalangeal joint, at the junction of the red and white skin	Stomachache, abdominal distension, borborygmus, diarrhea, constipation, hemorrhoids with fistula	pinching, pressing, kneading
	Gongsun (SP 4)	Anterior and inferior to the base of the 1st metatarsal bone	stomachache, vomiting, indigestion, abdominal pain, diarrhea, dysentery	pinching, pressing, kneading
	Sanyinjiao (SP 6)	3 cun above the tip of the medial malleolus, posterior to the center of the tibial border	insomnia, abdominal distension, anorexia, enuresis, unsmooth urination, women diseases	pressing, knocking with finger, grasping
Spleen Meridian of Foot-Taiyin	Diji (SP 8)	3 cun below Yinlingquan (SP 9)	abdominal pain, diarrhea, edema, unsmooth urination, seminal emission	grasping, pressing, kneading
	Yinlingquan (SP 9)	In the depression posterior and inferior to the medial condyle of the tibia	aching pain of the knee joints, unsmooth urination	knocking with finger, grasping, pressing, one-finger pushing
	Xuehai (SP 10)	2 cun above the medio-superior border of the patella	irregular menstruation, aching knees	grasping, pressing, knocking with finger
	Daheng (SP 15)	4 cun lateral to the navel	diarrhea and dysentery due to deficiency-cold, constipation, lower abdominal pain	one-finger pushing, stroking, kneading, grasping
Heart Meridian of Hand-Shaoyin	Jiquan (HT 1)	In the center of armpit	chest oppression and hypochondriac pain, coldness and numbness of the arm and elbow	grasping, flicking
	Shaohai (HT 3)	In the depression at the ulnarside of the elbow crease when the elbow is bent	Pain of the elbow joint, tremor and spasm of elbow	grasping, flicking

Continued

Meridian	Acupoint	Location	Indication	Manipulations
Heart Meridian of Hand-Shaoyin	Tongli (HT 5)	1 cun above Shenmen (HT 7)	palpitation, severe palpitation, vertigo, sore-throat, sudden loss of voice, difficulty to speak due to stiffness of the tongue, pain of wrist and arm	pinching, pressing, kneading, grasping
	Yinxi (HT 6)	0.5 cun above Shenmen (HT 7)	Heartache, severe palpitation, night sweating due to bone steaming, hemoptysis, nosebleeding and sudden loss of voice	pinching, pressing, kneading, grasping
	Shenmen (HT 7)	On the radial side of the tendon of m.flexor carpi ulnaris and at the transverse crease of the wrist.	Severe palpitation, severe palpitation, insomnia and amnesia.	grasping, pressing, kneading
Small Intestine Meridian of Hand-Taiyang	Shaoze (SI 1)	At the lateral to the ulnar side of the small finger, about 0.1 cun posterior to the corner of the nail	Fever, unconsciousness in apoplexy, lack of lactation and sore-throat	pinching
	Houxi (SI 3)	In the depression proximal to the 5th metacarpophalangeal joint, on the junction of the red and white skin	Stiffness and pain in the head and neck, deafness, sore-throat, toothache, cataract and spasmodic pain in the arm and elbow	pinching
	Wangu (SI 4)	In the depression between the base of the 5th metacarpal bone and hamate bone	headache, spasmodic pain in the shoulder, wrist and fingers, jaundice and febrile disease without sweating	pinching
	Yanglao (SI 6)	In the depression dorsal to the head of the ulna	Blurred vision and pain in the shoulder and waist	pinching, pressing, kneading
	Zhizheng (SI 7)	5 cun above the wrist, at the ulnar side of the forearm	Stiffness of neck and nape, spasm of fingers, headache and vertigo	grasping, pressing, kneading
Small Intestine Meridian of Foot-Taiyang	Xiaohai (SI 8)	In the depression between the olecaranon of the ulna and the ulna and tip of the medial epicondyle of the humerus	Toothache, pain in the neck and nape, aching pain in the upper limbs	grasping
	Jianzhen (SI 9)	1 cun posterior to the crease of the armpit	Aching pain in the shoulder joint, difficulty in movement and paralysis of the upper limbs	grasping, pressing, kneading, rolling

Continued

Meridian	Acupoint	Location	Indication	Manipulations
Small Intestine Meridian of Foot-Taiyang	Tianzong (SI 11)	In the centre of the depression of the infrascapular fossa	aching pain of the shoulder and back, difficult movement of the shoulder joint, and stiffness of the neck	one-finger pushing, rolling, pressing, kneading
	Bingfeng (SI 12)	In the centre of the superscapular fossa	Scapular pain, inability to raise the arm and aching numbness of the upper limbs	one-finger pushing, pressing, kneading, and rolling
	Jianwaishu (SI 14)	3 cun lateral to the lower border of the spinous process of the 1st thoracic vertebra	aching pain of the shoulder and back, stiffness of the neck and nape, cold pain in the upper limbs	one-finger pushing, rolling, pressing, kneading
	Jianzhongshu (SI 15)	2 cun lateral to Dazhui (GV 14)	cough, panting, pain in the shoulder and back, blurred vision	one-finger pushing, rolling, pressing, kneading
	Quanliao (SI 18)	Directly below the outer canthus, in the depression below the lower border of the zygomatic bone	distorted face	one-finger pushing, pressing, kneading
Bladder Meridian of Foot-Taiyang	Jingming (BL 1)	0.1 cun lateral to the inner canthus	Eye disorders	one-finger pushing, pressing
	Cuanzhu (BL 2)	In the depression proximal to the eyebrow	headache insomnia, pain in the orbital bone and redness of eyes	one-finger pushing, pressing, kneading
	Tianzhu (BL 10)	1.3 cun lateral to the Yamen (GV 15) and in the depression on the lateral side of the m. trapezius	headache, stiff neck, stuffed nose, and pain in the shoulder and back	one-finger pushing, pressing, grasping
	Dazhu (BL 11)	1.5 cun inferior to and lateral to the 1st thoracic vertebra	Fever, cough, stiff neck, aching pain in the scapula	one-finger pushing, rolling, pressing, kneading
	Fengmen (BL 12)	1.5 cun lateral to the 2nd thoracic vertebra	Common cold, cough, stiff neck and pain in the waist and back	one-finger pushing, rolling, pressing, kneading
	Feishu (BL 13)	1.5 cun inferior to and lateral to the 3rd thoracic vertebra	cough, panting, chest oppression, muscular overstrain in the back	one-finger pushing, rolling, pressing, kneading, flicking
	Xinshu (BL 15)	1.5 cun inferior to and lateral to the fifth thoracic vertebra	insomnia, , palpitation	one-finger pushing, rolling, pressing, kneading, flicking

Continued

Meridian	Acupoint	Location	Indication	Manipulations
	Geshu (BL 17)	1.5 cun inferior to and lateral to the seventh thoracic vertebra	vomiting, dysphagia, panting, cough and night sweating	one-finger pushing, rolling, pressing, kneading
	Ganshu (BL 18)	1.5 cun inferior to and lateral to the ninth thoracic vertebra	Hypochondriac pain, hepatitis and blurred vision	one-finger pushing, rolling, pressing, kneading, flicking
	Danshu (BL 19)	1.5 cun inferior to and lateral to the tenth thoracic vertebra	Hypochondriac pain, bitter taste in the mouth and jaundice	one-finger pushing, knocking with finger, pressing, kneading
	Pishu (BL 20)	1.5 cun inferior to and lateral to the eleventh thoracic vertebra	Distending pain in the stomach, dyspepsia and chronic infantile convulsion due to fright	one-finger pushing, knocking with finger, pressing, kneading, rolling, flicking
	Weishu (BL 21)	1.5 cun inferior to and lateral to the twelfth thoracic vertebra	Stomach disease, infantile vomiting of milk and indigestion	one-finger pushing, knocking with finger, pressing, kneading, rolling, flicking
Bladder Meridian of Foot-Taiyang	Sanjiaoshu (BL 22)	1.5 cun inferior to and lateral to the first lumbar vertebra	Borborygmus, abdominal distension, vomiting, and stiffness and pain in the waist and back	one-finger pushing, pressing, kneading, and rolling
	Shenshu (BL 23)	1.5 cun inferior to and lateral to the 2nd lumbar vertebra	Kidney asthenia, lumbago, seminal emission, irregular menstruation	one-finger pushing, pressing, kneading, rolling
	Qihaishu (BL 24)	1.5 cun inferior to and lateral to the third lumbar vertebra	lumbago	one-finger pushing, pressing, kneading, rolling
	Dachangshu (BL 25)	1.5 cun inferior to and lateral to the fourth lumbar vertebra	Pain in the waist and leg, lumbar muscular sprain, intestinal inflammation	one-finger pushing, pressing, kneading, rolling, flicking
	Guanyuanshu (BL 26)	1.5 cun inferior to and lateral to the fifth lumbar vertebra	Lumbago and diarrhea	one-finger pushing, pressing, kneading, and rolling
	Baliao	In the first, second, third and fourth sacral foramina	Pain in the waist and leg, disorders of the urinary and reproductive systems	knocking with finger, pressing, kneading, and rubbing

Continued

Meridian	Acupoint	Location	Indication	Manipulations
	Zhibian (BL 52)	3 cun lateral to and inferior to the fourth sacral foramina	Pain in the waist and thigh, flaccidity of the lower limbs, unsmooth urination, constipation	rolling, grasping, flicking, forking and pressing
	Yinmen (BL 37)	6 cun inferior to the centre of gluteal groove	sciatica, paralysis of the lower limbs and pain in the waist and back	knocking with finger, pressing, patting, rolling, grasping
Bladder Meridian of Foot-Taiyang	Kunlun (BL 60)	In the depression between internal malleolus and the tendo calcaneus	headache, stiff neck, lumbago and sprain of ankle	pressing, grasping, knocking with finger
	Shenmai (BL 62)	In depression at the lower border of the lateral malleolus	mania and epilepsy; aching pain in the waist and leg	pinching, knocking with finger, pressing
	Jinmen (BL 63)	In the depression lateral to the femur below Shenmai (BL 62)	Epilepsy, lumbago, pain in the lateral malleolus, pain in the lower limbs	pinching, knocking with finger, pressing
	Jinggu (BL 64)	In the red and white part and below the fifth metatarsal bone	epilepsy, headache, stiffness of neck, pain in the waist and leg, aching knees and spasm of feet	grasping, pinching
	Yongquan (KI 1)	In the depression of the sole	Migraine, hypertension and infantile fever	Rubbing, pressing, grasping
	Taixi (KI 3)	In the depression between internal malleolus and the tendo calcaneus	Sore-throat, toothache, insomnia, seminal emission, impotence and irregular menstruation	one-finger pushing, grasping, pressing, kneading
Kidney Meridian of Foot-Shaoyin	Dazhong (KI 4)	0.5 cun inferior to Taixi (KI 3) and at the medial border of the tendo calcaneus	Stiffness and pain of the waist and spine, pain of the heel, panting and hematemesis	one-finger pushing, pressing, kneading
	Shuiquan (KI 5)	1 cun directly below Taixi (KI 3)	irregular menstruation, dysmenorrheal, unsmooth urination, and blurred vision	pressing, kneading, knocking with finger
	Zhaohai (KI 6)	In the depression below the medial malleolus	irregular menstruation	Pressing
	Jiaoxin (KI 8)	2 cun above the medial malleolus and at the inner border of the tibia	irregular menstruation, diarrhea, constipation and pain of the scrotum	pressing, kneading

Meridian	Acupoint	Location	Indication	Manipulations
	Zhubin (KI 9)	5 cun above Taixi (KI 3)	Mania, epilepsy, painful hernia and pain of the ankle	knocking with finger, pressing, kneading, grasping
	Quze (PC 3)	On the transverse cubtial crease and at the ulnar side of the tendon of m. biceps brachii	Ache and tremor of the upper limbs	grasping, pressing, kneading
	Ximen (PC 4)	5 cun above the wrist crease and between tendon palmaris longus and tendon of flexor carpi radialis	Stomachache, palpitation, vomiting	grasping, pressing, kneading
Pericardium Meridian of Hand-Jueyin	Neiguan (PC 6)	2cun above the wrist crease and between tendon palmaris longus and tendon of flexor carpi radialis	stomachache, vomiting, palpitation, mental derangement	one-finger pushing, pressing, kneading, grasping
	Daling (PC 7)	In the middle of the wrist crease and between tendon palmaris longus and tendon of flexor carpi radialis	Stomachache, palpitation, stomachache, vomiting, epilepsy and pain in the chest and hypochondrium	pressing, kneading, flicking
	Laogong (PC 8)	In the palmar crease and between the second and third metacarpal bone	Palpitation and tremor	pressing, kneading, grasping
	Zhongzhu (TE 3)	In the depression at the lower border of the fourth and fifth between the metacarpal bone	Migraine, inflexibility of the fingers, and pain of the elbow and arm	knocking with finger, pressing, kneading, one-finger pushing
	Yangchi (TE 4)	On the transverse crease of the dorsum of wrist and on the ulnar side of the tendon of m. extensor digitorum communis	Pain of the shoulder and wrist, malaria, consumptive disease and deafness	one-finger pushing, pressing, kneading
Triple Energizer Meridian Of Hand-Shaoyang	Waiguan (TE 15)	2 cun above the dorsal crease of the wrist and between the radius and ulna	headache, pain and inflexibility of the elbow, arm and fingers	one-finger pushing, rolling, pressing, kneading
	Huizong (TE 7)	3 cun above the dorsal crease of the wrist and between the radius and ulna	Deafness, epilepsy and arm pain	rolling, pressing, kneading
	Jianliao (TE 14)	Inferior to the acromion and in the depression about 1 cun posterior to Jianliao (TE 14)	Aching pain of the shoulder and arm, difficult movement of the shoulder joint	one-finger pushing, pressing, kneading, rolling, grasping

Continued

Meridian	Acupoint	Location	Indication	Manipulations
	Fengchi (GB 20)	Between sternocleidomastoid muscle and trapezius muscle, parallel to Fengfu (GV 16)	Migraine, headache, common cold and stiff neck	pressing, grasping, one-finger pushing
	Jianjing (GB 21)	On the middle of the line between Dazhui (GV 14) and acromion	Stiff neck, pain of shoulder and back, difficulty to raise hands	grasping, rolling, one-finger pushing, pressing, kneading
	Juliao (GB 29)	On the middle of the line between anterior superior iliac spine and Greater trochanter of femur	Lumbago, leg pain, ache of hip joint and sacroiliitis	rolling, knocking with finger, pressing
	Huantiao (GB 30)	On the point 1/3 lateral and 2/3 median of the line between the Greater trochanter of femur and sacral hiatus	Lumbago, leg pain and paralysis	rolling, knocking with finger, pressing
Bladder Meridian of foot-Shaoyang	Fengshi (GB 31)	On the middle point lateral to the high and 7 cun above the popliteal crease	Paralysis, aching pain of the knee joints	rolling, knocking with finger, pressing
	Yanglingquan (GB 34)	In the depression anterior and inferior to capitulum fibulae	aching pain of the knee joints and hypochondriac pain	grasping, knocking with finger, pressing, kneading
	Waiqiu (GB 36)	On the anterior border of fibia and 7 cun above external ankle	Fullness in the chest, skin pain, obstruction, epilepsy and vomiting	rolling, pressing, kneading
	Guangming (GB 37)	5 cun above the external ankle and on the posterior border of the fibia	aching knees, pain of the lower limbs, pain of eyes, night blindness and breast distension	rolling, pulling and kneading
	Xuanzhong (GB 39)	3 cun above the external ankle and on the posterior border of the fibia	headache, stiff neck and ache of the lower limbs	grasping, and pressing
	Qiuxu (GB 40)	Anterior and inferior to the external ankle, in the depression lateral to the tendon of long extensor muscle of toe	Pain of the ankle joint, chest and hypochondrium	pressing, knocking with finger, grasping
	Zulinqi (GB 41)	On the dorsum of foot and 1.5 cun above the crease of the fourth and fifth toes	Scrofula, hypochondriac pain, foot swelling, pain and spasm	pinching, knocking with finger, pressing

Continued

Meridian	Acupoint	Location	Indication	Manipulations
Liver Meridian of Foot-Jueyin	Taichong (LR 3)	On the dorsum of foot, in the depression between the first and the second metatarsal bone	headache, vertigo, hypertension and infantile convulsion	grasping, pressing, kneading
	Ligou (LR 5)	5 cun above the internal ankle and on middle of the median side of the tibia	unsmooth urination, irregular menstruation, flaccidity of tibia	rolling, grasping, pressing, kneading
	Zhongdu (LR 6)	7 cun above the internal ankle and on the middle of the median side of the tibia	abdominal pain, diarrhea, hernia, uterine hematorrhagia and lochiorrhea	rolling, grasping, pressing, kneading
	Zhangmen (LR 13)	At the end of the eleventh rib	Pain of chest and hypochondrium, chest oppression	stroking, kneading, and pressing
	Qimen (LR 14)	Directly below the nipple and the sixth costal space	Chest and hypochondriac pain	stroking, kneading, and pressing
Ren Mai (Conception Vessel)	Guanyuan (CV 4)	3 cun below the navel	abdominal pain, dysmenorrheal and enuresis	one-finger pushing, stroking, kneading, and pressing
	Shimen (CV 5)	2 cun below the navel	abdominal pain, diarrhea	one-finger pushing, stroking, kneading, and pressing
	Qihai (CV 6)	1.5 cun below the navel	abdominal pain, irregular menstruation, enuresis	one-finger pushing, stroking, kneading, and pressing
	Shenque (CV 8)	In the middle of navel	abdominal pain, diarrhea	stroking, kneading, and pressing
	Zhongwan (CV 12)	4 cun above the navel	stomachache, abdominal distension, vomiting, and indigestion	one-finger pushing, stroking, kneading, and pressing
	Jiuwei (CV 15)	Below the xiphoid process and 7 cun above the navel	Pain of the heart and chest, regurgitation and epilepsy	pressing, kneading
	Danzhong (CV 17)	On the front midline and parallel to the fourth costal space	Cough, asthma, chest oppression and pain	one-finger pushing, stroking, pressing, kneading
	Tiantu (CV 22)	In the middle of suprasternal fossa	Asthma, cough and unsmooth expectoration	pressing, one-finger pushing

Continued

Meridian	Acupoint	Location	Indication	Manipulations
	Chengjiang (CV 24)	On the middle of mentolabial furrow	distorted face, toothache	pressing, kneading, pinching
	Changjiang (GV 1)	0.5 cun below the point of sacrum	diarrhea, constipation and proctoptosis	pressing, kneading, knocking with finger
	Yaoyangguan (GV 3)	Below the fourth lumbar vertebral spinous process	Pain of the waist and spine	rolling, one-finger pushing, pressing, kneading, rubbing and pulling
	Mingmen (GV 4)	Below the second lumbar vertebral spinous process	Pain of the waist and spine	rolling, one-finger pushing, pressing, kneading, rubbing and pulling
Du Mai (Governor Vessel)	Shenzhu (GV 12)	Below the third thoracic vertebral spinous process	Stiffness and pain of the knee and spine	rolling, one-finger pushing, pulling and pressing
	Dazhui (GV 14)	Below the seventh vertebral spinous process	Common cold, fever and stiff neck	one-finger pushing, rolling, pressing, kneading
	Fengfu (GV 16)	1 cun directly above the middle of the posterior hairline	headache and stiff neck	knocking with finger, pressing, kneading, one-finger pushing
	Baihui (GV 20)	7 cun directly above the middle of the posterior hairline	Headache, vertigo, coma, hypertension and prolapse of anus	pressing, kneading, one-finger pushing
	Renzhong	On the middle point 1/3 above and 2/3 below the nasaolabial groove	Convulsion and distorted face	pinching
Extraordinary Acupoints	Yintang (EX-HN 3)	On the middle of the line between the brows	headache, rhinitis and insomnia	mopping, one-finger pushing, pressing, kneading
	Taiyang (EX-HN 5)	In the depression 1 cun posterior to the point between the brow and the outer canthus	headache, common cold and eye problems.	pressing, kneading, mopping, one-finger pushing
	Yuyao (EX-HN 4)	Middle of the brows	Pain of the orbital bone, redness and pain of eyes, tremor of the eyelids	mopping, one-finger pushing and pressing

Continued

Meridian	Acupoint	Location	Indication	Manipulations
	Yaoyan (EX-B 7)	In the depression 3.3 cun lateral and below the fourth lumbar vertebral spinous process	Lumbar sprain and ache of the waist and back	rolling, pressing, grasping and rubbing
	Jiaji (EX-B 2)	0.5 cun below the first to the fifth thoracic and vertebral spinous process	Painful and stiff spine, visceral disease	rolling, pressing, pushing, one-finger pushing and rubbing
	Shiqizhui (EX-B 8)	Below the fifth lumbar vertebral spinous process	Lumbago and leg pain	Pulling, rolling, and pressing
	Shixuan (EX-UE 11)	Tips of the ten fingers, 0.1cun to the nails	coma	pinching
Extraordinary Acupoints	Heding (EX-LE 2)	In the depression on the middle of the upper border of patella	Swelling and pain of knee joint	pressing, kneading, knocking with finger
	Lanwei (EX-LE 7)	2 cun below Zusanli (ST 36)	Appendicitis and abdominal pain	pressing, grasping, kneading, knocking with finger
	Jianneiling	On the middle of the line between the crease anterior to the armpit and Jianyu (LI 15)	Ache of shoulder joint and difficulty in movement	one-finger pushing, rolling, grasping, pressing, kneading
	Qiaogong	The line between Yifeng (TE 17) and clavicular fossa	headache, vertigo	Pushing, kneading, grasping
	Dannang (EX-LE 6)	1 cun directly below Yanglingquan (GB 34)	Colic of gallbladder	pressing, kneading, knocking with finger

4

Commonly Used Examination Methods

4.1 Examination of the head and face

4.1.1 Inspection

Inspecting the spirit

The so-called spirit in TCM is a generalization of mental activities as well as the external manifestations of Qi, blood and viscera. Inspecting the state of spirit is helpful for understanding the condition of healthy Qi and changes of diseases.

To inspect visual expression is one of the aspect of spirit inspection. If the eyes of the patient are keen, bright and clear with quick response and normal speech, it indicates that the spirit is normal, the healthy Qi is not impaired, the functions of the viscera are not affected and the disease in question is not serious. If the eyes of the patient appear dull and were dispirited with slow response, weak breath or even unconscious ness, floccillation, or sudden faint with lockjaw and involuntary discharge of urine, it indicates that the spirit is lost, the healthy Qi is impaired, the disease in question is serious and the prognosis is unfavorable. If the disease is chronic and serious and the patient is very weak, but suddenly the pathological condition of the patient becomes much better, it is called false spirit, indicating a sudden spurt of vitality before death.

Inspecting facial expressions

Facial inspection mainly concentrates on the color and luster of the face. The external manifestations of the visceral Qi and blood mainly appear on the face. The changes of facial color and luster indicate different pathological changes inside the human body. Different facial colors indicate different diseases. While changes of facial luster demonstrate the state of essence and are helpful for deciding the state of disease and possible progress. Generally speaking, bright and lustrous facial color indicates that the disease is mild, Qi and blood are not impaired, and the prognosis is favorable. While dull and lusterless complexion indicates serious disease, impairment of essence and unfavorable prognosis.

For instance, inspection the facial expressions of the patient with trauma can tell whether the condition of the patient is serious or mild. If the patient can speak normally, the condition is mild; if the patient appears pale, indifferent or even unconscious, the condition is serious.

The shape of the head and face

Protrusion of frontal bone and temporal bone at both sides and flat vertex are often seen in patients with rickets. If a child turns his head to the affected side and his face to the healthy side, it indicates myogenic touticollis. Mild anterior bending of the head with rigidity is often seen in stiff neck and cervical spondylosis. Inability to close the eye of one side, disappearance of wrinkles, showing the teeth, deviation of the mouth corner to the healthy side and disappearance of nasolabial groove indicate facial paralysis. Paralysis of the lower part of the body and deviation of the mouth corner to the affected side indicate central neural facial distortion. Stiffness of the mandible at one side is characterized by deviation of the jaw to the affected side, loss of facial symmetry, prominence of the affected side and flatness of the healthy side. Stiffness of the mandible at both sides from childhood is marked by mal-development of the whole mandible and shrinkage of the jaw. Stiffness of the mandible from adulthood is marked by no obvious deformity but difficulty to open the mouth.

Inspecting the tongue

The state of the tongue reflects the changes of the spleen, the stomach and the body fluid.

1. The tongue of the normal people is usually slightly red.

Mild white tongue indicates weakness of Qi and blood or insufficiency of Yang Qi accompanied by cold.

Deep red tongue indicates heat syndrome or Yin syndrome. Freshly red tongue and deep red tongue all indicate heat. However, heat indicated by deep red tongue is more serious. Such changes of tongue are often seen in heat excess syndrome, fever due to infection, trauma or major operation.

Bluish and purplish tongue indicates unsmooth flow of Qi and blood after injury and stasis of blood. If there are regional purpura, it indicates mild blood stasis or local blood stasis. If the whole tongue is blue and purple, it shows that blood stasis is serious.

2. The normal tongue coating is thin, white and slippery. Inspecting tongue coating can tell whether the disease is internal or external. Changes of tongue coating can also indicate the condition of pathogenic factors and healthy Qi.

Scanty or no tongue coating indicates weakness of the spleen and stomach while thick and greasy tongue coating shows excessive dampness inside the body. Usually the thicker the tongue coating, the severer the disease. The changes of tongue coating can tell the progress of a disease. For instance, if tongue coating becomes thick, it indicates progress of a disease; if tongue coating becomes thin, it indicates improvement of a disease. Red tongue without coating indicates deficiency of stomach Qi or body fluid, often seen in old patients with fracture of neck of femur.

White tongue coating indicates cold. Thick white and slippery tongue coating indicates syndrome accompanied by cold dampness or cold phlegm. Thick white and greasy tongue coating indicates dampness and turbidity. Thin white and dry tongue coating indicates transformation of pathogenic dampness into heat and insufficiency of body fluid. Thick white and dry tongue coating indicates transformation of pathogenic dampness into dryness. Tongue coating as white as accumulating powder indicates infection after trauma and internal accumulation of heat toxin.

Yellow tongue coating indicates heat syndrome or external heat syndrome, usually seen in infection after trauma or transformation of blood stasis into heat. Change of tongue coating from yellow to gray and black indicates serious disease, usually seen in severe infection after trauma accompanied by high fever or loss of body fluid.

4.1.2 Palpation

Palpation, included in pulse taking examination, means to touch or feel certain part of the patient's body to differentiate cold, warmth, moisture, dryness, distension and pain.

Examination of infantile fontanel: The doctor may put his palms at both sides of the temple to examine the fontanel with the middle finger and index finger. Normally the artery in the anterior fontanel can be felt pulsating as that of the radial artery. The anterior fontanel is at the same level with the cranium. Protrusion of the anterior fontanel, excluding that appearing during crying, is often seen in high fever and bleeding inside the cranium. Retard closure of the anterior fontanel is often seen in rickets. Depression of the anterior fontanel is often seen in vomiting and diarrhea followed by loss of body fluid.

Examination to decide the length of mouth opening: The length from the upper teeth to the lower teeth is about the width of the middle, index and the fourth fingers when put together. Disorder of the mandible may narrow such a length or cause lockjaw.

Stiff muscle or rigid spasm can be felt in patients with stiffness of neck or cervical spondylosis.

Examination of traumatic injury: Traumatic injury without obvious changes should be examined carefully to see if there is depression in the cranium and whether there is fracture in the deep region of subcutaneous hematoma, or avulsion of scalp and cranial depression or deformity. Dislocation of mandible is often marked by emptiness of articular fossa and condyle anterior to it.

4.2 Examination of the chest and abdomen

4.2.1 Inspection

Inspection is made in order to see whether there is local redness, swelling, mass and visible veins. Hardness of the breast with obvious tenderness and fever is often caused by mastitis. Protrusion of veins accompanied by ascites, splenomegaly is usually caused by portal hypertension in liver disease. Infantile emaciation with swollen abdomen and visible veins is frequently caused by malnutrition. The changes of thoracic and abdominal shapes should also be taken into consideration in inspection. Barrel chest is often seen in emphysema and bronchial asthma. Flat chest is usually seen in people thin and tall or in people with pulmonary tuberculosis and the similar consumptive diseases. Chicken breast is often seen in rickets.

Deformity of spine can lead to changes of the thorax, such as tuberculosis of spine or humpback in the old that cause shortness of the thoracic vertebrae, narrowness between or overlapping of the ribs and deviation of the thorax to the spinal side. Deformity during physical development and other spinal diseases or muscular paralysis of muscles at one side of the spine may lead to scoliosis marked by protrusion of the thorax at one side of the spine and narrowness of the costal interstices, depression of the thorax at the other side of the spine marked by closeness or overlapping of ribs and imbalance of the two shoulders.

Abdominal depression and protrusion of the navel and abdomen when standing are often seen in gastroptosis. Abdominal peristaltic wave may be observed in patients with extreme emaciation. Obvious gastric or intestinal peristaltic wave can be seen in pyloric obstruction and intestinal obstruction.

4.2.2 Palpation

Tenderness is the focus of chest and abdominal palpation. Tenderness at certain region may reflect pathological changes of certain internal organs.

In cutaneous emphysema in the thoracic wall, something like holding snow or thread can be felt. Such feeling is due to breaking of lung or trachea.

Pinching test of the thorax: This method is used to see whether there is fracture. The patient is asked to sit or stand, the doctor pinch the thorax of the patient from both sides. If there is costal fracture, pain will be felt when pinched.

Abdominal wall reflex: The patient lies in supine position with the lower limbs bent and is asked to relax the abdominal muscle. The doctor quickly and mildly draws a line from the hypochondrium to the navel and abdomen with a stick to see whether there is muscular reflex. The reflex center of the upper abdominal wall is located in the 7~8 thoracic vertebrae, the reflex center of the middle abdominal wall is located in the 9~10 thoracic vertebrae and the reflex center of the lower abdominal wall is located in the 11~12 thoracic vertebrae. Loss of abdominal wall reflex can be found in extrapyramidal bundle injury. Loss of abdominal wall at a certain horizontal level suggests injury of spinal cord at the corresponding section.

Cremasteric reflex: A stick of match is used to draw the skin over the inner side of the thigh to induce contraction of the scrotum. If such a reflex has disappeared, it indicates extrapyramidal bundle injury. Disappearance of such a reflex at both sides can be seen in injury of 1~2 lumbar vertebrae.

4.3 Spine

4.3.1 Inspection

Inspection of the spine is to examine whether there is change of normal physiological curve and if there is spinal deformity. Normally there are four physiological spinal curves, namely neck curve, thoracic curve, lumbar curve and sacral curve. Cares should also be made to see whether there are abnormal changes of posture, such as scoliolosis, humpback, increased or decreased lumbar lordosis and wry pelvis.

Anatomically, scoliolosis can be functional and structural. Functional scoliolosis shows no structural deformity. The following method can be used to differentiate whether such scoliolosis is reversible. The patient is asked to pull the horizontal bar with both hands. If the spinal curve has disappeared, it is functional. Anterior bending of the spine test: When the spine is bent anteriorly for 80°, the functional curve disappears, but the structural curve still exists. Structural curve, irreversible and caused by disorders of vertebrae, ligament, intervertebral disc, nerve and muscles, cannot be rectified. Such curves, usually severe and fixated, appears prominent when the spine is turned. More serious curves are often accompanied by deformity of thorax. Such problems are usually caused by improper posture, non-symmetry of the lower limbs, deformity of the shoulders, breaking of the lumbar intervertebral fibers, infantile paralysis and chronic thoracic diseases. Deformity of the side due to improper posture usually disappears in supination or when the waist is bent.

In inspecting the spine, doctors should carefully observe the skin, body hair and soft tissues at both sides of the spine to see whether there are symptoms of swelling, congestion, blood stasis, contusion, muscular spasm, muscular atrophy, pigmented spots, flocci and mass. Different sized coffee spots over the waist and back indicate neurofibroma or proliferative fivrosis. Long body hair over the lumbosacral region indicates congenital fissure of sacral vertebrae. Swollen and distending soft tissues around the middle of the waist indicate spinal meningocele. Swelling in the triangular region at one side of the waist indicates wandering abscess.

4.3.2 Palpation

Palpation means to seek tenderness around the spinal region. Shallow tenderness indicates superficial disorders in the supraspinal and interspinal ligament. Deep tenderness and intermittent tenderness indicates deep disorders of vertebrae, small joints and intervertebral discs. Tenderness in sprain of lumbar soft tissues can be found in the affected region. For instance, interspinal tenderness can be found in interspinal ligament injury, supraspinal tenderness can be found in supraspinal ligament injury, lumbar tenderness can be found in lumbar myofascitis. If lumbar tenderness is mild or cannot be found and the patient feels comfortable when knocking the waist with the fist, it usually suggests retroverted uterus, nephroptosis and neurasthenia. Lumbar tenderness may reflect visceral disorders. For instance, tenderness at Xinshu (BL 15) in the right side suggests heart disease; tenderness at the right liver region and Danshu (BL 19) suggests liver and gallbladder disorders.

4.3.3 Motor examination

Normally the spine can bend forwards and backwards, to the left and to the right.

When examining the neck movement, doctors can ask patients to sit upright and keep the shoulders immobile when moving the neck. The neck bends anteriorly for 35°~45°, posteriorly for 35°~45°, moves to the right and left sides respectively for 45°, turns to the left and right sides respectively for 60°~80°.

The lumbar part keeps straight in a natural pose, bending anteriorly for 90°, posteriorly for 30°, turning to the left and right sides respectively for 30°, and moves to the right and left sides respectively for 30°.

Such examinations can tell whether there are symptoms of dyscinesia in order to exclude compensatory movement. Motor examination should be avoided in dealing with fracture lest spinal cord, nerves or vessels be impaired.

4.3.4 Special examination

Vertex percussion test: The patient is asked to sit straight with the head turning to the affected side. The doctor puts his left palm on the vertex of the patient and performs percussion with his right hand. If there is impairment of nerve root, the patient will feel pain or radiating pain. If there is sharp pain, it can be aggravated when pressed with both hands over the vertex.

Brachial plexus pulling test: The patient bends his neck anteriorly. The doctor supports one side of the patient's head with one of this hand and grasps the wrist of the patient with the other hand, then pulling towards the opposite direction. If the affected arm is painful or numb, it suggests pressure of the brachial plexus.

Deep breath test: The patient sits straight with both hands put on the knees. The doctor examines the pulsation of the radial artery in both hands first, and then asking the patient to bend the neck posteriorly as much as possible to breathe deeply and, at the same time, turn the head to the affected side. The doctor presses the shoulders of the patient and examines the pulsation of radial artery in both hands again. Under such a condition, usually the pulsation in the affected side will become weak or disappear while pain in the same side will become worsened. On the contrary, when the shoulders are raised and the head turned anteriorly, the pulsation will become normal and the pain will be relieved or improved. Such an examination is taken to find whether there is syndrome involving the neck, ribs and scalene.

Super-abduction test: This test is used to examine super-abduction syndrome to see whether the infraclavicular artery is pressed by coracoid process and smaller pectoral muscle. In conducting this test, the doctor abducts the affected limb of the patient over the head from the lateral side. If the radial artery pulsates weak or stops pulsation, it is a positive sign.

Neck rotation test: This test is used to examine the vertebral artery. The patient is asked to raise his head slightly to the posterior side and turns the neck automatically to the right and left sides. If there are symptoms of dizziness, it suggests insufficient supply of blood in the basilar artery. This test may induce vomiting or faint.

Neck bending test: The patient lies in supination. The doctor puts one of his hands at the occipital side and the other over the chest of the patient, and then bending the head of the patient anteriorly. If there appear lumbago and sciatica, they are regarded as positive signs. When the neck is bent anteriorly, the spinal cord will be raised 1~2cm and the nerve roots will be pulled, consequently leading to radiating pain. This test is usually used to examine protrusion of lumbar intervertebral disc.

Abdomen straightening test: The patient lies in supination and tries to straighten the abdomen so as to raise the waist and pelvis over the bed. If there are symptoms of radiating pain in the waist and lower limbs or cough, it suggests pressure of the lumbar nerve roots.

Leg raising and foot dorsum test: The patient lies in supination with both legs stretched straight, then raising the legs. The doctor examines the range of rising that does not cause pain (the angle between the raised leg and the bed). If the nerve root is pressed, pain in the regions with distribution of nerves will be caused when the legs are raised to the range below 60°. When the legs are lowered to 5~10°, the pain will disappear. If sciatica appears again when the foot dorsum is suddenly bent, it is a positive sign. The foot dorsum test is more significant than leg raising test in diagnosing lumbar intervertebral fiber breaking syndrome. Because positive signs can be caused by tension of the iliotibial tract and hamstring muscle when the legs are raised. However positive signs in foot dorsum test only indicate that the sciatic nerve is affected.

Femoral nerve pulling test: The patient lies in prone position. The doctor fixates the pelvis of the patient with one hand and holds the affected shank of the patient with the other hand, and then pulling the leg of the patient with great strength. Radiating pain in the anterior part of the thigh is a positive sign.

Pelvis rotating test: The patient lies in a supination. The doctor bends the hips and knees of the patient as much as possible to raise the buttocks of the patient over the bed and enable the waist of the patient to bend passively to the anterior direction. If pain appears in the lumbosacral part, it is a positive sign. Such a positive sign is usually seen in injury of lumbar soft tissue and lumbosacral vertebral disorder.

Pelvis separating and pressing test: The patient lies in supination. The doctor presses the wing of iliac crest of the patient from the opposite sides. This is called pelvis separating test. If the doctor presses the wing of ilium with both hands towards the central region, it is called pelvis pressing test. If there is pain, it suggests disorder of articulatio sacro-iliaca or pelvic fracture.

4-shaped test: The patient lies in supination, stretching the healthy lower limb straight and laterally bending the affected limb to put the foot over the knee of the healthy limb. The doctor presses the knee of the affected limb of the patient with one hand and presses the anterior superior iliac spine of the healthy limb of the patient with the other hand to rotate the articulatio sacro-iliaca. If there is pain, it suggests the disorder of articulatio sacro-iliaca.

Bed side test: The patient lies in supination and turns the buttock against the side of the bed, bending the knee of the healthy limb to fixate the pelvis. The doctor moves the affected limb of the patient to the edge of the bed and pulls as much as possible in order to move the articulatio sacro-iliaca. If there is pain in the articulatio sacro-iliaca, it suggests pathological changes.

Heel-buttock test: The patient lies in prone position and stretches the lower limbs. The doctor grasps the heel of the patient to bend the knee till the heel touches the buttock. If there is disorder in the lumbosacral joint, there will be pain in the lumbosacral region and the pelvis or even the waist will be raised during the test.

4.4 The upper limbs

4.4.1 The shoulders

clinically visceral diseases will cause pain in certain areas due to nerve reflex. So in dealing with shoulder pain, trials have to be taken to exclude visceral disorders. For instance, in diagnosing pain in the left shoulder, measures should be taken to exclude heart disease; in diagnosing pain in the right shoulder, cares should be taken to exclude liver and gallbladder disorders. Sometimes pain in the shoulders may be caused by cervical vertebral disorder.

Inspection

In examining the shoulders, the patient should take off the clothes over the shoulders. The doctor first examine symmetry between the two shoulders and observe the skin color, development of the deltoid muscle at both sides as well as the superclavicular and infraclavicular fossae to see whether there are symptoms of deformity, swelling, sinus, mass and dilation of veins. The back side should also be examined to see whether the scapulae at both sides are at the same level, the distance between the medial border of scapula and the spinal vertebrae is the same and the muscles at the upper and lower regions of the spine of scapula are atrophic. If there is asymmetry, further examination should be taken. If the scapula is prominent, it suggests congenital tall scapula disease. If the medial border of the scapula is protruding, it suggests paralysis of serratus anterior muscles. If the back of the shoulder is swollen in patients with acute injury, it suggests dislocation of shoulder joint or fracture of scapula. Bulge of deltoid muscle suggests dislocation of shoulder joint. Prominence of the lateral side of the clavicle suggests dislocation of clavicular joint or fracture of the external part of the clavicle. Shift of the affected shoulder towards the lower, anterior and medial sides suggests dislocation or fracture of sternoclavicular articulation. Besides, injury or paralysis of brachial plexus may cause muscular paralysis in the shoulder or shoulder drop.

Palpation

The purpose of palpating the shoulder with thumbs is to seek tenderness to see whether there are abnormal changes of the joint and whether there are snapping and friction sensation. Trials must be made to exclude fracture. Tenderness in the shoulder should be examined together with the functions of the shoulder joint to decide the location of a disorder. For instance, tenderness anterior and inferior to the acromion usually indicates disorder near the lesser tuberosity of humerus. Tenderness lateral to the acromion often indicates disorder near the greater tuberosity of humerus.

If the upper limbs are found not the same size and the muscles are atrophic, it should be measured. The length of the upper limbs to be measured is the distance between the acromion and the tip of the middle finger. To measure the diameter of the upper limbs, the part of the same size at both arms is chosen and the length between the two acromions or the oclecranon should be labeled.

Motor examination

The following are the normal ranges of shoulder joint movement:

Anteflexion movement: Normally the range of movement can reach 90°. The doctor fixates the shoulder of the affected side with one hand and asks the patient to raise the upper limbs anteriorly. The muscles involved in such a movement are the anterior part of deltoid muscle and coracobrachial muscle.

Retro-extension movement: Normally the range of movement can reach 45°. The doctor asks the patient to raise the upper limbs posteriorly and then abducts the upper limbs. The muscles involved in such a movement are broadest muscle of back and musculus teres major.

Abduction movement: Normally the range of movement can reach 90°. The patient is asked to abduct the upper limbs. The muscles involved in such a movement are deltoid muscle and supraspinous muscle.

Endoduction movement: Normally the range of movement can reach 45°. The patient is asked to bend the elbows and move the upper limbs medially. The muscle involved in such a movement is greater pectoral muscle.

Extorsion movement: Normally the range of movement can reach 30°. The patient is asked to bend the elbow for 90°. The doctor holds the elbow of the patient with one hand and wrist of the patient with the other to rotate the upper arms laterally. The muscles involved in such a movement are infraspinous muscle and musculus teres minor.

Adduction movement: Normally the range of movement can reach 80°. The patient is asked to bend the elbow for 90° and adduct the forearm to the front of the chest or to touch the subscapular muscle with the forearm from the back. The muscles involved in such a movement are subscapular muscle and broadest muscle of back.

Raising the upper arms: To raise the upper arms is a complicated action. Accomplishment of such an action indicates that the shoulder functions well.

Rotation movement: To rotate the upper arms around the acromiobrachial joint. Such an action can be done in corona plane, sagittal plane or transverse plane.

Special tests

Dugas syndrome test: The patient bends the elbow and puts the hand at the affected side on the shoulder at the opposite side and touches the elbow against the chest. If the patient can do such an activity, the function is normal. If the patient cannot do such an activity, it suggests dislocation of shoulder joint.

Straightedge test: Normally the acromion is located in the medial side of the line between the external condyle of humerus and greater tuberosity of humerus. In doing examination, the doctor can touch the lateral side of the patient's upper arm with the edge of a straightedge. If one end of the straightedge is put against the external condyle of humerus and the other end can touch against the acromion, it suggests dislocation of acromion.

Arm drop test: The patient stands up, passively abducts the affected limb for 90° and then slowly puts it down. If the arm cannot be put down slowly and suddenly drops to the side of the body, it is a positive sign, suggesting injury of supraspinous muscle.

Pain circle test: The patient is asked to abduct the shoulder or passively abduct the affected limb. When it is abducted to 60°~120°, the tendon of supraspinous muscle will cause friction below the acromion and pain in the shoulder. This is the positive sign, usually seen in myotenositis.

Tendon of supraspinous muscle breaking test: The patient is asked to abduct the shoulder to 30°~60°. Then the deltoid muscle in the affected side contracts, making it difficult to raise the upper limbs. When the shoulder is passively abducted over 60°, the affected limb can be raised up again. This is the positive sign, suggesting breaking or laceration of the tendon of supraspinous muscle.

Yergason test: The patient is asked to bend the elbow for 90°. The doctor holds the elbow of the patient with one hand and grasps the wrist of the patient with the other hand, asking the patient to bend the elbow and rotate the forearm posteriorly to see whether there is resistance. If the tendon of biceps muscle of arm is shifted, it suggests that the tendon of the long head of biceps brachii muscle is slipped; if pain is caused in the intertubercular sulcus, it suggests myotenositis of long head of biceps brachii.

4.4.2 Elbow

Inspection

The purpose for examining the elbow is to see whether there are symptoms of swelling and deformity.

In examining patients with obvious swelling and distension, the doctor must make it clear whether it is swelling within the joints or outside the joints, or swelling of the whole joint or just regional swelling, or traumatic swelling or pathological swelling (suppurative infection and nodules etc.). Retention of fluid inside the joints is manifested as disappearance of depression beside the olecranon. If there is excessive fluid retained in the joints, the joints will become obviously swollen and appear semi-flexed.

Limited swelling in trauma usually suggests regional injury. For instance, medial swelling of the elbow may suggest fracture of medial condyle of humerus, lateral swelling of the elbow may suggest fracture of external condyle of humerus or small head of the radius, posterior swelling of the elbow may indicate fracture of olecranon. Besides, swelling in contusion of regional soft tissue is often limited. Nerve palsy may lead to muscular atrophy.

Normally the elbow may manifest an angle of 5°~7° when stretched straight, usually slightly larger in women than in men. Enlarged angle indicates extraversion of the elbow while reduced angle or ulnar deviation of the forearm indicates introversion of the elbow.

If the shape of the elbow is changed, it may indicate fracture or dislocation. Dislocation of the elbow joint or supracondylar fracture usually causes semi-flexion of the elbow. Straight supracondylar fracture or posterior dislocation of the elbow joint is often marked by prominent posterior process of olecranon. In infantile of subluxation of capitulum radii, deformity of the forearm in pronation is often seen.

Palpation

Internal humeral condyles, external humeral condyles and olecranons are the landmarks in palpation of the elbow joint. These three points form the straight line and triangle of the elbow, the changes of which are significant in deciding whether there is dislocation or fracture of the elbow joint. The external condyle of humerus is attached with the extensor muscle group of the forearm. Obvious tenderness can be found there when there is external humeral epicondylitis (tennis elbow). The internal condyle of humerus is attached with flexor muscle group of the forearm and obvious tenderness can be found there when there is inflammation. The olecranon may have tenderness or become thick when there is fracture orbursitis. The head of radius can be felt at the radial fossa posterior to the elbow and the radial head can be felt moving when the forearm is turned. When there is fracture, this fossa will bulge with tenderness. The tuberosity of ulna anterior to the elbow is usually difficult to be felt and can only be sensed by heavily pressing the region anterior to the elbow with the thumb. There will be tenderness at this region when there is fracture. The ulnar nerve is located at the ulnar side posterior to the elbow. If the ulnar nerve is in disorder, local thickness accompanied by tenderness and numbness can be felt. Fracture of external condyle of humerus, medial epicondyle, small head of radius and olecranon will cause regional swelling and tenderness as well as friction of bones and abnormal activity. Limited abduction and adduction of the forearm suggests injury of the flexor and extensor of the forearm at the medial and lateral sides or injury of the lateral accessory ligament. Dislocation or fracture of the elbow joint can lead to abnormal changes of abduction and adduction.

Motor examination

The movement of the elbow joint is marked by flexion and extension. The main joint involved in such a movement is humeral and ulnar joint. Flexion is usually 140° and extension is about 0°~10°. Rotation of the forearm relies on the interaction between the interosseous membraneand the upper and lower joints of the ulna and radius. The pronation (with the palm downwards) is about 90° and the supination (with the palm upwards) is about 90°. Though the humeral and radial joint are involved in the flexion and rotation of the forearm, it is comparatively less important. When the elbow is straightened, it does not turn laterally. But when the lateral accessory ligament is injured, it will turn to the lateral side.

Special examinations

Mill test: The patient is asked to slightly bend the forearm, slightly clench the fist, flex the wrist joint as much as possible, then completely turn the forearm anteriorly and straighten the elbow. If there is pain in the lateral side of the humeral and radial joint when the elbow is straightened, it is a positive sign.

Forearm flexion and extensor tension test: The patient is asked to clench the fist and flex the wrist. The doctor presses the hand dorsum of the patient with his hand and asks the patient to stretch the wrist under the pressure. If there is pain in the lateral side of the elbow, it is a positive sign, suggesting inflammatory focus in the external condyle of humerus. Or the doctor may press the palm of the patient and ask the patient to flex his wrist under pressure. If there is pain in the medial side of the elbow, it is a positive sign, suggesting disorder of the medial condyle of humerus.

Forearm (adduction) test: This test is done to judge whether there is injury of the lateral accessory ligament in the elbow joint. The doctor and the patient sit face to face. The patient straightens his upper limbs forwards. The doctor holds the elbow of the patient with one hand to push the elbow laterally and grasps the wrist with the other to enable the forearm to turn medially. If the lateral accessory ligament is broken, adduction of the forearm will appear. If abduction of the forearm is caused when the doctor forces the forearm of the patient to perform abduction by holding the wrist and pulls the elbow joint medially, it suggests injury of medial accessory ligament.

4.4.3 Wrist, palm and fingers

Inspection

Comparison is made in inspecting the wrist and fingers to see whether there are signs of deformity, swelling of the soft tissues and muscular atrophy.

The hand maintains in natural clenching pose and the tension of all antagonistic muscles is balanced. The dorsiflexion of the wrist is about 15°, the thumb touches the index finger and the rest four fingers are in flexion. From the second to the fifth finger, the flexion of fingers gradually increases and the tips of fingers point to the navicular bone. When the hand is injured, the myodynamia becomes imbalanced and dysfunction of the hand will appear.

Rapidly clenching and stretching fingers indicates that the function of the hand is normal.

Distal fracture of radius will lead to silver fork deformity or bayonet shaped deformity. Distal fracture of ulnar joint will cause protrusion of styloid process of ulna at the dorsal side. The deformity caused by non-acute injury is damage of nerves and vessels. Injury of radial nerve can cause drop of the wrist, damage of the median nerve, failure of the thumb to oppose to the palm and abduct, inability of the thumb and index finger to flex and stretch, atrophy of major thenar, monkey paw deformity. Injury of ulnar nerve will make it impossible for the thumb to abduct, the rest fingers to adduct and abduct, the fourth and fifth metacarpophalangeal articulations to flex and distal interphalangeal articulations to stretch, consequently causing astrophy of interosseous muscles and minor thenar and paw like hand. Besides, paw like hand also can be found in patients with ischemic necrosis of the flexors in the forearm and ischemic spasm. Due to contraction of the interosseous muscles, the fractured end deviates to the dorsal side. Fracture of the proximal phalangeal bone or fracture of the middle finger (the fracture line is located in the distal end of the tendon of flexor digitorum and the fractured end) deviates to the palmar side. Fracture of the base of the fifth phalanx breaking of the distal part of the extensor tendon will lead to drop of the phalangette.

Cares should be taken to examine the region and range of soft tissue swelling. Bulge of the nasopharyngeal fossa usually indicates fracture of the navicular bone. Fusiform symmetrical swelling of the proximal interphalangeal articulations at both sides indicates rheumatic arthritis. Swelling along the tendons suggests tenovaginitis or peritendinitis. Clubbed fingers of the whole hand suggest pulmogenic heart disease, bronchiectasis or cyanotic congenital heart disease.

Tremor of fingers is often seen in hyperthyroidism, paralysis agitans and chronic alcoholism. In patients with paralysis agitans, tremor may disappear when he is moving and appear when he maintains static. To examine mild tremor, the doctor can ask the patient to close the eyes and stretch the hands anteriorly at a horizontal level with a piece of paper attached to the dorsum of the hand. If there is mild tremor, the paper will shake.

In diagnosis of babies less than three years old, inspecting the color of the fingerprint (superficial veins along the radial side of the palmar part of the index finger) can help diagnose diseases. The first section of the index finger is called wind-pass, the second section is called Qi-pass and the third section is called life-pass. The normal fingerprint appears light red within the wind-pass. If the fingerprint appears freshly red, it means invasion of pathogenic factors; if it appears purplish, it indicates fever; if it is blue, it indicates convulsion; if it is light-colored, it indicates cold. Appearance of the fingerprint in the wind-pass indicates mild disease, in the Qi-pass indicates serious disease, and in the life-pass indicates severe disease.

Palpation

The purpose of palpating the wrist, palm and fingers is to find tenderness, mass and pain under percussion. Tenderness in the styloid process of radius usually indicates tenovaginitis of the short and long extensor muscle of great toe and tenderness in the palmar side of the metacarpophalangeal articulation is often seen in tenovaginitis of the first, second, third and fourth fingers. Tenderness in the central region of wrist crease at the palmar side accompanied by radiating pain and numbness indicates carpal tunnel syndrome, suggesting pressure of the median nerve. Swelling and tenderness in the nasopharyngeal fossa suggest fracture of navicular bone. Tenderness at the distal radioulnar joint and prominence and flaccidity of the styloid process of ulna suggest separation of the distal radioulnar joint. Tenderness at the lateral side of the distal and proximal part of the interphalangeal bones or accompanied by lateral activity suggests injury of accessory ligament. Fracture of the wrist and palm is often characterized by obvious swelling, tenderness, deformity, friction of bones and axial pain under percussion.

Thecal cyst is usually marked by limited mass in the dorsal part of the wrist that can slightly move along the vertical direction of the muscle tendon, but cannot move horizontally.

Motor examination

This test is taken to examine the abduction, adduction, dorsal extension and palmar flexion of the wrist joint. The normal range of wrist joint movement: dorsal extension 35°~60°, palmar flexion 50°~60°, radial deviation 25°~30° and ulnar deviation 30°~40°.

Special examination

Fist clenching test: When the affected hand clenches into a fist (the thumb maintains inside while the rest four fingers outside), ulnar deviation of the wrist joint and pain in the region of styloid process of radius suggest tenosynovitis stenosans of radial styloid.

Wrist flexion test: Numbness and pain of the fingers when he wrist joint of the patient is extremely flexed suggests carpal tunnel syndrome.

Crush test of the triquetral cartillage of the wrist: This test is to judge whether the triquetral cartilage is injured. In examination, the patient is asked to flex the elbow to 90° with the palm turning downwards. The doctor holds the lower part with one hand and grasps the palm with the other to force the ulnar part of the patient to deviate passively. Then the wrist joint of the patient is flexed and extended. If the pain is obviously worsened, it is a positive sign.

4.5 Lower limbs

4.5.1 Hip

Inspection

The patient is asked to take off the coat and walk in order to see whether the anterior superior iliac spine at both sides are at the same level, whether the groin region is symmetrical in order to decide swelling of hip joint and severe injury of head of femur. Then the lower limbs are observed to see whether there are manifestations of excessive adduction, abduction and shrinkage.

Observation of the lateral side is to see if there is flexion deformity of the thigh, especially excessive protrusion of the lumbar vertebrae. Obvious anterior protrusion of the waist, posterior protrusion of the buttocks and flexion of the hip suggest dislocation of the hip joint or infantile congenital dislocation of the hip joint and flexing rigidity of the hip joint.

Observation of the back is made to see whether there are signs of atrophy of greatest gluteal muscle. Chronic disease of the hip joint may lead to disuse atrophy due to long-term lack of loading and dyscinesia. Sequela of infantile paralysis is usually followed by neural atrophy. Observation is also made of the transverse crease at both sides of the buttocks to see whether they are symmetrical. If the crease at one side is thickened, deepened and elevated, it suggests unilateral congenital dislocation of the hip joint. If the greater trochanter of femur at both sides protrudes laterally and the perineal region becomes thickened, it suggests bilateral congenital dislocation of the hip joint.

Percussion

The patient lies in supination. The doctor presses the point 2cm below the middle of inguinal ligament at both sides with the thumbs or performs percussion on the greater trochanter of femur or heel with the fist. If there is pain in the hip joint, it indicates disorder of the joint. When palpating the groin, the doctor should make sure whether there are symptoms of enlarged lymph nodes, local swelling and distension or tenderness. Superficial tenderness in the ateral greater trochanter of femur often suggests bursitis.

Pain in the hip joint must be carefully examined to decide its location. There are two ways to examine pain in rotation. One is straight rotation of the hip joint. It is used to examine whether there is friction pain in the articular surface. The other is flexing rotation of the hip joint. When the hip joint is flexed, the iliac and lumbar muscles are relaxed. If there appears pain when the joint is slightly rotated, it means friction pain of the articular surface, excluding referred pain in the iliac and lumbar muscles. If there is no pain in slight rotation but pain in quick rotation, it suggests disorder of the iliac and lumbar soft tissues.

If there are signs of asymmetry in the lower limbs and muscular atrophy, the length of the lower limbs should be measured from the anterior superior iliac spine to the medial condyle of femur or medial malleolus. The diameter of the lower limbs should be measured at the corresponding points at both limbs, labeling clear the distance between the decided points to the upper order or lower border of the patella.

Motor examination

This examination is to test the functional activities of the hip joint in flexion, posterior extension, adduction, abduction, intorsion and extorsion. The normal range of the hip joint in movement: flexion 145°, posterior extension 40°, abduction 30°~45°, adduction 20°~30°, extorsion 40° and intorsion 40°.

Special tests

Palm-heel test: The patient lies in supination with the lower limbs extended and the heel put on the palm of the doctor. Normally the lower limbs appear in a vertically median position. If there is fracture of the femur neck or dislocation of the hip joint or paraplegia, the heel will appear in extorsion.

Excessive extension of the hip joint test: The patient lies in pronation with the lower limbs extended. The doctor presses the posterior part of the sacrum of the patient to fixate the pelvis with one hand and lift the affected shank with the other hand to force the hip joint to extend excessively. If there is disorder in the hip joint or sacral and iliac joint, the pelvis will be raised and there will appear pain in the hip joint or sacral and iliac joint when it is extended excessively.

Flexion of the hip joint test: The patient lies in supination with the pelvis in anteversion and excessive flexion of the hip and knee joint at the healthy side. Then flexion deformity will appear. The angle between the thigh and the bed is the deformity angle.

Heel percussion test: The patient lies in supination with the lower limbs extended. The doctor lift the affected limb of the patient with one hand and knocks the heel of the patient with the other. If there is pain in the hip joint, it suggests disorder of the hip joint.

Genuflex and hip flexion and leg separation test: The patient keeps the lower limbs in flexion and extorsion with the soles opposing to each other, then performing the activity of abduction and adduction of the lower limbs. In patients with bone abductor syndrome, the legs cannot be completely separated and passive separation will cause pain.

4.5.2 Knees

Inspection

The inspection is made to see whether there is knee deformity. Normally the knee can only extend for 5° and there is a mild extorsion about 5°~8° in the thigh and shank. If the extorsion exceeds such a range, it is extorsion or intorsion deformity. Trial is also made to see whether there are signs of swelling and distension. Mild swelling and distension will make the sides of the knees prominent while serious mild swelling and distension will make lead to protrusion and enlargement of the whole knees. Mass above the synovial bursa may indicate bursitis and hydrarthrosis. Swelling of the condyle and epiphysis of the tibia and femur usually suggests bone tumor. The dyscinesia of the knee joint will quickly cause atrophy of the inner end of the quadriceps muscle of thigh.

Palpation

The patient lies in supination and extends the legs. In chondromalacia patellae, pressure will lead to slight shift of the patella and cause pain. In epiphysitis of tibial tubercle, hard mass can be palpated and there is obvious tenderness. In hypertrophy of subpatellar fat pad, hard mass can be sensed in the patellar ligaments at both sides. Tenderness between the interspace of the knee joint may be caused by injury of semilunar plate. If the accessory ligament is injured, tenderness can be found at the sides of the ligament. And tenderness can be found below the patella if the ligament below the patella is injured.

Motor examination

The normal range of knee joint movement is 145° of excessive flexion and 10° of excessive flexion. Limited passive movement of the knee joint suggests disorder of the knee joint. Examination of the active movement of the knee joint can tell the extension of the knee with the quadriceps muscle of the thigh and flexion of the knee with the hamstring muscles.

Special examination and nerve reflex

Patella floating test: The patient lies in a horizontal position and extends the affected limb. The doctor presses the suprapatellar bursal fluid above the patella into the cavity of the joint with one hand and repeatedly press the patella with the thumb of the other hand. Wave motion in the cavity of the joint indicates retention of fluid.

Lateral pressure of the knee joint test: The patient lies in supination with the affected limb extended and the quadriceps muscle of thigh relaxed, and then performing intorsion and extorsion of the knee joint. Normally there will be no lateral motion and pain. If the ligament is completely broken, lateral motion will appear; if the ligament is partly injured, pain will be caused.

Drawer test: The patient lies in supination and flexes the knee about 90° with the muscles relaxed and feet put on the bed in a horizontal position. The doctor holds the shanks of the patient to push and pull repeatedly. If the range of movement forwards is increased, it suggests injury of the crossing accessory ligament; if the range of movement backwards is increased, it suggests injury of the posterior crossing ligament.

Rotation and pinching test of the knee joint: This is a test commonly used to diagnosis injury of semilunar plate. The patient lies in supination with both limbs extended. In examining injury of semilunar plate, the doctor holds the ankle of the patient with one hand to flex the knee joint as much as possible, performing extorsion and of the knee and intorsion of the shank, gradually extending the knee joint to induce crush and friction in the interspace of the knee joint. Snapping and obvious pain are the positive signs. Extorsion and intorsion of the shank usually indicate injury of semilunar plate.

Grounding, lifting and pulling test: This test is used to differentiate injury of collateral ligament and breaking of semilunar plate. The patient lies in a prone position with the patellar joint extended and the knee flexed to 90°. The doctor fixates the thigh of the patient and holds the affected foot with both hands to press the knee joint and rotate the shank. Pain suggests injury of semilunar plate. If the interspace of the knee is enlarged when the shank is lifted and rotated and pain is caused, it suggests injury of the collateral ligament.

Patellar tendon reflex: The patient sits on the edge of the bed with both shanks hanging naturally, or lies on the bed. The doctor lifts the knee of the patient with the left hand to flex it about 20°~30°. Then the doctor slightly performs percussion on the tendon of quadriceps femoris below the knee and the center of knee is L_{2-4}.

4.5.3 Malleolus

Inspection

The purpose of inspection is to see whether there are signs of deformity, such as drop, intorsion and extorsion of foot, fatfoot and tallipes carvus as well as swelling, distension and subtaneous blood stasis.

Palpation

If the soft tissue over the ankle is thin, the tenderness is often the focus of disease. The tenderness in the ankle and foot is usually located in the interspace of the joints, the end of bones and the attaching point of tendons. Tenderness in the Achilles tendon often suggests disorder of the tendon proper or the membrane beside the tendon. Tenderness in the terminating point of the Achilles tendon suggests butsitis of the Achilles tendon. Tenderness below the heel among children of 8~12 years may be caused by epiphysitis of calcaneum. Tenderness median and posterior to the calcaneus may be caused by spur or fat pad. If it is anterior to the calcaneus, it may suggest pain of p;antar tascia. Tenderness medial and lateral to the calcaneus, it may suggest disorder of the calcaneus. Tenderness directly below the medial and external malleolus may suggest disorder of the subtalar joint.

Tenderness is often caused by swelling and distension. Swelling and mass of the soft tissues is often caused by synovium and tendon sheath. Hard mass usually indicates disorder of bones. Besides, examination of the artery over the dorsum of foot and posterior to the tibia is clinically significant in diagnosis.

Motor examination

The normal range of movement of the ankle joint: 20°~30° of dorsal extension, 40°~50° of flexion, 45° of intorsion and 25° of extorsion.

Special examination

Intorsion and extorsion of foot test: The doctor fixates the shank of the patient with one hand and holds the foot of the patient with the other to perform excessive intorsion and extorsion of foot. Pain in the same side suggests fracture of medial and external malleolus. Pain at both sides suggests injury of collateral ligament.

Ankle reflex test: The patient lies down with extorsion of the hip joint and flexion of the knee joint. The doctor pushes the sole of the patient with one hand to induce slight dorsal flexion of the ankle joint and performs percussion on the Achilles tendon of the patient with the other hand to induce flexion of metatarsal bones. If it is difficult to induce, the patient can be asked to knee down at the edge of the bed. Then the doctor pushes the sole of the patient to induce dorsal flexion with one hand and performs percussion on the heel and leg of the patient with the other. The center of reflex is in $S_{1~2}$.

Spasm of ankle often appears together with hyper-reflex of the Achilles tendon. In examination, the doctor can support the popliteal fossa of the patient with one hand and hold the foot of the patient with the other hand to cause sudden dorsal flexion of the ankle joint and then relieve it. In such a way, continuous extension and flexion of the Achilles tendon will be induced, suggesting injury of extrapyramidal bundle.

Babinski's sign: The doctor uses a stick with a blunt point to stroke the lateral edge of the sole from the back to the front. If there appears slow dorsal flexion of the big toe and mild extorsion of the rest toes, it suggests injury of extrapyramidal bundle.

Flicking toes test: The base of the toes is slightly flicked or dorsal part of the toes is pinched. Plantar flexion of the toes is a positive sign, suggesting injury of extrapyramidal bundle.

Review Questions

- Describe special tests for examining the waist.
- How to perform brachial plexus pulling test and what is its clinical significance?
- Describe tenderness around the knee joint in performing palpation examination.

5

Basic Exercises for Manipulation Practice

5.1 Characteristics and actions of manipulation exercises

5.1.1 Characteristics

Manipulation exercises are helpful for strengthening human body, preventing diseases, improving muscular strength and invigorating internal organs.

The manipulation exercises are designed to train the physical strength of the practitioners. In doing these exercises, the practitioners should pay great attention to the poses of steps and crotches, training the muscles and ligaments of the lower limbs as well as the abdominal, lumbar and back muscles through extending, flexing, lifting and lowering the lower limbs. Long-term training with such a method will strengthen the muscles and lower limbs.

Quite a number of exercises concentrate on training the palms. Usually the palms are pushed forwards slowly and forcefully by hypochondrium, turning and rotating to swirl the muscles on the forearm with the aid of instruments like barbell and dumbbell. Through adduction and abduction, the muscles on the palms and upper limbs are trained and strengthened.

In doing these exercises, trials have to be made to invigorate Qi, enrich essence and blood and adjust physiological condition, maintaining the spirit inside and integrating muscles. Mental concentration is quite helpful for improving the quality and functions of essence, Qi and blood. such a concentration can train the so-called intrinsic power which is beneficial both to life activities and rehabilitation.

In clinical practice, Tuina therapy is not only used to treat diseases, but also prevent diseases. The exercises used in training Tuina manipulations are proved to be effective for curing various diseases. For instance, the manipulations known as Qian Tui Ba Pi Ma (pushing eight horses forwards) and Dao La Jiu Tou Niu (pulling nine oxen backwards) are performed by pushing forwards the hands from the hypochondriac sides to direct Qi to flow to the Zhong Jiao (middle energizer). That is why they are helpful for strengthening the spleen and stomach, invigorating the stomach and intestines, improving appetite and promoting the production of Qi and blood.

5.1.2 Effect of Tuina exercises on the body

According to the theory of TCM, the exercises used to train Tuina manipulations are helpful for dredging the meridians, invigorating Qi and blood, soothing the limbs and skeleton and nourishing the viscera. The following are the findings made by modern scientific studies.

Promoting blood circulation

Blood and circulation system, including blood, heart and vessels, are responsible for transporting the nutrients and metabolites produced during the course of metabolism. Tuina manipulations can reinforce the cardiac muscles and strengthen the contractibility of the heart. Generally the heart pumps 60~70 ml of blood in each contraction. Long-term practice of the Tuina exercise can enable the heart to pump 80~100 ml blood in each contraction. The capacity of the heart in those who are practicing Tuina exercises is larger (about one third) than those who never do the exercises. To practice these exercises, one has to perform various poses, high and low, lifting and lowering, mild and forceful. That is why the heart is strengthened and invigorated.

Exercises for Tuina can increase white cells, red cells and hemoglobin in the blood, and therefore improving the states of nutrition and metabolism.

Effect of Tuina exercises on the respiratory system

The function of respiratory system is to absorb oxygen and excrete Carbon oxide to ensure metabolism. These exercises can consume more energy and discharge more Carbon oxide, and thus speeding up and improving respiration. For instance, those who often practice these exercises have improved their vital capacity and reduced their breath frequency to 8~12 times in a minute. Their breath is deep and slow, making it possible for respiratory organs to have more time to rest.

Effect of Tuina exercises on nerve system

These exercises can exert better regulating effects on the nerve system, since these exercises are either static or dynamic. The central nerve system rapidly and accurately becomes excited and inhibited with the motion of such exercises, and consequently improving the regulating function of the central nerve system and balancing the actions of the central nerve system, internal organs, the hands, eyes and body.

Effect of Tuina exercises on digestion system

Practice of these exercises can promote the production of digestive juice secreted from the glands, peristalsis of the gastric and intestinal tract, digestion and absorption of food. Besides, frequent practice of such exercises can enlarge the moving range of diaphragm and abdominal muscles, and therefore improving blood circulation in the stomach and intestines.

Effect of Tuina exercises on muscles and skeletal system

These excises can increase and thicken muscular fibers, increase myoglobin, strengthen muscles and skeleton as well as smooth the movement of joints. Besides, practice of these exercises can improve blood circulation and metabolism, reduce hyperosteogeny and degenerative changes of ligaments as well as delay senile changes of muscles, joints and bones.

Effect of Tuina exercises on endocrine system and skin

Practice of these exercises can improve the functions of corticoadrenal and metabolism of protein, fats, inorganic salts and water; promote metabolism of cells through tetraiodothyronine; accelerate the synthesis of protein and growth of bones through somatropin; stimulate the production of insulin; improve the oxidation of sugar and the excitation of coupling and parasympathetic nerves; regulate heart beat, respiration and blood pressure; improve the adaptation of the skin to changes of cold and heat; promote blood circulation and supply of oxygen.

5.2   Exercise of Yi Jin Jing (Change of tendons)

This exercise is used to improve the functions of the bones and tendons. It is practiced by means of static use of strength with natural breath which either normal or adverse. Normal breath is marked by sinking of the abdomen during breath while adverse breath is marked by bulging of the abdomen during breath. Normal breath is usually used at the early period of practice because adverse breath requires strenuous activity.

Before practice this exercise, the practitioner should wear loose and comfortable clothes and shoes, standing naturally with the mind concentrating on the lower abdomen, relaxing the muscles and maintaining calm. After or during the interval of practice, cares should be taken to avoid wind or to take certain activities such as walking or moving the joints, avoiding strenuous movement. The practice of this exercise can be done step by step. The time, frequency and intensity of practice should be monitored according to personal conditions. However, one should practice it at least once a day. For those weak in constitution, it is inadvisable to practice this exercise.

The first pose: Wei Tuo Xian Chu (Wei Tuo Presenting Pestle)

【Preparation】   Stand with both feet close to each other, relax the knees and hips, keep the neck erect, look straight forwards, slightly restrain the jaw and open the mouth, touch the tongue against the palate, relax the shoulders, naturally fall the arms with fingers touching each other, raise the chest and restrain the abdomen, straighten the back and waist, eliminate any avarice and breath naturally.

【Postures】

1. Move the left foot one step toward the left, slightly straighten the knees with the toes firmly touching the ground, abduct the shoulders to the horizontal level with the palms turning downwards.

2. Turn the palms forwards and slowly touch each other, bend the elbow, slowly adduct the arms and wrists with the fingers turned upwards.

3. Internally turn the arms with the tips pointing to the chest and Tiantu (CV 22).

4. Slowly separate the shoulders, keep the hands over the chest like carrying a ball, slightly fall the elbows, turn the palms internally, bend the fingers against each other with a distance about 4~5 cun, and slightly bend the body forwards.

5. Finishing: Take a deep breath of fresh air first, then slowly breath out and put down hands.

【Essentials】 Maintain the distance between the feet the same as that between the shoulders, relax the whole body, look forwards with the eyes half closed and half opened, raise the head, slightly open the mouth with the tongue touching the palate, breathe in quickly while breathe out slowly, mildly restrain the hip and lower abdomen, relax the popliteal fossa, and keep the mind calm.

【Notes】 The focus of this exercise is to train deltoid muscle, triceps brachii muscle, supinator muscle groups, extensor groups and anus in situ by internal and external sphincter. To practice this exercise can help patients smooth blood circulation and improve therapeutic effect. For patients with hemorrhoids and hypertension, this exercise can help them cure disease. For those who practice it for the first time, once 3 minutes is enough. One week later, 2 more minutes can be practiced. When the time has extended to 10 minutes each time, 1 more minute can be added each week. Usually it can be practiced once 30 minutes. However, it should be reduced for those who are weak.

The second pose: Heng Dan Xiang Mo Chu (Monster-Controlling Pestle)

【Preparation】 Same as that for Wei Tuo Xian Chu.

【Postures】

1. Move the left foot one step to the left, maintain a distance between the feet the same as that of the shoulders, turn the palms downwards, point the fingers forwards, straighten the elbows and look straight forwards.

2. Turn the palms to the chest and push forwards the strengthen exerted from the lateral side of the thumbs at the same level of the shoulders.

3. Move the hands away from each other with the strengthen exerted from the lateral side of the thumbs, straighten the arms with the shoulders, elbows and wrist at the same level, turn the palms downwards.

4. Straighten the knees, lift the heels with the front part of the soles touching the

ground, open the eyes and clench the teeth.

5. Finishing: Take a deep breath first, then slowly breathe out, put down the hands and heels, and then close the eyes for a while.

【Essentials】 Straighten the hands at the level of shoulders, lift the heels with the tip of the feet touching the ground, concentrate the mind on the palm and toes and open the eyes wide for the purpose of calming down.

【Notes】 This pose is taken right after the previous one (Wei Tuo Xian Chu) with the elbows slowly elevated to the level of the shoulders and the palms turned. The focus of this pose is to train deltoid muscle, triceps muscle of calf, extension toe muscle groups, quadriceps femoris muscle, anus in situ by internal and external sphincter, masseter muscles and orbicularis oculi muscle. Continuous practice of this exercise is good for strengthening health and balancing Qi activity. It can effectively improve the symptoms of cerebellar ataxia. The time of early practice is once 3 minutes. Once week later, it can be extended to once five minutes. When it has extended to 20 minutes, the time can be reduced. Usually 30 minutes a time is proper. For those who are weak, 15 minutes may be proper.

The third pose: Zhang Tuo Tian Men (Supporting the heaven gate with the palm)

【Preparation】 Same as that of Wei Tuo Xian Chu.

【Postures】

1. Move the left foot one step to the left, maintain a distance between the feet the same as that of the shoulders, keep the mind calm and breathe naturally.

2. Lift the hands to the chest, turn the wrist with the four fingers closely touching each other, turn the palms downwards with the fingers pointing to each other (about 1~2 cun).

3. Raise the hands over the head, turn the palms upwards with the distance of 1 cun between the tips of fingers, close the four fingers and abduct the thumbs, and form a square between the Hukou (part of the hand between the thumb and the index finger) of both hands.

4. Raise the head backwards, look at the dorsum of hands with both eyes, lift the heels and clench the teeth with vibration in the ears.

5. Finishing: Same as that for Wei Tuo Xian Chu.

【Essentials】 To look at the dorsum of hands may be difficult to do for the beginners. It should be practiced step by step. For the beginners, it is advisable not to raise the heels. To raise the heels, trials should be made to slightly move them laterally so as to enable blood and Qi to flow upwards. Besides, cares should be taken to relax the whole body in order to free the flow of Qi and blood. It is inadvisable to make strenuous movement of the arms because it cannot be lasted for a long time. The activities of lift the anus, clenching teeth and touching the palate with the tongue are helpful for smoothing the Du Mai (Governor Vessel).

【Notes】 This exercise focuses on training muscles on the limbs, deltoid muscle on the legs and levator ani flap. The practice of this exercise can evidently increase blood supply in the brain, improve blood vessels, refresh the mind and prolong life. However those with hypertension should not practice this exercise. For the beginners, once 3 minutes is enough. One week later, the practice can be extended to 5 minutes. Generally speaking 30 minutes once is proper. For those who are weak, 15 minutes once is advisable.

The fourth pose: Zhai Xing Huan Dou (Picking up star and changing constellation)

【Preparation】 Same as that for Wei Tuo Xian Chu.

【Postures】

1. Move the right foot one step forwards with a distance of a fist between the feet, make a fist of the left hand to Yaoyan (EX-B 7) and put the right hand against the right thigh.

2. Bend the left leg to squat with the tip of the right foot touching the ground and the heel raising 2 cun, keeping the body erect.

3. Close the fingers of the right hand, bend the wrist and raise it along the chest to the right side of the body, about the distance of a fist to the right side of the forehead.

4. Move the fingers slightly towards the right side, raise the head slightly tow the right side, stare at the palm with both eyes, breathe in quickly and breathe out slowly.

5. Finishing: Breathe in quickly and breathe out slowly, return to the state of preparation.

【Essentials】 Raise high one hand with fingers closed and wrist bent, about the distance of one fist to the forehead, move the elbow to the chest with fingers pointing laterally, head slightly deviated and shoulders relaxed, stare at the palms, touch the palate with the tongue, slightly open the mouth, breathe naturally, slightly restrain the buttocks, keep the front leg a load of about 30%~40% and the back leg 60%~70%, move the front foot half a step backwards when changing the step and vice versa.

【Notes】 This pose is more difficult to perform. Cares should be taken to concentrate the mind on the palms, not to intensify the muscles and perform it step by step. It focuses on training the tension of flexor muscle of wrist groups, triceps brachii muscle, flexors and extensors of the lower limbs and levator ani flap. For the beginners, once 2 minutes is enough. After one week, one more minute can be added. When it has extended to once 7 minutes, one more minute should be added each week. Generally speaking once 15 minutes is proper. For those who are weak, it is inadvisable to practice this exercise.

The fifth pose: Dao Zhuai Jiu Niu Wei (Pulling the tails of nine cows from the opposite direction)

【Preparation】 Same as that for Wei Tuo Xian Chu.

【Postures】

1. Move the left leg one step to the left with the tip of the foot restrained, bend the knees to squat, grasp the hands into fists to put against the waist, slightly bend the upper part of the body forwards, relax the shoulders, straighten the elbows, raise the head and look forwards.

2. Lift the fists to the chest and change into palms in a pose like holding a ball, straighten the waist, relax the shoulders, bend the elbows and look straight forwards.

3. Turn the palms to opposite sides, and move them separately till the elbows are straightened, relax the shoulders, bend the wrist and keep the shoulders, elbows and wrists at the same level.

4. Turn the body right with the fists against each other (below the shoulders), move the upper limbs at the same time, abduct the right upper limb, bend the elbow to a round position, grasp the fists, stare at the fists, turn internally and then rotate the left upper limb, straighten the upper part of the body, relax the waist and restrain the buttocks, and breathe naturally.

5. Finishing: Breathe in deeply and breathe out slowly, return to the state of preparation, change from the left to the right and vice versa.

【Essentials】 The front leg maintains the posture of a bow while the back leg keep the posture of an arrow. The front elbow is slightly bent in a half circle while the back elbow is slightly turned internally. The shoulders are relaxed and adducted. The eyes stare at the fists. The upper part of the body slightly bends forwards. The mouth slightly opens with the tongue touching the palate and natural breath. Qi is directed towards the lower abdomen. The body turns to the left when changing the step and vice versa.

【Notes】 The mind should be concentrated. This exercise is helpful for training supinator muscle groups and pronator groups of the arms as well as the five fingers. It is usually practiced with the right hand first. Activity of Qi is concentrated on Laogong (PC 8). For the beginners, once 3 minutes is enough. One week later, 1 more minute can be added. Usually once 8 minutes is enough.

The sixth pose: Chu Zhua Liang Chi (Showing fingers and displaying wings)

【Preparation】 Same as Wei Tuo Xian Chu.

【Postures】

1. Protecting the waist: Make the hands into fists and move to the sides of the waist with the palms turned internally.

2. Slowly lift the fists to the chest, change them into palms which are then turned upwards and pushed forward with the same level of the shoulders, slowly turn the hands with the thumbs touching each other and the four fingers closed and straightened, and look forwards with the head raised.

3. Raise the fingers upwards and laterally, bend the elbows, stare at the tips of the fingers, straighten the chest, touch the ground with the whole feet, relax the knees and

grasp the fists for 7 times.

【Essentials】 Grasp the fists to touch the waist, push the palms forward with the strength exerted from the lateral side of the thumb at the same level of the shoulders, open the eyes wide, concentrate the mind on the palms, grasp the fists 7 times. Breathe in when retreating the fist and breathe out when pushing the palms.

【Notes】 This exercise focuses on training flexors and extensors of the arms and the fingers. At the early period of practice, it can be performed quickly and gradually slowed down. For the beginners, once 1 minute is enough. One week later 1 more minute can be added till extended to 7 minutes. Usually once 15 minutes is advisable.

The seventh pose: Jiu Gui Ba Ma Dao (Nine ghosts pulling saber)

【Preparation】 Same as that of Wei Tuo Xian Chu.

【Postures】

1. Raise the right hand over the head with the palm turned upwards, straighten the elbow with the tips of fingers pointing to the left, press the left hand downwards with the palm turned down and the tips of the fingers pointing to the front.

2. Rotate the left arm and press back and downwards with the palm turned downwards and the tips of fingers pointing to the right.

3. Bend the elbow and rotate the wrist of right hand with the palm turned downwards around the neck, slightly bend the head and turn the left palm back.

4. Raise the neck forcefully and turn the head back with the right hand pressing downwards and the elbow lifting upwards, and look straight forwards with the five fingers pressing hard.

5. Finishing: Breathe in deeply and return to the preparation posture while breathing out. Such an activity is performed bilaterally with the same requirement.

【Essentials】 One arm stretches upwards while the other one downwards with the erected elbows. The tips of the fingers raised up point to the opposite side, and its palm turns upwards. Then turn the wrist and palm to clasp the neck and press it downward with the eyes looking to the opposite side. The finger tips of the hand pressing downwards point to the front with the palm facing the ground. And then press the back of the body with the tips of fingers pointing to the opposite side. Change from one side to another, and keep the breath smooth.

【Notes】 This exercise focuses on training the extensor muscles of upper limb (bracheial triceps), muscles of neck, levator scapulac muscles, palms and fingers.

Another method to practice this exercise is to lift the heels simultaneously. However, such a practice needs long-term training, otherwise problems will be caused. The first requirement is to sink Qi into Dan Tian (cinnabar field), without any lifting or sinking activity, and take costal breath in order to relax the neck, chest and shoulders. Only by doing so can Qi movement can be calm and the mind be concentrated on the back. For those with hypertension, this exercise is inadvisable. For the beginner, once 1 minute is enough. One week later, 1 more minute can be added. Generally speaking once 10 minutes is proper.

The eighth pose: San Pan Luo Di (Falling of three plates on the ground)

【Preparation】 Same as that for Wei Tuo Xian Wu.

【Postures】

1. Move the left leg one step to the left with a distance parallel to that of the shoulders, turn the tips of the feet to point inwards, bend the knees and squat akimbo.

2. Turn the palms upwards along the chest and slowly to the level of the shoulders and below the eyebrow with a distance about 1 Chi (1/3 meter) between two hands.

3. Turn the palms downwards and press slowly with parting fingers and the Hukou (tiger's mouth, a part of the hand between the thumb and the index finger) turned inwards to suspend over the knees (or put palms on the knees) and slightly bend forwards the upper part of the body.

4. Turn the upper part of the body backwards and erect it with the chest slightly straightened and the back bent like a bow, relax the shoulders, close the elbows to the body, look straight forwards, open the mouth, clench the teeth and lift the anus.

5. Finishing: Breathe deeply and return to the preparation posture.

【Essentials】 Keep the chest straight, bend and the back like a bow, slightly rotate the elbows inwards, look straight forwards, touch the palate with the tongue, slightly open the mouth, breathe smoothly through the nose, lift the anus, bend the knees 90° and concentrate the mind on the lower abdomen.

【Notes】 This exercise can smooth the flow of Qi and blood and strengthen arms and armpits, especially the quadriceps muscle of thigh, lumbar and back muscles. For the beginners, 2 minutes once is enough. One week later, 1 more minute is added. Usually once 8 minutes is proper.

The ninth pose: Qing Long Tan Zhua (Blue dragon showing its paws)

【Preparation】 Move the left leg one step to the left in a distance parallel to that of the shoulders, put the fists against the waist, stand straight and look forwards.

【Postures】

1. Push the left hand forwards to the upper right position with palm lifted over the head, slightly turn the body to the right side, relax the shoulders and erect the elbows without bending the wrists, put the right fist against the waist, look at the palm and stand hard on the ground.

2. Bend the left thumb to the center of the palm with eyes staring at the thumb.

3. Rotate the left arm inwards with the palm facing the ground, bend the waist and push the palm to the ground, erect the knees, raise the head and look forwards.

4. Lift the left palm to the waist along the left knee. Such an activity is done bilaterally with the same requirement.

【Essentials】 Keep the fists against the waist. Then push the left fist from the right side and change it into palm. Watch the palms and keep them below the eyebrow. Grasp the fist with force again, and make the shoulders relaxed and the elbow erected. Bend the waist, try to touch the ground and stand steadily while lift the palm to the waist along the knee.

【Notes】 This exercise focuses on strengthening the lung, liver, gallbladder and Dai Mai (Belt Vessel). It can soothe the liver and gallbladder, effective for treating liver and gallbladder diseases and women diseases. For the beginners, once 3 minutes is enough. One week later, 1 more minute is added. Usually once 10 minutes is advisable.

The tenth pose: E Hu Pu Shi (Hungry tiger pouncing on its prey)

【Preparation】 Same as that for Wei Tuo Xian Wu.

【Postures】

1. Move the left foot a big step to the left and slightly move the right foot to the left.

2. Put both hands forwards with the palms facing the ground, slightly lift the heels and raise the head.

3. Turn the front foot back and put the dorsum of foot on the heel, slightly withdraw the chest and abdomen, and raise the head.

4. Draw back the whole body with the buttock sticking out, straighten the elbows, look straight forward, move forward in about 2 cun clear the ground, then bend both elbows with the tip of right foot touching the ground as a hungry tiger on its prey.

5. Finishing: Breathe deeply while return to the preparation posture.

【Essentials】 Keep the head upright, neither too high nor too low, with the eyes staring ahead. When the elbows and knees are straightened, they should not appear stiff. When breathing in, the whole body contracts with the buttocks protruded and the chest and abdomen contracted. When breathing out, the body pushes forward. Keeping balance is essential when repeating the movement. Never try to hold the breath, breathing in deeply and quickly while breathing out slowly. When changing the posture, the requirement is the same.

【Notes】 This exercise can strengthen tendons and bones, improve the force of fingers, flexor and extensor muscles, and train the lumbo-abdominal muscles. The beginner can put the whole hand on the ground and, after a period of practice, use five fingers, then three fingers (thumb, fore finger and middle finger), then two fingers, and finally only one finger without other parts of the body touching the ground to support the body. Practice it 4 times for each side and add twice more each week. Usually once 10 minutes is advisable. Those who are weak should not practice this exercise.

The eleventh pose: Da Gong Ji Gu (Showing a pose in order to beat the drum)

【Preparation】 Same as that for Wei Tuo Xian Wu.

【Postures】

1. Move the left foot to the left in a distance parallel to that of the shoulders, slowly raise both palms from both sides, look forwards, relax the shoulders and erect elbows without bending the wrists, keep the body straight and the wrist, elbow, and shoulder at the same level.

2. Bend the elbow with clasped hands and hold the back of head. Do not protrude the abdomen and buttocks.

3. Bend the knees and squat.

4. Straighten the knees, bend the waist and head without lifting the heels, cover the ears with palms and hit the back of head with fingers alternatively for 24 times.

5. Finishing: Straighten the waist and relax the hands while breathing.

【Essentials】 Hold the head with two palms without moving the feet or bending the knees, then crouch down, keep the upper part of the body straight and upright, bend forward to put head between the legs, touch the palate with the tip of the tongue, and knock the back of the head with fingers for 24 times.

【Notes】 There are various ways to practice it, such as closing the feet, making a cross posture, or squatting. It is effective for strengthening the neck, waist, legs and buttock. For the beginners, once 3 minutes is enough. One week later, 1 more minute is added. Usually once 10 minutes is advisable.

The twelfth pose: Yao Tou Bai Wei (Shaking the head and tail)

【Preparation】 Same as that for Wei Tuo Xian Wu.

【Postures】

1. Raise both palms from the chest over the head with the eyes staring at the palms and straighten the body.

2. Clasp the hands, rotate the wrist with the palms turned upwards, straighten the elbows and look straight ahead.

3. Bend the body backwards with the eyes looking upward.

4. Then bend the body forwards, push the hands to touch the ground with erected head and staring eyes, straighten the heels without lifting from the ground.

5. Finishing: Return to the preparation posture with slow breath.

【Essentials】 Cross ten fingers, stretch the arms with the elbows straight, bend the body forwards, push the palms to the ground with straightened knees and elbows, raise the head high with staring eyes.

【Notes】 This exercise can relax the meridians and collaterals, strengthen the tendons and bones, reinforce the waist and arms. It is essential for practicing Yi Jin Jing. It is simple but effective for harmonizing the twelve meridians and extraordinary meridians to ensure smooth circulation of Qi and blood. For the beginners, once 3 times is enough. One week later, 2 more times is added. Usually once 15 times is advisable.

The twelve poses of Yi Jin Jing can be practiced in order or in parts according to individual condition.

5.3 Shao Lin Nei Gong (Shao Lin internal exercise)

This exercise is somewhat different from that of others. It emphasizes not on mental concentration, but on promotion of Qi with force. In practice, it requires great exertion from the armpits and firm touch of the ground with the toes and heels. The basic requirements are to straighten the lower limb, close the thighs with force, erect the body, protrude the chest, restrain the chest and jaw. The force is directed to the shoulders, arms, elbows, wrists and fingers with natural breath. Qi is guided to flow with the direction of force in the meridians. In practice, trials have to be made to breathe naturally and avoid holding the breath. Long-term practice is effective for improving digestion and sleep. Modern studies show that it can promote metabolism, digestion and nerve system.

The first pose: Zhan Shi (Standing pose)

[Postures]

1. Stand upright, move the left foot one step to the left to form a inner cross posture of the feet with the toes firmly touching the ground, and make great exertion to guide force to the feet.

2. Slightly protrude the chest, stretch the hands backwards, straighten the elbows, push the wrists without relaxing the shoulders and armpits, close the four fingers with the thumbs turned laterally, look straight ahead without moving the head, concentrate the mind and breathe naturally.

[Essentials]   Three-straightening and four-balancing

Three-straightening means to straighten the buttocks, waist and legs. Four-balancing means to keep the head, shoulders, palms and feet balanced. The feet are kept in an inward pose to exert great force. Other requirements are close the shoulders, erect the elbows, straighten the wrists, turn the palms, erect the fingers, protrude the chest, restrain the abdomen, touch the palate with the tongue, breathe naturally and look straight ahead.

[Notes]   This exercise focuses on training muscles on the inner side of the thighs, such as bones of toes muscle, Gracilis muscles, long adductor muscle, short adductor muscle and great adductor muscle, the muscles on the upper limbs, such as the latissimus dorsi muscle, teres major muscle and deltoid muscle managing the posterior extension of the arms, trapezius muscle responsible for closing the shoulders, long radial extensor carpal muscle in charge of dorsal extension of the wrist as well as musculus extensor pollicis longus and digital extensor muscles responsible for straightening the fingers.

This exercise is effective for promoting flow of Qi in the regular meridians and the four limbs to nourish all parts of the body so as to regulate the functions of the viscera, strengthen the body and remove pathogenic factors.

The second pose: Ma Dang Shi (Horse crotch)

[Postures]

1. Stand upright, move the left foot one step to the left, bend the knees to squat, slightly direct the knees and tips of the feet inwards, slightly protrude the heels externally to form an inward cross posture.

2. Stretch the hands back, extend the elbows and wrists, fork the thumbs, close the four fingers, or put the hands at the thighs with the part between the thumb and index finger turned upwards, straighten the chest, slightly restrain the abdomen, look straight ahead and breathe naturally.

【Essentials】 Lower the waist, bend the knees, straighten the chest, restrain the abdomen, look straight ahead and breathe naturally.

【Notes】 This exercise focuses on training the lower part of the body by means of bending the knees and turning the tips of the feet inwards with the coordination of semitendinosus muscle, semimembranous muscle, biceps femoris, sartorius muscle, Gracilis muscles and gastrocnemius muscles. Through the action of sacrospinous muscle, rectus muscle, external oblique muscle and transverse abdominal muscle, the chest is straightened and the gravitation is placed in between the legs. It is effective for strengthening the waist and kidney.

The third pose: Gong Jian Dang Shi (Arrow-like crotch)

【Postures】

1. Stand upright, turn the body to the right, move the right foot one step to the right, bend the knee of the front leg to squat, straighten the knee of the back leg with the heel touching the ground to from a arrow-like pose.

2. Slightly bend the upper part of the body forwards, slightly restrain the buttocks, stretch the arms back, extend the elbows and wrists, exert force from the root of the palms with the part between the thumb and index finger turned upwards, concentrate the mind and breathe naturally.

【Essentials】 Keep the front leg as a bow while the back leg as an arrow, straighten the chest, restrain the abdomen and breathe naturally.

【Notes】 This exercise focuses on training the lower part of the body. The front leg, and hip are bent through the actions of iliopsoas muscle, Rectus Femoris, tensor fasciae latae muscle, sartorius muscle, semitendinosus muscle,semimembranous muscle,biceps femorisand gastrocnemius muscles. The back leg is straightened through the action of quadriceps femoris muscle. After a period of practice, it can be practiced together with the exercise for training the upper part of the body.

The four pose: Mo Dang Shi (Moving crotch)

【Preparation】 Maintain a bow-like posture, bend the upper part of the body slightly forwards, slightly restrain the buttocks and put the palms against the waist.

【Postures】

1. Push the left palm to the up right direction, move the root of the palm and the lateral side of the arm slowly to the left side, rotate the body to the left side, change the right bow-like posture into left arrow-like posture, put the left palm against the waist.

2. Push the right palm to the up left side, move the root of the palm and the lateral side of the arm slowly to the right side, rotate the body to the right side, change the left

bow-like posture into right arrow-like posture, put the right palm against the waist.

【Essentials】 Keep the front leg as a bow while the back leg as an arrow, exert the upper limbs and slowly move the body.

【Notes】 Keep the front leg as a bow while the back leg as an arrow, change the upward turned palm into downward turned palm, bend the elbow and push it to the right or left side, exert the root of the palm and the lateral side of the arm with the action of muscles like deltoid muscle, supraspinatus, infraspinous muscle and teres minor, slowly move the body, change the right bow-like posture into left bow-like posture and vice versa.

The fifth pose: Liang Dang Shi (Display crotch)

【Preparation】 Same as that for Gong Jian Dang Shi.

【Postures】

1. Show the palms from the back to the upper side with the fingers opposed to each other, turn the palms upwards, look at the dorsum of palms and slightly bend the body forwards.

2. Turn to the right when changing the step, return the palms from the waist to the back in the same way at both sides.

【Essentials】 Raise the palms with eyes staring at the palms, change the step and turn to the right, then retreat the palms.

【Notes】 To raise the palms with the action of supraspinatus, deltoid muscle, trapezius muscle and serratus anterior muscle, retreat the palms and stretch them back when turning the body back.

The sixth pose: Bing Dang Shi (Closing crotch)

【Postures】

1. Stand upright, slightly protrude the heels laterally, close the tips of feet with the toes firmly touching the ground.

2. Stretch the elbows and wrist, slightly turn them to the back with the palms turned downwards, close the four fingers with the thumb turned laterally, and look straight ahead.

【Essentials】 Same as that for standing crotch.

The seventh pose: Da Dang Shi (Great crotch)

【Postures】

1. Move the left foot a great step to the left, straighten the knee and stand firmly.

2. Stretch the hands backwards with the part between the thumb and index finger turned upwards, close the four fingers, extend the elbow and wrist.

【Essentials】 Same as that for standing crotch.

The eighth pose: Xuan Dang Shi (Spiral crotch)

【Postures】

1. Move the left foot one big step to the left side, bend the knee, squat in a half way,

keep a distance between the feet longer than that of a crotch.

2. Stretch the hands backwards, erect the elbow and extend the wrist, close the four fingers with the thumb turned laterally.

【Essentials】 Same as that for horse crotch.

The ninth pose: Di Dang Shi (Low crotch)

【Postures】

1. Stand upright, close the tips of the feet with the toes firmly touching the ground, protrude the heel to from a inward cross posture.

2. Bend the knee to squat without touching the ground with the buttocks, make the hands into fists and raise them up, slightly bend the elbow with the palms opposed to each other, and look straight ahead.

【Essentials】 Bend the knee to squat without touching the ground with the buttocks, make the hands into fists and raise them up, slightly bend the elbow with the palms opposed to each other.

【Notes】 Bend the knee and hip with the action of semitendinosus muscle, semimembranous muscle, biceps femoris, sartorius muscle, Gracilis muscles, gastrocnemius muscles, iliopsoas muscle, Rectus Femoris, tensor fasciae latae muscleand sartorius muscle; maintain a low crotch with the action of quadriceps femoris muscle, gluteus maximus muscle, biceps femoris, semitendinosus muscle and semimembranous muscle.

The tenth pose: Zuo Dang Shi (Sitting crotch)

【Postures】

1. Cross the feet, squat with the knees crossed over each other, touch the ground with the lateral sides of the feet, slightly bend the upper part of the body forwards.

2. Turn the palms downwards, stretch the wrists, keep the body upright, and look straight ahead.

【Essentials】 Sit with the knees crossed over each other, touch the ground with the lateral sides of the feet.

【Notes】 Turn the hip joint externally with the action of gluteus medius muscle, gluteus minimus and piriformis.

Basic poses

The first pose: Qian Tui Ba Pi Ma (Pushing eight horses from the front)

【Preparation】 Stand in a required crotch.

【Postures】

1. Bend the elbows and put the palms at the rib-sides.

2. Keep the palms opposed to each other with the thumbs extended and four fingers closed, accumulate force over the shoulders, arms and finger tips, slowly move the arms anteriorly, slightly straighten the chest and retreat the arms without moving the head, look

straight ahead and breathe naturally.

3. Move the arms with the thumbs turned upright, slowly bend the elbows and turn them to the rib-sides.

4. Turn stretched palms into downward pressing palms, stretch the arms back and return to the original crotch.

【Essentials】 Accumulate force in the fingers and arms, slowly push the fingers, look straight ahead and breathe naturally.

【Notes】 Accumulate force in the fingers and arms, slowly push the arms with the action of triceps brachii muscle.

The second pose: Dao La Jiu Tou Niu (Pulling nine cows from the opposite direction)

【Preparation】 Stand in a required crotch.

【Postures】

1. Bend the elbows and put the palms at the rib-sides.

2. Push the palms along the rib-sides, gradually rotate the forearms internally, turn the part between the thumb and the index finger downwards when the arms are stretched, turn the thumbs laterally, straighten the wrist and elbows at the same level of the shoulders.

3. Bend the five fingers internally, change the palm into a fist like grasping something, turn the fist upwards to the rib-sides, slightly bend the body forwards and restrain the buttocks.

4. Press with the palm changed from upright position to downward pressing position, extend the arms backwards and return to the original crotch.

【Essentials】 Rotate and push the palms straightly, extend the elbows at the same level of the shoulders.

【Notes】 Push and internally rotate the forearm with the action of subscapularis muscle pectoralis major muscle the latissimus dorsi muscle and teres major muscle, turn the part between the thumb and the index finger downwards when the arms are stretched with the action of biceps brachii muscle, brachialis, brachioradialis and pronator teres.

The third pose: Dan Zhang La Jin Huan (Pulling the gold circle with one palm)

【Preparation】 Stand in a required crotch.

【Postures】

1. Bend the elbows and put the palms at the rid-sides.

2. Push the right hand forwards, gradually rotate the forearms internally, turn the part between the thumb and the index finger downwards when the arms are stretched, turn the thumbs laterally, accumulate force in the arms, straighten the wrist and elbows, keep the body straight, look straight ahead and breathe naturally.

3. Grasp the fingers into a fist, turn the wrist upwards, then change the fist into the palm and put it at the rib-side. The action of the left hand is the same with that of the right

hand.

4. Press with the palm bent downwards, stretch posteriorly the arms and return to the original crotch.

【Essentials】 Same as that for Dao La Jiu Tou Niu.

【Notes】 Same as that for Dao La Jiu Tou Niu.

The fourth pose: Feng Huang Zhan Chi (Flying wings of phoenix)

【Preparation】 Stand in a required crotch.

【Postures】

1. Bend the elbows and move them upwards slowly to the chest, and then cross the palms over the chest.

2. Change the palms from the upright position into downward pressing position, slowly separate them, stretch the arms like flying wings, close the four fingers with the thumbs turned laterally, look ahead, slightly bend the body forwards without raising the shoulders and breathe naturally.

3. Turn the wrists, bend the elbows, gradually change into a position that the centers of the palms facing each other and crossed in front of the chest.

4. Change the palms from the upright position into downward pressing position, stretch the arms posteriorly and return to the original crotch.

【Essentials】 Erect the palms and cross them, abduct them forcefully, and accumulate the force inside.

【Notes】 Change the palms from the upright position into downward pressing position with the action of radial flexor muscle of wrist, flexor carpi ulnaris, long palmar muscle, superficial flexor of fingers and deep flexor of fingers separate the arms to opposite sides with the action of deltoid muscle and supraspinatus.

The fifth pose: Ba Wang Ju Ding (Hegemon King raising the heavy quadripot)

【Preparation】 Stand in a required crotch.

【Postures】

1. Bend the elbows and turn them against the waist.

2. Turn the palms upwards and raise them slowly over the shoulders, then slowly turn the fingers internally with the parts between the thumb and index finger facing each other, the four fingers closed, the eyes looking ahead and natural breath.

3. Turn the wrist and palms upwards with the sides of the palms facing each other and the thumbs turned laterally, accumulate force downwards and gradually move the palms to the waist.

4. Change the palms from the upright position into downward pressing position at the waist side, extend the arms posteriorly as the original crotch.

【Essentials】 Raise the palms over the shoulders, then rotate the palms to face each other, stretch and raise the elbows, rotate the palms downwards to face each other.

【Notes】 Raise the palms over the shoulders, then rotate the palms with the action of long radial extensor carpal muscle short radial carpal extensor muscle, extensor carpi ulnaris and all the finger extensors, extend all the wrist joints and slowly raise the elbows.

The sixth pose: Shun Shui Tui Zhou (Pushing the boat along the torrents)

[Preparation]　Stand in a required crotch.

[Postures]

1. Bend the elbows and put the palms at the rib-sides.

2. Slowly push the erect palms forwards and abduct the palmar roots at the same time with the part between the thumb and index finger turned downwards, the four fingers closed and the thumbs forked laterally; turn the palms from the exterior side to the interior side with the fingers facing each other; straighten the elbows, bend the wrists without bending the head and the body.

3. Slowly rotate the five fingers to the left and right sides, then change the palm into erect position, close the four fingers, protrude the thumbs forcefully back, bend the elbows and put them at the rib-sides.

4. Change the palms from erect position to downward pressing position, stretch the arms and then return to the original crotch.

[Essentials]　Slowly push the palm in an erect position, turn the wrist to make the fingers facing each other, straighten the elbows like a boat.

[Notes]　To turn and rotate the forearms with the action of subscapularis muscle, pectoralis major muscle, the latissimus dorsi muscle teres major muscle, and the muscles on the upper limbs; to stretch the wrist joints back with the action of long radial extensor carpal muscle, short radial carpal extensor muscle, extensor carpi ulnaris and all the extensors.

The seventh pose: Huai Zhong Bao Yue (Embracing the moon)

[Preparation]　Stand in a required crotch.

[Postures]

1. Bend the elbows, turn the palms upwards and put them at the waist sides.

2. Lift the upward turned palms from the waist, change them into erect position and cross them over the chest, then slowly separate them to different sides, straighten the elbows with the fingers facing each other and the center of palms turned upwards parallel to the shoulders.

3. Turn the finger tips downwards and the center of palms inwards, slightly bend the upper part of the body forwards, keep the hands like holding something and slowly raise them from the upper to the lower and from the lower to the upper, finally cross them over the chest.

4. Change the palms from erect position to downward pressing position, stretch the arms back and return to the original crotch.

[Essentials]　Erect the palms and lift them to cross each other, then separate them to different sides with the centers facing the front and the tips of fingers pointing the ground, then turn the centers of the palms inwards, slightly bend the upper part of the body forwards, slowly raise the arms from the lower to the upper with the action of pectoralis major muscle, the latissimus dorsi muscle teres major muscle and biceps.

The eighth pose: Xian Ren Zhi Lu (Immortal guiding the way)

【Preparation】 Stand in a required crotch.

【Postures】

1. Bend the hands, turn the palms upwards and put them at the waist sides.

2. Turn the palm to the right side and lift it to the chest in a erect position with the four fingers closed and the thumb stretched, push the elbow and arm forwards with great force.

3. Push straight forwards, bend the wrist and grasp the fist, externally turn the forearm with adduction, put the erect palm at the waist. The action of the left palm is the same as that of the right palm.

4. Change the palm from erect position to downward pressing position, stretch the arms posteriorly and return to the original crotch.

【Essentials】 Erect the palm and lift it up to the chest with the center of the palm sunken, push with the force of arm and fingers, turn the wrist, grasp the fist and pull backwards.

【Notes】 Stretch the thumbs and push forwards with the force of the elbow and arm with the action of palmar interosseous muscles, musculus extensor pollicis longus and fidicinales.

The ninth pose: Ping Shou Tuo Ta (Holding the tower with even hand)

【Preparation】 Stand in a required crotch.

【Postures】

1. Bend the elbows and turn the palms upwards at the rib-sides.

2. Slowly push the erect palms with the thumbs turned laterally like holding something in the hands.

3. Stretch the thumbs laterally with the exertion of the four fingers, slowly bend the elbows to the rib-sides.

4. Change the palms from erect position to downward pressing position and return to the original crotch.

【Essentials】 Erect the palms and push forwards with the thumbs turned laterally and inferiorly, stretch the elbows like supporting something.

【Notes】 Rotate the forearm with the action of infraspinous muscle and teres minor, slowly push forwards.

The tenth pose: Yun Zhang He Wa (Turning the palm to fold tile)

【Preparation】 Stand in a required crotch.

【Postures】

1. Bend the elbows and put the erect palms at the waist sides.

2. Change the right palm from erect position into pressing position, push it with the force of the arm, relax the shoulder, stretch the elbow with the fingers pointing forwards and the center of the palm facing the ground.

3. Turn the right wrist to retreat the erect palm and change it into pressing position when nearing the chest and cross it with the right palm, then slowly push it forwards with the center of the palm facing the ground and finally put the erect right palm at the waist side.

4. Change the left palm into erect position and slowly retreat it, then change both palms into pressing position, stretch the arms posteriorly and return to the original crotch.

[Essentials] Erect the palm and push it forwards, relax the shoulder and straighten the elbow with the fingers pointing anteriorly.

[Notes] Push the palm with the action of pronator teres, pronator quadratus and brachioradialis.

The eleventh pose: Feng Bai He Ye (Wind blowing the lotus leaf)

[Preparation] Stand in a required crotch.

[Postures]

1. Bend the elbows and put the erect palm at the waist side.

2. Bend the elbows with the centers of the palms turned upwards, the four fingers closed and the thumbs stretched; push the palms to the chest where they are crossed and then separate to different sides; exert the lateral side of the thumbs to keep the hands at a even level; look ahead and breathe naturally.

3. Slowly close the erect palms with the right in the lower position and the left in the upper position, finally retreat the palms to the waist sides.

4. Change of the palms from erect position to the pressing position, stretch the arms back and return to the original crotch.

[Essentials] Erect, cross and push the palms; extend the elbows and keep the shoulders, elbows and wrists at the same level.

[Notes] Put the erect palms at the waist sides and keep the hands at a even level with the action of deltoid muscle and infraspinous muscle.

The twelfth pose: Liang Shou Tuo Tian (Supporting the sky with both hands)

[Preparation] Stand in a required crotch.

[Postures]

1. Bend the elbows and put the erect palms at the waist sides.

2. Turn the erect palms upwards and raise them with the centers turned upwards, exert the finger tips, relax the shoulders, straighten the elbows, look ahead like supporting something over the head.

3. Rotate the palm root externally with the four fingers closed, slowly lower it, change it into erect position when reaching the chest, and finally put it at the waist sides.

4. Change the palm from erect position to pressing position, stretch the arms back and return to the original crotch.

【Essentials】 Erect the palms with the centers facing upwards, exert the finger tips, relax the shoulders, straighten the elbows and look ahead.

【Notes】 Erect the palms and raise them with the action of deltoid muscle, supraspinatus, trapezius muscle and serratus anterior muscle.

The thirteenth pose: Dan Feng Chao Yang (Single phoenix facing the sun)

【Preparation】 Stand in a required crotch.

【Postures】

1. Bend the elbows and put the erect palms at the waist sides.

2. Change the left palm from erect position to pressing position, bend the elbows to the chest for left abduction, then slowly move them to the lower at the right side, finally bend the elbows and put them at the waist sides.

3. The action of the right hand is the same as that of the left hand, only the direction is opposite.

4. Change the palm from erect position to pressing position, stretch the arms back and return to the original crotch.

【Essentials】 Rotate the wrist, slowly move it downwards to form a semi-circle.

【Notes】 Change the palms from erect position to pressing position; abduct with the action of deltoid muscle supraspinatus and muscles of arm; slowly move it downwards with the action of pectoralis major muscle, the latissimus dorsi muscle, deltoid muscle and triceps brachii muscle.

The fourteenth pose: Hai Di Lao Yue (Scooping the moon from the bottom of sea)

【Preparation】 Stand in a required crotch.

【Postures】

1. Bend the elbows and put the erect palms at the waist sides.

2. Erect and slowly lift the palms to different sides from the chest, rotate the wrists with the centers of palms turned downwards, bend the waist forwards without bending the legs, gradually move the palms from the upper to the lower with the centers opposing to each other, appearing like holding something.

3. Move the arms with exertion of the palm center and fingers, slowly lift them to the chest, erect the palms and put them at the waist sides, look ahead.

4. Change the palm from erect position to pressing position, stretch the arms back and return to the original crotch.

【Essentials】 Erect and lift the palms over the chest, separate them, rotate the wrist, bend the waist, straighten the legs, turn the palms upwards like holding the moon, exert the arms and finger tips.

【Notes】 Push the arms to the opposite sides with the action of supraspinatus, deltoid muscle, serratus anterior muscle and trapezius muscle ; rotate the wrist and bend the body slightly with the action of pectoralis major muscle, latissimus dorsi muscle and musculus teres major.

The fiftieth pose: Ding Tian Bao Di (Supporting the sky and embracing the earth)

【Preparation】 Stand in a required crotch.

【Postures】

1. Bend the elbows and put the erect palms at the waist sides.

2. Erect the palms over the shoulders, turn the wrists, abduct the palm roots with the finger tips opposing to each other, slowly raise the palms, rotate the wrists, slowly separate them, bend the body forward, gradually close the palms with the thumbs turned laterally and the palms crossed.

3. Raise the palms to the chest and the waist sides like supporting something quite heavy, straighten the upper part of the body and look ahead.

4. Change the palm from erect position to pressing position, stretch the arms back and return to the original crotch.

【Essentials】 Erect and slowly lift the palms to different sides from the chest, rotate the wrists with the centers of palms turned downwards, bend the waist forwards without bending the legs, gradually move the palms from the upper to the lower with the centers opposing to each other, appearing like holding something.

【Notes】 Erect the palms over the shoulders and rotate the wrists with the action of long radial extensor carpal muscle, short radial carpal extensor muscle, extensor carpi ulnaris and finger extensors; stretch the wrist joints posteriorly and raise the elbows with the action of radial flexor muscle of wrist, flexor carpi ulnaris, long palmar muscle, superficial flexor of fingers and deep flexor of fingers and digitus primus flexor muscle; rotate the wrists and slowly separate them, bend the body forwards, cross the palms, slowly lift them with the action of sacrospinous muscle.

The sixteenth pose: Li Pi Hua Shan (Splitting hua shan mountain with great force)

【Preparation】 Stand in a required crotch.

【Postures】

1. Bend the elbows and cross them over the chest.

2. Erect the palms and slowly separate them, relax the shoulders, slightly bend the elbows with the four fingers closed, the thumb turned back and the palm center protruded forward.

3. Split three times with the arms without shaking the head, look ahead and put the palms at the waist sides after splitting.

4. Change the palms from erect position to pressing position, stretch the arms back and return to the original crotch.

【Essentials】 Erect and cross the palms, push them to different sides, split with great force and look ahead.

【Notes】 Erect, cross and push the palms to different directions with the action of trapezius muscle , the latissimus dorsi muscle, pectoralis major muscle, musculus teres major, subscapularis muscle and the muscles of the upper arms.

Review Questions
- Describe the functions of Tuina exercises.
- What are the requirements for Standing Crotch?

6 Manipulations for Tuina

Manipulations in Tuina are the standard techniques performed with the doctor's hands or other parts of the body for stimulating the affected parts of the patient. There are various types of manipulations because of varied stimulation, intensity and time, such as pushing manipulation, pressing manipulation and kneading manipulation. The combination of two more manipulations is called compound manipulation, such as pressing and kneading manipulation, pushing and stroking manipulation, etc. In infantile Tuina, there are some compound manipulations with special nomenclature, such as Da Ma Guo He (driving a horse to cross river) and Huang Feng Ru Dong (bee entering its hole) etc. Different manipulations bear different effect in dredging meridians, promoting Qi and blood circulation, smoothing joints and regulating viscera.

The manipulations should be performed continuously, forcefully, evenly, softly and thoroughly. That is to say manipulation should be performed gently for a continuous period of time with force according to individual condition. The basic manipulations can be classified into the categories of swaying, rubbing, vibrating, pressing, percussion and joint movement. Based on the tissues that are dealt with, manipulations are divided into soft tissue manipulations and joint setting manipulations. According to the application, manipulations can be categorized into stimulating, bone-setting and relaxing types. In this book, they are divided into two types, basic and compound.

The practice of Tuina manipulations concentrates on training the fingers, wrist and arms. The practitioner can practice it on sand bag first and then on human body. The sand bag is about 8 cun in length and 5 cun in width, containing clean sand and some small pieces of sponge, usually covered with cotton cloth for the benefit of washing. At the beginning, the bag can be fastened. With the progress of practice, the bag is gradually loosened. When the basic manipulations are well practiced on the bag, practitioners can do it on different parts of human body, such as head, face, neck, limbs, shoulders, back, waist, buttocks, chest and abdomen. The subject can take supine, prone, sitting or lateral recumbent positions.

Besides, practitioners have to try to train their fingers, wrists and arms by means of push-up, dumbbell and spring-grip dumb-bells. To practice these exercises for Tuina is also beneficial to mental cultivation of the practitioners.

6.1 Basic manipulations for adult Tuina

There are various kinds of manipulations with special techniques and dynamic form, which are the basic elements for composing compound manipulations.

6.1.1 Yi Zhi Chan Fa (One-finger pushing manipulation)

Exert force by swaying the forearm and direct it to the affected area or Acupoint with the tip or the whorl surface of the thumb. Such manipulation is called Yi Zhi Chan Fa (One-finger pushing manipulation). It is the typical manipulation of the school of one-finger pushing manipulation.

【Methods for performing manipulations】

Clench a hollow fist with suspended and flexed wrist and palm, and stretch the thumb straight naturally to cover the fist hole. Exert force on the body surface with the tip or the whorl surface of the thumb. Lower the shoulder, drop the elbow and suspend the wrist. Sway the forearm initiatively to bring the wrist swing inward and outward while flexing and extending the thumb joint to make the force on the Acupoint heavy and light, alternately with the frequency of 120~160 times per minute (see Fig. 6-1 on page 54).

【Essentials for performing manipulations】

1. Lowering shoulders: Relax the shoulder joints with the shoulder blades dropping naturally. Keep the armpit with the space of a fist. Avoid forcefully shrugging shoulders.

2. Dropping elbow: Lower the elbow joint naturally, slightly lower than the wrist. The elbow should not be adducted excessively.

3. Suspending wrist: Flex the wrist joint and suspend it naturally. Keep the wrist joint loose and try to flex to 90°.

4. Exert force of thumb: Fix it on the affected area or Acupoint naturally with the tip or whorl surface of the thumb, avoid forceful pressing.

5. Emptying palm: Keep the four fingers and the palm loose and make a hollow fist. Accumulate the power in the palm and shoot it from the fingers.

6. Pushing forcefully and moving slowly: It is essential for performing Yi Zhi Chan Fa (One-finger Pushing Manipulation) on the surface of the skin. Pushing forcefully means that the swaying is relatively quick, 120~160 times per minute. Moving slowly means to fix it on the surface of the skin with the tip or the whorl surface of the thumb that can move slowly along the meridian or a given path. Slipping or rubbing should be avoided.

【Cautions】

1. Concentrate the mind when operating the manipulation with correct postures. The shoulders, elbow and wrist should be kept relaxed, but not lax. Only when they are coordinated with the whole body can the manipulation be performed effectively.

2. There are two kinds of methods in performing Yi Zhi Chan Fa (One-finger

Pushing Manipulation): to be performed either with the thumb joint flexed or not flexed. If the practitioner's thumb joint is stiff or the treatment needs slight and soft stimulus, the manipulation can be done with the thumb joint flexed and extended. If the practitioner's thumb joint is flexible, manipulation is better performed with straight thumb joint.

3. Operating Yi Zhi Chan Fa (One-finger Pushing Manipulation) on the body surface should follow the principle of "pushing along the meridians and collaterals, and moving along the Acupoints" to select the Acupoints along the meridian.

Appendix: The evolvement of Yi Zhi Chan Fa (one-finger pushing manipulation)

1. Yi Zhi Chan Pian Feng Tui Fa (Lateral-pushing of the one-finger pushing manipulation) Exert force with the thumb-radius while straightening and adducting the thumb, and keep the palm and other fingers straight. Slightly flex the wrist joint, sway the forearm initiatively and the wrist joint gently. Such a manipulation is called Yi Zhi Chan Pian Feng Tui Fa (lateral-pushing manipulation of one-finger pushing manipulation, also called Shao Shang Force) (see Fig. 6-2 on page 55). It is suitable for performing on the craniofacial region because of its light stimulation.

2. Yi Zhi Chan Qu Zhi Tui Fa (One-finger pushing manipulation performed with flexed thumb) Flex the thumb with the force exerted from the radial border or the back of the interphalangeal joint of the thumb. Such manipulation is called Yi Zhi Chan Qu Zhi Tui Fa (one-finger pushing manipulation performed with flexed thumb) or Gui Tui Fa (genuflecting pushing manipulation). It is often applied to the nape and bone cleft of the joint because of its fixed and strong force. (see Fig. 6-3 on page 55)

3. Chan Fa (Twining manipulation or quick pushing manipulation) Reduce the area touched by the tip or the radial hump of the thumb and decrease the amplitude of swaying and the pressure on the body surface, increase the frequency up to 220~250 times per minute. Such manipulation is called twining manipulation or quick pushing manipulation which means continuous touch. It is commonly used to treat excess heat syndrome, furuncle and carbuncle and other external problems (see Fig. 6-4 on page 55).

6.1.2 Rolling manipulation

Use the ulnar dorsum to press the affected region. Sway the forearm to drive the wrist to extend and flex, and roll on the affected area. Such manipulation is called Gun Fa (rolling manipulation). It is the typical manipulation of the school of Gun Fa (rolling manipulation).

【Methods for performing manipulations】

The practitioner straightens the thumb naturally and makes a hollow fist. The little finger and the ring finger flex naturally to 90° and the flexed angle of the other two fingers reduces gradually to make the palm round along the palm surface. Press the affected area with the dorsum of the hand near the lateral side of the little finger. Sway the forearm initiatively to extend and flex the wrist in a wide range and rotate the forearm as well. Roll the ulnar side of the hand on the affected area continuously (see Fig. 6-5 on page 56). The swaying frequency is about 120 times per minute.

【Essentials for performing manipulations】

1. Lower shoulders and drop elbow with the wrist joint flexed naturally to 14°. Keep a space of a fist to the chest. Relax the wrist and make a hollow fist. Then fix on the affected area with the hand back.

2. The wrist joint extends and flexes about 120°, i.e. flexing the wrist joint to 80° while swaying outward about 40° backward to touch the affected area in turn with half of the hand. The forearm rotates outwards while swaying externally and inwards while swaying backward.

3. The stimulation should be done with light and heavy force alternately, rolling forward three times and rolling back once.

4. When applying Gun Fa (rolling manipulation), the frequency should be fixed. The speed should not be too quick.

5. Gun Fa (rolling manipulation) is often used together with passive limb movement of the patient. While one hand is performing Gun Fa (rolling manipulation), the other hand can help the patient do passive movement. The two hands should be coordinative. The passive movement should be soft, brief and causal.

【Cautions】

1. When performing Gun Fa (rolling manipulation), the amplitude of the wrist joint's extending-flexing movement should be maximized. Rotation of the forearm and insufficient extension and flexion of the wrist joint should be avoided.

2. Gun Fa (rolling manipulation) should be fixed; hauling, leaping or rotating-swaying is not allowed. Bumping between the hand and the body surface should be avoided.

3. Operating on the apophysial points of vertebral spinous process and other joints should be avoided because it may cause discomfort.

Appendix: The evolvement of rolling manipulation

1. Zhang Zhi Guan Jie Gun Fa (Rolling with palm and phalangeal joints) Press the affected area with apophysial points of palm and phalangeal joints. Replace the complex movement of extension and flexion of the wrist joint and the rotation of the forearm with simple movement of extension and flexion of the wrist joint. Such a manipulation is called Zhi Zhang Guan Jie Gun Fa (manipulation of rolling with palm and phalangeal joints). Compared with Gun Fa (rolling manipulation), it exerts greater pressure and stronger stimulation, so it is often applied on the areas with thick muscles, such as waist, buttock and lower extremities (see Fig. 6-6 on page 57).

2. Qian Bi Gun Fa (Manipulation of rolling with forearm) Exert force on the affected area with the lunar dorsum side of the forearm and roll to and fro. Such manipulation is called Qian Bi Gun Fa (manipulation of rolling with forearm) (see Fig. 6-7 on page 57). It has a large touching area with soft and comfortable stimulation, so it is often applied on patients who are heavy or the waist, buttock and lower extremities with larger area needed to be treated.

6.1.3 Rou Fa (Kneading manipulation)

Fix on the body surface with certain part of the finger and palm and knead in circles to rotate slowly and softly the subcutaneous tissues. Such manipulation is called Rou Fa (Kneading Manipulation). It is one of the commonly-used manipulations. According to different touching areas, it can be divided into Zhang Gen Rou Fa (palm-base kneading manipulation), Da Yu Ji Rou Fa (major thenar kneading manipulation) and Zhi Rou Fa (finger kneading manipulation).

[Methods for performing manipulations]

1. Da Yu Ji Rou Fa (Major thenar kneading manipulation) Exert force with major thenar and flex the wrist joint slightly to 120°~140°. Use the elbow joint as a pivot and sway the forearm initiatively to knead with major thenar and sway on the affected area. The frequency is about 120~160 times per minute (see Fig. 6-8 on page 57).

2. Zhang Gen Rou Fa (Palm-base kneading manipulation) Exert force with palm base. Flex the fingers naturally and stretch the wrist joint slightly backwards. Use the elbow joint which flexes slightly as a pivot and sway the forearm initiatively to knead with the palm base on the affected area. The frequency is about 120~160 times per minute. (see Fig. 6-9 on page 57)

3. Mu Zhi Rou Fa (Thumb kneading manipulation) Exert force with the whorl surface of the thumb while the other four fingers supporting on the suitable position with the wrist joint flexed slightly or straightened. The forearm rotates in a small amplitude with the thumb rotating on the affected area. The frequency is 120~160 times per minute (see Fig. 6-10 on page 58).

4. Zhong Zhi Rou Fa (Middle finger kneading manipulation) Exert force with the whorl surface of the middle finger. Use the elbow as a pivot with the middle finger joint straightened and the metacarpophalangeal joint flexed slightly. The forearm rotates in an initiative small amplitude with the whorl surface of the middle finger rotating on the affected area. The frequency is 120~160 times per minute. (see Fig. 6-11 on page 58)

Kneading with the index finger or with juxtaposed index finger, middle finger and ring finger is called Shi Zhi Rou (index finger kneading manipulation) and San Zhi Rou (three fingers kneading manipulation) respectively. Essentials for performing these two manipulations are the same as the ones for performing Zhong Zhi Rou (middle finger kneading manipulation).

【Essentials for performing manipulations】

1. In performing Rou Fa (kneading manipulation), the practitioner should lower the shoulders, drop the elbow and relax the wrist joint. The forearm sways in a small amplitude to rotate with force from the wrist joint.

2. In performing Rou Fa (Kneading manipulation), subcutaneous tissues should be activated to move together. The movement should be coordinative and rhythmic.

3. In performing Rou Fa (kneading manipulation), the pressure should be moderate, making the patient feel comfortable.

【Cautions】

1. In this manipulation, rubbing or slipping between the treated part and the body surface should be avoided.

2. The force should be passed through the relaxed wrist joint. When performing Rou Fa (kneading manipulation), the wrist joint should be relaxed with certain intensity, and avoiding excessive stiffness of the wrist.

6.1.4 Mo Fa (Circular-rubbing or stroking manipulation)

Use the finger surface or palm to touch the affected area and make rhythmic and circular movements. Such a manipulation is called Mo Fa (Circular Rubbing or Stroking Manipulation).

【Methods for performing manipulations】

1. Zhang Mo Fa (Palm-rubbing manipulation) Press on the body surface with the fingers juxtaposed, the palm straightened naturally and the wrist joint stretched slightly. Use the elbow joint as a pivot, and move the forearm initiatively to rub circularly with the palm on the affected area (see Fig. 6-12 on page 58). It can be performed either clockwise or counter-clockwise with the frequency of 100~120 times per minute.

2. Zhi Mo Fa (Finger-rubbing manipulation) Take the palm side of the index finger, middle finger, ring finger and the little finger as the touching area with the fingers juxtaposed, the palm straightened naturally and the wrist joint flexed slightly. Use the elbow joint as a pivot, and move the forearm initiatively to rub with the palm side of the fingers circularly on the affected area. It can be performed either clockwise or counter-clockwise with the frequency of 100~120 times per minute.

【Essentials for performing manipulations】

1. In performing Mo Fa (rubbing manipulation), the shoulders should be relaxed and the forearm should sway initiatively to enable the relaxed wrist joint to make circular movements. When performing Zhi Mo Fa (finger-rubbing manipulation), the wrist joint should be relaxed, avoiding excessive stiffness.

2. In performing rubbing manipulation, the force should be moderate and the frequency should be even. The manipulation should be light but not superficial; heavy but not stuck. Finger-rubbing manipulation is comparatively light and quick, while the palm-

rubbing is strong and slow.

【Cautions】

1. Such a manipulation should be done lightly and slowly.

2. The direction of the manipulation should be chosen according to the deficiency or excess syndrome of the patient's condition. Traditionally, clockwise Mo Fa (rubbing manipulation) is suitable for treating Xu Zheng (deficiency syndrome), while counterclockwise Mo Fa (rubbing manipulation) is suitable for treating Shi Zheng (excess syndrome). In the clinical operation, different kind of Mo Fa (rubbing manipulation) should be used according to the anatomical structure of the affected area and different pathological conditions.

3. When performing Mo Fa (rubbing manipulation), ointments with different kinds of function are often used according to symptoms, known as Gao Mo (rubbing manipulation with ointment) (See Gao Mo or rubbing manipulation with ointment). Medium, such as ginger and green onion juice, ever green ointment, or oil of turpentine, can also be used to reinforce the function of Mo Fa (rubbing manipulation).

4. Pay attention to the difference between Rou Fa (kneading manipulation) and Mo Fa (circular rubbing or stroking manipulation): when operating Rou Fa (kneading manipulation), fingers and palms should fixate on a certain part of the body surface to make the subcutaneous tissues to move with a comparatively strong force without friction between the body surface. While operating Mo Fa (circular rubbing or stroking manipulation), fingers and palms make circular rubbing with comparatively light force on the body surface without moving subcutaneous tissues. In the clinical operation, the two manipulations are often used together.

6.1.5 Ca Fa (To-and-fro rubbing manipulation)

Exert force on the affected area with the major thenar, palm base or minor thenar to perform straight to-and-fro rubbing movement. The warm effect induced by rubbing can penetrate into the deep layer through the body surface. Such a manipulation is called Ca Fa (To-and-fro rubbing manipulation). It can be divided into Zhang Ca Fa (To-and-fro rubbing manipulation with palm), Da Yu Ji Ca Fa (To-and-fro rubbing manipulation with major thenar) and Xiao Yu Ji Ca Fa (To-and-fro rubbing manipulation with minor thenar).

【Methods for performing manipulations】

1. Zhang Ca Fa (To-and-fro rubbing manipulation with palm) Keep the palm close to the skin while straightening the wrist joint. Take the shoulder joint as the pivot, and move the upper arm initiatively with the palm rubbing on the body surface to and fro along a straight line (see Fig. 6-13 on page 59). The frequency is 100~120 times per minute. It is often applied on chest, hypochondriac regions and abdomen.

2. Da Yu Ji Ca Fa (To-and-fro rubbing manipulation with major thenar) Keep the major thenar close to the body surface while straightening the wrist joint. Take the shoulder joint as the pivot, and move the upper arm initiatively with major thenar rubbing on the body surface to and fro along a straight line (see Fig. 6-14 on page 59). The frequency is 100~120 times per minute. It is often used to operate on chest, abdomen, back, lumbus and extremities.

3. Xiao Yu Ji Ca Fa (To-and-fro rubbing manipulation with palm minor thenar) Exert force on the body surface with minor thenar while keeping the palm straight and the wrist joint flat and straight. Take the shoulder joint as the pivot, and move the upper arm initiatively with minor thenar rubbing on the body surface to and fro along a straight line (see Fig. 6-15 on page 60). The frequency is 100~120 times per minute. It is often applied on shoulders, back, lumbus, stern, and lower extremities.

【Essentials for performing manipulations】

1. The rubbing route is better straight and long. No matter the direction of the rubbing is up and down or left and right, the route should be kept straight to and fro and the distance of rubbing should be lengthened without deflecting or halting, such as pulling a saw.

2. The palm should be kept close to the affected area. The pressing force should be monitor not to make the skin folded. The frequency should be kept even.

【Cautions】

1. When operating, the practitioner should breathe naturally without holding the breath.

2. Ca Fa (To-and-fro rubbing manipulation) can produce soft and warm stimulation. Zhang Ca Fa (To-and-fro rubbing manipulation with palm) exerts mild warming effect, while Xiao Yu Ji Ca Fa (To-and-fro rubbing manipulation with minor thenar) produces high heat effect, and Da Yu Ji Ca Fa (To-and-fro rubbing manipulation with major thenar) generates moderate warming effect. In clinical operation, each treatment is accomplished when the patient feels warm.

3. In operation, lubricant, such as ever green ointment or sesame oil, is often used on the affected area. It can protect the skin and lead the warmth deeply into the body.

4. Ca Fa (To-and-fro rubbing manipulation) is done directly on the body surface, so the operating room should be kept warm.

5. Ca Fa (To-and-fro rubbing manipulation) is better to be applied after other manipulations in order not to cause skin lesion.

6.1.6 Tui Fa (Pushing manipulation)

Exert force on the affected area or certain Acupoint with fingers, palm or other parts of the body, and make rectilinear or arc movement. Such a manipulation is called Tui Fa (pushing manipulation). It can be divided into Ping Tui Fa (flat pushing manipulation), Zhi Tui Fa (straight pushing manipulation), Xuan Tui Fa (spiral pushing manipulation), Fen Tui Fa (separate pushing manipulation) and He Tui Fa (coalescent pushing manipulation).

【Methods for performing manipulations】

1. Ping Tui Fa (Flat pushing manipulation) According to different operating parts, it can be divided into three kinds of manipulation: Mu Zhi Ping Tui Fa (flat pushing manipulation with thumb), Zhang Ping Tui Fa (flat pushing manipulation with palm), and Zhou Ping Tui Fa (flat pushing manipulation with elbow).

(1) Mu Zhi Ping Tui Fa (Flat pushing manipulation with thumb) Keep the thumb close to the body surface and support with the other four fingers. Flex and extend the elbow to bring the thumb to push slowly in a one way direction along the meridian or along the direction of muscular fiber. Repeat the manipulation 5 to 15 times continuously (see Fig. 6-16 on page 61).

(2) Zhang Ping Tui Fa (Flat pushing manipulation with palm) Press on the body surface with palm and exert force with the palm base (or the whole palm). Flex and extend the elbow to push the palm slowly along a certain direction. Repeat the manipulation 5 to 15 times continuously (see Fig. 6-17 on page 61).

(3) Zhou Ping Tui Fa (Flat pushing manipulation with elbow) Flex the elbow and exert force on certain part with the tip of the elbow (olceranon). Push slowly along the direction of muscular fiber in a straight line (see Fig. 6-18 on page 61).

2. Zhi Tui Fa (Straight pushing manipulation) Exert force on a certain part or Acupoint with the thumb radial border or the whorl surface of the index finger or middle finger. Push in a one way direction (see Fig. 6-19 on page 61). The frequency is about 200 times per minute.

3. Xuan Tui Fa (Spiral pushing manipulation) Push spirally on the Acupoint with the whorl surface of the thumb (see Fig. 6-20 on page 62). The frequency is about 200~240 times per minute.

4. Fen Tui Fa (Parting pushing manipulation) Keep close to the body surface with the whorl surface of two thumbs or palms. Push from the center part to the left or right side respectively in a one way direction (see Fig. 6-21 on page 62). The frequency is 120 times per minute.

5. He Tui Fa (Coalescent pushing manipulation) Keep close to the body surface with the whorl surface of two thumbs or palms. Push from either side of the Acupoint to the center of the Acupoint (see Fig. 6-22 on page 62).

【Essentials for performing manipulations】

1. Among Tui Fa (pushing manipulation), Ping Tui Fa (flat pushing manipulation) can exert comparatively stronger force. While pushing, certain pressure is needed. The force should be steady, the pushing speed should be slow and the movement should be done unilaterally.

(1) When operating Mu Zhi Ping Tui Fa (flat pushing manipulation with thumb), the elbow joint flexes and stretches within a small amplitude. The thumb, wrist and arm exert

force initiatively and push straight unilaterally towards the direction of the thumb tip within a short distance.

(2) When operating Zhang Ping Tui Fa (flat pushing manipulation with palm), exert force with the palm base (or the whole palm) while stretching the wrist joint slightly backwards. Use the shoulder joint as a pivot of the movement. Use the upper arm to exert force initiatively and flex and stretch the elbow joint so as to push the palm forward unilaterally.

(3) Zhou Ping Tui Fa (flat pushing manipulation with elbow) is performed by pushing with the strength of the whole body. So the stimulation induced is strong.

2. When performing Zhi Tui Fa (straight pushing manipulation), the wrist, palm and fingers move straight forwards with flexion and stretching of the elbow joint. Compared with Ping Tui Fa (flat pushing manipulation), its pressing force is lighter. The requirements of the movement are light, quick and continuous, just like sweeping dust with a broom. It is better not to make the skin of the affected part red.

3. When performing Xuan Tui Fa (spiral pushing manipulation), the joints of elbow and wrist should be kept relaxed. The thumb moves in a circle within a small range without make the subcutaneous tissues move. It is similar to Zhi Mo Fa (finger rubbing manipulation).

4. When performing Fen Tui Fa (separate pushing manipulation), the force of the two hands should be even. The movement should be mild and coordinate. The pushing movement to both sides can be operated in a straight line or in a curved line.

5. The essentials of performing He Tui Fa (coalescent pushing manipulation) are the same as that for performing Fen Tui Fa (separate pushing manipulation). But the operation should be done in an opposite direction. The Yin and Yang Acupoints located on the wrist and abdomen are often used together with this manipulation.

【Cautions】

1. When performing Tui Fa (pushing manipulation), the movement should be done along a straight line or a curved line unilaterally. To-and-fro movement should be avoided.

2. When performing the operation, the operating part should keep close to the body surface. The force used should be steady, even and moderate. The pushing speed should not be too quick.

3. When performing Tui Fa (pushing manipulation), the mediums, such as ever green ointment, talc powder, and juice of ginger or green onion, can be used on the operated part.

6.1.7 Mo Fa (Wiping manipulation)

Keep close to the skin with the whorl surface of the thumb and push up and down or left to right or along a curved path. Such manipulation is called Mo Fa (wiping manipulation). It is divided into Zhi Mo Fa (finger wiping manipulation) and Zhang Mo Fa (palm wiping manipulation).

【Methods for performing manipulations】

1. Zhi Mo Fa (Finger wiping manipulation)　Exert force on the body surface with the whorl surface of one thumb or two thumbs and support with the rest four fingers. The thumb moves to and fro slowly unilaterally up and down or left to right or a curved line (see Fig. 6-23 on page 63).

2. Zhang Mo Fa (Palm wiping Manipulation)　Exert force on the body surface with one or two palms and relax the wrist joint. The forearm and the upper arm exert force coordinately to move the palm to and fro slowly unilaterally up and down or left to right or a curved line (see Fig. 6-24 on page 63).

【Essentials for performing manipulations】

1. When performing Mo Fa (Wiping manipulation), the whorl surface of the thumb or the palm should be kept close to the body surface.

2. The force used in Mo Fa (Wiping manipulation) should be even, while the movement should be mild and slow. The operation route in the affected area should be longer. The manipulation should be light but not superficial, heavy but not stuck.

【Cautions】

1. The stimulation of Mo Fa (Wiping manipulation) is superficial. When performing this manipulation, subcutaneous tissues in the deep layer should not be affected.

2. Mo Fa (Wiping manipulation) is easily confused with Tui Fa (pushing manipulation). The movement of Tui Fa (pushing manipulation) is done unilaterally, while the movement of Mo fa (Wiping manipulation) can be done up and down, or in a straight line or in a curved line, appearing more flexible.

3. When Zhi Mo Fa (finger wiping manipulation) is applied to the head and face, the performing procedure is fixed.

6.1.8　Sao San Fa (Cleaning and dissipating manipulation)

Push and scrub to and fro along the meridians of Shaoyang over the temple with the thumb radial border and the tips of the other four fingers. Such a manipulation is called Sao San Fa (cleaning and dissipating manipulation).

【Methods for performing manipulations】

The practitioner holds the head of the patient with one hand and keeps close to the temple of the head with the thumb radial border and the tips of the other four fingers. Push and scrub to and fro behind the ear along the meridian of Shaoyang with slight force (see Fig. 6-25 on page 64). The frequency is about 250 times per minute.

【Essentials for performing manipulations】

1. The practitioner should lower the shoulders, drop the elbow, flex the elbow joint to 90~120 degrees, and keep the wrist joint relaxed.

2. Use the elbow joint as a pivot, sway the forearm initiatively to shake the wrist joint, and push and scrub to-and-fro on the temple with the operating finger.

【Cautions】

1. While performing Sao San Fa (cleaning and dissipating manipulation), the operating part of the fingers should be closely attached to the scalp with mild force. While pushing and scrubbing forward, the force should be slightly heavy; while returning, the force should be slightly light. The manipulation should be light but not superficial; heavy but not stuck.

2. While performing the manipulation, the hand holding the head should be fixated on the patient's head so as not to shake and cause discomfort.

3. While performing Sao San Fa (cleaning and dissipating manipulation), the movement should be done forward and backward along the meridians and the interval should not be too long.

6.1.9 Cuo Fa (Palm-twisting manipulation)

Clip a certain part of the body or extremity with both palms, and perform swiftly or alternately twisting and kneading to and fro with opposite force. Such a manipulation is called Cuo Fa (palm twisting manipulation).

【Methods for performing manipulations】

1. Jian Ji Shang Zhi Bu Cuo Fa (Palm twisting manipulation on shoulders and upper extremities) The patient is in a sitting position with relaxed and naturally dropped shoulders and arms. The practitioner stands by the patient with the upper body slightly inclining forward, clipping the front and back part of the patient's shoulder with two palms, performing swift twisting and kneading movement with opposite force, and at the same time, moving up and down from the upper extremity to the wrist (see Fig. 6-26 on page 64) 3 to 5 times.

2. Xie Lei Bu Cuo Fa (Palm twisting manipulation on hypochondrium) The patient is in a sitting position with the arms stretched slightly outside. The practitioner stands at the back of the patient and holds the hypochondrium of the patient with two palms. Twist several times from below the armpit to the waist.

3. Xia Zhi Cuo Fa (Palm-twisting manipulation on lower extremities) The patient is in a supine position with the knee flexed to about 60°. The practitioner stands on the side of the bed and clip both sides of the patient's thigh with two palms to rub from the upper to the calf.

【Essentials for performing manipulations】

1. While performing Cuo Fa (palm-twisting manipulation), the exertion of force should be symmetric and mild. The patient should keep the extremities relaxed.

2. The operation demands "rapid twisting and slow moving, which means the twisting movement should be swift while the up and down moving action should be slow.

【Cautions】

1. While in performing Cuo Fa (palm twisting manipulation), the force used should not be too heavy. Tight clipping will cause the manipulation stuck.

2. Cuo Fa (Palm twisting manipulation) is a supplementary manipulation. It is mainly applied to shoulders and upper extremities.

6.1.10 Zhen Fa (Vibrating manipulation)

It is performed by pressing a certain Acupoint or part of the body with the finger or palm, and vibrating swiftly and continuously. Such a manipulation is called Zhen Fa (vibrating manipulation). It is also called Zhen Chan Fa (vibrating and trembling manipulation). It can be divided into Zhi Zhen Fa (finger vibrating manipulation) and Zhang Zhen Fa (palm vibrating manipulation).

【Methods for performing manipulations】

1. Zhi Zhen Fa (Finger-vibrating manipulation) Drop the elbow and put the tip of the middle finger on the affected area. Straighten the finger and flex the elbow slightly. Put the index finger on the middle finger to add force. Exert force statically with the forearm and hand, and contract the muscles alternatively to direct the vibration produced by arm to the body through the middle finger (see Fig. 6-27 on page 65). The frequency of vibration is 300-400 times per minute.

2. Zhang Zhen Fa (Palm-vibrating manipulation) Stretch the wrist joint slightly backwards and extend the finger naturally. Press the patient's body gently with the palm (or overlapping the palms on the surface of the body) and flex the elbow slightly. Exert force statically with the forearm and hand, and contract the muscles alternatively to direct the vibration produced by the arm to the body through the palm (see Fig. 6-28 on page 65). The frequency of vibration is 300~400 times per minute.

【Essentials for performing manipulations】

1. While performing Zhi Zhen Fa (finger vibrating) and Zhang Zhen Fa (palm vibrating manipulation), the shoulder joint should be abducted for about 30 degrees, and the elbow joint should be flexed for about 140 degrees.

2. Exerting force statically means to tighten the muscles of the hand and forearm, but not to make any initiative movement. However, based on the tightened muscles of the hand and forearm, the initiative movement of the arm can maintain for a long time.

3. In performing this manipulation, the practitioner should highly concentrate his attention on the finger and palm.

【Cautions】

1. While performing Zhen Fa (vibrating manipulation), the muscle should exert force while keeping static. During the operating, the practitioner should breathe normally and avoid holding his breath.

2. The way of contracting muscles in performing Zhen Fa (vibrating manipulation)

consumes more strength. So the practitioner needs long-term training. The practice of Shao Lin Nei Gong (Shaolin Internal Exercise) can effectively improve the quality of Zhen Fa (vibrating manipulation).

6.1.11 Dou Fa (Shaking manipulation)

Hold the distal end of the patient's affected extremities with one hand or both hands to shake constantly up and down or from the left and to the right in a small amplitude. Such a manipulation is called Dou Fa (Shaking manipulation).

【Methods for performing manipulations】

Hold the distal end of the patient's upper or lower extremities (wrist or ankle). Lift the treated extremity to a certain angle (when taking a sitting position, the upper extremity should be in an abducted position of 60°; when taking a supine position, the lower extremity should be raised to form a 30° angle between the extremity and the bed). While pulling with slight force, shake constantly up and down in a small amplitude to cause the parenchyma of the affected extremity to shake and transmit to the proximal end of the extremity (see Fig. 6-29 on page 66).

【Essentials for performing manipulations】

1. The shaken extremities should be kept relaxed and straightened naturally. The practitioner should breathe normally and avoid holding the breath.

2. The amplitude of shaking should be small and the frequency should be rapid.

【Cautions】

1. When shaking the lower extremities, the amplitude of shaking can be wider than that of shaking upper extremities and the frequency should be lower for the lower extremities are heavier.

2. Dou Fa (Shaking manipulation) is often used as a finishing manipulation. Shang Zhi Dou Fa (Upper-extremities shaking manipulation) is commonly used.

6.1.12 An Fa (Point-pressing manipulation)

Press a certain Acupoint or part of the body surface with finger or palm and exert force gradually. Such a manipulation is called An Fa (Pressing Manipulation).

【Methods for performing manipulations】

1. Zhi An Fa (Finger pressing manipulation) Straighten the thumb and press the meridian on the body surface with the tip or whorl surface of the thumb, supported by the other four fingers. If the force of one thumb is not enough, the other thumb can be overlapped on it and press downward heavily with the thumb face (see Fig. 6-30 on page 66).

2. Zhang An Fa (Palm pressing manipulation) Press the body surface with palm base, thenar or the whole palm. If the force of one hand is not enough, both hands can be overlapped to press (see Fig. 31 on page 66).

【Essentials for performing manipulations】

1. The direction of pressing should be vertical. The force used should be steady and continuous, and be increased steadily to make the stimulation transmit sufficiently to the deep layer of the body tissues. Then the pressure is reduced gradually with the procedure of "light-heavy-light".

2. When performing An Fa (Pressing manipulation), if great stimulation is needed, the practitioner can incline his upper part of the body slightly forwards to increase the stimulation with his own gravity.

【Cautions】

1. Sudden violent force should be avoided lest side effect be caused.

2. The performance of An Fa (Pressing manipulation) is marked by changed rhythm. Attention should be paid to the difference between continuous pressure and pressing manipulation. In clinic, An Fa (Pressing manipulation) is frequently used together with Rou Fa (kneading manipulation) to form the compound manipulation of An Rou Fa (pressing and kneading manipulation).

6.1.13 Ya Fa (Suppressing manipulation)

Fix the thumb, palm or olceranon of the elbow joint on a certain Acupoint or part of the body surface and press downwards continuously. Such a manipulation is called Ya Fa (Suppressing manipulation).

【Methods for performing manipulations】

Suppress the body surface vertically with the whorl surface of the thumb, palm or the upper part of the forearm of the flexed elbow. While suppressing, gradual gliding also can be done on the body surface. The manipulation of suppressing with the upper part of the forearm of the elbow is called elbow suppressing manipulation (see Fig. 6-32 on page 67).

【Essentials for performing manipulations】

An Fa (Pressing manipulation) is similar to Ya Fa (Suppressing manipulation), so it is always simply called pressing. The former is more dynamic while the latter is static. The duration of An Fa (Pressing manipulation) is short while the duration of Ya Fa (Suppressing manipulation) is longer; the force of the former is light with small stimulation while the force of the latter is strong with great stimulation.

【Cautions】

1. When applying Ya Fa (pressing manipulation) on the dorsolumbar region, the strength should be moderate to avoid side effect.

2. The stimulation of elbow pressing manipulation is comparatively stronger, so it is usually applied to the muscles of waist and buttock for those who are strong.

6.1.14 Dian Fa (Point-pressing manipulation)

Press a certain Acupoint or part of the body with the tip of a finger or the interphalangeal joint. Such a manipulation is called Dian Fa (point-pressing manipulation). In clinic, it can be divided into Zhi Dian Fa (point-pressing manipulation with finger) and Zhou Dian Fa (point-pressing manipulation with elbow).

【Methods for performing manipulations】

1. Zhi Dian Fa (Point-pressing manipulation with finger)　Make a hollow fist, straighten the thumb and make it close to the middle interphalangeal joint of the middle finger. Exert force with the tip of the thumb, or with the interphalangeal joint of the thumb or with the tip of the middle finger supported by the overlapping the index finger on the middle finger. Press a certain Acupoint or part of the body with a steady force (see Fig. 6-33 on page 68).

2. Zhou Dian Fa (Point-pressing manipulation with elbow)　Flex the elbow and exert force with the olceranon. Incline the upper part of the body slightly forward, then press continuously with the elbow. The pressure from the practitioner's own gravity is transmitted through the shoulder joint and forearm (see Fig. 6-34 on page 68).

【Essentials for performing manipulations】

Dian Fa (Point-pressing manipulation) is developed from An Fa (pressing manipulation), and the essentials for performing manipulation are the same. But Dian Fa (point-pressing manipulation) is marked by smaller touching area and stronger stimulation.

【Cautions】

1. Dian Fa (Point-pressing manipulation) is marked by small touching area, strong and short period of stimulation. It is often used to relieve pain, also known as Zhi Zhen (finger needle). Rou Fa (kneading manipulation) is used after Dian Fa (Point-pressing manipulation) in order to smooth Qi and blood as well as to avoid the lesion of parenchyma of the operated part.

2. Dian Fa (Point-pressing manipulation) should be carefully applied to people who are old, weak or frail.

3. The part for exerting force in Zhou Dian Fa (point-pressing manipulation with elbow) and Zhou Ya Fa (suppressing manipulation with elbow) is different. The former exerts force with the sharp olceranon, and the later with blunt upper part of the forearm.

6.1.15　Nie Fa (Pinching manipulation)

Exert force symmetrically with the thumb and the other fingers to extrude the operated part. Such a manipulation is called Nie Fa (pinching manipulation). The manipulation applied to the spine is called Nie Ji (spine pinching), which is commonly used for treating children. (See the relative item of manipulation for infantile Tuina).

【Methods for performing manipulations】

Clip the operated part with the thumb and the index finger, middle finger or with the thumb and the other four fingers. Extrude symmetrically and release immediately after that. Repeat the manipulation mentioned above and move gradually (see Fig. 6-35 on page 68).

【Essentials for performing manipulations】

The force exerted with the thumb and the other fingers should be symmetrical, even, and soft. The movement should be continuous and rhythmical.

【Cautions】

1. The force should be exerted with the palm, not the tip of the finger.

2. When performing Nie Fa (pinching manipulation), much attention should be paid to the force of the finger, especially the combination of force between the thumb and other four fingers. The relative exercises for basic training will be helpful to improve the strength of the finger.

6.1.16　Na Fa (Grasping manipulation)

Exert force symmetrically with the thumb and the other four fingers to lift, pinch or clip the extremities or the skin. Such a manipulation is called Na Fa (grasping manipulation). It can be divided into San Zhi Na Fa (grasping manipulation with three fingers) and Wu Zhi Na Fa (grasping manipulation with five fingers).

【Methods for performing manipulations】

Relax the wrist joint and clip the operated part tightly with the thumb, index finger and middle finger or with the thumb and the whorl surface of the other four fingers. Lift the skin and repeat the performance of kneading and pinching continuously and alternatively in a form of forceful and gentle way (see Fig. 6-36 on page 69).

【Essentials for performing manipulations】

1. Relax the wrist joint and straighten the fingers. Clip the operated part with the fingers and exert force symmetrically to lift and pinch the skin and the subcutaneous tissues.

2. Perform the manipulation slowly, softly and evenly, fluctuating from light to heavy, and then from heavy to light. The performance of kneading and pinching should be continuous.

【Cautions】

1. When performing Na Fa (grasping manipulation), cautions should be taken not to clip the epidermis to avoid flexion of interphalangeal joints.

2. When performing Na Fa (grasping manipulation), according to the clinical needs, subcutaneous tissues should be pinched as much as possible. The slippage of the fingers on the body surface should be avoided.

3. Rou Mo Fa (kneading and rubbing manipulation) can be used after Na Fa (grasping manipulation) to smooth Qi and blood.

6.1.17　Nian Fa(Finger-twisting manipulation)

Hold the operated part with the thumb and the index finger, and twist while kneading and pinching symmetrically. Such a manipulation is called Nian Fa (finger-twisting manipulation).

【Methods for performing manipulations】

Exert force symmetrically and hold the operated part with the whorl surface of the thumb and the radial border of the index finger, then make a quicker twisting with force like twisting a thread (see Fig. 6-37 on page 69).

【Essentials for performing manipulations】

1. When performing Nian Fa (finger-twisting manipulation), the movement should be continuous, dexterous, soft and trenchant.

2. The frequency of Nian Fa (finger-twisting manipulation) is a bit quicker, while the movement on the operated part should be slow.

【Cautions】

Nian Fa (Finger-twisting manipulation) is a supplementary manipulation which is commonly applied to joints of fingers and toes.

6.1.18 Bo Fa (Plucking manipulation)

Press the operated part deeply with the thumb, and pluck back and forth. The direction of the movement should be perpendicular to the direction of the tendon and muscle. Such a manipulation is called Bo Fa (plucking manipulation) or flicking manipulation.

【Performing manipulations】

Extend the thumb, exert force with the tip or the whorl surface of the thumb, and support with the other four fingers. Press deeply until the patient feels aching and distending. Then pluck back and forth along the direction perpendicular to the direction of the tendon and muscle (see Fig. 6-38 on page 70). If the strength of one thumb is not enough, two thumbs can be overlapped.

【Essentials for performing manipulations】

1. When performing Bo Fa (plucking manipulation), the thumb should not rub and move on the body surface, but direct the subcutaneous muscular fiber or tendon and ligament to pluck together.

2. When performing Bo Fa (plucking manipulation), the force used should be increased gradually. The manipulation should be done according to the tolerance of the patient.

【Cautions】

1. Bo Fa (Plucking manipulation) is often performed on tenderness.

2. The stimulation of plucking manipulation is strong. So after performing the manipulation, kneading and rubbing manipulations can be used to smooth Qi and blood.

6.1.19 Pai Fa (Patting manipulation)

Pat on the body surface rhythmically with an empty palm. Such a manipulation is called Pai Fa (patting manipulation).

[Performing manipulations]

Coalesce the fingers and slightly flex the metacarpophalangeal joints so as to form an empty palm. Then pat the operated part rhythmically (see Fig. 6-39 on page 70). The frequency is 100~120 times per minute.

[Essentials for performing manipulations]

1. While performing Pai Fa (patting manipulation), the shoulder joint should be dropped and the wrist should be kept relaxed. The patting should be springy and steady. The palm should bounce up right away after patting on the operated part. The movement should be done with rhythm. The times of patting should not go beyond the desirable state that the skin appears reddish and congested.

2. The manipulation can be performed with one hand or with both hands.

[Cautions]

1. The palm should pat on the body surface flatly. Any dragging and whipping movement on the body surface should be avoided.

2. It is prohibited to apply to the patient who suffers from tuberculosis, serious osteoporosis, bone tumor, or coronary heart disease.

6.1.20 Ji Fa (Hitting manipulation)

Hit the operated part rhythmically with the palm base, the minor thenar, the back of a fist, the finger tip or a mulberry stick. Such a manipulation is called Ji Fa (hitting manipulation). It can be divided into Zhang Gen Ji Fa (hitting manipulation with palm base), Ce Ji Fa (hitting manipulation with the lateral side palm), Quan Ji Fa (hitting manipulation with a fist), Zhi Jian Ji Fa (hitting manipulation with finger tips) and Bang Ji Fa (hitting manipulation with a stick).

[Methods for performing manipulations]

1. Zhang Gen Ji Fa (Hitting manipulation the palm base) Hit the body surface with the palm base while stretching the fingers naturally and stretching the wrist joint slightly backward (see Fig. 6-40 on page 71).

2. Ce Ji Fa (Hitting manipulation with lateral side of palm) Hit the body surface with the minor thenar of both palms alternately while stretching the fingers naturally and the wrist joint slightly backward (see Fig. 6-41 on page 71).

3. Quan Ji Fa (Hitting manipulation with a fist) Hit the body surface with the dorsum of the fist (see Fig. 6-42 on page 71). The frequency is 3 to 5 times every time.

4. Zhi Jian Ji Fa (Hitting manipulation with finger tips) Hit the treated part with the tips of the fingers closing up like a plum blossom or a open claw (see Fig. 6-43 on page 71).

5. Bang Ji Fa (Stick-hitting Manipulation) Strike the body surface with a stick made of mulberry twigs. The force is exerted from the upper 1/2 part of the stick (see Fig.

6-44 on page 72).

【Essentials for performing manipulations】

1. The exertion of force in Ji Fa (hitting manipulation) should be rapid with a short duration. The hitting movement on the body surface should be vertical. The frequency should be even with rhythm.

2. When performing Zhang Gen Ji Fa (hitting manipulation with palm base), use the palm base as the force exerting point and strike with the force from the forearm. The amplitude of flirting could be a bit greater. Hitting can be done 3~5 times.

3. Ce Ji Fa (hitting manipulation with lateral side of palm) can be performed with one hand or both hands holding together. Concentrate on the elbow joint and make the forearm move initiatively. In striking, the minor thenar should be vertical with the direction of the muscular fiber, and the movement should be rapid with rhythm.

4. When performing Quan Ji Fa (hitting manipulation with a fist), the elbow joint is taken as the pivot. Make use of the force from the flexion and stretch the elbow joint and the forearm to strike. The force should be even.

5. When performing Zhi Jian Ji Fa (hitting manipulation with finger tips), relax the wrist joint and flex the elbow joint in a small amplitude. Tap the body surface with the tip of the finger at a rapid speed like rain drops.

6. When performing Bang Ji Fa (fitting manipulation with a stick), hold the 1/3 part of the lower part of the mulberry stick and move the forearm initiatively. Strike the affected area with the upper part of the mulberry twig rhythmically.

【Cautions】

1. When performing Ji Fa (hitting manipulation), attention should be paid to bouncing. The stick should bounce up immediately after it touches the affected area. Any halting, dragging or whipping should be avoided.

2. Strictly follow the indications of different Ji Fa (hitting manipulation). Violent striking should be avoided.

3. Quan Ji Fa (fitting manipulation with a fist) is mainly applied to Dazhui (GV 14) and the lumbosacral portion; Zhang Ji Fa (hitting manipulation with palm) is applied to Baihui (GV 20) and Huantiao (GB 30); Zhi Jian Ji Fa (hitting manipulation with finger tips) is applied to the head. The body of the stick, not the tip, should be used in performing stick hitting manipulation. The stick can be used to hit any part of the body except the lumbar and sacral regions. The body of the stick should be kept in the same direction as that of the muscular fibers.

6.1.21 Tan Fa (Flipping manipulation)

Press the back of the index finger tightly with the middle finger and spring rapidly to flip a certain part or Acupoint. Such a manipulation is called Tan Fa (flipping manipulation).

【Methods for performing manipulations】

Flex the index finger and press the back of the index finger tightly with the whorl surface of the middle finger. Then spring rapidly to hit the treated part (see Fig. 6-45 on page 72). The frequency is about 120~160 times per minute.

【Essentials for performing manipulations】

The manipulation should be performed evenly and continuously. The intensity of stimulation should be carefully monitored to avoid pain.

【Cautions】

It is often used as a supplementary manipulation applied to the head and face.

6.1.22 Yao Fa (Rotating manipulation)

It is a passive movement performed within the range of the joint or semi-joint. Such a manipulation is called Yao Fa (rotating manipulation). It is one of the common manipulations of Tuina and performed with different methods when applied to different parts.

【Methods for performing manipulations】

1. Jing Bu Yao Fa (Neck-rotating manipulation) The patient takes a sitting position with the neck relaxed. The doctor stands on the side of the patient, holds the patient's head posterior to vertex with one hand, and holds the lower jaw with the other hand. Then rotate the head clockwise and counterclockwise slowly for several times respectively with both hands giving force in opposite direction (see Fig. 6-46 on page 73).

2. Jian Bu Yao Fa (Shoulder-rotating manipulation) The patient takes a sitting position. There are three methods for performing this manipulation:

(1) Tuo Zhou Yao Jian Fa (Shoulder-rotating manipulation by supporting the elbow) The patient relaxes his shoulders and flexes his elbow. The doctor stands by the side of the patient, standing in an bow-like pose with the upper body inclining forward slightly, holding the upper part of the patient's shoulder blade with one hand to fix it, and the affected elbow with the other hand, rotating clockwise or counterclockwise for several times (see Fig. 6-47 on page 73).

(2) Wo Wan Yao Jian Fa (Shoulder-rotating manipulation by holding the elbow) The patient relaxes his shoulders with the upper extremities lowering naturally. The doctor holds the upper part of the patient's shoulder blade with one hand, and the affected elbow with the other hand, then rotating clockwise or counterclockwise for several times (see Fig. 6-48 on page 73).

(3) Da Fu Du Yao Jian Fa (Shoulder-rotating manipulation in a great amplitude) The patient lowers his upper extremities naturally. The doctor stands by the side of the patient in a T-shaped stance, holding the patient's wrist with one hand and supporting the patient's forearm with the dorsum of the other hand. Then the doctor turns the dorsum of his hand and raises the patient's wrist when lifting the patient's upper extremity to

160 degrees with the other hand slipping down to support the patient's shoulder. After a pause, the doctor uses both hands (the hand supporting the shoulder pressing slightly forward and the hand holding the wrist lifting slightly to extend the shoulder joint) to rotate the affected extremity backward in a great amplitude (see Fig. 6-49 on page 74). If the direction of rotation is opposite, then the manipulation is also performed in the opposite way.

3. Zhou Bu Yao Fa (Elbow- rotating manipulation) The patient takes a sitting position or supine position. The doctor holds the affected elbow with one hand, and holds the affected wrist with the other to rotate the elbow joint clockwise and counterclockwise for several times (see Fig. 6-50 on page 74).

4. Wan Bu Yao Fa (Wrist-rotating manipulation) The doctor holds the upper end of the affected wrist joint of the patient with one hand and the palm with the other, rotating the wrist joint clockwise and counterclockwise for several times respectively (see Fig. 6-51 on page 74) while pulling and extending the wrist joint.

5. Yao Bu Yao Fa (Waist-rotating manipulation) There are two methods for performing this manipulation:

(1) The patient takes a sitting position with the waist relaxed. The doctor stands behind the patient with one hand holding one side of the patient's waist and the other hand supporting the shoulder on the other side, bending the upper part of the patient's body in all directions with the force of both hands to rotate the waist clockwise and counterclockwise for several times (see Fig. 6-52 on page 75).

(2) The patient takes a supine position with the knee and hip flexed. The doctor presses the knees of the patient with one hand to make them coalescent, and holds the lower part of the patient's calves or two ankles with the other hand, then rotating the lower extremities to move the waist clockwise and counterclockwise for several times respectively (see Fig. 6-53 on page 75).

6. Kuan Bu Yao Fa (Hip-rotating manipulation) The patient takes a supine position with the affected hip and knee flexed and the healthy side of the extremity stretched straightly. The doctor stands beside the patient, supports the patient's knee with one hand and holds his heel with the other hand, flexing the patient's hip joint for 90 degrees with the force of both hands to rotate the hip joint clockwise and counterclockwise for several times (see Fig. 6-54 on page 75).

7. Xi Bu Yao Fa (Knee-rotating manipulation) The patient takes a supine position with the affected knee and hip flexed. The doctor supports the upper part of the knee to fix it with one hand, and holds the heel with the other hand to rotate the knee joint clockwise and counterclockwise for several times (see Fig. 6-55 on page 75).

8. Huai Bu Yao Fa (Ankle-rotating manipulation) The patient takes a supine position with the affected extremity stretching naturally. The doctor stands behind his foot and holds the lower part of his calf with one hand, and holds the foreside of the instep with the other hand to rotate the ankle joint clockwise and counterclockwise for several times (see Fig. 6-56 on page 75).

[Essentials for performing manipulations]

1. Movements of Yao Fa (rotating manipulation) should be moderate and mild with steady force. The frequency of the rotation should be slow and even, especially at the beginning.

2. The amplitude of the rotation should be gradually increased and adjusted according to individual conditions. Usually it should be kept within the limitation of normal physical joint movement.

[Cautions]

1. Yao Fa (Rotating manipulation) should not be done violently or violate the movement of normal physical activity. When performed for a patient with dysfunction of the joint, the manipulation should be adjusted according to the individual condition.

2. Yao Fa (Rotating manipulation) is forbidden to be used to treat patients with fracture or dislocation of joint. Neck-rotating manipulation is not allowed to be used to treat patients with vertebral artery type of cervical spondylosis and must be applied with great care to treat patients with vervical spondylotic myelopathy. For patients with excessive stiffness of cervical muscles, supine position is advisable.

3. Jian Guan Jie Yao Fa (Shoulder joint rotating manipulation) is often applied to improve the functions of the shoulder joint. The amplitude of movement is comparatively small in Tuo Jian Yao Fa (Shoulder rotating manipulation by supporting the elbow) and Wo Wan Yao Jian Fa (Shoulder rotating manipulation of by holding the wrist). It is suitable for treating the patients with pain in the shoulder joint or with obvious dyscinesia, such as early scapulohumeral periarthritis. Da Fu Du Yao Jian Fa (Rotating manipulation in a great amplitude) is suitable for the patient whose shoulder joint activity has already been improved, such as scapulohumeral periarthritis at convalescence.

6.1.23 Ba Shen Fa (Pulling-extending manipulation)

Fixate one end of a joint or an extremity, pull and extend the other end with constant force to enlarge the joint space. Such a manipulation is called Ba Shen Fa (Pulling-extending manipulation) or Qian Yin Fa (Traction manipulation). It can be applied to different joints.

[Methods for performing manipulations]

1. Jing Bu Ba Shen Fa (Pulling-extending manipulation of the neck) It can be divided into Zhang Zhi Tuo Ba Jing Shen Fa (pulling-extending manipulation with palm and finger supporting the neck), Zhou Tuo Ba Shen Fa (pulling-extending manipulation supported with elbow) and Yang Wo Wei Ba Shen Fa (pulling-extending manipulation in supine position).

(1) Zhang Zhi Tuo Jing Ba Shen Fa (Pulling-extending manipulation with palm and

finger supporting the neck) The patient takes a sitting position and the doctor stands behind him. The doctor supports the inferior aspect, Fengchi (GB20), of the patient's occipital bone with his thumbs, holds the inferior aspect of the angles of the lower jaws, and puts both of his forearms on the patient's shoulders, holding the patient's head up with both hands and pressing the patient's shoulders down at the same time with coordinate force to pull and extend the neck up slowly (see Fig. 6-57 on page 76).

(2) Zhou Bu Tuo Jing Ba Shen Fa (Pulling-extending manipulation with the elbow supporting the neck) The patient takes a sitting position with the head inclining slightly forward. The doctor stands behind the patient, holds the patient's chin with one hand crossing from the front part of the patient's neck, holding the patient's occiput with the part between the thumb and the four fingers of the other hand, then pulling and extending the neck up slowly along the direction of longitudinal axis of the cervical vertebrae with both hands simultaneously (see Fig. 6-58 on page 76).

(3) Yang Wo Wei Bo Shen Fa (Pulling-extending manipulation in supine position) The patient takes a supine position. The doctor sits at the front of the patient's head with one hand holding the patient's occiput and the other holding the patient's chin, then pulling and extending the neck along the direction of longitudinal axis of the cervical vertebrae with both hands simultaneously (see Fig. 6-59 on page 77).

2. Jian Bu Ba Shen Fa (Pulling-extending manipulation of the shoulder) There are two methods for operating this manipulation:

(1) Shang Ju Ba Shen Fa (Up-lifting pulling and extending manipulation) The patient sits on a stool with the affected extremity relaxed. The doctor stands behind, holds the patient's wrist with both hands and lifts it up gradually to the maximum limit, then pulling constantly around the longitudinal axis of the upper extremity in order to pull and extend the shoulder (see Fig. 6-60 on page 77).

(2) Wai Zhan Ba Shen Fa (Pulling-extending manipulation by abduction) The patient takes a sitting position with the relaxed affected extremity abducting for 45~60 degrees. The assistant stands by the healthy side holding the patient's body from the subaxillary regions to fix it with both hands. Then the doctor stands by the affected side and holds the patient's wrist with both hands and pulls gradually around the longitudinal axis of the upper extremity (see Fig. 6-61 on page 77).

3. Zhou Bu Ba Shen Fa (Pulling-extending manipulation of the elbow) The patient takes a sitting position. The doctor fixes the proximal end of the elbow joint of the affected extremity with one hand (or with the help of the assistant), and holds the distal end of the forearm with the other hand, then pulling and extending the elbow joint with both hands from opposite direction.

4. Wan Bu Ba Shen Fa (Pulling-extending manipulation of the wrist) The patient takes a sitting position. The doctor holds the proximal end of the wrist of the affected extremity with one hand, and holds the patient's palm and fingers with the other hand, then pulling and extending the wrist from opposite direction (see Fig. 6-62 on page 78).

5. Shou Zhi Ba Shen Fa (Pulling-extending manipulation of the fingers) The doctor holds the wrist of the affected finger with one hand, and fixes the affected finger between the flexed index and middle fingers, then pulling and extending from opposite direction (see Fig. 6-63 on page 78).

6. Yao Bu Ba Shen Fa (Pulling-extending manipulation of the waist) The patient takes a supine position. The assistant stands by the bed edge to hold the patient's subaxillary regions with both hands to fix the patient's body (or let the patient hold the bed edge with both hands). The doctor stands behind and holds the patient's ankles with both hands, and pulling back constantly with gradual force (see Fig. 6-64 on page 78).

7. Kuan Bu Ba Shen Fa (Pulling-extending manipulation of the hip) The patient takes a supine position while the doctor stands beside. The assistant holds the patient's anterior superior iliac spine with both hands to fix the patient's body when the patient bends his knees and hip. The doctor holds the patient's affected knee with one hand while the other hand supports the patient's popliteal fossa, chest and hypochondriac region with elbow to press on the calf of patient, with the coordination of hands, arms and body to pull back the hip joints around the vertical axis of the thigh.

8. Xi Bu Ba Shen Fa (Pulling-extending manipulation of the knee) The patient takes a supine position with the knee of the affected extremity flexed for 90 degrees. The doctor stands by the affected side and presses the lower part of the backside of the affected thigh with one knee, and holds the ankle with both hands, then pulling and extending the knee joint up around the longitudinal axis of the calf.

9. Huai Bu Ba Shen Fa (Pulling-extending manipulation of the ankle) The patient takes a supine position. The doctor holds the heel of the affected foot with one hand, and holds the toes with the other hand, then pulling the ankle around the longitudinal axis of the shin (see Fig. 6-65 on page 78).

〖Essentials for performing manipulations〗

1. The performance of Ba Shen Fa (pulling-extending manipulation) should be done stably and gently with the strength intensified gradually. When the traction reaches a certain degree, it should be kept steady for a while.

2. The angle of the traction should be well adjusted and the pulling should be done around the longitudinal axis of the extremity.

〖Cautions〗

1. Violent force and action against the direction of the physiological activities should be avoided.

2. When performing the Jing Bu Ba Shen Fa (pulling-extending manipulation of the neck), cares should be taken to avoid the carotid sinus on both sides of the neck.

6.1.24 Bei Fa (Back-carrying manipulation)

This manipulation means to carry the patient in order to pull and vibrate the lumbar vertebrae.

【Methods for performing manipulations】

The doctor and the patient stand back to back. The doctor loops the patient's elbows with his own, bends his waist, flexes his knees and sticks his buttocks to carry the patient up on his back and suspends the patient's feet, making the patient's body slip down slightly against the patient's lower back with his hip. The doctor waves his body till the patient's muscles relaxed, then taking a sudden action to straighten the knees, flex the coax and stick the hips (see Fig. 6-66 on page 79).

【Essentials for performing manipulations】

1. The patient should keep relaxed and breathe naturally. After being carried, the patient should rest the whole body on the back of the doctor with the head bending backward to draw and stretch the lumbar vertebrae with his lower part of body.

2. The actions of waving, straightening the knees and sticking the hips should be coordinated and done in continuity.

【Cautions】

Pay attention to the weight of the doctor and the patient, avoiding excessive heavy load or even injury of the doctor.

6.1.25 Ban Fa (Pulling manipulation)

This manipulation means to pull to the same direction or opposite direction with both hands to extend, flex or rotate the affected joints. It is a commonly used manipulation and there are different methods for performing this manipulation on the neck, waist or extremities.

【Methods for performing manipulations】

1. Jing Bu Ban Fa (Pulling manipulation of the neck) There are three methods commonly used for performing Jing Zhui Ban Fa (Manipulation of pulling the cervical vertebrae):

(1) Jing Bu Xie Ban Fa (Manipulation for obliquely-pulling the neck) The patient takes a sitting position with the head slightly bent forward or kept upright and the neck relaxed. The doctor stands behind the patient, holds the patient's head at the occiput with one hand and the chin with the other, then rotating the patient's head to the left side or the right side. When the head is turned to the restricted side where there is an elastic resistance, rotation should be stopped for a moment, and then a quick and controlled pulling is done in a small amplitude. Cracking sound is often heard during such an action (see Fig. 6-67 on page 80).

(2) Jing Zhui Xuan Zhuan Ding Wei Ban Fa (Pulling manipulation for rotating and

locating cervical vertebrae). The patient takes a sitting position with his head flexed forward for 15~30 degrees. Take pulling and rotating to the left side for example: the doctor stands behind the patient's left side while pressing the lateral side of the spinal process of the patient's affected cervical vertebrae with the right thumb, and holding the chin with the left hand to fix the patient's head while rotating slowly to the left side till there is an elastic resistance; then stopping rotation for a moment and taking a quick and controlled pulling action along the direction of the rotation within a small amplitude. Meanwhile, the thumb pressing the spinal process pushes and presses towards the opposite side (see Fig. 6-68 on page 81). Cracking sound is often heard if reduction of the joint is successful. Sometimes there is no sound, but the doctor can feel a flick under his thumb.

(3) Huan Shu Guan Jie Xuan Zhuan Ban Fa (Pulling and rotating manipulation on atlantoaxial joint)　The patient sits on a stool. The doctor stands behind the patient while pressing the second spinal process with the thumb of one hand, holding the patient's chin with the elbow of the other hand, and holding the occiput with the palm crossing behind the opposite ear, pulling the patient's neck slowly till the doctor can feel the affected spinal process gliding under his thumb, then keeping the angle and pulling up around the longitudinal axis of the cervical vertebrae. Then the doctor rotates the side with deflected spinal process till there is an elastic resistance. After a moment of pause, the doctor takes a quick and controlled pulling action within a small amplitude. Meanwhile, the thumb pressing the spinal process pushes and presses the other side of the spinal process (see Fig. 6-69 on page 81).

2. Xiong Zhui Ban Fa (Pulling manipulation of thoracic vertebrae)　There are two commonly used performing methods:

(1) Xiong Zhui Dui Kang Fu Wei Fa (Counter-reduction manipulation of thoracic Vertebrae)　The patient takes a sitting position with his fingers crossed behind the occiput. The doctor stands behind the patient with one foot stepping on the chair on which the patient sits, and puts his knee against the patient's spinal process of the thoracic vertebrae; stretching both hands between the upper arm and the forearm from the patient's armpits, and holding the lower part of the forearm, pressing the patient's forearm with both hands, and raising his forearm to bend the patient's neck slightly. At the same time, the doctor pulls the spine backward and upward. Pausing for a while, the doctor's both hands and arms exert force to take a quick and controlled pulling action within a small amplitude, then sustaining his knee suddenly. Cracking sound is often heard during such an action (see Fig. 6-70 on page 81).

(2) Xiong Zhui An Ya Fu Wei Fa (Pressing reduction of thoracic vertebrae)　The patient takes a supine position. The doctor folds his arms and puts pisiform bone of the palm base on the transverse process of the vertebra, asking the patient to breathe deeply. When the patient is inhaling, the doctor exerts force suddenly with the elbow joint to

press. Cracking sound is often heard during such a manipulation (see Fig. 6-71 on page 81).

3. Yao Bu Ban Fa (Pulling manipulation of the waist) There are three kinds of commonly used performing methods:

(1) Yao Zhui Xie Ban Fa (Obliquely pulling manipulation of the lumbar vertebrae) The patient takes a lateral position with the healthy leg below straightening naturally. The affected leg flexes at the hip joint. Its ankle is put on the popliteal fossa of the healthy leg. The doctor faces the patient, and puts both elbows (or the upper part of the forearm) on the patient's front part of the forearm or hip, then exerting opposite force slowly to pull the waist, and taking a quick and controlled pulling action within a small amplitude. Cracking sound is often heard during such a manipulation (see Fig. 6-72 on page 82).

(2) Yao Zhui Xuan Zhuan Ding Wei Ban Fa (Pulling manipulation for rotating and locating lumbar vertebrae) Take the manipulation for rotating and pulling the right side for example. The patient takes a sitting position with the waist relaxed. The assistant stands in front of the patient and fixes the patient's knee with both hands. The doctor stands behind the patient, presses the affected spinal process of the lumbar vertebrae with the left thumb, and the right hand, crossing from under the right axillary region, holds the patient's nape. Then the doctor presses his right palm downward to let the patient bow forwards until the doctor feels the affected process moving under his thumb. Keeping this position, taking the affected spinal process as the pivot, and bending the spine to the right side with the force from the right arm, the doctor rotates for a while, then pressing his right palm downward, raising his elbow and pushing the spinal process to the opposite direction with the thumb, followed by a quick and controlled pulling action within a small amplitude. Cracking sound is often heard during such a manipulation and the doctor can feel a flick under his thumb (see Fig. 6-73 on page 82).

When the manipulation is operated by one person, the patient can be asked to sit on the edge of the bed in order to fix his pelvis and lower extremities.

(3) Yao Bu Hou Shen Ban Fa (Pulling manipulation of the waist) The patient takes a supine position. The doctor stands beside the patient, and presses the patient's waist with one hand and holds the affected extremity or extremities, extending the lumbar vertebrae backward to take a quick and controlled backward pulling within a small amplitude (see Fig. 6-74 on page 83).

4. Jian Bu Ban Fa (Pulling manipulation of the shoulder) According to the movement of the shoulder joint, it can be performed in four directions: uplifting, adducting, backward extending and abducting.

(1) Jian Shang Ju Ban Fa (Pulling manipulation for uplifting the shoulder) The patient takes a sitting position with both arms dropping naturally. The doctor stands behind the patient, and fixes the patient's trunk with his body, holding the lower end of the affected forearm with one hand and raising slowly from the anterior flexion to

120~140 degrees. The other hand holds the part near the waist joint of the forearm, pulling upward gradually with both hands, then taking a quick and controlled upward pulling action within a small amplitude. The manipulation can be repeated for 3~5 times.

(2) Jian Nei Shou Ban Fa (Pulling manipulation for adducting the shoulder)　　The patient takes a sitting position and keeps the affected extremity flexed before the chest. The doctor stands close to the patient's back, flexes the affected shoulder with one hand, and holds the affected elbow with the other hand to pull inward, then taking a quick and controlled adducted pulling action within a small amplitude. The manipulation can be repeated for 3~5 times (see Fig. 6-75 on page 83).

(3) Jian Hou Shen (Nei Xuan) Ban Fa (Pulling manipulation for backward extending or adducting the shoulder)　　The patient takes a sitting position with the affected extremity dropping naturally. The doctor stands behind the side of the patient to fix the affected shoulder with one hand, and holds the wrist of the affected arm with the other hand, extending the affected arm backward and flexing the elbow with the back of the hand closing to the back, then taking a quick and controlled upward pulling action within a small amplitude. The manipulation can be repeated for 3~5 times. (see Fig. 6-76 on page 84).

(4) Jian Wai Zhan Ban Fa (Pulling manipulation for abducting the shoulder)　　The patient takes a sitting position and the doctor half-squats to the side of the patient's affected shoulder. The affected upper extremity is straightened and abducted. The doctor's one arm, by the affected upper arm and through the patient's axillary region, crosses with the other hand from the front side of the affected shoulder, pressing the affected shoulder, slowly standing up, swaging the upper arm of the patient gently and abducting the affected extremity. Finally a quick, controlled and abducted pulling action is taken within a small amplitude The manipulation can be repeated for 3~5 times (see Fig. 6-77 on page 84).

5. Zhou Bu Ban Fa (Pulling manipulation of the elbow)　　The patient takes a supine position. The doctor holds the lower end of the patient's upper arm with one hand, and holds the lower end of the patient's forearm with the other, flexing and stretching the elbow joint repeatedly, and then taking a controlled flexing, stretching and pulling action within a small amplitude The manipulation can be repeated for 3~5 times (see Fig. 6-78 on page 84).

6. Wan Bu Ban Fa (Pulling manipulation of the wrist)　　The doctor holds the lower end of the patient's forearm to fix with one hand, and holds the patient's palm to pull with the other hand, then flexing and stretching the wrist joint, followed by a controlled flexing or stretched pulling action within a small amplitude.

7. Di Ge Guan Jie Ban Fa (Pulling manipulation of sacro-iliac articulation)　　There are two commonly used methods to perform this manipulation:

(1) Di Ge Guan Jie Hou Shen Ban Fa (Backward extending and pulling manipulation of sacro-iliac articulation)　　The patient takes a prone position. The doctor stands by the

healthy side of the patient, presses the posterior and superior iliac spine with the palm base of one hand, and holds the lower part of the affected thigh with the other hand, flexing the knee joint of the affected side, and extending the affected leg backward. Then the patient is asked to cough, and the doctor takes a sudden controlled backward extending and pulling action to enlarge the amplitude of the back extension of the lower extremity to 3~5 degrees, and quickly pressing the posterior superior iliac spine.(see Fig. 6-79 on page 84).

(2) Di Ge Guan Jie Xie Ban Fa (Obliquely pulling manipulation of sacro-iliac articulation) The patient takes a supine position with the affected turned up and the healthy lower limb straightened, flexing the coxa slightly, and bending the knee and coxa of the affected side. The doctor pushes the patient's shoulder with one hand to make the upper body rotate backward, and presses the lateral side of the knee to make the waist rotate forward. When the spine is rotated, both hands of the doctor exert force cooperatively to take a quick controlled pulling action within a small amplitude (see Fig. 6-80 on page 85).

8. Xi Guan Ji Ban Fa (Pulling manipulation of the knee joint) There are two commonly used methods to perform this manipulations:

(1) Xi Guan Jie Shen Xi Ban Fa (Pulling manipulation for extending knee joint) The patient takes a supine position. The doctor stands at the side of the patient, presses the knee of the affected leg with one hand, and puts the other hand at the posterior side of the lower part of the affected calf, exerting force with both hands to stretch the knee, and then taking a quick controlled pulling action within a small amplitude (see Fig. 6-81 on page 85).

(2) Xi Guan Jie Qu Xi Ban Fa (Pulling manipulation for flexing knee joint) The patient takes a prone position. The doctor stands at the side of the patient, presses the posterior side of the buttock with one hand to fix the thigh, and holds the ankle of the affected leg with the other hand, flexing the knee joint of the affected leg, and taking a quick controlled pulling action within a small amplitude (see Fig. 6-82 on page 85).

9. Huai Bu Ban Fa (Pulling manipulation of the ankle) The patient takes a supine position. The doctor holds the patient's heel with one hand and holds the toes with the other hands, flexing and stretching the ankle joint, or turning the ankle joint outward or inward, and then taking a quick controlled pulling action within a small amplitude (see Fig. 6-83 on page 85).

【Essentials for performing manipulations】

1. When performing Ban Fa (Pulling manipulation), the manipulation should be performed within the limit of the normal physiological movement of the joints. Turning the joint to the limited degree is a critical step for successful performance of the manipulation.

2. The performance of Ban Fa (Pulling manipulation) should be quick and mild.

3. The patient should keep relaxed as much as possible. Sometimes, the patient needs to adjust his breath in order to cooperate with the doctor.

【Cautions】

1. When performing Ba Fa (Pulling manipulation), the strength should be controlled properly. Violent action should be avoided.

2. The amplitude of pulling should be monitored within the limit of the normal physiological movement of the joints and the pathological states.

3. Cracking sound implies successful reduction. But never try to achieve such a result on purposefully lest injury be caused.

4. Ban Fa (Pulling manipulation) should not be used to treat those with joint fracture, malposition and dislocation of the joints or tumor.

6.2　Compound Tuina Manipulation for Adults

Compound manipulation means two or more basic manipulations with similar characteristics in kinematics used together.

6.2.1　An Rou Fa (Pressing and kneading manipulation)

This manipulation is a combination of An Fa (Pressing manipulation) and Rou Fa (Kneading manipulation). It can be divided into two categories: Zhi An Rou Fa (pressing and kneading with fingers) and Zhang An Rou Fa (Pressing and kneading manipulation with palms).

【Methods for performing manipulations】

1. Zhi An Rou Fa (Pressing and kneading manipulation with fingers)　Exert force with the whorl surface of one or both thumbs and support with the rest four fingers, slightly suspend the waist joint, press and knead rhythmically with the thumb and the forearm (see Fig. 6-84 on page 86).

2. Zhang An Rou Fa (Pressing and kneading manipulation with palm)　Exert force with one palm base and straighten the other four fingers. The forearm swings initiatively to press and knead rhythmically, pressing and kneading with overlapped palms to increase stimulation. While performing the manipulation, the shoulder joint is used as the pivot, the upper extremity exerts force and brings the arm to press and knead rhythmically (see Fig. 6-85 on page 86).

【Essentials for performing manipulations】

1. An Rou Fa (Pressing and kneading manipulation) is an organic combination of An Fa (Pressing manipulation) and Rou Fa (Kneading manipulation).

2. The frequency of An Rou Fa (Pressing and kneading manipulation) is a bit slower than that of Rou Fa (Kneading manipulation), its manipulation should be performed rhythmically.

3. The doctor should lower his shoulder and drop his elbow. The relaxation of the shoulder, elbow and wrist joint enables the whole strength of the doctor to reach the deep layer of the patient's subcutaneous tissues.

【Cautions】

1. The strength of pressing is important. If the strength is too light, it is likely to be floating; while if it is too heavy, it is easily to get stuck.

2. The movement of Zhi An Rou Fa (Pressing and kneading manipulation with fingers) is quite similar to that of Na Fa (Grasping manipulation). The difference between them is that when performing An Rou Fa (Pressing and kneading manipulation), the function of the four fingers is to support; while performing Na Fa (Grasping manipulation), the thumb and the other four fingers exert force oppositely.

6.2.2 Na Rou Fa (Grasping and kneading manipulation)

This manipulation is a combination of Na Fa (Grasping manipulation) and part of Rou Fa (Grasping and kneading manipulation).

【Methods for performing manipulations】

The methods for performing this manipulation are similar to that for performing Na Fa (Grasping manipulation). The only difference is that the thumb and other fingers need to knead in rotation (see Fig. 6-86 on page 87).

【Essentials for performing manipulations】

1. When performing Na Rou Fa (Grasping and kneading manipulation), Na Fa (Grasping manipulation) is the main manipulation, and Rou Fa (Kneading manipulation) is used as a supplementary manipulation.

2. This manipulation is performed along the lateral side of the limbs, grasping and kneading at the same time. The frequency of moving should not be too quick.

【Cautions】

Na Rou Fa (Grasping and kneading manipulation) increases the rotating and kneading movement of the fingers and reduces the opposite force exerted by the thumb and other fingers, making the manipulation milder and smoother than grasping manipulation.

6.2.3 Tui Mo Fa (Pushing and rubbing manipulation)

The thumb performs Yi Zhi Chan Tui Fa (One-finger pushing manipulation), the other four fingers perform Zhi Mo Fa (Finger-rubbing manipulation). Such a compound manipulation is called Tui Mo Fa (Pushing and rubbing manipulation). It is often applied on the chest, abdomen and back.

【Methods for performing manipulations】

Exert force with the side of the thumb, swing the forearm to perform Yi Zhi Chan Tui Fa (One-finger pushing manipulation). At the same time, the other four fingers straighten and coalesce to perform Mo Fa (Rubbing manipulation). (see Fig. 6-87 on page 87)

【Essentials for performing manipulations】

When performing Zhi Mo Fa (Finger-rubbing manipulation), the essentials of lowering shoulder and dropping elbow are similar to those for performing Yi Zhi Chan Tui Fa (One-finger pushing manipulation). The amplitude of suspending the wrist is reduced, and the wrist joint flexes slightly with the thumb pressing on the Acupoint and the other four fingers exerting force with the bellies.

【Cautions】

1. When performing the manipulation, the thumb is put on the main Acupoint, while the other four fingers are put on the supplementary Acupoints.

2. Yi Zhi Chan Tui Fa (One-finger pushing manipulation) and Zhi Mo Fa (Finger-rubbing manipulation) should be performed cooperatively.

Review Questions

- What are the basic requirements for Tui Na Fa (Pushing and grasping manipulation)?
- Briefly describe the essentials for performing Gun Fa (Rolling manipulation), An Fa (Pressing manipulation), Rou Fa (Kneading manipulation), Tui Fa (Pushing manipulation) and Na Fa (Grasping manipulation).
- What are the cautions for performing Ban Fa (Pulling manipulation)?

7

Tuina Treatment for Adult Diseases

7.1 Disorders in oesteonosus and traumatism

7.1.1 Stiff neck

Stiff neck, also known as torticollis, is caused by stretched and spastic muscles around the nuchal region, especially sternomastoid muscles, trapezius muscles, levator muscle of scapula due to innate weakness of the body or tiredness, improper sleep posture, improper height or hardness of the pillow, which keep the muscles around head and neck in hyperextension or hyperflexion for a long time. Overstretched cervical muscles reduce the topical blood supply, cause anabolic disorder and accumulation of metabolic products, eventually causing spasm and soreness of cervical muscles. Constant working at the desk, sudden unconscious turning of head make the cervical muscles twitch and cause tropical bleeding, edema and exudation, consequently resulting in pain and rigidity. It also can be caused by cervical spasm due to metabolic disturbance of cervical muscles resulting from invasion of cold wind into the cervical region that leads to blood stasis, blockage of meridian and tropical contraction of vessels.

It is characterized by soreness, aching, stiff cervical vertebra, torticollis and compulsive body position etc. If the case is mild, it may heal in 4~5 days. If the case is severe, it will cause sharp pain radiating towards the head and upper limbs for weeks.

This disorder is often seen among young adults with higher morbidity among males than females, frequently occuring in winter and spring.

[Clinical manifestations]

In most cases, the patients wake up in the morning, suddenly feeling pain and discomfort around the cervical region with compulsive body posture. Usually the head turns towards the affected side. In severe cases, the pain radiates along the shoulders and back or unilateral upper arm. The symptoms mainly are spasmodic pain and rigidity on one side of the trapezius muscles, sternocleidomastoid or levator scapulae muscles around nuchal region. The symptoms could be either severe or mild when both sides are affected. Cervical motion is significantly limited and the head cannot be turned or bent freely. Movement of the neck will worsen the pain. Touching the muscles of the affected area causes severe pain, mild in daytime, severe at night. If it is caused by exogenous wind cold, the symptoms are more severe. If it is irritated by wind cold, it will cause cyanotic tongue or tongue with ecchymosis, thin lingual fur or thin and whitish fur, wiry pulse or tense pulse.

【Essentials for diagnosis】

1. Evident cervical hypermyotonia, often at sternocleidomastoid muscles, trapezius muscles, levator scapulae muscles, streak (code-like mass), tense or swelling muscle bundles.

2. There is evident tenderness, usually distributed at enthesis of muscles and muscle belly. Cases with sternocleidomastoid muscle spasm, tenderness can be found at sternocleidomastoid muscle belly and mastoid process. Cases with trapezius spasm, tenderness can be found at 1/3 of external extremity of clavicle or Jianjing (GB 21) or the side of cervicothoracic spinous process; Cases with levator scapulae muscle spasm, tenderness can be found at upper side of cervicothoracic spinous process and superior medial angle of scapula.

3. Restricted cervical movement, deviation of the head to the affected side, compulsive body posture, aggravation in movement.

4. Negative symptoms of nerve root compression after cervical examination.

5. No abnormal findings in X-ray examination.

【Treatment with Tuina therapy】

1. Therapeutic principles: smooth the meridians to activate blood, warm the meridians to dredge collaterals.

2. Location of Acupoints: Fengchi (GB 20), Bingfeng (SI 12), Jianjing (GB 21), Tianzong (SI 11), Jianzhongshu (SI 15), Jianwaishu (SI 14), Quchi (LI 11), Hegu (LI 4), Yanglingquan (GB 34) and nuchal region and shoulders.

3. Manipulations:

(1) The patient is asked to sit down and the doctors press and knead Tianzong (SI 11), Quchi (LI 11), Hegu (LI 4), Yanglingquan (GB 34), 30 seconds for each Acupoint. While pressing Tianzong (SI 11), the patient is asked to turn his neck, and move back and forward to relieve the spasm and pain so as to get ready for the next step.

(2) The doctor stands at the lateral side of the patient, holds his head with one hand, gently rubs around the affected region with palm for 3~5 times. Intensity should be monitored to the tolerance of the patient. Then rolling and one-finger-pushing methods are applied along the sides of neck and shoulders, first on the unaffected side, then on the affected side, 3~5 minutes altogether, until the pain is evidently relieved.

(3) The doctor uses the first finger pulp to rub or uses one-finger pushing method to rub Fengchi (GB 20), Bingfeng (SI 2), Jianjing (GB 21), Tianzong (SI 11), Jianzhongshu (SI 15), Jianwaishu (SI 14), ten seconds for each Acupoint, to dredge the meridian

passage and reduce the spasm.

(4) Use the pulps of the first 3 fingers of one hand to grasp and knead Fengchi (GB 20) for 30 seconds, rubbing the nuchal region with the same method 2~3 times. Use five fingers of both hands to lift and grasp Jianjing (GB 21) 2~3 times, and then gradually increase the strength to flick the tense muscles for 2~3 minutes to relax the spastic muscles completely.

(5) Ask the patient to relax the cervical muscles, hold the mandible with one hand while support the occiput with the other hand to lightly bend forwards the neck, adduct the mandible. Use both hands to lift the neck upward simultaneously, and rotate the neck slowly to the left and right for 10 times to mobilize the cervical joints. After the rotation, slightly bend forward the neck, pull the neck rapidly to the affected side. The manipulation should be steady and fast, the strength and angle of rotation should be monitored to the patient's tolerance. In order to avoid accident, violent pulling is forbidden.

(6) Use shaking manipulation to force the patient passively bend forward , stretch backward and rotate the patient's neck from the left to the right; then use minor thenar to perform percussion on the shoulder and back; use rubbing manipulation to rob the nuchal region, shoulder and back to induce local hyperthermia for 2~3 minutes.

【Cautions】

1. To treat this disorder, manipulation should be gentle and the strength should be gradually increased. In order to avoid accident, strong irritating manipulation and violent pulling are not advisable. The treatment should be started from the distal sites, gradually moving forward to the painful place.

2. For patients with severe pain, manipulation is used first to press his distal points to relieve the pain. Then other methods can be used to further the treatment.

3. The pillow should be moderate in height and hardness.

4. The patients with constant stiff neck should avoid tiredness and keep warm in the nuchal region.

7.1.2 Cervical Spondylopathy

Cervical Spondylopathy, also known as Cervical Spine Syndrome, is caused by retrograde degeneration of the cervical vertebrae, cervical hyperosteogeny and cervical injury, causing the internal or external disequilibrium of cervical vertebrae, relatively poor stability and changes of cervical function and structure that stimulate or press the cervical nerve root, carotid artery, spinal marrow or sympathetic nerve, consequently leading to a series of comprehensive syndromes. In mild cases, the patients will suffer from pain or numbness in the head, neck, shoulder and back; in severe cases, the patients may suffer from flaccid extremities, even urinary and fecal incontinence or paralysis. Clinical manifestations, such as vertigo and cardiopalmus can be seen when the pathological changes involve vertebral artery and sympathetic nerve.

Cervical spondylopathy belongs to the category of "Xiang Jin Ji (nuchal fascia snap)" "Xiang Jian Tong (neck and shoulder pain)" "Xuan Yun (vertigo)" in TCM. This is a common ailment among those over 40 years old, and frequently encountered in the middle-aged and the aged, more in males than in females. With the change of studying and working or living habits, it tends to affect people just over thirty.

【Clinical manifestations】

Cervical spondylopathy is a type of retrograde degeneration of the cervical vertebrae. Degeneration of intervertebral discs is the intrinsic factor of the problem, including various acute or chronic cervical injuries. According to the affected regions and symptoms, cervical spondylopathy is clinically divided into 6 types: cervical spondylosis, cervical spondylotic radiculopathy, cervical spondylotic myelopathy, vertebral artery type of cervical spondylosis, sympathetic type of cervical spondylosis and mixed type of cervical spondylosis.

1. Cervical type of cervical spondylosis This type is caused by excessive movement of cervical vertebrae, trauma or prolonged improper posture, which lead to paravertebral sprain, malposition of cervical movable segment and decreased state of cervical stability, eventually resulting in compensatory cataplasia of intervertebral discs. Such is the early stage of the compensatory cataplasia. At this stage, symptoms to be found include partially damaged intervertebral disc, anulus fibrosus, bulged intervertebral disc tissue, slight vertebrae hyperosteogeny, bulged and hyperplastic structure that have not compressed the nerves or vascular tissue but can irritate the sinus nerve sensory fiber among them. The sinus nerve sensory fiber then sends afferent impulses to the centrum, through the ways of segmental reflex, proximal segmental reflex to cause persistent stress of nuchal region and intermediate zone between scapulas as well as irritation in this area. Other symptoms are cyanotic tongue or tongue with ecchymosis, thin or whitish tongue coating, taut or tense pulse.

Symptoms: anteflexed cervical region, apparently reduced rotation extent, myotonic pains in splenius cervicis, semispinalis, trapezius; stiff neck, susceptibility to tiredness; aching distention in the shoulders, aggravation of symptom after overstrain and alleviation of symptoms after rest.

2. Cervical spondylotic radiculopathy This type is caused by hyperostosis of cervical vertebral joint and articular process, structural abnormalities between cervical vertebrae, soft tissue injury and swelling, which induce typical symptoms of mechanical pressure and chemical stimulus on the nerve roots.

Symptoms: paroxysmal or persistent vague pain or acute pain of the neck, shoulder and back; ache in the irritated or pressed nerve roots that radiates to the upper limbs, accompanied by stabbing pain or current passing numbness. The symptoms mentioned above become worsened when cervical movement and abdominal pressure increases.

Hyperalgesia, burning and lacerating pain may appear in the skin controlled by the nerve roots at acute stage; numbness of fingers, coldness of extremities accompanied by heaviness and weakness of the upper limbs, weakness in grasping or difficulty in holding things at later stage. Other symptoms include limited movement and rigidity of neck in varying degrees and turning of the head to the affected side which may result in aggravated radiating neuralgia and pain, wry neck with light redness of tongue, thin or whitish tongue coating, taut and tense pulse.

3. Cervical spondylotic myelopathy This type is caused by pressure of spinal marrow due to bulged cervical intervertebral discs, hyperostosis of posterior edge of corpus vertebrae, downward displaced vertebrae, thickened ligamenta flava, swollen soft tissue in vertebral canal; or caused by ischemic spinal marrow and degenerated necrosis, leading to abnormal sensation, movement, urination and defecation.

Symptoms: Symptoms of the upper limbs are usually not evident, sometimes only the feelings of heaviness or weakness; but symptoms of the lower limbs are obvious, including rigidity and weakness, distention, burning sensation, numbness and dyskinesia that exacerbate progressively. In severe cases, there often appear symptoms of inconvenient movement, unstable walk, dysfunction of urination and defecation, even paralysis, limited cervical movement and compulsive cervical stiffness, usually worsened after slight movement. Patients often show symptoms of distention of head, headache, vertigo, pale tongue, thin and whitish tongue coating, deep and thin pulse.

4. Vertebral artery type of cervical spondylosis This type is cause by vertebral degeneration and displacement of cervical intervertebral discs, osseous discontinuous twisting of transverse foramen; or by pressure of vertebral artery due to hyperostosis of posterior exterior edge of vertebrae and uncinate process; or by spasm of terminal branches of arteries due to irritated sympathetic plexus of vertebral arteries, leading to unilateral or bilateral insufficiency of blood supply.

Symptoms: persistent vertigo, nausea, tinnitus, deafness, decreased memory, numbness of the posterior part of the head, sometimes accompanied by blurred vision, poor vision, mental depression, hypodynamia, and lethargy. Over stretching or rotation of the head will cause acute episode, such as positional vertigo, nausea and vomiting. The patient may suddenly fall down when he is still conscious. Other symptoms are red tongue, thin and whitish tongue coating, taut and thin pulse.

5. Sympathetic type of cervical spondylosis This type is caused by abnormally increased excitability or inhibition of sympathetic nerves due to cervical hyperostosis, spastic prevertebral muscles, destabilized cervical vertebrae and sympathetic fibers irritated by mediators of inflammation or psychological factors, functional disorders of glands, blood vessels and viscera.

Symptoms: persistent headache or migraine, ocular distention, evident pain in frontal region and supraorbital bone, often accompanied by heaviness of head and vertigo, tinnitus and deafness, accelerated or reduced heartbeat, chest oppression or pain in precordial region; discomfort, dryness, foreign body sensation in throat, eructation; elevated blood pressure, coolness of extremities, topically dropped skin temperature, urtication due to cold exposure, red swelling of the skin, and increased pain, occasional redness in finger tip, fever and algesia. These symptoms may turn worsened when the patient is tired or mentally stressed and become alleviated after rest. Other symptoms include light-colored tongue, thin and yellowish tongue coating, taut and rapid pulse.

6. Mixed type of cervical spondylosis   This type is marked by the symptoms of the two types mentioned above. Clinically mixed type of cervical spondylosis is encountered more often than simple ones.

[Essentials for diagnosis]

When diagnosing the patients with cervical spondylosis, the doctor first has to ask about the etiological factors and history to distinguish the major symptoms and minor ones. Routine examinations for cervical spondylotic radiculopathy include orthotopic and lateral projection radiography, left anterior and right anterior oblique projection, hyperextension and hyperflexion radiogram, CT or MRI. Routine examinations for vertebral artery type of cervical spondylosis include rheo-encephalogram, electroencephalogram, vertebral arteriography when needed. Routine examinations for cervical spondylotic myelopathy include CT, MRI or myelography and electrocardiogram for sympathetic type of cervical spondylosis.

1. Cervical type of cervical spondylosis

(1) With history of cervical sprain and constant stiff neck.

(2) The routine symptoms are distention and soreness in upper inner angle of scapula and medial border of scapula. When this type occurs, there appear the symptoms of restricted cervical movement and cervical hypermyotonia, palpable streak mass and tenderness which can be found in levator scapulae, rhomboid muscle, infraspinatus muscle, teres major and teres minor.

(3) Neurologic check will not find definite location and physical sign.

(4) Negative brachial plexus neuropathy distraction test and vertexal percussion test.

(5) Rule out rheumatism of soft tissues of neck and shoulders and cervical trauma.

(6) Plain radiography shows retrograde degeneration, but lacks uniformity with the patient's symptoms found in X-ray examination.

2. Cervical spondylotic radiculopathy

(1) Tenderness can be found in intersegmental spaces, spinous process at its side and innervational area, cervical hypermyotonia, topical streak mass or tuberous substance.

(2) Clinical manifestations are consistent with that of cervical spondylotic radiculopathy.

(3) Positive findings in brachial plexus distraction test and vertexal percussion test, decreased biceps reflex or triceps reflex.

(4) X-ray Lateral projection shows decreased or disappeared physiological cervical lordosis, hyperplasia of posterior margin of vertebra and (or) small articular, relatively contracted intervertebral foramina. Orthotopic projection shows cervical scoliosis, intervertebral space of cervical vertebra narrowing. X-ray shows symptoms consistent with that of the affected nerve roots.

(5) Rule out the possibilities of intraspinal, nerve plexus, nerve stem disorders and tuberculosis of cervical vertebrae, tumor, thoracic outlet syndrome, scapulohumeral periarthritis and tennis elbow.

3. Cervical spondylotic myelopathy

(1) Central type is caused by spinal compression from top to bottom, eventually involving the whole body; while the peripheral type is from bottom to top, eventually involving the whole body.

(2) Hypertension of extremities, muscle weakness, incomplete paralysis of extremities. Lowering head will induce aggravated extremity symptoms.

(3) Evident sensory disturbance plane; sensory disturbance and imbalance normally refer to evident dysalgesia, thalposis disturbances, mild or normal dysaphia, severe sensory disorder of the lower limb and mild sensory disorder of the trunk.

(4) Impaired or absent abdominal reflex and cremasteric reflex; hyperreflexia of biceps tendon and triceps tendon, patella tendon, Achilles tendon, meanwhile trepidation sign and ankle clonus.

(5) Positive Hoffmann's sign and Babinski sign.

(6) X-ray lateral projection shows flattening or recurvatum of cervical physiological curve, proliferative posterior edge of vertebra, ligamentum nuchae ossification, narrowing of intervertebral spaces and vertebral canal sagittal diameter; CT or MRI reveals hyperostosis and (or) spinal cord pressure by soft tissues with pressed spinal incisure; myelography shows pressure of spinal cord and cerebrospinal fluid circulation disorder.

(7) Rule out intraspinal or extraspinal space-occupying lesion, spinal cord injury, amyotrophic lateral sclerosis, polyradiculitis and peripheral neuritis.

4. Vertebral artery type of cervical spondylosis

(1) Tenderness in the affected transverse segments.

(2) Symptoms of vertebral artery insufficiency such as cervical vertigo can be seen, manifesting as "cataplexy".

(3) Positive neck rotation test: vertigo appears when the neck is rotated to a certain angle, and disappears right after the position is changed.

(4) Abnormal rheo-encephalogram, electroencephalogram can be a clinical reference; vertebral artery pressure or twisting with vertebral arteriography can help make precise diagnosis.

(5) X-ray examination shows reduced or absent cervical curve, scoliosis deformity; hyperostosis in vertebral joint or articular process and hypertrophy of transverse process.

(6) Rule out arteriopathies such as aural vertigo, ocular vertigo, vertebral aneurysm, subclavian steal syndrome, intracranial tumor and neurosis.

5. Sympathetic type of cervical spondylosis

(1) With the history of chronic headache.

(2) Evident tenderness in bilateral transverse process of cervical vertebra.

(3) Signs and symptoms of sympathetic nerve functional disorder, such as vertigo, dizziness, tinnitus, tachycardia, bradycardia and precordial pain, can be seen. Horner's signs can be found in some cases.

(4) Normal or paranormal ECG.

(5) X-ray examination shows change of cervical curve, hyperostosis of vertebral body and vertebral joint and hypertrophy of transverse process.

(6) Rule out organic diseases related to the heart or eyes.

6. Mixed type of cervical spondylosis

It is marked by diagnostic points of two or more types of cervical spondylosis mentioned above.

【Treatment with Tuina therapy】

1. Therapeutic principles: soothing tendons to activate blood, reliving spasm to stop pain and releasing the adhesions.

2. Location of Acupoints: Fengchi (GB 20), Fengfu (GV 16), Jiaji (EX-B 2), Jianjing (GB 21), Tianzong (SI 11), Quchi (LI 11), Shousanli (LI 10), Hegu (LI 4), occiput posterior part, neck, shoulder, back and the affected upper limb.

3. Manipulations:

(1) Basic manipulations

1) The patient is in a sitting position, the doctor stands at the posterior and lateral side of the patient, holds his head with one hand, symmetrically grasping and kneading the soft tissue of the neck with the second and third finger of the other hand, repeating it for 3~5 times, gradually increasing the strength; then pushing with one finger to scrub the middle part and both sides of the neck for 5 minutes; rolling to press and knead with palms to relax the neck, shoulders, upper back and muscles of the upper extremities for 3~5 times.

2) To knead or use one-finger pushing method to rub Fengchi (GB 20), Fengfu (GV 16), Jiaji (EX-B2), Jianjing (GB 21), Tianzong (SI 11), Quchi (LI 11), Shousanli (LI 10), Hegu (LI 4), Ashi Acupoints for 10 seconds each.

3) It is then followed by pulling and extending the neck. The doctor puts his ulnar side of forearm on the shoulders of the patient and presses down, puts the thumbs on the upper part of Fengchi (GB 20), holds the patient's lower mandible with the rest four fingers and palms, asks the patient to squat down, then pushes up with his forearms and hands, bends forward and backward and rotates the patient's head in the mean time.

4) Grasping and rubbing the head with five fingers and the neck with three fingers;

lifting both sides of Jianjing (GB 21) for 2~3 minutes.

5) Grasping and kneading the affected limbs, especially on biceps brachii and triceps brachii, using fingers to pluck the subaxillary division of brachial plexus to make the patient feel numbness on his fingers. This manipulation should last for 2~3 minutes.

6) Pulling and shaking the upper limbs 2~3 times, taping the back and upper limbs to make the patient pleasant.

(2) Differentiation of diseases

1) Cervical type

The aim is mainly to relieve cervical pain and muscle convulsion by relaxing topical muscles and adjusting the cervical joints through flicking the tenderness and spastic cervical muscles.

If aching sensation remains in the superior medial angle or medial margin of scapula after the treatment, methods of pressing and kneading with fingers or one-finger pushing should be employed to relieve the tense muscular fibers from the affected segment on the transverse process and posterior tubercle gradually down to the location of pain.

2) Spinal cord type (cervicalspondylotic radiculopathy)

Using routine manipulation with one-finger pushing method and thumb-pressing and kneading with fingers along the route of radioactive neuralgia on the affected extremity to relieve the inflammatory reaction of nerve cord caused by pressed nerve root and stress of fascia strain due to reflex tonus of muscles; kneading and flicking the cervical tenderness to mobilize the local adherence and relieve tropical pain; using pulling method and rotating and pulling method to rectify the disorders of joints, to relieve the stimulation of the nerve root; rubbing the affected extremities up and down for 2~3 times, soothing the five fingers once to promote blood circulation, and to accelerate the dissipation and absorption of inflammation of affected nerves. Before performing the manipulation, the patient is required to be in a sitting position or recumbent position with persistent cervical traction, weighting 3~5 kg, for 20~30 minutes. The diameter of intervertebral foramen can be enlarged to relieve the pressure of affected nerve roots and spasm of cervical muscles so as to be ready for treatment.

3) Spinal cord type (cervical spondylotic myelopathy)

Before treatment, the patient is asked to be in a sitting position or recumbent position with persistent cervical traction weighting 3~5 kg for 40~60 minutes, so the intervertebral foramen can be enlarged and the spastic cervical muscles can be stretched to help relieve the mechanical pressure of cervical intervertebral discs and the spasm of cervical muscles. Fine adjusting method can be used to adjust cervical vertebrae while the cervical traction technique is employed to correct the cervical disorder and prevent the compensatory injury of soft tissues. The treatment on lower limbs should be the same as that of the upper limbs to relieve the symptoms of spasm, soreness and weakness.

4) vertebral artery type of cervical spondylosis

Routine manipulation with finger-rubbing manipulation is to rub around the orbita and both sides of the head by making a ∞-shape circle, and massage Taiyang (EX-HN 5), forehead and vertex, rubbing the forehead and the orbita, cleaning both sides of the head to restore consciousness, inducing resuscitation, promoting blood circulation in the head so as to eliminate symptoms of the head; using cervical oblique-pulling chiropractic method or rotating and pulling manipulation to relieve tension and spasm and prevent injury of cervical soft tissues; using shaking method to adjust the cervical muscles and joints; using traction method according to the individual condition, normally around 3 kg, to stretch the spastic cervical muscles and relieve the cervical spasm.

5) sympathetic type of cervical spondylosis

Using routine manipulation together with pushing and kneading manipulations to push up and down along the sides of the neck to relax the spastic anterior cervical muscles so as to relieve the irritated sympathetic nerve or sympathetic ganglia; using one-finger pushing method or thumb flicking method to manipulate along the anterior scalene muscle, pectoralis minor muscle, pectoralis major muscle and the ribs; using palm rubbing method to rub the left chest wall, massaging Neiguan (PC 6), Xinshu (BL 15) and Sanjiaoshu (BL 22) to adjust the abnormal heart rate and the excitability of the sympathetic nerve; shaking the head to relax the cervical muscle, adjust the disorder of cervical facet joints and alleviate the irritation of sympathetic nerve or sympathetic ganglia. For those who suffer from chronic headache, one-finger pushing method should be used to push from the posterior part of the occiput, along the Gall Bladder Meridian of Foot-Shaoyang to both temporal sides and the forehead; using lateral one-finger pushing method to treat the inner margins of the two orbits and wipe both sides of he head. For those whose vision is poor, one-finger pushing method can be used to push around the orbits; using lateral one-finger pushing method to stimulate the posterior margin of the eye sockets; rubbing the forehead and around orbit. If the patient has chronic sore-throat and foreign body sensation in the throat, one-finger pushing method can be used to push both sides of the trachea and the throat.

6) Mixed type of Vertebral spondylosis

Proper manipulations are used to deal with this kind of spondylosis according to the types of cervical disorders.

[Cautions]

1. When treating cervical spondylosis with Tuina, doctors must be aware whether it is at the acute stage or remission stage. The manipulations for the former is mild and soft while the manipulations for the latter is forceful and heavy.

2. Cervical spondylosis should be treated step by step with Tuina and passive movement should be slow and mild, avoiding any rough action.

3. Avoiding long time working at the desk, heading or holding heavy objects and avoiding improper body position.

4. The pillow should not be too high, too low, or too hard. It is better to have a small pillow under the nuchal region.

5. Collar brace can be worn during and 1~2 weeks after the treatment.

6. Keeping the neck and shoulder warm.

7. Functional cervical exercises during or after the treatment is necessary.

8. For progressive worsening cases of cervical spondylotic mydopathy, integrated treatment or surgery is suggested to take.

7.1.3 Acute Lumbar Sprain

Acute lumbar sprain refers to acute injury of lumbar muscles, fascia, ligaments, intervertebral articular and lumbosacral joints when working or doing exercise. It is normally caused by external force such as overloaded traction or wedge pressure. Acute lumbar sprain is a commonly encountered and multiple clinic disorder. It is incidental to young adults and laborers as well as those who lack physical work or work with improper posture. It occurs more often among males than females. If it is improperly treated or not treated in time, it may develop into a chronic disorder.

The causes of acute lumbar sprain are various, often related to overstrain, physical activity, health condition of the back and waist, tiredness and changes of weather or seasons. Most patients can clearly tell the position of their body when being injured and the location of the pain. The following factors are frequently responsible for acute lumbar sprain: ①improper posture of the waist (for instance, when the patient bends the waist to lift heavy objects, the center of gravity is shifted away from the central axis of the body and more pressure is put on the muscles due to lever effect, and consequently causing acute lumbar muscles sprain); ②tumbling over while walking on uneven road or tipping over while going downstairs, causing fascia sprain or laceration of fascia of lumbar muscles; ③imbalance of action while lifting objects that may shift the center of gravity, making the lumbar muscles contract violently and cause acute lumbar sprain; ④underestimation of a movement, such as pouring water, bending body, sudden standing up or even sneezing that may lead to acute lumbar sprain.

Acute lumbar sprain is clinically seen among acute injury of fascia of lumbar muscles, acute injury of lumbar ligaments and acute disorder of posterior lumbar joint.

[Clinical manifestations]

Acute injury of fascia of lumbar muscles Acute injury of fascia of lumbar muscles is a common lumbar injury. It is normally caused by lifting heavy objects with a sudden action or a stoop posture or sudden turning around with a stoop posture that may make the lumbar muscles and fascia contract and twist excessively or even lacerate. The degree of injury varies due to difference in exertion. The main symptoms are laceration of sacrospinal muscle from the starting point of sacrum or fascia laceration at the attachment point. Injury of fascia and vessels will inevitably cause stagnation of blood and obstruction of Qi, and eventually leading to swelling, pain and limited movement.

The clinical manifestations are feeling of tissue laceration, lumbar snap, lateral or bilateral lumbar pain, inability to straighten, bend or extend the waist, aggravation of pain when turning the body or sitting up, difficulty in moving the waist, stiffness of the waist, and aggravation when getting up from the bed, exerting force, coughing or sneezing. If the case is mild, the patient still can work but the symptoms will be worsened several hours later. In order to relieve the pain, the patient normally holds his waist with both hands. The pain is normally in the lumbosacral area, or in the lateral or bilateral side of the buttock and posterior side of the thigh with uncertain location and nature. The usual symptoms are swelling, distention, purple tongue with ecchymosis, thin fur, slow or wiry pulse.

Physical examination shows that, in the early stage, the pain may be caused by laceration of muscles, fascia and ligaments that may lead to protective spasm and reduced physiological lordosis. Anisomerous muscle spasm may cause physiological scoliosis. These symptoms will be alleviated or disappear automatically after the pain is relived.

There is local tenderness in most cases in lumbosacral joint, the tip of the third lumbar transverse process and postlaminar part of iliac crest. The tenderness is the place where the injured soft tissue is located and is one of the parts to be examined. It is also a protective reaction caused by the pain due to injury of sacrospinalis and gluteus maximus.

For those with acute lumbar muscle sprain, the lumbosacral orthophoria and lateral X-ray examination should be taken. If necessary, oblique position X-ray examination should also be taken. For those with usual soft tissue injury, X-ray examination will reveal any signs of pathologic fracture of lumbar isthmus, hyperostosis, tumor or tuberculosis.

【Essentials for diagnosis】

1. History of sudden lumbar injury.

2. Severe lower back pain, restricted movement, cough, aggravated pain when sneezing.

3. There are supraspinous, interspinous tenderness, and tenderness around intervertebral space and near cacroiliac joint; pain and spasm become worsened when being taped; deviation of spinous process, widened interspinal space and scoliolosis can be found.

4. Spasm of sacrospinalis and gluteus maximus are evident when the patient stands up and bends slightly forward.

5. Normally there are no signs of lower limb pain. Sometimes there is radiating pain in the buttocks, posterior part of the thigh, and the prelaminar internal part of the root of the thigh.

6. X-ray examination shows no abnormal changes or only straightened flexion or

lateral curvature of lumbar vertebrae, malformation or retrograde metamorphosis of osteoarthrosis.

Acute injury of lumbar ligaments The main lumbar ligaments are: anterior longitudinal ligaments, posterior longitudinal ligaments, ligamenta flava, interspinal ligaments, supraspinal ligaments, intertransverse ligaments and vertebral articular capsules and vertebral ligaments. The commonly seen ligament injuries are the injuries of supraspinal ligaments, interspinal ligaments and iliolumbar ligaments. The lumbar ligaments are normally protected by sacrospinalis, but when one bends over to move objects, the sacrospinalis is in a loosen state, the muscles of buttocks and posterior muscles of the thighs will contract, leading to injury of supraspinal ligaments and interspinal ligaments, especially the ligaments in the lumbosacral area. Moreover, lumbar injury can directly injure the lumbar ligaments. Concurrent fracture, dislocation and nerve damage are often seen in this type of injury. Other symptoms are reddish purple tongue, whitish and thin tongue coating, wiry and tense pulse.

The injuries of supraspinal ligaments, interspinal ligaments often take place when one is working with a bending posture. The patient usually hears a clear snap and feels lacerating pain in the waist, and immediately followed by sudden local pain appearing like lacerating, stabbing or cutting with the symptoms of local ecchymosis, swelling and difficulty to sit or lie down, often accompanied by radiating pain in the lower limbs, lumbar spasm, limited movement and aggravated pain when bending forward. There is evident tenderness in the injured spinous process or interspinal space. Local blocking therapy can relieve or eliminate the pain. The cases with lacerated supraspinal ligaments, interspinal ligaments and widened interspinous distance can be diagnosed by palpation. X-ray examination finds no abnormal changes in the injury of ligaments. For the cases of lacerated supraspinal ligament and interspinal ligaments, the interspinous space is usually widened.

[Essentials for diagnosis]

1. Evident history of injury.

2. The patient feels laceration in the injured lumbosacral area, acute pain, limitation of motion, aggravated pain when bending.

3. Evident supraspinous , interspinous tenderness and widened inerspinous space.

4. Pain can be relieved or eliminated by local blocking with procaine. Such a therapy also can be used to define the location and nature of the injury.

5. For severe cases, X-ray examination should be taken to see whether there is fracture or dislocation.

Acute synovial incarceration of posterior lumbar joint It is also called disorder of posterior lumbar joints or lumbar intervertebral articular syndrome. Lumbar posterior joint is composed of inferior articular process of epistatic vertebra and superior articular process of hypostatic vertebra. There is a right angle between the two articular processes, one is coronal, the other is sagittal. That is why there is a wide angle of lateral curvature or anteroposterior flexion and extension. Lumbosacral joint is a articular facet obliquely located between the coronal and sagittal processes. Since the upright plane gradually becomes horizontal, there are loose articular capsule and wide range of rotation, flexion and extension. When the lumbar part suddenly bends forward or rotates without preparation, the joint posterior space of lumbar vertebra stretches open, and then negative pressure takes place in the joint, sucking in the synovial membrane. If the antisternum suddenly stretches backward, the synovial membrane will be stuck in the articular facets, causing posterior lumbar articular synovial incarceration, or the cartilage displacement of the articular process facets, eventually resulting in severe pain in the lumbar region. If there exists asymmetric congenital lumbosacral articular process and one side of the joint moves obliquely, it may easily cause periosteum incarceration or displacement of articular process.

The cause of this disorder was unclear before, so most of the cases were misdiagnosed as acute injury of lumbar muscular fascia or acute lumbar fibrositis, delaying proper treatment and often leading to chronic lumbago. It is now regarded as a common clinical disorder, one of the common causes that lead to acute lumbago. It is commonly seen among young people, especially in males. It is caused by mild acute lumbar sprain or sudden standing up when bending the waist, consequently twisting the articular process and causing synovial incarceration and limited movement of antisternum.

Clinically the patient may have a history of lumbar sprain or sudden standing up when bending the waist. Usually severe pain appears right after injury of the waist, especially in movement. There is stiffness in the waist, and the functional activity is lost. Lumbar examination shows stiff flexed position, evident restricted back stretching movement without nerve root irritation sign. Palpation will not find spinal deviation of the affected antisternum. There is no sign of the change of spinous process intervals. There is evident tenderness in L4-5 or L5-S1 interspinal spaces and para vertebral body. X-ray examination shows asymmetrical rank of posterior joints in some cases, or posterior process and lateral curvature of lumbar vertebra and inequality in width of intervertebral spaces. Other symptoms are purple tongue with ecchymosis, thin and yellowish fur, sunken and tense pulse.

【Essentials for diagnosis】

1. History of acute lumbar sprain, or chronic lumbar strain.

2. Chief complaint: severe lumbar pain, aggravation when moving, abnormal change of physiological curve after occurrence of transposition of lumbar posterior joints or synovial incarceration and aggravation of pain when standing, sitting and over extending.

3. Tenderness in the spinous process or articular process gradually disappears when the symptoms of lumbar stiffness and tension are relieved.

4. Pain may become worsened when turning the body in bed. However the pain may become alleviated after mild movement or change of the body position. Usually it is difficult to lift the leg. But there are no signs of nerve stimulation.

5. Pain in lumbar area can be relieved after reduction or removal of incarceration.

【Treatment with Tuina therapy】

1. Therapeutic principles: Soothing tendons and activating blood.

2. Location of Acupoints: Shenshu (BL 23), Dachangshu (BL 25), Huantiao (GB 30), Yinmen (BL 37), Weizhong (BL 40), Chengshan (BL 57), Yanglingquan (GB 34), Kunlun (BL 60), Ashi points and dorsolumbar areas.

3. Manipulations:

(1) Acute injury of fascia of lumbar muscles

1) The patient is in a prone position. The doctor uses rolling method to press around the tenderness, then rolling along the direction of sacrospinal muscle fibers for 3~4 times, accompanied by passive movement of the waist. The range of manipulation is gradually increased and the strength of fingers is gradually intensified. Such a manipulation is performed for about 5 minutes.

2) The patient is in a prone position. The doctor uses rolling and kneading methods to press Shenshu (BL 23), Dachangshu (BL 25). Huantiao (GB 30), Yinmen (BL 37). Chengshan (BL 57), Yanglingquan (GB 34), Kunlun (BL 60) and Ashi points, grasp Weizhong (BL 40) till distention is felt, and then uses flicking method on the upper and lower part of the tenderness point for 5 minutes. This manipulation should be mild and deep, and performed for about 5 minutes.

3) The patient is in a prone position. The doctor rubs along the sacrospinal muscle fibers vertically on the affected side for 3 minutes till it becomes warm.

4) The patient is in a prone position with the affected side turned up, obliquely pulling the waist.

(2) acute injury of lumbar ligaments

1) Based on the treatment of acute injury of fascia of lumbar muscles, trials are taken to release adherence. The patient is in a standing or sitting position, the doctor stands behind, asking the patient to bend forward, using the two thumbs to feel and dissect the affected supraspinal ligament. The patient needs to rest on hard bed and avoid turning the waist or bending body. This procedure takes 5 minutes.

2) The patient is in a prone position, the doctor uses pressing and kneading methods to press along both sides of the spinal cord, flicking, pressing and kneading vertically on the affected supraspinal ligament with one thumb, and rubbing the governor vessel on the back for about 5 minutes till it becomes warm.

(3) Acute synovial incarceration of posterior lumbar joint

1) Based on the treatment of acute injury of fascia of lumbar muscles, trials are made to release the adherence.

2) Manipulations for bending, turning and pulling the waist are used.

【Cautions】

1. The patient is advised to take a rest after the treatment, avoiding bending and rotating the waist within a short period of time.

2. Acute symptoms can be relieved right after the treatment, but the pain and lumbar stiffness are not relieved. For this reason, the therapy for local conduction should be used to eliminate the symptoms.

3. Functional exercise of dorsolumbar extensor is useful for consolidating the therapeutic effect and preventing the disorder.

4. Keep the waist warm.

7.1.4 Chronic lumbar muscle strain

Chronic lumbar muscle strain is accumulated chronic injury of the muscles, fascia, ligament, bones and joints in the waist. It is caused by working with bowing or squatting position for a long time, frequently over exhaustion of the waist, fatigue and improper postures of the waist during working, or anatomical characteristics and defects of the waist. It may also be caused by acute waist injury that is not treated in time or properly, or by sequelae of repeated injury.

The causes of chronic lumbar muscle strain are long-term bowing or squatting, frequently over exhaustion of the waist, improper postures of the waist during working which may lead to the fascia strain of the lumbar muscles, or fascia relaxation, or chronic laceration, causing pain of the back hard to cure. It may also be caused by delayed treatment or incomplete treatment of acute contusion or repeated mild injury, giving rise to conglutination of fascia which may linger and gradually develop into chronic lumbar pain. It may also be caused by prenatal weakness with deficiency of kidney Qi and invasion of pathogenic wind, cold, and dampness factors into the muscles, tendons and meridians, leading to disharmony of tendons and meridians, spasm of muscles, tendons and fascia, obstruction of meridians and collaterals, and stagnation of Qi and blood, eventually causing chronic waist pain. Moreover, lumbar congenital abnormality or anatomical defects, such as lumbar sacralization, spondylolysis, lumbar spondylolisthesis, lumbar kyphosis deformity caused by fracture or dislocation may lead to imbalance of the lumbar myodynamia or fascia strain.

Waist strain, the most commonly encountered kind in lumbago, is clinically divided into lumbar muscle strain and ligament strain.

【Clinical manifestations】

Lumbar muscle strain mainly refers to the chronic exhausted injury of lumbar muscles. The chief complaint is pain of the waist, which is often vague, repeated and fluctuating, alleviated after rest and aggravated after exhaustion. It can be relieved after proper exercise or change of position. but it is difficult to bend the waist. The patient frequently pats the waist with both hands to relieve pain. A few patients may have distending pain in the upper part of the thigh. Weather change and fatigue will worsen the problem. Other symptoms are reddish tongue with thin and whitish tongue coating, floating and tense pulse.

The spine appears normal and shows no difficulty in bending backwards and forwards. Tenderness can be found in the sacrospinal muscle, back part of the iliac bone ridge, or lumbodorsal muscles posterior to the iliac bone on one or both sides. The pain will be worsened if the condition is serious with slight limited movement. Nerve system is normal in examination. X-ray test shows the physiological arc change in the spine, such as lumbar lateral curvature, disappearance of the lumbar lordosis, or congenital abnormalities, such as fifth lumbar sacralization, first lumbar sacralization, cryptomerorachisis, or hyperosteogeny.

In clinic, it should be distinguished from supraspinous ligaments strain.

【Essentials for diagnosis】

1. Long history of pain in the back and repeated onset.

2. Pain and ache of the waist, especially after heavy work or during rainy days.

3. Leg lifting test is normal and waist movement limitation is not evident.

4. X-ray test only shows congenital anomalies of lumbosacral spine or hyperosteogeny.

【Treatment with Tuina therapy】

1. Therapeutic principle: Soothing tendons and activating blood, warming meridians and dredging collaterals.

2. Location of Acupoints: Shenshu (BL 23), Dachangshu (SL 25), Guanyuanshu (BL 26), Zhibian (BL 52), Huantiao (GB 30), Weizhong (BL 40), waist, back, and lumbosacral region.

3. Manipulations:

(1) The patient takes a supine position. The doctor pushes, presses and kneads the sacrospinal muscles on both sides of the spine.

(2) Then the doctor knocks sacrospinal muscles with fingers of both hands for several times, then mainly presses the tenderness with the tip of the finger for five minutes.

(3) The doctor presses, kneads, vibrates the Acupoints of Shenshu (BL 23), Dachangshu (BL 25), Guanyuanshu (BL 26), Zhibian (BL 52), Huantiao (GB 30), Weizhong (BL 40) with the tips or bellies of both hands for half a minute each.

(4) The patient takes a supine position and the doctor rubs the Belt Vessel horizontally for 3 to 5 minutes.

【Cautions】

1. Keep proper posture, and correct habitual wrong posture in order to maintain normal physical arc of the spine.

2. Take more exercise to train the psoas muscles.

7.1.5 Retrograde spondylitis

Retrograde spondylitis, also called hyperplastic spondylitis, vertebral osteoarthritis, or senescent arthritis, refers to pathological changes of joints marked by degenerative change and hyperosteogeny of lumbar cartilages. It is common among the aged, more frequently to be found in males than in females, often occurring in an early period among those who are obese, physical workers or sportsmen. It is a kind of lumbar osteoarthritis with chronic pain in the wrist and leg.

This disease is either primary or secondary. Primary type is a physiological degenerative change among the aged because their tissues and organs are gradually becoming degenerative and the substance of bones has begun to show degenerative change. The manifestations of such changes are reduced water or gelation of tissues and organs with increased free calcium, leading to decline of the physiological function with varied hyperosteogeny on the margins of lumbar vertebral body, the degenerative changes of intervertebral discs, narrowing of vertebral space, contraction of intervertebral foramen, which stimulate and press the nerve root to cause pain in the waist and leg. The secondary type appears in various injuries, such as chronic inflammation, anemia, disorder of metabolism, or the endocrine disturbances which affect blood circulation and nutrition supply for chondral plate of bone joint, and eventually resulting in mucosal inflammation of cartilages and hyperosteogeny, consequently causing pain in the waist and leg.

The pathological mechanism of this disease is the change of cartilages and degenerative change of intervertebral discs. After the period of middle age, the elasticity of cartilages around the vertebral body decreases, and the margins, joint capsules and ligaments gradually develop protective hyperosteogeny. The fibrous tissues in nucleus pulposus increase with its original enlargement and gelatine state. After the period of middle age, the degenerative changes of nucleus pulposus gradually reaches the anaphase, so there are various changes of intervertebral disc atrophy, such as narrowing of vertebral space and smaller change of intervertebral foramen. Then the degenerative change of chondral plate is obvious with reduced fluid exchange, promoting the degeneration and necrosis of nucleus pulposus and annular fibrosus. The pressure on the posterior vertebral margin increases due to lever action. With the increase of age, the longer the vertebra experiences the pressure, the more the hyperosteogeny will appear. After the degenerative changes of intervertebral discs, the vertebral space becomes narrow and has lost its water support or hydraulic function. As a result, both tips of vertebral body will be shaken, impacted, and worn continuously. At the same time, the senile osteoporosis is brought about weakening the resistance of vertebral body to pressure.

【Clinical manifestations】

After middle age, lumbago gradually appears without any general symptoms. The period between the age of 45 and 55 is the peak of lumbago due to retrograde spondylitis. With the increase of age, the intervertebral disc turns to be atrophic with strengthened stability. Thus after the age of 60, lumbago gradually alleviates. Other symptoms are whitish or whitish and greasy tongue coating with deep and tense pulse or soft and moderate pulse.

Usually, lumbago is not severe, just a sort of aching in the waist and inflexible or bounding feeling in the waist. After getting up in the morning or standing up after a long period of sitting, the pain will become evident. However, it may disappear or relieve after some movement, but it can be worsened after overstrain. The pain can be radiated to the buttock and thigh. In the cold and rainy days or after cold attack, it will become severe. The symptoms are deformity of spine, decrease or disappearance of the physiological protrusion of lumbar, restricted movement of the spine; or the percussion pain in the lumbar spinous processes, tension and tenderness in psoas muscles on both sides, or tenderness in the superior gluteal nerves and sciatic nerves, even symptoms of stimulation in the sciatic nerves. Leg raising test is positive with decreased tendon reflex; bending neck and pressing abdomen test is positive. The X-ray test shows the degree of hyperosteogeny.

【Essentials for diagnosis】

1. Chronic pain in the lower waist and pain in the waist and leg.

2. There is no evident deformity of spinal column. If there is spondylolisthesis and the lumbar convexity will increase. Usually there is no evident limitation of waist movement or there is just slight limitation. Leg raising test is pseudo-positive.

3. There is no fixed tenderness in the waist. Or it may just be found in psoas muscles on both sides and L_3-L_4 and L_4-L_5 lumbar vertebrae.

4. X-ray test shows that hyperosteogeny is in the margin of the waist with the lip-shaped bony spur. The vertebral space become narrow or irregular and articular process is vague, accompanied by senile osteanabrosis.

【Treatment with Tuina therapy】

1. Therapeutic principles: Promoting Qi and activating blood, soothing tendons and dredging the collaterals.

2. Location of Acupoints: Mingmen (GV 4), Yaoyangguan(GV 3), Qihaishu (BL 24), Dachangshu (BL 25), Guanyuanshu (BL 26), Jiaji (EX-B 2), Weizhong (BL 40) Yanglingquan (GB 34), Chengshan(BL 57) and waist.

3. Manipulations:

(1) The patient takes a supine position. The doctor applies rolling manipulation to the place of pathological change and both sides of the waist for about 3~5minutes.

(2) The doctor presses Mingmen (GV 4), Yaoyangguan(GV 3), Qihaishu (BL 24), Dachangshu (BL 25), Guanyuanshu (BL 26), or press Jiaji (EX-B 2) with palm bases;

then rolls from the waist to buttock. If there is referred pain in the lower limbs, kneading, grasping, pressing and rubbing manipulations are used to manipulate from the back side of thigh down to leg with knocking with finger on Weizhong (BL 40), Chengshan (BL 57) and Yanglingquan (GB 34) combined with the activity of raising legs backwards for 10 minutes.

(3) Rub the waist and related region with warm compression.

【Cautions】

1. Lie on hard bed and keep the waist warm.

2. Take proper functional exercises, such as bending forwards, extending backwards or rotating the waist.

7.1.6 Third Lumbar Transverse Process Syndrome

The third lumbar transverse process syndrome refers to chronic lumbago with tenderness, also known as peripheral inflammation of the third lumbar transverse process, or bursitis of the third lumbar transverse process. It is a type of psoas muscular strain. Since the third lumbar vertebra is located in the center of the whole lumbar vertebrae, it is active in movements with longer transverse process, stronger resistance against pressure and higher incidence of strain, frequently leading to lumbago and buttock pain. This disease is mainly seen among young and middle-aged people, especially among those who are engaged in physical work.

The lumbar transverse processes is located at both sides of the waist without any protective osseous tissues. The third lumbar transverse process is the longest one, and the upper part of which is the starting point of psoas major and quadratus lumborum and connected with the transverse abdominal muscle and the deep fascia of latissimus dorsal. When the lumbar and abdominal muscles contract, the third lumbar transverse process experiences the strongest stress. As a result, the muscles attached to the third lumbar transverse process is apt to strain, leading to pathological changes as inflammatory swelling of the local tissue, hyperaemia and fluid exudation, and followed by secondary changes of hyperplasia of synovium, fibrous tissues and fibrocartilage, etc. In addition, prolonged stimulation of the branch of spinal nerve will lead to degenerative changes of nerve fibers, consequently causing lumbago, buttocks pain and lumbosacral spasm. Besides, exogenous pathological factors and trauma can also cause laceration of the peripheral muscular fascia of the third lumbar vertebra. Improper treatment may bring about such pathological changes as scar adhesion around the transverse process, fascia incrassation, tendon contracture and other corresponding symptoms.

【Clinical manifestations】

This problem is often characterized by fatigue, discomfort and pain that diffuses from the posterior part of the thigh to superior level of the popliteal fossa. It usually aggravates after fatigue and changes of weather, in the morning or when bending the waist. However, it may alleviate after some movement. In this syndrome, lumbago often lingers. In some patients, it may be characterized by intermittent ache, distension, and inertia with the pain radiating to the buttocks or the lateral side of the thigh. There is evident tenderness at the third lumbar transverse process. Sometimes indurations of fibrous nodules or funicular stripe can be felt. Numbness or allergy often appears beside the vertebral space of L_{2-3}. The lumbar muscular tension becomes weakened but the movement is basically normal. Other symptoms are light tender tongue, whitish tongue coating, thin and deep pulse.

Examination finds local tenderness in the third lumbar transverse process of the sacrospinal muscular peripheries. Sometimes fibrous soft tissue indurations can be felt, often causing reflex pain in the lower limbs. Leg lifting test is positive. X-ray examination shows that the third lumbar vertebra is evidently longer than usual and the transverse process in both sides is occasionally dissymmetrical or obliquely leaning backwards.

[Essentials for diagnosis]

1. Most patients have lumbar trauma history.

2. The pain is in one or both sides of the waist. Aggravation occurs in the morning or after fatigue and when bending the waist. In severe cases, pain may expand from the thigh to the lower limbs.

3. Evident pain is felt at the tip of the third lumbar vertebra transverse process and there is fibrous sclerosis of nodules.

4. X-ray examination shows that the third lumbar transverse process is longer than usual with shadow of calcification at the far edge or asymmetric transverse process at both sides.

[Treatment with Tuina therapy]

1. Therapeutic principles: promoting Qi and activating blood, soothing tendons and dredging collaterals.

2. Location of Acupoints: Huantiao (GB 30), Chengfu (BL36), Yinmen (BL 37), Weizhong (BL 40), Chengshan (BL 57), waist and back.

3. Manipulations:

(1) The patient takes a supine position while the doctor uses both palm bases or olecranons pushing repeatedly from the thoracic vertebrae to the lower part of the body and pressing the sacrospinal muscles in both sides of spine. At the same time, thumbs are used to press and knead Huantiao (GB 30), Chengfu (BL 36), Yinmen (BL 37), Weizhong(BL 40), and Chengshan (BL 57) for 5 minutes.

(2) The doctor uses one thumb to vertically flick the indurations of fibrous nodules or stripe funicular of third lumbar transverse process, then using the thumb or olecranon to knead and rub the same place for 3 minutes.

(3) The doctor uses his palm root to push, stroke, press and rub upwards and downwards along the sacrospinal muscle on the affected side. At the same time rolling

manipulation is used. Finally, pushing and rubbing manipulations are used to push and rub along the fiber of sacrospinal muscle combined with passive posterior extension of the waist. This treatment is continued for 2 minutes.

【Cautions】

1. Lie on hard bed during lesions and treatments.

2. Keep warm, avoid invasion of external pathogenic factors. Apply hot compress to enhance the therapeutic effect during treatments.

3. Avoid work that may exhaust the waist.

4. Rectify bad postures.

7.1.7 Lumbar intervertebral disc protrusion

Lumbar intervertebral disc protrusion, also known as ruptured lumbar annular fibrosus nucleus hernia, refers to lumbar pain syndrome caused by degeneration of lumbar intervertebral disc, partially or completely ruptured annular fibrosus, bulged or herniated nucleus due to external forces that may irritate the spinal cord and press the nerve root. This disorder is one of the common diseases among the patients with lumbar pain syndromes. It is frequently seen among young laborers. The incidence is high among workers aging from 20 to 40. The most commonly encountered lumbar disc protrusion often happens in the disc between L_4 and L_5, and sometimes in the disc between L_5 and S_1, occasionally in the disc between L_3 and L_4, and seldom in the disc between L_2 and L_3 or L_1 and L_2. The internal cause of the disease is the degeneration of lumbar intervertebral disc, or developmental defect of intervertebral discs; the external causes are injury, strain and invasion of pathogenic wind and cold.

Lumbar intervertebral disc is located between two consecutive vertebras, forming the weight-bearing joints of the vertebra and serving as the ginglymus of the spinal column. Intervertebral disc consists of annular fibrosus, nucleus pulposus and cartilages. Annular fibrosus is composed of tenacious interlaced elastic fibers in cartilage matrix and are connected tightly with the adjacent vertebras. Nucleus pulposus contains hydrous jell. The annular fibrosus and the soft board on the surface of the adjacent vertebras confine the nucleus pulposus in the global cavity. With the increase of age as well as the influence of pressing, pulling and twisting by external force, the intervertebral discs eventually degenerate, dehydrate, and lose their flexibility, making the intervertebral spaces narrow and the ligaments loose or causing fissures. These are the internal causes of lumbar disc protrusion.

Under the pressure of external force, the pressure on the back increases, easily causing rupture of the annular fibrosus and lateral protrusion of the nucleus pulposus, which may stimulate and press the spinal nerve or spinal cord and lead to evident neuralgic symptoms. In some cases, there is no evident history of injury and it is caused by cold attack, resulting in spasm of lumbar muscles and causing protrusion of the degenerated intervertebral discs and flattening of the nerve roots which then lead to hyperemia, edema and apomorphosis, or hyperplasia and hypertrophy of the peripheral tissues, or even adhesion with the protruding intervertebral discs. In most cases, lumbar disc protrusion is unilateral. If the nucleus pupsus protrudes from the longitudinal ligament and presses the spinal cord or nerve root, it will cause symptoms on the same side; if the nucleus pulposus protrudes from the longitudinal ligament and directly stimulates and presses the spinal cord, it will cause symptoms on both lower limbs or the alternating symptoms.

【Clinical manifestations】

There are five types of lumbar disc protrusions according to the protruding place, degree, direction, degree of degeneration, relationship with the nerve roots and the different imaging examinations, namely pathological type, location type, morphological type, clinical type, and the type differentiated according to TCM. But currently, it is classified mainly according to the direction of protrusion and the degree of the nucleus pulposus protrusion. The main symptoms are back pain, and the radioactive pain in the lower limb (ischiodynia).

Back pain normally is located in lumbosacral area. Usually there is local deep tenderness in the spaces of spinous processes between L_4-L_5, L_5-S_1, or L_3-L_4 radiating towards to the lower limb on the affected side. Ischiodynia is often unilateral and radiates along the thigh on the affected side down to the lateral side of the crural region, calcar pedis and lateral side of dorsum. If the protrusion of intervertebral disc is quite large or in the center of vertebral canal, it may cause bilateral pain. Coughing, sneezing and pushing hard while defecating may press the nerves and worsen the symptoms. Walking, bending, standing up from a sitting position may stretch the nerve roots and worsen the pain. The pain may be relieved when bending coax and knee and resting. The pain is frequently intermittent and seldom persistent. For those with intermittent pain, a good rest, especially sleeping in bed, may evidently reduce the pain. But it may recur after minor injury. For those with a long course of illness, there may be radiating numbness in their lower limbs, which pertains to the type of lumbago due to blood stagnation according to TCM, often characterized by pricking pain, fixed pain, unpressable pain, difficulty to bend in mild cases, inability to turn the waist in severe cases. Other symptoms are purple tongue with or without ecchymosis, deep and uneven pulse.

Clinical examination: Deformity of the waist. The waist appears stiff when it occurs. The patients may have functional scoliosis, reduction or disappearance of lumbar lordosis. Scoliolosis may be on the affected side or the healthy side. When the protrusion of intervertebral disc is on the medial inferior part of the pressed nerve roots, the spinal column will bend towards the healthy side, which can relieve pressure on the nerve root; when the protrusion of intervertebral disc is on the lateral superior side of the pressed nerve roots, the spinal column will bend toward the affected side, which can relieve the pressure on the nerve roots. To bend forward is evidently limited and to extend backwards is slightly limited. Lateral bending will cause pain or become limited according to the direction of the malformation. When it bends over to the concave side, the pain will be relieved; when it bends over to the prominent side, the pain will be worsened. In addition, there is evident tenderness. Neck bending test is positive; abdomen straightening test is positive; leg raising test is positive; tendon reflex is reduced or disappears.

X-ray examination: Routine orthotopic lateral side. The orthotopic film sometimes shows lumbar Scoliosis; the lateral film shows disappearance of the lumbar anterior protrusion, narrowed vertebral spaces and hyperosteogeny of the adjacent vertebras on the margin. The result of X-ray examination can be used referentially in diagnosing protrusion of intervertebral disc in order to rule out other pathological changes of the lumbar vertebras, such as pulmonary tuberculosis, tumor, bone fracture, or congenital deformity of lumbosacral vertebrae.

CT scan: Using CT to test the shape and caliber of lumbar spinal canal is a very significant way to help diagnose lumbar intervertebral disc hernia. It can clearly show the factors responsible for pressure on the lumbar and sacral nerve roots. The stereoscopic display can demonstrate the degree and area of the protrusion of intervertebral discs.

【Essentials for diagnosis】

1. The patients have a history of lumbar injury, chronic lumbar strain or pathogenic cold damp attack. Most of the patients suffer from chronic lumbago before the occurrence.

2. The incidence of the disease is high among young people.

3. Pain radiates down to the buttocks and lower limbs. Increase of the abdominal pressure like coughing and sneezing can worsen the pain.

4. Scoliosis, disappearance of physiological curvature, tenderness in the affected areas, downward radiating pain and confined lumbar movement.

5. The affected lower nerve innervated regions are hyperesthetic or dysesthetic. Atrophy may occur in those with a long course of disease. Leg raising test is positive; patella tendon and achilles tendon reflex is reduced or disappears; hallux dorsiflexion is weakened.

6. X-ray: Scoliosis, disappearance of anterior protrusion, hyperosteogeny in adjacent margins. CT and MRI show the areas and degree of protrusion of intervertebral discs.

【Treatment with Tuina therapy】

1. Therapeutic principles: Soothing tendons, activating meridians, releasing the adherence.

2. Location of Acupoints: Yaoyangguan (GV 3), Dachangshu (BL 25), Huantiao (GB 30), Juliao (GB 29), Chengfu (Bl 36), Yinmen (BL 37), Weizhong (BL 40), Chengshan (BL 57), Yanglingquan (GB 34), Juegu, Qiuxu (GB 40) and dorsolumbar part and lower limbs.

3. Manipulations:

(1) The patient is in a prone position, the doctor rolls, presses, kneads both sides of the spinal column, bladder region, buttocks and the lower limbs for 3~5 minutes, mainly focusing on the waist. Then the doctor overlaps his one hand over the other to press on the spinal column down to lumbosacral part for 5 minutes. Such a manipulation is to improve blood circulation and relieve dorsolumbar spasm and promote the absorption of the inflammation. This manipulation is performed for 5 minutes.

(2) The patient is in a prone position, the doctor uses his thumb pulp or olecranon to knead Yaoyangguan (GV 3), Dachangshu (BL 25), Huantiao (GB 30), Juliao (GB 29), Chengfu (BL 36), Yinmen (BL 37), Weizhong (BL 40), Chengshan (BL:57), Yanglingquan (GB 34), Juegu, Qiuxu (GB 40) and Ashi point for 5~10 minutes to relieve muscular spasm and alleviate pain.

(3) The doctor uses both thumb pulps or olecranon to knead the affected areas and push towards the healthy side for 3~5 minutes, relieving the stimulation and pressure of the protruded nucleus pulposus on the peripheral tissues.

(4) The patient is in a prone position, the doctor uses knocking, pressing, kneading and flicking method to massage from the waist to the affected sciatic innervation. Such a manipulation is to improve local circulation, promote the absorption of the inflammation caused by injury, help the atrophic muscles and paralyzed nerves restore their functions. This manipulation is performed for 1~3 minutes.

(5) The manipulations for bending, rotating and pulling the waist, posteriorly extending and pulling the unilateral limb as well as posteriorly extending and pulling both limbs are used to adjust the disorder of the joints and release the adherence to change the position of the protrusion and the nerves. When the pressure around the intervertebral discs is relieved, the pain will be alleviated and the normal functions will be restored.

【Cautions】

1. Sleeping on hard bed can reduce the pressure on the intervertebral discs.

2. Keep the waist warm, protect the dorsolumbar region from coldness and avoid cold food.

3. Pay attention to the posture when working, not to work for a long time with the waist bending over and avoid heavy load lest the degeneration of the intervertebral discs be worsened.

4. Stay in bed at the acute stage; appropriate rest is needed after the pain is alleviated; avoid fatigue.

5. Take food rich in calcium, such as milk, milk product and sea food, etc.

7.1.8 Chest and hypochondrium trauma

Chest and hypochondriac trauma is caused by injury, violent impact or extrusion that are not strong enough to cause rib fracture; or caused by abnormal posture and improper use of strength that may lead to the obstruction of Qi activity in the chest and hypochondrium, eventually resulting in tightness and referred pain and oppression in the chest. There are three types of chest and hypochondriac trauma, damage of Qi, damage of blood and damage of both Qi and blood. The type due to Qi damage is caused by indirect violent twisting, turning and pulling that may injure the joints and tissues in the chest without obvious local tenderness; the type due to blood damage is caused by direct violent attack that causes bleeding in the chest and stagnation of Qi with the symptoms of obvious and fixed tenderness; the type due to damage of both Qi and blood is caused by direct or indirect violence, such as extrusion accompanied by pulling and stretching, causing bleeding and extensive injury in the chest.

This disorder is commonly seen in clinic and can be effectively treated by Tuina therapy.

【Clinical manifestations】

The patients usually have evident history of injury. Injury usually causes pain in one side of the chest involving the shoulder and back. The pain is often worsened when coughing or breathing. Since the patient takes protective measures, there appear the signs of shallow respiration, accompanied by tachypnea and chest oppression. Impairment of Qi causes pain while injury of body causes swelling. Impairment of tendons and muscles and obstruction of Qi and blood will lead to the symptoms of bluish tongue, or tongue with ecchymosis, slightly thick tongue coating, slow and choppy pulse. For those with severe impairment of both Qi and blood, the symptoms will be pale tongue with ecchymosis, thin tongue coating, thin and choppy pulse. Clinical symptoms may vary due to different types of the disease.

Qi impairment type: It is characterized by wandering pain, no obvious local pain, referred pain during breathing or speaking, or inability to lie down and difficulty to lie in a prone position or turn the body in severe cases. For those with semiluxation of costovertebral joints, there may be tenderness in the affected joints.

Blood impairment type: It is characterized by fixed pain with obvious local swelling. If the muscles attached with sensory nerve endings are injured, evident swelling and tenderness can be found in the affected region. If there is laceration or spasm in the muscle groups of chest wall, swelling, tenderness and narrowed rib space can be found in the corresponding intercostal space.

Qi and blood impairment type: It is characterized by simultaneous appearance of the symptoms in both groups mentioned above with extensive pain and evident local tenderness. This type is clinically more frequently encountered than other types.

【Essentials for diagnosis】

Beside clinical physical examination, X-ray is the first routine test used to rule out dislocation of multiple joints and fracture of ribs.

1. Normally the patients have a history of injury. Careful inquiry should be done to make clear the cause of injury and decide the type it belongs to.

2. Use palpation to decide if there is evident tenderness or semiluxation of costovertebral joints as well as the location, degree and the affected area. The patient with Qi impairment type is always difficult to tell the location of the pain or there is just tenderness in small range of the affected part. Cyanotic ecchymosis, swelling and local tenderness can be found in blood impairment type as well as Qi and blood impairment type.

3. Referred pain appears when the patient is breathing and speaking. If it is severe, the patient cannot lie in a supine position and turns or bends his body because of unbearable pain.

4. Negative thoracic extrusion test.

5. Evident swelling and pain can be seen in patients with rib fractures, or accompanied by grafted rib malformation, bloody sputum, dyspnea and positive thoracic extrusion test.

6. Chest X-ray examination shows semiluxation of costovertebral joints, solitary or crinose transverse fracture or oblique fracture. It also shows pneumothorax, pulmonary contusion, hemothorax, subcutaneous or mediastinal emphysema, etc.

7. Ruling out simple intercostal neuralgia, pristine thoracic herpes zoster, tuberculosis of thoracic vertebra, tumor, pleurisy and costal chondritis, etc.

【Treatment with Tuina therapy】

1. Therapeutic principles: Activating blood to expel stasis, promote Qi flow to stop pain, soothing tendons and rectifying the functions.

2. Location of Acupoints: Danzhong (CV 17), Zhongfu (LU 1), Yunmen (LU 2), Zhangmen (LR 13), Qimen (LR 14), Dabao (SP 21), Riyue (GB 24), Acupoints on the unrinary bladder meridian on the back, sternocostal part and shoulder on the affected side.

3. Manipulations:

(1) The patient takes a supine position, the doctor uses thumb pulp to press Danzhong (CV 17), Zhongfu (LU 1), Yunmen (LU 2), Zhangmen (LR 13), Qimen (LR 14), Dabao (SP 21) and Riyue (GB 24) for 10 seconds each to dredge the meridians, promote Qi flow to stop pain and relieve local pain; then uses the palm to knead the sternocostal part for 3~5 minutes, gradually increasing the strength to relieve spasm and pain.

(2) The patient takes a sitting position, the doctor uses his palm to rub the areas of the back corresponding to pain in the chest; then uses one finger pushing method to push the bladder meridians of foot-Taiyang on the affected side of the back from upwards and downwards for 3~5 minutes; then uses the thumb pulp to knead the corresponding bladder meridian Acupoints to promote Qi flow and relieve pain.

(3) The patient is required to take a sitting position, relax the muscles and not to hold the breath. The doctor stands at the lateral and back side of the patient, facing the patient, grasping the upper part of the affected shoulder with one hand, holding the lateral side of the shoulder with the other, then pulling up the shoulder with both hands to draw the affected shoulder. When the patient is breathing in, the doctor pulls up in a small range. Such a manipulation is helpful for reduction if there is subluxation of costovertebral joint or incarceration of synovium. After the manipulation, the shoulder of the patient should be slowly put down.

(4) If the reduction is successfully done, thoracic expanding and pulling manipulation or anti-pulling manipulation can be used.

(5) Rub the bladder meridian on the back and the affected areas till it becomes warm. Such a manipulation is effective for warming meridians and activating the collaterals.

【Cautions】

1. In acute stage, heavy manipulations of Tuina therapy and thermotherapy should be avoided lest bleeding or exudation be caused. At the same time pain killers can be taken to stop pain.

2. For the cases with small joint disorder of thoracic vertebrae, the manipulation for expanding and pulling the chest or anti-pulling manipulation can be used.

3. During the treatment, the patient should sleep on hard bed and avoid heavy physical work.

7.1.9 Shifted sacroiliac joint

Shifted sacroiliac joint is mainly caused by violence, such as sudden falling on the side of buttocks. If this happens, the force is conducted upwards from the sacroiliac joint, and the impacting force from the body is conducted downward through the sacroiliac joint. In this case, the two forces are combined at the sacroiliac joint, pushing the iliac bone upwards and inwards and staggering the joint. Similarly, sudden loading on one side of the lower limb, such as leaping, tumbling, can also cause shifted sacroiliac joint.

Shifted sacroiliac joint is also caused by sprain resulting from holding heavy objects in a squatting position, leaning the body forward, tumbling down forward or backward that may make the sacroiliac joint over rotate, and thus pushing the iliac bone inwards and upwards. Displacement and pain can be caused by sudden contraction of the rectus abdominis muscle, leading to forward rotation of articular surface of iliac bone on sacrum. Such a rotation may shift the sacroiliac joint in an abnormal position and cause pain.

Shifted joint may happen during pregnancy and after childbirth because of endocrine change, that may loosen the sacroiliac joint due to twisting, pulling, impacting and tumbling.

Severe shifted sacroiliac joint can cause laceration of the muscles and ligaments around, reduce the stability of the joint, increase the possibilities of shifting the joint with heavy load or movement. Mild shifted joint may recover automatically. If shifted sacroiliac joint is not properly or timely treated, local bleeding and scarring might fill in the space of the joint, eventually causing difficult reduction and unstable joint, and consequently leading to refractory pain in the lower part of the back.

This disorder is one of the commonly seen cause responsible for lumbocrural pain. Incidence of the disease in young people is high, especially in females. Improper treatment will inevitably lead to refractory pain in the lower part of the back.

【Clinical manifestations】

Most of the patients have the history of injury, pain in the lower part of the back, and lateral or bilateral pain in the sacroiliac joints. There is lateral or bilateral alternating pain like sciatica. Other symptoms include spasm around the sacroiliac joint, restricted movement of lower limbs, incapability of loading, walking with a stick or a limp. Bending, turning, or lying on the back may worsen the pain. So the patients can neither wear shoes or socks nor talk aloud and cough because these activities can increase the abdominal pressure and cause pain in the affected sacroiliac joint. There will appear ache, weakness, radiating pain or numbness in the lower limbs. The patient feels that his lower limbs are extended or shortened, and uses his hand to prevent his affected limb from being shaken. The patient has to move the affected limb first when walking upstairs or downstairs, and needs others to help him get up or lie down on the bed. Other symptoms are pale tongue, whitish and thin tongue coating, wiry and tense pulse.

Examination finds swelling of the sacroiliac joint protruding from the healthy side, tenderness and percussion pain in the affected inner inferior angle of the posterior inferior iliac spine. Sometimes clustered nodules can be found. Besides palpation of the bilateral posterior superior iliac spine finds convex or concave in the affected posterior superior iliac spine. Comparing test of the lower limbs is done to observe different length of calcar pedis. Some scholars think that it is significant for diagnosis if the difference is more than 0.3 cm. If the difference is over 1 cm, definite diagnosis can be made. Normally it should not be more than 2 cm. Usually the affected lower limbs are shortened with convex of posterior superior iliac spine and backward displacement. Otherwise, the affected lower limbs are extended with concave of posterior superior iliac spine and forward displacement. Pelvic separation test, "4" figure test and bed edge test are all positive.

X-ray examination: Normally it shows no obvious change. Slight widened or narrowed interstitial space of the affected sacroiliac joint, wagged pubic symphysis may be seen in some patients. In old cases, hyperosteogeny can be found on the upper and lower edges of the sacroiliac joint.

This disorder should be differentiated from sprain of cacroiliac joint, prolapse of lumbar intervertebral disc and sacroiliac tuberculosis.

【Treatment with Tuina therapy】

1. Therapeutic principles: Dredging meridian and releasing the adherence.

2. Location of Acupoints: Shenshu (BL 23), Dachangshu (BL 25), Chengshan (BL 57), Baliao, Zhibian (BL 52), Huantiao (GB 30), Weizhong (BL 40), dorsolumbar areas and sacroiliac joint.

3. Manipulations:

(1) The patient takes a prone position, the doctor uses rolling, pressing and kneading manipulations to treat the sacrospinalis sacroiliac joint and buttocks for 5 minutes, and then using the manipulations of thumb pressing, kneading and knocking with fingers to manipulate Baliao, Huantiao (GB 30), Zhibian (BL 52) till the patient feels distending and aching.

(2) For those with lower limb pain, pinching, grasping, pressing, kneading manipulations should be used on the thigh or shank. The affected area is rubbed till it is warm. Sometimes wet compress also can be used.

(3) Ways to adjust displacement due to anterior rotation: ①the patient is required to lie on the healthy side on the edge of the bed with the leg on the healthy side straightened, bend the knee and coax. The doctor fixes the body by holding the affected shoulder with one hand, holding the affected knee to press forward and downward to replace the displaced sacroiliac joint with the other hand through leverage. ②The patient is in a dorsal position, the doctor stands at the affected side to bend the hip and knee joints to its maximum limit, then quickly stretching the knee and leg for 3~5 times.

【Cautions】

1. The symptoms may be relieved right after Tuina treatment, but the patient cannot move his waist or lower limbs grossly in 2 weeks because the ligament of sacroiliac joint needs some time to recover.

2. The patient must rest in bed and keep warm during the treatment.

7.1.10 Piriformis syndrome

Piriformis syndrome refers to a series of symptoms caused by laceration, congestion, exudation, edema, adhesion, spasm of piriformis due to direct or indirect injury; or symptoms manifesting mainly as sciatica due to invasion of wind, cold and dampness, such as local inflammatory exudation, edema, increased tension, irritation, and pressure on the sciatic nerves through the muscle. It can be called piriformis injury syndrome or piriformis spasticity syndrome. Clinical symptoms include pain in the buttocks extending along the posterior aspect of the thigh, anteriolateral of the calf, lateral malleolus, dorsum and toes. This syndrome is often seen among young people.

Abnormal changes of piriformis is casued by invasion of wind, cold and dampness which result in spasm and thickening of piriformis, nonspecific local inflammatory exudation, edema, local increased tension, irritation, and pressure of the sciatic nerves through the muscle belly or common peroneal nerve, consequently leading to sciatica.

【Clinical manifestations】

The patient usually has a history of injury due to sudden exertion when abducting the lower limbs, sudden adduction of the hip under great load or sudden exertion of the hip when performing internal rotation. Some patients were also attacked by cold on the hip. Symptoms are pain in one side or both sides of the buttocks extending along posterior aspect of the thigh, anteriolateral of the calf, lateral malleolus, dorsum and toes. Aggravation of pain often results from lameness, long walk, fatigue and bad weather. Besides, increased abdominal pressure due to, cough, defecation and sneezing may also worsen the pain.

There is evident tenderness in the piriformis at the affected buttocks side, which can cause cord-like spasm of the piriformis and radiating pain in the lower limp on the same side under pressure. When the symptoms remain for quite a long time, the muscles on the hip may develop mild atrophy. When the patient raises his leg, pain is evident when the angle is within 60 degrees and relived when the angle is over 60 degrees. Test of piriformis tension appears positive and no abnormal change is found in the X-ray examination of the pelvis.

In TCM, this syndrome is a tendon disorder of gallbladder meridian of foot-Shaoyang. Injuries on the tendons of the bladder meridian may cause contraction of the meridian, eventually resulting in pain in the hip. Lingering pain may cause stagnation of Qi and blood, obstruction of tendons, tendon spasm and leg ache. Other symptoms are light red tongue, whitish or thin and whitish tongue coating, wiry and tense pulse.

【Essentials for diagnosis】

1. The patient has a history of injury or cold attack on the hip.

2. Pain in the affected side of the hip, stiff buttock and lameness.

3. Tenderness on piriformis of affected side with cord-like spasm and radiating pain in the same side .

4. X-ray examination shows no abnormal changes.

【Treatment with Tuina therapy】

1. Therapeutic principles: Soothing tendons and dredging collaterals, activating blood to stop pain.

2. Location of Acupoints: Shenshu (BL 23), Dachangshu (BL 25), Huantiao (GB 30), Zhibian (BL 52), Juliao (GB 29), Chengfu, Weizhong, Yanglingquan (GB 34), Zusanli (ST 36), Chengshan, the lumbar region and hip.

3. Manipulations:

(1) The patient is in a prone position and the doctor stands on the affected side of the patient, applying rolling, pressing and kneading manipulations mainly on the surface projected area of the piriformis, performing the manipulations slowly and deeply with mild force for 5 minutes.

(2) The patient is in a prone position. The doctor applies rolling, pressing and

kneading around lumbar region and the third lumbar transverse process of the affected side, performing kneading manipulation for 3~5 minutes and, at the same time, pressing Shenshu (BL 23) and Dachangshu (BL 25) to relieve soreness and tension of muscles until relief of the sensation of soreness.

(3) The patient is in a prone position. The doctor applies pressing, kneading and flicking with finger bellies of both hands vertically on the tip of the third lumbar transverse process, then performing flicking manipulation with gradual intensification of strength. Palm-twisting and kneading manipulations are also used at the same time to relieve spasm and pain and resolve adhesion.

(4) The patient is in a prone position. The doctor applies nipping, grasping, pressing and kneading manipulations along the posterior aspect of the thigh and anteriolateral of the calf, performing pressing and kneading manipulations for 3~5 minutes in combination with the manipulations of knocking with finger, pressing and flicking Huantiao (GB 30), Zhibian (BL 52), Weizhong (BL 40) and Chengshan (BL 57) to soothe tendons, unblock collaterals and activate blood to resolve stasis.

(5) The doctor applies pressing, kneading and flicking manipulations on the governor vessel and bladder meridian of foot-Taiyang for 3~5 minutes with the patient's waist leaning backward, then rubbing the governor vessel and bladder meridian of foot-Taiyang and belt vessel in combination with hot-wet compress until thorough hot sensation is felt in local area.

【Cautions】

1. The patient is advised to wear wide belt to protect his waist from further injury.

2. Excessive extension, flexion and rotation of the waist are forbidden during treatment.

3. The patient should keep local regions warm and avoid fatigue.

7.1.11 Lumbospinal myofascitis

Lumbospinal myofascitis, also called functional lumbago or lumbar muscle strain, is one of the chronic syndromes of lumbago and skelalgia. It is marked by chronic injury of soft tissues such as back muscles, fascia and ligament, resulting in local aseptic inflammation and diffuse pain in one side or both sides of the lumbodorsal region.

According to TCM, lumbar myofascitis is mainly caused by deficiency of kidney Qi. Under the attack of wind, cold and damp, symptoms like obstruction of meridians and collaterals, stagnation of qi and blood, malnutrition of tendons and muscles may develop, causing lumbodorsal pain. That is why this disorder is called lumbago due to deficiency of kidney Qi. This disease is often seen in young people, sometimes without evident history of injury, and is closely related to occupation and working environment.

【Clinical manifestations】

Lumbospinal myofascitis is caused by excessive lumbar muscle fatigue due to long-term bending or working, improper habitual postures or fixed body position, resulting in continuous traction of muscles, fascia and ligament, and leading to increased internal pressure of the muscles, blood circulation disorder, insufficient supply of oxygen and nutrients and accumulation of lactates due to non-oxygen metabolism. If metabolites cannot be cleared away immediately, it will accumulate and cause inflammation and adhesion. If such a state lasts for a long time, it will result in degeneration, thickening and contracture of tissues, stimulating relevant nerves and causing chronic back pain. It may be caused by acute injury of the of lumbar soft tissues without immediate or complete treatment, consequently leading to further injury, local fibrosis or hyperplasia of local scarred tissues complicated by microcirculatory disorder and accumulation of lactates which press and stimulate the nerves and cause chronic back pain. It may also be caused by congenital abnormality like dissymmetry of lumbar facet joints, congenital spinal bifida, lumbar sacralization or lumbarization of the sacral vertebrae, causing different activity at both sides of the lumbrosacral region and unstable spinal cord, and eventually resulting in lumbrosacral tissue strain.

Clinically, it is marked by pain in one side or both sides of the lumbrosacral region. Repeated occurrence of the disease may produce lingering distending pain or soreness, sometimes mild and sometimes severe. Rest, proper exercises or frequent change of fixed postures may relieve the symptoms, while tiredness and bad weather may aggravate the disease. The patient sometimes may suffer from hypoesthesia and prefer warmth to cold, and often pound his back with both hands to relieve discomfort. Usually the waist can move normally without evident dysfunction. Sometimes there appears the sign of discomfort. The patient should not sit or stand for a long time, or keep bending his waist at work. Long-term bending may result in difficulty in stretching the waist. Sudden occurrence of the disease may aggravate all the symptoms with evident spasm, scoliosis in the lumbar region and dragging pain in the lower limbs. Other symptoms are red tongue, sometimes with ecchymosis, thin tongue coating and rapid pulse.

【Essentials for diagnosis】

1. The patient may have a history of trauma and cold attack, or have no history of trauma, but have a history of strain.

2. Symptoms are soreness or distending pain in the back, characterized by repeated occurrence, sometimes mild and sometimes severe, and inconspicuous restriction of lumbar movement.

3. According to different location of strain, tenderness may be extensive, but not evident and no radiating pain. Tenderness is often present at dorsal sacroiliac joint, dorsal sacrum and the transverse process of lumbar vertebrae. In mild cases, tenderness is not evident; while in severe cases, tenderness is present with spasm in the sacrospinal muscle at one side or both sides.

4. Physiological curvature of vertebra may lessen or disappear. For patients who

have contracted the disease for quite a long time, muscular atrophy on one side or both sides of the lumbrosacral region is evident and nodular or stripe-like lesion may be present in the lumbrosacral region.

5. In acute cases, the patient may present increased muscular tension in one side or both sides of the lumbrosacral region and obvious scoliosis, together with varied dysfunction.

6. In some cases, X-ray examination shows congenital abnormality of lumbosacral vertebrae and some old patients may present degenerative changes of the vertebra.

[Treatment with Tuina therapy]

1. Therapeutic principles: Soothing tendons and unblocking collaterals, warming meridians to activate blood, relieving spasm to stop pain.

2. Location of Acupoints: Shenshu (BL 23), Yaoyangguan (GV 3), Dachangshu (BL 25), Baliao, Zhibian (BL 52), Weizhong (BL 40), Yanglingquan (GB 34), Chengshan (BL 57), Kunlun (BL 60), Taixi (KI 3), lumbrosacral region and hip.

3. Manipulations:

(1) The patient is in a prone position. The doctor applies continual deep and mild rolling manipulation with the palm or palm base on the bladder meridian of foot-Taiyang on both feet. Repeat the manipulation for 3 to 5 times, particularly on the affected sites for relaxing local muscles and relieving local pain.

(2) Pressing and kneading, with both thumbs or tips of the elbows, Shenshu (BL 23), Yaoyangguan (GV 3), Dachangshu (BL 25), Baliao, Zhibian (BL 52) on both sides of the spinal column, and Weizhong (BL 40), Yanglingquan (GB 34), Yanglingquan (GB 34), Chengshan (BL 57), Kunlun (BL 60) and Taixi (KI 3). Performing the manipulation on each point for about 10 seconds until sensation of soreness and distention is felt. Such a treatment can increase pain threshold and relieve spasm and pain.

(3) Flicking with the thumb on the sites of pain, spasm or nodes. Repeating the manipulation for 3 to 5 times to relieve adhesion, increasing pain threshold and relieving spasm and pain.

(4) The doctor closes both hands together along the radial border and then grasps manipulation the index and middle fingers on Yaoyan (EX-B 7) at both sides. Repeat the manipulation for 2 to 3 times to relieve adhesion of the lumbrosacral soft tissue.

(5) The doctor stands beside the patient's head and pushes with one hand or both hands on the bladder meridian of foot-Taiyang at both sides. Repeating the manipulation for 2 to 3 times with mild force to relax lumbrosacral muscles.

(6) The patient is in a lateral position and faces the doctor. The doctor obliquely pulls each side of the lumbar region. Then the patient changes into a supine position. The doctor helps the patient bend coax and knee and applies arc-pushing manipulation on the lumbar region, repeating the manipulation clockwise and counterclockwise respectively for 2 to 3 times, holding the knees and rolling the waist for 2 to 3 times to relieve

disorders of posterior lumbar joint and lumbosacral joint.

(7) The patient is in a prone position. The doctor applies to-and-fro rubbing manipulation with the palm on the bladder meridian vertically at both sides of the back and lumbosacral region horizontally until the patient feels hot all over the region.

(8) The doctor holds empty fists and knocks alternately on the patient's back and lumbosacral region, repeating the manipulation downward for 2 to 3 times and finishing the whole treatment.

【Cautions】

1. The patient should protect himself from accidents during treatment with wide belt.

2. The patient is advised to sleep on a plank bed to prevent the spinal column from distortion.

3. The patient should have enough sleep and keep warmth of the affected region, and also restrict sexual life.

7.1.12 Scapulohumeral periarthritis

Scapulohumeral periarthritis is a disorder marked by extensive adhesion caused by aseptic inflammation of the articular capsule and surrounding tissues, or characterized by extensive congestion, exudation, edema, thickening and adhesion of the surrounding ligaments, tendons and articular capsules due to acute and chronic injury of the shoulder, resulting in nonspecific inflammation and restricting movement of the shoulder. The disorder is also called frozen shoulder, or shoulder periarthritis, or shoulder adhesion, or omalgia. But usually it is called periarthritis of shoulder. Clinically, it is marked by pain around the shoulder, dysfunction of motion and muscular atrophy in the late stage of the disorder. Scapulohumeral periarthritis is usually present on one side, rarely on both sides. It is often seen among people around 50, particularly among physical laborers. The occurrence of the disorder is higher in women than in men.

In TCM, this disorder is also called coagulation of the shoulder (shoulder periarthritis)or shoulder leakage of wind (omalgia). Tendons are attached to joints and connected with the bone governed by the kidney. From middle age, people begin to decline in kidney Qi. The deficiency of kidney Qi fails to produce sufficient essence to nourish marrow, resulting in loose bones and joints and tendon flaccidity due to the fact that insufficient marrow fails to nourish the liver. It may be caused by excessive motion, or traumatic injury, or impairment of tendons and joints, stagnation of Qi and blood and spasm of tendons. If the disorder lasts for quite a long time, it will cause stiffness of tendons and muscles, or blood stasis due to stagnation of Qi and blood, or obstruction of Qi and blood circulation. Obstructed meridians and collaterals may result in pain and eventually cause shoulder periarthritis.

【Clinical manifestations】

The onset of the disorder is slow and gradual. In some cases the onset may be sudden. Generally speaking, the patient has a history of chronic shoulder strain or cold, wind and damp attack. In some cases, it may be caused by acute shoulder strain, dislocation of shoulder, bone fractures of the upper limb, or fixation after dislocation of the shoulder. The main symptoms are pain, restricted motion and muscular atrophy.

In the early stage, soreness and pain of the shoulder are evident due to weather change, fatigue or cold. The usual symptoms are local aversion to cold, stiffness and fear of motion. Later on the symptoms may become aggravated and result in continuous pain over the whole shoulder, radiating to the cervix and elbow. Painful sensation in the daytime is mild but severe during the night, disturbing sleep and making the patient afraid of lying on the affected side. Severe pain may happen when the shoulder is pulled and dragged.

Early dysfunction is usually caused by pain, while late dysfunction by joint adhesion. When joint adhesion is present, pain is relieved remarkably but active motion and passive motion are restricted, resulting in difficulty in combing hair, dressing up, taking off clothes, washing face, standing akimbo and picking things up. After the disorder has taken place for a long time, atrophy may occur in deltoid muscle and supraspinatus. The extent of atrophy is related to the duration of the disorder.

Extensive tenderness of varied extent may occur around the shoulder on Jianliao (TE 14), Jianyu(LI 15), Bingfeng (SI 12), Jianzhen (SI 9) and deltoid muscle. Movements of the shoulder like anteflexion, backward extension, abduction, adduction, inward rotation and outward rotation are all limited, particularly when raising arms and rotating inward to touch the back. For patients with long duration of the disorder, muscular atrophy of the shoulder and convex acromion may develop. X-ray examination is mainly used to see whether bone lesion has developed. In most patients there are no signs of abnormality. In some cases, postmenopausal osteoporosis and irregular shadow of calcification over the surrounding soft tissue may be observed. The patient may present symptoms of pale or light red tongue with whitish or thin and whitish tongue coating, taut and tense, or tense and choppy pulse.

【Essentials for diagnosis】

1. The onset of the disorder is slow. The patient has a history of cold attack and chronic strain on the shoulder.

2. Tenderness is extensive and pain sites change with joint motion.

3. Dyscinesia is evident, leading to limitation of motion in all directions.

4. Long duration of the disorder may develop into muscular relaxation, stiffness and atrophy.

【Treatment with Tuina therapy】

1. Therapeutic principles: Activating blood to dispel stasis, soothing tendons to unblock collaterals, and loosing adhesion.

2. Location of Acupoints: Jianjing (GB 21), Jianyu (LI 15), Jianzhen (TE 14),

Tianzhong (SI 11), Binao (LI 14), Quchi (LI 11), shoulder joint and deltoid muscle.

3. Manipulations:

(1) The patient is in a sitting position. The doctor raises the affected arm to an angle of 60 degree and then performs pressing, kneading, circular rubbing or one-finger pushing manipulations on anterior, lateral and posterior sides of the shoulder and the upper arm. The manipulation is often combined with the activities of abduction, backward extension and passive rotation of the affected arm and for about 5 minutes.

(2) Rressing and kneading Jianjing (GB 21), Jianliao (TE 14), Jianyu (LI 15), Jianzhen (SI 9), Tianzong (SI 11), Binao (LI 14) and Quchi (LI 11), about one minute for each. Then pressing, kneading, knocking with finger and flicking the anterior side of the shoulder, short head of biceps, infraspinous muscle, teres major muscle and musculus teres minor of the posterior shoulder. The manipulations should be done slowly and deeply with mild force for about 2 minutes.

(3) Apply rolling, pressing, kneading, knocking with finger and traction manipulations alternately on the scapular and posterior shoulder; apply grasping, nipping, pressing and kneading manipulations on Jianjing (GB 21) and deltoid muscle. Perform the above manipulations for about 5 minutes.

(4) The doctor holds the affected shoulder with one hand and supports the elbow of the affected side with the other, then swinging the arm circularly in a gradual increasing amplitude, or swinging the shoulder in a great amplitude for about 1 minute.

(5) The doctor stands right behind the affected shoulder, putting one hand under the armpit of the affected side and keeping the elbow flexed with the other hand, then raising the affected arm with one hand and pushing the elbow inward with the other to loosen joint adhesion and increase range of motion.

(6) Rubbing around the shoulder until hot sensation is achieved and from the shoulder to the forearm for 3 to 5 times. Finally abducting the affected shoulder to a 60 degree angle and vibrating the shoulder.

【Cautions】

1. The patient should keep the shoulder warm and avoid wind, cold and damp.

2. The patient should reduce body activity during acute onset of the disorder to prevent increased inflammatory exudation; whereas in adhesion term, the patient should keep doing exercises.

7.1.13 Lateral humeral epicondylitis

Lateral epicondylitis is caused by sprain or chronic strain of the carpal extensor tendon resulting mostly from rotation of the forearm with improper exertion, injuring the radial aspect of extensor muscle of the wrist of the forearm, causing nonspecific inflammation, stimulating the nerve ending and periost, and leading to a series of clinic symptoms. It is also named tennis elbow, syndrome of external epicondyle of humerus, or bursitis bicipitoradialis. The main symptoms in clinic are swollen humeral epicondyle, pain and restricted movement. It occurs more on the right side than on the left side and is seen most frequently among workers who often rotate the forearm.

When the forearm rotates forwards and the wrist joint stretches backward suddenly and violently, radial aspect of extensor muscle of the wrist will contract, pulling the tendon area and leading to acute injury. Long-term rotation of the forearm will make the muscle of the radial aspect of the wrist maintain in a strained and pulled status, consequently leading to chronic strain. The pathological changes may be caused by the following factors: laceration in the tendon area of the extensor muscle of the wrist; bleeding, swelling and hematoma under the periost of the tendon area of the extensor muscle of the wrist, which will lead to periostitis and increase tension of subperiost; traumatic inflammation of annular ligament or fibrositis; bursitis bicipitoradialis or inflammation caused by pressure on humeroradial articular synovium.

This disease belongs to the category of tendon and joint injuries in TCM, The exterior of elbow joint is connected with the large intestine meridian of hand-Yangming. The acute and chronic overstrain can affect the tendon of the large intestine meridian. It may be caused by invasion of wind, cold, and dampness into the tendons, leading to stagnation of Qi and blood, adherence of tendons, spasm and pain of joints as well as difficult flexion and extension.

[Clinical manifestations]

Acute onset is usually marked by obvious sprain or history of sprain, no obvious injury and slow progress. The main symptoms are pain in the lateral aspect of the affected elbow, referred pain along the extensor muscle of the wrist, weakness of the forearm in rotation and grasping. It will become worsened after fatigue or in rainy days. When the forearm rotates and the wrist stretches backward, or when the patient performs the activity of lifting, pulling, holding or pushing, the pain will become worsened, especially when twisting a towel. Other symptoms are reddish tongue with white thin tongue coating, wiry and choppy pulse.

There is a slight local swelling and tenderness in the external condyle of humerus, even a small synovial bursa. Different tenderness reflects different injury of tissues. The tenderness in external condyle of humerus indicates the injury at the beginning of extensor carpi radialis brevis musculus; tenderness in the upper part of external condyle of humerus indicates that the injury is at the beginning of extensor carpi radialis long musculus; tenderness near the small radial head may be the hint of annular ligament and radial collateral ligament injury. The extensor muscle tension test and Miil test are all positive. X-ray examination usually shows no abnormal changes. But in some patients, the external condyle of humerus appears unsmooth and the density increases.

[Essentials for diagnosis]

1. History of acute injury or chronic strain.

2. Pain or tenderness in the anterior region of the external humeral epicondyle, dragging sensation of aching and distending pain in the radial aspect of the forearm.

3. It is difficult for the patient to carry things. The pain will get worsened when twisting a towel.

4. Positive result in Miil test.

【Treatment with Tuina therapy】

1. Therapeutic principles: Activating the blood and resolving stasis, soothing tendons and unblocking collaterals.

2. Location of Acupoints: Quchi (LI 11), Quze (PC 3), Shousanli ((LI 10), Hegu (LI 4), the anterior region of the external humeral epicondyle, the muscles of the radial aspect of the forearm.

3. Manipulations:

(1) The patient takes a supine position or a sitting position. The doctor rolls from the radial aspect of the elbow to the radial aspect of the forearm, and pressing, kneading and knocking with the thumb, and plucking Quchi (LI 11), Shousanli (LI 10), Hegu (LI 4) for about five minutes, one minute for each Acupoint.

(2) The doctor uses one-finger pushing, pressing and pointing manipulations on the anterior region of the external humeral epicondyle, flicking alternatively for 5 minutes.

(3) The doctor presses the tenderness on the anterior region of the external humeral epicondyle with the thumb of one hand while holding the epicondyle region of the external humeral epicondyle with the other four fingers of the hand, holding the wrist with the other hand to pull and stretch to the opposite direction for a while; then bending the elbow joint slowly to make the forearm rotate until the elbow impossible to be bent any further. After that, the forearm is quickly extended and pulled backwards for 3 times in succession so as to tear the bursa synovialis to absorb effusion.

(4) Press and knead from the anterior region of the external humeral epicondyle to the radial aspect of the extensor muscle of the wrist with the thumb, then scrubbing from the radial aspect of the forearm to humeral epicondyle until it is warm in the local area.

【Cautions】

1. During the period of treatment, avoid rotation of the forearm and stretching backwards the wrist.

2. The local area should be kept warm.

7.1.14 Carpal tunnel syndrome

Carpal tunnel syndrome is a series of clinical symptoms caused by factors like wrist strain, direct trauma, wrist bone fractures, dislocation, malunion, hyperosteogeny, ligament hypertrophy, ganglion and adipoma which lead to increased pressure on the median nerve and flexor digitorium through the tunnel. Clinically, this disease is mainly characterized by numbness of three and a half fingers, paresthesia of sensation, carpal atony, frequent occurrence among middle-aged or old people, especially among females.

According to TCM, this disease results from the obstruction of Qi and blood circulation due to acute trauma or chronic strain, blood stasis in meridians and collaterals, or invasion of pathogenic cold, dampness and wind into the muscle.

[Clinical manifestations]

The onset of this disease is slow. Some patients have an acute or chronic injury history. The early symptoms are soreness and distension of the wrist, gradually developing into symptoms of median nerve pressure with signs of paresthesia, numbness and stabbing pain in the thumb, index finger, middle finger and ring finger (three and a half fingers at the radial side) that radiate to the elbows and shoulders. The symptoms are severe at night and in the morning; aggravated when the temperature of the hand increases and when the hand becomes tired and droops; alleviated after moving, swinging and lifting the hands. Fingers at the affected side may feel distending, stiff and cold with pale or cyanotic color. Other symptoms are thin white tongue, or light red, whitish or thin and whitish tongue coatings, taut and tense or tense and unsmooth pulse.

There is obvious tenderness in the carpal tunnel radiating to the fingers. Stabbing pain like electronic shock can be felt in the thumb, index finger, middle finger and ring finger (three and a half fingers at the radial side) when carpal tunnel is knocked. The symptoms become worsened in 40 seconds when the wrist bends into a 90 degree angle. In the advanced stage, the symptoms seen are thenar atrophy, numbness, reduced muscular tension, loss or impairment of sensation in the fingers, and dysfunction of palm opposing function. The degree of muscular atrophy is related to the course of disease. X-ray examination shows no abnormal changes, ruling out bone lesion.

[Essentials for diagnosis]

1. Carpal pain accompanied by pain and numbness of three and a half finger at the radial side.

2. Anomalous skin sensation in the distribution area of median nerve.

3. Stabbing and electronic shock numbness is felt when carpal tunnel is knocked.

4. The test of flexing wrist is positive.

[Treatment with Tuina therapy]

1. Therapeutic principles: Activating blood to eliminate swelling, soothing tendons and unblocking collaterals.

2. Location of Acupoints: Daling (PC 7), Neiguan (PC 6), Quze (PC 3), Yuji (LU 10) and wrist.

3. Manipulations:

(1) Pressing and kneading Daling (PC 7), Neiguan (PC 6), Quze (PC 3), carpal tunnel, 1 minute for each Acupoint till soreness and distension are felt; pressing and kneading Yuji (LU 10).

(2) Pressing and kneading carpal tunnel with the thumb, vertically flicking

towards the flexor digitorum, combined with the performance of wagging and pulling manipulations alternatively for about 5 minutes.

(3) Grasping, pressing, kneading from the forearm flexor muscle to the wrist with the carpal as the focus to relax muscles of forearm for about 5 minutes.

(4) The affected elbow is bent into a 45° angle. The doctor fixes the wrist of the affected limbs with one hand, and then pushes and kneads from the wrist to antebrachium flexor with the other to push the extravasation to the forearm muscles so as to relieve pressure inside the tunnel. Such a manipulation is performed for about 2 minutes.

(5) The patient is in a sitting position with his antebrachium in pronation and his dorsum of hand turned upwards. The doctor holds the palm side of the patient's hand with four fingers of both hands, puts his thumbs on the back of the wrist, pressing the space at the back of the wrist with the finger tip of the thumbs, pulling the wrist and swaging it at the same time. While pressing with the thumbs, the doctor extends the wrist back to the maximum range, immediately bending the wrist and wagging repeatedly several times for about 5 minutes. Then rubbing the wrist joint to finish the treatment.

【Cautions】

1. After each treatment, hot-wet compress may be applied to the local areas, twice a day.

2. Avoid over using the wrist during treatment.

3. Keep the wrist warm. Cuff may be employed if necessary.

7.1.15 Sprain of wrist joint

Sprain of wrist joint is caused when the wrist joint is impacted by direct or indirect external force, or rotates beyond the endurance of the wrist ligament and thus injures the ligament, tendon and articular capsule around the wrist. It should be distinguished from direct or indirect violent injury of the wrist joint which can easily cause wrist fracture. In clinic treatment, the main symptoms are pain and swelling around the wrist joint and limited functional activities. It can be seen among people at different age, especially among young people who are active.

TCM holds that this disease is caused by injury of tendons that leads to stagnation of Qi and blood. So it pertains to the category of bone dislocation and tendon displacement. The wrist joint, a joint abundant in both Qi and blood, is the beginning of three hand Yin meridians and Yang meridians. Both acute and chronic trauma of the wrist joint will lead to injury of tendons and joint, causing looseness and spasm of tendons, adherence or dislocation of joints, restricted activity and pain due to stagnation of Qi and blood.

【Clinical manifestations】

Usually the patient has a history of obvious injury, such as falling down with the palm hitting on the ground, wrist sprain while working or taking sports activity, carrying heavy objects, or overwork with the wrist for a long time. In mild cases, the wrist just appears not quite agile, but there is no distinct pain. However, there may be pain in the wrist when it moves in a large range. In severe cases, pain occurs right after being injured and the wrist cannot move. There appear varied swelling and subcutaneous ecchymoma in the wrist. At first it appears bluish, and then turns purple and yellow or khaki. Acute injury may cause evident limitation in activities, or make it impossible to take any activities. But chronic injury does show distinct limitation in activities, or just shows limitation in turning to a certain direction. The symptoms become worsened after fatigue or in rainy days.

The symptoms of pain, tenderness and activity limitation in the injured area are helpful for diagnosis.

1. Tenderness: The tenderness is usually seen at the radial aspect of dorsale radialcarpl ligament if it is the injury of ligamentum carpi dorsale; if the tenderness is at the palm side of the ligamentum carpi volare, it is the injury of the ligamentum carpi volare; if the tenderness is at the radial aspect of the nasopharyngeanl fossa, it is the injury of the radial collateral ligament; if the tenderness is at the small head of the ulna, it is the injury of the collateral ulnar ligament; if is the tenderness at the space of radioulnar joint and radial collateral aspect of wrist joint, it is the injury at the triquetral cartilages.

2. Restricted activities: The injury of the ligamentum carpi dorsale results in activity limitation because of the pain in flexing and stretching movement with the wrist and palm. The injury of the ligamentum carpi volare results in limited activity because of the pain in backward stretching movement. The injury of the radial paraligament results in limited activity because of the pain in ulnar flexion movement. The injury of the ulnar paraligament results in limited activity because of the pain in radial flexion. The injury at the triquetral cartilages bone results in limited activity because of the pain in inward rotation. Other symptoms are reddish tongue with thin and whitish tongue coating, taut and unsmooth or unsmooth and tense pulse.

X-ray examination is important to diagnose sprain of wrist joint. Usually, there is no evident change in X-ray examination if it is a simple sprain of wrist joint. If the signs of swelling and subcutaneous ecchymoma are distinct, X-ray examination can rule out fracture or dislocation. In clinical practice it must be distinguished from the fracture of the distal end of the radius and ulna, fracture of scaphoid, fracture or dislocation of lunate bone, avulsion fracture of the dorsum of triangular bone, and aseptic necrosis of navicular and lunate bone.

【Essentials for diagnosis】

1. History of acute or chronic injury.

2. There is pain in the wrist joint and the pain is located in the injured place.

3. Arthrocele, indistinct signs in chronic injury, evident swelling and distension in acute injury; subcutaneous ecchymoma.

4. Restricted movement and function of the wrist.

5. Ruling out fracture or dislocation with X-ray examination.

【Treatment with Tuina therapy】

1. Therapeutic principles: Soothing tendons and activating blood, expelling phlegm and unblocking collaterals.

2. Location of Acupoints: Waiguan (TE 15), Yangxi (LI 5), Yanggu (SI 5), Yangchi (TE 4), Hegu (LI 4), Taiyuan (LU 9), Shaohai (HT 3), Chize (LU 5), Quchi (LI 11), Shenmen (HT 7), Lieque (LU 7), Daling (PC 7), Wangu (SI 4), Tongli (HT 5) and the injured area. These Acupoints are selected according to the injured area.

3. Manipulations:

Tuina therapy can only be applied after ruling out fracture or dislocation with X-ray. In acute injury, if swelling and subcutaneous ecchymoma are distinct, Tuina therapy should be applied 24 to 48 hours after the injury.

(1) Sprain on the palm side of the wrist: Shaohai (HT 3), Tongli (HT 5), Shenmen (HT 7) and other Acupoints on the heart meridian can be used; for sprain on the radial aspect of the wrist, Chize (LU 5), Lieque (LU 7), Taiyuan (LU 9) and other Acupoints on the lung meridian can be used; for sprain on the back side of the radial aspect of the wrist, Yangxi (LI 5), Hegu (LI 4) and other Acupoints on the large intestine meridian can be used. Other related Acupoints can be used to treat the sprain of other regions. Pressing manipulation and pointing manipulation can be applied alternatively with proper strength until the patient feels aching, one minute for each Acupoint.

(2) The patient takes a sitting position. The doctor applies pressing, kneading and plucking manipulations on the injured area. The manipulation should be done mildly and gently for 5 minutes around the injured area first, and then over the injured area.

(3) Passive movement: dorsiflexion, palmar flexion, bending and circular movement to the left and right, extending and shaking the wrist in order to relieve spasm and adhesion and improve the function of the wrist. Such a manipulation is performed for 5 minutes.

(4) Scrubbing the injured area of the wrist joint for 2 minutes till warmth penetrates deep inside the muscles.

【Cautions】

1. For acute injury with subcutaneous hemorrhage, ice compress should be used first to prevent bleeding.

2. For the severe injury, X-ray should be used to rule out fracture and dislocation.

3. Keeping warm and protecting the wrist with cuff during treatment.

4. If the case is complicated with dislocation and avulsion fracture, it should be treated in the same way as that used to deal with dislocation and fracture. Fixation should be continued for 6~8 weeks or after clinical union of fracture. Tuina therapy can be considered to restore the function of the joint.

7.1.16 Strain of iliotibial tract

Strain of iliotibial tract, also called snapping hip, is caused by long-term friction between the posterior iliotibial tract or the costal margin of gluteus maximus and great trochanterfemoral trochanter of femurs, or the snapping during slipping by the thickening of the costal margin of gluteus maximus and hip joint in flexion and walking. It is often seen in women and is frequently appears unilateral, sometimes involving both sides.

This disease pertains to the category of joint injury in orthopedics in TCM. Bi (hip joint) is the Xu Qiao (empty orifice) and the key place for passage of Zhen Qi (genuine Qi), blood and collaterals. It is caused by acute and chronic injuries, the stagnation of Qi and blood, or the tension and relaxing of collaterals, joints, tendons, and muscles for the tension makes pain while the relaxing involves snapping.

【Clinical manifestations】

Usually there is no obvious history of trauma. The patient just feels discomfort on the hip. Snapping sound in hip will be heard when the patient takes initiative movement of flexion, adduction, abduction, or stretching. However it may not occur if the movement is passive. If the discharge from the great trochanter increases due to bursitis, the patient will feel pain at the posterior side of great trochanter, and the pain will spread to the lateral side of the thigh. The patient will also feel aching, swollen, heavy and weak. When palpated, hardness or nodules on the tissues of the places that snapping sound can be felt. When the hip joint flexes and extends, snapping sound can be heard and rubbing between the iliotibial tract and great trochanter can be felt. X-ray examination shows normal image. The snapping sound will be heard when the patient moves. So it makes the patient feel nervous. The symptoms of this disease are reddish tongue with whitish thin fur, moderate, or wiry and taut pulse.

【Essentials for diagnosis】

1. No history of acute or chronic trauma.

2. Snapping sound in hip.

3. No pain, no activity dysfunction.

4. X-ray test is normal.

【Treatment with Tuina therapy】

1. Therapeutic principles: Relaxing muscles and tendons, promoting blood circulation, and dredging the meridian.

2. Location of Acupoints: Juliao (GB 29), Huantiao (GB 30), Chengfu (BL 36), Fengshi (GB 31), Biguan (ST 31) and great trochanter.

3. Manipulation:

(1) Press and knead Juliao (GB 29), Huantiao (GB 30), Chengfu (BL 36), Fengshi (GB 31), Biguan (ST 31) with thumb for one minute each. Knead great trochanter of

femur with palm base for 3 minutes.

(2) The patient is in a prone position. The doctor stands by the affected side pinching, grasping, pressing and kneading along the greatest gluteal muscle and iliotibial tract. At the same time, the doctor may use the passive activities of backward extending and abducting the hip-joint to relax the local muscle. The time for manipulation is about 3 minutes.

(3) The patient is in a lateral position with the affected side upward. The tensor fasciae latae muscle and lateral side of the thigh are pressed, kneaded, knocked with finger and plucked for 5 minutes. Then flicking manipulation is performed vertically to the nodules over the great trochanter of femur for 3 minutes.

(4) The patient is in a supine position. The doctor holds the knee of the affected side with one hand, and holds the lower end of the calf of the affected side with the other hand to flex the knee and hip for 10 to 15 times. Then palm-twisting manipulation is performed from upper end of the thigh to the knee. The manipulation should be repeated for 3 minutes.

(5) After application of the treatment mentioned above, the doctor rubs from the nodules to the lateral side of the thigh for 3 minutes until it is warm in the local area.

【Cautions】

1. Explain what this disease is to the patient to release the patient's pressure.
2. The local area should be kept warm in order not to catch cold.
3. Excessive activities of the hip, such as long time walking, should be avoided.

7.1.17 Osteoarthritis of knee joint

Osteoarthritis of knee joint is a kind of imbalanced and dysfunctional arthritis caused by the non-inflammatory and degenerative affection, such as hyperosteogeny or abrasion in tibial-femoral joint or patellofemoral joint, instead of soft tissue trouble. This disease is also called degenerative arthritis, osteoarthritis, hypertrophic arthritis, or senile gonarthritis. Major clinical symptoms are arthralgia, limited movement and joint deformity. The aged, especially women and obese people, are easy to be affected by it.

The cause of this disease is not clear now. Generally speaking, chronic accumulated injuries, mechanical traction and stimulation are believed to be the major causes. Since it is a senile disease, some people suppose that metabolism contributes to it. Etiologically, there are two kinds of osteoarthritis, primary and secondary. Primary osteoarthritis has something to do with aging. As one becomes older, hyperosteogeny results from degenerative connective tissues and wears cartilages. Secondary osteoarthritis is a result of cartilages damage caused by wound or malformation.

When the knee joint moves, hyperplasia stimulates joint contents or joint plate, and thus causing pain. Hyperplasia narrows the clearance joint. The exudation of synovia, caused by nonspecific inflammation, increases the pressure within the joint and results in swelling, fibrotic thickening of joint capsule as well as synovialis hypertrophy. After some time, the synovia decreases, the clearance becomes dry, attrition increases and cartilage of patella gets cracked as well as denudated. All the above factors may excite veins and nerves. As a result, the symptoms get worse and the muscles around the joint become adhesive and atrophic, consequently leading to inability to move.

Osteoarthritis is one of the bone obstruction diseases in TCM. The knee joint is the key place for tendons meeting and abundant in Qi and blood. The aging and weakness are usually accompanied by the deficiency of liver and kidney, and the disharmony of Qi and blood. So carelessness in movement may cause injury or give rise to invasion of wind cold or dampness into the knees, consequently leading to obstruction syndrome, swelling and pain. Looseness of bones will lead to spasm of tendons and joints.

[Clinical manifestations]

Osteoarthritis is a senile disease. It develops slowly and most patients have the records of knee joints injury because of overuse. At first, the knee joint becomes weak, then there appears aching sensation on one side while walking, eventually both sides are involved. The pain is either on the left or right, mild or serious. It may occur alternatively in both sides. When a patient changes his body position, such as getting up from bed, standing up from seat or going up or down stairs, the pain will be worsened. The pain may be improved after mild movement. But excessive movement will worsen the pain. With the development of disease, even a short walk will cause pain and the duration of pain gradually extends. The feeling of pain also changes into distending pain, stabbing pain and vague pain. There is stabbing pain inside the joint when the patient gets upstairs or downstairs. The tongue of the patient is slightly white or red, the coating is light whitish, and the pulse is unsmooth, taut and tense.

The knee joint is getting stiff and cannot straighten and bend freely, cracking while moving. There is obvious exudation. Both sides of the knee appear full and there is synovia in the knee cap. If the problem is severe, the knee will become stiff and cannot bend. In some cases, the knee fails to function well and part of the function has to be supplemented by the hip and ankle joints, and thus leading to disorders of the hip and ankle joints.

In tibial-femoral joint inflammation, there will appear tenderness in the sides of the knee and popliteal fossa. In patellofemoral joint inflammation, there is tenderness at the border of the patella and friction sound inside the patella. Also the floating patella test is positive. The femoral quadriceps become atrophic. ①Lab test: ESR is normal, ASO test and Rf are negative. ②X-ray examination: the middle apophysis of tibial condyle is noticeable; there is hyperosteogeny around the edge of the knee cap; the clearance between knee joints becomes narrow; and there is shadow of calcified ligament.

[Essentials for diagnosis]

1. Osteoarthritis is a senile disease. It develops slowly and most patients have a

history of knee joint injury due to overuse.

2. There is twinge inside the knee joint, especially when going up or down stairs.

3. Knee joint cannot move freely, there is friction inside the joint and the muscle becomes atrophic.

4. X-ray examination shows hyperosteogeny and obvious joint clearance narrowing.

5. Lab test is done to rule out rheumatism.

【Treatment with Tuina therapy】

1. Therapeutic principles: Soothing meridians to activate blood; relieving spasm to stop pain; smoothing joint.

2. Location of Acupoints: Dubi (ST 35), Xiyan (EX-LE 5), Heding (EX-LE 2), Xuehai (SP 10), Liangqiu (ST 34), Fengshi (GB 31), Weizhong, Yanglingquan (GB 34), Yinlingquan (SP 9), Chengshan (BL 57), the round of knee cap.

3. Manipulations:

(1) The patient takes in a supine position while doctor stands by, pinching, grasping, pressing, kneading repeatedly from the quadriceps femoris to the knee cap and both sides of knee cap, specially the two sides of the knee cap, then pressing and kneading the lateral side of calf for about 5 minutes.

(2) According to obvious tenderness, selectively pressing and kneading Dubi (ST 35), Xiyan(EX-LE 5), Heding (EX-LE 2), Xuehai (SP 10), Liangqiu (ST 34), Weizhong, Yanglingquan (GB 34), Yinlingquan (SP 9) or Chengshan (BL 57), 1 minute for each.

(3) The patient takes a prone position and the doctor stands by the affected side, pinching, grasping, pressing and kneading repeatedly the back of knee, the bottom of thigh and the top of calf. The key point is the back of knee, Weizhong (BL 40), and the knee joint should be straightened and bent during performance of manipulation. Finally Weizhong (BL 40) and Chengshan (BL 57) are pressed for about 5 minutes.

(4) The patient takes a prone position and flexes the knee to an angle of 45 degrees. The doctor presses and kneads the Xiyan (EX-LE 5) on both sides repeatedly, pushing with the thumb towards the ligament of knee cap. Then the doctor pushes the right Xiyan (EX-LE 5) with the right and the left Xiyan (EX-LE 5) with the left hand and, at the same time, pressing and kneading the edge around the knee cap and clearance with thumb or palm. While performing the manipulation, the doctor should pull the knee cap to expose the affected part. For example, when pressing and kneading the inner side of knee cap, the doctor should pull the cap inward; when pressing and kneading the lateral side of knee cap, the doctor should pull the cap outward; when pressing and kneading the lower part of knee cap, the doctor should pull the cap downward. In this way, the affected part can be exposed completely and the doctor can treat it more directly and effectively.

(5) The doctor rubs the sides of knee joint, the edge of knee cap and clearance until warm sensation is felt. Finally the doctor kneads and shakes the joint to end the treatment.

【Cautions】

1. Always keep the knee joint warm and foment with warm water about 45~50 degrees.

2. Take a rest and reduce the movement of knee joint when symptoms of pain and swelling appear.

3. Avoid heavy load to relieve the burden of the knee.

4. Exercise the knee regularly to prevent atrophy and adhesion.

5. Knead knee joint twice a day.

7.1.18 Injury of the collateral ligament of knee joint

Injury of collateral ligament of knee joint, including injury of tibia collateral ligament and fibular collateral ligament due to sudden valgus and varus stress, can be classified into three categories, partial laceration, complete breaking, embined knee meniscus or cruciate ligament. Serious cases may be accompanied by avulsion fracture. Clinically, it is characterized by collateral pain, blood stasis, swelling and limited activity.

1. Injury of tibia collateral ligament

The injury of tibia collateral ligament refers to mild valgus change of the knee joint physiologically when bent (about 130~150°) with poor stability. The attack on the knee joint is exogenous, making the leg suddenly turned externally and rotated externally, or causing sudden eversion and extorsion of the thigh when the foot is fixed, consequently injuring the collateral ligament of the knee joint. If the injury is worsened, it may even cause partial laceration and complete rupture.

Ligament injury will inevitably cause swelling and hemorrhage from the local capillaries. Ligament laceration is always found on the point of ligament attachment. Complete breaking is often complicated by laceration of meniscus and joint capsule and avulsion fracture of the medial condyle of the femur and tibia.

2. Injury of fibular collateral ligament

When the knee joint is bent in a semiflexed position, the fibular collateral ligament becomes loose with poor stability. When the thigh makes a sudden adduction and intorsion or makes a over external rotation, the knee joint will suddenly rotate internally, and consequently causing injury of fibular collateral ligament and laceration after a sudden traction. Or it may be caused by unsmooth ground when running and jumping, resulting in injury of the foot , excessive internal rotation of the knee joint and injury of the fibular collateral ligament. Besides, direct violence on the fibular collateral ligament also can cause the injury.

Injury of fibular ligament is either partial laceration and complete fragmentation. The latter usually is located in the capsule and the junction of muscular tendon and muscular fiber. If it is severe, cruciate ligament injury can be caused. When ligament laceration occurs in the fibular head, it can be accompanied by avulsion fracture, or even injury or pressure on the common personeal nerve when it is severe.

In clinical treatment, injury of tibial collateral ligament is frequently seen, usually caused by traumatic injury.

The knee is the meeting place of all tendons. Its interior part is the place where the tendons of three Yin meridians converge while the exterior is the region connected with the tendons of gallbladder meridian and stomach meridian. So acute and chronic sprain or injury of tendons and stagnation of Qi and blood will lead to muscular spasm and unsmooth flexion and extension, causing swelling and pain in the local area.

【Clinical manifestations】

The patient has a history of trauma. Pain appears in the affected side immediately after injury. Those with slight injury can move with foot tip or walk with a limp without obvious local swelling; those with severe injury cannot move with obvious local swelling and limited flexion and extension. Subcutaneous ecchymosis appears 2~3 days after injury and the size and degree of ecchymosis are related to the amount of bleeding. The color of ecchymosis appears bluish or cyanotic first, turns purplish and yellow after 5~7 days, and eventually changes into khaki yellow color. Then the swelling begins to abate and blood stasis is gradually absorbed. Other symptoms are lightly red tongue, whitish or thin and whitish tongue coating, wiry or taut and tense pulse.

Examination:

Injury of tibial collateral ligament: The tenderness is obvious in the medial side of the knee joint and usually located at the attaching point of femoral collateral ligament. The pain in the median side of the knee joint becomes worsened in lateral movement test. When the tibial collateral ligament is completely fragmented, the space of the fragmented ligament can be felt. The stretching and closing motions can be felt in lateral movement test. X-ray examination shows that there are no significant signs of partial laceration while the joint space becomes wider when the ligament is completely fragmented. If there is avulsion fracture, small pieces of bone can be seen. If there is injury of meniscus, CT or arthrography should be taken for diagnosis.

Injury of fibular collateral ligament: Tenderness is obvious in the lateral side of the knee joint and the tenderness is usually located in the point of lateral condyle of femur and small fibular head. The pain in the lateral side of the knee joint becomes severe in lateral movement test. Feelings of stretching and closing in the lateral side of the joint can be felt in lateral movement test. X-ray examination shows that there are no significant signs of partial laceration and the joint space becomes wider when the knee joint is in varus position. If it is complicated by avulsion fracture, small pieces of the small fibial head can be seen.

【Essentials for diagnosis】

1. Obvious history of knee joint injury.
2. Pain in the medial or lateral knee joint with the obvious tenderness in the affected

region.

3. Limited joint movement with worsened pain when knee joint extends.

4. Lateral movement test is positive.

5. X-ray examination shows that the articular space becomes wider while small pieces of bone can be seen in avulsion fractures.

【Treatment with Tuina therapy】

1. Therapeutic principles: Activating blood and dispelling stasis, dispersing swelling to stop pain, soothing tendons and dredging collaterals.

2. Location of Acupoints: Injury of tibial collateral ligament: Xuehai (SP 10), Ququan(LR 8), Yinlingquan (SP 9), Xiyan (EX-LE5), and the medial of knee joint. Injury of fibular collateral ligament: Xiyangguan (GB 33), Yanglingquan (GB 34), Dubi (ST 35), Liangqiu (ST 34) and the lateral side of the knee joint.

3. Manipulations:

Injury of tibia collateral ligament:

(1) The patient is in a supine position with the affected limb externally rotated and extended. The doctor applies grasping, pressing and kneading manipulations on the medial side of the thigh and knee repetitively, then pressing and kneading along the medial condyle of femurs to the medial condyle of tibia. The manipulations should be performed lightly and softly on the peripheral area of the injury first, and then on the affected area for about 10 minutes. Violent force should be avoided.

(2) Apply pressing and kneading manipulations with thumb on Xuehai (SP 10), Ququan (LR 8), Yinlingquan (SP 9) and Xiyan (EX-LE5) for 1 minute each.

(3) Apply pressing, kneading and flicking manipulations along the vertical direction of the ligament fibers to soothe the tendons combined with passive flexion and extension for about 3 minutes.

(4) Apply palm-rubbing manipulation on the affected area and rubbing manipulation along the direction of the ligament fibers to warm the deep region. Finally the knee joint is rubbed to accomplish the treatment. This manipulation is performed for about 3 minutes.

Injury of fibular collateral ligament:

(1) The patient lies on the healthy side with the affected limb slightly bent. The doctor applies pinching, grasping, pressing and kneading manipulations along the lateral side of the thigh and the shank. Then palm pressing and kneading manipulations are performed along the lateral condyle of femurs to the fibular head. The manipulations should be performed lightly and softly over the peripheral area first, and then over the local area for about 10 minutes. Violent force should be avoided.

(2) Pressing and kneading Yanglingquan (GB 34), Dubi (ST 35) and Liangqiu (ST 34) with the thumb for 1 minute each.

(3) Pressing, kneading and flicking along the vertical direction of the ligament fibers

with the thumb to soothe the tendons in combination with passive flexion and extension for about 3 minutes.

(4) Rubbing the affected region with the palm, and then rubbing along the direction of the ligament fibers till deep warmth is felt, and finally kneading the knee joint to finish the treatment. This manipulation is performed for about 3 minutes.

【Cautions】

1. Acute injury with bleeding and swelling should be treated with Tuina manipulations only 24~48 hours after injury according to the state of bleeding. Immediate application of ice compress is necessary when injury is caused.

2. In severe cases, X-ray examination is necessary to exclude bone fractures and complete fragmentation before application of Tuina manipulations.

3. Apply wet and hot compress after application of Tuina manipulations to accelerate the absorption of stasis and swelling.

4. To prevent the quadriceps femoris muscle from atrophy, exercise for training quadriceps femoris muscle in a supine position should be taken twice a day and 5 minute each.

5. To restore the function of knee joint, exercise for active flexion and extension of the knee joint as well as straightening and extending the leg in a supine position should be taken twice a day and 3 minute each.

7.1.19 Contusion and sprain of ankle joint

Contusion and sprain of ankle joint includes medial collateral ligament injury and lateral ligament injury. It refers to sudden onset of ankle joint damage which makes foot introrsus or valgus. This injury can be divided into partial incarceration, full fragmentation and avulsion fracture. The main clinical manifestations are pain of ankle joint, stasis, swelling and restricted movement.

1. Lateral ligament injury of ankle joint

There are three causes of lateral ligament injury of ankle joint: 1) Lateral malleolus is longer than medial malleolus and lateral ligament is weak, frequently leading to introversion; 2) the muscles responsible for valgus and dorsiflexion movement of foot (the third peroneal muscle) are not as strong as the ones responsible for introversion movement of the foot (anterior tibial); 3) the ankle joint is not firm, the fibers of ligament between the tibia and fibula slant laterally and inferiorly, and the articular surface of lateral malleolus appears oblique, making it easy for the lower part of fibia to move upward and outward. It also can be caused by injury of lateral ligament under strong tension due to sudden change of foot from dorsiflexion to introversion because of falling down when walking on uneven ground or going downstairs. In mild cases, periosteal laceration of ligament attachment and periosteal hemorrhage will be caused. In severe cases, partial or complete laceration of ligament will be caused, often accompanied by avulsion fracture and talar subluxation.

2. Medial collateral ligament injury of ankle joint

The main cause is sudden valgus change of ankle joint. If a person cannot stop stably when running or jumping and leans his body inward, he will inevitably sprain the lateral side of this ankle joint and lacerate the medial collateral ligament. If the eversion is continuously intensified, the medial collateral ligament will be avulsed, the inferior tibiofibular syndesmosis will be lacerated, or the lower part of tibia and fibula will be separated, or avulsion fractures of tibial side of the ankle will be caused.

Lateral collateral ligament is very common, especially among sportsmen.

Ankle is the pivot of foot where the three Yin and three Yang meridians of foot gather. Improper movement and overstretching often cause sprain and avulsion, leading to tendons of the Yang meridians loose and tendons of the Yin meridians spasmodic, extravasation of Qi and blood as well as stasis and swelling, restricted movement and pain.

[Clinical manifestations]

The patient has a history of injury. There will be pain and swelling in the affected side. In mild cases, the patient walks with a limp with mild local swelling; in severe cases, the patient cannot move with obvious local swelling, and restricted movement of the ankle joint. Ecchymosis will appear in two or three days after injury. If it is serious, ecchymosis can spread to the opposite side. The degree and size of ecchymosis has something to do with the degree of injury and the amount of hemorrhage. It appears bluish and purplish at first, turning purplish and yellowish five or seven days later, eventually changing into brown and yellow color. Then the tumefaction begins to abate and stasis of blood starts to be absorbed. The color of ecchymosis is important for deciding the duration of injury. Since ankle joint sprain is caused by stagnation of blood and Qi, the tongue is lightly reddish with thin and whitish coating and the pulse is taut or tense.

Injury of lateral ligament: There is obvious tenderness under the anterior part of the lateral malleolus where the anterior talus and fibula ligament is located, so it is also called injury of anterior talus and fibula ligament. Introversion will make the pain aggravated. When both of the anterior or middle talus and fibular ligaments are broken, a sense of opening and closing can be felt during the lateral movement test. When the lateral malleolus is avulsed, fragments of bone can be touched. X-ray test can make it certain if there is fracture and dislocation. If the ligament is broken, picture of forceful introversion position can reveal that the angle between the lower articular surface of tibia and upper articular surface is over 15°.

Injury of medial collateral ligament: There is obvious tenderness under the medial malleolus where the lower tibia and fibula ligaments are located. Valgus movement will make the pain aggravated. When the medial malleolus is avulsed, the fragments of bones can be touched. X-ray test can show whether there is fracture and dislocation. If the ligament is broken, the length between the lateral and medial ankles becomes broader than usual.

【Essentials for diagnosis】

1. There is obvious history of contusion and sprain.

2. The main clinical manifestations are ankle joint pain, swelling and tenderness in the injured area.

3. Joint movement is restricted and the pain will be aggravated when repeating the process of injury.

4. Exclude fracture and dislocation through X-ray test.

【Treatment with Tuina therapy】

1. Therapeutic principles: Eliminating swelling to stop pain, activating blood to eliminate stasis, dredging tendon and meridian.

2. Location of Acupoints: Lateral ligament injury: Zusanli (ST 36), Yanglingquan (GB 34), Jiexi (ST 41), Qiuxu (GB 40), Shenmai (BL 62), Jinmen (BL 63), anterior and inferior part of lateral malleolus. Medial collateral ligament injury: Sanyinjiao (SP 6), Shangqiu, Zhaohai (KI 6), Taixi (KI 3), inferior part of medial malleolus.

3. Manipulations:

Lateral ligament injury:

(1) The patient takes a supine position. The doctor applies pinching grasping, pressing and kneading manipulations from the leg to lateral malleolus repeatedly for about 5 minutes.

(2) Pressing and kneading with thumb or major thenar around the injured area anterior and inferior to the lateral malleolus; and then pressing and kneading the injured area with force for about 5 minutes. The manipulations should be performed mildly and softly.

(3) Applying pressing, kneading, knocking, pulling and one-finger pushing manipulations on Zusanli (ST 36), Yanglingquan (GB 34), Jiexi (ST 41), Qiuxu (GB 40), Shenmai (BL 62), Jinmen (BL 63), one minute for each point.

(4) The doctor uses one hand to hold the heel of the affected joint and the other hand to pull the toes for a while. During the process of pulling, the doctor should rotate the ankle joint gently and then perform introversion and valgus movement.

(5) Finally, the doctor uses backward and forward rubbing manipulation to treat the injured area until it is warm in the local region and then pushes the area up and down for about 5 minutes.

Medial collateral ligament injury:

(1) The patient lies on the healthy side with the affected limb straightened and the healthy limb flexed. The doctor applies pushing and pressing manipulations from the medial side of the leg and the medial malleolus down to the foot repeatedly for about 5

minutes.

(2) Apply pressing and kneading manipulations around the injured area. After the pain is relieved, apply pressing, kneading and knocking manipulations on the injured area gently for about 3 minutes.

(3) Apply pressing, kneading and one-finger pushing manipulations on Sanyinjiao (SP 6), Shangqiu, Zhaohai (KI 6), Taixi (KI 3), one minute for each point.

(4) Apply pulling and shaking manipulations. The doctor holds the heel of the affected leg with one hand and grasps the toes with the other to pull for a while. During the process of pulling, the doctor should rotate the ankle joint gently and perform introversion and valgus movement.

(5) Finally, apply backward and forward rubbing manipulation on the injured area until it is warm in the local area and then push the area up and down for about 2 minutes.

[Cautions]

1. If the injury is acute with tumefaction, Tuina therapy should be applied 24~48 hours later according to the state of hemorrhage. Ice application should be taken immediately after injury.

2. If it is serious, X-ray examination should be taken. Only when fracture and ligament fragmentation are excluded can Tuina therapy be applied.

3. During the acute period, the foot should be fixed to relax and the affected limb should be raised to abate swelling.

4. During the convalescence period, the patient is encouraged to do more exercises to flex and stretch the knee joint and ankle joint twice a day and 3 minutes a time, revolving the ankle joint clockwise and counter-clockwise respectively twice a day, and 3 minutes a time.

7.1.20 Dysfunction syndrome of the temporomandibular joint

The disturbance syndrome of temporomandibular joint, also called "snapping jaw" or snapping in the joint, is caused by the pathologic change of the surrounding capsule of temporomandibular joint, articular disk, ligament and muscle, or the joint itself. There is a series of syndromes, such as pain of the joint, snapping and inability to move. The pathologic factors of disturbance syndrome of temporomandibular joint have not been fully revealed. It is probably caused by violent hit, preference for hard food, asymmetrical development of joints, invasion of cold, periarthritis, frequent chewing at one side of the mouth and grinding the teeth or long time opening the mouth.

This syndrome often occurs in one side of the temporomandibular joints, occasionally involving both sides of the mouth, usually seen among people 20~40 years old.

[Clinical manifestations]

The patients of the disturbance syndrome of temporomandibular joint usually have the history of trauma or cold attack. It may be related to overexcitement or over restriction of the muscle around the joint, the disorder of occlusion and joint congenital deformity. The main clinical manifestation is the temporomandibular joint snapping, often caused by thickness due to articular disk spraining, folding or laceration. During movement, there is friction between articular tubercle and head of mandible, causing snapping which then results in uncomfortable feeling or pain. Sometimes snapping occurs during the beginning of opening and the end of closed entry while some occurs at the end of opening and the first stage of closed entry. The patient with joint cartilage and bone destruction will have continuous sound like breaking glass and paper during closed entry. The pain around the temporomandibular joint is not serious, just like aching.. The movement of chewing, opening mouth or forward mandibular extension will cause pain. In some cases, spasm of jaw-closing muscles may be found. Abnormal opening movement or restricted opening of mouth due to the pain may occur in some cases. In some other cases, over opening of the mouth is caused by looseness of ligament and capsule and over activity of lateral pterygoid muscle. Sometimes difficulty in opening the mouth is caused by half dropping of the temporomandibular joint. In some patients, lockjaw is caused by spasm of chewing muscles. Deviated opening of the mouth is caused by disorder of the temporomandibular joint. In some patients, symptoms of hearing problem, vertigo, headache and radiating pain may be caused by stimulation or pressure of auriculotemporal nerves and chorda tympani nerve by mandibular chondyle. And there are also some other symptoms caused by external pathogenic factor or trauma, such as reddish tongue or tongue with ecchymosis, or tongue with mild coating, thin and taut pulse.

[Essentials for diagnosis]

1. History of the impairment of temporomandibular joint or congenital dysfunction.

2. Abnormal facial looking due to long-term abnormity of the temporomandibular joint or habit of chewing with one side that lead to asymmetry of face and difficulty to gnash teeth.

3. Tenderness in one side or both sides of temporomandibular joint which may be found in sigmoid notch and the back of jaw nodular, or in the back part of the temporomandibular joint or articular tubercle and anterior of mandibular condyle.

4. Temporomandibular joint snapping when chewing or opening the mouth.

5. Difficulty to open the mouth or disturbance in opening the mouth. If one side is limited, the mandible will deviate to the affected side; if both sides are limited, the mandible will not deviate or just deviate to the side seriously limited.

6. X-ray examination shows congenital deformity, the temporomandibular joint devolution or semiluxation. It also can distinguish joint fracture, the degree of luxation and temporomandibular joint problems.

[Treatment with Tuina therapy]

1. Therapeutic principles: Soothing tendons to activate blood and adjusting tendons for reduction.

2. Acupoints and location: Shangguan (GB 3), Xiaguan (ST 7), Yifeng (TE 17), Jiache (ST 6), Hegu (LI 4) and one side or both sides of the temporomandibular joint.

3. Manipulations:

(1) The patient takes a sitting or supine position to get the affected side upward. The doctor presses Shangguan (GB 3), Xiaguan (ST 7), Yifeng (TE 17), Jiache (ST 6) and Hegu (LI 4) of the affected side for 10 minutes respectively to relieve the spasm and pain in the local area.

(2) The doctor uses finger-rubbing manipulationmajor thenar rubbing manipulation to knead around the temporomandibular joint and slowly move to the centre with gradual intensification of force. The purpose of such a manipulation is to relax local muscle and prepare for the next treatment. Such a manipulation is often performed for about 2~3 minutes.

(3) When the doctor uses finger pressing, kneading and one-finger pushing methods to knead the muscle and the temporomandibular joint, the patient is asked to close his mouth to make the masseter relaxed. When pressing on the capsule, the patient is asked to open the mouth to make the mandibular articulation open slightly for the convenience of performing manipulation, driving the strength to penetrate deep, smoothing meridians, activating collaterals and stopping pain. It lasts for about 3~5 minutes.

(4) The patient, with deviation of the mandible to the healthy side and abnormal occlusion of joint, takes a sitting position. The doctor stands behind the patient, using the thenar of one palm to press the patient's temple and mandibular condyle at the affected part while the other palm to press the mandible on the healthy side to make the patient open and close the mouth. Meanwhile, the doctor presses from the opposite direction with both hands to normalize occlusion. The duration is decided according to the patient's condition.

(5) The doctor uses finger rubbing manipulation to rub the temporomandibular joint slightly to regulate local the meridian Qi to relax the patient. It may last for 2~3 minutes.

(6) The patient with semiluxation of temporomandibular joint can be treated by reduction manipulation: The patient takes a sitting position while the doctor puts both thumbs on the patient's cheeks, other fingers pressing the inferior boarder of the mandible with slightly to drive the head of mandible to return to the articular fossa. If it is ineffective, the doctor can put the middle and index finger coated with antiseptic gauze of one hand into the mouth cavity to fix the inferior dental arch while the thumb on the bottom of the mandible holds the mandible and shakes it. Meanwhile, the doctor uses the other thumb to rub and knead the mandible for one minute, and then, asks the patient to open his mouth widely. Then the index and middle fingers in the mouth cavity press

down forcefully. After that, the doctor may take the fingers out of mouth quickly while the palm supports the mandible, lifting it posteriorly backwards and asking the patient to close the mouth. At this moment, the thumb pressing on the mandibular condyle pushes and presses it posteriorly backwards for reduction.

【Cautions】

1. To use reduction manipulation to treat the temporomandibular joint, cares should be taken to select proper manipulation. After reduction, a certain period of time is needed to loosen the mandible for taking food and treatment. Then measures should be taken to prevent re-dislocation. However, fixation should not be maintained for a long time.

2. Uncooked, cool, and hard food is forbidden, avoiding stimulation of the temporomandibular joint.

3. Keep the face warm and avoid cold stimulation.

4. Rectify improper chewing habit and avoid overstrain of the muscle on the affected side.

7.2 Diseases in internal medicine, gynaecology and otolaryngology

7.2.1 Stomachache

Stomachache refers to pain in the epigastric region. It is similar to gastrospasm, chronic and acute gastritis, gastric and duodenal ulcer, gastrointestinal neurosis and other functional disorders of the upper digestive tract in modern medicine.

【Clinical manifestations】

Clinically stomachache can be divided into two categories, stomachache due to stagnation of pathogenic factors and stomachache due to Zangfu-organ disorder. But whatever the cause is, it can result in blood stasis inside the body due to failure in treatment.

1. Stagnation of pathogenic factors

(1) Stomachache due to cold attack: It is characterized by sudden onset of vague or colic pain to be alleviated with warmth and worsened with cold, no thirst or preference for warm water, light and white tongue with coating, taut and tense pulse.

(2) Retention of food: It is marked by distention or even pain in the epigastric region, accompanied by belching, eructation with fetid odor, acid regurgitation or vomiting of indigested food, alleviation after vomiting and breaking wind, anorexia, unsmooth defecation, yellowish or whitish greasy coating and slippery pulse.

2. Zangfu-organ disorder

(1) Invasion of liver Qi into the stomach: It is marked by fullness in the stomach, distending pain involving the hypochondrium, frequent belching, unsmooth defecation,

depression, or pain due to emotional changes, thin whitish tongue coating and taut pulse,

(2) Deficiency cold of spleen and stomach: It is marked by vague stomachache, profuse clear saliva, preference for warmth and pressure, alleviation with warmth and pressure, aggravation on empty stomach, improvement of pain after taking food, poor appetite, lassitude, or even cold limbs, loose and thin stool, pale tongue, thin and whitish coating, weak soft pulse or slow pulse.

The syndromes mentioned above due to stagnation of pathogenic factors are often acute while the syndromes due to visceral disorders are often chronic. Clinically these symptoms never appear singularly. Usually two or more symptoms may appear simultaneously.

【Essentials for diagnosis】

1. Stomachache is often accompanied by oppression, distension, eructation and gastric upset.

2. Stomachache is often associated with emotion changes, improper diet, overstrain, and cold attack.

3. Through barium meal X-ray examination of upper digestive system and gastric endoscope, gastric duodenal mucositis and ulcer can be revealed.

4. If stool and vomitus test is positive, it suggests gastrointestinal hemorrhage.

5. B ultrasonic examination, liver function and gallbladder tract X-ray examination are helpful for differential diagnosis.

【Treatment with Tuina therapy】

1. Treatment principle: Regulating Qi and stopping pain.

2. Acupoints and location: Zhongwan (CV 12), Tianshu (ST 25), Qihai (CV 6), Zusanli (ST 36), Geshu (BL 17), Ganshu (BL 18), Pishu (BL 20), Weishu (BL 21), Sanjiaoshu (BL 22), Jianjing (GB 21), Shousanli (LI 10), Neiguan (PC 6), Hegu (LI 4) and hypochondriac region.

3. Operation:

(1) The patient takes a lateral recumbent position. The doctor gently uses one-finger pushing and rubbing manipulations to rub the epigastric region to direct warmth into the abdomen, then rubbing Zhongwan (CV 12), Qihai (CV 6), Tianshu (ST 25) and Zusanli (ST 36) for about 5 minutes.

(2) The patient takes a prone position. The doctor presses both sides of spine along the bladder meridian to Sanjiaochu (BL 22) for 4~5 times, then alternatively pressing Geshu (BL 17), Ganshu (BL 18), Pishu (BL 20), Weishu (BL 21) and Sanjiaoshu (BL 22) for about 5 minutes.

(3) The patient takes a sitting position, the doctor gasps and holds Jianjing (GB 21) from the arm down to the elbow, pressing comparatively hard on Shousanli (LI 10), Neiguan (PC 6) and Hegu (LI 4). Then the doctor rubs the shoulder and arm to smooth the meridians, wiping the rib-sides upwards and downwards. This manipulation is

performed for 5~6 times.

4. Manipulations determined according to syndrome differentiation:

(1) Stomachache due to cold attack: Strongly pressing Pishu (BL 20), Weishu (BL 21) for about 2 minutes; rubbing the left part of the back (T_7-T_{12}) until it becomes warm.

(2) Retention of food: Rubbing clockwise the abdomen, especially on Zhongwan (CV 12), Tianshu (ST 25), Weishu (BL 21), Dachangshu (BL 25), Baliao, Zusanli (ST 36) for 5 minutes.

(3) Stomachache caused by invasion of liver Qi: Gently pressing Tiantu (CV 22) down to Zhongwan (CV 12), specially Danzhong (CV 17); then rubbing and pressing Zhangmen (LR 13) and Qimen (LR 14); strongly pressing Ganshu (BL 18), Danshu (BL 19), Geshu (BL 17).

(4) Stomachache due to deficiency cold in the spleen and stomach: Gently rubbing Qihai (CV 6), Guanyuan (CV 4) and Zusanli (ST 36) for 2 minutes each. The duration can be prolonged at Qihai (CV 6); vertically rubbing the governor vessel on the back and horizontally rubbing the left side of the back (T_7-T_{12}), Shenshu (BL 23) and Mingmen (GV) until it is warm in the local area.

(5) Severe stomachache: Strongly pressing Pishu (BL 20) and Weishu (BL 21) for 2 minutes continuously. After the pain is relieved, it can be treated according to syndrome differentiation.

【Cautions】

1. Tuina therapy is not available for patients with gastrointestinal ulceration and hemorrhage.

2. The patient should have a regular daily life and pay more attention to mental state and diet.

3. Excessive drinking and eating or improper diet, wine and peppery foods are forbidden. It is better to take food that is easy to digest, avoiding alcohol and pungent food.

4. Patient with chronic stomachache should take liquid or semi-liquid diet for a certain period.

7.2.2 Diarrhea

Diarrhea may occur at any time, especially in summer and autumn. It is marked by frequent and sloppy stool, sometimes even appearing like water.. It is similar to intestinal inflammation, chronic enteritis, gastrointestinal neurosis and non-specific ulcerated colitis in Western medicine.

【Clinical manifestations】

1. Acute diarrhea acute diarrhea

(1) Attack of dampness: It is marked by sudden onset with thin and loose stool or mixed with mucus, ten times a day, accompanied by abdominal pain, borborygmus,

aching pain of the extremities, yellowish or whitish greasy tongue coating, soft or rapid and slippery pulse.

(2) Improper diet: It is marked by sudden onset with a history of improper diet, abdominal distension, diarrhea with rotten egg smell, foul belching, alleviation of pain after diarrhea, acid regurgitation, accompanied by thick greasy tongue coating, soft or rapid slippery pulse.

2. Chronic diarrhea

(1) Deficiency of spleen and stomach: This type of diarrhea usually occurs after taking greasy, oily food, marked by loose or watery stool, poor appetite; pale tongue with whitish tongue coating, slow and week pulse.

(2) Yang deficiency of kidney and spleen: Since it is a kind of diarrhea accompanied by pain around the umbilicus occurring at dawn and right after borboygmus. The pain is relieved after diarrhea. The other symptoms may include cold feeling in abdomen, aching and coldness in the waist and limbs, pale tongue with whitish coating, deep and thin pulse.

(3) Liver Qi over-restraining the spleen: It is often induced by excessive emotional changes, accompanied by abdominal pain, borborygums, full sensation in the chest and hypochondriac regions, belching, thin tongue coating, taut and thin pulse.

[Essentials for diagnosis]

1. Loose or watery feces, increased frequency, often accompanied by abdominal distension.

2. Sudden onset of acute fulminate diarrhea with short duration, accompanied by aversion of cold and fever.

3. Slow onset of chronic diarrhea with longer duration and frequent relapse and fluctuation in progress.

4. Improper diet, cold attack or emotional changes that can lead to the occurrence of diarrhea.

5. A few red blood cells and white blood cells can be seen in routine stool test, the bacteria culture of stool is either positive or negative.

6. Barium meal X-ray examination or intestinal endoscope should be done if necessary.

[Treatment with Tuina therapy]

1. Principle: Invigorating the spleen and harmonizing the stomach, warming the kidney to strengthen yang, soothing the liver to regulate Qi.

2. Acupoints and location: Zhongwan (CV 12), Tianshu (ST 25), Qihai (CV 6), Guanyuan (CV 4), Pishu (BL 20), Weishu (BL 21), Shenshu (BL 23), Dachangshu (BL 25) and Changjiang (GV 1).

3. Operation

(1) The patient takes a lateral recumbent position. The doctor pushes now gently and

then strongly from Zhongwan (CV 12) down to Qihai (CV 6) and Guanyuan (CV 4) for 5~6 times. The abdomen is rubbed counter-clockwise for about 8 minutes.

(2) The patient takes a prone position. The doctor rolls from Pishu (BL 20) to Dachangshu (BL 25), 1 minute each; then pressing Pishu (BL 20), Weishu (BL 21), Dachangshu (BL 25) and Changjiang (GV 1) repeatedly for about 3~4 times; finally rubbing the left side of the back until it is warm for about 10 minutes.

4. Manipulations determined according to syndrome differentiation

(1) Diarrhea caused by cold and dampness: Rubbing Shenque (CV 8), Qihai (CV 6) until the abdomen becomes warm; pressing and rubbing Zusanli (ST 36) and Neiguan (PC 6) for 1 minute each; rubbing the left side of the back and lumbosacral region till it turns warm.

(2) Diarrhea caused by improper diet: Rubbing the abdomen clockwise.

(3) Gastricsplenic deficiency: Gently rubbing Guanyuan (CV 4) and Zusanli (ST 36), 2 minutes each. Qihai (CV 6) can be rubbed for a longer period of time. The whole abdomen is rubbed anticlockwise, mainly focusing on the epigastric region. The lower abdomen is rubbed clockwise.

(4) Yang deficiency in both the spleen and kidneys: Gently rubbing Qihai (CV 6) and Guanyuan (CV 4) for 3 minutes each; vertically rubbing the govern vessel on the back; transversely rubbing Shenshu (BL 23), Mingmen (GV 4) and Baliao.

(5) Liver Qi over restraining the spleen: Gently pressing and kneading Zhangmen (LR 13) and Qigmen (LR 14) for about 5~10 minutes; obliquely backward and forward rubbing hypochondrium region until it is slightly warm; rubbing Ganshu (BL 18), Danshu (BL 19), Geshu (BL 17), Taichong (LR 3) and Xingjian (LR 2).

【Cautions】

1. Abstain from starch and fat food, avoid food difficult to digest.
2. Keep warm, avoid overstrain and pay attention to mental state and diet.

7.2.3 Constipation

Constipation is a disease due to dry stools that causes difficulty defecation, prolonged defecation, or unsmooth defecation. It may occur alone or may be complicated with other diseases. Constipation is mainly caused by dysfunction of the large intestine, leading to retention of feces in the intestines and excessive absorption of fluid in the stool.

【Clinical manifestations】

The manifestations include dry stools, difficulty in defecation (once every three to five or even seven to eight days); or normal frequency of defecation with dry feces; difficulty in defecation in spite of desire to discharge. Prolonged constipation will lead to abdominal distension, stomachache, vertigo, anorexia, uncomfortable sleep, even hemorrhoids and anal fissure.

1. Accumulation of heat in the stomach and intestines: Dry stool, fullness in the abdomen, flushed face, warm feeling in the body, dry mouth, restlessness, or foul breath, sores on lips, red tongue with yellow or dry yellow coating, slippery and forceful pulse.

2. Stagnation of Qi: Constipation without dry feces, abdominal distension involving the hypochondrium, frequent belching, poor appetite, mental depression, irritability, restlessness, thin whitish tongue coating and taut pulse.

3. Deficiency of Qi and blood:

(1) Constipation due to Qi deficiency: Difficult defecation, weakness to defecate, profuse sweating and short breath after defecation, defecation without dry feces, pale tongue with thin, whitish coating, weak and soft pulse.

(2) Constipation due to blood deficiency: Dry stool, grayish complexion, vertigo, palpitation, pale tongue, and thin pulse.

4. Constipation due to the stagnation of Yin cold: Difficult defecation, pale complexion, cold limbs, cold pain in abdomen, soreness and cold on the back, profuse and clear urine, pale tongue with whitish coating, deep and slow pulse.

【Essentials for diagnosis】

1. Defecation is prolonged once every two or more days.

2. Dry stool like nuts accompanied by abdominal distension, lassitude and poor appetite.

3. Intestinal organic diseases should be ruled out.

【Treatment with Tuina therapy】

1. Principle: Regulating intestine and Qi to promote defecation.

2. Acupoint: Zhongwan (CV 12),Tianshu (ST 25),Daheng (SP 15),Guanyuan (CV 4),Ganshu (BL 18), Pishu (BL 20), Weishu (BL 21), Shenshu (BL 23), Dachangshu (BL 25), Baliao, Changjiang (GV 1), abdomen and back position.

3. Operation:

(1) The patient takes a supine position, the doctor gently rubs Zhongwan (CV 12),Tianshu (ST 25) and Daheng (SP 15) with one-finger pushing method, 1 minute for each Acupoint; then rubs the abdomen clockwise with the palm for about 8 minutes.

(2) The patient takes a prone position. The doctor rubs gently along the bilateral side of the spine from Ganshu (BL 18) and Pishu (BL 20) to Baliao for about 5 minutes; then gently presses and rubs Shenshu (BL 23), Dachangshu (BL 25), Baliao and Changjiang (GV 1) twice or three times.

(3) The doctor finally rubs the back of the patient with rolling manipulation for about 5 minutes.

4. Treatment based on syndrome differentiation

(1) Accumulation of heat in the stomach and intestines: Rubbing horizontally Baliao until it is warm inside; pressing and rubbing Zusanli (ST 36) and Dachangshu (BL 25) until aching and distending feeling is felt.

(2) Stagnation of Qi: Pressing and rubbing Zhongfu (LU 1), Yunmen (LU 2), Danzhong (CV 17), Zhangmen (LR 13), Qimen (LR 14), Feishu (BL 13), Ganshu (BL 18) and Geshu (BL 17) until aching and distending feeling is felt. But heavy stimulation should be avoided. Rubbing horizontally backward and forward the chest until it is warm; obliquely rubbing backward and forward the hypochondriac region until it becomes slightly warm.

(3) Deficiency of Qi and blood: Rubbing the upper part of the chest, the left back and Baliao points in sacral region until it is warm; pressing and rubbing Zusanli (ST 36) and Zhigou (TE 6) 1 minute each.

(4) Stagnation of Yin cold: Horizontally rubbing the shoulder, back region and Shenshu (BL 23), Mingmen (GV 4) and Baliao points in the lumbosacral region until it is warm; rubbing vertically the governor vessel until it is warm.

[Cautions]

1. Help the patient to develop the habit of regular defecation.

2. Adjust diet, drink more hot water and eat more vegetables and fruits, avoid pungent and rich food.

3. Take some outdoor activities. If the condition allows, the patient may do some exercise to strengthen the abdominal muscle so as to promote defecation.

7.2.4 Hypertension

Hypertension is a very common disease, also called "primary hypertension", marked by increasing blood pressure. In the later period it can cause pathological changes of the heart, kidney and brain, etc. Its occurrence often associates with age, occupation and family history.

Primary hypertension is defined as the major syndrome of frequent elevation of blood pressure, which accounts for 80%-90% in clinical patients. Secondary hypertension is one of the syndrome occurring during the course of other diseases. As a symptom in other diseases, it may be present or not, temporary or protracted, accounting for 10%-20% in clinical treatment. Generally speaking, 140 mmHg of systolic pressure or diastolic pressure$\geqslant$90 mmHg can be diagnosed as hypertension.

[Clinical manifestations]

The clinical manifestations of hypertension varies greatly. Some patients show no subjective symptoms and hypertension is often found by accident. The common symptoms are vertigo, headache, red face and eyes, bitter taste in mouth, palpitation, constipation, reddish tongue and taut pulse.

Clinically it can be divided into two types, slow progressive and rapid progressive. Usually the former one occurs more frequently.

1. Slow progressive hypertension

(1) The symptoms include headache, dizziness, insomnia, memory failure, dysphoria,

lassitude, palpitation and so on. The severity of the symptoms is irrelevant to the level of hypertension.

(2) The state of this type at the advanced stage is concerned with the pathological changes of the heart, brain and kidneys.

2. Rapid progressive hypertension

(1) It occurs suddenly and develops rapidly.

(2) It commonly occur among young people and those below 40, marked by significant elevation of blood pressure and diastolic pressure over 130~140 mmHg.

(3) Pathological changes of the kidney and heart occur several months or 1~2 years later.

(4) This type of hypertension is subject to cerebrovascular disease, heart failure and acute renal insufficiency.

[Essentials for diagnosis]

1. According to the standard made by WHO/ISH and hypertension prevention manual (October 1999), hypertension is defined as systolic blood pressure ≥ 140 mmHg and diastolic blood pressure ≥ 90 mmHg without taking antihypertension drugs for adults over 18.

2. The patient who has a hypertension history and takes antihypertension drugs also can be diagnosed as hypertension even though the blood pressure is under 140/90 mmHg.

[Treatment with Tuina therapy]

1. Principle: Smoothing the liver to tranquilize mind, resolving phlegm and descending turbid Yin.

2. Acupoint and location: Qiaogong, Yintang (EX-HN 3), Faji, Taiyang (EX-HN 5), Baihui (GV 20), Fengchi (GB 20), Touwei, Gongsun (SP 4), Cuanzhu (BL 2), Dazhui (GV 14), Guanyuan (CV 4), Qihai (CV 6), Shenque (CV 8), Zhongwan (CV 12), Daheng (SP 15), Shenshu (BL 23), Mingmen (GV 4), Yongquan (KI 1), head and face, neck and nape.

3. Operation

(1) The patient takes a sitting position, the doctor pushes and rubs Qiaogong for about 1 minute; pushing from Yintang (EX-HN 3) to the hairline, along the eyebrows to Taiyang (EX-HN 5), and then around the eye socket from Yintang (EX-HN 3) to Jingming (BL 1); rubbing the forehead from one side of Taiyang (EX-HN 5) to the other; using clean and dissipating manipulations to rub the Gallbladder meridian of foot-shaoyang; rubbing the forehead, face and Jiaosun, Jingming (BL 1) and Taiyang (EX-HN 5) about 3 minutes; grasping the vertex and, using just three fingers, rubbing Dazhui (GV 14) at neck and nape region; pressing and kneading Baihui (GV 20) and Fengchi (GB 20); pushing from Fengfu (GV 16) down to Dazhui (GV 14). The same operation is performed on the bilateral courses of the bladder meridian about 4 minutes. Finally

the operation is continued to the face with separate manipulation from the forehead to Yingxiang (LI 20) back and forth for about 3~5 minutes.

(2) The patient takes a recumbent position. The doctor rubs the abdomen clockwise and at the same time presses the six Acupoints mentioned above for about 10 minutes.

(3) Rubbing Shenshu (BL 23), Mingmen (GV 4) and the Governor vessel until it is warm in the local area; rubbing vertically Yongquan (KI 1)on the bottom of foot until it is warm.

【Cautions】

1. Live a regular life, avoid overstrain, do exercise under the instruction of the doctor and abstain from greasy food and strong alcohol.

2. Avoid emotional stimulation.

Tuina therapy is suitable for treating slow progressive hypertension and can be used as the supplementary treatment for rapidly progressive hypertension.

7.2.5 Coronary heart disease

Coronary heart disease, also known as ischemic heart disease, refers to imbalance of blood supply and demand between coronary artery blood flow and heart muscle, leading to the damages of heart muscle. The cause of coronary artery circulation obstruction may be functional, such as coronary vasospasm, and organic, such as coronary atherosclerosis.

【Clinical manifestations】

The clinical manifestations are paroxysmal or constant crush pain or sharp pain in the precordial region, even arrhythmia, shock, or heart failure. Sometimes it may have no obvious symptoms and signs, but ECG examination may reveal signs of heart muscle ischemia.

1. Obstruction of chest Yang: Colic pain, or alternate pain and distress involving the left shoulder and arm, dark colored nail, purplish and grayish tongue and lips, or vomiting of sputum and salvia, blood stasis spot at the edge of tongue, light or greasy whitish tongue coating, taut or thin and slippery pulse.

2. Declination of Yang Qi: Chest oppression or vague pain with short respiration, vertigo, palpitation, lassitude, aversion to cold, cold limbs, pale complexion, perspiration after movement, light-colored and plump tongue with teeth imprints at edge, deep and thin or knotted and intermittent pulse.

【Essentials for diagnosis】

1. Paroxysmal or constant pressing pain or sharp pain in the chest or showing no symptoms at all.

2. Heart muscle ischemia signs revealed in ECG examination.

3. Obstruction of chest Yang: Marked by chest pain involving the left shoulder and arm, blood stasis spot at the edge of tongue, light or greasy whitish tongue coating, taut or thin and slippery pulse.

4. Declination of Yang Qi: Marked by vertigo, palpitation, lassitude, aversion to cold, cold limbs, pale complexion, perspiration after movement, light-colored and plump tongue with teeth imprints at edge, deep and thin or knotted and intermittent pulse.

【Treatment with Tuina therapy】

1. Principle: Nourishing heart to warm Yang, removing obstruction to stop pain.

2. Acupoint and location: Danzhong (CV 17), Xinshu (BL 15), Jueyingshu (BL 14), Neiguan (PC 6), the chest region where the conception vessel runs and the back region where the governor vessel and the bladder meridian of foot-Taiyang pass by.

3. Operation

(1) The patient takes a sitting or supine position. The doctor pushes and presses Danzhong (CV 17) and Neiguan (PC 6); horizontally rubs the chest until it is warm. The manipulation is performed for about 3~5 minutes.

(2) The patient takes a sitting or prone position. The doctor pushes and presses Xinshu (BL 15) and Jueyingshu (BL 14), obliquely rubbing the back till it is warm for about 3~5 minutes.

(3) The patient takes a sitting position. The doctor uses the digital pads of the thumbs to push and rub Qiaogong for about 3~5 minutes.

4. manipulations determined according to differentiation

(1) Obstruction of chest Yang: Forcefully push from Feishu (BL 13) to Geshu (BL 17) with reducing techniques.

(2) Declination of Yang Qi: Gently rub Xinshu (BL 15) and Jueyingshu (BL 14) for about 10~20 minutes with reinforcing techniques.

【Cautions】

1. The patient should maintain a regular life and pay attention to mental cultivation and diet.

2. Patients at the remission stage or with mild disease can be effectively treated by Tuina therapy; patients during acute attack of with serious disease have to be treated with both Tuina therapy and other necessary medicines.

7.2.6 Headache

Headache is marked by pain in the upper part of the head due to pathological changes inside or outside the cranium. It is a commonly encountered subjective symptom and can be found in many different acute or chronic diseases. There are four causes of headache, intracranial pathologic changes, extracranial pathologic changes, general diseases and neurosis.

Headache discussed in this chapter is the primary symptom pertaining to internal medicine in TCM. If the headache is secondary symptom caused by injury, wound or some other diseases, it will disappear after the main symptoms are eliminated.

【Clinical manifestations】

1. Headache due to wind cold: Caused by wind and cold, marked by involvement of the nape and back, aversion to wind and cold, aching limbs and joints, preference for wrapping the head, no thirst, light and whitish tongue coating, floating or tense pulse.

2. Headache due to wind heat: Marked by distending headache, or even splitting pain in the head, aversion to wind, fever, reddish complexion and eyes, thirst and preference for drinking, reddish and sore throat, yellowish urine, reddish tongue tip and light yellow coating, floating and rapid pulse.

3. Headache due to summer-heat: Marked by binding pain, abdominal distension, anorexia, lassitude, heaviness, and pain in the body, feverish body and spontaneous sweating, dysphoria, thirst, greasy coating, soft and rapid pulse.

4. Headache due to hyperactivity of liver Yang: Marked by headache and dizziness, especially in both sides, dysphoria, restless sleep, reddish complexion, dry and bitter taste, hypochondriac distension, reddish tongue and light yellowish or scanty tongue coating, taut and strong or taut, thin and rapid pulse.

5. Headache due to phlegm and turbid substance: Marked by distension headache, fullness sensation in the chest and diaphragm, anorexia, lassitude, profuse saliva and fluid, vomiting, whitish and greasy tongue coating and slippery pulse.

6. Headache due to blood deficiency: Marked by headache, vertigo, aggravation of pain after overstrain, languor, dark complexion, poor appetite, palpitation, short respiration, light tongue, thin and limp or unsmooth pulse.

7. Headache due to kidney deficiency: Marked by severe pain, languor, tinnitus and vertigo, amnesia and insomnia, weakness of waist and limbs, seminal emission and leukorrhagia. Headache due to Yang deficiency is marked by cold limbs, light and plump tongue, sink thin and limp pulse; headache due to Yin deficiency is marked by dry mouth with scanty fluid, reddish tongue, thin and rapid pulse.

8. Headache due to blood stasis: Marked by repeated occurrence, difficulty to heal, fixed location, puncturing pain (or with a history of traumatic injury of the head), with purple and dark tongue and unsmooth pulse.

【Essentials for diagnosis】

1. The main symptom is headache, involving the forehead, tempus, vertex and occiput or the whole head, characterized by flicking pain, stabbing pain, distending pain, vertigo or vague pain. It may occur suddenly or recur frequently and linger. It may last for several minutes, hours, days or weeks.

2. There is history of sudden onset or repeated occurrence due to invasion of exogenous pathogenic factors or endogenous ones.

3. It is necessary to take blood routine test, blood pressure test, cerebrospinal fluid test and EEG test as well as Doppler, cranial and cerebral CT and MRI test if possible, in order to rule out organic disease and decide diagnosis.

【Treatment with Tuina therapy】

1. Principle: Dredging meridians, prompting Qi and blood flow.

2. Acupoint and location: Yintang (EX-HN 3), Touwei (ST 8), Taiyang (EX-HN 5), Yuyao (EX-HN 4), Cuanzhu (BL 2), Yangbai, Baihui (GV 20), Sishencong, Jianjing (GB 21), Fengchi (GB 20), the head, face, nape and neck regions.

3. Operation

(1) The patient takes a sitting position. The doctor uses one-finger pushing method to push down through the neck, where the bladder meridian of foot-Taiyang runs, for about three minutes, applying pressing manipulation on Fengchi (GB 20), Fengfu (GV 16), Tianzhu (BL 10), then applying Na Fa (grasping method) on Fengchi (GB 20) and Jianjing (GB 21), 1 minute for each, finally applying the same manipulation along the neck where the bladder meridian of foot-taiyang runs for 4~5 times.

(2) The patient takes seating position. The doctor uses one-finger pushing method to push from Yintang (EX-HN 3), the hairline up to Touwei (ST8) and Taiyang (EX-HN 5) for 3~4 times. At the same time, Yintang (EX-HN 3), Yuyao (EX-HN 4), Taiyang (EX-HN 5) and Baihui (GV 20) are pressed. Then grasping method with five fingers is used to grasp from vertex to Fengchi (GB 20). Then grasping method with three fingers is used with three fingers to grasp the bladder meridian of foot-taiyang down to Dazhui (GV 14) for 3~4 times.

4. Manipulations determined according to Syndrome differentiation

(1) Headache due to cold and wind: Rolling the neck and back for about 2~3 minutes. At the same time Feishu (BL 13) and Fengmen (BL 12) are pressed and rubbed; then Jianjing (GB 21) at both sides is grasped and the bladder meridian at both sides of the back are rubbed until it is warm.

(2) Headache due to wind and heat: Pressing and rubbing Dazhui (GV 14), Feishu (BL 13), Fengmen (BL 12), one minute each; then grasping Jianjing (GB 21), Quchi (LI 11), Shousanli(LI 10), Hegu (LI 4) until there is aching and distending feeling in the local area; knocking the back until it becomes warm.

(3) Headache due to the summer-dampness: Pressing and rubbing Dazhui (GV 14) and Quchi (LI 11), grasping Jianjing (GB 21) and Hegu (LI 4); knocking the bilateral courses of the bladder meridian until the skin turns red; pinching Yintang (EX-HN 3) and neck until it turns red.

(4) Headache due to hyperactivity of liver Yang: Pushing Qiaogong up and down for 20 times each side; cleaning and dissipating tempus where the gallbladder meridian runs, pressing and rubbing Jiaosun (TE 20), Taichong (LR 3) and Xingjian (LR 2) for about 10 times; rubbing Yongquan (KI 1) until it turns warm.

(5) Headache due to phlegm and turbid substance: Pushing and rubbing the abdomen, specially Zhongwan (CV 12), and Tianshu (ST 25); pressing and rubbing Pishu (BL 20), Weishu (BL 21), Dachangshu (BL 25); rubbing the left back horizontally until it is warm; pressing and rubbing Zusanli (ST 36), Fenglong (ST 40) and Neiguan (PC 6).

(6) Headache due to blood deficiency: Rubbing the abdomen for 6~8 minutes, especially Qihai (CV 6), Zhongwan (CV 12) and Guanyuan (CV 4); rubbing the left back horizontally and the governor vessel vertically until it is warm; pressing and rubbing Xinshu (BL 15), Geshu (BL 17), Zusanli (ST 36) and Sanyinjiao (SP 6) until it is slightly aching and distending.

(7) Headache due to kidney deficiency: Rubbing in circle the abdomen for six-eight minutes, especially Qihai (CV 6) and Guanyuan (CV 4); rubbing the governor vessel horizontally and pressing Shenshu (BL 23) and Mingmen (GV 4) and waist until warmth is felt.

(8) Headache due to blood stasis: Pressing and kneading Taiyang (EX-HN 5), Cuanzhu (BL 2), forehead and tempus where the gallbladder runs; rubbing the forehead and both sides of Taiyang (EX-HN 5) until it is warm.

【Cautions】

1. Tuina therapy is not available for intracerebral diseases, such as cerebrovascular disease at the acute stage, cerebral contusion, and encephalic traumatic hematoma.

2. Patients with headache due to exogenous pathogenic factors must keep warm, avoiding wind and cold and taking sufficient rest.

3. Patients with headache due to hyperactivity of liver Yang should frequently test blood pressure, pay attention to the undulation of blood pressure and its influence on the heart.

4. Patients with headache due to blood deficiency and kidneys deficiency should avoid excessive sexual intercourse.

5. Stopping smoking and drinking is helpful for healing different types of headache.

7.2.7 Insomnia

Insomnia is a disease in which the patient cannot sleep normally, including inadequate sleep, insufficient depth of sleep and refreshment. In mild cases, the patient is hard to sleep, or difficult to sleep soundly. In serious cases, the patient cannot fall asleep all the night. This disorder may occur alone or together with other disorders like headache, vertigo, palpitation and amnesia. In Western medicine, insomnia is usually involved in neurosis and menopause syndromes.

【Clinical manifestations】

Insomnia is either of deficiency or of excess. Deficiency type is mostly caused by insufficiency of blood while excess type is often caused by fire transformed from liver, internal disturbance due to phlegm heat and stomach obstruction.

1. Deficiency of heart and spleen: It is characterized by dreaminess, shallow sleep, even sleeplessness all the night, palpitation, amnesia, languor, poor appetite, lusterless complexion, light-colored tongue and coating, thin and weak pulse.

2. Hyperactivity of fire due to Yin deficiency: It is characterized by restlessness, insomnia, vertigo, tinnitus, dry mouth with scanty fluid, nocturnal seminal emission, amnesia, palpitation, lumbago with reddish tongue, thin and rapid pulse.

3. Insomnia due to phlegm heat disturbing inside: It is characterized by insomnia, dreaminess, restlessness, irascibility, chest oppression, dizziness and heaviness of head, distension of the ribs at both sides, poor appetite, thirst and preference for drinking, reddish eyes, bitter taste in the mouth, yellowish and reddish urine, constipation, reddish tongue, yellowish and greasy tongue coating, taut and slippery rapid pulse.

4. Insomnia due to fire transformed from liver stagnation: It is characterized by insomnia, irritability, anorexia, thirst and preference for drinking, reddish eyes, a bitter taste in the mouth, yellowish and reddish urine, constipation, reddish tongue, yellowish tongue coating, taut and rapid pulse.

[Essentials for diagnosis]

1. The only symptom is sleeplessness and the secondary symptoms include difficulty to sleep, shallow sleep, liability to waking up during sleep, dreaminess, difficulty to fall asleep after waking up, discomfort after waking up, tiredness and fatigue in the daytime.

2. The symptoms mentioned above occur three times a week and last for over one month.

3. It is not part of the symptoms of any physical diseases and mental disorders.

[Treatment with Tuina therapy]

1. Principle: Regulating viscera and tranquilizing the mind.

2. Acupoint and location: Yintang (EX-HN 3), Shenting (GV 24), Taiyang (EX-HN 5), Jingming (BL 1), Cuanzhu (BL 2), Yuyao (EX-HN 4), Jiaosun (TE 20), Baihui (GV 20), Fengchi (GB 20), Jianjing (GB 21), Zhongwan (CV 12), Qihai (CV 6), Guanyuan (CV 4), Xinshu (BL 15), Ganshu (BL 18), Pishu (BL 20), Weishu (BL 21), Shenshu (BL 23), Mingmen (GV 4), head, face, neck, shoulder and abdomen.

3. Operation

(1) The patient takes a seating or supine position. The doctor applies one-finger pushing and kneading manipulations from Yintang (EX-HN 3) up to Shenting (GV 24), pushing from Yintang (EX-HN 3) to Taiyang (EX-HN 5) through the eyebrows, and then using pushing the orbit with one finger. The time of operation is about 5 minutes.

(2) Then pressing and kneading from Yintang (EX-HN 3) downwards, along the nose and Quanliao (SI 18) to the front of ears; pressing and rubbing Yintang (EX-HN 3), Shenting (GV 24), Jingming (BL 1), Cuanzhu (BL 2), Taiyang (EX-HN 5). The time of operation is about 5 minutes.

(3) Applying pressing and rubbing manipulations to Jingming (BL 1) and Yuyao (EX-HN 4) with both hands for about 3 minutes.

(4) Cleaning and dissipating the bilateral courses of the gallbladder meridian; pressing Jiaosun (TE 20); grasping with five fingers from vertex and then with three fingers to the occipital bone; pressing and grasping Jianjing (GB 21) for about 3 minutes.

(5) Rubbing the abdomen clockwise, pressing and rubbing Zhongwan (CV 12), Qihai (CV 6) and Guanyuan (CV 4). The time of operation is about 5 minutes.

4. Manipulations determined according to syndrome differentiation

(1) Insomnia due to deficiency of both the heart and spleen: Pressing and rubbing Xinshu (BL 15), Ganshu (BL 18), Weishu (BL 21), Xiaochangshu (BL 27) and Zusanli (ST 36), 1 minute for each Acupoint; rubbing the left side of the back horizontally and the governor vessel vertically until it is warm in the local area.

(2) Insomnia caused by hyperactivity of fire due to Yin deficiency: Pushing Qiaogong from one side to the other; rubbing Shenshu (BL 23) and Mingmen (GV 4).

(3) Insomnia due to phlegm heat: Rolling both sides of the spine vertically, especially Pishu (BL 20), Weishu (BL 21), Xinshu (BL 15) with a soft and gentle force; then pressing and rubbing the Acupoints mentioned above for about 5 minutes; wiping, pressing and rubbing Zhongwan (CV 12), Qihai (CV 6), Tianshu (ST 25), Shenque (CV 8), Zusanli (ST 36) and Fenglong (ST 40); horizontally rubbing the left side of the back and Baliao Acupoint until it is warm in the local area.

(4) Insomnia due to fire transformed from liver stagnation: pressing and rubbing Ganshu (BL 18), Danshu (BL 19), Qimen (LR 14), Zhangmen (LR 13) and Taichong (LR 3), 1~2 minutes for each Acupoint; rubbing hypochondriac region with the palm for about 1 minute.

【Cautions】

1. Insomnia is often seen in neurasthenia. However, it also can be caused by some organic diseases and must be carefully differentiated.

2. Avoid smoking, drinking alcohol, tea and coffee as well as reading sentimental books and seeing sentimental films before sleeping. Wash feet with warm water everyday.

3. Do some physical work and exercises to train the body. .

4. Balance the activities of work and rest, avoid excessive sexual intercourse, live a regular life with the habit of sleeping early and getting up early. .

5. Advise the patient to eliminate anxiety and keep a happy and optimistic mind.

7.2.8 Apoplexy sequelae

Apoplexy sequela, also called hemiplegia or paraplegia, refers to muscular atrophy, languor and inability to move freely half of the limb, accompanied by distorted face and difficulty in speaking. It is usually seen in encephalopathy and other mental diseases. Clinically it is similar to other mental and spinal cord diseases such as tumor, encephalitis and trauma.

【Clinical manifestations】

1. Hemiparalysis: Its main symptoms include paralysis of the upper limb or lower limb at one side, distorted face, stiff tongue and difficulty in speaking. The early symptoms are languor, lack of consciousness or slight stiffness and limited movement which gradually develop into stiffness and spasm, deformity of limbs and postures.

2. Distorted face: It is marked by distorted mouth and deviation of the nasolavial groove to the healthy side, air leakage in bulging the cheeks and inability to wrinkle, frown and close the eyes.

Examination

1. Hemiparalysis: It is characterized by increased muscular tension of the limbs, spasm and deformed joint, reduced consciousness, dysfunction in movement ability, hyperactivity of the biceps, triceps, knee and Achilles tendon in flexion. However the healthy side is normal.

2. Blood pressure: Increased blood pressure due to cerebral hemorrhage and cerebral thrombosis; positive meningeal irritation signs in subarachnoild hemorrhage; signs of nerve system due to cerebral embolism.

3. Cerebrospinal fluid test: Cerebrospinal fluid in cerebral hemorrhage and subarachnoild hemorrhage is bloody; while it is normal in patients with cerebral thrombosis and cerebral embolism.

【Essentials for diagnosis】

1. The patient has a history of hypertension, cardiac disease, headache and vertigo.

2. Sudden loss of consciousness or the occurrence of paraplegia with distorted face, stiff tongue and difficulty in speaking.

【Treatment with Tuina therapy】

It should be treated early. Usually manipulations can be used to treat it two weeks after occurrence.

1. Principle: Dredging meridians, prompting Qi flow and activating blood.

2. Acupoints and the location: Tianzong (SI 11), Ganshu (BL 18), Danshu (BL 19), Geshu (BL 17), Shenshu (BL 23), Huantiao (GB 30), Yanglingquan(GB 34), Weizhong(BL 40), Chengshan(BL 57), Fengshi (GB 31), Futu (ST 32), Xiyan(EX-LE 5), Jiexi (ST 41), Chize (LU 5), Quchi (LI 11), Shousanli (LI 10), Hegu (LI 4), Yintang (EX-HN 3), Jingming (BL 1), Taiyang (EX-HN 5), Jiaosun(TE20), Fengchi (GB 20), Fengfu (GV 16), Jianjing (GB 21), back, limbs, face and head.

3. OperationTuina therapy

(1) The patient takes a prone position; the doctor presses the back upwards and downwards, hitting, pressing and rubbing Tianzong (SI 11), Ganshu (BL 18), Danshu (BL 19), Geshu (BL 17) and Shenshu (BL 23); then rolling along the bilateral sides of rachis down to the buttock, back of the thigh and calf, especially both sides of the lumbar vertebrae as well as the Acupoints of Huantiao (GB 30), Weizhong(BL 40), Chengshan (BL 57) and Achilles' tendon. At the same time the waist and the hip joint are stretched backwards. The time of operation is about 5 minutes.

(2) The patient lies on the healthy side with the affected side turned up. The doctor rolls from the lateral side of the thigh to the lateral side of the calf, focusing especially on

the hip joint and knee joint. The time of operation is about 3 minutes.

(3) The patient takes a supine position. The doctor stands besides him, rolling the affected leg from the anterior superior iliac spine to the anterior side of the thigh and from the ankle joint to the dorsum of foot; then hitting, pressing and rubbing Futu (ST 32), Xiyan (EX-LE 5), Jiexi (ST 41). Meanwhile, the hip joint, knee joint and ankle joint are moved passively. Then grasping manipulation is applied to the affected leg, Weizhong (BL 40), Chengshan (BL 57), the thigh and knee joint. The time of operation is about 5~10 minutes.

(4) The patient takes a recumbent position. The doctor rolls from the affected arm to the forearm, especially the elbow joint. At the same time, the affected limb and elbow joint are moved passively in extension and flexion. Then pressing and rubbing Chize (LU 5), Quchi (LI 11), Shousanli (LI 10) and Hegu (LI 4); the affected wrist, palm and fingers are rolled with palms and fingers with passive extension and flexion of the wrist joint and fingers. At the same time twisting manipulation can be used over the finger joints. The time of operation is about 5 minutes.

(5) The patient takes a sitting position. The doctor rolls around the shoulder blade and both sides of the nape and neck, passively raising the affected the arm, abducting and adducting the shoulder joint, grasping from the shoulder to wrist and moving the shoulder, elbow and wrist joint. Finally twisting manipulation is used to treat the shoulder and wrist. The time of operation is about 3 minutes.

(6) The doctor wipes from Yintang (EX-HN 3) to Taiyang (EX-HN 5) and, at the same time, pressing and rubbing Jingming (BL 1) and Taiyang (EX-HN 5); then cleaning and dissipating manipulations are performed at the tempus position where the gallbladder meridian runs. At the same time, pressing and rubbing manipulations are performed on Jiaosun (TE20). The time of operation is about 2 minutes.

Distorted face: One-finger pushing manipulation is applied to Yintang (EX-HN 3), Yangbai (GB 14), Jingming (BL 1), Sibai (ST 2), Yingxiang (LI 20), Xiaguan (ST 7), Jiache (ST 6) and Dicang (ST 4), accompanied by gentle kneading manipulation. Then one-finger pushing manipulation is applied to Fengchi (GB 20) and the nape region; grasping manipulation is applied to Fengchi (GB 20) and Hegu (LI 4).

【Cautions】

1. The course of apoplexy sequela directly influences rehabilitation. So early treatment is very important. Generally speaking, Tuina therapy can be resorted when the pathological condition becomes stable.

2. If the course of apoplexy is within half a year, the treatment should focus on activating blood to eliminate stasis; if the course is over half a year, the treatment should focus on nourishing Qi and blood to strengthen healthy Qi, consolidate the base of life the root, invigorate the tendons and reinforce the bones. The essentials for operation are the same. The patient should try to move the affected limbs more to restore its functions.

3. The patient should keep a stable mood and live a regular life, avoiding smoking, alcohol, hot and fat food, keeping the body clean, taking measures to prevent and deal with bedsore. At the same time, other rehabilitative methods, such as Chinese herbal medicine, acupuncture and physical therapy, can also be resorted.

4. During the convalescent phase, the patient should do general exercise and take some light activity, such as rolling balls, holding loops, pulling the truckle, stretching the shoulder, waving the hands, extending and flexing quadriceps muscle of the thigh, kicking in jumping, rubbing and rolling to soothe the tendons. However, cares should be taken to avoid overstrain.

7.2.9 Dysmenorrhea

Dysmenorrhea refers to the periodical abdominal pain or lumbago, even unbearable pain before or after the menstrual period. It is often accompanied by pale complexion, vomiting, dripping clammy sweating and cold limbs. So it is also called "menstrual abdominal pain", often seen among unmarried young women.

Dysmenorrhea may start from menarche, related to disorder of autonomic nerve and uterus spasm, or imperfect uterus growth, narrow cervix of uterus and over-flexion of uterus which affect smooth circulation of blood. Secondary dysmenorrhea often follows the organic disease of genital organ, such as inflammation and myoma of uterus.

【Clinical manifestations】

The main clinical manifestations are lower abdominal pain, sometime involving the whole abdomen or lumbosacral region, and dropping pain in the vulvae and anus. If the pain is serious, it may cause pale complexion, dripping clammy sweating, cold limbs, even coma and prostration during menstruation. It can be differentiated as of deficiency type or excess type according to the time and the nature of pain. Dysmenorrhea before the menstruation is excess in nature while dysmenorrhea after menstruation is deficiency in nature. If it is not palpable, it is excess in nature; if it is palpable, it is deficiency in nature. If it becomes alleviated with warmth, it is caused by cold; if it becomes worsened with warmth, it is caused by heat. If the pain is more serious than distention and becomes alleviated after discharge of blood clots, it is caused by blood stasis; if distention is more serious than pain, it is caused by Qi stagnation.

1. Qi stagnation and blood stasis: It is characterized by non-palpable abdominal distension and pain one or two days before or during menstruation, scanty menorrhea or unsmooth menstruation with purple and blackish clots, alleviation after discharge of blood clots, often accompanied by discomfort in the chest and hypochondriac region, distension of breasts, darkish tongue even with spots, thin and wiry pulse.

2. Stagnation of cold dampness: It is characterized by cold pain in the lower abdomen several days before or during menstruation, alleviation with warmth, aggravation under pressure, blackish menorrhea with blood clots, or aversion to cold and body pain, whitish and greasy tongue coating, thin and tense pulse.

3. Deficiency of Qi and blood: It is characterized by vague pain after or during menstruation, alleviation under pressure, light or thin menorrhea, lassitude, lusterless complexion, anorexia and loose stool, light tongue with thin coating, weak and thin pulse.

4. Deficiency of liver and kidney: It is characterized by vague pain one or two days after menstruation, lumbago, scanty thin and blackish menorrhea, or accompanied by tinnitus, vertigo, giddiness, wrist or lumbar pain, sense of dropping in the abdomen, tidal fever, reddish cheeks, light tongue with thin whitish or yellowish coating, deep and thin pulse.

[Essentials for diagnosis]

1. Lower abdominal pain involving the waist and sacrum, even coma before or after or during menstruation, often appearing periodically.

2. Commonly seen among young and unmarried women.

3. Exclude abdominal pain due to organic pathological changes of pelvis.

[Treatment with Tuina therapy]

1. Principle: Regulating Qi and blood, warming meridians to dispel cold.

2. Acupoint: Qihai (CV 6), Guanyuan (CV 4), Shenshu (BL 23), Baliao, abdomen, lower abdomen, waist and back.

3. Operation

(1) The patient takes a supine position, and the doctor rubs the lower abdomen, then applying one-finger pushing, pointed pressing and rubbing manipulations to Qihai (CV 6) and Guanyuan (CV 4), 5 minutes for each Acupoint.

(2) The patient takes a prone position, the doctor rolls the bilateral sides of the spine column and wrist, then applying one-finger pushing and pointed pressing manipulations to Shenshu (BL 23) and Baliao until ache and distension are felt, finally rubbing the wrist and Baliao points until it turns warm. The time for operation is about 5 minutes.

4. Manipulations determined by syndrome differentiation

(1) Dysmenorrhea due to Qi stagnation and blood stasis: Pressing and rubbing Zhangmen (LR 13), Qimen (LR 14), Ganshu (BL 18) and Geshu (BL 17) first, then grasping Xuehai (SP 10) and Sanyinjiao (SP 6) until it is aching and distending.

(2) Dysmenorrhea due to stagnation of cold dampness: Firstly vertically rubbing the governor vessel over the back, and then horizontally rubbing Shenshu (BL 23) and Mingmen (GV 4) until it becomes warm, finally pressing and rubbing Xuehai (SP 10) and Sanyinjiao (SP 6).

(3) Dysmenorrhea due to deficiency of Qi and blood: Firstly vertically rubbing the Governor vessel over the back, then horizontally rubbing the back till it is warm, and finally wiping, pressing and kneading Zhongwan (CV 12), Pishu (BL 20), Weishu (BL 21) and Zusanli (ST 36).

(4) Dysmenorrhea due to deficiency of liver and kidney: First vertically rubbing the

governor vessel over the back, then horizontally rubbing Shenshu (BL 23) and Mingmen (GV 4) until it is warm, finally pressing and kneading Zhaohai (KI 6), Taixi (KI 3), Ganshu (BL 18), Shenshu (BL 23) and Yongquan (KI 1).

(5) Special treatment for dysmenorrhea of excess type: If there are deflected spinous process and slight tenderness at the fourth lumbar vertebrae or other lumbar vertebrae (mainly at the fourth lumbar vertebra), the doctor should use rotating and obliquely pulling manipulations to correct the deflected spinous process, vertically rubbing the governor vessel and horizontally rubbing Baliao points until it is warm.

This treatment should be taken twice one week before menstruation and continued for three successive months. Six times make up one course of treatment.

【Cautions】

1. Keep warm, avoid cold, and keep clean and hygienic during the menstrual period.
2. Take proper rest and avoid overstrain.
3. Keep peaceful mind and avoid fury and anxiety.
4. The late result of Tuina therapy in treating dysmenorrhea due to organic diseases is unsatisfactory.

7.2.10 Menopause syndrome

Menopause syndrome refers to a series of symptoms marked by autonomic nerve disorder and metabolic disturbance due to hypofunction of ovary and estrogen from reproductive age to old age.

Menopause syndrome is closely related to physiological characteristics before and after menopause. When a woman is around 49 years old, her kidney Qi gradually declines and the thoroughfare vessel and conception vessel become weak. During this period of time, the balance between Yin and Yang may be destroyed due to various internal and external factors, such as frequent superabundance or deficiency of Yin and Yang, melancholic personality, chronic disease, or the changes of family and social environment. Since the "kidney is the prenatal base of life", imbalance between Yin and Yang in the kidney will affect other Zangfu-organs and eventually involves the kidney. So the cause of menopause syndrome is the changes of the kidney, often involving the heart, liver, spleen and multiple meridians.

【Clinical manifestations】

Menopause syndrome usually occurs among women aging from 45~55 with psychic impairment and ovariotomy or radioactive treatment history. In diagnosis, cares should be taken to make sure whether there are changes in life and work. The early symptoms are tidal fever, perspiration and emotional change. The tidal fever runs from the chest to the head, neck and face, and then followed by sweating. After sweating, fever will abate. Such a fluctuation may last for several seconds or several minutes. The times of occurrence in a day is irregular. The emotional changes are manifested as irritation, anger, sadness and crying without any reason or loss of self-control. Other symptoms are vertigo, headache, insomnia, palpitation, lumbago, back pain and disorder of menstruation. The symptoms in the advanced stage are dry and hot sensation in the vagina, pruritus vulva, frequent and urgent urination or urinary incontinence, itchy skin and so on.

Examinations

1. Gynecology examination: Atrophy of vagina and uterus as well as reduced secretion in the cervix of uterus and vagina in the advanced stage.

2. Lab examination: Exfoliative cytoscopy of vagina test indicates that estrogen has decreased, ESH has increased and E2 has decreased.

〖Essentials for diagnosis〗

1. The clinical manifestations of menopause syndrome are complicated, the chief complaint is promiscuous and there are few signs. For this reason, it is easy to be confused with other diseases. So great cares must be taken to diagnose this syndrome and rule out other organic diseases.

2. Menopause syndrome often occurs among women over 40 years old with the symptoms of irregular menstruation or menopause, tidal fever, sweating, palpitation, irritability, insomnia or melancholy.

3. Varied atrophy of genital organs and other second sex signs.

4. Estrogen decreases in urine and blood while ESH and luteotropic hormone evidently increase.

5. Cervix of uterus and uterine body become smaller and the vaginal fornix becomes shallow.

6. Cervix of uterus contracts while endometrium becomes atrophic.

7. Vaginal mucosa becomes thin and lacks cells of superficial layer.

8. Increased PH level in the vagina.

9. Vagina is dry and loses elasticity.

〖Treatment with Tuina therapy〗

1. Principle: Balancing Yin and Yang, regulating the thoroughfare vessel and conception vessel.

2. Acupoint and location: Danzhong (CV 17), Zhongwan (CV 12), Qihai (CV 6), Guanyuan (CV 4), Zhongji (CV3). Waist and back region: Jueyinshu (BL 14), Geshu (BL 17), Ganshu (BL 18), Pishu (BL 20), Shenshu (BL 23), Mingmen (GV 4), Governor Vessel, the first line of the bladder meridian. Head, face, neck and nape region: Taiyang (EX-HN 5), Cuanzhu (BL 2), Sibai (ST 2), Yingxiang (LI 20), Baihui (GV 20), Fengchi (GB 20) and Jianjing (GB 21).

3. Operation

(1) The patient takes a recumbent position, the doctor applies one-finger pushing manipulation to Danzhong (CV 17), Zhongwan (CV 12), Qihai (CV 6), Guanyuan (CV 4) and

Zhongji (CV 3), 2~3 minutes for each Acupoint; then rubbing and kneading the stomach region and the lower abdomen clockwise for 5 minutes.

(2) The patient takes a prone position, the doctor applies one-finger pushing or pressing and kneading manipulations to Jueyinshu (BL 14), Geshu(BL 17), Ganshu (BL 18), Pishu (BL 20), Shenshu (BL 23) and Mingmen (GV 4), 2 minutes for each Acupoint; then rubbing the governor vessel and the first line of bladder meridian and Shenshu (BL 23) and Mingmen (GV 4) until it is warm inside.

(3) The patient takes a sitting position, the doctor pinches and grasps Fengchi (GB 20) and neck for 2 minutes; kneads and holds the head (from the front hairline to the back hairline) for 5~10 times; pushes with one finger and rubs with the thenar at the forehead for about 5 minutes; then rubs both sides of the forehead, eye socket and alae nasi for 5~10 times; presses and rubs Taiyang (EX-HN 5), Cuanzhu (BL 2), Sibai (ST 2), Yingxiang (LI 20) and Baihui (GV 20), about half a minute for each Acupoint; finally grasps Jianjing (GB 21) for 5~10 times.

4. Manipulations determined with syndrome differentiation

(1) Menopause syndrome due to deficiency of liver Yin and kidney Yin: Kneading and pressing Zhishi (BL 52), Xuehai (SP 10), Yinlingquan (SP 9), Sanyinjiao (SP 6), Taixi (KI 3), Taichong (LR 3), about half a minute for each Acupoint; then pushing both sides of Qiaogong alternately.

(2) Menopause syndrome due to disharmony between the heart and kidney: Kneading and pressing Tongli (HT 5), Neiguan (PC 6), Hegu (LI 4), Feishu (BL 13), Xinshu (BL 15), Xuehai (SP 10), Sanyinjiao (SP 6) and Taixi (KI 3), about half a minute for each Acupoint; then rubbing and stroking Yongquan (KI 1) until it is warm inside.

(3) Menopause syndrome due to deficiency of spleen and kidney Yang: Kneading and pressing Tianshu (ST 25), Quchi (LI 11), Hegu (LI 4), Zusanli (ST 36), Yanglingquan (GB 34), Fenglong (ST 40), Xuanzhong (GB 39), Weizhong(BL 40), Chengshan (BL 57) and Kunlun (BL 60), half a minute for each Acupoint; then vibrating Guanyuan (CV 4) and horizontally rubbing Baliao points until it is warm inside.

(4) Menopause syndrome due to deficiency of both the heart and spleen: Kneading and pressing Laogong (PC 8), Tongli (HT 5), Neiguan (PC 6), Hegu (LI 4), Xinshu (BL 15), Xuehai (SP 10), Zusanli (ST 36), Yinlingquan (SP 9), Xuanzhong (GB 39) and Sanyinjiao (SP 6), half a minute for each Acupoint; then rubbing and stroking Yongquan (KI 1) until it is warm inside.

(5) Menopause syndrome due to deficiency of both Yin and Yang: Kneading and pressing Hegu (LI 4), Zusanli (ST 36), Yanglingquan (GB 34), Xuehai (SP 10), Yinlingquan (SP 9), Sanyinjiao (SP 6), Taixi (KI 3), Taichong (LR 3) and Xuanzhong (GB 39), half a minute for each Acupoint; then rubbing and stroking Yongquan (KI 1) until it is warm inside.

(6) Menopause syndrome due to deficiency of blood: Kneading and pressing

Laogong (PC 8), Tongli (HT 5), Neiguan (PC 6), Hegu (LI 4), Xinshu (BL 15), Xuehai (SP 10), Zusanli (ST 36), Xuanzhong (GB 39), Sanyinjiao (SP 6) and Taichong (LR 3), half a minute for each Acupoint; then rubbing and stroking Yongquan (KI 1) until it is warm inside.

(7) Menopause syndrome due to liver stagnation and spleen deficiency: Kneading and pressing Neiguan (PC 6), Zusanli (ST 36), Yanglingquan (GB 34), Fenglong (ST 40), Xuanzhong (GB 39), Sanyinjiao (SP 6) and Taichong (LR 3), half a minute for each Acupoint; then rubbing and stroking Yongquan (KI 1) and horizontally rubbing Baliao points until it is warm inside.

(8) Menopause syndrome due to weakness of thoroughfare vessel and conception vessel: Kneading and pressing Hegu (LI 4), Zusanli (ST 36), Yanglingquan (GB 34), Yinlingquan (SP 9), Sanyinjiao (SP 6), Taixi (KI 3) and Taichong (LR 3), half a minute for each Acupoint; then vibrating Guanyuan (CV 4) and horizontally rubbing Baliao point; finally rubbing and stroking Yongquan (KI 1) until it is warm inside.

(9) Menopause syndrome due to stagnation of Qi and sputum: Kneading and pressing Zhigou (TE 6), Hegu (LI 4), Zusanli (ST 36), Tiantu (CV 22), Fenglong (ST 40), Sanyinjiao (SP 6), Taixi (KI 3) and Taichong (LR 3), half a minute for each Acupoint; then horizontally rubbing Baliao points until it is warm inside.

【Cautions】

1. Every woman must experience menopause period which is a normal physiological phase. The doctor should encourage the patient to take a positive attitude toward this disorder of autonomic nerve and help them relieve anxiety.

2. The curative effect of Tuina therapy on this syndrome is certain.

7.2.11 Impotence

Impotence refers to inability to erect penis or incomplete erection during sexual intercourse among young peope or people of prime of life due to deficiency, fright and damp heat. Western medicine holds that impotence is one of sexual dysfunctions among males, often accompanied by early emission, seminal emission, sexual hypoesthesia or asexuality due to disorder of cerebral cortex, central nerve system disorder and pathological changes of genital organ.

【Clinical manifestations】

1. Mingmen fire declination: It is characterized by inability to erect penis, thin and cold sperm, vertigo, tinnitus, dizziness, lassitude, whitish complexion, lumbago and limp knees, aversion to cold and cold limbs, light tongue with whitish coating, thin and deep pulse.

2. Deficiency of heart and spleen: Symptoms include inability to erect penis, lassitude, insomnia, lusterless complexion, anorexia, light tongue with whitish and greasy coating and thin pulse.

3. Downward migration of damp heat: Symptoms include flaccid penis, stench scrotum, weakness of lower limbs, yellow and brown urine, dripping urination, reddish tongue with yellowish and greasy coating, soft and rapid pulse.

4. Impairment of the kidney by terror and fear: Symptoms include inability to erect penis, or incomplete erection, cowardliness and suspiciousness, palpitation insomnia, light and greasy tongue coating, wiry and thin pulse.

【Essentials for diagnosis】

1. Major clinical manifestation of impotence is inability to erect penis, or incomplete erection, resulting in inability to conduct sexual intercourse.

2. Impotence is either primary or secondary, organic or functional. The manifestation of primary impotencies is failure to insert penis into vagina. The manifestation of secondary impotence is failure to continue sexual intercourse after insertion of penis into vagina. The manifestation of organic impotence is failure to erect penis at any time, neither during excitement (for example, during sleep and fullness of bladder) nor spontaneous erection. The manifestations of functional impotence is failure to conduct sexual intercourse after spontaneous erection.

3. Impotence is mainly caused by psychological factors. So the usual manifestations of the patients are nervousness, fear, melancholy, anxiety and distress.

4. To exclude functional impotence, other manifestations and causes have to be taken into consideration, such as secondary diabetes. In this case, routine blood and glucose in urine tests should be done.

【Treatment with Tuina therapy】

1. Principle: Invigorating kidney and strengthening Yang.

2. Acupoints and location: Shenque (CV 8), Qihai (CV 6), Guanyuan (CV 4), Zhongji (CV 3), Xinshu (BL 15), Pishu (BL 20), Shenshu (BL 23), Mingmen (GV 4), Yaoyangguan (GV 3), Sanyinjiao (SP 6), abdomen, waist and lower part of the body.

3. Operation

(1) The patient takes a recumbent position. The doctor kneads Shenque (CV 8) for about 5 minutes, then using one finger to push Qihai (CV 6), Guanyuan (CV 4) and Zhongji (CV 3) 2 minutes each, kneading the lower abdomen until it is warm, and finally vibrating the lower abdomen with palm.

(2) The patient takes a prone position, the doctor presses and rubs Xinshu (BL 15), Pishu (BL 20), Shenshu (BL 23) and Mingmen (GV 4), 2 minutes for each Acupoint; then rubs Yaoyangguan (GV 3) until it is warm inside.

(3) Pressing, kneading and rubbing Sanyinjiao (SP 6) with fingers, 2 minutes for each Acupoint; then pinching the legs alternately for about 3~5 minutes.

4. Manipulations determined according to syndrome differentiation

(1) Impotence due to Mingmen fire declination: Pressing and rubbing Shenshu (BL 23) and Mingmen (GV 4), 5 minutes for each Acupoint; vertically rubbing the governor

vessel and the bilateral lines of the bladder meridian; horizontally rubbing Shenshu (BL 23), Mingmen (GV 4) and Baliao points until it is warm inside.

(2) Impotence due to deficiency of the heart and spleen: Pressing and rubbing Neiguan (PC 6), Zusanli (ST 36) and Xuehai (SP 10), about 1~2 minutes for each Acupoint; pressing and kneading Xinshu (BL 15) and Pishu (BL 20), 3~5 minutes for each Acupoint.

(3) Impotence due to downward migration of damp heat: Pressing and rubbing Tianshu (ST 25), Fenglong (ST 40), Zusanli (ST 36), Yinlingquan (SP 9), Dachangshu (BL 25) and Pangguangshu (BL28), 2 minutes for each Acupoint; kneading the abdomen for about 5 minutes.

(4) Impotence due to impairment of the kidney by terror and fear: Rubbing the forehead about 10 times; pressing and kneading Taiyang (EX-HN 5), Shenmen (HT 7), Daling (PC 7) and Dannang (EX-LE 6), 1~2 minutes for each Acupoint; grasping and pinching the upper limbs alternately for about 2 minutes.

[Cautions]

1. Help the patient eliminate fear and keep a peaceful mood.
2. Encourage the patient to have confidence, especially mutual care between husband and wife.
3. Balance the activities of rest and work, actively participate in physical training.
4. Live a regular life and stop smoking and drinking.
5. Keep a peaceful mind, abstain masturbation and reduce sexual intercourse.

7.2.12 Toothache

Toothache, a frequently encountered syndrome in oral problems, can be induced or aggravated by cold, hot, sour and sweet tastes, usually seen in decayed tooth, pulpitis periodontitis and dental allergy in Western medicine.

[Clinical manifestations]

Toothache can occur at any age and in any season.

1. Toothache due to wind heat: Symptoms include recurrence of toothache with wind, aggravation with heat, alleviation with cold and gum swelling, accompanied by fever, aversion to cold, thirst, reddish tongue with whitish and dry coating and floating pulse.

2. Toothache due to stomach fire: Symptoms include acute toothache and gum swelling, even transude blood and pus, cheek swelling, headache, thirst, bad smell, constipation, yellowish and greasy tongue coating, surging and rapid pulse.

3. Toothache due to deficiency fire: Symptoms include vague or slight toothache, light reddish and slight swelling of gum, even atrophy of gum due to long-term duration, inability to bite due to slackness, severe pain in the afternoon, lumbar and back pain, vertigo, dizziness, thirst without any desire to drink water, reddish and tender tongue without coating, thin and rapid pulse.

【Essentials for diagnosis】

The problem with the symptoms mentioned above can be diagnosed as toothache.

1. Toothache due to wind heat: The main symptom is toothache which is aggravated by heat and alleviated by cold. Other symptoms are gum swelling, fever, aversion from cold, thirst, reddish tongue with whitish and dry coating, floating and rapid pulse.

2. Toothache due to stomach fire: The main symptom is acute toothache marked by gum swelling, even cheek swelling, headache, thirst, bad smell, constipation, yellowish and greasy tongue coating, full and rapid pulse.

3. Toothache due to deficiency fire: The main symptom is vague or slight toothache marked by light reddish and slight swelling of gum, even atrophy due to long-term duration, inability to bite slackness, severe pain in the afternoon, lumbar and back pain, vertigo, dizziness, thirst without desire to drink water, reddish and tender tongue without coating, thin and rapid pulse.

【Treatment with Tuina therapy】

1. Treatment principle: Dispelling wind and clearing away fire, subsiding swelling to stop ache.

2. Points and positions: Hegu (LI 4), Xia guan(ST 7), Jiache(ST 6), Neiting(ST 44), Taixi (KI 3), Xingjian (LR 2), Taichong (LR 3), facial region.

3. Operation

(1) Hitting, pressing and rubbing Neiting, Taixi (KI 3), Xingjian (LR 2) and Taichong (LR 3) with forceful strength for about 3 minutes.

(2) Pushing with one finger and pressing Xiaguan (ST 7) and Jiache (ST 6) for about 3 minutes.

(3) Pressing, kneading, pinching and grasping Hegu (LI 4) for about 1 minute.

(4) Finally pinching, grasping, pressing and grasping the local area of toothache.

4. Manipulations determined according to syndrome differentiation

(1) Toothache due to wind heat: Pushing Taiyang (EX-HN 5) with one finger, grasping Fengchi (GB 20), Quchi (LI 11) and Waiguan (TE 15).

(2) Toothache due to stomach fire: Apart from application of manipulations mentioned above, the manipulations for pressing and rubbing Erjian (TE 2), Sanjian (LI 3) and Neiting (ST 44) are also used.

(3) Toothache due to deficiency fire: Apart from application of manipulations mentioned above, the manipulations for pushing with one-finger, pressing and rubbing Taixi (KI 3) and Xingjian (LR 2) are also used.

【Cautions】

1. Whatever the cause is, the patient must gargle and brush teeth after meal.

2. During the course of treatment, the manipulation must focus on one spot. Any

sorts of friction must be avoided lest swelling be caused.

3. Decayed tooth, pulpitis periodontitis are acute inflammatory diseases and should be treated simultaneously by manipulations and drugs.

7.2.13 Deafness

Deafness is a symptom of abnormal changes of hearing. Its major manifestation is failure of hearing, often due to tinnitus. According to Western medicine, damage of acoustic nerve or congenital dysaudia due to auditory disease or certain drugs can cause deafness.

【Clinical manifestations】

1. Excess syndromes

Main symptoms: Sudden onset of deafness or sense of distension, continuous tinnitus in the ears which cannot be alleviated by pressing, accompanied by distension in the head, flushed complexion, dry throat, upset and irritability, wiry pulse due to superabundance fire in the liver and gallbladder; and aversion to cold, fever with floating pulse due to exogenous wind factor attack.

2. Deficiency syndrome

Main symptoms: Deafness due to long-term illness, tinnitus like cicada chirping, alleviation with pressure and aggravation with overstrain, accompanied by vertigo, soreness and weakness of the waist and knees, lassitude, seminal emission, leukorrhagia, thin and weak pulse due to deficiency of kidney Q, night sweat, reddish tongue with scanty fluid, thin and rapid pulse due to deficiency of liver Yin and kidney Yin. .

【Essentials for diagnosis】

1. Poor hearing accompanied by tinnitus and slight vertigo.

2. Deafness is often caused by anger, overstrain, exogenous factors; or toxic drugs, aging, weakness and malnutrition.

3. There are no obvious changes of drum membrane, or there are just opacity, invagination, thickening, adhesion and calcification.

4. Hearing examination shows deafness due to failure of sound perception or sound conduction.

5. Deafness should be differentiated from auditory distension, blockage, vertigo and acoustic neuroma.

【Treatment with Tuina therapy】

1. Principle: Dredging orifices and invigorating ears, clearing the liver to reduce fire.

2. Points and location: Ermen (TE 21), Tinggong (SI 19), Tinghui (GB 2), Yifeng (TE 17), Baihui (GV 20), Yamen (GV 15), Fengchi (GB 20), Fengfu (GV 16), head and the surrounding areas.

3. Operation

(1) Pinching and grasping the five meridians: Pinching, grasping, pressing and

rubbing the nape and neck region; then pressing and rubbing Baihui (GV 20), Yamen (GV 15), Fengchi (GB 20) and Fengfu (GV 16) for about 5 minutes.

(2) Pushing unilateral side of Ermen (TE 21), Tinggong (SI 19) and Tinghui (GB 2) with one finger; pressing and rubbing Yifeng (TE 17) for about 5 minutes.

(3) Pushing and rubbing manipulations: Using the index fingers and middle fingers to hold the ears and push backward and forward until it is warm inside for about 5 minutes.

(4) Vibrating the ears with palms.

4. Treatment based on syndrome differentiation

(1) Deafness due to predominant fire in the liver and gallbladder: Pressing Taichong (LR 3), Xingjian (LR 2), Danshu (BL 19) and Sanjiaoshu (BL 22) until sore and distending sensation is felt; rubbing the hypochondriac regions for about 1 minute; grasping the inner muscles of the thigh for about 2 minutes.

(2) Deafness due to wind attack: Rolling the neck and back regions for about 2~3 minutes; then pressing and rubbing Taiyang (EX-HN 5), Dazhui (GV 14), Feishu (BL 13) and Fengmen (BL 12); pinching Jianjing (GB 21) on both sides; horizontally rubbing bladder meridian at both sides until it is warm inside; pinching Jianjing (GB 21) on both sides; hitting the bladder meridian at both sides until it is slightly red.

(3) Deafness due to deficiency kidney Qi: Pressing and rubbing Qihai (CV 6), Guanyuan (CV 4), 1 minute for each Acupoint; vertically rubbing the governor vessel; horizontally rubbing Shenshu (BL 23), Mingmen (GV 4) and Baliao points until it is warm inside.

(4) Deafness due to deficiency of liver Yin and kidney Yin: Pressing and rubbing Shenshu (BL 23), Qihai (CV 6), Guanyuan (CV 4) and Sanyinjiao (SP 6), 2 minutes for each Acupoint; gently rubbing the waist and Yongquan (KI 1) until it is warm inside.

【Cautions】

1. Tuina therapy is effective to increase the flow blood in the brain, improve the blood and oxygen supply for the injured acoustic nerve, enforce the elasticity of the blood vessels, reduce obstruction and restore the function of acoustic nerve. But the effect in treating deafness due to damage of drum membrane is unsatisfactory.

2. The causes of deafness are various and complicated. So before treatment, trials have to be taken to make the diagnosis accurate and treat primary disease at the same time. The treatment of cervical deafness is discussed in the chapter dealing with cervical vertebral disorders.

3. Regular life and peaceful mind are very important for curing deafness. So the patient should avoid overstrain, adjust mental state and keep the acoustic meatus clean.

7.2.14 Depression syndrome

Depression syndrome is a general term for the diseases caused by depressed mind and stagnation of Qi, usually marked by depressed mind, dysphoria, distension and fullness in the chest, distending pain in the hypochondriac region, or irritability and frequent weeping or globus hystericus.

Depression syndrome is a general term for various related diseases, including dysfunction of viscera, blood stasis, phlegm retention, indigestion, and fire stagnation caused by invasion of six exogenous pathogenic factors, improper diet and stagnations of phlegm. In Western medicine, it pertains to the category of neurasthenia, hysteria, psychopathy and menopause syndrome. Tuina therapy is mainly used to deal with depression due to stagnation of Qi.

【Clinical manifestations】

1. Depression of liver Qi: Symptoms include depressed mind, chest oppression, frequent signing, distending pain in the hypochondriac region or pain without fixed location, anorexia, stomachache, vomiting, frequent eructation, impeded defecation, light whitish and greasy coating, wiry and tense pulse.

2. Qi stagnation transforming into fire: Symptoms include bad temper, chest oppression, bitter taste and dryness in the mouth, red eyes, tinnitus, belching and acid regurgitation, constipation, reddish tongue with yellowish coating, wiry and rapid pulse.

3. Stagnation of Qi and phlegm: Symptoms include depressed mind, globus hystericus in the throat unable to be swallowed or vomited, chest distension and oppression, light whitish coating, wiry and slippery pulse.

4. Insufficient nutrition of the heart and mind: Symptoms include emotional upset and trance, even frequently crying and laughing, light whitish coating, wiry and thin pulse.

5. Deficiency of heart and spleen: Symptoms include frequent contemplation and consideration, vertigo, lassitude, palpitation, timidity, insomnia, amnesia, anorexia, lusterless complexion, light tongue with whitish coating and thin pulse.

6. Deficiency of heart and kidney Yin: Symptoms include vertigo, tinnitus, palpitation, insomnia, upset and irritability, soreness and weakness in the waist and knees, seminal emission, irregular menstruation, reddish tongue with scanty coating, wiry, thin and rapid pulse.

【Essentials for diagnosis】

1. The main manifestation is mental fluctuation, accompanied by quick or retard thinking.

2. This disease is recurrent, the patient's mind appears normal during episodes of attack.

3. There are no positive symptoms involving the body and nerve system in lab examinations.

【Treatment with Tuina therapy】

1. Treatment principle: Soothing the liver to regulate Qi, relieving depression to eliminate phlegm.

2. Acupoint and location: Ganshu (BL 18), Pishu (BL 20), Weishu (BL 21),

Zhangmen (LR 13), Qimen (LR 14), back, hypochondriac and rib regions and abdomen.

3. Operation

(1) The patient takes a prone position. The doctor rolls along the bladder meridian on both sides for about 5 minutes, pushing with one finger, pressing and rubbing Ganshu (BL 18), Pishu (BL 20) and Weishu (BL 21), 2 minutes for each Acupoint.

(2) The patient takes a supine position. The doctor presses and rubs Zhangmen (LR 13) and Qimen (LR 14), about 1 minute for each Acupoint; then rubbing the hypochondriac and abdominal regions for about 3 minutes.

4. Treatment based on syndrome differentiation

(1) Stagnation of liver Qi: Pointing and pressing Taichong (LR 3) and Xingjian (LR2), about 2 minutes for each Acupoint; rubbing the hypochondriac and rid regions for about 1 minute.

(2) Qi stagnation transforming into fire: Pointing and pressing Danshu (BL 19) and Sanjiaoshu (BL 22), about 2 minutes for each Acupoint; then grasping the internal muscles of the thigh for about 5 minutes.

(3) Stagnation of Qi and phlegm: Pointing and pressing Feishu (BL 13), Danshu (BL 19) and Tiantu (CV 22), about 2 minutes for each Acupoint; then rubbing Zhongwan (CV 12) with palm for about 3 minutes.

(4) Insufficient nutrition of the heart and mind: Pressing and rubbing Xinshu (BL 15) and Zusanli (ST 36), about 2 minutes for each Acupoint; grasping the muscles over the lateral and anterior sides of the lower body for about 5 minutes.

(5) Deficiency of the heart and spleen: Pressing and rubbing Xinshu (BL 15), Neiguan (PC 6), Waiguan (TE 15) and Zusanli (ST 36) with finger, about 1 minute for each Acupoint; then rubbing Zhongwan (CV 12) with palm for about 3 minutes.

(6) Deficiency of heart and kidney Yin: Pressing and rubbing Shenshu (BL 23), Qihai (CV 6), Guanyuan (CV 4) and Sanyinjiao (SP 6) with finger, about 2 minutes for each Acupoint; then rubbing Yongquan (KI 1) until it is warm inside.

【Cautions】

1. Depression syndrome is often caused by emotional disorder. So treatment should focus on mental aspect, helping the patient relieve anxiety.

2. Keep the room quiet and noiseless, avoid strong light.

3. Take vegetables, fish, meat, dairy products and bean products, avoid pungent and fatty foods as well as smoking and drinking.

4. Balance the activities of work and rest and have enough sleep.

7.2.15 Irregular menstruation

Irregular menstruation is a common gynecological disease. It is also the general term for menstrual disorders. It is characterized by abnormal changes of menstrual period, quantity, color and quality, including advanced, delayed or irregular menstruation.

Advanced menstruation means that menstruation occurs one week earlier than usual; delayed menstruation means that menstruation occurs one week later than usual, even forty or fifty days later than usual; irregular menstruation means that menstruation occurs without a fixed period, it may be advanced or delayed.

In modern medicine, irregular menstruation is thought to be caused by disorder of estrogen excretion, dysfunction of autonomic nerve, emotional stimulation, cold and fatigue and other diseases.

【Clinical manifestations】

Irregular menstruation is mainly characterized by abnormal changes of menstrual period, quantity, color and quality. Abnormal changes of menstrual period are marked by advanced, delayed, irregular, shorted or prolonged menstruation. Abnormal quantity is marked by excessive or scanty menstruation. Abnormal changes of menstrual color are marked by thick or thin menstruation with blood clots or bad smell. Irregular menstruation also can be accompanied by discomfort in the lower abdomen, distension or pain in the breast or hypochondriac distension and pain, headache, vomiting and unsmooth urination and defecation.

1. Advanced menstruation: Menstruation occurs earlier than usual, even twice in one month. If it is due to excess heat, it is marked by excessive thick and purple menstruation, chest oppression, light and yellowish tongue coating, floating and rapid pulse. If it is due to Yin deficiency and blood heat, it is marked by scanty menstruation, flushed face and hot palm, reddish tongue with yellowish coating, thin and rapid pulse. If it is caused by liver stagnation transforming into heat, it is marked by menstruation with clots, distension and pain in the chest, breasts and lower abdomen, irritability and wiry pulse. If it is due to Qi deficiency, it is marked by scanty and thin menstruation, lassitude and palpitation, dropping and distending sense in the lower abdomen, light-colored tongue and weak pulse.

2. Delayed menstruation: Menstruation occurs later than usual. If it is due to excessive cold, it is marked by scanty and blackish menstruation, colic in the lower abdomen to be alleviated with warmth, bluish complexion and cold limbs, light-colored tongue with whitish coating, deep and tense pulse. If it is due to cold, it is marked by scanty and light-colored menstruation, abdominal pain to be alleviated by pressure and warmth, pale complexion, light-colored tongue with white coating, deep and slow pulse. If it is due to Qi stagnation, it is marked by scanty menstruation, lower abdominal distension and pain, depressed mind, discomfort and fullness in the chest to be alleviated after sighing, yellowish tongue coating, taut and unsmooth pulse. If it is due to blood deficiency, it is marked by lower abdominal pain, sallow complexion, dry skin, palpitation, giddiness, light-colored tongue with thin coating, weak and thin pulse.

3. Disordered menstruation: Early or delayed menstruation. If it is caused by liver stagnation, it is marked by unsmooth menstruation, distension and pain in the chest, breasts and lower abdomen, depression, chest oppression and taut pulse. If it is due to kidney deficiency, it is marked by scanty, thin and light-colored menstruation, blackish complexion, vertigo and tinnitus, soreness and weakness in the lower back and knees, frequent urination at night, light-colored tongue and coating, deep and weak pulse.

[Essentials for diagnosis]

1. Advanced menstruation: Menstruation occurs 7 days or even half a month earlier than usual, over twice in a month.

2. Delayed menstruation: Menstruation is delayed more than 35 days for over two periods. B ultrasonic examination should be taken to rule out organic diseases of uterus and ovary.

3. Disordered menstruation: Menstruation is advanced or delayed more than 7 days for over two periods. B ultrasonic examination should be taken to rule out other organic diseases. Basic body temperature test, vagina smear test and cervical mucous crystal examination should be taken to examine the function of ovary.

[Treatment with Tuina therapy]

1. Principle: Regulating the Qi and blood, soothing liver and adjusting Qi.

2. Acupoints and location: Guanyuan (CV 4), Qihai (CV 6), Zhongji (CV 3), Pishu (BL 20), Ganshu (BL 18), Shenshu (BL 23), Sanyinjiao (SP 6), Taichong (LR 3), Taixi (KI 3), abdomen, waist and back, lower part of body.

3. Operation

(1) The patient is in a supine position. The doctor pushes with one finger or rubs Qihai (CV 6), Guanyuan (CV 4) and Zhongji (CV 3), 1 minute for each Acupoint till Qi is obtained; then kneading the lower abdomen clockwise for about 10 minutes.

(2) The patient takes a prone position. The doctor pushes with one finger along the bilateral lines of the bladder meridian, especially Pishu (BL 20), Ganshu (BL 18) and Shenshu (BL 23), for about 3~5 minutes; then pressing and rubbing Pishu (BL 20), Ganshu (BL 18) and Shenshu (BL 23), 1 minute for each Acupoint till Qi is obtained.

(3) The patient takes a supine positon. The doctor presses with thumbs and kneads Sanyinjiao (SP 6), Taichong (LR 3) andTaixi (KI 3), 1 minute for each Acupoint till soreness and distension are felt.

4. Manipulations determined according to syndrome differentiation

(1) Heat blood: Pressing and kneading Dadun (LR 1), Xingjian (LR 2), Yinbai (SP 1), Sanyinjiao (SP 6), Jiexi (ST 41) and Xuehai (SP 10), 1 minute for each Acupoint till Qi is obtained; pressing and kneading with thumbs, index fingers or middle fingers around Ganshu (BL 18), Weishu (BL 21) and Dachangshu (BL 25) for about 3~5 minutes.

(2) Cold blood: Pressing Shenque (CV 8) for 3~5 minutes till it is warm in the lower abdomen; then rubbing the governor vessel, Shenshu (BL 23) and Mingmen (GV 4) for about 1~2 minutes until the warmth penetrates into the skin.

(3) Deficiency of Qi and blood: Pressing Zhongwan (CV 12) and Qihai (CV 6), 3

minutes for each Acupoint until it becomes warm; then pressing and rubbing Zusanli (ST 36) and Sanyinjiao (SP 6), 3 minutes for each Acupoint until Qi is obtained; next pressing and kneading with fingers over Pishu (BL 20) and Weishu (BL 21), 1 minute for each Acupoint; finally rubbing Pishu (BL 20) and Weishu (BL 21) until the warmth penetrates into the body.

(4) Liver depression: Pressing and kneading Zhangmen (LR 13) and Qimen (LR 14) for about 2 minutes; then pressing and kneading Geshu (BL 17) and Ganshu (BL 18) for about 3~5 minutes.

(5) Deficiency of kidney: Pressing Guanyuan (CV 4) for about 3~5 minutes until the warmth penetrates deeply into the abdomen; then pressing and kneading the bilateral sides of Yongquan (KI 1) for about 1 minutes; vertically rubbing the sole of foot repeatedly until the warmth penetrates into it; finally rubbing the governor vessel and the bilateral courses of the bladder meridian repeatedly for about 5~7 times; then rubbing Shenshu (BL 23), Mingmen (GV 4) and Baihuanshu (BL 30) until the warmth penetrates into the body.

【Cautions】

1. Tuina manipulation is applicable before and after the menstruation. Cares should be taken to adjust the diet, avoid crapulence, fatty, cold, uncooked and spicy foods.

2. Pay attention to changes of weather and avoid cold and excessive heat.

3. Keep a delighted mind, avoid extreme changes of emotions.

4. Rest more and avoid overstrain and excessive sexual intercourse.

Review Questions

- Describe how to diagnose and treat cervical Spondylopathy, acute Lumbar Sprain, chronic lumbar muscle strain, lumbar disc protrusion, piriformis Syndrome, lumbospinal myofascitis, scapulohumeral periarthritis and injury of the collateral ligament of knee joint.
- Describe how to diagnose and treat stomachache, constipation, headache, insomnia, menopause syndrome, depression syndrome and irregular menstruation.

8

Tuina Therapy for Commonly Encountered Infantile Diseases

8.1 Basic manipulations for infantile Tuina

8.1.1 Pushing manipulation

Exert force on the treated area or certain Acupoint. The manipulation performed by pushing straight forward or making rotational movements on the point with the pad of the thumb or the pads of the index and middle fingers is known as pushing manipulation, which can be further categorized, according to different operating methods, into straight pushing manipulation, rotational pushing manipulation, separate-pushing manipulation and combined pushing manipulation.

【Methods for performing manipulations】

Straight pushing manipulation: Push one way straight on the Acupoint with the radial aspect of the thumb or the pads of the index and middle fingers (see Fig. 8-1 on page 147).

Rotational pushing manipulation: Make clockwise or counterclockwise rotational movements on the Acupoint with the pad of the thumb (see Fig. 8-2 on page 148).

Separate-pushing manipulation: Push from a point to both sides respectively or make such movements in the form of the Chinese character "八" (eight) with the radial aspects or pads of the thumbs or the pads of the index and middle fingers (see Fig. 8-3 on page 148).

Combined pushing manipulation: Straighten the thumbs with the other fingers separated, and push from two sides of a point to its center with palms or the whorl surface of both thumbs (see Fig. 8-4 on page 148).

【Essentials for performing manipulations】

Straight pushing manipulation: Relax the shoulder, elbow and wrist. Straighten the thumb, or straighten the index and the middle finger; perform adducting or abducting movements with the redial aspect of the thumb; flex and extend the elbow while performing with the index and the middle finger. During the operation, the movements should be done quickly and continuously with a frequency of 250~300 times per minute.

Rotational pushing manipulation: Relax the shoulder, elbow and wrist. Rub the body surface with the pad of the thumb without pulling the subcutaneous tissue to move. The operation should be done with steady and mild force at a speed of 160~200 times per minute.

Separate-pushing manipulation: Push from a point to both sides with both hands, and coordinate the movements with steady and mild force. The movements should be dexterous and gentle. The operation can be done either along a straight line or along curved body surface at a frequency of 120~160 times per minute.

Combined pushing manipulation: The operation is similar to that of separate-pushing manipulation. It is done in the opposite direction of separate-pushing manipulation with a comparatively small range of motion.

【Cautions】

1. When performing straight pushing, the practitioner should pay attention to the operating direction and regulate the force and speed to gain different reinforcing and reducing effects.

2. Apply certain amount of shallot juice, ginger juice or sesame oil to prevent injury of the skin and improve the effect of the therapy.

3. Straight pushing should be done in stable motions with even force.

8.1.2 Kneading manipulation

Kneading manipulation is performed by fixing the thenar or whorl surface of the middle finger or thumb on a certain part or point and making circular movements. Kneading manipulation can be further categorized according to different operating methods into middle finger kneading manipulation, thumb kneading manipulation and thenar kneading manipulation.

【Methods for performing manipulations】

1. Finger kneading manipulation: Fix the pad or fingertip of one, or two or three fingers on the treated area or point, directing the subcutaneous tissue to make soft and circular movements in small amplitude.

2. Palm base kneading manipulation: Fix the palm base on the treating point, relax the wrist, press downward with force, use the elbow as a pivot, sway the forearm initiatively and direct the force-exerting point to make soft and circular movements in small amplitude.

3. Thenar manipulation: Fix the great thenar on the treated point, relax the wrist, sway the forearm initiatively and direct the skin with the movements of the wrist to make soft and fast circular movements.

【Essentials for performing manipulations】

1. The practitioner should relax the shoulder, elbow and wrist, and keep the fingers naturally forked.

2. The manipulation should be done with steady and even force in a certain rhythm.

The practitioner should keep the rhythm.

3. The kneading movement should be performed from small to big amplitude. The frequency is 200~300 times per minute.

【Cautions】

1. During the operation, the practitioner should fix the force-exerting point and make movements with mild force. Local slippage and friction are forbidden.

2. Strong force is not applied in this manipulation.

8.1.3 Pressing manipulation

Pressing manipulation is performed by pressing a certain part or point with the fingers or palm, steadily exerting force. It is divided into finger pressing and palm pressing manipulation.

【Methods for performing manipulations】

1. Palm pressing manipulation: Straighten the wrist, relax the five fingers by straightening, attach the palm surface or palm base to the treated part, press the point vertically for a certain period of time and then relax. Repeat such a manipulation again and again.

2. Finger pressing manipulation: Press the treated part vertically with the whorl surface of the thumb or middle finger. The rest of the manipulations are similar to palm pressing manipulation.

【Essentials for performing manipulations】

1. Drive Qi down to Dan Tian (lower abdomen) instead of holding the breath forcibly.

2. Press still with steadily increasing force.

【Cautions】

1. The practitioner should keep his hands attached to the treated area after pressing instead of removing his hands suddenly. Strong force is forbidden.

2. During the operation of palm pressing, the contact area is large, requiring strong pressure but mild stimulation.

3. The contact area is small in the performing finger pressing with mild force.

8.1.4 Mo Fa (Circular rubbing manipulation)

Circular rubbing manipulation is performed by fixing the palm surface or the pad of the thumb, index or middle finger on a certain part or point, using the wrist together with the forearm to make clockwise or counterclockwise movements.

【Methods for performing manipulations】

1. Palm rubbing manipulation: Extend the fingers naturally and slightly bend the wrist joint, attach the palm surface slightly on the treated area, relax the wrist joint, use the forearm and the wrist and palm to perform clockwise or counterclockwise rubbing.

2. Finger rubbing manipulation: Extend the index, middle finger, ring finger and small finger, bend the wrist joint slightly, attach the pads of the fingers on the treated area or point, use the forearm and the wrist to perform circular movements.

【Essentials for performing manipulations】

1. The practitioner should relax the shoulder, elbow and wrist with the elbow slightly flexed.

2. During the operation of palm rubbing, the practitioner should relax the wrist joint and extend the palm naturally; while in finger rubbing, the practitioner should slightly bend the wrist as well as the fingers.

3. The manipulation should be performed in slow and coordinated motions with moderate force at a frequency of 120~160 times per minute.

【Cautions】

1. Avoid affecting the subcutaneous tissue during rubbing.

2. The fingers should also make circular movements in accordance with the manipulation. Tapping and striking are not allowed.

8.1.5 Nipping manipulation

Nipping manipulation is done by hitting a point or area with the nail of the thumb.

【Methods for performing manipulations】

The practitioner should hold a hollow fist with the thumb extended, fix the nail of the thumb on the treated point or area, and then perform pressing or kneading with gradual intensification (see Fig. 8-5 on page 150).

【Essentials for performing manipulations】

1. The force should be made vertically with gradual intensification. The practitioner can also make force at intervals to increase stimulation. The selection of Acupoints should be accurate.

2. Usually the manipulations is performed 4~5 times in one treatment. Frequent and long-term application is not advisable. Strong force is applied in emergency until the patient becomes conscious.

【Cautions】

Nipping manipulation is one of the manipulations with strong stimulation. Therefore, frequent and long-term application is not advisable. To avoid injury of the skin, the practitioner can put thin cloth onto the treated area or point. Kneading manipulation is often operated after nipping to alleviate stimulation, local pain and discomfort.

8.1.6 Pinching manipulation

Pinching manipulation is done by holding the limbs or grasping the skin with the pads of the thumb, index and middle finger, squeezing with opposite force, pinching and releasing repeatedly.

【Methods for performing manipulations】

For children, this manipulation is mainly performed by pinching the spine.

1. Three-finger pinching: Support the skin with the thumb, press forward with the index and middle finger; then grasp and lift the skin with the three fingers simultaneously with opposite force; perform the lifting and pinching manipulations with both hands alternately and move forward, pinching and releasing repeatedly. (see Fig. 8-6 on page 150)

2. Two-finger pinching: Bend the index and support the skin with the radial aspect of the middle knuckle of the flexed index finger. Press forward with the thumb and then use opposite force to lift and pinch with the thumbs and index fingers of both hands that alternately move forward (see Fig. 8-7 on page 150).

【Essentials for performing manipulations】

1. Exert force with the forearm hanging still and pinch steadily and softly with the wrist and metacarpophageal joint.

2. The manipulation should follow be done in order: First, grasp and lift up the skin, and then pinch and press forward. The practitioner is supposed to repeat such a way of manipulation for several times.

3. The manipulation is done slowly and rhythmically with mild and even force. The movements should be soft and dexterous.

【Cautions】

1. The manipulation should be performed continuously without halting or skipping. The amount of the skin pinched and the force used should be proper.

2. During pinching operation, twisting and rotating operation must be avoided. The practitioner should avoid nipping and pressing the skin with fingernails. When pinching forward, the manipulation should be performed in a straight line without deflection.

8.1.7 Circularly pushing manipulation

Circularly pushing manipulation is performed by pushing on certain points in an arc or rotary way with the whorl surface of the thumb or middle finger.

【Methods for performing manipulations】

Attach the whorl surface of the thumb or the middle finger to the treated area and push in an arc or rotary way. (see Fig. 8-8 on page 151).

【Essentials for performing manipulations】

1. Extend the wrist joint naturally, straighten the thumb with other fingers slighted curved, open the Hukou (thumb web, the part between the thumb and the index finger) and use the radial aspect of the tip of the thumb as the force-exerting point. Or exert force with the tip of the middle finger while the other four fingers are slightly curved.

2. Wave the metacarpophangeal joint or wrist joint to lead the thumb or middle finger to push in an arc or rotary way.

3. The operation should be done with mild force. The rubbing is only sensed by the surface of the skin. The frequency is often monitored at 80~120 times per minute.

【Cautions】

1. Deep muscular tissues should not be involved in the operation. The force applied is lighter than that of the pushing manipulation and circular rubbing manipulation.

2. Lubricant can be applied during the operation to protect the skin of the infant patients.

8.1.8 Pounding manipulation

Pounding manipulation is performed by striking certain Acupoints with the tip of the middle finger or the interphalangeal joints of the flexed index and middle fingers.

【Methods for performing manipulations】

Relax the shoulder, elbow and wrist. Then wave the wrist to lead the tip of the finger to strike the Acupoints. The finger is lifted up instantly after striking. Generally 5 to 20 times of striking is done in one treatment. (see Fig. 8-9 on page 152).

【Cautions】

1. During the operation, relax the interphalangeal joints and flex and extend the wrist joint initiatively.

2. The selection of the treated area or Acupoints should be accurate. The striking should be elastic.

3. Violent force should be avoided. The practitioner should clip his nails in advance to avoid injury of the skin.

8.2 Compound manipulations for infantile Tuina

8.2.1 Huang Feng Ru Dong (Wasp entering the hole)

【Methods for performing manipulations】

Support the head of the infant gently with one hand and keep it in a comparatively fixed position. Then attach the tip of the middle finger of the other hand to the area below the nares, wave the wrist to repeat kneading movements with the middle finger for about 50~100 times. (see Fig. 8-10 on page 152)

【Action】

The manipulation is effective for inducing sweat, ventilating the lung and relieving stuffy nose. It is used to treat fever caused by exogenous pathogenic wind cold, an hidrosis, nose stuffiness and difficult breath due to acute or chronic rhinitis.

8.2.2 Manipulation of Shuang Feng Zhan Chi (Two phoenixes spreading wings)

【Methods for performing manipulations】

The practitioner presses the ears of the infant from both sides with the thumbs and middle fingers of both hands and lifting for 3~5 times; then uses the tip(s) of the thumb(s) of one hand or both hands to press the brow, Taiyang (EX-HN 5), Tinghui, Renzhong, Chengjiang(CV 24) and Jiache (ST 6). Each Acupoint is pressed 3~5 times.

【Action】

This manipulation is effective for relieving wind and dispersing cold, warming the lung and dredging meridian passage, relieving cough and reducing phlegm. It is used to treat upper respiratory tract diseases like attack by exogenous pathogenic wind cold and cough with excessive phlegm (see Fig. 8-11 on page 152).

8.2.3 An Xuan Zou Cuo Mo (Twisting and rubbing like plucking string)

【Methods for performing manipulations】

Seat the infant in a chair or in the parent's arms, cross the patient's forearms onto the opposite shoulder respectively. Then sit in front of the infant, twist and rub the hypochondriac areas downwards to both sides of the lower abdomen with both palms for 50~500 times. (see Fig. 8-12 on page 153)

【Action】

This manipulation is effective for regulating Qi to dissipate phlegm and invigorating the spleen to promote digestion. It is used to treat phlegm accumulation, chest stuffiness, cough, panting, abdominal pain, abdominal distention and dyspepsia etc.

8.2.4 Yuan Hou Zhai Guo (Manipulation of ape picking fruits)

【Methods for performing manipulations】

Seat the infant patient in a chair or let him lie on the back, and then sit in front of the infant. Pinch the skin above the Luoshigu with the thumbs and index fingers of both hands, pinching and releasing alternately for a number of times. (see Fig. 8-13 on page 153)

【Action】

The manipulation is effective for invigorating the spleen to dissipate phlegm. It is used to treat food retention, cold phlegm, alternate attacks of chill and fever.

8.2.5 Manipulation of Shui Di Lao Yue (Scooping the moon from the bottom of water)

【Methods for performing manipulations】

The doctor puts the infant in a chair or lets the infant lie on the back, and then sits in front of the infant, holding the infant's four fingers and turn the palm upward, dropping cool water in the center of the palm, and performing rotationally pushing with the whorl surface of the other thumb; then pushing from the infant's little finger base with the edge of the palm. During the operation, the doctor should blow cool air to the palm while pushing. This manipulation should be repeated for 3~5 minutes (see Fig. 8-14 on page 153).

【Action】

The manipulation can induce cold and cool effect, and is effective for clearing away heat, cooling blood and tranquilizing the mind to relieve dysphoria. It is used to treat excess heat syndrome such as fever, coma, heat in the blood, dysphoria, and constipation.

8.2.6 Manipulation of Da Ma Guo Tian He (Beating the horse to cross the heaven river)

【Methods for performing manipulations】

Seat the infant patient sitting in a chair or let him lie on the back, and then sit in front of the infant patient. Support the infant patient's four fingers with the palm facing upward. Put the pad of the other middle finger on the patient's Neilaogong point, and then flick and beat with the index, middle and ring fingers from Acupoint Zongjin, along Tianheshui to Hongchi. This manipulation should be repeated for 20~30 times (see Fig. 8-15 on page 154).

【Action】

This manipulation is effective for clearing away heat and cooling blood. It is used to treat fever, dysphoria, coma, delirious speech, numbness and twitch in the upper limbs.

8.2.7 Manipulation of Yun Tu Ru Shui (Carrying earth into water)

【Methods for performing manipulations】

Seat the infant in a chair or let him lie on the back, and then sit in front of the infant patient. Use one hand to hold the infant patient's four fingers (index, middle finger, ring finger and little finger) and turn the palm upward. Then push with the radial aspect of the other thumb from Acupoint Pitu along the edge of the palm, by way of Xiaotianxin and Zhangxiaohengwen, to Shenshui at the tip of little finger. Repeat this manipulation for 100~300 times in one direction (see Fig. 8-16 on page 154).

【Action】

The manipulation is effective for clearing away heat in the spleen and stomach, promoting diuresis, stopping diarrhea and nourishing kidney water. It is used to treat frequent and hot urination, abdominal distension and diarrhea.

8.2.8 Manipulation of Yun Shui Ru Tu (Carrying water into earth)

【Methods for performing manipulations】

Seat the infant in a chair or let him lie on the back, and then sit in front of the infant patient. Use one hand to hold the infant patient's four fingers (index, middle finger, ring finger and little finger) and turn the palm upward. Then push with the radial aspect of the other thumb from Acupoint Shenshui along the edge of the palm, by way of Zhanghengwen and Xiaotianxin, to Pitu at the tip of the thumb. Repeat the operation 100~300 times in one direction (see Fig. 8-17 on page 155).

[Action]

This manipulation is effective for strengthening the spleen to help transformation and transportation moistening dryness to relieve constipation. It is used to treat indigestion, poor appetite, constipation, abdominal distention and diarrhea, etc.

8.3 Specific acupoints for infantile tuina

Specific points here refer to the points used only in infantile Tuina therapy. (see Fig. 8-18, 8-19, 8-20 on page 155, 156, 157) They have locations not only in the form of "point", but also in the form of "course" and "area", as is said in the saying that all the meridians and collaterals in children converge in the hands. In order to make it easier to learn how to apply these points, the information in the item "times" is only for infants aging from 6 months to 1 year, just as a clinical reference. During clinical operation, there are some factors that should be taken into consideration to increase or reduce the times of performance, such as age, constitution and state of illness. Usually the specific points on the upper limbs are applied for both boys and girls. Practitioners often perform on the left hand. The following is the order of the operation in infantile Tuina therapy: the head and face, the upper limbs, the chest and abdomen, the lower limbs. The order can be determined according to the condition of disease and the posture of the infant during the treatment.

8.3.1 Kangong

Location: The transverse line from the medial end to the lateral end of the eyebrow.

Manipulation: Push the points respectively from the medial ends of the eyebrows to the lateral ends with both thumbs, known as pushing Kangong or pushing eyebrow arc. Repeat the manipulation 30~50 times.

Action: Dispersing wind to relieve exterior syndrome, restore consciousness to improve vision, and relieve headache.

Indication: Exogenous fever, headache, redness and pain of eyes, convulsion and myopia.

Application: It is used together with the manipulations for pushing Cuanzhu (BL 2) and kneading Taiyang (EX-HN 5) to treat fever in exterior syndrome and headache. When applied to treat redness and pain of the eyes, it is often used together. with the manipulations for clearing Ganjing (liver meridian), kneading Xiaotianxin (small heaven center) and clearing Tianheshui (heaven water).

8.3.2 Tianmen (Heaven gate)

Location: The line from the midpoint between the two eyebrows to the anterior hairline.

Manipulation: Push the point straight upward with the pads of both thumbs alternately, known as opening Tianmen (heaven gate), or pushing Cuanzhu (BL 2). Repeat the manipulation 30~50 times.

Action: Inducing sweat to relieve exterior syndrome, resuscitating the brain to activate spirit.

Indication: Headache, cold, vertigo, night cry and insomnia.

Application: It is often used together with the manipulations for pushing Kangong and kneading Taiyang (EX-HN 5) to treat fever, headache, absence of sweating and common cold due to wind cold. When applied to treat convulsion and restlessness, it is often used together with the manipulations for clearing Ganjing (liver meridian), pounding Xiaotianxin (small heaven center), kneading Wuzhijie (fiver finger sections) and Baihui (GV 20).

8.3.3 Taiyang (EX-HN 5)

Location: In the depression beside the lateral end of the eyebrow.

Manipulation: Kneading the point with the distal ends of the middle finger or thumb, known as kneading Taiyang (EX-HN 5). The reinforcing manipulation is done by kneading toward the eye, while the reducing manipulation is performed by kneading toward the back of the ear. Pushing the point straight backward with the radial aspect of the thumb is called pushing Taiyang. Repeat the manipulation 30~50 times respectively.

Action: Relieve the exterior, improve vision and relieve headache.

Indication: Headache, vertigo, cold, fever, redness and pain of eyes.

Application: To treat exogenous headache of exterior excess type, the manipulation for reducing purpose is used. To treat headache due to exterior deficiency and interior injury, the manipulation for reinforcing purpose is used. Pushing Taiyang is mainly used to treat exogenous fever.

8.3.4 Erhougaogu (Prominent bone behind the ear)

Location: In the depression inferior to the mastoid process behind the eye and superior to the posterior hairline.

Manipulation: Kneading the point with the tip of the thumbs or middle fingers is called kneading Erhougaogu. Repeat the manipulation 30~50 times.

Action: Dispel wind and relieve the exterior, ease the mind and remove restlessness.

Indication: Headache, dysphoria and common cold.

Application: It is used together with the manipulations for pushing Cuanzu(BL2), Kangong and kneading Taiyang (EX-HN5), often used to together with the manipulations for opening Tianmen, pushing Kangong and kneading Taiyang. The four Acupoints mentioned above are usually called the four major manipulations for infantile Tuina.

8.3.5 Tianzhugu (Cervical column)

Location: The line from the midpoint of the posterior hairline to Dazhui (GV 14).

Manipulation: Pushing the point straight downward with the pads of the thumb or the index and middle fingers. Repeat the manipulation 100~500 times.

Action: Descending the adverse flow of Qi to stop vomiting, expelling wind to remove cold.

Indication: Nausea, vomiting, cold, fever, sore-throat and stiff nape.

Application: For vomiting and nausea, the manipulation is often used together with the manipulations pushing from Hengwen (transverse crease) to Banmen (major thenar) and kneading Zhongwan (CV 12). For fever in exterior syndrome, rigidity and pain of nape, it is commonly used together with the manipulations of grasping Fengchi (GB 20) and kneading Ershanmen (double gate).

8.3.6 Rugen (ST 18)

Location: 0.2 cun below the breast.

Manipulation: Kneading the point with the tip of the middle finger. Repeat the manipulation 20~50 times.

Action: Relieve chest distress to regulate Qi, stop cough and resolve phlegm.

Indication: Chest oppression, cough and chest pain.

Application: See Rupang (the Acupoint lateral to the breast).

8.3.7 Rupang (Region lateral to the breast)

Location: 0.2 cun lateral to the breast.

Manipulation: Kneading the Acupoint with the tip of the middle finder. Repeat the manipulation 20~50 times.

Action: Relieving chest distress to regulate Qi, stopping cough and resolving phlegm.

Indication: Chest oppression, wheezing, cough and vomiting.

Application: It is mainly used to treat chest oppression, cough, wheezing and vomiting. Clinically, Rugen (ST18) and Rupang are often used in combination, operated with the index and middle fingers together.

8.3.8 Xielei (Hypochondrium)

Location: Hypochondriac regions from the level of armpits to Tianshu (ST 25).

Manipulation: Rubbing the hypochondriac regions with both palms across under the armpits to Tianshu (ST 25) is called Cuo Mo Xielei (rubbing and stroking the hypochondrium). Repeat the manipulation 50~100 times.

Action: Guide Qi to flow downward, resolve phlegm and relieve chest oppression.

Indication: Chest oppression, phlegmatic dyspnea and pain in the hypochondriac region.

Application: This manipulation is effective for opening and descending. It is used to treat chest oppression and abdominal distension due to indigestion, phlegm accumulation and adverse flow of Qi.

8.3.9 Fu (Abdomen)

Location: Abdomen.

Manipulation: Rubbing the abdomen means to push along the border of costal arch, or from Zhongwan (CV 12) to the umbilicus and toward both sides of the abdomen. Rubbing the abdomen with the palm or the four fingers is called Mo Fu (rubbing the abdomen) (see Fig. 8-21 on page 159). Repeat the operations 100~200 times for 5 minutes.

Action: Invigorating the spleen and regulating stomach, and regulate Qi to promote digestion.

Indication: Diarrhea, abdominal distension, abdominal pain, constipation, nausea and vomiting.

Application: Rubbing and kneading the abdomen in clockwise circles (reducing method) is used to treat excess syndrome such as infantile diarrhea, constipation, abdominal distension and anorexia; while the counterclockwise movement (reinforcing method) is used to treat deficiency syndrome such as spleen deficiency and diarrhea. Rubbing manipulation is often used in combination with the manipulations for pinching the spine and kneading Zusanli. The manipulation for separately pushing abdominal Yin and Yang is used in combination with the manipulations for pushing from Hengwen (transverse crease) to Banmen (major thenar) and pushing Tianzhugu (cervical column) to treat dyspepsia due to improper diet. This manipulation is also used as a method of infantile healthcare.

8.3.10 Qi (Umbilicus)

Location: On the umbilicus.

Manipulation: Rubbing the point with the fingers or palm is called rubbing umbilicus. Kneading the point with the tip of the thumb or the middle finger, or with palm base is called kneading umbilicus. Knead the point 100~300 times and rub it 3~5 minutes.

Action: Counterclockwise rubbing and kneading can warming Yang to dispel cold and invigorate Qi and blood; clockwise rubbing and kneading can promote digestion to eliminate stagnation.

Indication: Abdominal pain, constipation, abdominal distension, food retention and diarrhea etc.

Application: Clinically, this manipulation is used in combination with the manipulations for rubbing abdomen, pushing upwards Qijiegu (from the fourth lumbar vertebra to the end of coccyx) and kneading Guiwei (coccyx). Rubbing and kneading umbilicus counterclockwise can treat deficiency syndrome and cold syndrome such as infantile diarrhea, borygmus and abdominal pain. Rubbing and kneading umbilicus clockwise can treat excess syndrome such as infantile constipation and abdominal distention.

8.3.11　Dantian (Lower abdomen)

Location: On the lower abdomen, 2 or 3 cun below the umbilicus.

Manipulation: Kneading or rubbing the point respectively is called kneading Dantian (lower abdomen) or rubbing Dantian. Knead Dantian 50~100 times or rub it for 5 minutes.

Action: Reinforcing the kidney to strengthen the body resistance, warming and reinforcing kidney Yang, and separating purity from turbidity.

Indication: Enuresis and abdominal pain.

Application: Combined with the manipulations for reinforcing Shenjing (kidney meridian), pushing Sanguan (triple pass) and kneading Wailaogong (EX-UE8), it is often used to treat abdominal pain and enuresis due to congenital deficiency and cold accumulation in the lower abdomen.

8.3.12　Dujiao (Side of abdomen)

Location: 2 cun below the umbilicus and 2 cun lateral to Shimen (CV 5).

Manipulation: Grasping with the thumb, index and middle finger is called grasping Dujiao and pressing with the tip of the middle finger is called pressing Dujiao. Repeat the manipulation 3~5 times.

Action: Relieve abdominal pain.

Indication: Abdominal pain and diarrhea.

Application: It is used to treat abdominal pain due to various factors, especially effective for treating cold pain and abdominal pain due to improper diet. It is advisable to apply this manipulation after other manipulations lest that the baby's crying affect the performance of manipulations.

8.3.13　Feishu (BL 13)

Location: 1.5 cun lateral to the spinous process of the third thoracic vertebra.

Manipulation: Kneading the point with the tip of the index and middle fingers of one hand, or the tip of both thumbs is called kneading Feishu (BL 13). Pushing downward separately along the inner edge of the scapulae with the thumbs is called pushing Feishu (BL 13), or pushing scapulae. Repeat the kneading manipulation 50~100 times and the pushing manipulation 100~300 times.

Action: Separate pushing the scapulae is effective for descending the lung Qi and relieving cough. Kneading Feishu (BL 13) is effective for regulating lung Qi and improving deficiency.

Indication: Cough, asthma, chest oppression, chest pain, wheezing, sore-throat, cold, fever, and back pain etc.

Application: It is used to treat infantile respiratory diseases in combination with the manipulations for pushing and kneading Danzhong (CV 17), kneading Rugen (ST 18) and Rupang (region lateral to the breast), pushing Feijing (lung meridian), circularly pushing Neibagua, kneading Tiantu (CV 22), kneading Zhangxiaohengwen (small palmar transverse crease) and pushing Xiaohengwen (small transverse crease).

8.3.14 Jizhu (Spinal column)

Location: On the spine, the segment between Dazhui (GV 14) and Changqiang (GV 1).

Manipulation: Pinching the spine upward is called Nie Ji (pinching along the spine), which is often performed by lifting the skin of the spine once after every three times of pinching. Pushing the spine straight downward with the pads of the index and middle fingers is called Tui Ji (pushing the spinal column). Repeat the pushing manipulation 100~300 times and pinching manipulation 3~5 times.

Action: Pinching along the spine is effective for balance Yin and Yang, regulating Qi and blood, harmonizing Zangfu-organs, dredging the meridians and cultivating Yuan Qi (primordial Qi). Pushing the spinal column is effective for clearing away heat.

Indication: Diarrhea, abdominal pain, vomiting, constipation, fever and night crying.

Application: Nie Ji (pinching along the spine) is one of the commonly used manipulations for infantile healthcare. In clinic, it is often used in coordination with the manipulations for reinforcing Pijing (spleen meridian), reinforcing Shenjing (kidney meridian), pushing Sanguan (triple pass), rubbing the abdomen in circles, pressing and kneading Zusanli (ST 36) to treat diseases due to congenital deficiency and acquired insufficiency.

Pushing along the spinal column, combined with clearing Tianheshui (heaven river water), reducing Liufu (six Fu-organs) and pushing Yongquan (KI 1), is used to treat infantile fever.

8.3.15 Qijiegu (Seven lumbrosacral vertebrae)

Location: On the spine, the part from the 4th lumbar vertebra to the end of the coccyx, or Changqiang (GV 1).

Manipulation: Pushing the spine upward with the radial side of the thumb or the pads of the index and middle fingers is called pushing lumbrococcygeal vertebrae upward; and pushing downward is called pushing lumbrococcygeal vertebrae downward (see Fig. 8-22 on page 160). Repeat the manipulation 100~300 times.

Action: Warming Yang to relieve diarrhea, and purging heat to promote defecation.

Indication: Diarrhea, constipation and fever.

Application: pushing lumbrococcygeal vertebrae upward is effective for warming Yang to relieve diarrhea, which is usually used for diarrhea due to deficiency and cold and abdominal pain. Clinically, it is often used in combination with the manipulations for reinforcing the large intestine, pushing Sanguan (triple pass), pressing and kneading Baihui (GV 20), and kneading Dantian (lower abdomen). The manipulation is not advisable to treat diarrhea due to heat and dampness, otherwise it may cause abdominal distension or other problems in infants.

Pushing lumbrococcygeal vertebrae downward is effective for purging heat to promote defecation. It is used to treat constipation due to heat accumulation in the intestine and fever.

8.3.16 Guiwei (Coccyx)

Location: At the end of the coccyx.

Manipulation: Kneading the Acupoint with the tip of the thumb or the middle finger is called kneading Guiwei. (see Fig. 8-23 on page 161) Repeat the manipulation 100~300 times.

Action: Regulating the function of the large intestine.

Indication: Constipation, diarrhea and enuresis.

Application: Guiwei is just the location of Changqiang (GV 1). Kneading it is effective for regulating Qi in the governor vessel. This Acupoint is moderate in nature and can stop diarrhea and promote defecation. It is often used together with the manipulations for pinching along the spine and pushing lumbrococcygeal vertebrae to treat diarrhea and constipation.

8.3.17 Pijing (Spleen meridian)

Location: On the radial border of the thumb and from the tip to the root.

Manipulation: Flex the thumb of the infant patient, and then push along the radial border of the thumb towards the wrist. This is called reinforcing Pijing (spleen meridian), which is considered as a reinforcing manipulation. Pushing from the opposite direction is called clearing Pijing (spleen meridian), which is considered as a clearing manipulation (see Fig. 8-24 on page 161). Repeat these manipulations 100~500 times.

Action: Reinforcing Pijing (spleen meridian) is effective for invigorating the spleen and regulating stomach, and replenishing Qi and blood. Clearing Pijing (spleen meridian) is effective for eliminating damp heat and resolving phlegm to stop vomiting.

Indication: Diarrhea, constipation, abdominal distension, dysentery, anorexia and jaundice due to damp heat.

Application: Reinforcing Pijing (spleen meridian) is used to treat poor appetite, emaciation caused by weakness of the spleen and stomach as well as deficiency of Qi and blood. The spleen and stomach of children are generally delicate, so in many cases reinforcing Pijing (spleen meridian) is frequently used.

8.3.18 Ganjing (Liver meridian)

Location: The whorl surface of the distal interphalangeal joint of the index finger.

Manipulation: Pushing from the finger tip to the root is considered as a reinforcing manipulation. Pushing from the opposite direction is considered as a clearing manipulation. Repeat these manipulations 100~500 times.

Action: Clearing Ganjing (liver meridian) is effective for clearing the liver to reduce fire, expelling wind to relieve spasm and removing restlessness.

Indication: Conjunctive congestion, bitter taste in the mouth, dry throat, convulsion, restlessness, and feverish sensation over five centers.

Application: Clearing Ganjing (liver meridian) is often used in combination with the manipulations for clearing Xinjing (heart meridian) and Tianheshui (heaven river water) to treat conjunctive congestion with swelling and pain, convulsion and restlessness due to ascending pathogenic fire of the liver. Ganjing (liver meridian) should be cleared rather than reinforced. When the liver is deficient and needs to be reinforced, reinforcing Shenjing (kidney meridian) is applied.

8.3.19 Xinjing (Heart meridian)

Location: The whorl surface of the distal interphalangeal joint of the middle finger.

Manipulation: Pushing from the finger tip to the root is considered a reinforcing method, called reinforcing Xinjing (heart meridian). Pushing from the opposite direction is considered a clearing method, called clearing Xinjing (heart meridian). Repeat the manipulation 100~500 times.

Action: Clearing Xinjing (heart meridian) is effective for clearing the heart to purge the heart fire. Reinforcing Xinjing (heart meridian) is effective for nourishing the heart to calm the mind.

Indication: Orolingual ulceration, short and hot urination, coma due to high fever and feverish sensation over the palms and soles.

Application: Clearing Xinjing (heart meridian) is used to treat coma due to high fever, reddened face, oral ulceration, and short and hot urination due to excessive heart fire. The manipulation is usually applied together with the manipulations for clearing Tianheshui (heaven river water) and small intestine. It is advisable to apply clearing this manipulation on Xinjing (heart meridian) because reinforcing manipulation can stir up heart fire.

8.3.20 Feijing (Lung meridian)

Location: The ungual whorl surface of the distal part of the ring finger.

Manipulation: Pushing from the finger tip to the transverse crease of the distal interphalangeal joint is considered as a reinforcing manipulation; pushing in the opposite direction is considered as a clearing manipulation. Repeat the manipulation 100~500 times.

Action: Reinforcing Feijing (lung meridian) is effective for nourishing lung Qi. Clearing Feijing (lung meridian) is effective for dispersing the lung to clear away heat, dispersing wind to relieve the exterior and resolving phlegm to stop cough.

Indication: Cold, cough, panting, wheezy phlegm, spontaneous sweating, night sweat, pale face, prolapse of the rectum, enuresis and constipation.

Application: Reinforcing Feijing (lung meridian) is used for treating deficiency cold syndrome of the lung meridian marked by deficiency of lung Qi, cough, panting, spontaneous sweating and aversion to cold. Clearing Feijing (lung meridian) is used for treating excess heat syndrome of the lung meridian marked by fever due to common cold, cough, panting, and wheezy phlegm.

8.3.21 Shenjing (Kidney meridian)

Location: The ungual whorl surface of the distal part of the small finger.

Manipulation: Pushing from the finger root towards the tip is considered a reinforcing method; pushing in the opposite direction is considered a clearing method. Repeat the manipulation 100~500 times.

Action: Reinforcing Shenjing (kidney meridian) is effective for replenishing the kidney and brain, warming and nourishing the primordial Qi. Clearing Shenjing (kidney meridian) is effective for clearing away damp ness and heat in the lower energizer.

Indication: Congenital defect, weakness due to lingering illness, diarrhea, enuresis, cough, panting, redness of the eye and painful urination.

Application: Reinforcing Shenjing (kidney meridian) is used to treat congenital deficiency, weakness due to lingering illness, chronic diarrhea resulted from kidney deficiency, profuse urine, enuresis, spontaneous sweating and shortness of breath. Clearing Shenjing (kidney meridian) is applied for retention of damp heat in the urinary bladder, and painful urination with dark urine. Clinically, Shenjing (kidney meridian) is often stimulated with reinforcing method. If the clearing method is needed, then the method for clearing Xiaochang (small intestine) is applied.

8.3.22 Xiaochang (Small intestine)

Location: On the ulnar side of the little finger and the line from the finger tip to the root.

Manipulation: Pushing from the finger tip to its root is considered as a reinforcing method known as reinforcing Xiaochang (small intestine). Pushing to the opposite direction is considered as a clearing method, called clearing (small intestine). Repeat the manipulation 100~300 times.

Action: Clearing away pathogenic heat to induce diuresis, separating purity from turbidity, nourishing Yin and improving deficiency.

Indication: Hot and difficult urination, watery diarrhea, boils in the mouth and tidal fever in the afternoon.

Application: Clearing Xiaochang (small intestine) is effective for separating purity from turbidity. It is often used to treat difficult urination with scanty and brown urine. When used together with clearing Tianheshui (heaven river water), it can clear away heat and promote urination. If heat from the heart meridian is transmitted into the small intestine, it can be treated by application of this manipulation and the one for clearing Tianheshui (heaven river water) for reinforcing the the effect of clearing away heat and promoting urination. If there is deficiency cold in the lower energizer with frequent urination and enuresis, it can be treated by reinforcing Xiaochang (small intestine).

8.3.23 Dachang (Large intestine)

Location: On the radial border of the index finger, from the finger tip to the margin of the web between the index finger and thumb.

Manipulation: Pushing from the finger tip to the wed margin is considered as a reinforcing method, known as reinforcing Dachang (large intestine). Pushing to the opposite direction is considered as a clearing method, known as clearing Dachang (large intestine). Repeat the manipulation 100~300 times.

Action: Reinforcing Dachang (large intestine) is effective for warming the middle energizer and astringing the intestine to stop diarrhea. Clearing Dachang (large intestine) is effective for clearing away heat, eliminating dampness and promoting defecation.

Indication: Diarrhea, dysentery, constipation and abdominal pain.

Application: Reinforcing Dachang (large intestine) is often used for diarrhea due to deficiency and cold. Clearing Dachang (large intestine) is frequently applied for retention of the damp heat or retention of food in the intestine, feverish sensation of the body, abdominal pain, dysentery, diarrhea due to damp heat and constipation.

8.3.24 Shending (Tip of the small finger)

Location: On the tip of the little finger.

Manipulation: Pressing and kneading the point with the tip of the thumb or index finger is called kneading Shending (tip of the small finger). Repeat the manipulation 100~500 times.

Action: Astringing primordial Qi and consolidating the exterior to stop perspiration.

Indication: Spontaneous perspiration, night sweating and infantile metopism.

Application: Kneading Shending (tip of the small finger) is effective for spontaneous sweating, night sweating or lingering massive sweating.

8.3.25 Sihengwen (Four transverse creases)

Location: On the palmar surface, at the midpoint of the transverse creases of the 1st interphalangeal joints of the index, middle, ring and little fingers.

Manipulation: Pressing and kneading the point with the nail of the thumb is called nipping Sihengwen; pushing the creases from the index finger to the little finger is known as pushing Sihengwen. Repeat the nipping manipulation on each point 5 times or do pushing creases 100~300 times.

Action: Nipping this point is effective for abating fever, relieving vexation and dissipating mass. And pushing the point can regulate the middle energizer to promote flow of Qi, regulate Qi and blood and relieve abdominal flatulence.

Indication: Indigestion, abdominal distention, abdominal pain, disharmony of Qi and blood, panting and fissure on the lip.

Application: Clinically, it is often used to treat infantile malnutrition, abdominal distention, disharmony of Qi and blood and indigestion. It is often used together with the manipulation for reinforcing Pijing (spleen meridian) and kneading Zhongwan (CV 12). Pricking the point with filiform needle or a three-edged needle to cause bleeding is effective in treating infantile malnutrition.

8.3.26 Xiaohengwen (Small transverse crease)

Location: On the palmar surface, the transverse crease of metacarpal interphalangeal joints of the index, middle, ring and little finger.

Manipulation: Nipping the crease with the nail of the thumb is called nipping Xiaohengwen (small transverse crease); pushing the crease with the side of the thumb is called pushing Xiaohengwen (small transverse crease). Nipping the crease of each finger for five times, or pushing 100~300 times.

Action: Reducing fever, relieving distention and removing stasis.

Indication: ulceration of the lip, boils in the mouth, abdominal distention, fever and restlessness etc.

Application: Pushing and nipping the point can treat retention of heat in the spleen and stomach, ulceration of the lip, and abdominal distention etc. Clinically, pushing Xiaohengwen (small transverse crease) is effective in treating pulmonary dry rales.

8.3.27 Zhangxiaohengwen (Small palmar transverse crease)

Location: On the palmar surface, at the root of the little finger, on the ulnar end of transverse crease.

Manipulation: Pressing and kneading the point with the tip of the thumb or middle finger is called kneading Zhangxiaohengwen (small palmar transverse crease). Repeat the manipulation 100~500 times.

Action: Clearing away heat and dissipating mass, soothing chest oppression, dispersing lung and resolving phlegm to stop cough.

Indication: Orolingual ulcer, salivation, pneumonia, phlegm retention and panting etc.

Application: As an important point for treating whooping cough and pneumonia, it is mainly used in treating cough, asthma and orolingual ulcers. Clinically, kneading Zhangxiaohengwen (small palmar transverse crease) is effective in treating pulmonary wet rales.

8.3.28 Weijing (Stomach meridian)

Location: At the junction of red and white skin of the greater thenar.

Manipulation: Pushing from the thumb root to the palmar root is considered as a reinforcing method, called reinforcing Weijing (stomach meridian). Pushing to the opposite direction is considered as a clearing method, known as clearing Weijing (stomach meridian). Repeat the manipulation 100~500 times.

Action: The manipulation of clearing Weijing (stomach meridian) is effective for clearing away damp heat in the middle energizer, regulating the stomach to direct adverse Qi downwards, reducing stomach fire and relieving restlessness and thirst. The manipulation for reinforcing Weijing (stomach meridian) is effective for invigorating the spleen and stomach to promote transportation and transformation.

Indication: Nausea, vomiting, belching, no appetite, abdominal distention, halitosis, and constipation.

Application: This manipulation is often used to treat nausea, vomiting and abdominal distension due to retention of damp heat or disharmony of stomach Qi, together with the manipulations for clearing Pijing (spleen meridian), pushing Tianzhugu (cervical column) and pushing from Hengwen (transverse crease) to Banmen (major thenar). This method can be also used to treat excess syndrome such as fever, polydipsia and constipation with the manipulations for clearing Dachang (large intestine), pushing Liufu (six Fu-organs), kneading Tianshu (ST 25) and pushing Qijiegu (lumbrosacral vertebrae) downwards. The manipulations for reinforcing Weijing (stomach meridian) is often used to treat deficiency cold syndrome such as weakness of the spleen and stomach, indigestion and anorexia with the manipulations for reinforcing Pijing (spleen meridian), kneading Zhongwan (CV 12), stroking, pressing and kneading Zusanli (ST 36).

8.3.29 Banmen (Major thenar)

Location: on the surface of the greater thenar.

Manipulation: Kneading the point with the finger tip is called kneading Banmen (major thenar). Pushing from finger root to the transverse crease of the wrist is called pushing manipulation from Banmen (major thenar) to Hengwen (transverse crease) and the opposite is known as pushing manipulation for from Hengwen (transverse crease) to Banmen (major thenar). Repeat the kneading manipulation 30~50 times or pushing manipulation 100~300 times.

Action: Promoting digestion and eliminating food retention, and stopping diarrhea and vomiting.

Indication: anorexia, indigestion, vomiting, diarrhea, abdominal distension, panting, and belching.

Application: Kneading Banmen (major thenar) is mostly used for treating retention of milk, anorexia or belching, abdominal distension, diarrhea and vomiting with the manipulations for circularly pushing Neibagua and rubbing Zhongwan (CV 12). Pushing from Banmen (major thenar) to Hengwen (transverse crease) can stop diarrhea, while pushing from Hengwen (transverse crease) to Banmen (major thenar) can stop vomiting.

8.3.30 Neilaogong (Inner part of palm)

Location: on the center of the palm, at the midpoint between the middle and ring fingers when these two fingers flex.

Manipulation: Kneading the point with the tip of the middle finger is called kneading Neilaogong (inner part of palm). Nipping the point from the root of the little finger to Neilaogong (inner part of palm) via Zhangxiaohengwen (small palmartransverse crease) and Xiaotianxin (small heaven center) is called circularly pushing Neilaogong (inner part of palm). Repeat the kneading manipulation 100~300 times, or pushing manipulation 10~30 times.

Action: Clearing away heat and relieving dysphoria, and clearing away asthenia heat.

Indication: Fever, polydipsia, aphthae, blood in the stool, gum ulcer, interior heat with dysphoria.

Application: Kneading Neilaogong (inner part of palm) is used for treating the disorders due to heat in the heart meridian, such as orolingual ulcers, fever and polydipsia. Circularly pushing Neilaogong (inner part of palm) is a compound manipulation, including circularly pushing Zhangxiaohengwen (small palmar transverse crease), kneading Xiaotianxin (small heaven center) and circularly pushing Neilaogong (inner part of palm). It is especially suitable for dealing with deficiency heat in the heart meridian and kidney meridian.

8.3.31 Xiaotianxin (Small heaven center)

Location: In the depression of the junction between the greater and small thenar eminences.

Manipulation: Kneading the point with the tip of the middle finger is called kneading Xiaotianxin (small heaven center). Pinching with the nail of the thumb is called pinching Xiaotianxin (small heaven center). Pounding the point with the tip of the middle finger or the interphalangeal joint of the middle finger is called pounding Xiaotianxin (small heaven center). Repeat kneading manipulation 100~300 times, pinching and pounding manipulations 5~20 times respectively.

Action: Clearing away heat, relieving convulsion, promoting urination and improving vision.

Indication: Spasm, night crying, hot and difficult urination, conjunctival congestion with pain, orolingual ulcers and strabismus.

Application: Kneading Xiaotianxin (small heaven center) is mainly used for symptoms caused by retention of heat in the heart meridian, such as conjunctival congestion with pain, orolingual ulcers, fear and restlessness; or scanty dark urine caused by transmission of heat of the heart meridian into the small intestine. Additionally, the manipulation is also effective for treating infantile uroschesis. The manipulations for pinching and pounding Xiaotianxin (small heaven center) are mainly used for night crying.

8.3.32 Neibagua

Location: The region 2/3 from the center of the palm to the crease at the root of the middle is divided into eight portions and orientations according to the structure of Bagua (eight diagrams used for calculation, prediction and other mysterious purposes in ancient China).The one facing Xiaotianxin (small heaven center) is Kan, the one facing the root of middle finger is Li; while the one located in the middle of the semi-circle between the lateral side of the thumb and Kan is Zhen, and the middle point of the semi-circle lateral to the little fingers is Dui. Altogether there are eight orientations, namely Qian, Kan, Gen, Zhen, Xun, Li, Kun and Dui.

Manipulation: Move the thumb tip from Qian to Kan through Dui once, mildly passing by Li. Such a manipulation is called clockwise moving Neibagua (see Fig. 8-25 on page 165). If it moves from Dui to Qian, it is known as counter-clock wise moving Neibagua. Such manipulations are performed 100~300 respectively.

Action: Clockwise pushing of Neibagua is effective for soothing the chest to regulate Qi, stopping cough to remove sputum, promoting digestion and stopping asthma.

Indication: Chest oppression, cough, panting, vomiting, diarrhea, abdominal distension, anorexia, hiccup, fever and aversion to cold.

Application: It can be used to treat chest oppression, cough, abdominal distension and anorexia, often used together with rubbing Banmen (major thenar). Counter-clockwise rubbing of Neibagua can relieve dyspnea due to sputum and vomiting, often used together with pushing Danzhong (CV 17) and Tianzhu (BL 10).

8.3.33 Zongjin (Great tendon)

Location: At the midpoint of the palmar transverse crease of the wrist.

Manipulation: Pressing and kneading the point is called kneading Zongjin (great tendon). Nipping it with the nail of the thumb is called nipping Zongjin (great tendon). Repeat the kneading manipulation 100~300 times and nipping manipulation 3~5 times.

Action: Clearing away heat from the heart meridian, removing obstruction, relieving spasm and regulating Qi activity in the body.

Indication: Orolingual ulcers, tidal fever, night crying and toothache.

Application: Kneading Zongjin (great tendon) is often combined with the manipulation for clearing Tianheshui (heaven river water) and Xinjing (heart meridian) to treat heat syndrome of excess type marked by orolingual ulcers, tidal fever and night crying. This manipulation should be performed quickly with stronger force.

8.3.34 Dahengwen (Major transverse crease)

Location: On the palmar transverse crease of the wrist when the palm is turned up, the radial end close to the thumb is known as Yangchi (pool of Yang) and the ulnar end close to the small finger is called Yinchi (pool of Yin).

Manipulation: Pushing separately from the midpoint of the palmar transverse crease of the wrist, where Zongjin (great tendon) is located, towards both sides with the two thumbs is called separate-pushing Dahengwen (major transverse crease), also known as separate Yin and Yang. Pushing jointly from Yinchi and Yangchi towards Zongjin (great tendon) is called joining Yin and Yang.

Action: Balancing Yin and Yang, regulating Qi and blood to promote digestion, expel phlegm and relieve spasm.

Indication: Alternate fever and chill, diarrhea, vomiting, food retention, lingering fever, restlessness, chest oppression and cough.

Application: Separating Yin and Yang is mostly used for alternation of fever and chill, restlessness due to imbalance of Yin and Yang and disharmony of Qi and blood; or retention of milk and food, abdominal distention, diarrhea and vomiting. During operation, the practitioner should apply stronger manipulation on Yinchi for heat syndrome of excess type, or on Yangchi for cold syndrome of deficiency type. Joining Yin and Yang is effective for cough and chest oppression.

8.3.35 Zuoduanzheng (Left upright)

Location: At the radial side of the nail root of the middle finger, on the junction of the red and white skin.

Manipulation: Pinching the point with the nail of the thumb is called pinching Zuoduanzheng. Kneading the point with the whorl surface of the thumb is called kneading Zuoduanzheng. Repeat the pinching manipulation 5 times or kneading manipulation 50 times.

Action: Elevating Yang to stop diarrhea.

Indication: Watery diarrhea and dysentery.

Application: Kneading Zuoduanzheng is used in combination with the manipulation for reinforcing Dachang (large intestine) and pushing upwards Qijiegu (lumbrosacral vertebrae) to treat watery diarrhea and dysentery.

8.3.36　Youduanzheng (Right upright)

Location: At the ulnar side of the nail root of the middle finger, on the junction of red and white skin.

Manipulation: Pinching the point with the nail of the thumb is called pinching Youduanzheng. Kneading the point with the whorl surface of the thumb is called kneading Youduanzheng. Repeat the pinching manipulation 5 times or kneading manipulation 50 times.

Action: Descending the adverse flow of Qi to stop vomiting.

Indication: Stopping vomiting, descending the adverse flow of Qi and stop bleeding.

Application: Kneading Youduanzheng is mainly used for nausea, vomiting and other symptoms caused by upward attack of stomach Qi. Pinching Youduanzheng is commonly used to treat infantile convulsion, together with the manipulation for clearing Ganjing (liver meridian). The point is also effective for treating epistaxis by winding the third section of the middle finger with a thin thread and then letting the child lie in bed quietly.

8.3.37　Wuzhijie (Interphalangeal joints of five fingers)

Location: On the dorsum of the hand and the first interphalangeal joints of the five fingers.

Manipulation: Pinching the point with the nail of the thumb is called pinching Wuzhijie (interphalangeal joints of fiver fingers). Kneading and rubbing it with the thumb and index finger is called kneading Wuzhijie (interphalangeal joints of fiver fingers). Repeat the pinching manipulation 3~5 times, or kneading and rubbing the points 30~50 times.

Action: Relieving convulsion to calm the mind, expelling wind phlegm, smoothing joint movement and dredging orifices.

Indication: cough, wind phlegm, salivation and terrified restlessness, etc.

Application: Pinching Wuzhijie (interphalangeal joints of fiver fingers) is mainly used for terrified restlessness, commonly combined with clearing Ganjing (liver meridian). Kneading Wuzhijie (interphalangeal joints of fiver fingers) is chiefly used for chest oppression, asthmatic breathing and cough together with the manipulations of circularly pushing Neibagua, pushing and kneading Danzhong (CV 17).

8.3.38　Ershanmen (Double gate)

Location: On the dorsum of the hand and in the depression on both sides of the root of the middle finger.

Manipulation: Pinching the point with the nail of the thumb is called pinching Ershanmen. Pressing and kneading it with the lateral side of the thumb is called kneading Ershanmen. Repeat the nipping manipulation 5 times, or kneading manipulation 100~300 times.

Action: Relieving the exterior syndrome diaphoresis, reducing fever to relieve asthma.

Indication: cold, fever, adiaphoresis, and asthmatic breathing etc.

Application: Pinching or kneading Ershanmen is an effective manipulation for inducing sweating. Kneading the point is often used to treat common cold due to wind cold, but the operation should be quick and slightly forceful. Together with the manipulations for kneading Shending (tip of the small finger), reinforcing Pijing (spleen meridian) and Shenjing (kidney meridian), it is suitable for children with common cold due to constitutional weakness.

8.3.39 Shangma (Climbing upon the horse)

Location: On the dorsum of the hand and in the depressions proximal to the metacarpophalangeal joints of the ring and little fingers.

Manipulation: Kneading the point with the tip of the thumb is called kneading Shangma. Nipping it with the nail of the thumb is called nipping Shangma. Repeat the nipping manipulation 3~5 times or kneading manipulation 100~300 times.

Action: Nourishing kidney Yin to strengthen kidney, promoting circulation of Qi to remove obstruction and inducing diuresis for treating stranguria.

Indication: Hot and difficult urination, abdominal pain, enuresis, indigestion, asthma and toothache.

Application: Clinically kneading Shangma is more frequently used for hyperactivity of Yang due to deficiency of Yin, tidal fever, irritability, night sweating, toothache and hot and difficult urination. It is effective to treat pulmonary infection with lingering dry rales with weak constitution. If it cannot be healed, the manipulation for kneading Xiaohengwen (small transverse crease) can be used for supplementation. When treating wet rales, it can be used together with the manipulations for kneading Zhanghengwen (palmar transverse crease).

8.3.40 Weiling (Powerful and magic)

Location: On the dorsum of hand and in the depression between the second and third metacarpal bones.

Manipulation: Nipping the point is called nipping Weiling. Repeat the manipulation 3~5 times or until the child wakes up.

Action: Resuscitating the brain and activating spirit.

Indication: Acute convulsion, sudden syncope and coma and headache.

Application: The manipulation is mainly used in combination with nipping Renzhong (philtrum) and Shixuan (EX-UE 11) to treat syncope and coma.

8.3.41 Jingning (Essence and tranquility)

Location: On the dorsum of the hand and in the depression between the 4th and 5th metacarpal bones.

Manipulation: Nipping this point is called nipping Jingning. Repeat this manipulation 3~5 times or until the child wakes up.

Action: Promoting flow of Qi, removing stagnation and resolving phlegm.

Indication: Retention of food and phlegm, wheezing, asthmatic breathing, dry vomiting, infantile malnutrition and convulsion.

Application: Nipping Jingning is often used for treating retention of food and phlegm, wheezing, asthmatic breathing, dry vomiting and infantile malnutrition. It is not advisable to select the point for the children with constitutional weakness. If it must be used, it is usually used together with the manipulations for reinforcing Pijing (spleen meridian), pushing Sanguan (triple pass) and pushing along the spine to avoid damage of primordial Qi.

When this manipulations is used to treat acute coma, it is often used together with the manipulation for nipping Weiling in order to strengthen its effect in resuscitating the brain and invigorating the spirit.

8.3.42 Boyangchi (Pool of Yang on the arm)

Location: On the dorsum of the hand and 3 cun posterior to Yiwofeng (a cave of wind).

Manipulation: Nipping the point with the nail of the thumb is called nipping Boyangchi, and kneading it with the tip of a finger is called kneading Boyangchi. Repeat the nipping manipulation 3~5 times or kneading manipulation 100~300 times.

Action: Promoting defecation and urination and stopping headache.

Indication: Constipation, hot and difficult urination, cold and heartache.

Application: Prolonged kneading on the point is quite effective for constipation. It is forbidden to select this point for lingering diarrhea. When it is used to treat common cold, headache and painful urination with scanty dark urine, the point is often used together with other points for relieving the exterior syndrome and benefiting urination.

8.3.43 Yiwofeng (A cave of wind)

Location: On the dorsum of the hand and on the midpoint of the transverse crease of the wrist.

Manipulation: Kneading the point with the tip of a finger is called kneading

Yiwofeng. Repeat the manipulation 100~300 times.

Action: Warming the middle energizer to promote Qi circulation, relieving arthralgia and smoothing joint movement, and dispersing Qi stagnation of the interior and exterior.

Indication: Abdominal pain, borborygmus, wind cold, acute and chronic convulsion, and difficult joint movement.

Application: Kneading Yiwofeng is frequently applied to treat abdominal pain caused by cold or food retention, often used together with the manipulations for grasping Dujiao (side of abdomen), pushing Sanguan (triple pass) and kneading Zhongwan (CV 12). It is also effective for Bi (obstruction) syndrome due to obstruction of the meridians by cold or for common cold due to wind cold.

8.3.44 Sanguan (Triple pass)

Location: On the radial aspect of the forearm and the line between Yangchi and Quchi.

Manipulation: Pushing from the transverse crease of the wrist to that of the elbow with the bellies of the index and middle fingers is called pushing Sanguan. (see Fig. 8-26 on page 168) Repeat the manipulation 100~300 times.

Action: Warming Yang to dispel cold, nourishing Qi to activate blood circulation, inducing sweat to relieve the exterior syndrome.

Indication: Abdominal pain, diarrhea, aversion to cold, lassitude of limb, weakness due to illness, wind cold and all other deficiency and cold syndromes.

Application: Sanguan is warm and hot in nature. It can be used to treat all kinds of syndromes caused by deficiency and cold. Clinically it is used to treat the disorders caused by deficiency of Qi and blood, weakness of Mingmen fire and deficiency cold in the kidney as well as the symptoms due to deficiency of Yang Qi, such as cold limbs, pale complexion, poor appetite, indigestion, vomiting and diarrhea. For this purpose, it can be used together with the manipulations for reinforcing Pijing (spleen meridian) and Shenjing (kidney meridian), kneading Dantian (lower abdomen), pushing along the spine and rubbing the abdomen in circles.

8.3.45 Liufu (Six Fu-organs)

Location: On the ulnar aspect of the forearm and the line between Yinchi and the transverse crease of the elbow.

Manipulation: Pushing from the transverse crease of the elbow to that of the wrist with the belly of the thumb, or bellies of the index and middle fingers is called pushing Liufu (see Fig. 8-27 on page 168). Repeat the manipulation 100~300 times.

Action: Clearing away heat and cooling blood.

Indication: High fever, polydipsia, convulsion, sore throat and constipation.

Application: Liufu is cold in nature and can be used to treat heat syndrome of excess type including attack of blood by febrile pathogenic factors, retention of heat in Zang-organs, high fever, restlessness, thirst and mumps. When used together with reinforcing Pijing (spleen meridian) (spleen meridian), it is effective for stopping sweating. When used to treat children with chronic loose stool and diarrhea due to spleen deficiency, it should be performed carefully.

Pushing Liufu and pushing Sanguan (triple pass) are the major manipulations for inducing cold and heat. They can be used alone or together. For children with constitutional deficiency of Qi and aversion to cold, the manipulations for pushing Sanguan is used alone; for children with high fever, restlessness, thirst and eruption, pushing Liufu is performed lone. When used together, the two manipulations can balance Yin and Yang, prevent extremely cold and extremely heat from impairing healthy Qi. For treating the syndrome complicated by both cold and heat with heat in predominance, the manipulation for pushing Liufu is performed 3 times and the manipulation for pushing Sanguan is performed once. If cold is in predominance, then the manipulation for pushing Sanguan is performed 3 times while the one for pushing Liufu is performed once.

8.3.46 Tianheshui (Heaven river water)

Location: Along the midline of forearm from Zongjin (great tendon) to Hongchi (PC 3).

Manipulation: Pushing from the transverse crease of the wrist to that of the elbow is called clearing Tianheshui (heaven river water). Repeat the manipulation 100~300 times.

Action: Clearing away heat to relieve the exterior syndrome, reducing heart fire, relieving restlessness and moistening dry tissues.

Indication: All heat symptoms, such as exogenous fever, tidal fever, internal heat, restlessness, thirst, orolingual ulcers, cough, wheezing phlegm and sore throat.

Application: Tianheshui (heaven river water) is slightly cool and mild in nature. It is mainly used to treat heat syndromes. It can clear away heat without damage of Yin, often used to deal with feverish sensation in the palms and soles, restlessness, dry throat, orolingual ulcers and night crying. This manipulation is also used together with the manipulations for pushing Cuanzhu (BL 2), pushing Kangong and kneading Taiyang (EX-HN 5)to treat fever due to common cold, headache, aversion to wind, slightly sweating, sore-throat and other symptoms related to exterior syndrome of wind heat. It is very effective in clearing away heat from Wei phase and Qi phase.

8.4 Commonly encountered infantile diseases

8.4.1 Characteristics in treating infantile diseases

Infantile Tuina is an important branch of Chinese Tuina. Infantile Tuina is an external therapy based on the basic theories of TCM. It is used, with full considerations of children's physiological and pathological characteristics, to prevent diseases and improve mentality in view of infantile physical and mental development by performing manipulations on certain Acupoints.

Infantile Tuina attaches great importance to infantile physiological and pathological characteristics. Physically, the infantile viscera are delicate, immature and under fast development and growth. At birth, infantile Zang-organs and Fu-organs are still delicate because the body structure is incomplete and the body functions are immature. According to the theory of "immature Yang and immature Yin" in TCM, Yin is not enough and his Yang has not fully developed in children. That is to say, a child is under development and growth in both body structure and physiological functions. The younger a child is, the faster he grows, and the more desperate he is for nutrients. Pathological characteristics include susceptibility to illness marked by rapid changes. However, since infantile visceral Qi is pure and flexible, infantile disease is easier to cure. With comparatively weak constitution, a child is susceptible to illness as the environment changes. And what is more, because his inability to adjust himself to the weather changes and control his diet, he is easily to be attacked by the six pathogenic factors in the exterior and impaired by improper food in the interior. Clinically, diseases concerning the spleen and lung are frequently seen. Generally speaking, changes of cold, heat, deficiency and excess in children are more complicated than that in adults. If not well treated, a mild pathological change will turn severe and even dangerous. However, as mentioned above, infantile visceral Qi is pure and tend to recover soon, which indicates that a child's body is vigorous with quick responses and has a strong ability to heal and restore itself in the course of illness. Therefore, accurate diagnoses will is important for better recovery and reduction of sequela. Infantile Tuina is based on the four diagnostic methods and eight principles of TCM to make diagnosis. Among the four examinations, inquiry is often made indirectly due to children's inability to express themselves. Although elder children can speak, they are not able to describe their conditions accurately. Besides, a child's Qi, blood and meridians are not fully developed, it is hard to tell the pulse condition. Smell examination can be applied to obtain some information, but it cannot fully reveal the real condition. Only inspection examination is capable of making accurate diagnosis, and in particular, the inspection of the fingerprint should be used more often.

Since exogenous factors and improper food are the main causes that lead to infantile illness, syndrome differentiation mainly concentrates on distinguishing Yang syndrome, excess syndrome and heat syndrome. That is why the manipulations frequently used are those that are effective for relieving the exterior and promoting digestion. Besides apart from the some frequently used meridian Acupoints and extraordinary Acupoints, most of the Acupoints applied in infantile Tuina are specific points, usually located below the elbows, different from that in adults. The distribution of these special distributions makes it convenient for clinical treatment.

Tuina therapy for infants requires soft and mild exertion of force and accurate location of Acupoints. Usually in infantile Tuina, pushing and kneading manipulations are performed with high frequency, stroking manipulation is performed for a longer period of time, nipping manipulation is performed quickly with strong force and low frequency, often followed by kneading manipulation. Besides, pressing and kneading manipulations are usually used as supplementary ones.

When performing infantile Tuina, the practitioner should pay attention to the following points: (1) trim his nails; (2) keep his hands warm in cold days; (3) perform the manipulations flexibly. Clinically manipulations are performed in three ways: ① apply manipulations on the head and face first, next on the upper limbs, then on the chest, the abdomen and finally the lower limbs; ② apply manipulations on principal points first, and then on subordinate points; ③ apply manipulations on subordinate points first, and then on principal points (like pinching spine). Whichever order is taken, strong manipulations like pinching, grasping and nipping are normally performed at the end of treatment, for these strong manipulations might make the infant to cry and affect the following treatment; ④ according to variations in age and constitution, and seriousness of the case, Tuina is normally performed within 20 minutes. The time of performing manipulations can be monitored according to different conditions, usually once a day and twice in treating acute illness, such as high fever; ⑤ manipulations on the Acupoints of the upper limbs are usually performed on the left side for both males and females, however manipulation can be performed on either side when dealing with other points symmetrical location; ⑥ a medium such as talcum powder should be used during application of the manipulations to prevent excoriation and improve curative effect; ⑦ it is better to apply manipulations one hour after a meal because manipulations cannot take full effect when children are hungry or full.

8.4.2 Cough

Cough is one of common symptoms of the respiratory diseases. It may occur in any season, but mostly in winter and spring with a high occurrence among infants. Cough to be discussed in this chapter only refers to acute and chronic bronchitis with cough as the main symptom.

Cough is divided into exogenous cough and endogenous cough, mostly involving the lung and spleen. The lung is a delicate organ, opening into the nose and connected with the skin in exterior. The lung governs the surface of the body and therefore tends to be attacked by exogenous pathogenic factors, leading to stagnation of Lung Qi, dysfunction of the lung in depurating and descending activities and adversely upward flow of Lung Qi. As a result, cough is caused. If the lung is attacked by pathogenic dryness, the throat will become obstructed, pulmonary fluid will be scorched, phlegm and sputum will turn thick and Lung Qi will flow adversely upwards, consequently resulting in cough. Cough due to internal impairment is often caused by constitutional weakness, or adversely upward flow of Lung Qi due to deficiency of Lung Yin, or retention of fluid due to dysfunction of the spleen and stomach that disturbs the pulmonary collaterals.

It is believed in Western medicine that physical and chemical stimulus, infection and allergy are the exogenous pathogenic factors of cough, while poor body resistance, weak immunity and allergic constitution are the endogenous factors. Infants are weak in immunity of respiratory tract, cough reflex, contractibility of the smooth muscle in the respiratory tract and cilia movement, making it difficult for them to eliminate dust and other foreign substances inhaled. That is why they frequently suffer from infection of respiratory tract.

【Clinic manifestations】

1. Cough due to wind cold: Frequent cough with clear and thin phlegm, stuffy nose, running nose, or aversion to cold, no sweating, headache and body pain, thin whitish coating, floating tense pulse and red dactylogram.

2. Cough due to wind heat: Cough with thick yellow phlegm, sticky nasal discharge, aversion to wind, slight sweating, fever, thirst, sore-throat, yellow urine, dry stool, red tip of the tongue, thin yellow tongue coating, superficial rapid pulse, bright red or purple dactylogram.

3. Endogenous cough: Prolonged cough, feverish sensation in the body, dry cough with scanty phlegm, or cough with profuse phlegm, anorexia, lassitude, emaciation, reddish tongue with scanty coating, weak and rapid pulse and light purple dactylogram.

【Treatment with Tuina therapy】

1. Cough due to wind cold

Therapeutic methods: Expelling wind to dispel cold and dispersing the lung to stop cough.

Formula: Push Cuanzhu (BL 2) and Kangong, then knead Taiyang (EX-HN 5), Erhougaogu, push and knead Danzhong (CV 17), knead Rugen (ST 18), Rupang and Feishu (BL 13), separate-push the scapulae, clear Feijing (lung meridian) and circularly push Neibagua.

Explanation of the formula: Pushing Cuanzhu (BL 2) and Kangong, and kneading Taiyang (EX-HN 5) and Erhougaogu can function to disperse the wind and relieve the exterior to stop headache. Kneading Danzhong (CV 17), Rugen and Rupang can resolve phlegm and regulate Qi circulation, and disperse the lung to stop cough. Pushing and kneading Feishu (BL 13) and separate-pushing the scapulae can regulate the function of the lung and Qi circulation, and resolve phlegm to stop cough. Clearing Feijing (lung meridian) is effective for dispersing the wind and relieving the exterior, and dispersing the lung to stop cough. Circularly pushing Neibagua can regulate Qi and resolve phlegm. For wind-cold syndromes with adiaphoresis and clear nasal discharge, the operation should be done by nipping and kneading Ershanmen, and kneading Yingxiang (LI 20), Huangfengrudong, and Wailaogong (EX-UE 8). For patients with asthma, phlegm, and wet or dry rales, he practitioner should add manipulations such as pushing XiaoHengwen (transverse crease), kneading Zhangxiaohengwen (small palmar transverse crease) and Shuangfengzhanchi.

2. Wind-heat cough

Therapeutic methods: dispersing wind and clearing away heat, and dispersing the lung to stop cough.

Formula: Push Cuanzhu (BL 2) and Kangong, knead Taiyang (EX-HN 5), push and knead Danzhong (CV 17), knead Rugen (ST 18) and Rupang, push the spine, knead Feishu (BL 13), clear Feijing (lung meridian) and Tianheshui (heaven river water), and circularly push Neibagua.

Explanation of the formula: Pushing Cuanzhu (BL 2) and Kangong and kneading Taiyang (EX-HN 5) is effective for dispersing wind and relieving the exterior. Kneading Danzhong (CV 17), Rugen (ST 18) and Rupang (side of breast) can regulate Qi flow and resolve phlegm to stop cough. Clearing Feijing (lung meridian) can disperse wind, relieve the exterior and disperse the lung to stop cough. Clearing Tianheshui (heaven river water) is effective for clearing away heat and relieving the exterior. Circularly pushing Neibagua can soothe the chest and hypochondrium, regulate Qi flow and resolve phlegm.

For syndromes with excessive phlegm and asthma, add manipulations for rubbing Fenglong (ST 40) and dorsal areas related to the stomach and spleen. For syndromes with dry rales in the lung, add manipulations for kneading Xiaohengwen (small transverse crease); for wet rales in the lung, add manipulations for kneading Zhangxiaohengwen (palmar transverse crease). For syndromes with cough, constipation and feverish sensation in the body, add manipulations for restraining Liufu (six Fu-organs), nipping and clearing Dachang (large intestine).

3. Endogenous cough

Therapeutic methods: Invigorating the spleen to nourish the lung, stopping cough and resolving phlegm.

Formula: Reinforce Pijing (spleen meridian) and Feijing (lung meridian), circularly push Neibagua, push and knead Danzhong (CV 17), knead Rugen (ST 18), Rupang, Zhongwan (CV 12) and Feishu (BL 13), and press and knead Zusanli (ST 36).

Explanation of the formula: Reinforcing Pijing (spleen meridian) and pressing and kneading Zusanli (ST 36) have the effect of invigorating the stomach and spleen and resolve phlegm. Reinforcing Feijing (lung meridian) can benefit lung Qi. Circularly pushing Neibagua, pushing and kneading Danzhong (CV 17), kneading Rupang (side of breast) and Rugen (ST 18) can regulate Qi flow, stop cough and resolve phlegm. Kneading Zhongwan (CV 12) can invigorate the stomach and spleen. Kneading Feishu (BL 13) is effective for regulating lung Qi to stop cough.

For patients with cough due to Yin deficiency, add manipulation of kneading Shangma. For weakness and dyspnea due to prolonged cough, add manipulations of reinforcing Shenjing (kidney meridian), pushing Sanguan (triple pass) and pinching the spine. For patients with excessive phlegm, add manipulations of kneading Fenglong (ST 40)and Tiantu (CV 22).

[Nursing]

1. During treatment, patients are forbidden to take the following food: uncooked, cold, sour, and sweet food as well as fish and pungent diet lest cough be worsened.

2. Patients should have adequate sleep, drink more water and avoid wind and cold to prevent recurrence of severe common cold.

3. Measures should be taken to improve living environment, keep ventilation of the room and avoid stimulations of dust and smoke.

8.4.3 Fever

Fever refers to abnormal rise of body temperature, and is one of the most common symptoms of infants. Clinically, exogenous fever can be caused by excessive heat in the lung and spleen, Yin deficiency with heat in the body, and deficiency of Qi. Generally speaking, exogenous fever refers to common cold and can occur in any season, particularly in spring and winter. The younger the patients are, the more vulnerable they are to run fever. Weak infants tend to run fever when falling ill.

Fever is mainly caused by weak constitution and susceptibility to pathogenic factors. Without careful nursing, infants vulnerable to wind cold and wind heat tend to run fever. Fever can also be caused by excessive heat in the lung and stomach, weak constitution, malnutrition, Yin deficiency due to lingering disease, Yin deficiency with heat in the body due to consumption of Yin fluid, weakness of the stomach and spleen, Qi deficiency due to lingering disease and Yang floating outside.

It is believed in Western medicine that infants are weak in immunity and are susceptible to fever due to infection of upper respiratory tract. That is why children tend to run fever. Besides, the content of water in children's body is more than that in adults' body. Thus vigorous infantile metabolism leads to comparatively excessive discharge of water, frequently causing metabolic disorder of water, consequently leading to elevation of body temperature.

[Clinical manifestations]

1. Exogenous fever: If it is marked by fever, diaphoresis, aversion to cold, headache, general pain, stuffy nose, running nose, cold limbs, thin and whitish tongue coating and fresh red finger veins, it is caused by pathogenic wind and cold. If it is marked by fever, slight perspiration, yellow or thick nasal discharge, sore-throat, dry mouth, thin and yellowish tongue coating, red and purple finger veins, it is caused by pathogenic wind and heat.

2. Excessive heat in the lung and stomach: It is marked by high fever, excessive perspiration, thirst with desire to drink water, anorexia, flushed face, shortness of breath, constipation, restlessness, red tongue with yellowish dry coating and dark purple finger veins.

3. Fever due to Yin deficiency: It is marked by afternoon fever, feverish sensation in the palms and soles, night sweating, red cheek, anorexia, emaciation, rapid and thin pulse, red tongue with slight coating or without coating and purple finger veins.

4. Fever due to Qi deficiency: It is marked by low fever due to fatigue, weak and low voice, tiredness, no desire to speak, spontaneous perspiration, anorexia, emaciation, diarrhea after meal, pale tongue with whitish thin fur, weak pulse and pale finger veins.

【Treatment with Tuina therapy】

1. Exogenous fever

Therapeutic methods: Clearing heat to relieve the external and dispersing exogenous pathogenic factors.

Formula: Push Cuanzhu (BL 2) and Kangong, circularly push Taiyang (EX-HN 5), clear Tianheshui (heaven river water) and Feijing (lung meridian). For patients with wind cold syndrome, add manipulations of pushing Sanguan (triple pass), kneading Ershanmen (double gate), grasping Fengchi (GB 20) and pushing Tianzhugu (cervical column). For patients with wind heat syndrome, clear Tianheshui (heaven river water), pushing along the spine and kneading Dazhui (GV 14). For patients with cough and wheezing phlegm, add manipulations of pushing and kneading Danzhong (CV 17), kneading Feishu (BL 13), circularly pushing Neibagua (inner part of palm), pushing Xiaohengwen (small transverse crease), kneading Fenglong (ST 40), clearing Ganjing (liver meridian), kneading Xiaotianxin (small heaven center), nipping and kneading Wuzhijie (interphalangeal joints of fiver fingers). For patients with running nose, add manipulation of Huang Feng Ru Dong (Wasp Entering Hole). For patients with high fever and restlessness, add manipulation of Da Ma Guo Tian He (Beating the Horse to Cross the Heaven River). For patients with convulsion, restlessness and difficulty in sleeping, add manipulations of clearing Ganjing (liver meridian), nipping and kneading Xiaotianxin (small heaven center).

Explanation of the formula: Pushing Cuanzhu (BL 2) and Kangong, and circularly pushing Taiyang (EX-HN 5) can disperse wind and relieve the exterior. Clearing Feijing (lung meridian) can disperse the lung and clear away heat and disperse wind to relieve exterior. Clearing Tianheshui (heaven river water) is effective for clearing away heat and relieving the exterior, reducing fire and relieving dysphoria. For patients with wind cold syndrome, add manipulations of pushing Sanguan (triple pass), kneading Ershanmen (double gate), grasping Fengchi (GB 20) and pushing Tianzhugu (cervical column), which can induce sweat and relieve the exterior. For patients with wind-heat syndrome, add manipulations of pushing downward the spine and kneading Dazhui (GV 14), which can clear away heat and relieve the exterior.

2. Excessive heat in the lung and stomach

Therapeutic methods: Clearing away internal heat and regulating Qi to promote digestion.

Formula: Clear Feijing (lung meridian), Weijing (stomach meridian) and Dachang (large intestine), knead Banmen (major thenar), circularly push Neibagua, clear Tianheshui (heaven river water), reducing fire from Liufu (six Fu-organs) and knead Tianshu (ST 25). For patients with constipation, add manipulations of pushing downward Qijiegu (lumbrosacral vertebrae), rubbing the abdomen clockwise in circles, kneading Boyangchi and rubbing hypochondriac region.

Explanation of the formula: Clearing Feijing (lung meridian) and Weijing (stomach meridian) (stomach meridian) is effective for clearing away excessive heat in the lung and stomach meridians. Clearing Dachang (large intestine) and kneading Tianshu (ST 25) can dispel obstruction in the intestine to promote defecation and reduce fire. Clearing Tianheshui (heaven river water) and reducing fire from Liufu (six Fu-organs) can help relieve dysphoria. Kneading Banmen (major thenar) and circularly pushing Neibagua (inner part of palm) can regulate Qi and promote digestion.

3. Internal heat due to Yin deficiency

Therapeutic methods: Nourishing Yin to clear away heat.

Formula: Knead Shangma (climbing upon horse), clear Tianheshui (heaven river water), perform the manipulation of scooping the moon from the bottom of water, reinforce Pijing (spleen meridian) and Feijing (lung meridian), knead Zusanli (ST 36) and push and rub Yongquan (KI 1). For patients with spontaneous perspiration and night sweating, add manipulations of kneading Shending (tip of the small finger), pinching the spine and reinforcing Shenjing (kidney meridian). For patients with dysphoria and insomnia, add manipulations of clearing Ganjing (liver meridian), kneading Baihui (GV 20), pushing Cuanzhu (BL 2), nipping and kneading Wuzhijie (interphalangeal joints of fiver fingers), and pounding Xiaotianxin (small heaven center).

Explanation of the formula: Kneading Shangma (climbing upon horse), pushing and rubbing Yongquan (KI 1) and performing scooping the moon from the bottom of water can nourish Yin and clear away heat due to deficiency syndrome. Clearing Tianheshui (heaven river water) can clear away heat, reduce fire and relieve dysphoria. Reinforcing Pijing (spleen meridian) and Feijing (lung meridian) and kneading Zusanli (ST 36) can invigorate the spleen and stomach, supplement Qi, nourish blood and clear away heat.

4. Fever due to Qi deficiency

Therapeutic methods: Invigorating the spleen to nourish Qi and clearing away heat.

Formula: Reinforce Pijing (spleen meridian) and Feijing (lung meridian), circularly push Neibagua (inner part of palm) , rub the abdomen, knead Zusanli (ST 36), Pishu (BL 20)and Feishu (BL 13), clear Tianheshui (heaven river water) and nip the spine.

Explanation of the formula: Reinforcing Pijing (spleen meridian) and Feijing (lung meridian), kneading Zusanli (ST 36), Pishu (BL 20) and Feishu (BL 13), and rubbing the abdomen can invigorate the spleen and lung, supplement Qi, nourish blood and clear away heat. Circularly pushing Neibagua (inner part of palm) and separate pushing Yin and Yang can balance Yin and Yang as well as regulate Qi and blood. Clearing Tianheshui (heaven river water) is effective for clearing away heat and reducing fire. Nipping the spine is effective for balancing Yin and Yang as well as Qi and blood. It can also supplement Qi and clear away heat.

For patients with abdominal distention or anorexia, add manipulations of kneading Banmen (major thenar), rubbing Zhongwan (CV 12) and separate pushing the abdomen. For patients with loose stool, add manipulations of rubbing the abdomen counterclockwise, reinforcing Dachang (large intestine), pushing upwards Qijiegu (from the fourth lumbar vertebra to the end of coccyx) and pushing from Banmen (major thenar) to Hengwen (transverse crease). For patients with nausea and vomiting, add manipulations of pushing Tianzhugu (cervical column), pushing from Hengwen (transverse crease) to Banmen (major thenar), pushing Zhongwan (CV 12) and kneading Youduanzheng (right upright).

【Nursing】

1. The room should be ventilated and the air in the room should be kept clean.
2. The patient should take food rich in nutrients and not greasy.
3. Great attention should be paid to changes of body temperature. The patient should frequently take shower with warm water for inducing sweating and lowering body temperature.

8.4.4 Asthma

Asthma is one of the most commonly encountered respiratory symptoms among infants. Clinically, it is characterized by difficult breath, prolonged exhalation, wheezy sound from the throat, opening the mouth with the shoulders elevated, and even difficulty in lying on the back. Asthma usually occurs in spring and winter and is often caused by sudden changes of weather and inappropriate diet.

The causes of asthma can be internal or external. Internal causes are related to the lung, spleen and kidney. The deficiency of lung Qi may fail to protect the body from the attack of exogenous pathogenic factors; phlegm and adverse flow of lung Qi may develop, eventually causing asthma. The deficiency of spleen Qi may affect digestion and absorption, and thus causing stagnation of phlegm in the lung. If the lung fails to disperse Qi, asthma will be caused. The deficiency of kidney Qi may affect the acceptance and storage of Qi in the lung, consequently resulting in asthma. If infants are attacked by wind cold, have taken inappropriate diet or touched strange things, phlegm may occur and block respiratory tract and lead to asthma. Frequent occurrence of asthma may consume lung Qi. Lingering asthma may affect the kidney, resulting in deficiency of kidney Yang and failure to receive Qi.

It is believed in Western medicine that asthma is caused by allergens (such as pollen, paint, fish and shrimp), which contract small smooth muscles of bronchia. Fatigue, excitement and weather change can also induce asthma.

[Clinical manifestations]

1. Asthma due to cold: Symptoms are cold, panting, difficulty in breathing, wheezy sound from the throat, opening the mouth with the shoulders rising, difficulty in lying on the back, thin and whitish phlegm with bubbles, diaphoresis, pale face, cold limbs, preference to hot drinks, long voiding of clear urine, light red tongue with thin and whitish tongue coating, superficial and rapid pulse and light red finger veins.

2. Asthma due to heat: Symptoms are cough, short breath, holding breath, breathing with wheezy sound, thick and yellow phlegm, flushed face, fever, fullness and oppression over the chest, restlessness, thirst with preference to cold drink, yellow and hot urine, dry stool, red tongue with thin and yellow tongue coating, floating and rapid pulse, and dark red finger veins.

3. Asthma due to Yang deficiency and failure to receive Qi of the kidney: Symptoms are panting, difficulty in breathing, breathing with wheezy sound, green and grey face, no thirsty feeling, fatigue, anorexia, opening the mouth with the shoulders rising, short breath even in sitting position, limbs feeling cold, soreness and weakness in lumbar region and legs, frequent urination, thin and white fur, weak pulse and whitish finger veins.

[Treatment with Tuina therapy]

1. Asthma due to cold

Therapeutic methods: Descending Qi to relieve asthma, dispersing the lung to dispel cold.

Formula: Clear Feijing (lung meridian), push and knead Danzhong (CV 17), knead Tiantu (CV 22), stroke and rub Xielei (hypochondrium), knead Feishu (BL 13), circularly push Neibagua, press and knead Fengchi (GB 20), push Sanguan (triple pass), knead Wailaogong (EX-UE8), Rupang and Rugen (ST 18), push the spine and press and knead Sanyinjiao (SP 6).

Explanation of the formula: Clearing Feijing (lung meridian), pushing and kneading Danzhong (CV 17), kneading Tiantu (CV 22), stroking and rubbing Xielei (hypochondrium), and kneading Feishu (GB 20) can promote Qi circulation and descending the adverse flow of Qi. Circularly pushing Neibagua, pressing and kneading Fengchi (GB 20), and pushing Sanguan (triple pass) can dispel wind cold and disperse the lung to relieve asthma. Kneading Wailaogong (EX-UE8), Rupang and Rugen (ST 18), pushing the spine, pressing and kneading Sanyinjiao (SP 6) can disperse the lung, relieve asthma and resolve phlegm.

2. Asthma due to heat

Therapeutic methods: Clearing away heat to descend Qi and dispersing lung to relieve asthma.

Formula: Clear Tianheshui (heaven river water) and Feijing (lung meridian), pinch Zongjin (great tendon), clear Dachang (large intestine), push Liufu (six Fu-organs), Tianzhu (BL 10) and the spine, knead Fenglong (ST 40) and Feishu (BL 13) and circularly push Neibagua (inner part of palm).

Explanation of the formula: Clearing Tianheshui (heaven river water) and Feijing (lung meridian) can clear away lung heat and descend Qi to relieve asthma. Pinching Zongjin (great tendon), clearing Dachang (large intestine) and pushing Liufu (six Fu-organs) can clear away heat, reduce fire, and descend Qi. Separately pushing Danzhong (CV 17), pushing Tianzhu (BL 10) and the spine, kneading Fenglong (ST 40) and Feishu(BL 13) and circularly pushing Neibagua can soothe the chest to descend the adverse flow of Qi, resolve phlegm and relieve asthma.

3. Asthma due to failure to receive Qi of the kidney complicated by Yang deficiency

Therapeutic methods: Receiving Qi to relieve asthma and invigorating the spleen to warm Yang.

Formula: Reinforce Feijing (lung meridian), push Xiaochang, push and knead Danzhong (CV 17), knead Tiantu (CV 22), push Sanguan (triple pass), stroke and rub Zhongwan (CV 12), knead Dantian and Shenshu (BL 23), reinforce Pijing (spleen meridian), circularly push Neibagua, knead Rupang (side of the breast), Rugen (ST 18), Zhongwan (CV 12) and Feishu (BL 13) and press and knead Zusanli (ST 36).

Explanation of the formula: Reinforcing Feijing (lung meridian) and pushing Xiaochang can strengthen the kidney to help receive Qi. Pushing and kneading Danzhong (CV 17), kneading Tiantu (CV 22), pushing Sanguan (triple pass) and Anxian Cuomo (stroke and rub like feeling thread) can lower adverse of Qi. Rubbing Zhongwan (CV 12), kneading Dantian (lower abdomen) and Shenshu (BL 23), and reinforcing Shenjing (kidney meridian) and Pijing (spleen meridian) can benefit the spleen and kidney and help receive Qi. Circularly pushing Neibagua, kneading Rupang, Rugen (ST 18), Zhongwan (CV 12) and Feishu (BL 13), pressing and kneading Zusanli (ST 36) can nourish the spleen, lower adverse of Qi and resolve phlegm.

【Nursing】

1. The patient with weak constitution and rickets should take measures to improve the state of nutrition.

2. The patient should keep warm and avoid attack from exogenous pathogenic factors.

3. The patient should take less spicy and roasted food lest food retention be caused.

4. When asthma attacks, the patient should rest. However if it does attack, the patient should do more outdoor exercises to strengthen the body.

8.4.5 Vomiting

Vomiting is one of the commonly encountered symptoms of infants and is caused by adverse flow of Qi, leading to discharge of contents from the stomach. It can be found in many different diseases. The infantile stomach is delicate and the cardia is loose. If an infant is fed with excessive milk or in a wrong position, he may inhale too much air and vomit some milk. This is a normal reaction.

TCM regards the stomach as the sea of water and food and holds that Stomach Qi normally flows downwards. Infantile stomach is delicate. That is why infants often vomit. Infantile vomiting is usually caused by invasion of exogenous pathogenic factors into the spleen and stomach, or irregular feeding, excessive eating of uncooked and cold food and fruit as well as excessive oily and rich food that is retained in the stomach. It can also be caused by traumatic injury, terror, adverse flow of Qi that affects the spleen and stomach in transportation and transformation.

It is believed in Western medicine that vomiting is an instinctual reflection of the body to discharge harmful materials from the stomach. However, frequent and intense vomiting may affect normal intake of food, causing dehydration, electrolyte disorders, imbalance between acid and alkali as well as malnutrition. Infantile vomiting is often accompanied by other diseases. So it is necessary to inquire details about the patient in order to make accurate diagnosis.

【Clinical manifestations】

1. Vomiting due to cold: It is marked by vomiting after overeating, intermittent vomiting, vomitus with slight sour smell, pale complexion, cold limbs, abdominal pain to be relieved by warmth, loose stools, pale tongue, thin and whitish tongue coating and red finger veins.

2. Vomiting due to heat: It is marked by vomiting right after meal, sour and stinking vomitus, restlessness, feverish sensation in the body, thirst, stinking or dry stools, brownish yellow urine, dry and red lips, yellowish and greasy tongue coating and purple finger veins.

3. Vomiting due to indigestion: It is marked by frequent vomiting, foul breath, anorexia, abdominal distention and pain, sour and stinking stools, red tongue with thick and greasy tongue coating, slippery pulse and purple or red finger veins.

4. Vomiting due to fright: It is marked by sudden vomiting after fright or frequent spitting of clear saliva, nervousness, uneasiness, poor sleep, proneness to cry, bluish nose bridge and finger veins and irregular pulse.

【Treatment with Tuina therapy】

1. Vomiting due to cold

Therapeutic methods: Harmonizing stomach to descend Qi, warming middle energizer to dispel cold.

Formula: Knead Zhongwan (CV 12), reinforce Pijing (spleen meridian) and Weijing (stomach meridian), push from Hengwen (transverse crease) to Banmen (major thenar), push Tianzhugu (cervical column), knead Wailao gong and push Sanguan (triple pass).

Explanation of the formula: Kneading Zhongwan (CV 12), reinforcing Pijing (spleen meridian) and Weijing (stomach meridian) can strengthen the spleen to harmonize the stomach, relieve the adverse flow of Qi to stop vomiting and warm the middle energizer to dispel cold. Kneading Tianzhugu (cervical column) is effective for clearing away cold to stop vomiting. Pushing from Hengwen (transverse crease) to Banmen (major thenar) can stop vomiting of different causes. Kneading Wailaogong (EX-LE 9) and pushing Sanguan (triple pass) can strengthen the middle energizer to warm Yang and dispel cold.

2. Vomiting due to heat

Therapeutic methods: To cleat away heat and relieve adverse flow of Qi; harmonize stomach to stop vomiting.

Formula: Clear the spleen and stomach, push Liufu (six Fu-organs), clear Dachang (large intestine), push from Hengwen (transverse crease) to Banmen (major thenar), circularly push Neibagua, and push Tianzhugu (cervical column) and push downwards Qijiegu (lumbrosacral vertebrae).

Explanation of the formula: Clearing the spleen and stomach combined with pushing Tianzhugu (cervical column) can clear away heat in the middle energizer, harmonize and descend adverse flow of Qi to stop vomiting. Pushing Liufu (six Fu-organs) can clear away heat. Circularly pushing Neibagua and pushing from Hengwen (transverse crease) to Banmen (major thenar) can regulate Qi, harmonize the stomach to stop vomiting. Pushing downwards Qijiegu (from the fourth lumbar vertebra to the end of coccyx) and clearing Dachang (large intestine) can clear away heat and promote defecation to descend stomach Qi.

3. Vomiting due to indigestion

Therapeutic methods: Promoting digestion to relieve food retention, harmonizing the middle energizer to stop adverse flow of Qi.

Formula: Reinforce Pijing (spleen meridian), knead Zhongwan, press and knead Zusanli (ST 36), knead Banmen (major thenar), circularly push Neibagua, separately push the abdomen, push from Hengwen (transverse crease) to Banmen (major thenar) and An Xuan Zou Cuo Mo (stroke and rub like feeling a piece of thread).

Explanation of the formula: Reinforcing Pijing (spleen meridian), kneading Zhongwan (CV 12) and pressing and kneading Zusanli (ST 36) can invigorate the spleen and harmonize the stomach to reinforce the function of the middle energizer in transformation and transportation. Circularly pushing Neibagua and kneading Banmen (major thenar) can promote digestion to resolve food retention and sooth the chest to regulate Qi. Separately pushing the abdomen and pushing from Hengwen (transverse crease) to Banmen (major thenar) can stop adverse flow of Qi to relieve vomiting, An Xuan Zou Cuo Mo is effective for invigorating the spleen to promote digestion, regulating Qi and resolving the phlegm.

4. Vomiting due to fright

Therapeutic methods: To relieve fright and stop vomiting.

Formula: Press and knead Tiantu (CV 22), knead Rupang (side of breast), clear Ganjing (liver merdian), knead Xiaotianxin (small heaven center), pinch and knead Wuzhijie (interphalangeal joints of fiver fingers), separately push the abdomen, push Tianzhugu (cervical column), circularly push Neibagua, push from Hengwen (transverse crease) to Banmen (major thenar) and knead Youduanzheng (right upright).

Explanation of the formula: Pressing and kneading Tiantu (CV 22) and Kneading Rupang (side of breast) can stop adverse flow of Qi to relieve vomiting. Pinching and kneading Wuzhijie (interphalangeal joints of fiver fingers), clearing Ganjing (liver meridian) and kneading Xiaotianxin (small heaven center) can relieve fright and disperse the liver. Separately pushing the abdomen and pushing Tianzhugu (cervical column) can stop adverse flow of Qi to relieve vomiting. Pushing from Hengwen (transverse crease) to Banmen (major thenar), circularly pushing Neibagua and kneading Youduanzheng (right upright) can promote digestion to resolve food retention, relieve fright and tranquilize the mind.

[Nursing]

1. Adjust diet to avoid overeating, starving, or eating excessive hot or cold food.

2. Serious vomiting may cause temporary stoppage of breath. Great cares should be taken to observe the condition of the patient to prevent inhalation of vomitus and cause respiratory disorders like pneumonia.

3. Frequent vomiting may cause dehydration and acidosis and should be treated by integrated traditional Chinese and Western medicine.

8.4.6 Diarrhea

Infantile diarrhea refers to frequent defecation with thin or watery stools. It is often seen in the infants less than one year old and usually occurs in summer and autumn.

Diarrhea is either chronic or acute. It is mainly related to dysfunction of the spleen, small intestine and large intestine because the spleen dominates transportation and transformation of food, the small intestine separates the clear from the turbid and the large intestine dominates transportation of the waste. Diarrhea tends to consume Qi and blood. Delayed treatment will affect absorption of nutrients as well as growth and development of the body, and even causing dehydration due to deficiency of Qi.

According to Western medicine, internal causes of diarrhea include underdevelopment of the digestive system, unsatisfactory regulation of the nerve system, insufficient secretion of gastric acid and digestive enzymes as well as inactive digestive enzymes. External causes include irregular diet, or cold attack, intestinal infection of E.coli, viruses or fungi. Severe diarrhea may result in disorder of water and electrolytes, dehydration and acidosis.

[Clinical manifestations]

1. Diarrhea due to pathogenic cold dampness: It is marked by frothy loose stool without foul smell, profuse clear urine, vomiting, chest oppression, poor appetite, borborygmus, abdominal pain, slight fever, chills, cold limbs, no thirst, white greasy tongue coating, soft pulse and red finger veins.

2. Diarrhea due to pathogenic damp heat: It is marked by thin or sticky yellow diarrhea, hot and scanty urine, thirst, restlessness, high fever, reddish tongue with greasy yellow coating, rapid pulse and dark purplish finger veins.

3. Diarrhea due to indigestion: It is marked by abdominal distention and fullness in the abdomen, pain relieved after defecation, massive and sour stools, anorexia, thirst, poor appetite, restless sleep during night, feverish sensation of the palms and soles, thick tongue coating, slippery pulse and dark purplish finger veins.

4. Diarrhea due to deficiency of the spleen: It is marked by lingering diarrhea, sloppy stools after meal or after eating greasy food, white-colored stool without stinking smell but mixed with undigested food, sallow complexion, lassitude, cold limbs, light-colored tongue with white coating, soft pulse and light red finger veins.

5. Diarrhea due to Yang deficiency of the spleen and kidney: It is marked by watery and frequent diarrhea with undigested food in it, sallow complexion, cold limbs, white tongue coating, thin pulse and light reddish finger veins.

No matter what kind of diarrhea it is, if it serious, it will exhaust Yin inside while drive Yang to float outside. So when diarrhea occurs, it must be carefully diagnosed and treated.

[Treatment with Tuina therapy]

1. Diarrhea due to pathogenic cold dampness

Therapeutic methods: Warming the middle energizer to disperse cold and invigorating the spleen to stop diarrhea.

Formula: Reinforce Pijing (spleen meridian) and Dachang (large intestine), knead Wailaogong (EX-LE 9) and Zuoduanzheng (left upright), push Sanguan (triple pass), rub the abdomen, knead Zhongwan (CV 12), push upwards Qijiegu (lumbrosacral vertebrae), knead Guiwei (coccyx), and press and knead Zusanli (ST 36).

Explanation of the formula: Pushing Sanguan (triple pass) and kneading Wailaogong (EX-LE 9) can warm Yang and disperse cold. Reinforcing Pijing (spleen meridian), kneading Zhongwan (CV 12), rubbing the abdomen and pressing and kneading Zusanli (ST 36) can invigorate the spleen to expel dampness and warm the middle energizer to disperse cold. Reinforcing Dachang (large intestine), kneading Zuoduanzheng (left upright), pushing Qijiegu (lumbrosacral vertebrae) and kneading Guiwei (coccyx) can elevate Yang to stop diarrhea.

For patients with abdominal pain and borborygmus, manipulations for kneading Yiwofeng (a cave of wind) and grasping Dujiao (side of abdomen) can be used. For patients weak in constitution, the manipulation for pinching the spine can be used. For patients with terror and nervousness, the manipulations for clearing Ganjing (liver meridian) and pinching and kneading Wuzhijie (interphalangeal joints of fiver fingers) can be used.

2. Diarrhea due to pathogenic damp heat

Therapeutic methods: Clearing heat and dampness, regulating the middle energizer to stop diarrhea.

Formula: Clear the spleen and stomach, clear Xiaochang (small intestine) and Dachang (large intestine), push Liufu (six Fu-organs), knead Tianshu (ST 25) and Guiwei (coccyx), and push downward Qijiegu (lumbrosacral vertebrae).

Explanation of the formula: Clearing the spleen and stomach can clear away heat in the middle energizer. Kneading Tianshu (ST 25) and clearing Dachang (large intestine) can clear damp heat in the intestines and Fu-organs. Clearing Xiaochang (small intestine) and pushing Liufu (six Fu-organs) can clear away heat to promote urination. Kneading Guiwei (coccyx) is effective for regulating the intestines to stop diarrhea. Pushing downward Qijiegu (lumbrosacral vertebrae) can clear away heat and promote defecation.

3. Diarrhea due to indigestion

Therapeutic methods: To promote digestion and relieve food retention, normalize the middle energizer and reinforce transportation.

Formula: Grasp Dujiao (side of abdomen), reinforce Pijing (spleen meridian), clear Dachang (large intestine), circularly push Neibagua, knead Banmen (major thenar) and Zongjin (great tendon), rub the abdomen, and knead Tianshu (ST 25) and Guiwei (coccyx).

Explanation of the formula: Grasping Dujiao (side of abdomen) can promote digestion and relieve food retention. Reinforcing Pijing (spleen meridian) and kneading Zhongwan (CV 12) can invigorate the spleen to reinforce transportation. Kneading Banmen (major thenar), circularly pushing Neibagua and rubbing the abdomen can invigorate the spleen, harmonize the stomach and promote digestion to relieve food retention. Clearing Dachang (large intestine) and kneading Tianshu (ST 25) can regulate the intestines and relieve food retention. Kneading Guiwei (coccyx) can regulate the intestines to stop diarrhea.

4. Diarrhea due to deficiency of the spleen

Therapeutic methods: Invigorating the spleen to nourish Qi and warming Yang to stop diarrhea.

Formula: Reinforce Pijing (spleen meridian) and Dachang (large intestine), push Sanguan (triple pass), rub the abdomen, knead Tianshu (ST 25) and umbilicus, push upwards Qijiegu (lumbrosacral vertebrae), knead Dantian (lower abdomen) and Guiwei (coccyx), pinch the spine and perform the manipulation of carrying water into earth.

Explanation of the formula: Reinforcing Pijing (spleen meridian) and Dachang (large intestine) can invigorate the spleen and promote Qi, strengthen the intestines and solidify stools. Pushing Sanguan (triple pass), kneading Dantian (lower abdomen) and Tianshu (ST 25), rubbing the abdomen, kneading umbilicus and pinching the spine can warm Yang and invigorate the middle energizer. Kneading Guiwei (coccyx) and pushing upwards Qijiegu (lumbrosacral vertebrae) can warm Yang to stop diarrhea. Manipulation of carrying water into earth can invigorate spleen to stop diarrhea.

For patients with Yang deficiency of the kidney, add manipulation of kneading Wailaogong (EX-LE 9). For patients with abdominal distention, add manipulation of circularly pushing Neibagua. For patients with lingering diarrhea, add manipulation of kneading Baihui (GV 20).

【Nursing】

1. The food should be hygienic.

2. The food should be taken regularly, avoiding excessive hot or cold food.

3. The patient should take plain food and avoid greasy food. Diapers should be changed regularly and the body of the patient should be turned frequently to prevent recessive urethral infection or secondary pneumonia.

8.4.7 Anorexia

Anorexia refers to long-term poor appetite or even refusal to take food in infants. Similar symptoms caused by exogenous pathogenic factors or internal injuries are different. Anorexia is often seen in 1 to 6 year old infants and may occur in any season. Infants living in cities often suffer from this problem.

Anorexia is related to dysfunction of the spleen and stomach as well as improper habit in taking food. It may be caused by improper diet and feeding; or by long-term partiality in diet that causes dysfunction of the spleen and stomach; or by frequent deficiency of Yin or insufficiency of Yin due to febrile disease that leads to lack of nourishment and moisture; or by prenatal weakness or weakness after illness that affects the functions of the spleen and stomach. Besides, terror and mental disappointment may disturb the flow of Qi, cause liver depression and damage the spleen, consequently leading to anorexia.

According to Western medicine, anorexia may be caused by inadequate intake of protein and calorie, lack of vitamin B and some trace elements, or excessive intake of protein, sugar, fat, vitamin D or Vitamin A. Besides, forced taking food may reduce children's interest in taking food; frequent feeding may disturb infantile habit in taking food. In addition, nervousness, anxiety and excitement of children may also affect appetite.

【Clinical manifestations】

1. Anorexia due to dysfunction of the spleen in transportation and transformation: It is marked by poor appetite, no interest in food, pale complexion, physical leanness, light-colored tongue whitish and thin or greasy coating and slow pulse.

2. Anorexia due to insufficiency of stomach Yin: It is marked by poor appetite, preference for drinking water, dry mouth and tongue, lusterless complexion, dry stools, scanty urine, lusterless skin, red tongue with scanty fluid, scanty or patched coating, smooth and thin pulse.

3. Anorexia due to deficiency of the spleen and stomach: It is marked by no appetite, sallow complexion, physical leanness, lassitude, listlessness, frequent perspiration, stools with undigested food in it, thin and whitish tongue coating and weak pulse.

4. Anorexia due to liver depression and Qi stagnation: It is marked by no appetite, mental depression, abdominal distension, chest oppression, eructation, hypochondria fullness, frequent sighing, light-colored tongue with exfoliating tongue, taut and slow pulse.

[Treatment with Tuina therapy]

1. Dysfunction of the spleen in transportation and transformation

Therapeutic methods: To regulate the spleen and reinforce its function in transportation and transformation.

Formula: Clear and reinforce Pijing (spleen meridian), clear Dachang (large intestine), knead Banmen (major thenar), push Sihengwen (four transverse creases), knead Tianshu (ST 25), rub the abdomen, knead Zhongwan (CV 12), press and knead Zusanli (ST 36) and push Dahengwen (major transverse crease).

Explanation of the formula: Clearing Pijing (spleen meridian) can invigorate the spleen and clear dampness. Clearing Dachang (large intestine) can clear away heat and promote defecation. Pushing Dahengwen (major transverse crease) and kneading Banmen (major thenar) can promote digestion to relieve food retention. Rubbing abdomen, kneading Tianshu (ST 25) and Zhongwan (CV 12), pressing and kneading Zusanli (ST 36) can invigorate the spleen to harmonize the stomach. Pushing Sihengwen (four transverse creases) can regulate the middle energizer to promote Qi circulation.

2. Insufficiency of stomach Yin

Therapeutic methods: To nourish stomach Yin.

Formula: Reinforce Pijing (spleen meridian), circularly push Neibagua, knead Banmen (major thenar) and Shangma (climbing upon horse), clear Dachang (large intestine) and Tianheshui (heaven river water), perform the manipulations of Shui Di Lao Yue (scooping the moon from the bottom of water) and Yun Tu Ru Shui (carrying earth into water), and knead Pishu (BL 20) and Weishu (BL 21).

Explanation of the formula: Clearing Tianheshui (heaven river water) and Dachang (large intestine), performing the manipulations of scooping the moon from the bottom of water and carrying earth into water can clear away heat in the stomach and intestines. Reinforcing Pijing (spleen meridian), kneading Pishu (BL 20) and Weishu (BL 21) can invigorate the spleen and stomach. Kneading Shangma (climbing upon horse) is effective for nourishing Yin to relieve symptoms of dryness. Circularly pushing Neibagua and kneading Banmen (major thenar) can promote Qi flow and digestion.

3. Weakness of the spleen and stomach

Therapeutic methods: Invigorating the spleen to nourish Qi.

Formula: Reinforce Pijing (spleen meridian) and Weijing (stomach meridian), circularly push Neibagua, perform the manipulation of Yun Shui Ru Tu (carrying water into earth), push Sanguan (triple pass), rub Zhongwan (CV 12) and the abdomen, knead Dantian (lower abdomen), Pishu (BL 20) and Weishu (BL 21), pinch the spine and knead Zusanli (ST 36).

Explanation of the formula: Reinforcing Pijing (spleen meridian) and Weijing (stomach meridian), and performing Yun Shui Ru Tu (carrying water into earth) can strengthen the spleen and stomach. Pushing Sanguan (triple pass) and kneading Dantian (lower abdomen) can warm Yang and invigorate Qi. Kneading Pishu (BL 20) and Weishu (BL 21), pinching the spine, kneading Zusanli (ST 36) and rubbing Zhongwan (CV 12) can invigorate the spleen to promote digestion. Circularly pushing Neibagua and rubbing the abdomen can promote Qi flow and digestion.

4. Liver depression and Qi stagnation

Therapeutic methods: To promote Qi flow and disperse the liver.

Formula: Clear Ganjing (liver meridian), reinforce Pijing (spleen meridian), circularly push Neibagua, knead Banmen (major thenar), perform An Xuan Zou Cuo Mo (twisting and rubbing like plucking string), and knead Ganshu (BL 18), Pishu (BL 20) and Weishu (BL 21).

Explanation of the formula: Clearing Ganjing (liver meridian), performing An Xuan Zou Cuo Mo (twisting and rubbing like plucking string) and kneading Ganshu (BL 18) can disperse the liver to promote Qi flow. Reinforcing Pijing (spleen meridian) and kneading Pishu (BL 20) and Weishu (BL 21) can invigorate spleen and harmonize the stomach. Circularly pushing Neibagua and kneading Banmen (major thenar) can promote Qi flow and digestion.

【Nursing】

1. Feed infants regularly and properly and correct wrong feeding habit.
2. Never force infants to take food.
3. Feed infants with a variety of food that is easy to digest.

8.4.8 Constipation

Constipation refers to difficulty in defection and prolonged intervals or unsmooth defecation. The morbidity of infantile constipation is 3%~8%, of which 90%~95% is functional constipation. The morbidity of constipation in cities is higher than that in the country, more frequently affecting girls than boys.

Infantile constipation is either excess or deficiency in nature and is related to pathological changes of the stomach and intestines as well as the state of Qi, blood and body fluid. Constipation of excess type may be caused by dryness and heat in the stomach and intestines as well as failure to body fluid to transport downwards due to excessively taking spicy and greasy food or impairment of Yin due to febrile disease. Or it may be caused by deficiency of blood and body fluid to moisten the large intestines resulting from stagnation of Qi and dysfunction of the stomach and intestines in transmission due to food retention and lack of necessary exercises. Long-term constipation may, due to obstruction of Fu-organs and failure of turbid Qi to descend, cause abdominal distension and pain, vertigo, distension of head, reduced appetite and restless sleep. Long-term constipation may lead to hemorrhoids and anal rupture.

According to Western medicine, constipation may be functional or due to intestinal deformity. Clinically functional constipation is commonly encountered. The causes of constipation are irregular life and defecation that cause weak reflexioin of bowel movement and intestinal myasthenia; excessive intake of fine food that produces little waste or insufficiency of carbohydrates; anal disorders like hemorrhoids or anal fissure that cause pain in defecation and retention of feces; malnutrition problems, such as rickets, that may lead to dysfunction of the intestines weakness or palsy of the abdominal muscles.

[Clinical manifestations]

1. Constipation of excess type: It is marked by dry stool, difficulty in defection, scanty and brown urine, flushed face and feverish body, fullness in the chest and hypochondriac region, abdominal distension and pain, poor appetite, dry mouth, restlessness, reddish tongue with yellow coating, rapid pulse and bluish finger veins.

2. Constipation of deficiency type: It is marked by difficult defecation, shortness of breath and perspiration after defecation, loose stools, pale complexion, listlessness, lassitude, whitish tongue with thin coating, weak and thin pulse and light finger veins.

[Treatment with Tuina therapy]

1. Constipation of excess type

Therapeutic principles: Clearing away heat to promote defecation, promoting Qi flow to relieve food retention.

Formula: Clear Dachang (large intestine) and Weijing (stomach meridian), circularly push Neibagua, press and knead Boyangchi (pool of Yang on the arm), push Liufu (six Fu-organs), rub the abdomen, knead Tianshu (ST 25), perform An Xuan Zou Cuo Mo (twisting and rubbing like plucking string), push downward Qijiegu (lumbrosacral vertebrae), knead Guiwei (coccyx) and press and knead Zusanli (ST 36). For patients with flushed face, feverish body, dry mouth and restlessness, manipulations for pushing the spine and Shui Di Lao Yue (scooping the moon from the bottom of water) are used in addition. For patients with fullness in the chest and abdominal distension, manipulations for separately pushing the abdomen and pushing Sihengwen (four transverse creases) are used in addition.

Explanation of the formula: Clearing Dachang (large intestine) and Weijing (stomach meridian) and pushing Liufu (six Fu-organs) can clear away heat and eliminate dampness. Pressing and kneading Boyangchi (pool of Yang on the arm), pushing Downwards Qijiegu (lumbrosacral vertebrae) and kneading Guwei (coccyx) can promote Qi flow to improve defecation. An Xuan Zou Cuo Mo (twisting and rubbing like plucking string) can promote Qi flow to relieve food retention. Rubbing the abdomen, kneading Tianshu (ST 25) and pressing and kneading Zusanli (ST 36) can invigorate the spleen to promote digestion.

2. Constipation of deficiency type

Therapeutic principles: Replenishing Qi and nourish blood, nourishing Yin to moisten dryness.

Formula: Reinforce Pijing (spleen meridian), clear Dachang (large intestine), knead Shangma (climbing upon horse), press and knead Boyangch (pool of Yang on the arm), push Sanguan (triple pass), knead Shenshu (BL 23)and Guiwei (coccyx), pinch the spine and press and knead Zusanli (ST 36). For patients with Qi deficiency, add manipulations of kneading Guanyuan (CV 4) and Yun Shui Ru Tu (carrying water into earth). For patients with deficiency of Yin and blood, add manipulations of kneading Zhigou (TE 6) and Geshu (BL 17).

Explanation of the formula: Reinforcing Pijing (spleen meridian), pushing Sanguan (triple pass), pinching the spine and pressing and kneading Zusanli (ST 36) can invigorate the spleen to replenish Qi, harmonize the middle energizer and promote defection. Kneading Guiwei (coccyx), pressing and kneading Boyangchi (pool of Yang on the arm) and clearing Dachang (large intestine) can promote Qi flow to help defecation. Kneading Shangma (climbing upon horse) and Shenshu (BL 23) can nourish Yin, moisten intestines and promote defecation.

【Nursing】

1. To maintain a habit of regular defecation.

2. To increase intake of fruits, vegetables and coarse food, avoiding spicy and greasy food.

3. To have a certain amount of outdoor exercises.

8.4.9 Night Crying

Night crying means that infants tend to cry at night or cry regularly at night without any abnormal changes in the daytime. In mild cases, infants still can sleep after crying; in serious cases, infants are crying over night, even in the daytime. This problem may last from several days to several months and is commonly seen among infants under 1 year.

Night crying is related to the dysfunction of the spleen, stomach and heart. The spleen pertains to Taiyin and infants are usually weak in constitution and the spleen. Invasion of cold into the spleen or endogenous cold in the spleen will lead to coagulation of cold and stagnation of Qi and blood due to combination of exogenous and endogenous cold, consequently causing abdominal pain and making infants cry. Night crying may be caused by impairment of the spleen and stomach due to retention of food in the stomach and intestines resulting from improper feeding, leading to discomfort of the stomach and making infants crying at night. It may also be caused by dysphoria due to invasion of heat into the stomach and spleen resulting from excessive intake of greasy food by the mother. Or it may be caused by strange noise or objects that disturbs the mind of the infants due to the fact that infants are insufficient in spirit and heart Qi.

According to Western medicine, night crying of infants is caused by disorders of the digestive system and malnutrition. Disorders of the digestive system are often intestinal infection and functional disorder of the intestines which cause convulsion of the smooth muscle in the intestines and abdominal pain. That is why infants are crying at night. Malnutrition, deficiency of trace elements, rickets and infantile tetany all can cause night crying.

【Clinical manifestations】

1. Deficiency cold in the spleen: It is marked by intermittent crying at night with low and weak voice, pale complexion, preference for lying in pronation and warm compress over the abdomen, cold limbs, poor appetite, watery stools, bluish urine, pale lips, light red tongue and finger veins, thin and slow pulse.

2. Retention of milk and food: It is marked by restlessness and crying at night, feverish sensation in the palms, soles and heart, anorexia, vomiting of milk, acid regurgitation, abdominal distention, sour and stinking stools, red tongue with thick and greasy coating, purple finger veins and slippery pulse.

3. Retention of excessive heat in the heart meridian: It is marked by loud crying, dislike of lamp light, flushed face, red lips, feverish sensation in the stomach and the whole body, restlessness, scanty and brown urine, constipation, red tip of the tongue with yellow coating, red and purple finger veins, rapid and strong pulse.

4. Fright and fear: It is marked by sudden crying at night as if seeing strange things, dysphoria, occasional fear, preference for staying in the mother's arms, sudden pale or sudden bluish complexion, normal tongue and pulse, blue finger veins.

【Treatment with Tuina therapy】

1. Deficiency cold in the spleen

Therapeutic methods: To warm the middle energizer and invigorate the spleen.

Formula: Reinforce Pijing (spleen meridian), push Sanguan (triple pass), perform the manipulation of Yun Shui Ru Tu (carrying water into earth), rub the abdomen, knead Zhongwan (CV 12) and pinch the spine.

Explanation of the formula: Reinforcing Pijing (spleen meridian), performing Yun Shui Ru Tu (carrying water into earth), rubbing the abdomen and kneading Zhongwan (CV 12) can invigorate the spleen and warm the middle energizer. Pressing Sanguan (triple pass) can warm Yang Qi and promote its circulation. Pinching the spine can regulate Qi and blood and cultivate primordial Qi.

2. Retention of milk and food

Therapeutic methods: Promoting digestion to relieve food retention.

Formula: First clear and then reinforce Pijing (spleen meridian), clear Dachang (large intestine), knead Banmen (major thenar), push Sihengwen (four transverse creases), rub the abdomen, knead Zhongwan (CV 12) and Tianshu (ST 25), perform An Xian Zou Cuo Mo (pressing string and stroking) and pinch the spine.

Explanation of the formula: Clearing and reinforcing Pijing (spleen meridian) can invigorate the spleen and clear away dampness. Clearing Dachang (large intestine) and pushing downwards Qijiegu (lumbrosacral vertebrae) can clear away heat to promote defecation. Kneading Banmen (major thenar), performing the manipulation of Yuan Hou Zhai Guo (Ape Picking Fruits) and An Xuan Zou Cuo Mo (pressing string and stroking) can promote digestion and relieve food retention. Rubbing the abdomen, kneading Zhongwan (CV 12) and Tianshu (ST 25) and pinching the spine can invigorate the spleen and normalize the stomach. Pushing Sihengwen (four transverse creases) can regulate the middle energizer and promote Qi flow.

3. Excessive heat in the heart meridian

Therapeutic methods: Clearing away heat from the heart.

Formula: Cleat heart meridian, knead Zongjin (great tendon) and Neilaogong (inner part of palm), perform Shui Di Lao Yue (scooping the moon from the bottom of water), and push the spine.

Explanation of the formula: Clearing heart meridian, kneading Zongjin (great tendon) and Neilaogong (inner part of palm), and performing the manipulation of Shui Di Lao Yue (scooping the moon from the bottom of water) can clear the heart, reduce fire to relieve restlessness. Clearing Xiaochang (small intestine) can clearing away heat to promote urination. Clearing Tianheshui (heaven river water) and pushing the spine can clear away heat to relieve restlessness.

4. Fright and fear

Therapeutic methods: Removing fear and tranquilize the mind.

Formula: Push Cuanzhu (BL 2), clear Ganjing (liver meridian), pound Xiaotianxin (small heaven center), pinch Weiling (powerful and magic) and Jingning (essence and tranquility), and knead Wuzhijie (interphalangeal joints of fiver fingers).

Explanation of the formula: Pushing Cuanzhu (BL 2), pounding Xiaotianxin (small heaven center), kneading Wuzhijie (interphalangeal joints of fiver fingers), pinching Weiling (powerful and magic) and Jingning (essence and tranquility) can remove fear and tranquilize mind. Clearing Ganjing (liver meridian) can disperse the liver, relieve depression and tranquilize mind.

【Nursing】

1. The patient should wear proper clothes. If the patient is troubled by cold in the spleen, measures should be taken to keep warm and prevent cold; if the patient is troubled by heat in the heart, it is inadvisable to keep warm.

2. The patient should be fed with proper food regularly, avoiding taking excessive

cold or hot food.

3. Pregnant women and breast feeding women should avoid taking cold, hot and spicy food.

4. Keep the room quiet lest the infant be frightened.

8.4.10 Enuresis

Enuresis refers to involuntary urination of children over three during sleep. Similar symptoms in children under 3 cannot be diagnosed as enuresis, since they are still weak in the central nerve system and are still unable to control urination.

Enuresis should be treated as early as possible. Delayed treatment will affect physical and mental development of infants.

Enuresis is related to the dysfunction of the lung, spleen and kidney, especially the kidney. Normal urination depends on normal function of the bladder and the triple energizer. In terms of Qi transformation in the triple energizer, the upper energizer centers around the lung, the middle energizer around the spleen and the lower energizer around the kidney. The dysfunction of any of these three organs will cause enuresis. In TCM, the liver is responsible for dredging and regulating activities while the kidney governs closure and storage. Stagnated heat in liver meridian affect the kidney in closure and storage, leading to disorder of the kidney in managing the activities of opening and closing and abnormal changes of the bladder in storage.

According to modern medicine, infantile urination is under the control of vegetative nerve system. But the cerebral cortex of infants is still unable to regulate this nerve system. When infants are over three, the cerebral cortex begins to control urination. If the cerebral cortex fails to inhibit spinal central nerve to monitor urination, the bladder forces the detrusor to contract and discharge urine.

[Clinical manifestations]

The main symptom is involuntary urination, especially in rainy days or when the infant is tired in the daytime, once a night or even twice or several times a night if the problem is serious. Sometimes the infant may have enuresis even in the daytime. Infants with long-term enuresis are characterized by sallow complexion, decline of intelligence, dispiritedness, vertigo, back pain and cold limbs. Elder children may feel shy or nervous.

1. Deficiency of kidney Qi: It is marked by enuresis in the night, once or twice or even more in a single night. The complaints of elder children are lassitude, weakness of the lumber region and legs, cold limbs, profuse and clear urine, or accompanied by vertigo, aversion to cold, preference for sleeping in curled position, light-colored tongue with thin and whitish coating, weak, deep and thin pulse.

2. Deficiency of lung Qi and spleen Qi: It is marked by enuresis during sleep with scanty urine, lusterless complexion, shortness of breath, spontaneous perspiration, poor appetite, loose stools, emaciation, light-colored tongue with thin and whitish coating, weak and slow pulse.

3. Stagnation of heat in the liver meridian: It is marked by enuresis with yellow, scanty and brown urine, inability to control urination, impatience, feverish sensation in the palms, soles and heart, flushed face, red lips, frequently drinking water, even red eyes, red tongue with yellow and greasy coating, rapid and taut pulse.

【Treatment with Tuina therapy】

1. Deficiency of kidney Qi

Therapeutic methods: Nourish Qi to reinforce kidney, strengthen kidney to arrest enuresis.

Formula: Reinforce Shenjing (kidney meridian) and Xiaochang (small intestine), push Sanguan (triple pass), press and knead Baihui (GV 20), knead Dantian (lower abdomen) and Guiwei (coccyx), press and knead Shenshu (BL 23), rub lower lumbar region, and press and knead Sanyinjiao (SP 6).

Explanation of the formula: Reinforcing Shenjing (kidney meridian) and Xiaochang (small intestine), pressing and kneading Shenshu (BL 23), kneading Dantian (lower abdomen) and Guiwei (coccyx) and rubbing lower lumbar region can warm and nourish kidney Qi, reinforce fire in Mingmen (life gate) and strengthen the kidney to arrest enuresis. Pressing and kneading Baihui (GV 20) and pushing Sanguan (triple pass) can warm yang. Pressing and kneading Sanyinjiao (SP 6) can regulate water passage.

2. Deficiency of the lung Qi and spleen Qi

Therapeutic methods: Replenishing Qi to arrest enuresis.

Formula: Reinforce Pijing (spleen meridian) and Feijing (lung meridian), press Baihui (GV 20), rub Zhongji (CV3) and Pangguangshu (BL28) and knead Zusanli (ST 36).

Explanation of the formula: Reinforcing Pijing (spleen meridian) and Feijing (lung meridian) and Pressing and kneading Zusanli (ST 36) can nourish the spleen and lung to nourish Qi. Pressing and kneading Baihui (GV 20) and pushing Sanguan (triple pass) can warm yang. Kneading Zhongji (CV 3) and pressing and kneading Pangguangshu (BL 28) can regulate Qi transformation in the bladder and strengthen water passage.

3. Stagnation of heat in the liver meridian

Therapeutic methods: Clearing the liver to reduce fire.

Formula: Clear Ganjing (liver meridian) and Xinjing (heart meridian), reinforce Pijing (spleen meridian), knead Xiaotianxin (small heaven center), and knead Shangma (climbing upon horse), Sanyinjiao (SP 6) and Yongquan (KI 1). For patients with loose stools, add the manipulations for reinforcing Dachang (large intestine) and rubbing the abdomen. For patients with poor appetite, add the manipulation of circularly pushing Neibagua. For patients with perspiration, add the manipulation for kneading Shending (tip of the small finger).

Explanation of the formula: Clear Ganjing (liver meridian) and Xinjing (heart meridian) can clear away heat to relieve restlessness. Kneading Xiaotianxin (small heaven center), Shangma (climbing upon horse), Sanyinjiao (SP 6) and Yongquan (KI 1) can strengthen the kidney to control fire and direct fire to move downwards. Reinforcing Pijing (spleen meridian) can invigorate the spleen.

【Nursing】

1. Help the children maintain a habit of regular urination and avoid fatigue.

2. Increase intake of nutrients, have more rest and avoid drinking water two hours before sleep and taking liquid food.

3. Parents should wake up infants to urinate in the night and help them maintain a good living habit.

4. Parents should try to relieve nervousness and anxiety of children.

8.4.11 Infantile Myogenic Torticollis

Infantile myogenic torticollis is marked by deviation of the head to the affected side, or the head leaning forward, or the face turning to the healthy side due to spasm and contraction of sternocleidomastoid muscle. Surgery may be considered if the condition lasts over 1 year and deformity is obvious.

Infantile myogenic torticollis is caused by fibrotic spasm of the sternocleidomastoid on the affected side. Hyperplasia of fibroblasts and degeneration of muscular fibers are evident and are eventually replaced by connective tissue. The real cause is still uncertain.

1. It is generally believed that infantile myogenic torticollis is caused by malposition of the fetus during delivery, resulting in bleeding due to pressure of the sternocleidomastoid muscle by the birth canal or obstetric forceps. The formation of hematoma brings on spasm of the sternocleidomastoid muscle.

2. It is also believed that myogenic torticollis is caused by malposition of the fetus in the uterus, preventing blood from flowing to the sternocleidomastoid muscle on the other side and leading to ischemic fibrosis of the muscle, myofibroma, even necrosis and fibrohyperplasia, and consequently causing muscular contraction and myogenic torticollis.

3. It is still believed that myogenic torticollis is not caused during childbearing, but resulted from deviation of the fetus' head to one side in the uterus that prevents blood from flowing to the sternocleidomastoid muscle on the other side, eventually causing ischemic changes of the muscle.

【Clinical manifestations】

1. After birth, fusiform mass appears on one side of the neck. Later on the sternocleidomastoid muscle on the affected side gradually becomes contracted and the part that protrudes appears like a cord.

2. The head deviates to the affected side while the face turns to the healthy side.

3. In a few cases, hard mass can be found around the point of attachment of the sternocleidomastoid muscle at the affected side near the clavicle.

4. Long-term duration of myogenic torticollis will affect facial development at the affected side, leading to corresponding changes of the face at the healthy side and consequently causing asymmetry. At the advanced stage, it is usually accompanied by compensatory scoliosis.

【Treatment with Tuina therapy】

Therapeutic methods: Soothing the tendons and dredging the collaterals, softening and resolving hard mass.

Formula:

1. Put the child in a supine position. Apply pushing and kneading manipulations on the sternocleidomastoid muscle of the affected side with the whorl surface of the thumb, or the index and middle fingers for 4~5 minutes.

2. Knead and nip the sternocleidomastoid muscle with mild force for 3~5 minutes.

3. The doctor holds the shoulder of the patient on the affected side with one hand, while grasps the top of the patient's head with the other, moving the patient's head gradually toward the shoulder of the healthy side, and simultaneously lengthening the sternocleidomastoid muscle on the affected side. This manipulation is performed for several times and monitored to the tolerance of the patient.

4. Grasp and knead the sternocleidomastoid muscle at the affected side. This manipulation is performed 3~5 minutes.

5. Grasp Jianjing (GB 21) 5~6 times with mild force.

Explanation of the formula: Pushing, kneading, grasping and nipping the sternocleidomastoid muscle at the affected side can soothe tendons, dredge collaterals, activate blood, promote local blood circulation, relieve muscular convulsion and abate detumescence. Stretching and pulling the sternocleidomastoid muscle at the affected side can improve and restore normal movement of the neck.

【Nursing】

1. Parents should frequently try to pull and stretch the sternocleidomastoid muscle of the baby at the affected side.

2. Measures can be taken to turn the head of infants to the deformed side in daily life, such as feeding, pillow or toys that can attract infants and are helpful for rectifying the position of neck.

8.4.12 Infantile subluxation of radial head

Infantile subluxation of radial head, a commonly encountered injury of elbow in clinical treatment, is cause by improper position of radial head and annular ligament, often occurring among children under 5.

The anterior and lower part of humeroradial ligament is weak. The carpitulum radii leans to the anterior, posterior and distal directions, deviating from the longitudinal axis of radium. The sagittal diameter in supination is comparatively longer and the capitulum radii is slightly away from the radius notch of ulna in extreme pronation. Its lateral border is lower and in a comparatively distal position. When the elbow of an infant is stretched and pulled, such as putting on clothes and grasping the elbow by others when falling down, the space of humeral and radial joint will be widened, the negative pressure in the joint will increase and the articular capsule and annular ligament will be absorbed into the space. As a result, the radial head will be stuck by the annular ligament, consequently causing subluxation of radial head.

【Clinical manifestations】

It is commonly encountered among children with a history of injury of the affected limb. It is characterized by pain in the elbow at the affected side, semi-bending position of the elbow joint, pronation of the forearm, pain in the small head of radius, local swelling and deformity, inability of the affected hand to take anything or move the elbow. There are no abnormal changes of humeral condyle and olecranon. X-ray shows no pathologic changes.

【Treatment with Tuina therapy】

Therapeutic methods: Soothing tendons and rectifying subluxation to stop pain.

The parent holds the child in a sitting position, the doctor stands at the opposite side. Take the right side for example. The doctor puts the left thumb on the lateral side of the humeral head, holds the wrist with the right hand, slowly rotating the forearm backwards. Reduction will be accomplished during supination. If it does not work, the doctor may push the forearm to the distal point to conduct supination, or push the forearm to the proximal point to drive the annular ligament into its proper position. In performing such a manipulation, a clear sound can be heard. Then the pain disappears immediately and the elbow can be moved freely. Or the elbow is bent 90° to rotate the forearm backwards for reduction. After reduction, the pain in the elbow disappears immediately and the child can move his elbow freely.

【Nursing】

1. For cases without evident swelling and distension, it can simply be treated by hanging the wrist from the neck for 2~3days without applying any medicines.

2. Avoid pulling or pushing the affected limb lest habitual dislocation be caused.

Review Questions

- Briefly describe the performance and actions of Tui Fa (pushing manipulation), Mo Fa (stoking manipulation), Yun Tu Ru Shui (carrying earth into water) and Da Ma Guo Tian He (beating horse to cross heaven river).
- Describe the location, performance and actions of Kangong (Kan palace), Tianmen (heaven gate), Er Hou Gao Gu (prominent bone behind the ear), Fu (abdomen), Jizhu (spinal column), Qijiegu (from the fourth lumbar vertebral to the end of coccyx), Pijing (spleen meridian), Sihengwen (four

transverse creases), Zhang Xiao Heng Wen (small palmar transverse crease), Shangma (climbing upon horse), Liufu (six Fu-organs) and Tianheshui (heaven river water).
- Briefly describe manipulations used to treat cough, fever, diarrhea, anorexia, night crying, enuresis, myogenic torticollis and infantile subluxation of radial head.

9 Self-Healthcare Tuina

9.1 The effect of self-healthcare Tuina on human body

Self-heathcare Tuina means that people use some basic manipulations to work on certain parts of their body in order to achieve pretreatment or improve and strengthen their constitution.

Self-heathcare Tuina can stimulate all the meridians and Acupoints, regulate the functions of some vital tissues and organs to promote the body resistance. It also can activate Zheng Qi (healthy Qi) to promote the production, transformation and circulation of Qi and blood as well as improve immunity.

Self-healthcare Tuina can be classified into various categories with rich manipulations, suitable for people of different age to preserve health, prevent and treat diseases

9.2 The methods of Self-healthcare Tuina

9.2.1 Soothing the liver to regulate Qi

The liver is the residence of Po (soul) and pertains to wood in the theory of Wu Xing (five elements), characterized by constant moving and ascending. The main physiological functions of the liver are to maintain free flow of Qi and store blood, regulating Qi flow, smoothing meridians and collaterals, ensuring normal physiological function of various Zang-organs and Fu-organs, promoting flow of Qi, blood and body fluid, strengthening the functions of the spleen and stomach in transportation and transformation. The liver is closely connected with the eyes, dominates over the tendons and manifests its functional states on the nail, related to anger in emotions and tears in fluids. If liver Qi is sufficient, the tendons will be strong, the nails will be firm and the eyes will be bright. Deficiency of liver Qi will result in soft and weak tendons and blurred vision. The liver and gallbladder are connected with each other because the liver meridian of foot-Jueyin and gallbladder meridian of foot-Shaoyang are internally and externally related to each other. Thus frequently application of the manipulations for soothing the liver and smoothing the gallbladder is an efficient way to prevent and treat diseases.

Rubbing intercoastal region: Taking a sitting position, putting both hands horizontally under the armpits with fingers forked (the distance between the fingers is equal to that between the ribs), pushing to the right side with the left hand to the sternum, and then pushing to the left side with the right hand to the sternum, alternately from the upper to the navel for 9 times. The fingers should touch the intercoastal region closely and the force exerted should be stable and even until warmth is felt.

Kneading Danzhong (CV 17): Taking a sitting position, juxtaposing the four fingers and putting them on Danzhong (CV 17), kneading it clockwise and counterclockwise for 36 times respectively with relatively forceful strength.

Rubbing the hypochondriac regions: Taking a sitting position, putting the hands over the chest at the sides of the nipples with the left hand over the right hand, rubbing horizontally along the ribs and gradually shifting downward to the floating ribs, then putting the right hand over the left side and performing the same movement again. Repeat the same process until warm feeling in the hypochondriac regions is felt.

Plucking Yanglingquan (GB 34): Taking a sitting position, putting the thumbs on Yanglingquan (GB 34) at both sides, assisted with the rest fingers; pressing and kneading the point for one minute, and then plucking the tendons at the local area for 3~5 times until aching and numb feeling radiates like electric shock.

Nailing Taichong (LR 3): Taking a sitting position, pressing Taichong (LR 3) with the tips of thumbs forcefully for about one minute till aching and numb feeling is felt; then kneading the point gently with the whorl surface of the thumbs.

Rubbing the lower abdomen: Taking a sitting or supine position, putting the hands below hypochondriac regions, rubbing forcefully along an oblique line to the lower abdomen and pubis for 36 times.

Pointing and pressing Zhangmen (LR 13): Putting the tips of the middle fingers on Zhangmen (LR 13), pressing the point for about one minute with slightly strong force till aching and numb feeling is felt.

Kneading Qimen (LR 14): Taking a sitting or supine position, putting the palm base of the left hand on the right Qimen (LR 14), kneading it forcefully clockwise and counterclockwise for 36 times respectively, then changing the other hand to repeat the same manipulation.

Grasping the lumbar muscles: Taking a sitting or supine position, holding the lumbar muscles bilaterally with the margin of the web between the thumbs and index fingers to grasp the muscles from the lumbar region to the sacral region for 36 times.

Moving the eyes: Taking a sitting position, looking ahead with upright position of the body while the eyeballs rotate clockwise slowly for 9 times; then opening the eyes widely and staring forward for a while. Repeat the rotation counterclockwise for 9 times.

9.2.2 Tranquilizing the heart and calming the mind

The main physiological function of the heart is to dominate over blood and vessels, which is considered as the key of life activity. Only when the function of dominating blood and vessels works normally can blood circulates smoothly in the vessels to nourish the body and maintain the normal physiological activities. The heart is connected with the small intestine via meridians inside the body. The condition of the heart is shown through the aspects of spirit, consciousness, mental activities, motor movement, pulse states and tongue condition. Sufficient heart Qi and abundant blood in the vessels are manifested as vigorous spirit, sound mental activities, agile movement, moderate and forceful pulse as well as light reddish tongue with moist coating. Insufficient heart Qi may cause low spirit, slow reaction, irregular pulse, dark purple or pale tongue. Thus, the manipulation for tranquilizing the heart and calming the mind can effectively prevent and cure disease of the heart.

Strengthening the heart meridian: Take a sitting position with the feet kept apart in a distance as the width of the shoulders, relax the body and stretch the hands naturally; sway the waist to lead the elbows and the hands toward the opposite directions. When the hand reaches the front, pat the chest with the palm. When the hand reaches the back, pat the center of the back with the dorsum of hand. At the initial stage, pat the body gently. The strength can be increased if there is no uncomfortable reaction. Repeat the same manipulation for about 36 times.

Rubbing the chest: Put the right hand on the area between the breasts with fingers pointing downward to the side of the abdomen. Push first downward to the area below the left breast and rub the heart area, and then return to the initial position. Then withdraw the hand to the area below the right breast to repeat rubbing in circles. Push and rub in this way to form a figure of "∞"(horizontal 8) for 36 times.

Plucking Jiquan (HT 1): Put four fingers of the right hand on the left greater pectoral muscle and press with the palm root for a few minutes. Then, hold the anterior part of the armpit with the margin of the web between the index and thumb, put the middle finger on Jiquan (HT 1) to hook the tendon there and pluck outward to induce aching and numb feeling which may radiate like electric shock.

Pinching Zhongchong (PC 9): Clip the tip of middle finger of the left hand with the thumb and index finger of the right hand, that is the location of Zhongchong (PC 9). Press and pinch the tip of left middle finger forcefully for 9 times. Then change the other hand and perform the same procedure.

Kneading Xuehai (SP 10) : Take a sitting position, put hands above the knee joints respectively. Press Xuehai (SP 10) with the tips of the thumbs for about 1 minute, then knead gently and slowly for 36 times.

Grasping the heart meridian: Put the thumb of the right hand under the left armpit and the rest other four fingers on the medial aspect of the upper arm, grasp, press and knead simultaneously. Then shift the hands bit by bit to Shenmen (HT 7). Repeat the same procedure up and down for 9 times. Then change the hand to perform the same procedure on the right arm.

Kneading Shenmen (HT 7): Take a sitting position, put the middle finger over the index finger of the right hand to knead Shenmen (HT 7) on the left hand for about 1 minute. Then change the hand and repeat the same procedure on the opposite side.

Squeezing Neiguan(PC 6): Take a sitting position, press Neiguan(PC 6) on the left side with the thumb of the right hand, the other four fingers assist to squeeze the point from the back of the wrist. Press and squeeze for 9 times. Then change the hand and perform the same manipulation on the right side.

Beating heaven drum: Press the hands on the ears with the bottom of the palms pointing to the front with the five fingers pointing to the back. Hit the occiput region with the index, middle and ring fingers for 3 times, and then move the hands away suddenly. Repeat the same procedure for 9 times.

Stirring the sea: Rotate the tongue to rub the outside and inside of the gum, from the right to the left and the left to the right for 9 times respectively. Swallow the saliva excreted in three times.

9.2.3 Strengthening the spleen and regulating the stomach

The main physiological function of the spleen are transportation and transformation of nutrients which are the important functions of the spleen in digesting, absorbing, transporting and transforming nutrient substances and promoting the metabolism of water. The internal organs and health of the body depend on the function of the spleen. In TCM, the spleen is called "acquired foundation" because the spleen controls the blood and keeps it circulating in the vessels. Inside the body, the spleen is related to the stomach via meridians internally and externally. On the body surface, the spleen manifests its conditions through the muscle of the limbs, lips and taste in the mouth. When the spleen functions well in transportation and transformation, the food nutrient is absorbed continuously, Qi and blood are constantly produced, the body is well nourished, the lip are red and lustrous. If the spleen does not function well, it will cause emaciation, muscular atrophy and weakness, tastelessness or abnormal taste in the mouth, pale lips without luster. The manipulation for strengthening the spleen and regulating the stomach can effectively prevent and treat disorders of the spleen and stomach.

Rubbing the epigastric region: Put the left or the right hand on Zhongwan (CV 12). Rub the epigastric region counterclockwise in circles for 36 times from small circle to large circle. Then perform the same rubbing movement clockwise for 36 times from big circle to small circle.

Pushing and waving the stomach: Lie down on the back with the lower limbs flexed, put the hands over Zhongwan (CV 12) one over the other. Take abdominal respiration, pushing upward and waving the abdomen with the root of palms when breathing out and relaxing the hands when breathing in. Repeat the whole procedure for 36 times.

Separating Yin and Yang: Take a sitting position, or lie down on the back. Put the hands on the xipoid process with fingers pointing to each other. Perform pulling manipulation from the front midline to the hypochondriac regions along the rib arcs and shift to the lower abdomen. Repeat the whole procedure for 9 times.

Pressing Zusanli (ST 36): Put the thumbs, index fingers or middle finger on Zusanli (ST 36), press and knead with slightly forceful strength for about 3 minutes until aching and distending feeling in the local area is felt.

Kneading Tianshu (ST 25): Take a sitting position, or lie down on the back. Press and knead Tianshu (ST 25) with the index fingers and middle fingers simultaneously clockwise and counterclockwise for 36 times respectively.

Pressing epigastric region: Juxtapose the four fingers of the left or the right hand and put them on Zhongwan (CV 12). Take abdominal respiration, press downward when breathe in and knead in circles when breathe out. Repeat the whole procedure for 36 times.

Kneading Xuehai (SP 10): Take a sitting position, knead Xuehai (SP 10) with the thumbs clockwise and counterclockwise for 36 times respectively.

9.2.4 Dispersing the lung and relieving superficies

The main physiological function of the lung is to dominate over Qi and respiration. It is the chief organ for exchanging air between the interior and exterior of the body. The body inhales fresh air and exhales waste air to promote the production of Qi and adjust the movement of Qi so as to ensure normal metabolism of the human body. The lung is also responsible for the activities of "dispersing, descending, and regulating water passage". The normal function of the lung ensures normal respiration, nutrition and water metabolism. If the function of the lung is abnormal, it will lead to difficulty in breath, stuffiness in the chest, cough, asthmatic breath, and even edema. The lung is connected with the large intestine via meridians and collaterals. The condition of the lung is manifested through luster of skin or the changes of nose. Thus, the manipulation of dispersing the lung and promoting Qi may effectively prevent and treat diseases of the lung.

Soothing the influential Acupoint of Qi: Put the hands, one over the other, on Danzhong (CV 17) between the nipples, rubbing up and down for 36 times.

Freeing Qi flow: Take a sitting position, put the right hollow palm over the right breast, pat with proper force and move to the left horizontally, back and forth for 9 times; then, cross the hands with fingers and put them above or below the breasts, transversely rub back and forth forcefully for 36 times. Finally, hold the side of body with the margin of the web between the thumb and index fingers, rub up and down from the hypochondriac regions to the ilium for 36 times until warm feeling at the local area is felt.

Vibrating the chest: Take a sitting position, hold greater pectoral muscle of the left side and grasp with the right hand for 9 times, repeat the same manipulation on the right side with the left hand. Then, cross the fingers, hold the nape with the elbow flexed horizontally. Try to extend the elbows backward as much as possible when breathing out. Repeat the same procedure for 9 times.

Kneading Zhongfu (LU 1): Take a sitting position, cross the hands in front of the chest. Put the tips of middle fingers on Zhongfu (LU 1) at both sides. Knead the point with slightly forceful strength clockwise and counterclockwise for 36 times respectively.

Hooking Tiantu (CV 22): Hook Tiantu (CV 22) with the tip of index finger and knead for 1 minute.

Regulating the triple energizers: Take a sitting position, or lie down on the back. Cross the fingers and put the hands horizontally on Danzhong (CV 17) with the palm base over the medial borders of the breasts. Push from Danzhong (CV 17) to Guanyuan (CV 4) with stronger force. Repeat the same procedure for 36 times.

Removing obstruction from the lung meridian: Take a sitting position or standing position, put the right hand above the left breast and rub in circles till it is warm in the local area. Then rub backward and forward along the front of the shoulder, anterior border of medial aspect of the arm, and radial side of the wrist and dorsum of the index finger (the course of the lung meridian) for 36 times. Then repeat the same procedure with the left hand on the right side.

Pinching Hegu (LI 4): Take a sitting position, press Hegu (LI 4) with the thumb and index finger of the right hand for about 1 minute. Then perform the same procedure with the left hand on the other side.

Ruving Yingxiang (LI 20): Take a sitting position, put the greater thenar of both hands or radial sides of the index fingers on Yingxiang (LI 20). Rub the local area up and down with rapid breath until warmth is felt.

9.2.5 Strengthening the kidney and benefiting essence

The kidney is the most important organ in the human body. In TCM, it is considered as "the root of congenital foundation" and is the power source of life. The major function of the kidney is to store essence, control reproduction and development and regulate the metabolism of body fluid, transporting the clear part of the body fluid to the lung to be further distributed to various parts of the body and transmitting the turbid part to the bladder to be discharged out of the body. In addition, the function of the kidney in accepting Qi is important to respiration. The condition of the kidney is often revealed through firmness of bones, luster of hair, spiritual status and hearing. This manipulation can strengthen and consolidate kidney functions, effective for preventing and curing the disorders of the kidney system.

Rubbing Yongquan (KI 1): Take a sitting position with the legs crossed, rub both hands till they are hot, then rub back and forth from Sanyinjiao (SP 6) to the toe until the skin is hot; and then rub Yongquan (KI 1) with both hands respectively until it is warm inside. The rubbing movement should be even in proper rhythm.

Rubbing kidney regions: Put the hands over Shenshu (BL 23), rub and turn for 36 times in circles with both hands simultaneously (rubbing clockwise is reinforcing and counterclockwise is reducing). It is not advisable to apply reducing method on Shenshu (BL 23). If one has the problems of kidney deficiency or lumbago, it is necessary to increase the times of turning activity.

Kneading Mingmen (GV 4): Put the index finger and middle finger on Mingmen (GV 4) and knead the point in circles clockwise and counterclockwise for 36 times respectively.

Rubbing lumbosacral region: Lean the body forward slightly, flex the elbow, put two palms on the sides of the lower back. Then, rub the sacral region up and down with the whole palm or small thenar until it is warm in the local area.

Rubbing Guanyuan (CV 4): Take Guanyuan (CV 4) as the centre of a circle, rub Guanyuan (CV 4) in circles clockwise or counterclockwise with the left and right hands for 36 times respectively. Then press Guanyuan (CV 4) inward and downward for 3 minutes with the rhythm of respiration.

Rubbing the lower abdomen: From the area below hypochondriac regions to the pubis, two hands push and rub repeatedly along an oblique course until it is warm in the local area.

Vibrating the ears: First, put both hands over the ears, rub and push for 36 times. Then, hold the earlobes with the thumbs and index fingers and shake for 36 times. After that, insert the index finger into the ear tracts, vibrate for several times rapidly, and pull out the fingers suddenly. Repeat the whole procedure for 9 times.

Contracting the anus and perineum: Relax the body in a quiet environment, take abdominal respiration (breathe in with the abdomen protruded and breathe out with the abdomen contracted.). During the expiration, slightly contract the anus and perineum. During inspiration, relax the abdomen, Repeat the whole procedure for 36 times.